A Charlton Standard Catalogue

Canadian Coins

D1768844

60th EDITION, 2006
DIAMOND ANNIVERSARY

Editions 1 to 30
by J. E. Charlton

Editions 31 to 60
by W. K. Cross

The Charlton Press

TORONTO, ONTARIO • PALM HARBOR, FLORIDA

ABOUT PRICING IN THIS CATALOGUE

The purpose of this catalogue is to give the most accurate, up-to-date retail prices for all Canadian coins. To this end, we have from the very inception of this catalogue used a pricing panel of established experts who have submitted the most current market values from across Canada. These individual market results are drawn from both dealer and collector activity as well as recent auction results and are averaged to reflect the current marketplace for Canadian coins.

A necessary word of caution: no catalogue can or should propose to be a fixed price list. This catalogue should be considered as a guide, showing the most current retail prices possible for the collector and dealer alike. The prices in this catalogue are in Canadian dollars. The U.S. price equivalent at the time of publication, is the catalogue price multiplied by 0.800

Library and Archives Canada Cataloguing in Publication

Canadian coins (Charlton Press)
Canadian coins : a Charlton standard catalogue

Annual
60th ed.-
Continues: Charlton standard catalogue of Canadian coins
ISSN 1716-0782
ISBN 0-88968-297-6 (60th edition)

1. Coins, Canadian--Catalogs.   2. Coins, Canadian--Collectors and collecting. I. Title

CJ1864.S82   737.4971'029   C2005-902187-X

**Printed in Canada
in the Province of Quebec**

EDITORIAL

Editor	W. K. Cross
Editorial Assistant	Jean Dale
Graphic Technician	Davina Rowan
Photography	Scott Cornwell

VERY SPECIAL MENTION

Jim Charlton must be given special credit for his work over the years which made this catalogue possible.

SPECIAL MENTION

We would like to thank the following individuals for answering requests or supplying information which assisted in putting the 60th edition together. At 560 pages we needed all the help we could muster.

Cameron Bevers
Sandy Campbell
Louis Chevrier
Brian Cornwell
Mark Drake

Joe Iorio
Ian Laing
Charles Moore
Stan Wright

The Charlton Press

Editorial Office
P.O. Box 820, Postal Station Willowdale B
North York, Ontario M2K 2R1
Tel.: (416) 488-1418 Fax: (416) 488-4656
Tel.: (800) 442-6042 Fax.: (800) 442-1542
www.charltonpress.com
email: chpress@charltonpress.com

FOREWARD

Fifty-five years, sixty editions and hundreds of contributors have gone into making this Anniversary Edition the encyclopaedia of Canadian numismatics.

However, with this Sixtieth Edition dramatic changes have taken place within the catalogue. Prior to the advent of third party grading services, the recording of population data for coins by date, variety and grade was virtually nonexistent, except for the efforts of a few dedicated individuals who manually kept track of what they saw and collected. Grading services with their population reports have changed they way we look at the availability of collectable coins.

Previously it was sometimes nearly impossible to establish that specific coins even existed in a specific grade. The natural trend in the Standard Catalogue was to price each coin in all grades, whether we knew they existed or not. In some cases we were pricing the imaginary, for not all coins have been seen in all grades. All that has changed with the 60th edition. If a coin in a specific grade has not been recorded by a recognized grading service, no corresponding price will appear in the pricing table.

This now leads us to questions that need to be addressed and decisions made regarding the different grading standards and the methods by which the results are recorded (Population Reports). While there are only two Canadian grading services, the United States supports over ten, with three, PCGS, NGC and ANACS recognized as major firms.

Grading standards, while differing between companies, also vary between countries. The standards between Canadian grading companies differ, and the standards between the Canadian and United States companies also differ. Thus, uniformity does not exist among all companies.

Now, the second major change that is happening in the numismatic field is the tremendous growth of auctions, both traditional and Internet, with of course the on-line auctions growing at an explosive rate. With over 7,000 bits of information available daily on just one auction site alone, a decision had to be reached as to the reliability and meaningfulness of the data being gathered from these on-line auctions. This generation of pricing data cannot be ignored.

Historically our pricing data was gathered from submissions by dealers across Canada. With the 60th edition the basis changed to auctions, both traditional and Internet, dealer advertisements and website price lists. The Internet has become predominant and now accounts for well over 85% of the pricing information available. A common thread between all these sources – on-line auction, dealers prices lists, etc. – was required to supply continuity to the data base. With this in mind the logical choice for the Canadian market was to price the coins in this catalogue based on those which have been graded by International Coin Certification Services (ICCS).

William K. Cross
The Charlton Press

TABLE OF CONTENTS

INTRODUCTION

The Charlton Standard Catalogue of Canadian Coins is an illustrated, descriptive price catalogue for the principal types of commercial and commemorative coins used in Canada over the years, including pre-Confederation coinages. As a standard catalogue, it provides an accurate overview and introduction to Canadian numismatics and current market values. Each major variety of all issues of Canadian coins is listed, illustrated and priced. Several minor varieties that have a wide appeal to collectors, such as Arnprior dollars, are also included. Historical introductions provide important background information for each series, and relevant technical information is provided wherever available.

The new reader should find in this catalogue all the basic information needed to identify and evaluate individual coins as he or she embarks upon an old and widely enjoyed hobby. Continuing and expanding upon the completely revised and enlarged text introduced in the 32nd edition, readers will find herein more historical information, technical data and statistics than has ever before been compiled for a Canadian coin catalogue. A summary of the principal foreign coins used during the French and British regimes is included, as well as local, pre-decimal issues. The decimal series is complete for the provinces of British North America and Canada from its inception to the present, and also includes patterns, essais and test tokens.

This edition is just the latest in our continuing efforts to bring readers the best possible reference book for one of Canada's most popular and profitable pastimes. Welcome, then, to this new edition of the 'Charlton Standard Catalogue of Canadian Coins' and to the exciting field of Canadian numismatics.

THE COLLECTING OF CANADIAN DECIMAL COINS
PAST AND PRESENT

Today, the majority of those collecting Canadian numismatic material specialize in the decimal coin series. The collecting popularity of decimal coins is a relatively recent phenomenon, however. When Canada's first coin club was formed in Montreal in 1862, there was little interest in either coins or paper money. Eighty years later this was still the case. Most collectors specialized in Canadian tokens, the private coppers that served for so long as a medium of exchange in the absence of official coins. Decimal coins were mostly collected by type. One or two examples of each design were sufficient, and there was little concern regarding the relative scarcity of the various dates and varieties.

The current preoccupation with collecting decimal coins by date and variety arose in the 1940's, under the influence of U.S. dealer Wayte Raymond. Shortly after World War II and on into the 1950's, Canadian pioneers J. Douglas Ferguson, Fred Bowman, Sheldon Carroll and Leslie Hill attempted to establish the relative rarities of the decimal coins issued up to that time.

In 1950 collectors in the Ottawa area joined with scattered groups and individuals to form the Canadian Numismatic Association. Its official publication, and annual conventions beginning in 1954, served to bridge the miles and facilitate the exchange of information and ideas.

Two years after the C.N.A. was formed, the Charlton Standard Catalogue made its appearance. Early editions were modest paperback pamphlets with line drawings, but they were a serious attempt to list and price Canadian coins, tokens, paper money and some medals. The first hard-cover edition of 128 pages appeared in 1960. By 1971 it had grown to 200 pages, and by 1978 so much additional numismatic information was available that it was decided the needs of collectors could best be met by splitting the catalogue into separate, specialized works.

The 27th (1979) Edition became the 'Standard Catalogue of Canadian Coins,' now issued yearly. This was followed by the annual edition of the 'Charlton Standard Catalogue of Canadian Government Paper Money,' the 'Standard Catalogue of Canadian Colonial Tokens,' and the 'Charlton Standard Catalogue of Canadian Bank Notes.' A new series, 'Canadian Historical Medals,' is under development.

BUILDING A COLLECTION

Decimal coin collections can be formed in a variety of ways. Coins may come from pocket change, family hoards, the bank, the mint or from other collectors. In general, older coins no longer circulate and the excitement of searching through change for missing dates has been diminished by the withdrawal of most silver coins from circulation.

Collecting is a matter of individual taste. Some people collect by design type, others concentrate on one or two denominations or monarchs, while some brave souls try to collect the entire decimal series. Regardless of which path you choose, there is a variety of coin boards, envelopes and other supplies available to help house and organize your collection. For reasons of security many collectors keep their best coins in a bank vault.

Another decision that must be made when building a collection is the minimum state of preservation one will accept when buying coins. As a general rule, it is advisable to buy the best condition coins one can afford.

AGE - RARITY - DEMAND - CONDITION - VALUE

The value of a coin on the numismatic market is dictated by a complex mixture of factors. One feature that those unfamiliar with coins often mistakenly believe to be of great importance is age. That age is a minor contributor to value is illustrated by the fact that the 1969 Large Date variety 10 cents is worth far more than the 1870 10-cent piece, a coin nearly 100 years older!

Basically, a coin's value is determined by a combination of supply and demand. The 1870 50-cent piece does not command as high a premium as the 1921 coin of the same denomination because there are many more 1870s than 1921s available.

Finally, the state of preservation of a coin markedly influences its value. It is not unusual for an uncirculated (brand new) George V silver coin, for example, to sell for 100 times what a coin of the same date and denomination would bring in well-worn condition.

GRADING CANADIAN COINS

Canadian coins, as with coins of any other country, can be distinguished from each other by a simple comparison of their coin type, denomination, and date of issue. Coins of the same type, denomination and date can be further identified from each other by each coin's "condition" or state of preservation.

Coin conditions vary considerably. They range from the poorest state where the date and other details can barely be determined to the best states where details are as sharp and clear as they were the moment the coin was minted. Generally coin conditions are divided into one or two categories, namely, circulated condition or uncirculated condition. Examples of circulated coins are those that you might find in pocket change. These coins have varying degrees of surface wear as a result of human handling or use as "money" in our world of commerce. Uncirculated coins (also called mint state coins) differ from circulated coins in that they must have absolutely no visible signs of wear on any part of the coin's surface. However uncirculated coins are not necessarily flawless. The majority will still have small marks, as opposed to wear, which are a result of contact with other coins received when they were distributed by the mint to our banking system in large bags.

Once a coin's condition is understood it can be assigned one of a number of circulated or uncirculated "grades" according to grading standards accepted by the coin industry in Canada. Early standards for grading Canadian coins that appeared in the first Charlton catalogue in 1952 used terms like Very Good and Extremely Fine to describe some of these grades. Since that time coin grading has been considerably refined. Today there are ten officially recognized grades for circulated coins and a further ten to designate all of the uncirculated grades, although only five of the latter are in general use.

Since 1979 the Charlton Standard Catalogue has utilized a grading system similar to that accepted by the American Numismatic Association for United States coinage in 1977. Some of the following general text has been reproduced from "The Official ANA Grading Standards for United States Coins". We wish to express our appreciation to the American Numismatic Association for allowing us to do so.

ADJECTIVAL AND NUMERICAL GRADING SYSTEMS

New coin collectors and investors are often confused when they read or hear about an adjectival grading scheme on the one hand and a numerical system on the other. There is no need for this confusion. Both systems use the same grade definitions. They simply refer to them by different labels.

Adjectival grading, as the name implies, uses adjectives to describe coin grades. This scheme has been in use since the earliest days of Canadian numismatics and is therefore the traditional grading nomenclature. The following adjectives represent most of the officially accepted grades (from poorest quality to best) in use today: About Good (AG), Good (G), Very Good (VG), Fine (F), Very Fine (VF), Choice Very Fine (Choice VF), Extremely Fine (EF), Choice Extremely Fine (Choice EF), About Uncirculated (AU), Choice About Uncirculated (Choice AU)), Typical Uncirculated (Unc. or BU), Select Uncirculated (Select Unc.), Choice Uncirculated (Choice Unc.), Gem Uncirculated (Gem Unc.) and Perfect Uncirculated (Perfect Unc.).

The numerical grading system is a modern day development by comparison. It was devised by Dr. William Sheldon in the late 1940's. Sheldon's numerical grading scale used numbers ranging from one to seventy. All circulated grades were assigned numbers in the range of 1 to 59 while the numbers from 60 to 70 were reserved for the uncirculated grades. His intent was to have a grading scheme that would interrelate coin grades and coin prices for each grade. He accomplished this by assigning specific numbers from these ranges to each of the traditionally used adjectival grades. A summary of these adjectival grades with his numerical designation follows:

About Good-3, Good-4, Very-Good 8, Fine-12, Very Fine-20, Choice Very Fine-30, Extremely Fine-40, Choice Extremely Fine-45, About Uncirculated-50, Choice About Uncirculated-55, Typical Uncirculated-60, Select Uncirculated-63, Choice Uncirculated-65, Gem Uncirculated-67, Perfect Uncirculated-70.

The basis of his actual number selection was the relative prices of early American copper coins in each of the various grades. For example, in the late 1940's, a typical uncirculated coin (MS-60) was determined to be about 7½ times the price of a typical Very Good (VG-8) example of the same kind and so on.

The numerical system has now been extended beyond early American copper coins to include most areas of North American numismatics. Sheldon's number assignments no longer have any relevance to current coin pricing. Today a typical MS-60 coin might easily be priced 50 to 100 times more than a typical VG-8 coin of the same kind! Unfortunately this only adds to the confusion of those graders who expect his number assignments to have some special pricing or other scientific meaning.

COIN GRADING AND HUMAN NATURE

Before actually trying to understand all of the rules relating to coin grading, it is equally important to appreciate the human elements that often surround the act of grading a coin. Inexperienced coin graders are often dismayed by the seemingly large number of grading arguments, some very heated, that arise within this industry. Why are there differences of opinion in the field of grading coins? There are numerous reasons, but the most common are as follows:

Grading coins can never be completely scientific in all areas. A great deal of human judgement is also involved. One may weigh a coin and also obtain its specific gravity by mechanical devices and the result will be factual if accurate equipment is used carefully. There are no scientific means available to measure the surface condition – the amount of wear – of a coin.

In grading coins, considerations such as striking, surface of the planchet, the presence of heavy toning (which may obscure certain surface characteristics), the design, and other factors each lend an influence. A panel containing a dozen of the foremost numismatic industry leaders justifiably could have some **slight** difference of opinion on the precise grade of some coins.

However, it is not **slight** differences which concern us here: it is serious or major differences. The term "overgrading" refers to describing a coin as a grade higher than it actually is. For example, if a coin in AU (About Uncirculated) grade is called Uncirculated, it is overgraded. If a coin in Very Fine grade is called Extremely Fine, it is overgraded.

What induces overgrading? Here are some of the factors:

Buyers Seeking Bargains. The desire to get a bargain is part of human nature. If a given Uncirculated coin actively traded at $100 is offered at $70, it will attract a lot of bargain seekers. These same buyers would reject an offering such as: "I am offering this stock which trades on the New York Stock Exchange for $100 for just $70 cash," or "I am offering $100 bills for $70 each."

In coins, as in any other walk of life, you get what you pay for. If a coin which has a standard value of $100 is offered for $70 there may be nothing wrong, but chances are the piece is overgraded.

False Assumptions. Buyers often assume falsely that any advertisement which appears in a numismatic publication has been approved by that publication. Actually, publishers cannot be expected to examine coins and approve of all listings offered. A person who has no numismatic knowledge or experience whatsoever can have letterheads and business cards printed and, assuming he has good financial and character references (but not necessarily numismatic expertise), run large and flashy advertisements. Months or years later it is often too late for the deceived buyer to get his money back. The solution to this is to learn how to grade coins and think for yourself. Examine the credentials of the seller. Is he truly an expert in his field? How do you know? What do collectors with more experience think of this seller? To what professional organizations does this dealer belong? It is usually foolish to rush and spend your hard-earned money with a coin seller who has no professional credentials and whose only attraction is that he is offering "bargains." Think for yourself!

The Profit Motive. Sellers seeking an unfair markup may overgrade. For purposes of illustration, let us assume that a given variety of coin is worth the following prices in these grades: AU $75, and Uncirculated $150. A legitimate dealer in the course of business would buy, for example, an AU coin at $50 or $60 and sell it retail for $75, thus making a profit of $15 to $25. However, there are sellers who are not satisfied with the normal way of doing business. They take shortcuts. They pay $50 or $60 for the same AU coin which is worth $75 retail, but rather than calling it AU they call it "Uncirculated" and sell it for $150. So, instead of making $15 to $25 they may make $90 to $100!

Inexperience or error on the part of the seller may lead to incorrect grading — both overgrading and undergrading.

LIGHTING AND MAGNIFICATION

The same coin can have a different appearance depending upon the lighting conditions and also the amount of magnification used to examine it. For purposes of standardization, we recommend that a magnifying glass of four to eight power be used. This is sufficient to reveal all the differences and peculiarities necessary to grade the coin accurately. At the same time it is not too much magnification. Under extensive magnification — 10 power or more — even the finest coin may show marks and imperfections in an exaggerated fashion. You may wish to keep a stronger magnifying glass on hand, however, for examination of minute die details.

It is also desirable to use a magnifying glass of sufficient width so that a fairly large amount of the coin's surface can be studied at one time.

Recommended for grading is a 200 watt incandescent light bulb approximately three feet (one metre) from the coin (or a 50 watt bulb at about half the distance, or other equivalents). Incandescent light furnishes a pinpoint light source and enables surface characteristics to be studied in more detail. Fluorescent light, which spreads illumination from diffused origin, is apt to conceal minute differences. "Tensor" type lamps, popular at coin conventions, furnish a high intensity pinpoint light source and are satisfactory for grading.

To grade a coin, hold it between your fingertips (over a soft surface to prevent damage in the event of dropping) at an angle so that light from the bulb reflects from the coin's surface into your eye. Turn or rotate the coin horizontally so that different characteristics can be observed in better detail. You will want to examine the edge also.

Lamp wattage and magnifying intensities are less critical with circulated grades. They are very important, however, for Uncirculated and Proof coins where judgment is dependant upon relatively small differences in surface appearance.

NATURAL COLOURATION OF COINS

Knowledge of the natural colour which coinage metals acquire over a period of years is useful to the collector. To an extent, a coin's value is determined by the attractiveness of its colouration. Also, certain types of unnatural colour might indicate that a coin has been cleaned or otherwise treated.

The basic coinage metals used in Canada are alloys of copper, nickel, silver and gold. Copper tends to tone the most rapidly. Gold is the least chemically active and will tone only slightly and then only over a long period of years.

Copper. Copper is among the most chemically active of all coinage metals. When a copper coin is first struck, it emerges from the dies with a brilliant pale orange surface.

Once a freshly minted copper coin enters the atmosphere it immediately begins to oxidize. Over a period of years, especially if exposed to actively circulating air, if placed in contact with sulfides, the coin will acquire a glossy brown surface. In between the brilliant and glossy brown stages it will be part red and part brown.

An Uncirculated coin with full original mint brilliance, usually slightly subdued in colouration, is typically described as Brilliant Uncirculated (our example here is for a typical Uncirculated or MS-60 coin); a Choice piece would be called Choice Brilliant Uncirculated, and so on. One which is part way between the brilliant and brown surface hues would be called Red and Brown Uncirculated. Specimens with brownish surfaces can be called Brown Uncirculated. Particularly valuable coins can have the colouration described in more detail. Generally, in any category of grading, the more explanation given, the more accurate the description.

Early copper coins with full original mint brilliance are more valuable than Red and Brown Uncirculated or Brown Uncirculated pieces. The more original mint brilliance present, the more valuable a coin will be. The same is true of Proofs.

Circulated copper coins are never fully brilliant, but are toned varying shades of brown.

Nickel. Uncirculated nickel coins when first minted are silver/gray in appearance, not as bright as silver but still with much brilliance. Over a period of time nickel coins tend to tone a hazy gray. Circulated nickel coins have a gray appearance.

Silver. When first minted, silver coins have a bright silvery-white surface. Over a period of time silver, a chemically active metal, tends to tone deep brown or black. Uncirculated and Proof silver pieces often exhibit very beautiful multi-coloured iridescent hues after a few years. The presence of attractive toning often increases a silver coin's value. Advanced collectors will often prefer attractive toned coins. Beginners sometimes think that "brilliant is best." Circulated silver coins will often have a dull gray appearance, sometimes with deep gray or black areas.

Gold. When first struck, gold coins are a bright yellow-orange colour. As gold coins are not pure gold but are alloyed with copper and traces of other substances, they do tend to tone over a period of time. Over a period of decades, a gold coin will normally acquire a deep orange colouration, sometimes with light brown or orange-brown toning "stains" or streaks in certain areas (resulting from improperly mixed copper traces in the alloy). Light toning does not affect the value of a gold coin.

Very old gold coins, particularly those in circulated grades, will sometimes show a red oxidation. Gold coins which have been recovered from treasure wrecks after centuries at the sea bottom will sometimes have a minutely porous surface because of the corrosive action of sea water. Such pieces sell for less than specimens which have not been so affected. Care must be taken to distinguish these from cast copies which often have a similar surface.

HANDLING AND STORAGE OF COINS

As a coin collector you are commissioned by posterity to handle each coin in your possession carefully and to preserve it in the condition in which it was received.

When examining a coin you should hold it by its edges and over a cloth pad or other soft surface. In this way if it accidentally falls no harm will be done. A coin should never be touched on either of its faces, obverse or reverse, for the oil and acid in one's skin will eventually leave fingerprints - if not soon, then years later. Also, one should avoid holding a coin near one's mouth while talking as small drops of moisture may land on the coin's surface and later cause what are commonly referred to as "flyspecks" - tiny pinpoints of oxidation.

Coins should be sorted in a dry location free of harmful fumes. The presence of sulfur in the atmosphere, a situation caused by certain types of coal combustion and also by industrial processes, sometimes will impart to silver coins in particular a yellowish or blackish toning. Dampness will result in oxidation or, in extreme instances, surface corrosion. Dampness can be best avoided by moving coins to a drier location. If this is not possible, then a packet of silica gel (available in drugstores or photography supply stores) put in with the coins will serve to absorb moisture and may alleviate the problem. Also, the storage of coins in airtight containers will help.

The more a coin is exposed to freely circulating air, the more tendency it has to change colour or tone. Storage of coins in protective envelopes and hard plastic holders will usually help prevent this.

CLEANING COINS

Experienced numismatists will usually say that a coin is best left alone and not cleaned. However, most beginning collectors have the idea that "brilliant is best" and somehow feel that cleaning a coin will "improve" it. As the penchant for cleaning seems to be universal, and also because there are some instances in which cleaning can actually be beneficial, some important aspects are presented here.

All types of cleaning, "good" and "bad," result in the coin's surface being changed, even if only slightly. Even the most careful "dipping" of a coin will, if repeated time and time again, result in the coin acquiring a dullish and microscopically etched surface. It is probably true to state that no matter what one's intentions are, for every single coin actually improved in some way by cleaning, a dozen or more have been decreased in value. Generally, experienced numismatists agree that a coin should not be cleaned unless there are spots of oxidation, pitting which might worsen in time, or unsightly streaking or discolouration.

PROCESSING, POLISHING AND OTHER MISTREATMENT OF COINS

Many methods have been attempted to give a coin the appearance of being in a higher grade than it actually is. Numismatists refer to such treatments as "processing." Being different from cleaning (which can be "good" or "bad"), processing is never beneficial.

Types of processing include polishing and abrasion which removes metal from a coin's surface, etching and acid treatment, and "whizzing," the latter usually referring to abrading the surface of the coin with a stiff wire brush, often in a circular motion, to produce a series of minute tiny parallel scratches which to the unaided eye or under low magnification often appear to mimic mint lustre. Under high magnification (in this instance a very strong magnifying glass should be used) the surface of a whizzed coin will show countless tiny scratches. Also, the artificial "mint lustre" will usually be in a uniform pattern throughout the coin's surfaces, whereas on an Uncirculated coin with true mint lustre the sheen of the lustre will be different on the higher parts than on the field. Some whizzed coins can be extremely deceptive. Comparing a whizzed coin with an untreated coin is the best way to gain experience in this regard.

Often one or more methods of treating a coin are combined. Sometimes a coin will be cleaned or polished and then by means of heat, fumes, or other treatment, an artificial toning will be applied. There are many variations.

When a coin has been polished, whizzed, artificially retoned, or in any other way changed from its original natural appearance and surface, it must be so stated in a description. For example, a coin which was Extremely Fine but whizzed to give it the artificial appearance of Uncirculated should be described as "Extremely Fine, whizzed." An AU coin which has been recoloured should be described as "AU, recoloured." The simple "dipping" (without abrasion) of an already Uncirculated or Proof coin to brighten the surface does not have to be mentioned unless such dipping alters the appearance from when the coin was first struck (for example, in the instance of a copper or bronze coin in which dipping always produces an unnatural colour completely unlike the coin when it was first struck.)

FRATERNAL AFFILIATION

Over the years, coin clubs have sprung up in many Canadian communities. In addition, both Canada and the United States have national organizations which hold annual conventions. Coin clubs constitute one of the most attractive features of present-day collecting. They offer beginning collectors the opportunity for good fellowship and the encouragement and knowledge of more experienced collectors. The larger groups maintain lending libraries and publish a journal or newsletter on a regular basis. Memberships and other information can be obtained from:

The Canadian Numismatic Association
4936 Yonge Street, Suite 601
North York, Ontario
Canada M2N 6S3

The American Numismatic Association
818 N. Cascade Avenue
Colorado Springs, Colorado
U.S.A. 80903-3279

Ontario Numismatic Association
Post Office Box 33
Waterloo, Ontario
Canada N2J 3Z6.

COIN CERTIFICATION SERVICE

In recent years there has been an increase in the number of North American companies that offer third party professional coin grading services. Another service offered is that of rendering an opinion whether a particular coin is genuine or counterfeit. Most of these companies operate along similar lines, that is, a coin is submitted by its owner for an independent grading and/or authentification assessment, an opinion is offered along with a certificate and a fee is charged on a per coin basis. These services are widely used by collectors and investors who recognize their grading skills are not at an expert's level. Most dealers also make use of such services because their clients often demand that the coins they buy have an official certificate with them. To date the most popular U.S. coin grading services appear to be The Professional Coin Grading Service (PCGS) located in California, and The Numismatic Guaranty Corporation (NGC) located in Florida. These two services specialize in U.S. coinage. In Canada the only such service for coins is that offered by International Coin Certification Service (ICCS) in Toronto.

International Coin Certification Service (ICCS)
2010 Yonge Street, Suite 202
Toronto, Ontario, M4S 1Z9
Canada
Tel.: (416) 488-8620 Fax: (416) 488-6371

Professional Coin Grading Service (PCGS)
P.O. Box 9458, Newport Beach
California 92658, U.S.A.
Tel.: (800) 447-8848 or (949) 833-0600
www.pcgs.com

Numismatic Guaranty Corporation of America (NGC)
P.O. Box 4776, Sarasota
Florida 34320, U.S.A.
Tel.: (941) 360-3990 Fax: (941) 360-2553
www.ngccoin.com

Canadian Coin Certification Service (CCCS)
Box 57119, Centre Maxi
Longueil, Quebec J4L 4T6 Canada
Tel.: (450) 448-3662
www.canadiancoincertification.com

FOREIGN COINS IN CANADA

Strictly speaking, Canada (rather, the areas that now form Canada) did not have a coinage struck for its specific use until the mid-19th century. After 1820, some provincial governments issued their own coppers, but this was without imperial government sanction until the 1850s. Thus, for some two centuries Canada relied on foreign coins to provide the lifeblood for her commerce. The importance of foreign coins in our currency history has not been given the emphasis it deserves in Canadian catalogues. Certainly it is difficult to deal with this subject. None of the foreign coins that were once so important here can strictly be called Canadian. This includes the coins of the French regime, some of which have been listed in past catalogues. To simply list some French issues is both misleading and illogical. The Spanish-American dollar, for example, was a more important coin in our overall currency history than any French (or British) coin ever was. A more realistic listing must include coins of France, Great Britain, Spain and Spanish America, Portugal and the United States.

It has been decided to attempt to list the most important foreign coins that circulated in Canada, regardless of their country of origin. In order to qualify for listing a coin must have circulated in colonial Canada in reasonable quantity. The many coins that filtered into North America in small quantities through trade cannot be listed.

NOTE: The prices listed below for broad types of coins, which may encompass several separate types and a span of many years, are for the most commonly encountered form of the coin only. Readers are advised to see specialized foreign catalogues for specific varieties, dates and prices.

COINS OF FRANCE

During the French regime (c.1600-1760), French imperial coins were intermittently shipped to New France by the king or were imported by local merchants. Occasionally these were supplemented by general colonial coinages not intended for circulation in France. But, as New France was just one of the recipients of the colonial issues, they cannot be considered to have been minted specifically for Canada. French coins became less important in Canada after 1760. The silver ecus and ½ ecus, however, remained in commercial use well into the next century.

Between 1680 and the early 1720's, French coins were subject to considerable variation in the rates at which they were to be officially current. We will not attempt to detail these changes or "reformations" for each coin. A single example is sufficient to make the point. One of the few French coins with its original value actually stated on it is the "mousquetaire" or 30-denier piece minted between 1710 and 1713. Its initial rate of 30 deniers was lowered to 27 deniers in 1714 and to 22 deniers the next year. It remained at that level until the wild inflation of John Law (1720-1721), when it soared to 60 deniers and quickly fell back to 45 deniers. In 1724 its rate was returned to 27 deniers and in 1732 it was lowered to 24 deniers. It continued at that level in New France until the Conquest.

By 1726 the French government realized the folly of frequent changes in the value of coins and generally the currency was stabilized.

MINT MARKS ON FRENCH COINS. Numerous mints produced French coins. Only for issues produced by a small number of mints will the listings by mint be separated. The following mint marks were employed on coins that circulated in quantity in New France and British Canada:

A - Paris	K - Bordeaux	S - Reims	& - Aix
B - Rouen	L - Bayonne	T - Nantes	AA - Metz
C - Caen	M - Toulouse	V - Troyes	BB - Strasbourg
D - Lyon	N - Montpellier	W - Lille	)(- Besancon
E - Tours	O - Riom	X - Amiens	a cow - Pau
G - Poitiers	P - Dijon	Y - Bourges	
H - LaRochelle	Q - Perpignan	Z - Grenoble	
I - Limoges	R - Orleans	9 - Rennes	

COPPER COINS

DENIER TOURNOIS. Along with the copper double and liard, the denier was one of the predominant coins in circulation in New France up to the early 1660's. The denier, although rated at 1 denier in France, circulated as a 2-denier piece in New France. The merchants saw a chance for a quick profit and imported these coins in large quantities. This resulted in an oversupply prompting the government at Quebec to ban the denier altogether in 1664.

Type and Denomination	VG	F	VF	EF
1589-1649, Denier, Henri IV, Louis XIII or XIV	35.	50.	125.	275.

DOUBLE TOURNOIS. In 1664 the Order of the Sovereign Council which demonetized the denier allowed the double to remain in circulation but reduced its value to 1 denier to curb its excessive importation. It had formerly circulated at 4 deniers in New France.

Type and Denomination	VG	F	VF	EF
1589-1647, Double, Henri IV, Louis XIII or XIV	25.	40.	100.	225.

LIARD. Until the Order of Sovereign Council of 1664, the liard passed in New France as a 6-denier piece. After 1664 its value was reduced to 2 deniers to discourage its excessive importation.

Type and Denomination	VG	F	VF	EF
1643-1774, Liard, Louis XIV or XV, (13 types)	40.	65.	150.	350.

½ **SOL COINAGE OF 1710-1712.** The first coinage of this denomination in copper took place in 1710-1712. When first issued it was rated at 6 deniers.

Type and Denomination	VG	F	VF	EF
1710-1712, ½ Sol, Louis XIV	30.	50.	90.	250.

COPPER COINAGE OF 1719-1724. This coinage consisted of a liard, a ½ sol and a sol. The middle denomination (the half sol) was shipped to New France in large amounts in 1720.

Type and Denomination	VG	F	VF	EF
1719-1724, ½ Sol	25.	35.	75.	200.

Type and Denomination	VG	F	VF	EF
1719-1724, Sol	25.	50.	85.	250.

COLONIAL 9 DENIER COINAGE 1721-1722. This was a special colonial issue imported by a private trading company, the Company of the Indies. Following difficulties in circulating their new coins, the company attempted to have them transferred to the government of New France. This was not successful, so most of the coinage was returned to France in 1726 with only 8,000 plus pieces put into circulation in New France. These coins were also sent to other French colonies.

Type and Denomination	VG	F	VF	EF
1721B, 9 Deniers	175.	400.	800.	2,000.
1721H, 9 Deniers	90.	175.	400.	800.
1722H, 2 over 1	125.	300.	550.	1,000.
1722H, Normal Date	90.	175.	400.	800.
1722H, Brass		Extremely Rare		

BILLON SOLS MARQUES COINAGES

The most important coinages in circulation during the French regime were a group of billon (low grade silver) pieces collectively called sols (or sous) marques. They often constituted the smallest denomination coins because copper was generally unpopular with the colonists. There were no fewer than six coinages of sols marques; the coinages of 1709-1713 and 1738-1764 also had double sol denominations.

COUNTER STAMPED DOUZAINS (1640). During the Middle Ages a new French coin called a gros tournois made its appearance. It was about the size of a 25-cent piece and made of good silver. By the first part of the 17th century this coin had become a billon piece called a douzain. The douzain or sol was rated at 12 deniers. In 1640 the French government called in all douzains and counterstamped them with a small fleur-de-lis in an oval to change their rating to 15 deniers. The term sol marque (marked sol) came from the fact that these coins were counterstamped. It later came to apply to all sols.

Type and Denomination	VG	F	VF	EF
Counterstamped Douzain (1640)	40.	75.	150.	–

COINAGE OF 1641. The next billon coin in the series was a new design dated 1641. It was initially rated at 15 deniers and supplemented the douzains counterstamped the year before. Its relation to these coins is clearly shown by its design (both obverse and reverse) containing a fleur-de-lis in an oval, in imitation of the counterstamp on the earlier issue.

Type and Denomination	VG	F	VF	EF
1641, 15 Deniers	125.	300.	600.	1,350.

COINAGE OF 1658. The douzain of 1658 was rated at 12 deniers in France but was given a rating of 20 deniers when it made its first appearance in New France in 1662. A 6-denier piece was also struck, but there is no reason to believe that denomination circulated in quantity in the colony.

Type and Denomination	VG	F	VF	EF
1658 Douzain	150.	300.	600.	1,350.

COINAGE OF 1692-1698. Beginning in 1692 and continuing through 1698, a new issue of sols marques was made. The designs were new, but instead of being struck on fresh blanks, many were struck over previous issues of sols. It is sometimes possible to detect parts of the undertypes on the overstruck coins. The new issue was rated at 15 deniers when it first came out.

Type and Denomination	VG	F	VF	EF
1692-1698, 15 Deniers, Billion, (4 types)	20.	35.	60.	125.

Note: Extremely fine prices are indications only. These coins are rarely found in this condition. If an example does appear for sale, it will more than likely trade at a much higher price.

"MOUSQUETAIRE" ISSUES OF 1709-1713. This issue consisted of a 15-denier piece and a 30-denier piece. The name mousquetaire is believed to have come from the cross on the reverse of the coins, which resembled the crosses on the cloaks of the legendary musketeers.

Type and Denomination	VG	F	VF	EF
1710-1713, 15 Deniers, Billion	150.	275.	500.	1,000.

Type and Denomination	VG	F	VF	EF
1709-1713, 30 Deniers, Billion	85.	150.	300.	650.

COINAGE OF 1738-1756. The final billon coinage used in New France was that of 1738-1756, consisting of a sol and a double sol. The double sol has often been mistakenly referred to as "the" sol marque. First, there is no single sol marque; some six coinages are involved. Second, the sol or sou was by 1738 a coin about the size of our present small cent. The larger coin so often called a sou marque is in fact a double sol.

SOL (SOU) 1739-1748. This coin was rated at 12 deniers in both France and New France.

Type and Denomination	VG	F	VF	EF
1739-1748, Sol, (14 different mint marks)	80.	150.	275.	600.

Note: Extremely fine prices are indications only. These coins are rarely found in this condition. If an example does appear for sale, it will more than likely trade at a much higher price.

DOUBLE SOL (2 SOUS) 1738-1756. Although this type was struck until 1764, large shipments to Quebec and Cape Breton ended in 1756. It is unlikely that any dated later than 1756 circulated extensively in New France. This coin was rated at 24 deniers.

Large quantities of contemporary counterfeits were made of the double sol, particularly of the dates 1740, 1741, 1742, 1750, 1751, 1755 and 1760. Differences in the rendition of the crown are the easiest way to tell the genuine from the counterfeit.

 Original

 Typical Counterfeit

Type and Denomination	VG	F	VF	EF
1738-1756, Double sol, (29 different mint marks)	75.	100.	150.	300.
1740-1756, Double sol, counterfeit	40.	60.	100.	150.

SILVER COINS

½ ECU. The half ecu was not routinely imported into French America; nevertheless, it did circulate in considerable quantity. It is assumed that these coins came primarily from issues of Louis XIV and XV. The ecu, a large silver coin about the size of the Canadian silver dollar, was imported into French America in significant quantities. Most types of ecu minted between 1640 and the 1750's probably circulated in Canada. The ecu and its half continued in use after the fall of New France, when they became known as the French crown and half crown.

Heavily worn old French crowns and half crowns were legally overvalued in Lower Canada, where bank notes were often redeemed in such coin, depreciating the notes outside the colony. Corrective action could not be delayed after the Act of Union, and in 1842 the old French silver was finally demonetized.

Type and Denomination	VG	F	VF	EF
1645-1715, ½ Ecu, Louis XIIII	65.	100.	225.	700.
1715-1774, ½ Ecu, Louis XV	30.	45.	110.	350.

ECU. The ecu, a large silver coin about the size of the Canadian silver dollar, was imported into French America in significant quantities. The ecu continued in use after the fall of New France, when it was called the French crown. Most types of ecu minted between 1640 and the 1750s probably circulated in Canada.

Type and Denomination	VG	F	VF	EF
1641-1643, Ecu, (60 Sols), Louis XIII		Very Rare		
1643-1715, Ecu, Louis XIII, (4 major bust varieties)	100.	200.	400.	900.
1715-1774, Ecu, Louis XV, (7 major bust varieties)	50.	75.	125.	300.

Colonial Coinage of 1670

In 1670 a special coinage of silver 5-sol and 15-sol pieces was produced for circulation in the French colonies in the New World. On the reverse was "GLORIAM REGNI TVI DICENT" meaning "They shall speak of the glory of Thy kingdom" and taken from the 145th Psalm of the Bible. Despite their fame, these coins barely qualify as "Canadian." Period documents suggest that they probably were intended for the West Indies rather than New France. Authorities in the West Indies were anxious to obtain a subsidiary silver coinage for payment of day labourers and artisans, who were being paid in goods. In New France these coins were not particularly wanted because they could not be used for buying goods in France; they were not legal tender there. In any case it is quite clear that these coins had a very limited circulation in French America.

Date and Denomination	Quantity Minted	VG	F	VF	EF
1670A, 5 Sols	200,000	800.	1,500.	2,400.	4,500.

Date and Denomination	Quantity Minted	VG	F	VF	EF
1670A, 15 Sols	40,000	15,000.	24,000.	40,000.	—

Reduced Silver Coinages of 1674 - 1709

In the late 17th and early 18th centuries the French government was in a rather precarious financial condition. As a money-raising scheme it struck seven coinages with reduced silver content (approximately .800 fine) at the same time as the regular .917 fine silver types were being produced. Most of the reduced fineness types were sent to New France in quantity.

4 SOLS ISSUES OF 1674-1677. By 1679 there were so many of these coins in circulation in New France that they were being used in payment by the bagful. An ordinance passed in that year lowered their value to 3 sols 6 deniers and placed strict limits on the quantity that could be used for any one payment.

Date and Denomination	VG	F	VF	EF
1674-1677, 4 Sols	25.	45.	80.	250.

4 SOLS ISSUES OF 1691-1700. This coin was the successor to the previous reduced silver 4-sol piece and was struck over it.

Date and Denomination	VG	F	VF	EF
1691-1700, 4 Sols	30.	50.	100.	200.

5 SOLS, 1702-1704. The next reduced silver coinage used in New France was a piece of approximately the same weight as the old 4-sol pieces, but which was called a 5-sol piece instead.

Date and Denomination	VG	F	VF	EF
1702-1704, 5 Sols, (27 mint marks)	15.	35.	65.	175.

10 SOLS, 1703-1708. This 10-sol piece is from the same series as the 5-sols.

Date and Denomination	VG	F	VF	EF
1703 to 1708, 10 Sols, (17 mint marks)	25.	50.	100.	250.

20 SOLS DE NAVARRE, 1719-1720. Twenty sols silver coins with the denomination shown as XX S were struck during an inflationary period, but were reduced to 18 sols by later edicts. They are the first of three coin types recognized by British authorities after the fall of New France as "French Ninepenny pieces". They circulated in Quebec and Nova Scotia.

Date and Denomination	VG	F	VF	EF
1719-1720, 20 Sols (29 different mint marks)	30.	75.	175.	350.

LIVRE OF 1720. In 1720, during the wild inflation brought about by the schemes of John Law, a special coin was produced in pure silver and issued at the over-valued rating of one livre. The Company of the Indies imported a quantity of these coins into French America in 1722. This is the second of three coin types known as the "French Ninepenny piece".

Date and Denomination	Quantity Minted	VG	F	VF	EF
1720A, Livre	6,918,583	75.	200.	400.	750.

SIXTH ECU DE FRANCE, 1720-1723. These coins were struck over the XX sols de Navarre of 1719-1720, and many show portions of the undertype. Their rating eventually settled at 18 sols, and they are the third of three types known collectively as "French ninepenny pieces."

Date and Denomination	VG	F	VF	EF
1720-1723, 1/6 Ecu (27 different mint marks)	25.	60.	175.	375.

SMALL SILVER LOUIS OF 1720. In 1720 a new coin called a small silver louis (petit louis d'argent) was brought into Canada. Its initial rating was 60 sols, but this was soon reduced to 40 sols.

Date and Denomination	F	VF	EF	AU
1720, Small Silver Louis	30.	90.	250.	350.

GOLD COINS

THE GOLD LOUIS. The only French gold coin to see significant circulation in French North America was the gold louis (louis d'or). Louis d'or were regularly sent over and saw use even after the Conquest. Any of the types struck between the 1640s and the 1750s potentially circulated here in quantity.

Type of 1680   Type of 1723-1725

Type and Denomination	VG	F	VF	EF
1643-1715, Louis d'or, Louis XIIII	300.	600.	900.	1,500.
1723-1725, Louis d'or, Louis VX, "mirlitons" (26 mint marks)	400.	750.	1,100.	1,700.
1726-1739, Louis d'or, Louis XV, "lunettes" (30 mint marks)	275.	400.	550.	900.

COINS OF GREAT BRITAIN

For most of the British colonial period (1760-1870) the British government was hardly better than the French government had been at supplying Imperial coins for use in Canada. British coinage was struck infrequently during the last half of the 18th century, and England and her colonies alike suffered from the lack of coin.

A major alteration took place in the British coinage in 1816. The silver coinage was reduced to a subsidiary status (along with the coppers) by lowering the amount of silver it contained to bring the bullion value of the coins below the face value. This left gold as the sole standard coinage and marks the beginning of the British gold standard. The coinage of silver was begun on a large scale and British coins gradually became more available. In 1825-1826 a serious attempt was made to establish Imperial coins as the principal coinage of the colonies and to drive out the Spanish-American coins. This attempt largely failed in British North America. Nevertheless, at various times some British coins did achieve a significant circulation here, particularly in Nova Scotia. That province came the closest to adopting sterling coinage: when it was decided to institute a decimal currency in 1859, the dollar was rated so as to allow the continued circulation of British coins. The 2-shilling piece (florin) became a 50-cent piece, the shilling became a 25-cent piece and so on. The halfpenny and shilling also saw much use in Upper and Lower Canada and later in the united Province of Canada.

COPPER COINS

Halfpenny

GEORGE II ISSUES. These coins, along with the George III halfpenny listed next, formed the most important part of the British North American copper currency until the War of 1812. After that time they were supplemented by the tokens issued by local merchants and others. Until the first bank tokens were issued, they formed the only copper currency sanctioned by the British government.

Halfpennies of the United Kingdom have a seated Britannia reverse, while Irish halfpennies have a harp reverse.

Date and Denomination	VG	F	VF	EF	AU	UNC
George II, 1740-1754, U.K. ½d	5.	9.	25.	120.	200.	400.
George II, 1736-1760, Irish ½d	6.	10.	30.	150.	250.	500.

GEORGE III ISSUES. The majority of the coins of this issue that circulated in both Great Britain and North America were contemporary counterfeits. Halfpennies issued during later reigns circulated to a lesser extent in British North America.

Genuine Issue

Typical Counterfeit

Date and Denomination	VG	F	VF	EF	AU	UNC
George III, 1770-1775, U.K. ½d, genuine	4.	7.	20.	100.	175.	300.
George III, 1770-1775, U.K. ½d, counterfeit	7.	17.	60.	200.	–	–
George III, 1766-1782, Irish ½d	5.	8.	25.	80.	150.	400.

Penny

COINAGE OF 1831. A special shipment of copper coins dated 1831 was sent to Canada in 1832. These could only be circulated at local currency rates, and consequently most were promptly returned to Britain at a profit. The penny was not at that time a frequently used denomination in British North America. Farthings of this issue were also struck for Canada (despite absence of demand for this denomination) but lost en route, together with part of the halfpence.

Date and Denomination	VG	F	VF	EF	AU	UNC
William IV, 1831, Penny	6.	15.	50.	150.	300.	600.
William IV, 1831, Halfpenny	4.	10.	20.	60.	115.	225.

SILVER COINS

British silver coins became more important in circulation in some parts of British North America after about 1830. The intermediate denominations were the most common.

Six Pence

Type and Denomination	VG	F	VF	EF	AU	UNC
William IV, Six Pence	4.	12.	40.	115.	165.	225.
Victoria (Young Head) 1838-1866 Six Pence	4.	8.	20.	85.	140.	200.

Shilling

Type and Denomination	VG	F	VF	EF	AU	UNC
William IV, Shilling	5.	15.	35.	140.	225.	350.
Victoria (Young Head) 1838-1863 Shilling	4.	11.	30.	115.	175.	275.

Florin

This denomination probably saw use in Nova Scotia during the 1850s and 1860s. In 1861 the florin, shilling and sixpence were imported into British Columbia.

Type and Denomination	VG	F	VF	EF	AU	UNC
Victoria (Gothic Head) 1851-1887 Florin*	7.	18.	60.	175.	300.	450.

*On these coins the date is on the obverse in the form of Roman numerals.

Halfcrown

Type and Denomination	VG	F	VF	EF	AU	UNC
George IV, Halfcrown (3 types)	12.	25.	50.	200.	300.	500.
William IV, Halfcrown	14.	30.	65.	250.	350.	600.
Victoria (Young Head), 1839-1850 Halfcrown	10.	22.	60.	235.	325.	550.

Bank of England Silver Tokens

The Bank of England issued captured Spanish-American dollars, restruck as five shilling/dollar pieces over the period 1804 to 1811 although all are dated 1804. The Bank also issued two types of three shilling and one shilling sixpence tokens. The Bank tokens were deficient in silver content in relation to sterling coin, and fell to their bullion value after a recall period. They continued to provide a substantial portion of the silver currency of Prince Edward Island, at enhanced ratings, until the 1840's.

Type and Denomination	VG	F	VF	EF	AU	UNC
George III, 5 shillings/dollar, 1804	70.	130.	240.	550.	800.	1,200.
George III, 3 shillings bank token, 1811-1816	14.	30.	60.	100.	150.	240.
George III, 1s6d bank token 1811-1816	10.	18.	42.	75.	110.	180.

GOLD COINS

GEORGE III ½ GUINEA. The ½ guinea was usually rated at 10 shillings 6 pence in Great Britain.

Type and Denomination	VG	F	VF	EF	AU	UNC
George III, ½ Guinea, 1787-1800	85.	165.	225.	350.	500.	750.

GEORGE III GUINEA, 1761-1813. The guinea or 21-shilling piece was one of the principal gold coins to circulate in British North America.

Type of 1765-1773

Type and Denomination	VG	F	VF	EF	AU	UNC
George III, Guinea	175.	200.	275.	550.	750.	1,000.

½ **SOVEREIGN.** The ½ sovereign was the successor to the ½ guinea and probably saw enough circulation in British North America and the Dominion of Canada to warrant its inclusion in this listing.

Type and Denomination	F	VF	EF	AU	UNC
George III, ½ Sovereign	100.	200.	500.	600.	800.
George IV, ½ Sovereign	140.	300.	700.	900.	1,100.
William IV, ½ Sovereign	150.	350.	800.	1,000.	1,400.
Victoria (Young Head), ½ Sovereign	100.	150.	250.	350.	500.

SOVEREIGN. The sovereign was perhaps the most widely used gold coin in Canada. It was used extensively by banks and the government for redeeming paper money right up to the 20th century.

Type and Denomination	F	VF	EF	AU	UNC
George III, Sovereign	200.	350.	750.	900.	1,200.
George IV, Sovereign	175.	300.	950.	1,100.	1,400.
William IV, Sovereign	175.	300.	1,000.	1,200.	1,600.
Victoria (Shield), Sovereign	BV	BV	225.	275.	400.

COINS OF PORTUGAL

During the 18th and early 19th centuries, several types of gold coins issued by Portugal found their way into British North America and were used extensively here.

MOIDORE. This coin had a denomination of 4,000 reis in Portugal and bore on its reverse the Cross of Jerusalem. It was struck from the reign of Alfonso VI (1656-1683) to the reign of John V (1706-1750).

Type and Denomination	VG	F	VF	EF
Alfonso VI to John V, Moidore	275.	375.	500.	800.

6,400 REIS (½ JOE). This coin, with a formal denomination of 6,400 reis, was introduced in the 1720's, along with a 12,800 reis coin of similar design. The king of Portugal at the time was John (Joao) V and from his name on the coins, Johannes V, came the nickname "Joe" for the 12,800 reis coin and "½ Joe" for the 6,400 reis coin. The "½ Joe" was also applied to the 6,400 reis coins issued in subsequent reigns. The larger coin was not issued in later reigns and "Joe" was eventually used for the 6,400 reis denomination.

Type and Denomination	VG	F	VF	EF
John V to John VI, 1706 - 1826 "½ Joe" (6,400 reis)	350.	450.	650.	1,000.

12,800 REIS (JOE). This was a coin of 12,800 reis issued during the reign of John V (see above).

Type and Denomination	VG	F	VF	EF
John V, "Joe" 1724 - 1732 (12,800 reis)	1,000.	2,000.	3,000.	5,000.

COINS OF SPAIN, SPANISH AMERICA
AND FORMER SPANISH COLONIES

This group of coins was more important in the currency history of what is now Canada for a longer period of time than any other foreign coinage. It was the Spanish-American dollar that served as the basis for the United States dollar, upon which in turn was based the decimal dollar of the Province of Canada in 1858.

COINS OF SPAIN

The Spanish metropolitan coinage is relatively unimportant compared with that of her New World colonies, excepting only the pistareen and, to a lesser extent, the half pistareen. These were nicknames given the reduced standard 2- and 1-real pieces minted only in Spain and which enjoyed wide circulation in British North America in the first half of the 19th century.

Type and Denomination	VG	F	VF	EF	AU
18th Century, Spanish Pistareen	35.	65.	90.	120.	200.
18th Century, Spanish Half Pistareen	50.	80.	110.	150.	250.

COINS OF SPANISH AMERICA

The coinage of Spain's colonies emanated from the following principal mints: Potosi in Bolivia, Santiago in Chile, Sante Fe do Bogota and Popayan in Colombia (Nueva Granada), Guatemala in Guatemala, Mexico City in Mexico and Lima and Cuzco in Peru. Minting of Spanish-American coins began in the early 16th century with the coins being of conventional round appearance. These were replaced about 1580 by the "cob" series: crude-appearing coins hand-struck on irregular blanks hewn from bars of refined bullion.

The cob series was finally superseded by round coins in 1732. The round gold issues bore the portrait of the reigning Spanish monarch from the first; however, the silver did not carry portraits until 1772. In the intervening 40 years the reverses featured the "two world" or "pillar" design, consisting of two crowned hemisphere between the crowned pillars of Hercules.

The Spanish-American series came to an end in the 1820's as Spain's colonies successfully revolted and became independent. Nevertheless, the Spanish-American coins had been minted in such great quantities that they continued to exert an important influence for decades. Probably the most important coinages for Canada are those struck under the rulers Charles III (1760-1788), Charles IV (1788-1808) and Ferdinand VII (1808-1821).

1 REAL

Type and Denomination	VG	F	VF	EF	AU
Philip V to Charles III, 1 Real, Pillar Type	10.	20.	50.	100.	250.
Charles III to Ferdinand VII, 1 Real, Bust Type	7.	15.	25.	85.	150.

2 REALES

Type and Denomination	VG	F	VF	EF	AU
Philip V to Charles III, 2 Reales, Pillar Type	20.	50.	80.	175.	325.
Charles III to Ferdinand VII, 2 Reales, Bust Type	10.	20.	40.	150.	250.

4 REALES

Type and Denomination	VG	F	VF	EF
Philip V to Charles III, 4 Reales, Pillar Type	150.	250.	450.	750.
Charles III to Ferdinand VII, 4 Reales, Bust Type	50.	80.	150.	500.

8 REALES. This is by far the most important foreign coin to circulate in Canada. It was known and appreciated all over the civilized world and was the principal end product of the vast amounts of silver mined in the New World. The 8-real piece had the nickname dollar (even though it was not a decimal coin) due to its similarity in size to the European thalers and daalders. It is the famous "piece-of-eight" of pirate lore. The first 8-real pieces were produced in 1556 at the Mexico City mint.

Type and Denomination	VG	F	VF	EF
Philip V to Charles III, 8 Reales (Dollar), Pillar Type	100.	150.	300.	450.
Charles III to Ferdinand VII, 8 Reales, Bust Type	35.	55.	80.	175.

GOLD COINS

2 ESCUDOS. This gold coin was popularly known as the Spanish pistole and, next to the doubloon (see below), was the most widely used Spanish-American gold coin in Canada.

Type and Denomination	VG	F	VF	EF
Charles III to Ferdinand VII, 2 Escudos	200.	400.	550.	1,000.

4 ESCUDOS

Type and Denomination	VG	F	VF	EF
Charles III to Ferdinand VII, 4 Escudos	450.	750.	1,200.	2,000.

8 ESCUDOS (DOUBLOON). The most important gold coin in Canada was the 8-escudo piece or doubloon. It circulated widely, but was especially popular in the Atlantic provinces. After the Spanish colonies gained their independence, these coins were called "Royal" doubloons (as opposed to "Patriot" doubloons discussed below).

Type and Denomination	VG	F	VF	EF
Charles III to Ferdinand VII, 8 Escudos (Doubloon)	600.	700.	1,000.	1,500.

COINS OF FORMER SPANISH COLONIES

By 1826 Spain had lost all her colonies in the New World. This ushered in new coinages on the existing standards by each of the former colonies. They were accepted and circulated alongside the coins of the Spanish-American series. Probably only two denominations are necessary in this listing – the silver dollar and the gold doubloon.

8 REALES (DOLLAR). The most important dollars of former Spanish colonies to circulate in Canada are undoubtedly those of Mexico.

Type and Denomination	VG	F	VF	EF	AU	UNC
1820s to 1840s, Mexican 8 Reales (Dollar)	20.	30.	50.	90.	150.	200.

8 ESCUDOS (DOUBLOON). In the case of the doubloon it is more difficult to single out any one former colony's coinage as being the most important for Canada. Therefore a general listing is given. Contemporary sources refer to such doubloons as "Patriot" doubloons to distinguish them for the "Royal" doubloons of the Spanish-American series. It is known that "Patriot" doubloons were specifically imported into such provinces as Nova Scotia.

Typical "Patriot" Doubloon from Chile

Type and Denomination	VG	F	VF	EF	AU	UNC
1817- 1830s, "Patriot" 8 Escudos (Doubloon)	450.	500.	650.	1,000.	2,000.	—

COINS OF THE UNITED STATES

It is to the United States coinage that we owe our present decimal currency system. By the 1850s trade links between British North America and the U.S. were so strong and her coinage so commonplace here that the proponents of a currency akin to that of the U.S. instead of Great Britain prevailed.

The U.S. coinage on a decimal basis began in the 1790s and it has circulated here to varying degrees ever since. A great influx of U.S. silver coins took place during the 1850s and 1860s, after the proportion of silver contained in the 5-, 10-, 25- and 50-cent pieces was reduced. Previous to that time, U.S. large cents came across the border in quantity and large numbers of half dollars were imported to help pay for work on such projects as the Rideau Canal. The larger denominations of U.S. gold coins were important in Canada well into the twentieth century because they were widely imported by banks and the government for use in backing and redeeming paper money.

COPPER COINS

ONE CENT

Many varieties exist in the size of letters, placement of letters, and the size of date and number of stars.

Type and Denomination	VG	F	VF	EF	AU	UNC
1816-1836, Coronet Head	24.	36.	80.	175.	300.	450.
1837-1857, Braided Hair	20.	24.	32.	70.	160.	275.

SILVER COINS

HALF DIME – CAPPED BUST

Type and Denomination	VG	F	VF	EF	AU	UNC
1829-1837	40.	45.	85.	150.	275.	400.

HALF DIME – SEATED LIBERTY

Type and Denomination	VG	F	VF	EF	AU	UNC
1837-1838, No stars on obverse	45.	70.	135.	250.	500.	800.
1838-1859, Stars on obverse	15.	18.	25.	45.	150.	200.
1853-1855, Arrows at date	13.	15.	25.	60.	150.	250.
1860-1873, Legend on obverse	15.	18.	25.	40.	90.	175.

DIME – CAPPED BUST

Type and Denomination	VG	F	VF	EF	AU	UNC
1809-1837	23.	30.	80.	250.	475.	800.

DIME – SEATED LIBERTY

Type and Denomination	VG	F	VF	EF	AU	UNC
1837-1838, No stars on obverse	50.	100.	400.	700.	1,000.	1,500.
1838-1853, Stars on obverse	15.	18.	25.	60.	150.	400.
1853-1855, Arrows at date	13.	15.	20.	60.	160.	450.
1856-1860, Stars on obverse	13.	15.	24.	50.	150.	350.
1860-1873, Legend on obverse	15.	16.	27.	50.	100.	200.

QUARTER DOLLAR – CAPPED BUST

Type and Denomination	VG	F	VF	EF	AU	UNC
1815-1828, Motto over eagle	90.	135.	350.	850.	1,500.	2,500.
1831-1838, No motto	60.	70.	115.	300.	800.	1,050.

QUARTER DOLLAR – SEATED LIBERTY

Type and Denomination	VG	F	VF	EF	AU	UNC
1838-1853	25.	35.	50.	80.	250.	650.
1853, Rays around eagle	25.	35.	60.	200.	375.	1,250.
1854-1855, Arrow at date, no rays around eagle	25.	35.	50.	100.	300.	600.
1856-1865, No motto above eagle	25.	35.	50.	80.	200.	400.
1866-1873, Motto above eagle	55.	110.	145.	200.	300.	600.

HALF DOLLAR – CAPPED BUST

Type and Denomination	VG	F	VF	EF	AU	UNC
1807-1836, many minor varieties	50.	55.	65.	110.	275.	675.
1836-1837, "50 CENTS"	50.	55.	100.	160.	450.	1,000.
1838-1839, "HALF DOL."	50.	55.	100.	160.	500.	1,100.

HALF DOLLAR – SEATED LIBERTY

Type and Denomination	VG	F	VF	EF	AU	UNC
1839-1853, No motto above eagle	35.	55.	65.	140.	250.	500.
1853, Arrows at date; Rays around eagle	40.	60.	125.	300.	650.	2,000.
1854-1855, Arrows at date; No rays around eagle	30.	45.	70.	135.	360.	700.
1856-1866, No motto above eagle	25.	40.	60.	100.	200.	475.
1866-1873, "IN GOD WE TRUST" above eagle	35.	55.	65.	100.	200.	475.

GOLD COINS

FIVE DOLLARS - HALF EAGLE

Type and Denomination	F	VF	EF	AU	UNC
1834-1838, Classic Head	325.	400.	600.	1,000.	3,500.
1839-1866, Coronet Head	225.	275.	300.	400.	1,700.
1866-1908	200.	220.	230.	250.	350.

TEN DOLLARS - EAGLE

Type and Denomination	F	VF	EF	AU	UNC
1838-1865, Coronet Head 2 Varieties	325.	400.	500.	750.	5,000.
1866-1907	280.	310.	325.	350.	400.

TWENTY DOLLARS - DOUBLE EAGLE

Type and Denomination	F	VF	EF	AU	UNC
1849-1866, Coronet Head 3 Varieties	600.	750.	875.	1,100.	4,100.
1866-1876	600.	625.	650.	750.	1,150.
1877-1907	575.	600.	625.	650.	700.

LOCAL PRE-DECIMAL COINS

Although it is sometimes stated that the first coins produced for local use in Canada were the 1858-1859 decimal coins for the Province of Canada, this is not the case. A small but important group of local coinages was produced prior to the adoption of decimal currency. These coinages were at first specially modified Spanish-American silver coins, but coppers were added to this group in the 1850s.

NEW FRANCE (FRENCH REGIME)

COUNTERSTAMPED SPANISH-AMERICAN COINS

During the last part of the 17th century, the quantity of Spanish-American silver coins in circulation in New France increased. This increase was due primarily to the illegal trade in furs which the colonists were carrying on with the Dutch and English. At that time such coins circulated at a value that depended upon their weight; the more worn the coin was, the lower it was valued compared to unworn pieces. Since many Spanish-American coins in New France had varying amounts of wear, their use in commerce was difficult. Colonial authorities were not anxious to see these coins used in preference to French coins, but the latter were so scarce that they relented. In the early 1680s treasury officials weighed a quantity of these coins and counterstamped each with a fleur-de-lis. Underweight coins also received a Roman numeral counterstamp (from I to IV) to indicate the amount by which the weight was deficient. The coins could then be compared to a table to determine the exact value at which they were current.

Unfortunately for collectors, no surviving examples of this interesting local issue are known.

NOVA SCOTIA, NEW BRUNSWICK, PRINCE EDWARD ISLAND

For the pre-decimal coinage of Colonial New Brunswick, Nova Scotia and Prince Edward Island, see the 'Charlton Standard Catalogue of Canadian Colonial Tokens.'

HISTORY OF CANADIAN DECIMAL COINS

The decimal coins which we take so much for granted today have a history that stretches back into the last century and beyond. During the 1700s, the single most important coin in North America was the Spanish-American dollar, a large silver coin produced in great quantities by mints in Mexico, Peru and other parts of the New World. The Spanish- American dollar was not a decimal coin; its formal denomination was 8 reales. It was nicknamed dollar in deference to its resemblance in size to German thalers and other large European coins of similar name. This Spanish-American coin was so important in the United States that when the U.S. adopted a decimal system of dollars and cents in the 1790s, their silver dollar was made with the same amount of silver as the Spanish-American dollar.

In British North America in the first half of the 19th century each colony used a system of accounting which consisted of pounds, shillings and pence. However, the coins actually in circulation were mostly Spanish-American and U.S. As trade with the United States increased in the 1840s and 1850s, the British North American colonies (provinces) were naturally drawn toward the adoption of a currency system more like that of the U.S. than Great Britain.

All through the 1850s British North America struggled with the problem of currency standards. The Province of Canada, under Francis Hincks, took the lead in fighting for a decimal system. Acts passed in 1851 and 1853 stipulated that public accounts be kept in dollars and cents, but no coins were issued under their provisions. An 1857 act provided a broader base for a decimal currency system. It directed that both government and private accounts be kept in dollars, cents and mills. A decimal coinage followed in 1858-1859, based upon a dollar equal to the U.S. gold dollar.

Other British North American provinces soon followed the Province of Canada's lead. New Brunswick and Nova Scotia adopted decimal systems in 1859-1860, Newfoundland followed suit in 1864 and Prince Edward Island went decimal in 1871. Thus, even before Confederation the use of decimal coins was firmly established.

NOVA SCOTIA

In the years immediately preceding the adoption of a decimal currency system in Nova Scotia in 1859, British coins formed an important part of the circulating currency, much more so than in the other British North American provinces. Consequently, the Nova Scotia government chose a decimal dollar equal to one-fifth of a pound sterling (i.e. $5 = £1), allowing British silver coins to conveniently fit into the new system and continue circulating. The British 2-shilling piece (florin) became a 50-cent piece, the shilling became a 25-cent piece and the sixpence became a 12 1/2-cent piece. The only coins the province needed to have specially produced were a cent, and to make change for the sixpence and half crown, a half cent.

HALF CENT
Victoria 1861 - 1864

The half cent was coined with the same diameter as the British farthing and utilized the same obverse. Pattern pieces incorporated the royal crown and a wreath of roses (see NS-1 to NS-3 and NS-5 in the chapter on Patterns). However, a local campaign in favour of the provincial flower, the mayflower, resulted in the adoption of a design using the royal crown surrounded by a wreath of both roses and mayflowers.

LAUREATED PORTRAIT, 1861-1864.

Designer and Engraver:
  Obv.: Leonard C. Wyon
  Rev.: Leonard C. Wyon
      from a model by C. Hill
Composition: .95 copper, .04 tin, .01 zinc
Weight: 2.84 grams
Diameter: 20.65 mm
Edge: Plain
Die Axis: ↑↑

Date and Mint Mark	Mintage	VG-8	F-12	VF-20	EF-40	AU-50	MS-60 Br	MS-63 Rd/Br	MS-65 Rd
1861	400,000	7.	10.	15.	25.	50.	75.	250.	5,000.
1864	400,000	7.	10.	15.	25.	60.	100.	225.	—

Note: Br = Brown; Rd/Br = Red/Brown; Rd = Red

ONE CENT
Victoria 1861 - 1864

The cent was minted with the same diameter as the British halfpenny and used the same obverse. The reverse designs are similar to those used for the half cent, including pattern pieces with a wreath of roses (see NS-4 and NS-6 in the chapter on Patterns).

The circulation issues of this denomination have two distinct reverses. The first (1861) has much detail in the crown and a large rosebud at the lower right part of the wreath. On the second reverse (1861-1864) the crown has a narrower headband and generally less detail, the rosebud at the lower right is smaller, and the rosebud and certain other parts of the design come closer to the lettering and the raised line just inside the rim denticles.

MINTAGE FIGURES, 1861-1862. The mintage figures of 800,000 for 1861 and 1,000,000 for 1862 have puzzled collectors for many years since the 1862-dated coins are scarcer. The probable explanation is that some, perhaps most, cents struck in 1862 were from dies dated 1861. Therefore, the mintages for the two years have been combined.

LAUREATED PORTRAIT, 1861-1862.

Designer and Engraver:
   Obv.: Leonard C. Wyon
   Rev.: Leonard C. Wyon
          from a model by C. Hill
Composition: .95 copper, .04 tin, .01 zinc
Weight: 5.67 grams
Diameter: 25.53 mm
Edge: Plain
Die Axis: ↑↑

| Large Rosebud | Small Rosebud |

Date and Mint Mark	Mintage	VG-8	F-12	VF-20	EF-40	AU-50	MS-60 Br	MS-63 Rd/Br	Ms-65 Rd
1861 Large bud	1,800,000	5.	7.	10.	25.	60.	150.	250.	–
1861 Small bud	Included	5.	7.	15.	40.	70.	175.	400.	5,000.
1862	Included	65.	95.	200.	300.	400.	4,000.	–	–
1864	800,000	5.	7.	10.	25.	60.	225.	750.	–

*Most of the cents issued in 1862 were dated 1861.

NEW BRUNSWICK

When New Brunswick adopted a decimal dollar in 1860, it chose the same rating for its dollar and ordered the same denominations as the Province of Canada: cents in bronze and 5-, 10- and 20-cent pieces in silver. The effective date for the decimal currency act was November 1, 1860 but, like Nova Scotia, New Brunswick had to wait until early 1862 before the first coins arrived from England. In the meantime, the government introduced other decimal coins as a temporary expedient. Thus, in late 1861 and early 1862 some 500,000 Province of Canada cents and a quantity of United States small denomination silver coins were put into circulation in the province.

HALF CENT
Victoria 1861

This denomination was not required by the province since its dollar and hence British coins went at a different rating than in the sister province of Nova Scotia. Nevertheless, the Royal Mint became confused and struck a half cent for New Brunswick. Over 200,000 of these coins came off the presses before the error was discovered. Most of the mintage was returned to the melting pot. The circulation strikes that survived are thought to have become mixed with the Nova Scotia half cents and sent to Halifax.

The obverse is that of the British farthing and the reverse is a royal crown and a rose/mayflower wreath very similar to that used for Nova Scotia.

LAUREATED PORTRAIT, 1861.

Designer and Engraver:
    Obv.: Leonard C. Wyon
    Rev.: Leonard C. Wyon
              from a model by C. Hill
Composition: .95 copper, .04 tin, .01 zinc
Weight: 2.84 grams
Diameter: 20.65 mm
Edge: Plain
Die Axis: ↑↑

Date and Mint Mark	Mintage	VG-8	F-12	VF-20	EF-40	AU-50	MS-60 Br	MS-63 Rd/Br	MS-65 Rd
1861	222,800*	150.	200.	300.	400.	500.	800.	2,000.	—

*most were melted prior to issue.

Note: Br = Brown; Rd/Br = Red/Brown; Rd = Red

ONE CENT Victoria
1861 - 1864

The New Brunswick 1-cent pieces have the British halfpenny obverse and a reverse similar to that used for the Nova Scotia cent.

For the 1864 issue two styles of 6 were used in the date: a figure with a round centre in its loop and a short top, and a figure with a more oval centre and a longer top.

LAUREATED PORTRAIT, 1861-1864.

Designer and Engraver:
Obv.: Leonard C. Wyon
Rev.: Leonard C. Wyon
from a model by C. Hill
Composition: .95 copper, .04 tin, .01 zinc
Weight: 5.67 grams
Diameter: 25.53 mm
Edge: Plain
Die Axis: ↑↑

Short 6

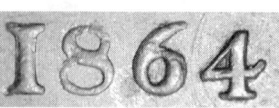

Tall 6

Date and Mint Mark	Mintage	VG-8	F-12	VF-20	EF-40	AU-50	MS-60 Br	MS-63 Rd/Br	MS-65 Rd
1861	1,000,000	6.	8.	18.	30.	60.	175.	450.	5,000.
1864 Short 6	1,000,000	6.	9.	15.	35.	85.	250.	500.	–
1864 Tall 6	Included	7.	10.	18.	35.	75.	275.	600.	–

FIVE CENTS
Victoria 1862 - 1864

The production of New Brunswick's first silver decimal coinage had to await the completion of the bronze coinage. Consequently, it could not commence until 1862. The 5-cent piece designs were basically those of the Province of Canada with an appropriately modified obverse legend. Two styles of 6 were employed in dating the 1864 issue: a small 6 and a large 6.

LAUREATED PORTRAIT, 1862-1864.

Engraver: Obv.: Leonard C. Wyon
Composition: .925 silver, .075 copper
Weight: 1.16 grams
Diameter: 15.49 mm
Edge: Reeded
Die Axis: ↑↓

Small 6   Large 6

Date and Mint Mark	Mintage	VG-8	F-12	VF-20	EF-40	AU-50	MS-60	MS-63	MS-65
1862	100,000	75.	150.	250.	550.	1,500.	3,250.	–	–
1864 Small 6	100,000	100.	150.	250.	500.	1,000.	–	–	–
1864 Large 6	Included	150.	250.	500.	1,000.	2,000.	–	–	–

TEN CENTS
Victoria 1862 - 1864

The designs for the New Brunswick 10-cent piece were adapted from existing Province of Canada designs. The reverse was used without modification and the obverse involved changing the legend only.

The 1862 issue is usually collected as two varieties. One has a normal date and the other has an obviously double-punched 2.

LAUREATED PORTRAIT, 1862-1864.

Engraver: Obv.: Leonard C. Wyon
Composition: .925 silver, .075 copper
Weight: 2.32 grams
Diameter: 17.91 mm
Edge: Reeded
Die Axis: ↑↓

Normal Date   Double-punched 2

Date and Mint Mark	Mintage	VG-8	F-12	VF-20	EF-40	AU-50	MS-60	MS-63	MS-65
1862	150,000	75.	150.	300.	600.	1,200.	2,500.	5,000.	13,500.
1862 D-P 2	Included	100.	200.	500.	1,000.	2,000.	–	10,000.	–
1864	150,000	75.	125.	250.	650.	1,250.	–	–	–

TWENTY CENTS
Victoria 1862 - 1864

The New Brunswick 20-cent piece has an unusual reverse design once rejected for the Province of Canada (see PC-4 in the chapter on Patterns). The reverse adopted by the Province of Canada differs in style from that chosen by New Brunswick, while using the same elements. This stylistic difference, plus the fact a die for the New Brunswick 20-cent piece of 1862 was used to strike one side of George W. Wyon's obituary medalet, suggests that it was George Wyon and not Leonard Wyon who engraved this reverse. The obverse utilizes the Province of Canada 20 cents portrait with a special legend for New Brunswick.

LAUREATED PORTRAIT, 1862-1864.

Designer:
  Obv.: Leonard C. Wyon
Engraver:
  Obv. Leonard C. Wyon
  Rev.: Possibly Geo. W. Wyon
Composition: .925 silver, .075 copper
Weight: 4.65 grams
Diameter: 23.27 mm
Edge: Reeded
Die Axis: ↑↓

Date and Mint Mark	Mintage	VG-8	F-12	VF-20	EF-40	AU-50	MS-60	MS-63	MS-65
1862	150,000	25.	45.	100.	300.	500.	2,000.	6,000.	−
1864	150,000	30.	50.	90.	250.	1,250.	2,500.	4,500.	−

PRINCE EDWARD ISLAND

ONE CENT
Victoria 1871

Prince Edward Island adopted a decimal currency system in 1871. Its dollar was given the same rating as those of the provinces of Canada and New Brunswick. The only coinage in the new system was bronze cents in 1871. The island entered Confederation two years later. The provincial government experienced considerable difficulty placing its cents in circulation. It took almost ten years to deplete the stock and the last of it was sold at a 10 percent discount.

The reverse was prepared specifically for the Prince Edward Island government, incorporating the seal of the island and a Latin phrase, "PARVA SUB INGENTI," meaning "The small beneath the great." The seal shows a large oak tree, representing England, sheltering three young oak trees, representing the three counties on the island.

Because of pressure to produce domestic coin, the Royal Mint in London made arrangements with Heaton's Mint in Birmingham to strike P.E.I. cents. For some unknown reason Heaton's familiar "H" mint mark is absent from the coins.

LAUREATED PORTRAIT, 1871.

Designer and Engraver:
Obv.: Leonard C. Wyon, from a portrait model by Wm. Theed
Rev.: Leonard C. Wyon
Composition: .95 copper, .04 tin, .01 zinc
Weight: 5.67 grams
Diameter: 25.40 mm
Edge: Plain
Die Axis: ↑↑, ↑↓

Date and Mint Mark	Mintage	VG-8	F-12	VF-20	EF-40	AU-50	MS-60 Br	MS-63 Rd/Br	MS-65 Rd
1871 Medal	2,000,000	3.	5.	10.	20.	55.	125.	175.	650.
1871 Coinage	Included	4.	6.	12.	25.	65.	150.	225.	750.

Note: Br = Brown; Rd/Br = Red/Brown; Rd = Red

NEWFOUNDLAND

Since Newfoundland remained separate from Canada until 1949, it has a much larger decimal coin series than the other pre-Confederation British colonies. The island adopted decimal currency in 1863, hoping to have coins on the new standard in circulation in 1864. The most important coin in Newfoundland had been the Spanish-American dollar or 8-real piece, so the government set its dollar equal in value to this coin. This made the new decimal cent equal to the British halfpenny and $4.80 equal to £1 sterling.

ONE CENT
Victoria 1865 - 1896

Beginning in 1864, several designs were considered for the Newfoundland cent. The first tendency was to use the same designs as New Brunswick. Pattern dies are known for an 1864 Newfoundland cent with the royal crown, rose/mayflower design (see NF-1 in the chapter on Patterns). This design was rejected in favour of a royal crown and wreath of pitcher plant (the provincial flower) and oak, with unusual broad, bold lettering and date. The obverse incorporated the British halfpenny portrait with the legend "VICTORIA QUEEN," also in the same bold type (see NF-6 in the chapter on Patterns). However, it was decided that this legend was inappropriate and the cents struck for circulation in 1865 used the obverse legend "VICTORIA D:G:REG:."

An interesting variation in die axes occurs on this denomination. For all dates except 1872 the dies are in the medal arrangement (↑↑) but on the 1872s they are coinage arrangement (↑↓). The most reasonable explanation for this difference is that the Heaton Mint, which struck the 1872 cents, did not receive specific instructions regarding which die arrangement to use and chose the same arrangement as for the silver. The error was corrected in 1876 when Heaton's next coined cents for Newfoundland.

LAUREATED PORTRAIT, 1865-1876.

Designers:
    Obv.: Leonard C. Wyon
    Rev.: Horace Morehen
Engraver:
    Rev.: Thomas J. Minton
Composition: .95 copper, .04 tin, .01 zinc
Weight: 5.67 grams
Diameter: 25.53 mm
Edge: Plain
Die Axis:
    1865, 1873-1896: ↑↑
    1872: ↑↓

Heaton Mint issues have an "H" mint mark at the bottom of the wreath (1872, 1876). Royal Mint strikings have no mint mark.

Date and Mint Mark	Mintage	VG-8	F-12	VF-20	EF-40	AU-50	MS-60 Br	MS-63 Rd/Br	MS-65 Rd
1865	240,000	6.	7.	15.	30.	150.	300.	700.	4,000.
1872H	200,000	4.	7.	12.	35.	75.	125.	225.	600.
1873	200,000	6.	10.	25.	80.	225.	625.	2,000.	–
1876H	200,000	5.	12.	20.	80.	225.	500.	1,000.	–

Note: Br = Brown; Rd/Br = Red/Brown; Rd = Red

VARIETIES OF 1880. Three date varieties exist for 1880. The first has a narrow 0 in the date, while the second and third have a wide 0, in different positions.

1880 Narrow O   1880 Wide O

Date and Mint Mark	Mintage	VG-8	F-12	VF-20	EF-40	AU-50	MS-60 Br	MS-63 Rd/Br	MS-65 Rd
1880 Narrow 0	400,000	250.	400.	650.	1,000.	1,500.	3,000.	–	–
1880 Wide, Low 0	Included	5.	7.	15.	40.	90.	–	–	–
1880 Wide 0	Included	4.	15.	35.	100.	275.	250.	500.	–
1885	40,000	50.	95.	135.	275.	550.	–	2,500.	–
1888	50,000	60.	100.	125.	300.	500.	–	4,000.	–
1890	200,000	5.	15.	25.	75.	250.	700.	1,500.	–
1894	200,000	5.	10.	18.	40.	175.	300.	900.	–
1896	200,000	5.	7.	14.	30.	100.	200.	500.	3,000.

Note: A dash (–) in a pricing column indicates no coin has been assigned that grade.

ONE CENT
Edward VII 1904 - 1909

The reverse design is a modification of the Victorian reverse, substituting the Imperial State crown for the St. Edward's crown. The obverses of most Edward VII denominations were those of the corresponding Dominion of Canada coinage; however, the Newfoundland cent has a distinctive design. The bust is very large and the letter size in the legend correspondingly small.

CROWNED PORTRAIT, 1904-1909.

Designer and Engraver:
    Obv.: G. W. DeSaulles
Engraver:
    Rev.: W. H. J. Blakemore modifying existing coinage tools
Composition: .95 copper, .04 tin, .01 zinc
Weight: 5.67 grams
Diameter: 25.53 mm
Edge: Plain
Die Axis: ↑↑
The Birmingham Mint issue (1904 only) has an "H" mint mark at the bottom of the wreath. Royal Mint strikings have no mint mark.

Date and Mint Mark	Mintage	VG-8	F-12	VF-20	EF-40	AU-50	MS-60 Br	MS-63 Rd/Br	MS-65 Rd
1904H	100,000	10.	18.	40.	75.	200.	500.	1,000.	–
1907	200,000	3.	6.	10.	40.	150.	300.	700.	4,000.
1909	200,000	3.	6.	10.	30.	75.	150.	225.	600.

ONE CENT
George V 1913 - 1936

The reverse for the cents of this reign is that established for the Edward VII series and the obverse is that of the Dominion of Canada cents.

CROWNED PORTRAIT, 1913-1936.

Designer and Engraver:
Obv.: Sir E. B. MacKennal
Composition:
1913-1920: .95 copper, .04 tin, .01 zinc
1926-1936: .955 copper, .030 tin, .015 zinc
Diameter:
1913,1929-1936: 25.53 mm
1917-1920: 25.40 mm
Edge: Plain
Die Axis:↑↑1913,1929-1936

Ottawa Mint issues (1917-1920) have a "C" mint mark at the bottom of the wreath, Royal Mint strikings have no mint mark.

Date and Mint Mark	Mintage	VG-8	F-12	VF-20	EF-40	AU-50	MS-60 Br	MS-63 Rd/Br	MS-65 Rd
1913	400,000	3.	4.	5.	10.	40.	60.	85.	400.
1917C	702,350	3.	4.	5.	10.	40.	125.	400.	2,500.
1919C	300,000	3.	4.	5.	15.	60.	300.	800.	−
1920C	302,184	3.	4.	8.	20.	75.	450.	1,250.	−
1929	300,000	3.	4.	5.	8.	35.	75.	150.	750.
1936	300,000	3.	4.	5.	6.	20.	40.	100.	300.

Note: Br = Brown; Rd/Br = Red/Brown; Rd = Red

ONE CENT
George VI 1938 - 1947

In 1937 the Newfoundland government reviewed the question of converting to a small cent, similar to those used in Canada and the United States. The smaller coin was less expensive to produce and Newfoundlanders objected to the reverse design of the large cent, in which their provincial flower was forced into an unnatural configuration.

The reverse design adopted for the new coins was a very lifelike rendition of the pitcher plant in bloom. The plant is native to Newfoundland, and is one of the insectivores of the plant kingdom. The large leaves are pitcher-like receptacles, the inner surfaces being covered with downward-sloping bristles. Insects are attracted onto their leaves by a sweet sticky syrup at the bottom and the bristles help prevent their escape. The digestible portions of the insects are then absorbed by the plant.

During World War II, Newfoundland cents were coined at Ottawa rather than in England to avoid the risks of transatlantic shipping. In 1940 and 1942 the "C" mint mark was omitted in error.

CROWNED PORTRAIT, 1938-1947.

Designer and Engraver:
   Obv.: Percy Metcalfe
   Rev.: Walter J. Newman
Composition: .955 copper, .030 tin,
        .015 zinc
Weight: 3.24 grams
Diameter: 19.05 mm
Edge: Plain
Die Axis: ↑↑

Royal Canadian Mint issues (1940-47) have a "C" mint mark to the right of CENT on the reverse (except for the 1940 and 1942 issues, which have none). The Royal Mint issue (1938) has no mint mark.

Date and Mint Mark	Mintage	VG-8	F-12	VF-20	EF-40	AU-50	MS-60 Br	MS-63 Rd/Br	MS-65 Rd
1938	500,000	1.	1.	2.	4.	10.	30.	75.	500.
1940	300,000	2.	3.	5.	18.	60.	75.	150.	500.
1940 Re	Included	45.	65.	80.	150.	300.	750.	–	–
1941C	827,662	1.	1.	1.	3.	10.	30.	125.	–
1941C DD	Included	15.	25.	40.	100.	200.	300.	600.	–
1942	1,996,889	1.	1.	1.	3.	15.	45.	150.	–
1943C	1,239,732	1.	1.	1.	3.	10.	35.	125.	–
1944C	1,328,776	2.	3.	18.	35.	100.	200.	–	–
1947C	313,772	1.	2.	8.	23.	35.	150.	300.	–

FIVE CENTS
Victoria 1865 - 1896

Work on the coinage tools for the silver began later than for the cent, so there are no legend wording varieties for this denomination. The first pattern is a bronze striking of the adopted obverse (derived from the New Brunswick obverse by substitution of "NEWFOUNDLAND" for "NEW BRUNSWICK") and the Canada/New Brunswick reverse with a maple wreath and royal crown (see NF-2 in the chapter on Patterns). A later pattern, in silver, has an arabesque design similar to the adopted design, except the arches are thinner (see NF-8 in the chapter on Patterns).

VICTORIA OBVERSE PORTRAIT VARIETIES

PORTRAIT: NF1
Two well defined strands of hair at top of brow, below top leaf of laurel crown. **Dot before and after Newfoundland on obverse.**

NF-1 will be found on the following dates: 1865; 1870; 1873

PORTRAIT: NF2
Two weakly defined strands of hair at top of brow, below top leaf of laurel crown. **No dot before and after Newfoundland on obverse:**

NF2 will be found on the following dates: 1865; 1870; 1872H; 1873; 1873H; 1876H; 1880; 1881; 1885; 1888

VICTORIA OBVERSE PORTRAIT VARIETIES

PORTRAIT: NF3
Three well defined strands of hair at top
of brow, below top leaf of laurel crown.
Dot after Newfoundland on obverse:

NF3 will be found on the following dates:
1882H; 1888; 1890; 1894; 1896

VICTORIA REVERSE VARIETIES

There are no major reverse varieties for the five cent silver coins. There is however a variation in the punch numbers used between 1865 and the balance of the issue: 1865 has a Roman numeral I in the date, while 1870 to 1896 has an Arabic 1 in the date.

LAUREATED PORTRAIT, 1865-1896.

Designer and Engraver:
    Obv.: Leonard C. Wyon
    Rev.: Leonard C. Wyon
Composition: .925 silver, .075 copper
Weight: 1.18 grams
Diameter: 15.49 mm
Edge: Reeded
Die Axis: ↑↓

Heaton Mint issues have an "H" mint mark either on the obverse under the bust (1872-1876), or on the reverse under the date (1882). Royal Mint strikings have no mint mark.

Date, Mint Portrait	Mintage	VG-8	F-12	VF-20	EF-40	AU-50	MS-60	MS-63	MS-65
1865, NF1	80,000	55.	100.	300.	375.	–	–	–	–
1865, NF2	Included	–	–	–	–	–	–	–	–
1870, NF1	40,000	100.	175.	300.	800.	–	–	–	–
1870, NF2	Included	–	–	–	–	–	–	–	–
1872H, NF2	40,000	50.	100.	175.	350.	700.	–	–	–
1873, NF1	40,000	–	–	–	–	–	–	–	–
1873, NF2	Included	125.	250.	700.	–	–	–	–	–
1873H, NF2	Included	1,200.	1,800.	3,500.	6,000.	–	–	–	–
1876H, NF2	20,000	150.	300.	400.	750.	–	–	–	–
1880, NF2	40,000	60.	125.	250.	400.	1,000.	–	–	–
1881, NF2	40,000	60.	125.	250.	650.	1,300.	–	–	8,500.
1882H, NF3	60,000	35.	50.	125.	250.	500.	1,500.	3,000.	–
1885, NF2	16,000	300.	400.	550.	1,200.	2,000.	–	–	–
1888, NF2	40,000	–	–	–	–	–	–	–	–
1888, NF3	Included	80.	200.	350.	–	–	–	–	–
1890, NF3	160,000	15.	30.	75.	175.	600.	1,750.	–	–
1894, NF3	160,000	15.	30.	65.	150.	500.	1,750.	–	–
1896, NF3	400,000	7.	14.	35.	100.	450.	1,500.	3,000.	–

Note: For a coin in Good-4 (G-4) condition, use as an indication 50% of the Very Good-8 (VG-8) price.

FIVE CENTS
Edward VII 1903 - 1908

The obverse for this denomination is that of the Dominion of Canada issues. The reverse, a new design by George W. DeSaulles, is one of the last coinage designs he did before his death.

CROWNED PORTRAIT, 1903-1908.

Designer and Engraver:
    George W. DeSaulles
Composition: .925 silver, .075 copper
Weight: 1.18 grams
Diameter: 15.49 mm
Edge: Reeded
Die Axis: ↑↓

The Birmingham Mint issue of 1904 has an "H" mint mark below the oval at the bottom on the reverse. Royal Mint issues have no mint mark.

Date and Mint Mark	Mintage	VG-8	F-12	VF-20	EF-40	AU-50	MS-60	MS-63	MS-65
1903	100,000	6.	12.	35.	85.	300.	750.	2,000.	–
1904H	100,000	4.	8.	25.	60.	150.	250.	400.	800.
1908	400,000	6.	10.	25.	65.	175.	350.	850.	–

Note: A dash (–) in a pricing column indicates no coin has been assigned that grade.

FIVE CENTS
George V 1912 - 1929

The obverse is the same as for the Dominion of Canada issue and the reverse is the same as the Newfoundland Edward VII issue.

CROWNED PORTRAIT, 1912-1929.

Designer and Engraver:
Obv.: Sir E. B. MacKennal
Rev.: George W. DeSaulles
Composition: .925 silver, .075 copper
Weight:
1912: 1.18 grams
1917-1929: 1.17 grams
Diameter:
1912-1919: 15.49 mm
1929: 15.69 mm
Edge: Reeded
Die Axis: ↑↑

The Ottawa Mint issues (1917-1919) have a "C" mint mark below the oval at the bottom on the reverse. Royal Mint strikings have no mint mark.

Date and Mint Mark	Mintage	VG-8	F-12	VF-20	EF-40	AU-50	MS-60	MS-63	MS-65
1912	300,000	2.	3.	8.	30.	80.	150.	300.	600.
1917C	300,319	2.	4.	10.	40.	150.	450.	–	–
1919C	100,844	6.	12.	30.	150.	600.	1,500.	4,000.	–
1929	300,000	2.	3.	5.	20.	80.	200.	300.	900.

FIVE CENTS
George VI 1938 - 1947

While considering the replacement of the large cent, the Newfoundland government also contemplated dropping its "fish scale" silver 5-cent piece in favour of a nickel coin similar to Canada's. At that time, because of a strong conservative element, it was decided to change only the cent. The reverse design was continued from the previous reign and the obverse used the standard portrait for British colonial coinages.

The 1946C issue is an anomaly. Published official mint reports, as well as unpublished mint accounting records, do not indicate any mintage of this denomination during 1946. It appears that this scarce issue was actually coined during 1947. The mintage figures given for the years 1946 and 1947 must be considered unofficial although they are believed to have come from a mint officer many years ago.

CROWNED PORTRAIT, 1938-1947.

Designer and Engraver:
Obv.: Percy Metcalfe
Rev.: George W. DeSaulles
Composition:
1938-1944: .925 silver, .075 copper
1945-1947: .800 silver, .200 copper
Weight: 1.17 grams
Diameter:
1938: 15.69 mm
1940-1947: 15.49 mm
Edge: Reeded
Die Axis: ↑↑

Royal Canadian Mint issues (1940-47)
have a "C" mint mark below the oval
at the bottom on the reverse. The Royal
Mint issue (1938) has no mint mark.

Date and Mint Mark	Mintage	VG-8	F-12	VF-20	EF-40	AU-50	MS-60	MS-63	MS-65
1938	100,000	2.	3.	4.	5.	35.	125.	300.	900.
1940C	200,000	2.	3.	4.	5.	25.	100.	200.	2,000.
1941C	612,641	2.	3.	4.	6.	12.	20.	40.	400.
1942C	298,348	2.	3.	4.	5.	15.	25.	60.	325.
1943C	351,666	2.	2.	3.	4.	12.	25.	40.	325.
1944C	286,504	2.	2.	3.	8.	30.	85.	250.	1,250.
1945C	203,828	2.	2.	3.	5.	12.	30.	50.	250.
1946C	2,041	400.	500.	600.	800.	1,200.	–	–	4,000.
1947C	38,400	3.	5.	9.	25.	60.	100.	250.	500.

TEN CENTS
Victoria 1865 - 1896

Like the 5 cents, the 10 cents exists as a bronze pattern with the adopted obverse (derived from the New Brunswick obverse by substituting "NEWFOUNDLAND" for "NEW BRUNSWICK") and the Canada/New Brunswick reverse (see NF-3 in the chapter on Patterns). As well there is a silver pattern with very thin arches in the arabesque design on the reverse (see NF-9 in the chapter on Patterns).

VICTORIA OBVERSE PORTRAIT VARIETIES

The portraits of Victoria for the Newfoundland coinage are easily identifiable by the use of the 'periods' before and after 'Newfoundland' in the obverse legend.

PORTRAIT: ND1
Two leaves at top of laurel crown; uppermost rising into legend band. **Dot before and after Newfoundland on obverse.**

ND1 will be found on the following dates: 1865; 1870; 1873

PORTRAIT: ND2
Three leaves at top of laurel crown; uppermost leaf well into legend band. **Dot before but not after Newfoundland on obverse.**

ND2 will be found on the following dates: 1870; 1872H; 1873; 1876H; 1880; 1885; 1894

PORTRAIT: ND3
Two leaves at top of laurel crown. Top leaf barely touches legend band. **Dot before and after Newfoundland on obverse.**

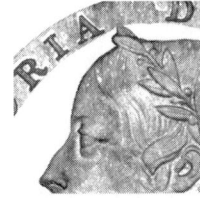

ND3 will be found on the following dates: 1882H; 1885; 1888; 1890; 1894; 1896

VICTORIA REVERSE VARIETIES

As with the silver five cents, there are no major reverse die varieties. Again, the Roman numeral 1 appears on two dates, 1865 and 1870, and the Arabic 1 on 1872 to 1896.

LAUREATED PORTRAIT, 1865-1896.

Designer and Engraver:
Rev.: Leonard C. Wyon
Engraver: Obv.: Leonard C. Wyon
Composition: .925 silver, .075 copper
Weight: 2.36 grams
Diameter: 17.98 mm
Edge: Reeded
Die Axis: ↑↓
Heaton Mint issues have an "H" mint mark either on the obverse under the bust (1872-1876), or on the reverse under the date (1882). Royal Mint strikings have no mint mark.

Date, Mint Portrait	Mintage	VG-8	F-12	VF-20	EF-40	AU-50	MS-60	MS-63	MS-65
1865-ND1	80,000	35.	60.	160.	400.	750.	2,000.	3,500.	7,500.
1870-ND1	30,000	250.	350.	650.	–	–	–	–	–
1870-ND2	Included	250.	500.	750.	–	–	–	–	–

1871H NEWFOUNDLAND/CANADA MULE. A rare variety exists because an 1871H Dominion of Canada reverse die was muled, apparently accidentally, with an "H" Newfoundland obverse die. All known examples are in well-worn condition.

1871H Newfoundland/Canada Mule

1880 Second 8 over 7

Date, Mint Portrait	Mintage	VG-8	F-12	VF-20	EF-40	AU-50	MS-60	MS-63	MS-65
1871H Mule	40,000				Extremely Rare				
1872H-ND2	Included	25.	60.	125.	250.	600.	–	2,500.	4,500.
1873-ND1	20,000	–	–	–	–	–	–	–	–
1873-ND2	Included	75.	150.	300.	–	–	–	–	–
1876H-ND2	10,000	60.	125.	275.	600.	–	–	–	6,500.
1880-ND2	10,000	60.	125.	250.	600.	1,250.	–	4,000.	–
1882H-ND3	20,000	60.	100.	250.	850.	–	–	–	–
1885-ND2	8,000	125.	225.	500.	–	–	–	–	–
1885-ND3	Included	–	–	–	–	–	–	–	–
1888-ND3	30,000	65.	125.	325.	1,500.	–	–	–	–
1890-ND3	100,000	15.	30.	75.	200.	1,000.	–	–	–
1894-ND2	100,000	–	–	–	–	–	–	–	–
1894-ND3	Included	13.	25.	100.	250.	700.	–	–	–
1896-ND3	230,000	11.	20.	40.	150.	700.	–	–	–

Note: All examples of the 1880 issue are from dies in which the second 8 of the date is punched over a 7.

TEN CENTS
Edward VII 1903 - 1904

The obverse is that used for the Dominion of Canada issues. The reverse is a new design by George W. DeSaulles.

CROWNED PORTRAIT, 1903-1904.

Designer and Engraver:
George W. DeSaulles
Composition: .925 silver, .075 copper
Weight: 2.36 grams
Diameter: 17.96 mm
Edge: Reeded
Die Axis: ↑↓

The Birmingham Mint issue of 1904 has an "H" mint mark below the oval at the bottom on the reverse. The Royal Mint issue (1903) has no mint mark.

Date and Mint Mark	Mintage	VG-8	F-12	VF-20	EF-40	AU-50	MS-60	MS-63	MS-65
1903	100,000	10.	30.	100.	300.	800.	–	–	–
1904H	100,000	5.	12.	35.	125.	200.	350.	600.	1,500.

TEN CENTS
George V 1912 - 1919

The obverse is the same as for the Dominion of Canada issues. The reverse is a continuation of the Newfoundland Edward VII designs.

CROWNED PORTRAIT, 1912-1919.

Designer and Engraver:
Obv.: Sir E. B. MacKennal
Rev.: George W. DeSaulles
Composition: .925 silver, .075 copper
Weight:
1912-1917: 2.36 grams
1919: 2.33 grams
Diameter:
1912: 17.96 mm
1917-1919: 18.03 mm
Edge: Reeded
Die Axis: ↑↑

Ottawa Mint issues (1917-1919) have a "C" mint mark below the oval at the bottom on the reverse. The Royal Mint issue (1912) has no mint mark.

Date and Mint Mark	Mintage	VG-8	F-12	VF-20	EF-40	AU-50	MS-60	MS-63	MS-65
1912	150,000	2.	5.	12.	55.	175.	250.	500.	1,000.
1917C	250,805	3.	5.	15.	60.	275.	650.	1,500.	–
1919C	54,342	4.	10.	30.	90.	175.	300.	500.	1,000.

TEN CENTS
George VI 1938-1947

The obverse for this denomination used Percy Metcalfe's standard portrait of George VI for British colonial coinages and the existing Edward VII/George V reverse. The 1946C issue was probably coined in 1947 (see preceding comments on the 1946C 5 cents); the mintage figures for 1946 and 1947 must be considered unofficial.

CROWNED PORTRAIT, 1938-1947.

Designer and Engraver:
Obv.: Percy Metcalfe
Rev.: George W. DeSaulles
Composition:
1938-1944: .925 silver, .075 copper
1945-1947: .800 silver, .200 copper
Weight: 2.33 grams
Diameter: 18.03 mm
Edge: Reeded
Die Axis: ↑↑

Royal Canadian Mint issues of 1941-47 have a "C" mint mark below the oval at the bottom on the reverse. The Royal Mint issue (1938) and the Royal Canadian Mint issue of 1940 have no mint mark.

Date and Mint Mark	Mintage	VG-8	F-12	VF-20	EF-40	AU-50	MS-60	MS-63	MS-65
1938	100,000	2.	2.	4.	15.	50.	300.	600.	—
1940	100,000	2.	2.	4.	15.	50.	175.	300.	—
1941C	483,630	2.	2.	3.	6.	20.	60.	125.	500.
1942C	292,736	2.	2.	3.	6.	20.	100.	300.	1,000.
1943C	104,706	2.	2.	3.	8.	30.	90.	350.	—
1944C	151,471	2.	2.	18.	35.	150.	450.	1,500.	—
1945C	175,833	2.	2.	3.	6.	25.	75.	200.	—
1946C	38,400	3.	6.	12.	25.	60.	100.	400.	—
1947C	61,988	2.	4.	6.	15.	55.	150.	350.	1,000.

TWENTY CENTS
Victoria 1865 - 1900

The first pattern known for the Newfoundland 20-cent piece is a bronze striking with the adopted obverse (derived from the New Brunswick obverse) and a reverse from a die for the 1864 New Brunswick 20 cents (see NF-4 in the chapter on Patterns). Later patterns in silver have an arabesque design similar to that finally adopted. The first (see NF-10 in the chapter on Patterns) has very thin arches and corresponds to similar 5-cent and 10-cent patterns. The second stands alone and has arches more like the adopted design and a raised line just inside the denticles (see NF-13 in the chapter on Patterns).

This denomination proved popular with Newfoundlanders and was minted on a regular basis throughout the remainder of Victoria's reign. With the passing years, however, it became increasingly unpopular with Canadians (due to its similarity to their 25-cent piece) and was replaced with a 25-cent coin during World War I.

VICTORIA OBVERSE PORTRAIT VARIETIES

PORTRAIT: NT1
Two leaves at top of laurel crown, with the rear leaf being very thin. Knot of hair at the back of the head touches the legend band. Prominent upper lip. **Dot before and after Newfoundland on obverse.**

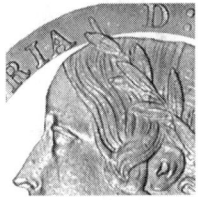

NT1 will be found on the following dates: 1865; 1870; 1872H; 1873; 1876H; 1880; 1881; 1885; 1894; 1896 (all varieties)

PORTRAIT: NT2
Two leaves at top of laurel crown; both distinctive and well into legend band. Knot of hair at the back of the head enters legend band. Repressed upper lip. **Dot before and after Newfoundland on obverse.**

NT2 will be found on the following dates: 1882H; 1888; 1890; 1894; 1896 (all varieties); 1899 (all varieties); 1900

VICTORIA REVERSE VARIETIES

As with previous denominations there are no major reverse varieties. Use of the Roman numeral 'I' in the date was extended from 1865 to 1880. The Arabic '1' appears in dates from 1881 to 1900.

LAUREATED PORTRAIT, 1865-1894.

Designer:
    Obv.: Leonard C. Wyon
    Rev.: Horace Morehen
Engraver:
    Obv.: Leonard C. Wyon
    Rev.: Leonard C. Wyon
Composition: .925 silver, .075 copper
Weight: 4.71 grams
Diameter: 23.19 mm
Edge: Reeded
Die Axis: ↑↓

Heaton Mint issues have an "H" mint mark on the obverse under the bust (1872 to 1876), or on the reverse under the date (1882). Royal Mint strikings have no mint mark.

Date, Mint Portrait	Mintage	VG-8	F-12	VF-20	EF-40	AU-50	MS-60	MS-63	MS-65
1865-NT1	100,000	25.	45.	125.	350.	850.	–	4,000.	–
1870-NT1	50,000	35.	70.	175.	500.	–	–	4,000.	8,000.
1872H-NT1	90,000	20.	35.	85.	300.	–	–	–	–
1873-NT1	40,000	35.	75.	200.	600.	–	–	–	–
1876H-NT1	50,000	30.	75.	150.	425.	1,100.	–	3,000.	–
1880-NT1	30,000	35.	70.	200.	500.	–	–	–	–
1881-NT1	60,000	20.	40.	150.	425.	–	–	–	–
1882H-NT2	100,000	12.	30.	70.	275.	850.	–	–	–
1885-NT1	40,000	25.	45.	150.	425.	–	–	–	–
1888-NT2	75,000	15.	25.	75.	325.	650.	–	–	–
1890-NT2	100,000	12.	25.	75.	325.	–	–	–	–
1894-NT1	100,000	15.	30.	70.	300.	–	–	–	–
1894-NT2	Included	20.	30.	125.	650.	–	–	–	–

Note: A dash (–) in a pricing column indicates no coin has been assigned that grade.

VARIETIES OF 1896 AND 1899.

1896	1896	1899	1899	1899
Small 96 (S)	Large 96 (L)	Small 99 (S)	Hooked 99 (H)	Large 99 (L)

Date, Mint Portrait	Mintage	VG-8	F-12	VF-20	EF-40	AU-50	MS-60	MS-63	MS-65
1896, S96-NT1	125,000	12.	20.	60.	225.	700.	–	–	–
1896, S96-NT2	Included	12.	20.	80.	225.	650.	–	–	–
1896, L96-NT1	Included	15.	25.	75.	300.	900.	–	–	–
1896, L96-NT2	Included	12.	20.	100.	300.	900.	–	–	–
1899, S99-NT2	125,000	8.	40.	75.	300.	–	–	–	–
1899, H99-NT2	Included	35.	65.	200.	450.	–	–	–	–
1899, L99-NT2	Included	10.	18.	50.	225.	750.	–	–	–
1900-NT2	125,000	10.	15.	45.	175.	500.	2,000.	–	–

TWENTY CENTS
Edward VII 1904

Coins of this denomination were required on only one occasion during Edward's short reign, making the 1904 issue a one-year type.

CROWNED PORTRAIT, 1904.

Designer and Engraver:
Obv.: George W. DeSaulles
Rev.: W. H. J. Blakemore, copying DeSaulles' design for the reverse of 5¢ and 10¢ pieces
Composition: .925 silver, .075 copper
Weight: 4.71 grams
Diameter: 23.19 mm
Edge: Reeded
Die Axis: ↑↓

This issue was coined by The Birmingham Mint and bears an "H" mint mark below the oval at the bottom on the reverse.

Date and Mint Mark	Mintage	VG-8	F-12	VF-20	EF-40	AU-50	MS-60	MS-63	MS-65
1904H	75,000	18.	50.	85.	275.	1,000.	4,000.	–	–

TWENTY CENTS
George V 1912

Like its Edwardian predecessor, the George V 20 cents is a one-year type. The reverse established for the previous reign was reused.

CROWNED PORTRAIT, 1912.

Designer and Engraver:
    Obv.: Sir E. B. MacKennal
Composition: .925 silver, .075 copper
Weight: 4.71 grams
Diameter: 23.19 mm
Edge: Reeded
Die Axis: ↑↑

Date and Mint Mark	Mintage	VG-8	F-12	VF-20	EF-40	AU-50	MS-60	MS-63	MS-65
1912	350,000	3.	6.	15.	60.	150.	400.	600.	1,500.

TWENTY-FIVE CENTS
George V 1917 - 1919

The second time 20-cent pieces were required during George V's reign was toward the end of World War I. By that time, however, arrangements had been made for the Ottawa Mint to produce Newfoundland's coins. Canada took a dim view of the 20 cents because it circulated in Canada as well, and was confused with the Canadian 25 cents. The Canadian government convinced the Newfoundland government to drop the 20 cents and adopt a 25 cents, struck on the same standard as the corresponding Canadian coin. Indeed, the obverse of the new coin was identical to that for the Canadian 25 cents.

CROWNED PORTRAIT, 1917-1919.

Designer and Engraver:
    Obv.: Sir E. B. MacKennal
Engraver:
    Rev.: W. H. J. Blakemore, modifying
    the 20¢ reverse
Composition: .925 silver, .075 copper
Weight: 5.83 grams
Diameter: 23.62 mm
Edge: Reeded
Die Axis: ↑↑

This denomination was coined by the Ottawa Mint and bears a "C" mint mark below the oval at the bottom on the reverse.

Date and Mint Mark	Mintage	VG-8	F-12	VF-20	EF-40	AU-50	MS-60	MS-63	MS-65
1917C	464,779	3.	5.	7.	20.	75.	225.	450.	—
1919C	163,939	3.	6.	15.	35.	150.	600.	1,800.	—

FIFTY CENTS
Victoria 1870 -1900

The 50-cent piece was the last denomination to be added to the Victorian coinage, coming in 1870. Its laureate portrait is stylistically unlike anything used for the rest of the British North America. This denomination became popular on the island and assumed even greater importance after the failure of the Commercial and Union Banks of Newfoundland during the financial crisis of 1894.

VICTORIA OBVERSE PORTRAIT VARIETIES

PORTRAIT: NH1
Four leaves at top of laurel crown; the upper-most leaf enters the legend band between the 'E' and 'I' in DEI. Prominent upper lip. **No dot before or after Newfoundland on obverse.**

NH-1 will be found on the following dates:
1870; 1872H; 1873; 1874; 1876H; 1880; 1881; 1885; 1888; 1894; 1896; 1898

PORTRAIT: NH2
Four leaves at top of laurel crown, with none entering the legend band. Repressed upper lip. **No dot before or after Newfoundland on obverse.**

NH2 will be found on the following dates:
1882H; 1896; 1898; 1899; 1900

VICTORIA REVERSE VARIETIES

No major die varieties exist for the Newfoundland fifty cent coins. However, in 1880 or 1881 the reverse die was modified with the design being rendered more delicate. The 1865 to 1880 fifty cent coins have wide thick loops, and 1881 to 1898 have thin loops.

LAUREATED PORTRAIT, 1870-1900.

Designer and Engraver:
Leonard C. Wyon
Composition: .925 silver,
.075 copper
Weight: 11.78 grams
Diameter: 29.85 mm
Edge: Reeded
Die Axis: ↑↓

 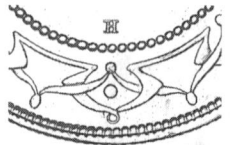

Heaton Mint issues have an "H" mint mark either on the obverse under the bust (1872-1876) or on the reverse under the date (1882). Royal Mint strikings have no mint mark.

All examples of the 1880 issue are from dies in which the second 8 of the date is punched over a 7.

Small W

Large W over Small W

Date, Mint Portrait	Mintage	VG-8	F-12	VF-20	EF-40	AU-50	MS-60	MS-63	MS-65
1870-NH1	50,000	30.	75.	225.	925.	–	–	–	–
1872H-NH1	48,000	25.	60.	100.	450.	–	–	–	–
1873-NH1	32,000	75.	150.	300.	950.	2,500.	–	–	–
1874-NH1	80,000	40.	80.	225.	750.	–	–	–	–
1876H-NH1	28,000	50.	85.	250.	800.	–	–	–	–
1880-NH1	24,000	50.	100.	350.	850.	–	6,500.	15,000.	–
1881-NH1	50,000	35.	70.	225.	800.	1,750.	3,500.	–	–
1882H-NH2	100,000	20.	35.	125.	400.	750.	2,500.	5,000.	–
1885-NH1	40,000	40.	75.	200.	750.	1,750.	–	–	–
1888-NH1	20,000	75.	150.	350.	750.	–	–	–	–
1894-NH1	40,000	15.	40.	125.	500.	–	–	–	–
1896, SW-NH2	60,000	15.	30.	125.	400.	1,000.	–	–	–
1896, LW/SW-NH1	Included	15.	30.	125.	400.	1,000.	–	–	–
1898, SW-NH1	79,607	25.	30.	200.	600.	–	–	–	–
1898, SW-NH2	Included	12.	25.	90.	300.	1,250.	–	–	–
1898, LW/SW-NH1	Included	15.	25.	100.	300.	1,200.	–	–	–

Note: A dash (–) in a pricing column indicates no coin has been assigned that grade by a Canadian Grading Company.

VARIETIES OF 1899.

Narrow 9s with thick sides
and oval centres

Wide 9s with thin sides
and round centres

Date, Mint Portrait	Mintage	VG-8	F-12	VF-20	EF-40	AU-50	MS-60	MS-63	MS-65
1899, N9-NH2	150,000	12.	25.	90.	250.	850.	–	–	–
1899, W9-NH2	Included	12.	30.	125.	350.	1,200.	–	–	–
1900-NH2	150,000	12.	25.	90.	250.	750.	2,000.	–	–

FIFTY CENTS
Edward VII 1904 - 1909

The obverse for this denomination is that of the Dominion of Canada issues.

CROWNED PORTRAIT, 1904-1909.

Designer and Engraver:
  Obv.: George W. DeSaulles
  Rev.: W. H. J. Blakemore,
      copying DeSaulles' design
      for 5¢ and 10¢ pieces
Composition: .925 silver,
      .075 copper
Weight: 11.78 grams
Diameter: 29.85 mm
Edge: Reeded
Die Axis: ↑↓ ↑↑

The Birmingham Mint issue (1904) has an "H" mint mark below the oval at the bottom on the reverse. Royal Mint issues have no mint mark.

Date and Mint Mark	Mintage	VG-8	F-12	VF-20	EF-40	AU-50	MS-60	MS-63	MS-65
1904H	140,000	5.	10.	25.	65.	200.	400.	1,000.	3,000.
1907	100,000	5.	10.	25.	75.	225.	425.	1,500.	–
1908	160,000	5.	10.	25.	60.	150.	350.	1,000.	–
1909	200,000	5.	10.	25.	75.	175.	400.	1,400.	–

FIFTY CENTS
George V 1911 - 1919

The obverse for the Newfoundland 50-cent piece is the same as that for the 1912-1936 Dominion of Canada coins. That legend contains "DEI GRA" (see Dominion of Canada George V one-cent section) indicating that the modification of the Canadian obverses was made during 1911, prior to commencing the production of the Newfoundland issue for the year. The reverse continued the Edwardian design.

In 1917-1919 nearly 1,000,000 50 cents were struck and many were used to replace the discontinued government "cash notes" for making relief payments to the poor. The need for silver for this purpose diminished in 1920, when a new issue of government paper money was made.

CROWNED PORTRAIT, 1911-1919.

Designer: Obv.: Sir E.B. MacKennal
Composition: .925 silver, .075 copper
Weight:
  1911: 11.78 grams
  1917-1919: 11.66 grams
Diameter:
  1911: 29.85 mm
  1917-1919: 29.72 mm
Edge: Reeded
Die Axis: ↑↑

Ottawa Mint issues (1917-1919) have a "C" mint mark below the oval at the bottom on the reverse. The Royal Mint issue has no mint mark.

Date and Mint Mark	Mintage	VG-8	F-12	VF-20	EF-40	AU-50	MS-60	MS-63	MS-65
1911	200,000	4.	6.	15.	35.	100.	300.	750.	—
1917C	375,560	4.	6.	15.	35.	90.	200.	550.	—
1918C	294,824	4.	6.	15.	35.	75.	200.	500.	—
1919C	306,267	4.	6.	15.	50.	150.	400.	1,500.	—

TWO DOLLARS
Victoria 1865 - 1888

In the original planning for the Newfoundland coinage a gold dollar was considered. However, it was decided that such a coin would be so small it could be easily lost by the fishermen, so a 2-dollar denomination was chosen instead. The initial bronze pattern combines the adopted obverse (derived from the New Brunswick 10 cents obverse and identical to the Newfoundland 10 cents obverse) with the crown and maple wreath of the Canada/New Brunswick 10 cents reverse (see NF-5 in the chapter on Patterns). The adopted reverse has more conventional letters and the unusual feature of expressing the denomination three ways: 2 dollars, 200 cents, 100 pence, the last being the equivalent value in sterling (British money). Newfoundland was the only British colony with its own gold issue.

VICTORIA OBVERSE PORTRAIT VARIETIES

PORTRAIT: NTD1
Young head portrait. **Dot before and after Newfoundland on obverse.**

NTD1 will be found on the following dates:
1865; 1870

PORTRAIT: NTD2
Mature head portrait. **Dot before Newfoundland on obverse.**

NTD2 will be found on the following dates:
1870; 1872; 1880; 1881; 1885; 1888

VICTORIA OBVERSE PORTRAIT VARIETIES

PORTRAIT: NTD3
Older portrait. **Dot before and after Newfoundland on obverse.**

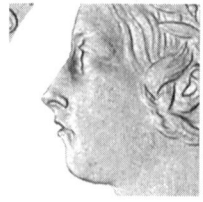

NTD3 will be found on the following dates:
1882H; 1888

LAUREATED PORTRAIT, 1865-1888. No major die varieties exist for the Newfoundland two dollar coins.

Designer and Engraver:
  Obv.: Leonard C. Wyon
  Rev.: Leonard C. Wyon
Composition: .917 gold, .083 copper
Weight: 3.33 grams
Diameter: 17.98 mm
Edge: Reeded
Die Axis: ↑↓

The Heaton Mint issue (1882) has an "H" mint mark below the date on the reverse. London Mint strikings have no mint mark.

Date, Mint Portrait	Mintage	F-12	VF-20	EF-40	AU-50	MS-60	MS-63	MS-65
1865-NTD1	10,000	225.	350.	500.	600.	1,750.	−	−
1870-NTD1	10,000	250.	350.	550.	800.	−	−	−
1870-NTD2	Included	225.	325.	450.	600.	2,000.	10,000.	−
1872-NTD2	6,000	275.	450.	600.	900.	−	−	−
1880-NTD2	2,500	1,300.	1,700.	2,000.	3,000.	8,000.	−	−
1881-NTD2	10,000	200.	300.	375.	500.	2,250.	−	−
1882H-NTD3	25,000	200.	275.	300.	375.	650.	3,500.	10,000.
1885-NTD2	10,000	200.	300.	350.	425.	750.	3,000.	−
1888-NTD2	25,000	−	−	−	−	−	−	−
1888-NTD3	Included	175.	275.	325.	350.	750.	4,000.	−

PROVINCE OF CANADA

LARGE CENTS
Victoria 1858 - 1859

After the decision to adopt decimal coins was approved, a number of designs, sizes and compositions were considered for the cent. The first trials used a reverse design consisting of 19 maple leaves placed side by side, radiating from the centre (see PC-1 to PC-3 in the chapter on Patterns). However, a serpentine motif of 16 maple leaves was adopted and trial pieces were struck in a cupro-nickel alloy. Later, it was decided the new cents would be bronze.

The adopted obverse design shows a youthful, idealized bust of the queen wearing a laurel wreath in her hair. In fact, by the late 1850s the Queen was quite pudgy and decidedly older looking than the coinage portraits suggested.

The government optimistically ordered approximately 10,000,000 1-cent pieces, which proved to be much more than the province could absorb. At the time both Canada East and Canada West were inundated with the copper tokens issued by banks and individuals. The bank tokens were heavier than the thin cents (which weighed 1/100 lb. avoirdupois) which slowed their public acceptance. The majority of the mintage remained unissued in the original boxes. In 1861 part of it was sent to the New Brunswick government to provide a temporary supply of decimal coins while the province awaited the arrival of its own issues, but the bulk of the stock went to the Bank of Upper Canada, the governments's bank. Until 1866, when it closed its doors, the Bank of Upper Canada experienced considerable difficulty in reducing its stock of cents, even when it offered to sell them at 20 percent below face value.

A stock of several million Province of Canada cents was inherited by the Dominion of Canada government in 1867 and it proceeded to issue them as Dominion currency.

LAUREATED PORTRAIT, 1858.

Designer and Engraver:
Leonard C. Wyon
Composition: .95 copper, .04 tin, .01 zinc
(except for the rare brass)
Weight: 4.54 grams
Diameter: 25.4 mm
Edge: Plain
Die Axis: ↑↑, ↑↓

Date and Mint Mark	Mintage	VG-8	F-12	VF-20	EF-40	AU-50	MS-60 Br	MS-63 Rd/Br	MS-65 Rd
1858 Medal	421,000	80.	100.	150.	200.	275.	500.	1,500.	3,000.
1858 Coinage	Included	–	–	–	1,500.	–	–	–	–

VARIETIES 1859. Since the coining of cents did not begin until the latter part of 1858, production continued throughout most of 1859, with most coins bearing an 1859 date. The first 1859s were undoubtedly overdates, on which a special wide 9 punch was employed to alter the second 8 to a 9, produced from several 1858-dated dies.

The majority of the 1859 dies were not overdates: they were dated with a narrow 9 punch. Many such dies were made and numerous re-punching varieties exist. Only those most widely collected are listed here.

Double-punched Narrow 9 #1: Resembles and is often designated "narrow 9 over 8." Actually it is a double-punched narrow 9, confused by the presence of a die defect causing a small "tail" at the lower left of the 9.

Double-punched Narrow 9 #2: Traces of the original 9 at the left.

A very rare variety of the plain, narrow 9 exists in brass, which can be identified by its distinctive yellow colour.

Overdate,
Wide 9 over 8

Plain, Narrow 9

Date and Mint Mark	Mintage	VG-8	F-12	VF-20	EF-40	AU-50	MS-60 Br	MS-63 Rd/Br	MS-65 Rd
1859 W9/8 Medal	9,579,000	40.	55.	75.	150.	250.	500.	1,500.	–
1859 W9/8 Coinage	Incl.	–	–	–	–	–	–	–	–
1859 N9, Bronze	Incl.	5.	10.	12.	20.	30.	65.	175.	2,000.
1859 N9, Brass	Incl.	4,000.	5,000.	–	–	–	–	–	–

Double-punched Narrow 9 #1
Resembles narrow 9 over 8

Double-punched Narrow 9 #2
Traces of original 9 at left

Date and Mint Mark	Mintage	VG-8	F-12	VF-20	EF-40	AU-50	MS-60 Br	MS-63 Rd/Br	MS-65 Rd
1859 D-P N9#1	Included	200.	300.	450.	600.	1,500.	2,500.	–	–
1859 D-P N9#2	Included	85.	125.	175.	250.	500.	600.	2,500.	–

FIVE CENTS
Victoria 1858

The 5-cent piece chosen by the Province of Canada was a small silver coin, half the weight of the 10-cent piece and similar to the United States half dime. The obverse depicts an idealized, youthful laureated Victoria and the reverse features a maple wreath of 21 leaves surmounted by St. Edward's crown.

The first dies bore small, widely spaced digits in the date. Later strikings carried larger digits punched over the small figures, making the digits closer together.

LAUREATED PORTRAIT, 1858.

Designer and Engraver:
Leonard C. Wyon
Composition: .925 silver, .075 copper
Weight: 1.16 grams
Diameter: 15.5 mm
Edge: Reeded
Die Axis: ↑↓

1858 Small Date
Digits widely spaced

1858 Large Date over Small Date
Digits closely spaced

Date and Mint Mark	Mintage	VG-8	F-12	VF-20	EF-40	AU-50	MS-60	MS-63	MS-65
1858 SD	1,460,389	20.	40.	60.	100.	175.	375.	675.	3,500.
1858 LD/SD	Included	150.	250.	400.	650.	900.	–	–	–

TEN CENTS
Victoria 1858

In design, the Province of Canada 10-cent pieces resemble the 5-cent pieces. An interesting variety occurred through a dating blunder in which a 5 punch was used to repair a defective first 8. The top of the 5 can be seen rising above the first 8, as these numbers were punched simultaneously.

LAUREATED PORTRAIT, 1858.

Designer and Engraver:
   Leonard C. Wyon
Composition: .925 silver, .075 copper
Weight: 2.32 grams
Diameter: 18.0 mm
Edge: Reeded
Die Axis: ↑↓

1858
First 8 and 5 punched simultaneously

Date and Mint Mark	Mintage	VG-8	F-12	VF-20	EF-40	AU-50	MS-60	MS-63	MS-65
1858	1,216,402	30.	60.	100.	150.	200.	400.	1,000.	3,000.
1858 8 over 5	Included	1,000.	1,500.	2,500.	4,500.	6,000.	–	–	–

Note: For the price of a coin in Good-4 (G-4) condition, use as an indication 50 - 60% of the Very Good-8 (VG-8) price.

TWENTY CENTS
Victoria 1858

This unusual denomination was chosen as a bridge between two currency systems. It apparently deferred to the pounds, shillings, pence basis of the Halifax currency system while naming the new issue in the dollar, cents, mills system. The relationship between the two systems meant 20 cents was equivalent to a shilling in Halifax currency, and it was assumed that consequently the new coin would be found useful. This assumption proved unfounded because there had been no coin representing a shilling in the old system; the British shilling coin was worth just over 20 percent more than a shilling in Halifax currency. Furthermore, the size and weight of the 20-cent piece led to confusion with both British shillings and U.S. 25-cent pieces. As one would expect, the government had difficulty introducing the 20-cent piece and by 1860 it was decided to replace it with a 25-cent coin as the opportunity arose.

The replacement of the 20-cent piece with a 25-cent coin came after Confederation. The Dominion government actively withdrew the 20-cent pieces and at various times from 1885 onward sent them back to the Royal Mint in London for melting and recoining as 25-cent pieces.

LAUREATED PORTRAIT, 1858.

Designer and Engraver:
  Leonard C. Wyon
Composition: .925 silver, .075 copper
Weight: 4.65 grams
Diameter: 23.3 mm
Edge: Reeded
Die Axis: ↑↓

Date and Mint Mark	Mintage	VG-8	F-12	VF-20	EF-40	AU-50	MS-60	MS-63	MS-65
1858	730,392	65.	95.	150.	250.	450.	1,000.	2,250.	14,000.

CANADA

CIRCULATING COINAGE

ONE CENT
Victoria 1876 - 1901

The large cents produced in 1858-1859 for the Province of Canada were inherited by the Dominion of Canada government at the time of Confederation. It was decided to issue them as Dominion cents. Nearly ten years were required to use up the stock; the first cents struck for the Dominion came out in 1876. An 1876 pattern cent (see DC-1 in the chapter on Patterns) with the laureated obverse of 1858-1859 suggests that initially it was intended the Dominion cents be the same design as those of the Province of Canada. However, the obverse of the pieces actually issued bore a diademed head adapted from that used for the Jamaica halfpenny and the Prince Edward Island cent. The government also took the opportunity to increase the weight to 1/80th of an avoirdupois pound, the same as the British halfpenny.

VICTORIA OBVERSE PORTRAIT VARIETIES

The portrait varieties of Victorian coins have been part of Canadian numismatics since James Haxby's series of articles first appeared in the Canadian Numismatic Journal, Vol. 13, Number 12, in December 1968. In these articles Jim introduced six different portraits appearing on Canadian and Newfoundland coins between 1858 and 1901.

Identification and pricing has always been a major problem. Identification of the varieties becomes challenging as wear first blurs, and then erodes, crucial diagnostic details. Digital images and the ability to manipulate these images may help to resolve the identification problem.

With the 58th edition we started to build pricing tables for the Victorian portrait varieties. Pricing reflects the numbers reported by ICCS in their Population Report of 2005. The Report, released in January 2005, counts the number of each denomination by date and variety graded by ICCS on a cumulative basis from April 1988 to December 2005.

PORTRAIT: C1
Rounded chin and nose.

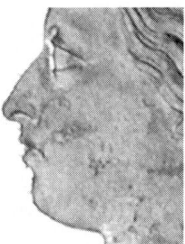

C1 will be found on the following dates:
1876H; 1881H; 1882H; 1884; 1886

VICTORIA OBVERSE PORTRAIT VARIETIES

CANADA ONE CENT - C

PORTRAIT: C2
Doubling of chin and pointing of nose.

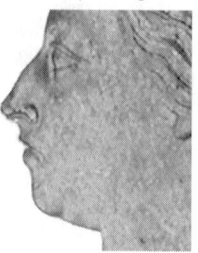

C2 will be found on the following dates:
1882H; 1884; 1886; 1887; 1888;
1891; 1892

PORTRAIT: C3
Strong doubling of chin coupled with
strong cheek accent lines. Nose has a
pinched look.

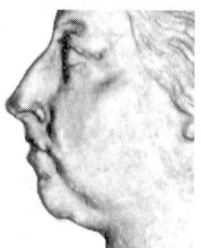

C3 will be found on the following dates:
1890H; 1891; 1892

PORTRAIT: C4
The chin is again rounded with the doubling
reduced dramatically. The cheek accents are
removed, with the nose lines less harsh.

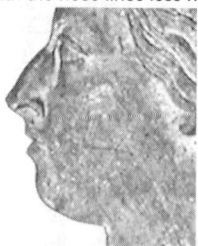

C4 will be found on the following dates:
1892; 1893; 1894; 1895; 1896; 1897;
1898H; 1899; 1900; 1900H; 1901

VICTORIA REVERSE VARIETIES

Three varieties of the reverse, from independently engraved master tools, are known to exist: the Provincial Leaves reverse (1876-1882), the Large Leaves reverse (1884-1891), and the Small Leaves reverse (1891-1901). Only in 1891 are two reverses employed for a single year's coinage (see page 64).

DIADEMED PORTRAIT, PROVINCIAL LEAVES DESIGN, 1876-1882.

Designer and Engraver:
Obv.: Leonard C. Wyon
Rev.: Provincial and Large Leaves –
    Leonard C. Wyon;
    Small Leaves Reverse –
    G.W. DeSaulles
Composition: .95 copper, .04 tin
    .01 zinc
Weight: 5.67 grams
Diameter: 25.4 mm
Edge: Plain
Die Axis: ↑↑

Heaton Mint issues of 1876-1882 and The Birmingham Mint issues of 1890, 1898 and 1900 have an "H" mint mark on the reverse under the date. Royal Mint strikings have no mint mark.

Date, Mint Portrait	Mintage	VG-8	F-12	VF-20	EF-40	AU-50	MS-60 Br	MS-63 Rd/Br	MS-65 Rd
1876H-C1	4,000,000	4.	5.	9.	15.	40.	80.	250.	2,500.
1881H-C1	2,000,000	6.	8.	15.	25.	50.	110.	300.	2,500.
1882H-C1	4,000,000	6.	10.	15.	25.	50.	150.	400.	2,500.
1882H-C2	Included	4.	5.	10.	20.	30.	75.	225.	2,500.

DIADEMED PORTRAIT, LARGE LEAVES DESIGN, 1884-1891.

Designer: Obv.: Leonard C. Wyon
    Rev.: Leonard C. Wyon
Composition: .95 copper, .04 tin
    .01 zinc
Weight: 5.67 grams
Diameter: 25.4 mm
Edge: Plain
Die Axis: ↑↑

Date, Mint Portrait	Mintage	VG-8	F-12	VF-20	EF-40	AU-50	MS-60 Br	MS-63 Rd/Br	MS-65 Rd
1884-C1	2,500,000	50.	80.	100.	125.	160.	500.	750.	–
1884-C2	Included	5.	7.	10.	18.	40.	110.	300.	2,500.
1886-C1	1,500,000	12.	25.	35.	50.	100.	300.	600.	–
1886-C2	Included	7.	12.	18.	35.	75.	175.	450.	–
1887-C2	1,500,000	5.	8.	12.	22.	45.	110.	300.	2,500.
1888-C2	4,000,000	5.	8.	10.	15.	30.	60.	160.	2,000.
1890H-C3	1,000,000	10.	15.	25.	50.	90.	250.	500.	2,500.

VARIETIES OF 1891. Three major varieties of the 1891 cent are known. The first two have the Large Leaves reverse. The broad, flat leaves have very little detail and the bottom leaf runs into the rim denticles. The third variety has the Small Leaves reverse, which has slightly smaller leaves with much more detail. The bottom leaf ends well short of the rim denticles. The first variety has a large date; the second and third varieties have a small date.

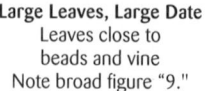

Large Leaves, Large Date	Large Leaves, Small Date
Leaves close to	Leaves close to
beads and vine	beads and vine
Note broad figure "9."	Note narrow figure "9."

Date and Mint Mark	Mintage	VG-8	F-12	VF-20	EF-40	AU-50	MS-60 Br	MS-63 Rd/Br	MS-65 Rd
1891 LL LD-C2	800,000	10.	15.	30.	50.	110.	200.	550.	4,000.
1891 LL LD-C3	Included	10.	15.	25.	50.	110.	200.	550.	3,000.
1891 LL SD-C2	Included	100.	135.	200.	300.	600.	1,100.	2,500.	–
1891 LL SD-C3	Included	100.	150.	200.	350.	600.	1,250.	2,750.	–

DIADEMED PORTRAIT, SMALL LEAVES DESIGN, 1891-1901

Small Leaves, Small Date: Leaves far from beads and vine; note narrow figure "9."

Date, Mint Portrait	Mintage	VG-8	F-12	VF-20	EF-40	AU-50	MS-60 Br	MS-63 Rd/Br	MS-65 Rd
1891 SL SD-C2	Included	75.	85.	125.	175.	300.	600.	1,200.	–
1891 SL SD-C3	Included	70.	100.	135.	200.	300.	500.	1,000.	–
1892-C2	1,200,000	15.	30.	45.	65.	100.	150.	500.	3,500.
1892-C3	Included	8.	12.	20.	30.	60.	100.	300.	3,000.
1892-C4	Included	6.	10.	20.	30.	60.	150.	300.	3,500.
1893-C4	2,000,000	4.	7.	12.	15.	30.	75.	200.	2,000.
1894-C4	1,000,000	15.	20.	35.	50.	90.	125.	300.	1,750.
1895-C4	1,200,000	8.	12.	18.	30.	60.	125.	300.	2,000.
1896-C4	2,000,000	4.	6.	9.	15.	30.	75.	200.	2,000.
1897-C4	1,500,000	4.	7.	10.	15.	35.	85.	300.	2,000.
1898H-C4	1,000,000	10.	15.	25.	35.	70.	200.	400.	3,000.
1899-C4	2,400,000	5.	7.	10.	14.	25.	75.	150.	1,200.
1900-C4	1,000,000	10.	15.	25.	45.	90.	150.	500.	4,000.
1900H-C4	2,600,000	4.	5.	7.	10.	25.	75.	100.	750.
1901-C4	4,100,000	4.	5.	7.	10.	25.	50.	100.	1,600.

ONE CENT
Edward VII 1902-1910

IMPERIAL STATE CROWNED PORTRAIT, SMALL LEAVES DESIGN, 1902-1910. The Victorian small leaves reverse design was carried forward into the Edward VII coinage..

Designer and Engraver:
Obv.: George W. DeSaulles
Composition: .95 copper, .04 tin, .01 zinc
Weight: 5.67 grams
Diameter: 25.4 mm
Edge: Plain
Die Axis: ↑↑

The Birmingham Mint issue of 1907 has an "H" mint mark on the reverse above the wreath, below the date. London Mint strikings (1902-1907) and Ottawa Mint strikings (1908-1910) have no mint mark.

Date and Mint Mark	Mintage	VG-8	F-12	VF-20	EF-40	AU-50	MS-60 Br	MS-63 Rd/Br	MS-65 Rd
1902	3,000,000	3.	4.	5.	10.	15.	35.	70.	400.
1903	4,000,000	3.	4.	5.	10.	15.	40.	70.	700.
1904	2,500,000	4.	5.	7.	12.	20.	55.	150.	800.
1905	2,000,000	5.	7.	10.	15.	25.	75.	150.	1,350.
1906	4,100,000	3.	4.	5.	10.	20.	60.	250.	1,500.
1907	2,400,000	3.	4.	6.	12.	25.	50.	175.	2,000.
1907H	800,000	13.	22.	35.	50.	80.	200.	600.	2.500.
1908	2,401,506	4.	5.	7.	14.	25.	50.	125.	1,200.
1909	3,973,339	2.	3.	5.	8.	20.	50.	100.	1,400.
1910	5,146,487	2.	3.	4.	7.	15.	45.	90.	1,400.

ONE CENT - LARGE
George V 1911 - 1920

IMPERIAL STATE CROWNED PORTRAIT, SMALL LEAVES DESIGN, 1911. The obverse introduced in 1911 broke a tradition set by the coins of the previous two reigns in which the Latin phrase "DEI GRATIA" (or an abbreviation for it) was included in the monarch's titles. Omission of the phrase aroused public criticism during which the coins were labelled "Godless."

Designer and Engraver:
Obv.: Sir E. B. MacKennal
Rev.: W. H. J. Blakemore
Composition: .95 copper, .04 tin, .01 zinc
Weight: 5.67 grams
Diameter: 25.4 mm
Edge: Plain
Die Axis: ↑↑

Date and Mint Mark	Mintage	F-12	VF-20	EF-40	AU-50	MS-60 Br	MS-63 Rd/Br	MS-65 Rd
1911	4,663,486	2.	3.	5.	15.	35.	65.	650.

IMPERIAL STATE CROWNED PORTRAIT, SMALL LEAVES, MODIFIED DESIGN, 1912-1920. The coinage tools were modified during the year 1911, and cents with "DEI GRA:" in the legend appeared in 1912. The reverse also marked a departure from the previous reigns with the inclusion of "CANADA" in the legend. It had formerly been part of the obverse legend on this denomination.

Composition:
1912-1919:
.95 copper, .04 tin, .01 zinc
1919-1920:
.955 copper, .030 tin, .015 zinc

Specifications:
Same as 1911 issue

Date and Mint Mark	Mintage	F-12	VF-20	EF-40	AU-50	MS-60 Br	MS-63 Rd/Br	MS-65 Rd
1912	5,107,642	2.	3.	5.	15.	35.	75.	750.
1913	5,735,405	2.	3.	6.	15.	40.	100.	950.
1914	3,405,958	3.	4.	6.	16.	50.	150.	950.
1915	4,932,134	2.	3.	6.	15.	40.	90.	900.
1916	11,022,367	1.	2.	4.	10.	30.	95.	600.
1917	11,899,254	1.	2.	3.	7.	30.	75.	800.
1918	12,970,798	1.	2.	4.	8.	20.	75.	700.
1919	11,279,634	1.	2.	3.	7.	25.	60.	600.
1920	6,762,247	1.	1.	2.	7.	30.	85.	1,500.

ONE CENT - SMALL
George V 1920 - 1936

As a matter of economy the Canadian government introduced in 1920 a small cent similar in size and composition to that of the United States. The large cents were not immediately withdrawn, but were allowed to circulate until the late 1930s. The small coins lacked rim denticles, the first instance of this in the Canadian decimal series. The obverse design was retained while a new reverse design, featuring two maple leaves, was used.

IMPERIAL STATE CROWNED PORTRAIT, TWO MAPLE LEAVES DESIGN, 1920-1936.

Designer: Obv.: Sir E. B. MacKennal
Rev.: Fred Lewis
Engraver: Obv.: Sir E. B. MacKennal
Rev.: W. H. J. Blakemore
Composition: .955 copper, .030 tin, .015 zinc
Weight: 3.24 grams
Diameter: 19.05 mm
Edge: Plain
Die Axis: ↑↑

Date and Mint Mark	Mintage	VG-8	F-12	VF-20	EF-40	AU-50	MS-60 Br	MS-63 Rd/Br	MS-65 Rd
1920	15,483,923	–	1.	2.	3.	9.	20.	50.	1,000.
1921	7,601,627	1.	1.	3.	7.	15.	65.	200.	–
1922	1,243,635	16.	20.	30.	50.	100.	325.	1,200.	–
1923	1,019,022	35.	40.	55.	85.	175.	400.	1,500.	–
1924	1,593,195	7.	9.	13.	25.	65.	200.	1,000.	3,000.
1925	1,000,622	30.	35.	40.	60.	120.	250.	700.	5,000.
1926	2,143,372	5.	6.	10.	20.	55.	150.	900.	–
1927	3,553,928	2.	2.	4.	10.	20.	60.	200.	3,000.
1928	9,144,860	–	1.	1.	3.	10.	30.	125.	3,500.
1929	12,159,840	–	1.	1.	3.	10.	35.	100.	2,000.
1930	2,538,613	3.	4.	6.	10.	25.	90.	200.	3,500.
1931	3,842,776	1.	2.	3.	8.	20.	60.	200.	3,000.
1932	21,316,190	–	–	1.	2.	8.	20.	60.	2,000.
1933	12,079,310	–	–	1.	2.	8.	30.	70.	1,750.
1934	7,042,358	–	–	1.	3.	8.	25.	75.	1,750.
1935	7,526,400	–	–	1.	3.	10.	25.	60.	750.
1936	8,768,769	–	–	1.	3.	8.	25.	60.	300.

COINAGE USING GEORGE V DIES 1936. In December,1936, the reigning King, Edward VIII, abdicated in favour of his brother, who became George VI. This placed a great strain upon the Royal Mint in London. It was well along in the preparation of the tools for the British Commonwealth coinage obverses, including those for Canada. All this work had to be scrapped and new obverse tools made for George VI.

In 1937, during the delay involved in the preparation of new obverses in London, the Royal Canadian Mint was forced to strike from 1936 dies quantities of all denominations, except the 5-cent and 50-cent piece. The dies for the 1, 10, and 25 cent pieces are said to have been marked with a tiny dot on the reverse. This was to indicate that the coins were struck in a year different from that borne on the dies and with the bust of the late King.

The 1936 dot cent is an extreme rarity; only three, all in mint state, are at present known. Numerous circulated examples of this rarity have come to light over the years; however, none has been satisfactorily authenticated. It seems unlikely that any genuine 1936 dot cents ever circulated, despite the supposedly official mintage of almost 700,000 pieces.

1936 with raised dot below date
struck in 1937

Date and Mint Mark	Mintage	F-12	VF-20	EF-40	AU-50	MS-60 Br	MS-63 Rd/Br
1936 Dot	Incl. in 1936		Heritage Belzberg Sale 2003 - $230,000 U.S.F.				

ONE CENT
George VI 1937 - 1952

In the early part of 1937 the Royal Mint in London decided to speed up the production of the new coinage tools for Canadian coinages by having some of the work done by the Paris Mint. Included in this work was the reverse for the cent. The model was sent to Paris for conversion into master coinage tools.

The reverse of the new cent continued the trend toward modernization of the Canadian coinage designs begun in 1935 with the voyageur silver dollar.

UNCROWNED PORTRAIT, "ET IND:IMP:", MAPLE TWIG, 1937-1947. The initial obverse (1937-1947) bore a legend containing the Latin abbreviation "ET IND:IMP:," indicating the king was the Emperor of India.

Designer and Engraver:
Obv.: T. H. Paget
Rev.: G. E. Kruger-Gray
Composition:
1937-1942:
.955 copper, .030 tin, .015 zinc
1942-1952:
.980 copper, .005 tin, .015 zinc
Weight: 3.24 grams
Diameter: 19.05 mm
Edge: Plain
Die Axis: ↑↑

Date and Mint Mark	Mintage	EF-40	AU-50	MS-60 Br	MS-63 Rr/Br	MS-64 Rd	MS-65 Rd.
1937	10,090,231	2.	3.	5.	15.	60.	150.
1938	18,365,608	1.	2.	3.	15.	50.	125.
1939	21,600,319	1.	2.	3.	10.	30.	60.
1940	85,740,532	1.	2.	3.	10.	35.	85.
1941	56,336,011	1.	3.	10.	50.	150.	600.
1942	76,113,708	1.	2.	10.	40.	175.	1,250.
1943	89,111,969	1.	2.	5.	35.	150.	500.
1944	44,131,216	1.	3.	15.	90.	500.	2,000.
1945	77,268,591	1.	2.	3.	20.	150.	600.
1946	56,662,071	1.	2.	3.	10.	40.	200.
1947 Bl 7	31,093,901	1.	2.	3.	9.	30.	125.

MAPLE LEAF ISSUE, 1947. The granting of independence to India resulted in a dilemma for the Royal Canadian Mint in the early part of 1948. New obverse coinage tools with "ET IND: IMP:" omitted would not arrive for several months, yet there was a pressing need for all denominations of coins. The mint satisfied this demand by striking coins dated 1947 and bearing an obverse with outmoded titles. To differentiate this issue from the regular strikings of 1947, a tiny maple leaf was placed after the date.

Blunt 7, Near maple leaf

Designers, engravers, physical and chemical specifications: Same as 1937 issues

Pointed 7, Near maple leaf

Date and Mint Mark	Mintage	EF-40	AU-50	MS-60 Br	MS-63 Rd/Br	MS-64 Rd	MS-65 Rd
1947 ML Bl 7	43,855,448	4.	6.	10.	30.	125.	250.
1947 ML Pt 7	Included	1.	2.	3.	8.	50.	175.

UNCROWNED PORTRAIT, MODIFIED OBVERSE LEGEND, MAPLE TWIG DESIGN, 1948-1952. Following the arrival of the master tools with the new obverse legend lacking "ET IND: IMP:" in 1948, the 1947 Maple Leaf coinage was suspended. For the remainder of the year coins were produced with the new obverse and the true date 1948. This obverse was employed for the rest of the reign.

Designers, Engravers, and Specifications:
Same as 1937 issues

VARIETIES OF 1948 AND 1949. Two master matrices were employed during the years 1948 and 1949. The obverse legend when centered by the "A" of GRATIA in relation to the denticles is found to be displaced.

"A" Points to Denticle   "A" Points between Denticles

Date and Mint Mark	Mintage	EF-40	AU-50	MS-60 Br	MS-63 Rd/Br	MS-64 Rd	MS-65 Br
1948 'A' points	25,767,779	1.	2.	15.	40.	150.	375.
1948 'A' between	Included	2.	3.	20.	30.	250.	900.
1949 'A' points	33,128,933	50.	65.	100.	450.	750.	–
1949 'A' between	Included	1.	2.	3.	12.	45.	125.
1950	60,444,992	1.	1.	2.	12.	50.	100.
1951	80,430,379	1.	1.	2.	15.	70.	250.
1952	67,631,736	1.	1.	2.	5.	40.	125.

ONE CENT
Elizabeth II 1953 to date

The portrait model for the new Queen Elizabeth coinages was prepared in England by a sculptress, Mrs. Mary Gillick. The relief of this model was too high, with the result that the centre portion containing two lines on the shoulder (representing a fold in the Queen's gown) did not strike up well on the coins. This first obverse variety has been commonly termed the "no shoulder strap" variety by many collectors. Later in 1953, Royal Canadian Mint authorities decided to correct the defects in the obverse design. Thomas Shingles, the Mint's Chief Engraver, lowered the relief of the model, and strengthened the shoulder and hair detail. This modified obverse (often called the "shoulder strap" variety due to the resemblance of the lines to a strap) was introduced before the end of the year and became the standard obverse. By mistake the No Shoulder Fold obverse was used to produce some of the 1954 cents for the Proof-like sets and a small quantity of 1955 cents for circulation.

Many collectors have difficulty differentiating the two varieties on slightly worn cents. The best way is to note that the "Is" on the No Shoulder Fold variety are flared at the ends and that an imaginary line drawn up through the centre of the "I" in "DEI" goes between two rim denticles. On the Shoulder Fold variety the "I's" are nearly straight sided and a line drawn up through the "I" of "DEI" runs into a rim denticle.

The reverse was a continuation of the George VI reverse.

LAUREATE PORTRAIT, MAPLE TWIG DESIGN, 1953-1964

Designer and Engraver:
    Obv: Mary Gillick
    Rev.: G. E. Kruger-Gray
Engraver:
    No Shoulder Fold Obverse:
        Thomas Shingles, using the Gillick
        portrait model;
    Shoulder Fold Obverse:
        Thomas Shingles, modifying
        existing NSF coinage tools
Composition: .980 copper, .005 tin,
        .015 zinc
Weight: 3.24 grams
Diameter: 19.05 mm
Edge: Plain
Die Axis: ↑↑

VARIETIES OF 1953 AND 1955.

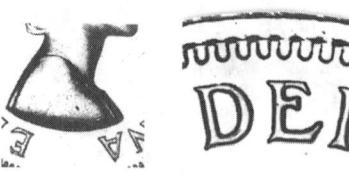  

No Shoulder Fold Obverse
Note flared ends of "Is", and "I" in
DEI points between two rim denticles.

Shoulder Fold Obverse
Note straight-sided "Is", and "I"
in DEI points at a rim denticle.

Date and Mint Mark	Mintage	VF-20	EF-40	AU-50	MS-60 Br	MS-63 Rd/Br	MS-64 Rd	MS-65 Rd
1953 NSF	67,806,016	–	–	–	1.	2.	20.	70.
1953 SF	Included	3.	4.	8.	15.	40.	100.	500.
1954 SF	22,181,760	–	–	–	2.	9.	35.	300.
1955 SF	56,403,193	–	–	–	1.	2.	20.	100.
1955 NSF	Included	200.	350.	550.	1,250.	1,750.	4,500.	–
1956	78,685,535	–	–	–	1.	2.	15.	75.
1957	100,601,792	–	–	–	1.	2.	15.	65.
1958	59,385,679	–	–	–	1.	1.	15.	50.
1959	83,615,343	–	–	–	1.	1.	12.	50.
1960	75,772,775	–	–	–	1.	1.	12.	50.
1961	139,598,404	–	–	–	1.	1.	10.	50.
1962	227,244,069	–	–	–	1.	1.	10.	50.
1963	279,076,334	–	–	–	1.	1.	10.	40.
1964	484,655,322	–	–	–	1.	1.	10.	40.

Note: Elizabeth II small cents, except for the 1953 SF and 1955 NSF, grading EF-40 and lower, at present, are not collectable.

TIARA PORTRAIT, MAPLE TWIG DESIGN, 1965-1966. In 1964 the British government decided to introduce a more mature portrait of Queen Elizabeth for domestic and Commonwealth coinages. The new portrait model, by Arnold Machin, features the Queen wearing a tiara instead of a laurel wreath. A copy of the model was forwarded to Canada and was incorporated into the obverses for 1965.

Designer and Engraver:
Obv.: Arnold Machin
Rev.: G. E. Kruger-Gray
Composition: .980 copper, .005 tin, .015 zinc
Weight: 3.24 grams
Diameter: 19.05 mm
Thickness: 1.55 mm
Edge: Plain
Die Axis: ↑↑

VARIETIES OF 1965. During 1965, difficulties were encountered in striking the cents, resulting in the introduction of a second variety obverse. The first variety has small beads at the rim and a flat field; the second variety has large rim beads and a field that slopes up at the rim. Another way to distinguish the two obverses is by the location of the "A" in "REGINA" relative to the rim beads: on the small beads obverse it points between two beads, whereas on the large beads obverse it points at a bead. In addition, two reverses differing in the style of 5 in the date were used in 1965. The obverses and reverses were employed in all possible combinations, creating four varieties for the year.

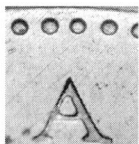   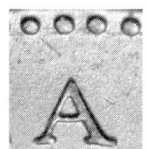

Small Beads Obverse   Large Beads Obverse
A of REGINA points between beads   A of REGINA points at bead

Pointed 5	Blunt 5
Top right of 5	Top right of 5
comes to a point	is nearly square

Date and Mint Mark	Mintage	AU-50	MS-60 Br	MS-63 Rd/Br	MS-64 Rd	MS-65 Rd
1965 Variety 1 (SB,P5)	304,441,082	1.	2.	4.	15.	100.
1965 Variety 2 (SB,B5)	Included	–	1.	1.	10.	40.
1965 Variety 3 (LB, B5)	Included	–	1.	1.	10.	40.
1965 Variety 4 (LB, P5)	Included	15.	20.	50.	100.	225.
1966	183,644,388	–	1.	1.	10.	40.

TIARA PORTRAIT, CENTENNIAL DESIGN, 1967. Alex Colville's design of a rock dove was selected for the 1967 cent reverse, struck in commemoration of Canada's centennial of Confederation. The event was marked by a special design for each denomination coined for circulation, plus a special $20 gold piece for collectors only. The obverse of the cent is the same as that for the 1966 issue.

Specifications:
Same as 1965 issue.

Date and Mint Mark	Mintage	MS-60 Br	MS-63 Rd/Br	MS-64 Rd	MS-65 Rd
1967 Confederation	345,140,645	1.	1.	10.	40.

TIARA (LARGE) PORTRAIT, MAPLE TWIG DESIGN RESUMED, 1968-1978

Specifications:
Same as 1965 issue.

Date and Mint Mark	Mintage	MS63 Rd	MS64 Rd	MS-65 Rd	MS-66 Rd	MS-67 Rd
1968	329,695,772	1.	2.	3.	–	–
1969	335,240,929	1.	2.	3.	–	–
1970	344,145,010	1.	2.	3.	–	–
1971	298,228,936	1.	2.	3.	–	–
1972	451,304,591	1.	2.	3.	–	–
1973	457,059,852	1.	2.	3.	–	–
1974	692,058,489	1.	2.	3.	–	–
1975	642,618,000	1.	2.	3.	–	–
1976	701,122,890	1.	2.	3.	–	–
1977	453,050,666	1.	2.	3.	–	–
1978	911,170,647	1.	2.	3.	–	–

MODIFIED TIARA PORTRAIT, MAPLE TWIG DESIGN, 1979. As part of a general standardization of the coinage, the portrait of the Queen was made smaller beginning with the 1979 coinage. The purpose was to make the size of the portrait proportional to the diameter of the coin, regardless of the denomination.

Designers and Engravers:
  Obv.: Arnold Machin, Walter Ott
  Rev.: G. E. Kruger-Gray
Composition: .980 copper, .005 tin,
              .015 zinc
Weight: 3.24 grams
Diameter: 19.05 mm
Thickness: 1.55 mm
Edge: Plain
Die Axis: ↑↑

Date and Mint Mark	Mintage	MS-63 Rd	MS-64 Rd	MS-65 Rd	MS-66 Rd	MS-67 Rd
1979	753,942,953	1.	2.	3.	–	–

MODIFIED TIARA PORTRAIT, MAPLE TWIG DESIGN, REDUCED WEIGHT, 1980-1981. In 1978 the Mint struck pattern pieces, dated 1979, with a considerably reduced weight and a diameter of 16 mm. The change was prompted by the rising price of copper which had resulted in the 1-cent piece being coined at a loss. Unfortunately, the diameter of the pattern was the same as that for the tokens used by the Toronto Transit Commission and this was enough to result in the cancellation of plans for the new 16 mm cent. The mint struck cents of the old size and design during 1979. However, in 1980 it introduced a coin of the same design as before, but with a decreased diameter and thickness resulting in a diminished weight.

Designer and Engraver:
  Obv.: Arnold Machin
  Rev.: G. E. Kruger-Gray
Composition: .980 copper, .005 tin,
              .015 zinc
Weight: 2.8 grams
Diameter: 19.00 mm
Thickness: 1.38 mm
Edge: Plain
Die Axis: ↑↑

Date and Mint Mark	Mintage	MS-63 Rd	MS-64 Rd	MS-65 Rd	MS-66 Rd	MS-67 Rd
1980	911,800,000	1.	2.	3.	–	–
1981	1,209,468,500	1.	2.	3.	–	–

TIARA PORTRAIT, MAPLE TWIG DESIGN, 1982-1989. In December of 1981 the Ministry of Supplies and Services announced that the Royal Canadian Mint would be modifying Canada's one-cent coin. The design was changed from a round to a twelve-sided piece. Also the rim denticles were removed and replaced with beads.

Designers and Engravers:
  Obv.: Arnold Machin
  Rev.: G. E. Kruger-Gray
Composition: .980 copper, .005 tin, .015 zinc
Weight: 2.5 grams
12-sided: 19.1 mm
Thickness: 1.45mm
Edge: Plain
Die Axis: ↑↑

1983 Near Beads   1983 Far Beads

Date and Mint Mark	Mintage	MS-63 Rd	MS-64 Rd	MS-65 Rd	MS-66 Rd	MS-67 Rd
1982	876,036,898	1.	2.	3.	–	–
1983 Near Beads	975,510,000	1.	2.	3.	–	–
1983 Far Beads	Included	1.	2.	3.	–	–
1984	838,225,000	1.	2.	3.	–	–

VARIETIES OF 1985

Blunt Five   Pointed Five

Date and Mint Mark	Mintage	MS-60	MS-63 Rd	MS-64 Rd	MS-65 Rd	MS-66 Rd	MS-67 Rd
1985 BL5	771,772,500	–	1.	2.	3.	–	–
1985 PT5	Included	15.	25.	40.	60.	–	–
1986	788,285,000	–	1.	2.	3.	–	–
1987	774,549,000	–	1.	2.	3.	–	–
1988	482,676,752	–	1.	2.	3.	–	–
1989	1,066,628,200	–	1.	2.	3.	–	–

CROWNED PORTRAIT, MAPLE TWIG DESIGN, COPPER, 1990-1996. In line with changes in Great Britain and other Commonwealth countries, Canada in 1990 introduced a new portrait for Canadian coins. This crowned portrait of Queen Elizabeth II is the first effigy of the queen designed by a Canadian, Dora de Pédery-Hunt. The diamond crown is completely circular, decorated with symbolic roses, shamrocks and thistles. It was made for George IV and worn by Queen Victoria for many of her formal portraits. Today it is worn by Queen Elizabeth for her opening of Parliament. In 1992 the reverse design was modified to include the bracket dates 1867-1992 for the 125th birthday of Canada.

1990-1991 and 1993-1996

1867-1992

Designers and Engravers:
Obv.: Dora de Pédery-Hunt,
Ago Aarand
Rev.: G. E. Kruger-Gray
Composition: .980 copper, .005 tin,
.015 zinc
Weight: 2.5 grams
12-sided: 19.1 mm
Thickness: 1.45mm
Edge: Plain
Die Axis: ↑↑

Date and Mint Mark	Mintage	MS-63 Rd	MS-64 Rd	MS-65 Rd	MS-66 Rd	MS-67 Rd
1990	218,035,000	1.	2.	3.	–	–
1991	831,001,000	1.	2.	3.	–	–
1867-1992	673,512,000	1.	2.	3.	–	–
1993	808,585,000	1.	2.	3.	–	–
1994	639,516,000	1.	2.	3.	–	–
1995	624,983,000	1.	2.	3.	–	–
1996	445,746,000	1.	2.	3.	–	–

CROWNED PORTRAIT, MAPLE TWIG DESIGN, COPPER PLATED ZINC, 1997-2003: In 1997 a decision was made to change the composition of the one cent coin from copper to copper plated zinc. The twelve sided design was not conducive to copper plating, which resulted in the reintroduction of the round design.

In 2002, in celebration of the Golden Jubilee of Elizabeth II's ascension to the throne, double dates, 1952-2002, were added to the obverse.

1997 to 2001 and 2003

Double dates 1952 2002

Designers and Engravers:
Obv.: Dora de Pédery-Hunt
Ago Aarand
Rev.: G. E. Kruger-Gray
Composition: Copper plated zinc
Weight: 2.25 grams
Diameter: 19.05 mm, round
Thickness: 1.45mm
Edge: Plain
Die Axis: ↑↑

Date and Mint Mark	Mintage	MS-63 Rd	MS-64 Rd	MS-65 Rd	MS-66 Rd	MS-67 Rd
1997	549,868,000	1.	2.	3.	–	–
1998	999,578,000	1.	2.	3.	–	–
1999	1,089,625,000	1.	2.	3.	–	–
2000	771,908,206	1.	2.	3.	–	–
2001	919,358,000	1.	2.	3.	–	–
1952-2002	715,502,000	1.	2.	3.	–	–
2003	92.219,775	1.	2.	3.	–	–

Note: In 2002 two varieties of composition were used in the production of the one cent coin: one copper plated zinc, the other copper plated steel. The official distribution was 80% plated zinc, and 20% plated steel. Naturally, the steel core 2002 will respond to a magnet.

UNCROWNED PORTRAIT, MAPLE TWIG DESIGN, COPPER PLATED ZINC, 2003-2004. In celebration of the Jubilee of the coronation of Queen Elizabeth II in 1953, a new portrait is seen on Canadian Coins.

Designers and Engravers:
Obv.: Susanna Blunt
      Susan Taylor
Rev.: G. E. Kruger-Gray
Specifications: Same as 1997 issue

Date and Mint Mark	Mintage	MS-63 Rd	MS-64 Rd	MS-65 Rd	MS-66 Rd	MS-67 Rd
2003	56,877,144	1.	2.	3.	–	–
2004	645,220,000	1.	2.	3.	–	–
2005	N/A	1.	2.	3.	–	–

CROWNED PORTRAIT, MAPLE TWIG DESIGN, MULTI-PLY PLATED STEEL, 1999-2003. To reduce costs, the Royal Canadian Mint developed a new multi-ply plated steel process which allows for the production of plated steel blanks. The acid based process electroplates a thin coating of nickel, then copper, onto a steel core. Sets of new multi-ply plated steel coinage, from one cent through fifty cents, were provided to the vending industry in early 1999 for testing purposes, in response to their requests for actual coins rather than test tokens. Naturally, samples found their way into collectors' hands resulting in a brisk trade. So that the demand would not get out of hand, resulting in failure of the testing procedures, the Mint issued sets of "P" coins for collectors. The new composition coins are marked with the letter "P" (plated) for identification purposes.

Designers and Engravers:
Obv.: Dora de Pédery-Hunt
      Ago Aarand
Rev.: G. E. Kruger-Gray
Composition: .940 steel, .045 copper
               .015 nickel
Weight: 2.35 grams
Diameter: 19.05
Thickness: 1.45 mm
Edge: Plain
Die Axis: ↑↑

Date and Mint Mark	Mintage	MS-63 Rd	MS-64 Rd	MS-65 Rd	MS-66 Rd	MS-67 Rd
1999P	Issued for testing	15.	20.	25.	–	–
2000P	Issued for testing		Only One Known			
1952-2002P	114,212,000	1.	2.	3.	–	–
2003P	235,936,799	1.	2.	3.	–	–

Note: There is no firm evidence that a Business Strike 2001P exists. We have listed it hoping that confirmation will surface; however, this may not be possible as this coin was also issued in Brilliant Uncirculated Sets of that year, which are often opened and sold as single coins.

UNCROWNED PORTRAIT, MAPLE TWIG DESIGN, MULTI-PLY PLATED STEEL, 2003-2005.

Designers and Engravers:
Obv.: Susanna Blunt, Susan Taylor
Rev.: G. E. Kruger-Gray
Composition: .940 steel, .045 copper
.015 nickel
Weight: 2.35 grams
Diameter: 19.05 mm
Thickness: 1.45 mm
Edge: Plain
Die Axis: ↑↑

Date and Mint Mark		Mintage	MS-63 Rd	MS-64 Rd	MS-65 Rd	MS-66 Rd	MS-67 Rd
2003P		354,994,666	1.	2.	3.	–	–
2004P		134,906,000	1.	2.	3.	–	–
2005P	Circulation Issue	N/A	1.	2.	3.	–	–
2005P	RCM Mint Roll, 50 coins	N/A	5.	–	–	–	–
2005P	First Strike	5,000	15.	–	–	–	–

FIVE CENTS
Victoria 1870 - 1901

The first 5-cent pieces for the Dominion of Canada were introduced in 1870. The initial designs were identical to those used for the Province of Canada in 1858. During the reign of Queen Victoria, five obverse varieties, differing primarily in the facial features, were employed. Three varieties of the reverse are known: the Wide Rim reverse (1870), the Narrow Rim, 21 Leaves reverse (1870-1881, 1890-1901) and the Narrow Rim, 22 Leaves reverse (1882-1889).

VICTORIA OBVERSE PORTRAIT VARIETIES

PORTRAIT: F1
The hair to the side of the ear has an 'S' curl to the braid.

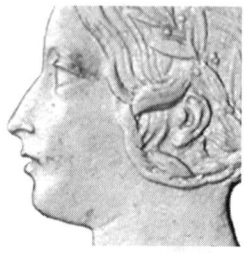

F1 will be found on the following dates:
1870 W

PORTRAIT: F2
The hair to the side of the ear has a faint 'S' curl to the braid.

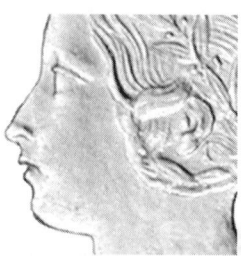

F2 will be found on the following dates:
1870 N; 1871; 1872H; 1874H S; 1874 L;
1875H S; 1875 L; 1880H; 1891; 1892;
1893; 1894; 1896; 1897 W; 1897 N;
1897 N/W; 1898; 1899; 1900 W; 1900 N;
1901

VICTORIA OBVERSE PORTRAIT VARIETIES

PORTRAIT F3
The hair to the side of the ear curves up and is then flat to the ear.

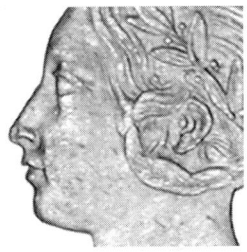

F-3 will be found on the following dates:
1880H; 1881H

PORTRAIT: F4
The braid to the side of the ear is flat and curves upward from the ear.

F4 will be found on the following date:
1882H

PORTRAIT: F5
The braid over the ear is very prominent with almost no visible strands.

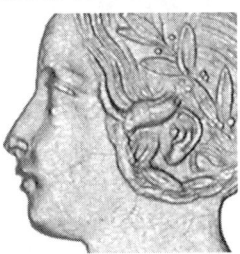

F5 will be found on the following dates:
1883H; 1884 N; 1884 F; 1885 S; 1885 5/5;
1885 L; 1886 S; 1886 L; 1887; 1888; 1889;
1890H; 1891; 1892

VICTORIA REVERSE VARIETIES

1870 Wide rim, 21 leaves reverse
1870-1881 Narrow rim, 21 leaves reverse
1882-1889 Narrow rim, 22 leaves reverse
1890-1901 Narrow rim, 21 leaves reverse

21 LEAVES, WIDE RIM DESIGN, 1870.

1870 Wide Rims (W)

Designer and Engraver: Leonard C. Wyon
Weight: 1.16 grams
Edge: Reeded

Composition: .925 silver, .075 copper
Diameter: 15.50 mm
Die Axis: ↑↓

Date, Mint Portrait	Mintage	VG-8	F-12	VF-20	EF-40	AU-50	MS-60	MS-63	MS-65
1870 W-F1	2,800,000	25.	40.	75.	100.	200.	350.	1,000.	6,500.

21 LEAVES, NARROW RIM DESIGN, 1870-1881. Before the coinage of 1870 was complete, new master tools for the 5-cent piece were introduced, with the result that two varieties were created for the year. The first has wide rims (including unusually long rim denticles) on the obverse and reverse and the second has more conventional narrow rims.

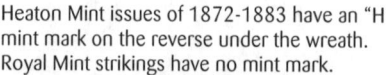

1870 Narrow Rims (N)

Heaton Mint issues of 1872-1883 have an "H" mint mark on the reverse under the wreath. Royal Mint strikings have no mint mark.

Date, Mint Portrait	Mintage	VG-8	F-12	VF-20	EF-40	AU-50	MS-60	MS-63	MS-65
1870 N-F2	Included	25.	40.	75.	125.	200.	375.	900.	5,000.
1871-F2	1,400,000	25.	40.	75.	125.	200.	400.	1,000.	3,000.
1872H-F2	2,000,000	18.	30.	60.	100.	250.	600.	2,000.	6,500.

VARIETIES OF 1874H AND 1875H. In 1874 and 1875 two sizes of digits were used for dating the dies. In addition to date sizes, the style of the 4 and 5 differ in their respective dates. The four of 1874 has either a plain 4 or a crosslet 4, while the five of 1875 has either a short top 5 or a long top 5.

1874H Small Date (S)	1874H Large Date (L)
(Plain 4)	(Crosslet 4)

1875H Small Date (S)	1875H Large Date (L)
Short top on 5	Long top on 5

Date, Mint Portrait	Mintage	VG-8	F-12	VF-20	EF-40	AU-50	MS-60	MS-63	MS-65
1874H S-F2	800,000	30.	70.	150.	250.	375.	600.	1,500.	4,000.
1874H L-F2	Included	25.	60.	125.	200.	375.	800.	2,000.	5,000.
1875H S-F2	1,000,000	225.	300.	550.	850.	1,600.	2,500.	10,000.	–
1875H L-F2	Included	350.	500.	875.	1,500.	2,750.	5,000.	15,000.	–
1880H-F2	3,000,000	10.	18.	35.	125.	275.	–	–	–
1880H-F3	Included	10.	18.	40.	100.	200.	500.	1,250.	5,000.
1881H-F3	1,500,000	12.	20.	35.	100.	250.	500.	1,250.	–

22 LEAVES DESIGN, NARROW RIM, 1882-1889. In the 1884 'punch' variety we find a spacing difference between the 8 and the 4. Besides the punch spacing, the cross ends of the fours differ – a pointed end and a blunt end.

VARIETIES OF 1884

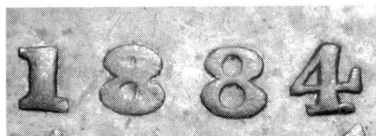 

1884 Near 4, Pointed (N)	1884 Far 4, Blunt (F)

Date, Mint Portrait	Mintage	VG-8	F-12	VF-20	EF-40	AU-50	MS-60	MS-63	MS-65
1882H-F4	1,000,000	16.	30.	60.	115.	250.	600.	1,200.	3,000.
1883H-F5	600,000	30.	65.	135.	275.	675.	1,500.	3,000.	–
1884 N-F5	200,000	150.	250.	550.	1,100.	2,500.	–	–	–
1884 F-F5	Included	125.	275.	450.	1,200.	3,000.	6,000.	12,000.	25,000.

VARIETIES OF 1885 AND 1886. During the year 1885, two markedly different styles of 5 were used in the date. One is the small 5 seen on the 1875H issue; the other is the larger 5 used in the denomination "5 CENTS." There is also an overdate 5 over 5. Coins of 1886 occur with either a small 6 or a large 6 for the final digit of the date. The uppermost part of the inner portion of the small 6 comes to a point, whereas that area on the large 6 is almost square.

1885 Small 5 **(S)**	1885	1885 Large 5 **(L)**
Short top on 5	Small 5 over	Large top on 5
	large 5	

1886 Small 6 **(S)**   1886 Large 6 **(L)**

Date, Mint Portrait	Mintage	VG-8	F-12	VF-20	EF-40	AU-50	MS-60	MS-63	MS-65
1885 S-F5	1,000,000	20.	30.	75.	150.	300.	2,000.	4,000.	–
1885 5/5-F5	Included	75.	125.	250.	600.	1,500.	–	–	–
1885 L-F5	Included	25.	45.	65.	150.	300.	–	–	–
1886 S-F5	1,700,000	15.	30.	40.	100.	200.	600.	1,800.	4,500.
1886 L-F5	Included	18.	30.	40.	85.	200.	600.	1,800.	4,000.
1887-F5	500,000	30.	60.	100.	200.	350.	600.	1,000.	4,000.
1888-F5	1,000,000	10.	18.	35.	75.	100.	300.	650.	1,500.
1889-F5	1,200,000	35.	55.	100.	200.	300.	800.	2,400.	–

21 LEAVES, NARROW RIM DESIGN RESUMED, 1890-1901.

Date, Mint Portrait	Mintage	VG-8	F-12	VF-20	EF-40	AU-50	MS-60	MS-63	MS-65
1890H-F5	1,000,000	12.	22.	40.	100.	200.	300.	600.	2,500.
1891-F2	1,800,000	10.	15.	25.	60.	120.	300.	700.	–
1891-F5	Included	10.	15.	30.	60.	100.	250.	600.	3,500.
1892-F2	860,000	11.	20.	40.	100.	200.	500.	1,000.	4,000.
1892-F5	Included	10.	20.	40.	100.	200.	–	–	–
1893-F2	1,700,000	9.	13.	25.	65.	100.	300.	600.	3,500.
1894-F2	500,000	25.	55.	100.	160.	350.	600.	1,500.	6,000.
1896-F2	1,500,000	9.	15.	30.	60.	150.	250.	650.	2,500.

VARIETIES OF 1889.

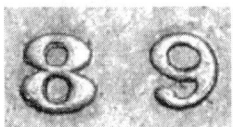
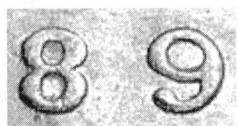

| 1897 Wide 8 **(W)** | 1897 Narrow 8 **(N)** | 1897 Narrow over Wide 8 **(N/W)** |

Date, Mint Portrait	Mintage	VG-8	F-12	VF-20	EF-40	AU-50	MS-60	MS-63	MS-65
1897 W-F2	1,319,280	10.	20.	45.	100.	150.	275.	600.	–
1897 N-F2	Included	9.	12.	25.	50.	125.	250.	600.	2,400.
1897 N/W-F2	Included	10.	20.	45.	100.	200.	750.	2,000.	–
1898-F2	580,400	20.	30.	65.	125.	250.	600.	1,200.	5,000.
1899-F2	3,000,000	8.	12.	25.	50.	100.	225.	450.	1,250.

VARIETIES OF 1900. Two sizes of the date are seen on the 1900 issue. The large date has been referred to most often as the Round 0s variety and the small date as the Oval 0s variety, but there is a greater difference in the 9s. The large date has a Wide 9 as on the 1898 issue and the small date has a Narrow 9 as on the 1899 and 1901 issues.

| 1900 Large Date Wide 0s and 9 **(W)** | 1900 Small Date Narrow 0s and 9 **(N)** |

Date, Mint Portrait	Mintage	VG-8	F-12	VF-20	EF-40	AU-50	MS-60	MS-63	MS-65
1900 W-F2	1,800,000	33.	60.	90.	200.	350.	500.	1,000.	3,000.
1900 N-F2	Included	8.	12.	23.	45.	100.	200.	450.	1,500.
1901-F2	2,000,000	8.	12.	20.	50.	90.	300.	450.	1,500.

FIVE CENTS
Edward VII 1902 - 1910

In 1902, the coronation year for Edward VII, the Royal Mint was extremely busy producing new coinage tools and striking the new coins and medals. One compromise this necessitated involved the reverse of the Canadian 5-cent piece. It had been intended to transfer both the word "CANADA" from the obverse to the reverse legend and to replace the old St. Edward's crown, showing depressed arches at the top, with the Imperial State crown, showing raised arches at the top. Instead, the mint had to settle for making the legend change only. The following year the crown was changed. The 1903H issue had a reverse with 21 leaves, but a modified design with 22 leaves was instituted for the London issue. The Mint, Birmingham issue has an "H" mint mark on the reverse under the wreath. The London Mint has no letter.

IMPERIAL STATE CROWNED PORTRAIT, ST. EDWARD'S CROWN, 21 LEAVES DESIGN, 1902

Designer and Engraver:
George W. DeSaulles
Composition: .925 silver, .075 copper
Weight: 1.16 grams
Diameter: 15.50 mm
Edge: Reeded
Die Axis: ↑↓

VARIETIES OF 1902. Two sizes of "H" appear on the 1902 Heaton Mint issue of this denomination. One is a small, narrow "H" not seen on any other Canadian coins and the other is a large, wide "H" similar to that on the 1903H.

1902 Large H	1902 Small H

Date and Mint Mark	Mintage	VG-8	F-12	VF-20	EF-40	AU-50	MS-60	MS-63	MS-65
1902	2,120,000	3.	4.	7.	13.	25.	50.	70.	200.
1902H Large H	2,200,000	3.	5.	9.	18.	32.	50.	75.	300.
1902H Small H	Included	10.	18.	40.	65.	100.	125.	200.	500.

IMPERIAL STATE CROWNED PORTRAIT, 21 LEAVES DESIGN, 1903. The 1903 issue for the Heaton Mint was essentially the same as the 1902 coinage with the St. Edward's crown replaced by the Imperial State crown. This design was employed for only the one year at the Heaton Mint.

Designer and Engraver:
probably George W. DeSaulles

Specifications:
Same as 1902 issue.

Date and Mint Mark	Mintage	VG-8	F-12	VF-20	EF-40	AU-50	MS-60	MS-63	MS-65
1903H Large H	2,640,000	25.	50.	75.	135.	275.	450.	1,500.	—
1903H Small H	Included	4.	8.	14.	30.	75.	125.	400.	—

IMPERIAL STATE CROWNED PORTRAIT, IMPERIAL STATE CROWN, 22 LEAVES DESIGN,

1903-1910. In a move unprecedented in Canadian coinage the Royal Mint produced a coin (the 5-cent piece) that bore a somewhat different design than that used by its sub-contractor, Ralph Heaton, in 1903. The 1903 Royal Mint issue features a new wreath with 22 instead of 21 leaves.

Designer and Engraver:
Obv.: George W. De Saulles
Rev.: W. H. J. Blakemore
Composition: .925 silver, .075 copper
Weight: 1902-1910: 1.16 grams
       1910: 1.17 grams
Diameter: 15.50 mm
Edge: Reeded
Die Axis: 1903-1907: ↑↓
       1908-1910: ↑↑

Date and Mint Mark	Mintage	VG-8	F-12	VF-20	EF-40	AU-50	MS-60	MS-63	MS-65
1903	1,000,000	6.	12.	25.	60.	135.	225.	500.	950.
1904	2,400,000	4.	6.	13.	35.	90.	250.	650.	3,000.
1905	2,600,000	3.	5.	12.	25.	65.	175.	375.	1,250.
1906	3,100,000	3.	4.	8.	18.	50.	125.	325.	1,250.
1907	5,200,000	3.	4.	7.	15.	35.	75.	175.	800.

VARIETIES OF 1908. In 1908, different sized punches were used, resulting in small 8 and large 8 varieties.

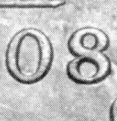 

      1908 Small 8   1908 Large 8

Date and Mint Mark	Mintage	VG-8	F-12	VF-20	EF-40	AU-50	MS-60	MS-63	MS_65
1908 Small 8	1,197,780	8.	16.	35.	55.	100.	125.	200.	1,000.
1908 Large 8	Included	35.	50.	125.	225.	350.	600.	1,200.	3,600.

VARIETIES OF 1909 AND 1910. In 1909 the existing reverse was modified to create a variety in which the maple leaves have sharp points along their edges, causing them to resemble holly leaves. Both the Maple Leaves and the Holly Leaves reverses saw use in 1909 and 1910.

Maple Leaves Reverse (1903-1910)   Holly Leaves Reverse (1909-1910)
     Round leaves   Pointed leaves

Date and Mint Mark	Mintage	VG-8	F-12	VF-20	EF-40	AU-50	MS-60	MS-63	MS-65
1909 Maple	1,890,865	5.	9.	18.	45.	120.	250.	750.	1,750.
1909 Holly	Included	20.	30.	65.	150.	275.	800.	2,000.	—
1910 Maple	5,580,325	16.	30.	55.	150.	300.	600.	1,750.	3,500.
1910 Holly	Included	3.	4.	9.	15.	30.	75.	125.	600.

FIVE CENTS - SILVER
George V 1911 - 1921

IMPERIAL STATE CROWNED PORTRAIT, 'GODLESS', 22 LEAVES DESIGN, 1911. The new obverse introduced in 1911 was criticized by the public because the Latin phrase "DEI GRATIA" (or an abbreviation for it), indicating that the King ruled by the grace of God, was omitted. The coinage tools were modified during the year and a new obverse with "DEI GRA:" included in the legend appeared on the 1912 issue. The Maple Leaves design reverse was that of the previous reign.

Designer and Engraver:
Obv.: Sir E. B. MacKennal
Rev.: W. H. J. Blakemore
Composition: .925 silver, .075 copper
Weight: 1.17 grams
Diameter: 15.50 mm
Edge: Reeded
Die Axis: ↑↑

Date and Mint Mark	Mintage	VG-8	F-12	VF-20	EF-40	AU-50	MS-60	MS-63	MS-65
1911	3,692,350	3.	5.	8.	15.	45.	80.	125.	300.

IMPERIAL STATE CROWNED, 'DEI GRATIA', 22 LEAVES DESIGN, 1912-1921. During 1920-1921 plans moved forward for the replacement of the small silver 5-cents piece with a larger coin of pure nickel, the same size as the U.S. nickel. The enabling legislation was passed in May 1921 and thereafter no more circulating 5-cent pieces were coined in silver. The mint melted some 3,022,665 coins of this denomination. The presumed composition of this melt was almost all the 1921 mintage and a portion of the 1920 mintage, thus explaining the rarity of the 1921 date today. Only about 400 1921s are believed to have survived. A few are Specimen coins, issued to collectors in sets and the rest are thought to be circulation strikes sold to visitors to the Mint in the early months of 1921.

Composition:
1912-1919: .925 silver, .075 copper
1920-1921: .800 silver, .200 copper
Edge: Reeded
Die Axis: ↑↑

Date and Mint Mark	Mintage	VG-8	F-12	VF-20	EF-40	AU-50	MS-60	MS-63	MS-65
1912	5,863,170	3.	4.	7.	15.	35.	75.	225.	1,000.
1913	5,588,048	3.	4.	8.	12.	25.	40.	65.	200.
1914	4,202,179	3.	4.	8.	12.	35.	75.	200.	1,500.
1915	1,172,258	15.	25.	40.	80.	200.	350.	700.	2,000.
1916	2,481,675	5.	8.	15.	30.	85.	150.	300.	1,500.
1917	5,521,373	3.	4.	5.	10.	25.	50.	100.	500.
1918	6,052,289	3.	4.	5.	9.	20.	40.	75.	300.
1919	7,835,400	3.	4.	6.	9.	20.	35.	75.	300.
1920	10,649,851	3.	4.	5.	9.	20.	40.	75.	300.
1921	2,582,495*	3,500.	4,250.	5,500.	8,000.	11,000.	−	−	60,000.

*Almost all 1921 5¢ are believed to have remained unissued and were returned to the melting pot in 1922.

FIVE CENTS - NICKEL
George V 1922 - 1936

IMPERIAL STATE CROWNED, 'DEI GRATIA', TWO MAPLE LEAVES DESIGN, 1922-1936. The new Canadian nickel 5-cent piece was introduced in 1922 after two years of planning. The silver coin it replaced was allowed to circulate until the 1930s, when a more active withdrawal program was instituted.

Designer and Engraver:
Obv.: Sir E. B. MacKennal
Rev.: W. H. J. Blakemore
Composition: 1.00 nickel
Weight: 4.54 grams
Diameter: 21.21 mm
Edge: Plain
Die Axis: ↑↑

Date and Mint Mark	Mintage	VG-8	F-12	VF-20	EF-40	AU-50	MS-60	MS-63	MS-65
1922 Near Rim	4,763,186	1.	2.	3.	12.	35.	65.	125.	850.
1922 Far Rim	Included	2.	4.	8.	25.	45.	65.	125.	750.
1923	2,475,201	–	1.	5.	20.	70.	125.	400.	–
1924	3,066,658	–	1.	5.	15.	50.	125.	275.	3,500.
1925	200,050	95.	125.	165.	300.	800.	2,000.	6,000.	–

VARIETIES OF 1926. It was the usual practice in the George V 5-cent series to complete the date at the matrix stage, eliminating the necessity of dating every reverse die and thereby assuring that there would be no difference in the positioning of the date digits on a given year's coinage. A notable exception occurred in 1926, when the reverse punch (bearing a 6 which nearly touched the maple leaf) was retired before the conclusion of the coinage. The second variety had the 6 slightly farther from the maple leaf.

1926 Near 6
The 6 almost touches
the maple leaf

1926 Far 6
The 6 is farther from
the maple leaf

Date and Mint Mark	Mintage	VG-8	F-12	VF-20	EF-40	AU-50	MS-60	MS-63	MS-65
1926 Near 6	933,577	4.	10.	25.	85.	250.	500.	1,200.	–
1926 Far 6	Included	175.	275.	375.	700.	1,250.	2,000.	2,500.	6,000.
1927	5,285,627	–	1.	5.	20.	45.	90.	175.	2,000.
1928	4,588,725	–	1.	5.	20.	45.	75.	125.	500.
1929	5,562,262	–	1.	5.	20.	45.	95.	175.	2,500.
1930	3,685,991	–	2.	5.	20.	35.	150.	300.	2,500.
1931	5,100,830	–	2.	6.	20.	60.	200.	600.	–
1932	3,198,566	–	2.	5.	20.	50.	150.	1,200.	3,500.
1933	2,597,867	–	2.	8.	30.	85.	250.	1,000.	–
1934	3,827,304	–	2.	5.	22.	60.	150.	450.	–
1935	3,900,000	–	2.	5.	18.	45.	175.	350.	1,500.
1936	4,400,450	–	1.	3.	15.	35.	75.	150.	500.

FIVE CENTS
George VI 1937 - 1942

UNCROWNED PORTRAIT, BEAVER DESIGN, NICKEL, 1937-1942. In 1937 Canada introduced new coinage designs for the lower denominations, in keeping with a trend towards modernization begun in 1935 with the silver dollar. The reverse of the 5-cent piece depicts a beaver on a rock-studded mound of earth rising out of the water. At the left is a log on which the beaver has been chewing. The master tools for this reverse were produced at the Paris Mint because the Royal Mint in London was pressed for time.

Designer and Engraver:
　　Obv.: T. H. Paget
　　Rev.: G. E. Kruger-Gray
Composition: 1.00 nickel
Weight: 4.54 grams
Diameter: 21.21 mm
Edge: Plain
Die Axis: ↑↑

Date and Mint Mark	Mintage	EF-40	AU-50	MS-60	MS-63	MS-65
1937 Dot	4,593,263	3.	6.	15.	25.	200.
1938	3,898,974	18.	45.	90.	200.	3,500.
1939	5,661,123	9.	25.	60.	125.	400.
1940	13,820,197	4.	10.	25.	50.	400.
1941	8,681,785	5.	15.	40.	75.	1,250.
1942 Nickel	6,847,544	4.	10.	20.	40.	325.

UNCROWNED PORTRAIT, BEAVER DESIGN, TOMBAC, 1942. Nickel is an important component of stainless steel and other alloys needed for producing war materials, so World War II put a great strain upon Canada's nickel producers. By 1942 it was decided that nickel would have to be suspended as a coinage material for the duration of the war and experiments were initiated to find a substitute metal for the 5-cent piece. This led to the adoption of a 12-sided coin made of tombac, a kind of brass. The idea had come from the British 3-penny piece first issued in 1937. The tombac 5-cent was given its shape so that when tarnished it would still not be confused with 1-cent pieces.

Designer: Royal Canadian Mint staff,
　　　　　　modifying existing designs
Engraver: Thomas Shingles, modifying
　　　　　　Royal Mint coinage tools
Composition: .88 copper, .12 zinc
Weight: 4.54 grams
12-sided: 21.3 mm (opposite corners)
　　　　　　20.0 mm (opposite sides)
Edge: Plain
Die Axis: ↑↑

Date and Mint Mark	Mintage	EF-40	AU-50	MS-60	MS-63	MS-65
1942 Tombac	3,396,234	3.	4.	5.	25.	150.

UNCROWNED PORTRAIT, VICTORY DESIGN, TOMBAC, 1943-1944. In 1943 a new reverse design came into use for this denomination. Its purpose was to help promote the war effort. The idea for the design came from Churchill's famous "V" sign and the V denomination mark on the U.S. 5-cent pieces of 1883-1912. A novel feature was the use of an International Code message meaning, "We Win When We Work Willingly." It was placed along the rim on the reverse instead of denticles. The original master matrix was engraved entirely by hand by Royal Canadian Mint Chief Engraver Thomas Shingles. The obverse was the same as that for 1942, except rim denticles were added.

Designer and Engraver:
Obv.: Thomas Shingles, modifying existing design and tools
Rev.: Thomas Shingles
Composition: .88 copper, .12 zinc
Weight: 4.54 grams
12-sided: 21.3 mm (opposite corners)
20.9 mm (opposite sides)
Edge: Plain
Die Axis: ↑↑

Date and Mint Mark	Mintage	EF-40	AU-50	MS-60	MS-63	MS-65
1943	24,760,256	1.	2.	5.	15.	150.
1944	8,000			Only one known		

Note: 1. A 1943 5¢ Torch and V design struck on a nickel planchet was certified as an error coin by Numismatic Guarantee Corporation of America during 2001.

2. Most of the 1944 5¢ tombac remained unissued and were melted; only one is known to have survived. This coin was auctioned at the ANA Sale in 1999 for $38,500. USF.

UNCROWNED PORTRAIT, VICTORY DESIGN, STEEL, 1944-1945. War demands for copper and zinc forced a suspension in the use of tombac for the 5-cent piece and the institution of plated steel. The steel was plated with nickel and then returned to the plating tank for a very thin plating of chromium. The chromium was hard and helped retard wear. Unfortunately it was necessary to plate the strips prior to the blanks being punched out. This resulted in the edges of the blanks (and hence the coins) being unplated and vulnerable to rusting.

Some collectors have noted steel 5-cent pieces which have a dull gray colour instead of the normal bluish-white colour. This is the result of some of the strips being plated with nickel only and not nickel and chromium. Such coins do not ordinarily command a significant premium.

Composition: Steel with .0127 mm plating of nickel and .0003 mm plating of chromium

Specifications: Same as 1943 issue

Date and Mint Mark	Mintage	EF-40	AU-50	MS-60	MS-63	MS-65
1944	11,532,784	1.	2.	3.	10.	45.
1945	18,893,216	1.	2.	3.	10.	45.

UNCROWNED PORTRAIT, "ET IND:IMP:', BEAVER DESIGN RESUMED, NICKEL, 1946-1947.
After the end of World War II, the Mint returned to the issue of nickel 5-cent pieces of the beaver design. However, it was decided to retain the 12-sided shape, because it had become popular. The obverse was a continuation of that of 1943-1945.

Designer and Engraver:
  Obv.: Thomas Shingles, modifying
        existing design and tools
  Rev.: Thomas Shingles, modifying
        existing design and tools
Composition: 1.00 nickel
Weight: 4.54 grams
12-sided: 21.3 mm (opposite corners)
       20.9 mm (opposite sides)
Edge: Plain
Die Axis: ↑↑

Date and Mint Mark	Mintage	EF-40	AU-50	MS-60	MS-63	MS-65
1946	6,952,684	3.	7.	30.	45.	500.
1947	7,603,724	2.	5.	15.	30.	300.

MAPLE LEAF ISSUE OF 1947. The granting of independence to India created a dilemma for the Royal Canadian Mint in the early part of 1948. The new obverse coinage tools (with "ET IND: IMP:" omitted) would not arrive for several months, yet there was a great need for all denominations of coins. Therefore, the mint struck coins dated 1947 and bearing the obverse with the outmoded titles. To differentiate this issue from the regular strikings of 1947, a tiny maple leaf was placed after the date.

1947 Maple Leaf issue, struck in 1948.

Specifications: Same as 1946-1947
            issues.

VARIETIES OF 1947.

1947 Maple Leaf

1947 Dot

Date and Mint Mark	Mintage	VF-20	EF-40	AU-50	MS-60	MS-63	MS-65
1947 ML	9,595,124	1.	2.	5.	15.	30.	200.
1947 Dot	Included	40.	90.	200.	250.	425.	1,500.

UNCROWNED PORTRAIT, 'DEI GRATIA', BEAVER DESIGN, NICKEL, 1948-1950. Following the arrival of the master tools with the new obverse legend lacking "ET IND: IMP:" in 1948, the 1947 Maple Leaf coinage was suspended from production. For the remainder of the year coins were produced with the new obverse and the true date, 1948.

Designer and Engraver:
  Obv.: Thomas Shingles, modifying existing design and tools
  Rev.: Thomas Shingles, modifying existing design and tools
Composition: 1.00 nickel
Weight: 4.54 grams
12-sided: 21.3 mm (opposite corners)
            20.9 mm (opposite sides)
Edge: Plain
Die Axis: ↑↑

Date and Mint Mark	Mintage	VF-20	EF-40	AU-50	MS-60	MS-63	MS-65
1948	1,810,789	−	5.	12.	25.	40.	175.
1949	13,736,276	−	2.	4.	10.	20.	125.
1950	11,950,520	−	2.	4.	6.	20.	150.

UNCROWNED PORTRAIT, COMMEMORATIVE DESIGN, NICKEL, 1951. In 1950 plans were made to strike a coin to commemorate the isolation and naming of the element nickel by the Swedish chemist A.F. Cronstedt in 1751. The three Canadian commemorative coins issued up to that time had been silver dollars, but the 5-cent piece was selected for use in 1951 because it was the only denomination struck in nickel. The design was chosen from entries submitted to the Mint in an open competition, the first of its type in Canada for a coinage that was actually issued. The winning design depicts a nickel refinery, with low buildings flanking a smoke stack in the centre. The obverse is the same as that for the 1948-1950 issues.

Some members of the public became confused and believed that the dates 1751-1951 should have read 1851-1951. This caused hoarding of these coins in the mistaken belief that they would become extremely valuable.

Designer and Engraver:
  Obv.: Thomas Shingles, modifying existing design and tools
  Rev.: Stephan Trenka
Composition: 1.00 nickel
Weight: 4.54 grams
12-sided: 21.3 mm (opposite corners)
            20.9 mm (opposite sides)
Edge: Plain
Die Axis: ↑↑

Date and Mint Mark	Mintage	VF-20	EF-40	AU-50	MS-60	MS-63	MS-65
1951 Comm.	8,329,321	−	1.	2.	3.	10.	250.

UNCROWNED PORTRAIT, BEAVER DESIGN RESUMED, STEEL, 1951-1952. The Korean War placed strong demand on nickel, forcing suspension of production of the commemorative nickel 5-cent piece before the end of 1951. In its place steel coins of the beaver design were struck. It was found during trials that the beaver design was not as easy to strike in steel as in nickel, so new, lower relief coinage tools were prepared for both obverse and reverse. By mistake, a High Relief obverse die was used to strike a small proportion of the 1951 steel coinage, resulting in two varieties for the year. Aside from the difference in relief, the High and Low Relief obverses differ in the position of the last A of "GRATIA" relative to the rim denticles. On the High Relief variety the "A" points to a rim denticle; on the Low Relief variety it points between denticles. The entire 1952 issue was coined with the Low Relief obverse.

Designer and Engraver:
Obv.: Thomas Shingles, modifying existing design and tools
Rev.: Thomas Shingles, modifying existing models
Composition: Steel with .0127 mm plating of nickel and .0003 mm plating of chromium
Weight: 4.54 grams
12-sided: 21.3 mm (opposite corners) 20.9 mm (opposite sides)
Edge: Plain
Die Axis: ↑↑

A in GRATIA
points to a rim denticle

1951 High Relief
Obverse

A in GRATIA points
between rim denticles

1951 Low Relief
Obverse

Date and Mint Mark	Mintage	VG-8	F-12	VF-20	EF-40	AU-50	MS-60	MS-63	MS-65
1951 High Relief	4,313,410	350.	600.	825.	1,500.	2,250.	–	–	–
1951 Low Relief	Included	–	–	–	1.	2.	4.	15.	175.
1952	10,891,148	–	–	–	1.	2.	4.	10.	100.

FIVE CENTS:
Elizabeth II 1953 to date

LAUREATED BUST, BEAVER DESIGN, STEEL, 1953-1954. Two obverse varieties, termed the No Shoulder Fold and Shoulder Fold obverses, saw use during 1953 (see 1-cent Elizabeth II, 1953 to date, for full explanation). On the 5-cent piece these varieties are best distinguished on worn coins by observing the styles of the letters in the obverse legends: they are more flared (particularly the E and I of "DEI") on the No Shoulder Fold variety. The Reverse was also modified in 1953 resulting in Far and Near Maple Leaf varieties.

Designer and Engraver:
    Obv.: Mary Gillick
Engraver: No Shoulder Fold Obverse:
    Thomas Shingles, using the
    Gillick portrait model
    Shoulder Fold Obverse:
    Thomas Shingles, modifying
    existing NSF coinage tools
Composition: Steel with .0127 mm
    plating of nickel and .0003 mm
    plating of chromium
Weight: 4.54 grams
12-sided: 21.3 mm (opposite corners)
    20.9 mm (opposite sides)
Thickness: 1.90 mm
Edge: Plain
Die Axis: ↑↑

No Shoulder Fold Obverse
note flared ends of "I"s

No Shoulder Fold
Obverse

Far Maple Leaf

Shoulder Fold Obverse
note straight-sided "I"s

Shoulder Fold Obverse
note straight-sided "I"s

Near Maple Leaf

Date and Mint Mark	Mintage	VF-20	EF-40	AU-50	MS-60	MS-63	MS-64	MS-65
1953 NSF, far	16,635,552	–	1.	2.	4.	10.	20.	90.
1953 NSF, near	Included	750.	850.	1,250.	2,000.	4,000.	–	–
1953 SF, near	Included	1.	2.	3.	10.	12.	25.	100.
1953 SF, far	Included	400.	700.	1,200.	1,500.	4,000.	–	–
1954 SF	6,998,662	–	2.	3.	6.	15.	20.	75.
1954 NSF	Included	Only One Known in VF-20						

LAUREATED BUST, BEAVER DESIGN, NICKEL, 1955-1962. The mint returned to production in nickel for the 5-cent piece in 1955. The obverse and reverse designs were continued from the previous year.

Designers, Engravers and Specifications:
Same as 1953 issues.

Composition: 1.00 nickel

Date and Mint Mark	Mintage	AU-50	MS-60	MS-63	MS-64	MS-65
1955	5,355,028	2.	4.	10.	20.	60.
1956	9,399,854	2.	4.	7.	25.	75.
1957	7,387,703	2.	3.	10.	20.	75.
1958	7,607,521	2.	3.	10.	15.	60.
1959	11,552,523	–	1.	10.	15.	60.
1960	37,157,433	–	1.	10.	15.	60.
1961	47,889,051	–	1.	5.	15.	60.
1962	46,307,305	–	1.	5.	15.	60.

LAUREATED BUST, ROUND, BEAVER DESIGN, NICKEL, 1963-1964. For strictly economic reasons the production of round 5-cent pieces was resumed in 1963 for the first time since 1942. It was cheaper to make round coins because the collars for the coining presses lasted longer.

1964 Extra Water Line

Engraver: Thomas Shingles
Weight: 4.54 grams
Edge: Plain
Die Axis: ↑↑

Composition: 1.00 nickel
Diameter: 21.21 mm
Thickness: 1.75 mm

Date and Mint Mark	Mintage	AU-50	MS-60	MS-63	MS-64	MS-65
1963	43,970,320	–	1.	5.	15.	30.
1964	78,075,068	–	1.	5.	15.	30.
1964 XWL	Included	30.	45.	85.	–	–

Note: Five cent coins in lower grades currently do not command a premium over face value.

TIARA PORTRAIT, ROUND, BEAVER DESIGN, NICKEL, 1965-1966. A new obverse with the Queen showing more mature facial features and wearing a tiara was introduced on all denominations in 1965.

Designer and Engraver:
Obv.: Arnold Machin

Specifications: Same as 1963-1964 issues

VARIETIES OF 1965.

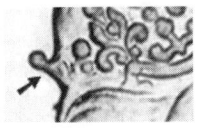 1965 Small Beads
Attached Jewel

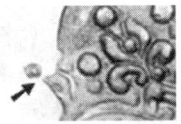 1965 Large Beads
Detached Jewel

Date and Mint Mark	Mintage	VF-20	EF-40	AU-50	MS-60	MS-63	MS-64	MS-65
1965 Small beads	84,876,018	–	–	–	1.	5.	15.	40.
1965 Large beads	Included	50.	100.	200.	750.	1,500.	–	–
1966	27,976,648	–	–	–	1.	5.	15.	30.

Note: A dash (–) in the pricing column of the "Mint State" grades indicates that no example has been graded by a Canadian grading company.

TIARA PORTRAIT, ROUND, CENTENNIAL DESIGN, NICKEL, 1967. A reverse design showing a hopping rabbit was selected for the 1967 5-cent piece. It was by Alex Colville, who also designed the reverses of the other Confederation commemoratives issued for circulation. The obverse was a continuation of the 1965-1966 design.

Designer:
  Rev.: Alex Colville
Engraver:
  Rev.: Myron Cook
Specifications: Same as 1963-1966
    issues.

Date and Mint Mark	Mintage	MS-60	MS-63	MS-64	MS-65
1967	36,876,574	1.	5.	15.	30.

TIARA PORTRAIT, ROUND, BEAVER DESIGN RESUMED, NICKEL, 1968-1978. During 1977 a change in the matrix resulted in new punches and thus new dies creating a variety in the seven's for that year. The seven's vary in distance from Canada and are also different in type size.

Designer and Engraver:
  Obv.: Arnold Machin
  Rev.: G. E. Kruger-Gray
Composition: 1.00 nickel
Weight: 4.54 grams
Diameter: 21.21 mm
Thickness: 1.80 mm
Edge: Plain
Die Axis: ↑↑

Date and Mint Mark	Mintage	MS-63	MS-64	MS-65	MS-66	MS-67
1968	99,253,330	1.	2.	3.	–	–
1969	27,830,229	1.	2.	3.	–	–
1970	5,726,010	1.	2.	3.	–	–
1971	27,312,609	1.	2.	3.	–	–
1972	62,417,387	1.	2.	3.	–	–
1973	53,507,435	1.	2.	3.	–	–
1974	94,704,645	1.	2.	3.	–	–
1975	138,882,000	1.	2.	3.	–	–
1976	55,140,213	1.	2.	3.	–	–

VARIETIES OF 1977.

1977 High 7   1977 Low 7

Date and Mint Mark	Mintage	MS-63	MS-64	MS-65	MS-66	MS-67
1977 High	89,120,791	1.	2.	3.	–	–
1977 Low	Included	20.	45.	150.	–	–
1978	137,079,273	1.	2.	3.	–	–

MODIFIED TIARA PORTRAIT, ROUND, BEAVER DESIGN, NICKEL, 1979-1989. Beginning on the 1979 coinage and as part of a general standardization of the coinage, the portrait of the Queen was made smaller. The purpose was to make the size of the portrait proportional to the diameter of the coin, regardless of the denomination.

Designer and Engraver:
    Obv.: Arnold Machin, Walter Ott
    Rev.: G. E. Kruger-Gray
Composition:
    1979-1981: 1.00 nickel
    1982-1989: .75 copper, .25 nickel
Weight: 4.54 grams
Diameter: 21.21 mm
Thickness: 1.75 mm
Edge: Plain
Die Axis: ↑↑

Date and Mint Mark	Mintage	MS-63	MS-64	MS-65	MS-66	MS-67
1979	186,295,825	1.	2.	3.	–	–
1980	134,878,000	1.	2.	3.	–	–
1981	99,107,900	1.	2.	3.	–	–
1982	105,539,898	1.	2.	3.	–	–
1983	72,596,000	1.	2.	3.	–	–
1984	84,088,000	1.	2.	3.	–	–
1985	126,618,000	1.	2.	3.	–	–
1986	156,104,000	1.	2.	3.	–	–
1987	106,299,000	1.	2.	3.	–	–
1988	75,025,000	1.	2.	3.	–	–
1989	141,435,538	1.	2.	3.	–	–

Note: Circulating coinage grading below MS-63 at the present time is not collectable.

CROWNED PORTRAIT, ROUND, BEAVER DESIGN, NICKEL, 1990-1991. A new obverse portrait of the Queen wearing a diamond diadem and jewellery was introduced on all denominations in 1990.

Designers and Engravers:
Obv.: Dora de Pédery-Hunt
Ago Aarand
Rev.: G. E. Kruger-Gray
Composition: Cupro-nickel
.75 copper, .25 nickel
Weight: 4.6 grams
Diameter: 21.2 mm
Thickness: 1.76 mm
Edge: Plain
Die Axis: ↑↑

Date and Mint Mark	Mintage	MS-63	MS-64	MS-65	MS-66	MS-67
1990	42,537,000	1.	2.	3.	–	–
1991	10,931,000	1.	2.	3.	–	–

CROWNED PORTRAIT, COMMEMORATIVE FOR THE 125TH ANNIVERSARY DESIGN, NICKEL, 1867-1992. The reverse design was modified to include the bracket dates 1867-1992 for the 125th birthday of Canada

Designers, Engravers and Specifications:
Same as 1990 issues

Date and Mint Mark	Mintage	MS-63	MS-64	MS-65	MS-66	MS-67
1867-1992	53,732,000	1.	2.	3.	–	–

CROWNED PORTRAIT, ROUND, BEAVER DESIGN, COPPER NICKEL, 1993-2001. In 1993 the practice of using a single date was resumed. The transition from rim denticles to beads, which began in 1982 on the one cent piece, was carried out on the five cent piece in 1993. The Winnipeg Mint Mark (W) is found only on coins from the "Oh Canada!" and "Tiny Treasures" sets issued by the Numismatic Department of the Mint.

Designers, Engravers and Specifications:
Same as 1990 issues

5¢ 1996 Far 6

"6" Far from "D"
in Canada

5¢ 1996 Near 6

"6" Near "D"
in Canada

VARIETIES OF 1996.

Date and Mint Mark	Mintage	MS-63	MS-64	MS-65	MS-66	MS-67
1993	86,877,000	1.	2.	3.	–	–
1994	99,352,000	1.	2.	3.	–	–
1995	78,780,000	1.	2.	3.	–	–
1996 Far 6	36,686,000	2.	3.	10.	–	–
1996 Near 6	Included	1.	2.	3.	–	–
1997	27,354,000	1.	2.	3.	–	–
1998	156,873,000	1.	2.	3.	–	–
1999	124,861,000	1.	2.	3.	–	–
2000	105,868,000	1.	2.	3.	–	–
2001	30,035,000	1.	2.	3.	–	–

CROWNED PORTRAIT, ROUND, BEAVER DESIGN, MULTI-PLY PLATED STEEL, 1999-2003. In 2000 the Royal Canadian Mint began issuing circulating 5-cent coins struck on their new multi-ply plated steel blanks. The process is acid based and electroplates a thin coating of nickel, then copper, then nickel again to a steel core.

1999P to 2001P and 2003P

Double dates 1952 2002P

Designers and Engravers:
Obv.: Dora de Pédery-Hunt
      Ago Aarand
Rev.: G. E. Kruger-Gray
Composition: .945 steel, .035 copper, .02 nickel
Weight: 3.95 grams
Diameter: 21.10 mm
Thickness: 1.76 mm
Edge: Plain
Die Axis: ↑↑

"P" Mint Mark

Date and Mint Mark	Mintage	MS-63	MS-64	MS-65	MS-66	MS-67
1999P	Issued for testing	6.	12.	25.	–	–
2000P	4,899,000	5.	15.	40.	–	–
2001P	136,656,000	1.	5.	25.	–	–
1952-2002P	134,361,000	1.	2.	3.	–	–
2003P	31,388,921	1.	2.	3.	–	–

UNCROWNED PORTRAIT, ROUND, BEAVER DESIGN, MULTI-PLY PLATED STEEL, 2003-2005.

Designers and Engravers:
Obv.: Susanna Blunt, Susan Taylor
Rev.: G. E. Kruger-Gray
Specifications: Same as 1999P issue

Date and Mint Mark	Mintage	MS-63	MS-64	MS-65	MS-66	MS-67
2003P	61,392,180	1.	2.	3.	–	–
2004P	123,085,000	1.	2.	3.	–	–
2005P	N/A	1.	2.	3.	–	–

TEN CENTS
Victoria 1870 - 1901

The initial designs for the Victoria 10-cent pieces issued by the Dominion government were identical to the 1858 Province of Canada issue. During the reign, six obverse portraits were used. They differed primarily in the features of the Queen's face. A detailed description and listing by year follow on the next pages. Two major varieties of the reverse exist; only in 1891 were both used for the same year's coinage (see page 103).

VICTORIA OBVERSE PORTRAIT VARIETIES

PORTRAIT: T1
The legend has large narrow letters. The two top leaves of the laurel crown are both well defined. The primary leaf does not touch the 'I' in 'Dei'.

T1 will be found on the following dates:
1870 N0; 1870 W0; 1871; 1871H;
1872H; 1874H; 1875H; 1880H; 1881H

PORTRAIT: T2
The legend has large narrow letters. The two top leaves in the laurel crown are well defined. The primary leaf touches the lower pointed serif of the 'I' in 'DEI'; the secondary leaf is fat.

T2 will be found on the following dates:
1880H; 1881H

VICTORIA OBVERSE PORTRAIT VARIETIES

PORTRAIT: T3

The legend has large narrow letters. The top two leaves of the laurel crown are well defined. The primary leaf touches the lower serif of the 'I' in 'DEI'; and the secondary leaf is thin.

T3 will be found on the following dates:
1882H; 1883H

PORTRAIT: T4

The legend has small wide letters. Of the two top leaves of the laurel crown the primary leaf is fully outlined but weak in definition, the secondary leaf is cut with the top missing, only a small portion of it protruding from behind the primary.

T4 will be found on the following dates:
1884; 1885; 1886 (all varieties)

PORTRAIT: T5

The legend has large letters. Of the two top leaves of laurel crown, the primary leaf, which is ill-defined, is complete, the secondary leaf appears as only a small point.

T5 will be found on the following dates:
1885; 1886 (all varieties); 1887; 1888; 1889; 1890H; 1891 21 Lvs; 1891 22 Lvs; 1892; 1892 2/1; 1893 (all varieties)· 1894; 1896; 1890

PORTRAIT: T6
The legend has large narrow letters. Of the top
two leaves of the laurel crown, both the primary
and the large secondary are well defined with
the primary barely touching the 'I' in 'DEI'.

T6 will be found on the following dates:
1892; 1892 2/1; 1893 (all varieties);
1894; 1896; 1898; 1899 S9; 1899 L9;
1900; 1901

LAUREATED PORTRAIT, 21 MAPLE LEAVES DESIGN,1870-1881.

Designer and Engraver:
    Leonard C. Wyon
Composition: .925 silver, .075 copper
Weight: 2.33 grams
Diameter: 18.03 mm
Edge: Reeded
Die Axis: ↑↓

Heaton Mint issues of 1871-1883 and
1890 have an "H" mint mark on the
reverse under the wreath. Royal Mint
strikings have no mint mark.

VARIETIES OF 1870. Two styles of 0 appear in the date of the 1870 issue. The Narrow 0 with sides
of equal thickness is more common than the Wide 0, on which the right-hand side is thicker.

1870 Narrow "0" **(N)**
Sides of equal thickness

1870 Wide "0" **(W)**
Right side is thicker

Date, Mint Portrait	Mintage	VG-8	F-12	VF-20	EF-40	AU-50	MS-60	MS-63	MS-65
1870 N-T1	1,600,000	35.	60.	100.	175.	250.	600.	1,500.	6,000.
1870 W-T1	Included	50.	100.	175.	300.	450.	900.	3,000.	6,000.
1871-T1	800,000	45.	75.	150.	300.	475.	900.	2,000.	6,000.
1871H-T1	1,870,000	45.	75.	175.	300.	450.	900.	2,500.	–
1872H-T1	1,000,000	175.	250.	500.	750.	1,250.	2,500.	4,000.	–

MINTAGE FIGURES 1874H AND 1875H. Through a clerical error part of the mintage of 1874H-dated coins was assigned to the next year's production figures. Therefore, the mintage figures for the two years, 600,000 and 1,000,000, respectively, have been combined.

Date, Mint Portrait	Mintage	VG-8	F-12	VF-20	EF-40	AU-50	MS-60	MS-63	MS-65
1874H-T1	1,600,000	20.	40.	75.	175.	250.	475.	1,500.	3,500.
1875H-T1	Included	375.	650.	1,200.	2,250.	3,500.	–	–	–
1880H-T1	1,500,000	25.	50.	100.	175.	275.	650.	2,000.	4,000.
1880H-T2	Included	30.	60.	125.	225.	400.	1,000.	–	–
1881H-T1	950,000	30.	50.	100.	200.	300.	–	–	–
1881H-T2	Included	30.	55.	110.	225.	300.	750.	–	7,000.

LAUREATED PORTRAIT, 22 MAPLE LEAVES DESIGN, 1882-1901. Another leaf was added to the maple wreath design of 1870-1881.

Date, Mint Portrait	Mintage	VG-8	F-12	VF-20	EF-40	AU-50	MS-60	MS-63	MS-65
1882H-T3	1,000,000	30.	50.	100.	200.	300.	1,000.	2,000.	–
1883H-T3	300,000	100.	175.	325.	650.	900.	1,500.	3,500.	–
1884-T4	150,000	325.	600.	1,100.	2,500.	5,000.	9,000.	18,000.	–
1885-T4	400,000	75.	175.	350.	900.	1,750.	–	–	–
1885-T5	Included	200.	400.	800.	1,600.	2,500.	3,500.	–	–

VARIETIES OF 1886. For the 1886 coinage three distinctly different styles of 6 were used: a small 6, a large 6 with a point on its tail, and a large 6 with a large knob on its tail.

    1886 Small 6   1886 Large, Pointed 6   1886 Large, Knobbed 6

Date, Mint Portrait	Mintage	VG-8	F-12	VF-20	EF-40	AU-50	MS-60	MS-63	MS-65
1886 S6-T4	800,000	40.	75.	150.	300.	600.	–	–	–
1886 S6-T5	Included	50.	90.	200.	450.	1,000.	–	–	–
1886 Pt6-T4	Included	150.	225.	450.	900.	1,500.	–	–	–
1886 Pt6-T5	Included	175.	225.	500.	1,000.	1,750.	–	–	–
1886 Kn6-T4	Included	60.	100.	200.	500.	1,200.	–	–	–
1886 Kn6-T5	Included	120.	175.	350.	700.	1,400.	–	–	–
1887-T5	350,000	75.	150.	300.	600.	1,200.	2,000.	5,500.	–
1888-T5	500,000	20.	40.	80.	175.	250.	500.	1,250.	3,500.
1889-T5	600,000	900.	1,750.	2,500.	5,000.	10,000.	20,000.	45,000.	–
1890H-T5	450,000	35.	65.	125.	250.	400.	750.	2,000.	4,000.

VARIETIES OF 1891, 1892 AND 1893. The two major reverse varieties seen on this denomination differ in the number of leaves in the wreath. The first (1870-1881 & 1891) has 21 leaves and the second (1882-1901) has 22 leaves. The 21-leaf reverse in 1891 occurs with small digits in the date, whereas the 22-leaf reverse in 1891 has a large date.

One 1891 large date die was carried over into 1892 and the 1 was overdated with a 2. Aside from the overpunching, the 1892 over 1 differs from the non-overdate 1892s in the style of the 9. The overdate has the large 9 of the 22 leaves, 1891 variety, and the non-overdates have the small 9 of the 21 leaves, 1891 variety.

Dating varieties continued into 1893. In that year one or two dies were dated with a large 9 and round-top 3, while the rest were dated with a medium 9 and a flat-top 3.

VARIETIES OF 1891, 1892 AND 1893.

1891 - 21 Leaves, Small Date   1891 - 22 Leaves, Large Date

1892 - 2 over 1, Large 9   1892 Normal Date, Small 9

1893 Round-top 3, Large 9   1893 Flat-top 3, Large 9

The last two digits of the date are added to the punch or die by hand. The hand punching of the "Round Top" 3 digit was weak, either by lack of force or possibly because the punch itself was broken.

Date, Mint Portrait	Mintage	VG-8	F-12	VF-20	EF-40	AU-50	MS-60	MS-63	MS-65
1891 21L-T5	800,000	35.	60.	120.	250.	375.	750.	1,500.	4,000.
1891 22L-T5	Included	35.	60.	120.	250.	375.	750.	2,000.	4,500.
1892-T5	520,000	30.	60.	125.	250.	400.	–	–	–
1892-T6	Included	40.	70.	125.	250.	–	–	–	–
1892 2/1-T5	Included	275.	450.	850.	1,750.	–	–	–	–
1892 2/1-T6	Included	275.	450.	850.	1,750.	3,500.	–	–	–
1893 R3-T5	Included 1,200.		2,000.	4,000.	7,000.	10,000.	–	–	–
1893 R3-T6	Included 1,200.		2,000.	4,000.	7,000.	10,000.	–	–	–
1893 F3-T5	500,000	50.	100.	200.	325.	650.	–	–	–
1893 F3-T6	Included	70.	120.	250.	450.	750.	1,250.	–	–
1894-T5	500,000	45.	75.	150.	275.	500.	–	–	–
1894-T6	Included	45.	75.	150.	275.	500.	–	2,000.	–
1896-T5	650,000	20.	40.	65.	125.	200.	–	–	–
1896-T6	Included	20.	40.	65.	125.	500.	1,000.	1,500.	–
1898-T5	720,000	20.	35.	70.	125.	200.	–	–	–
1898-T6	Included	20.	35.	70.	125.	200.	500.	1,200.	4,000.

VARIETIES OF 1899. During the production of the 1899 10-cent pieces, two styles of 9 were used for dating the dies: a small, narrow 9 and a large, wide 9. The upper centre of the wide 9 is almost round, compared with the tall, rectangular centre of the narrow 9.

    1899 Small 9s   1899 Large 9s

Date, Mint Portrait	Mintage	VG-8	F-12	VF-20	EF-40	AU-50	MS-60	MS-63	MS-65
1899 S9-T6	1,200,000	18.	30.	60.	115.	175.	400.	800.	2,000.
1899 L9-T6	Included	35.	55.	100.	200.	325.	800.	1,200.	4,000.
1900-T6	1,100,000	15.	30.	50.	100.	150.	300.	600.	1,500.
1901-T6	1,200,000	15.	25.	50.	100.	150.	275.	550.	2,000.

TEN CENTS
Edward VII 1902 - 1910

IMPERIAL STATE CROWNED PORTRAIT, MAPLE LEAVES DESIGN, 1902-1910. The reverse first employed for the 10-cent pieces of this reign was adapted from the 22-leaf Victorian reverse. The Imperial State crown replaced the St. Edward's crown at the top and the word "CANADA" was transferred from the obverse legend.

Designer and Engraver:
Obv.: George W. DeSaulles
Rev.: **Victorian Leaves Reverse:**
1902-09: G.W. DeSaulles
Broad Leaves Reverse:
1909-1910:
W. H. J. Blakemore
Composition: .925 silver, .075 copper
Weight: 1902-1910: 2.32 grams
1910: 2.33 grams
Diameter: 18.03 mm
Edge: Reeded
Die Axis: 1902-1907: ↑↓
1908-1910: ↑↑

The Mint, Birmingham, issues (1902-1903) have an "H" mint mark on the reverse under the wreath. Royal Mint issues have no mint mark.

Date and Mint Mark	Mintage	VG-8	F-12	VF-20	EF-40	AU-50	MS-60	MS-63	MS-65
1902	720,000	10.	20.	45.	100.	175.	500.	1,000.	4,000.
1902H	1,100,000	7.	12.	25.	50.	85.	175.	300.	900.
1903	500,000	20.	40.	80.	300.	600.	1,200.	2,500.	5,000.
1903H	1,320,000	10.	20.	50.	100.	165.	350.	650.	2,000.
1904	1,000,000	15.	30.	60.	125.	200.	375.	750.	4,500.
1905	1,000,000	12.	36.	75.	150.	275.	750.	1,750.	4,500.
1906	1,700,000	8.	16.	35.	75.	150.	350.	1,000.	3,250.
1907	2,620,000	7.	14.	35.	70.	150.	325.	600.	3,000.
1908	776,666	14.	30.	70.	140.	190.	300.	500.	1,250.

VARIETIES OF 1909. In 1909 an entirely new model was prepared for this denomination. The variety thus created has been called the Broad Leaves variety because of its broad leaves with strong, detailed venation.

1909 Victoria Leaves   1909 Broad Leaves

Date and Mint Mark	Mintage	VG-8	F-12	VF-20	EF-40	AU-50	MS-60	MS-63	MS-65
1909 Victorian	1,697,200	8.	25.	55.	125.	200.	500.	1,250.	—
1909 Broad	Included	14.	30.	65.	130.	300.	800.	1,750.	5,000.
1910	4,468,331	6.	12.	25.	50.	75.	160.	375.	1,500.

TEN CENTS
George V 1911 - 1936

IMPERIAL STATE CROWNED PORTRAIT, "GODLESS", MAPLE LEAVES DESIGN, 1911. The obverse combined with the 1911 reverse aroused criticism because it lacked reference to the King's ruling "by the grace of God." The coinage tools were modified during 1911 and a new legend containing the Latin abbreviation "DEI GRA." appeared on the 1912 and subsequent issues. The first reverse was a continuation of the Broad Leaves design introduced in 1909. It was replaced during 1913 (see below).

Designer and Engraver:
Obv.: Sir E. B. MacKennal
Rev.: W. H. J. Blakemore
          (Small Leaves Reverse)
Composition: .925 silver, .075 copper
Weight: 2.32 grams
Diameter: 18.03 mm
Edge: Reeded
Die Axis: ↑↑

Date and Mint Mark	Mintage	F-12	VF-20	EF-40	AU-50	MS-60	MS-63	MS-65
1911	2,737,584	12.	25.	50.	75.	150.	275.	500.

IMPERIAL STATE CROWNED PORTRAIT, "DEI GRATIA", MAPLE LEAVES DESIGN, 1912-1936.

Composition:
  1912-1919: .925 silver, .075 copper
  1920-1936: .800 silver, .200 copper

Specifications:
  Same as 1911 issue

Date and Mint Mark	Mintage	F-12	VF-20	EF-40	AU-50	MS-60	MS-63	MS-65
1912	2,234,557	4.	10.	40.	90.	275.	600.	2,500.

VARIETIES OF 1913. The reverse that replaced the Broad Leaves design during 1913 has smaller leaves with less venation. It is from a completely new model.

1913 Broad Leaves   1913 Small Leaves

Date and Mint Mark	Mintage	F-12	VF-20	EF-40	AU-50	MS-60	MS-63	MS-65
1913 Small	3,613,937	4.	9.	25.	75.	175.	500.	1,500.
1913 Broad	Included	250.	500.	1,000.	3,500.	8,000.	–	–
1914	2,549,811	4.	9.	25.	70.	300.	600.	1,500.
1915	688,057	16.	35.	100.	250.	475.	1,000.	3,000.
1916	4,218,114	3.	7.	20.	60.	100.	225.	700.
1917	5,011,988	2.	5.	15.	40.	70.	125.	400.
1918	5,133,602	2.	4.	12.	40.	75.	100.	400.
1919	7,877,722	2.	4.	12.	40.	65.	125.	400.
1920	6,305,345	2.	4.	15.	45.	80.	150.	500.
1921	2,469,562	3.	8.	22.	50.	110.	250.	600.
1928	2,458,602	2.	5.	15.	40.	75.	175.	600.
1929	3,253,888	2.	5.	15.	40.	75.	150.	400.
1930	1,831,043	3.	6.	18.	50.	75.	150.	600.
1931	2,067,421	2.	5.	16.	40.	75.	150.	375.
1932	1,154,317	4.	10.	30.	60.	100.	200.	600.
1933	672,368	5.	15.	40.	80.	200.	400.	1,500.
1934	409,067	8.	25.	70.	125.	350.	650.	1,500.
1935	384,056	8.	25.	60.	160.	375.	650.	1,500.
1936	2,460,871	2.	4.	12.	40.	50.	100.	250.

COINAGE USING GEORGE V DIES 1936. Early in 1937, while the Royal Canadian Mint was awaiting the arrival of the master tools for the new coinage for George VI, an emergency coinage of 10-cent pieces dated 1936 and from George V dies is said to have taken place. To mark the special nature of the coinage the dies bore a small raised dot on the reverse under the wreath.

Although the mintage of the 1936 dot variety is claimed to be nearly 200,000, only five examples seem to survive today. All are specimen strikes, adding to the suspicion that circulation strikes were either never produced or were all melted. No genuine circulation strike has been confirmed.

  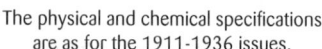

The physical and chemical specifications are as for the 1911-1936 issues.

1936 With Raised Dot Below Date, struck in 1937

Date and Mint Mark	Mintage	SPECIMEN
1936 Dot	191,237	Belzberg Sale 2003 – $74,750 USF

TEN CENTS
George VI 1937 - 1952

COINAGE OF GEORGE VI 1937-1952. The new reverse design introduced in 1937 was destined to become one of the most loved and most controversial of Canada's coinage designs. It features a "fishing schooner under sail," as the official proclamation states. Proud Nova Scotians, believing the ship represents the famous fishing and racing schooner "Bluenose" have continually pressed for official acknowledgment. It was not until March 15th, 2002 that the design was officially recognized to be that of the Bluenose. Available information indicates that the designer, Emanuel Hahn, used that ship as his primary model. The original master tools for the reverse were prepared at the Paris Mint. To improve the wearing qualities of the date, larger size digits were introduced in 1938.

UNCROWNED PORTRAIT, 'ET: IND: IMP:', BLUENOSE DESIGN, 1937-1947. The initial obverse bore a legend containing the Latin abbreviation "ET IND: IMP:" to indicate that the King was the Emperor of India.

Designer and Engraver:
    Obv.: T. H. Paget
    Rev.: Emanuel Hahn
Composition: .800 silver, .200 copper
Weight: 2.33 grams
Diameter: 18.03 mm
Edge: Reeded
Die Axis: ↑↑

Date and Mint Mark	Mintage	VF-20	EF-40	AU-50	MS-60	MS-63	MS-65
1937	2,500,095	3.	4.	10.	20.	30.	200.
1938	4,197,323	4.	10.	30.	60.	85.	550.
1939	5,501,748	3.	9.	20.	50.	75.	500.
1940	16,526,470	2.	4.	8.	25.	35.	175.
1941	8,716,386	4.	10.	20.	45.	70.	300.
1942	10,214,011	2.	6.	18.	40.	60.	250.
1943	21,143,229	2.	5.	12.	20.	35.	250.
1944	9,383,582	2.	6.	12.	30.	45.	250.
1945	10,979,570	2.	5.	8.	20.	35.	200.
1946	6,300,066	3.	7.	15.	35.	60.	200.
1947	4,431,926	4.	10.	18.	35.	55.	200.

MAPLE LEAF ISSUE 1947. The granting of independence to India posed a problem for the Royal Canadian Mint in the early part of 1948. The new obverse coinage tools (with the Latin phrase "ET IND: IMP:" omitted to indicate that the King was no longer the Emperor of India) would not arrive for several months, yet there was a need for all denominations of coins. The mint satisfied the demand by striking coins dated 1947 bearing the obverse with the outmoded titles. To differentiate this issue from the regular strikings of 1947, a tiny maple leaf was placed after the date.

1947 Maple Leaf Issue
struck in 1948

Date and Mint Mark	Mintage	VF-20	EF-40	AU-50	MS-60	MS-63	MS-65
1947 Maple Leaf	9,638,793	3.	5.	8.	18.	25.	125.

UNCROWNED PORTRAIT, 'DEI GRATIA', BLUENOSE DESIGN, 1948-1952. Following the arrival of the master tools with the obverse legend omitting "ET IND: IMP:" production of the 1947 Maple Leaf coinage was suspended. For the remainder of the year coins were produced with the new obverse and the true date, 1948. This obverse was employed for the rest of the reign.

Designer and Engraver:
    Obv.: T. H. Paget
    Rev.: Emanuel Hahn
Composition: .800 silver, .200 copper
Weight: 2.33 grams
Diameter: 18.03 mm
Edge: Reeded
Die Axis: ↑↑

Doubled Die 1951 10¢

Date and Mint Mark	Mintage	VF-20	EF-40	AU-50	MS-60	MS-63	MS-65
1948	422,741	12.	22.	30.	60.	75.	300.
1949	11,336,172	2.	4.	6.	15.	20.	135.
1950	17,823,075	2.	3.	5.	10.	15.	150.
1951	15,079,265	1.	2.	3.	9.	15.	150.
1951 DD	Included	6.	10.	25.	60.	90.	–
1952	10,474,455	1.	2.	4.	9.	12.	100.

TEN CENTS
Elizabeth II 1953 to Date

LAUREATED PORTRAIT; BLUENOSE DESIGN, 1953-1964. Two obverse varieties, termed the No Shoulder Fold and the Shoulder Fold obverses, saw use during 1953 (see 1-cent Elizabeth II 1953 to date for full explanation). On heavily circulated 10-cent pieces these varieties are most easily distinguished by observing the lettering styles in the legend. The No Shoulder Fold obverse has thicker letters with more flared ends (note the ls). The use of the George VI reverse was continued.

Designer and Engraver:
    Obv.: Mary Gillick
Engraver:
    Obv.: **No Shoulder Fold:**
        Thomas Shingles, using the
        Gillick portrait model;
    Shoulder Fold:
        Thomas Shingles, modifying
        existing NSF coinage tools
Composition: .800 silver, .200 copper
Weight: 2.33 grams
Diameter: 18.03 mm
Thickness: 1.16
Edge: Reeded
Die Axis: ↑↑

No Shoulder Fold Obverse
1953, note the flared ends
of the letters.

Shoulder Fold Obverse
1953-1954, the ends of the
letters are not as flared.

Date and Mint Mark	Mintage	AU-50	MS-60	MS-63	MS-64	MS-65
1953 NSF	17,706,395	3.	7.	12.	20.	100.
1953 SF	Included	3.	9.	15.	45.	250.
1954	4,493,150	5.	9.	16.	35.	150.
1955	12,237,294	3.	5.	10.	20.	80.
1956	16,732,844	3.	4.	10.	15.	75.
1957	16,110,229	2.	3.	8.	12.	35.
1958	10,621,236	2.	3.	8.	15.	40.
1959	19,691,433	–	3.	8.	15.	40.
1960	45,466,835	–	2.	5.	10.	40.
1961	26,850,859	–	2.	5.	10.	40.
1962	41,864,335	–	2.	5.	10.	40.
1963	41,916,208	–	2.	5.	10.	40.
1964	49,518,549	–	2.	5.	10.	40.

TIARA PORTRAIT, BLUENOSE DESIGN, 1965-1966. A new obverse with the Queen showing more mature facial features and wearing a tiara was introduced on all denominations in 1965.

Designer and Engraver:
    Obv.: Arnold Machin
    Rev.: Emanuel Hahn
Composition: .800 silver, .200 copper
Weight: 2.33 grams
Diameter: 18.03 mm
Thickness: 1.16
Edge: Reeded
Die Axis: ↑↑

Date and Mint Mark	Mintage	MS-60	MS-63	MS-64	MS-65
1965	55,965,392	2.	5.	10.	40.
1966	34,330,199	2.	5.	10.	40.

TIARA PORTRAIT, CENTENNIAL DESIGN, 1967. A reverse design showing a mackerel was chosen as part of the group of commemorative designs for the centennial of Confederation. During the year, the rising price of silver forced a reduction in the silver content to .500 from .800. The two varieties are not distinguishable by appearance. The obverse is the same as on the 1965-1966 issues.

Designers and Engravers:
  Obv.: Arnold Machin
  Rev.: Alex Colville, Myron Cook
Composition: .800 silver, .200 copper
             .500 silver, .500 copper
Weight: 2.33 grams
Diameter: 18.03 mm
Thickness: 1.16 mm
Edge: Reeded
Die Axis: ↑↑

Date and Mint Mark	Mintage	MS-60	MS-63	MS-64	MS-65
1967 .800 silver	32,309,135	2.	5.	7.	50.
1967 .500 silver	30,689,080	2.	5.	7.	50.

TIARA PORTRAIT, BLUENOSE DESIGN RESUMED, 1968. During 1968 the use of silver in circulation coins was discontinued. Nickel was used in its place. The nickel coins are darker and are attracted to a magnet. About half of the 1968 nickel 10-cent pieces were coined at the Philadelphia Mint in the United States because of the pressure of other work at the Royal Canadian Mint. The Philadelphia and Ottawa issues differ only in the number and shape of the grooves in the edge of the coins; the grooves have square bottoms on the Philadelphia coins and V-shaped bottoms on the Ottawa strikings.

Designers and Engravers:
  Obv.: Arnold Machin
  Rev.: Emanuel Hahn
Composition: .500 silver, .500 copper
             1.00 nickel
Weight: 2.33 g silver, 2.07 g nickel
Diameter: 18.03 mm
Thickness: 1.16 mm
Edge: Reeded
Die Axis: ↑↑, ↑↓

Philadelphia Mint
Edge grooves have
flat bottoms

Royal Canadian Mint
Edge grooves have
V-shaped bottoms

Date and Mint Mark	Mintage	MS-60	MS-63	MS-64	MS-65
1968 Silver, Medal	70,460,000	–	5.	10.	30.
1968 Silver, Coinage	Included		Only One Known		
1968 Nickel, Philadelphia Mint	85,170,000	–	1.	2.	5.
1968 Nickel, Ottawa Mint	87,412,930	–	1.	2.	5.

NOTE: Lower grade silver coins, which do not have price listings, will have their value based on silver bullion on the day of purchase or sale. These lower grades do not have a numismatic premium at this time.

TIARA PORTRAIT, MODIFIED BLUENOSE DESIGN, 1969-1978. The 1969 Large Schooner-Large Date design is a rare variety. A small quantity was struck early in the year before it was discovered that the original design had deteriorated so much as to be unfit for further use. A completely new model with a noticeably smaller schooner and small date replaced the original master matrix in early 1969. The obverse is as on the 1965-1968 issues.

Designers and Engravers:
    Obv.: Arnold Machin
    Rev.: Emanuel Hahn, Myron Cook
Composition: 1.00 nickel
Weight: 2.07 grams
Diameter: 18.03 mm
Thickness: 1.16 mm
Edge: Reeded
Die Axis: ↑↑

VARIETIES OF 1969. As of January 2005, only fifteen examples of the rare large date variety have been found.

      1969 Large Date   1969 Small Date

Date and Mint Mark	Mintage	VF-20	EF-40	AU-50	MS-60	MS-63	MS-64	MS-65
1969 Large Date	Included	11,000.	15,000.	20,000.	25,000.	–	–	–
1969 Small Date	55,833,929	–	–	–	–	1.	2.	5.

Date and Mint Mark	Mintage	MS-63	MS-64	MS-S65	MS-66	MS-67
1970	5,249,296	1.	2.	5.	–	–
1971	41,016,968	1.	2.	5.	–	–
1972	60,169,387	1.	2.	5.	–	–
1973	167,715,435	1.	2.	5.	–	–
1974	201,566,565	1.	2.	5.	–	–
1975	207,680,000	1.	2.	5.	–	–
1976	94,724,000	1.	2.	5.	–	–
1977	128,056,000	1.	2.	5.	–	–
1978	170,366,431	1.	2.	5.	–	–

MODIFIED TIARA PORTRAIT, BLUENOSE DESIGN, 1979-1989. With the 1979 issue a general standardization of the coinage was started. The portrait of the Queen was reduced to make it proportional to the diameter of the coin, regardless of the denomination.

Designers and Engravers:
    Obv.: Arnold Machin, Walter Ott
    Rev.: Emanuel Hahn,
Composition: 1.00 nickel
Weight: 2.07 grams
Diameter: 18.03 mm
Thickness: 1.16 mm
Edge: Reeded
Die Axis: ↑↑

VARIETIES OF 1980. In the general makeover, the type style came under review, with a finer style being selected.

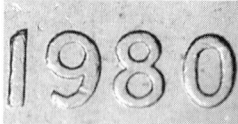

1980 Bold Type, Wide 0   1980 Fine Type, Narrow 0

Date and Mint Mark	Mintage	MS-63	MS-64	MS-65	MS-66	MS-67
1979	236,910,479	1.	2.	5.	–	–
1980 Wide '0'	169,910,479	5.	10.	30.	–	–
1980 Narrow '0'	Included	1.	2.	5.	–	–
1981	123,912,900	1.	2.	5.	–	–
1982	93,960,898	1.	2.	5.	–	–
1983	111,501,710	1.	2.	5.	–	–
1984	119,080,000	1.	2.	5.	–	–
1985	142,800,000	1.	2.	5.	–	–
1986	168,620,000	1.	2.	5.	–	–
1987	147,309,000	1.	2.	5.	–	–
1988	162,998,558	1.	2.	5.	–	–
1989	198,693,414	1.	2.	5.	–	–

CROWNED PORTRAIT, BLUENOSE DESIGN, NICKEL, 1990-1992. A new obverse portrait of the Queen wearing a diamond diadem and jewellery was introduced on all denominations in 1990.

In 1992 the reverse design was modified to include the bracket dates 1867-1992 for the 125th birthday of Canada.

1990 and 1991

Designers and Engravers:
Obv.: Dora de Pédery-Hunt
       Ago Aarand
Rev.: Emanuel Hahn
Composition: Nickel
Weight: 2.07 grams
Diameter: 18.03 mm
Thickness: 1.25 mm
Edge: Reeded
Die Axis: ↑↑

Double dates 1867 1992

Date and Mint Mark	Mintage	MS-63	MS-64	MS-65	MS-66	MS-67
1990	65,023,000	1.	2.	5.	–	–
1991	50,397,000	1.	2.	5.	–	–
1867-1992	174,476,000	1.	2.	5.	–	–

CROWNED PORTRAIT, BLUENOSE DESIGN, NICKEL, 1993-2000. In 1993 the practice of using a single date was resumed. The transition to beads from rim denticles which began in 1982 on the one-cent piece, was completed on the ten-cent piece in 1993. The Winnipeg Mint Mark (W) is found only on coins from the Brilliant Uncirculated sets, "Oh Canada!" and "Tiny Treasures" sets issued by the Numismatic department of the Mint and these are covered in the collector sets: see pages 405 and 408-409.

Designers, Engravers and Specifications:
Same as 1990 issues

Date and Mint Mark	Mintage	MS-63	MS-64	MS-65	MS-66	MS-67
1993	135,569,000	1.	2.	5.	–	–
1994	145,800,000	1.	2.	5.	–	–
1995	123,875,000	1.	2.	5.	–	–
1996	51,814,000	1.	2.	5.	–	–
1997	43,126,000	1.	2.	5.	–	–
1998	203,514,000	1.	2.	5.	–	–
1999	258,462,000	1.	2.	5.	–	–
2000	160,798,000	1.	2.	5.	–	–

CROWNED PORTRAIT; BLUENOSE DESIGN, MULTI-PLY PLATED STEEL, 1999-2003. In 2001 the Royal Canadian Mint began issuing circulating coinage struck from their new multi-ply plated steel blanks. The process is acid based and electroplates a thin coating of nickel, then copper, then nickel again onto a steel core. Prior to 2001, "P" coinage was only issued to the vending industry for testing purposes. The 1999P and 2000P ten-cents originated from this source.

In 2002 all circulating coinage carried the double dates 1952-2002, to commemorate the 50th anniversary of the reign of Queen Elizabeth II, and this was also the year Royal Canadian Mint officially acknowledged the schooner that has graced the reverse of the Canadian ten cent coin since 1937 (except for 1967 and 2001) as the Bluenose.

1999P to 2001P and 2003P

Double dates 1952 2002P

Designers and Engravers:
Obv.: Dora de Pédery-Hunt
Ago Aarand
Rev.: Emanuel Hahn
Composition: Multi-Ply Plated steel;
.920 steel, .055 copper,
.025 nickel
Weight: 1.75 grams
Diameter: 18.03 mm
Thickness: 1.22 mm
Edge: Serrated
Die Axis: ↑↑

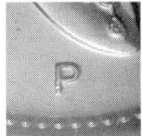

Date and Mint Mark	Mintage	MS-63	MS-64	MS-65	MS-66	MS-67
1999P	Issued for testing	6.	12.	25.	–	–
2000P	Issued for testing	1,250.	1,500.	2,000.	–	–
2001P	46,265,000	1.	2.	5.	–	–
1952-2002P	251,278,000	1.	2.	5.	–	–
2003P	162,398,000	1.	2.	5.	–	–

CROWNED PORTRAIT, INTERNATIONAL YEAR OF THE VOLUNTEER DESIGN, MULTI-PLY PLATED STEEL, 2001. This coin was issued for circulation in multi-ply plated steel to commemorate the 7.5 million Canadian volunteers who work towards making this country a better place for all. The Volunteer ten cents was also issued in sterling silver: see page 257.

Designers and Engravers:
  Obv.: Dora de Pédery-Hunt
  Rev.: RCM Design, Stan Witten

Specifications:
  Same as 1999P issue.

Date and Mint Mark	Mintage	MS-63	MS-64	MS-65	MS-66	MS-67
2001P	224,714,000	1.	2.	5.	–	–

UNCROWNED PORTRAIT, BLUENOSE DESIGN, MULTI-PLY PLATED STEEL, 2003-2005.

Designers and Engravers:
  Obv.: Susanna Blunt, Susan Taylor
  Rev.: Emanuel Hahn
Composition: Multi-Ply Plated steel;
  .920 steel, .055 copper,
  .025 nickel
Weight: 1.75 grams
Diameter: 18.03 mm
Thickness: 1.22 mm
Edge: Reeded
Die Axis: ↑↑

Date and Mint Mark		Mintage	MS-63	MS-64	MS-65	MS-66	MS-67
2003P		Included	1.	2.	5.	–	–
2004P		211,924,000	1.	2.	5.	–	–
2005P	Circulating Issue	N/A	1.	2.	5.	–	–
2005P	Mint Roll, 50 Coins	N/A	8.	–	–	–	–
2005P	First Strike	5,000	15.	–	–	–	–

TWENTY-FIVE CENTS
Victoria 1870 - 1901

VICTORIA OBVERSE PORTRAIT VARIETIES

The Province of Canada did not issue this denomination so new coinage tools were required for the Dominion of Canada issue. During Victoria's reign, five obverse and two reverse device varieties were employed. Detailed descriptions of the obverses, and corresponding date listings, follow on the next two pages. The basic design for the reverse is the same as all other silver denominations: crossed boughs of sweet maple, tied at the bottom by a ribbon and surmounted by St. Edward's crown.

PORTRAIT: Q1
Two waves meet slightly below the crown at top of brow.

Q1 is found on the following dates:
1870; 1871; 1871H; 1872H

PORTRAIT: Q2
A wave, which breaks into three, joins the brow slightly below the crown.

Q2 will be found on the following dates:
1870; 1871; 1871H; 1872H; 1874H;
1875H; 1880H (all varieties); 1881H;
1885 (all varieties); 1886

VICTORIA OBVERSE PORTRAIT VARIETIES

PORTRAIT: Q3
A single wave of hair and crown meet at top of brow.

Q3 will be found on the following date: 1882H.

PORTRAIT: Q4
Crown sits on a good strand of hair at top of brow.

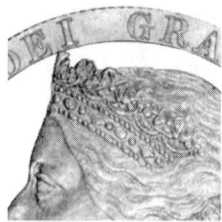

Q4 will be found on the following dates: 1883H; 1886 6/6

PORTRAIT: Q5
No hair on brow beneath crown. Three waves to crown back from top of brow.

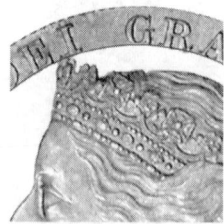

Q5 will be found on the following dates: 1886 N8; 1886 W8; 1886 6/3; 1887; 1888 N8; 1888 W8; 1889; 1890H; 1891; 1892; 1893; 1894; 1899; 1900; 1901

VICTORIA REVERSE VARIETIES

Short stem ends   Long stem ends

CROWNED PORTRAIT, 22 MAPLE LEAVES, SHORT STEM ENDS DESIGN, 1870-1886.

Designer and Engraver:
Leonard C. Wyon
Composition: .925 silver, .075 copper
Weight: 5.81 grams
Diameter: 23.62 mm
Edge: Reeded
Die Axis: ↑↓

Heaton Mint issues of 1871-1883 and 1890 have an "H" mint mark on the reverse under the wreath. Royal Mint strikings have no mint mark.

Date, Mint Portrait	Mintage	VG-8	F-12	VF-20	EF-40	AU-50	MS-60	MS-63	MS-65
1870-Q1	900,000	35.	60.	150.	225.	400.	850.	1,700.	–
1870-Q2	Included				Extremely rare				
1871-Q1	400,000	100.	250.	350.	700.	900.	–	–	–
1871-Q2	Included	35.	65.	150.	300.	550.	–	–	–
1871H-Q1	748,000	75.	150.	375.	650.	900.	–	–	–
1871H-Q2	Included	35.	75.	225.	450.	700.	1,500.	3,000.	–
1872H-Q1	2,240,000				Very rare				
1872H-Q2	Included	20.	30.	60.	150.	250.	900.	2,000.	6,000.
1874H-Q2	1,600,000	15.	20.	60.	150.	275.	600.	1,200.	8,500.
1875H-Q2	1,000,000	550.	900.	2,000.	4,000.	8,000.	–	–	–

VARIETIES 1880H AND 1885. Two styles of 0 were utilized for dating the dies for the 1880 issue of the denomination. Both the Narrow 0 and the Wide 0 occur alone, but in addition there is a scarce variety with the Narrow 0 punched over the Wide 0. The narrow over the wide O is difficult to identify in worn condition.

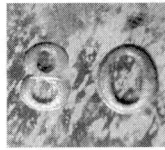

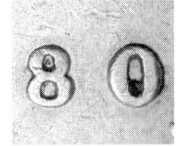

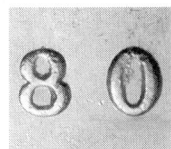

1880H Wide 0   Narrow 0   1880H Narrow 0
                        over wide 0

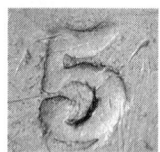 1885 Curved top 5    1885 Re-engraved Straight top 5

Date, Mint Portrait	Mintage	VG-8	F-12	VF-20	EF-40	AU-50	MS-60	MS-63	MS-65
1880H W0-Q2	400,000	200.	450.	700.	1,250.	2,500.	–	–	–
1880H N/W-Q2	Included	200.	450.	750.	1,500.	2,500.	4,000.	8,500.	–
1880H N0-Q2	Included	75.	175.	400.	750.	1,500.	2,500.	5,500.	–
1881H-Q2	820,000	35.	75.	175.	350.	650.	2,250.	6,000.	–
1882H-Q3	600,000	45.	85.	175.	400.	750.	2,000.	4,000.	8,000.
1883H-Q4	960,000	30.	60.	125.	250.	450.	850.	1,700.	–
1885-Q2	192,000	175.	400.	750.	1,500.	2,500.	–	10,000.	–
1885 RED-Q2	Included	200.	400.	800.	1,600.	3,000.	–	–	–

VARIETIES OF 1886. An 1886 variety has surfaced on which there appears to be a repunched six. The six used for repunching is slightly smaller than the original 6.

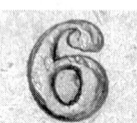

1886 6/6

Date, Mint Portrait	Mintage	VG-8	F-12	VF-20	EF-40	AU-50	MS-60	MS-63	MS-65
1886-Q2	540,000	45.	85.	175.	500.	750.	–	–	–
1886, 6/6-Q4	Included	100.	200.	300.	700.	1,500.	–	–	–
1886-Q5	Included	70.	125.	250.	600.	1,200.	3,000.	6,000.	–

CROWNED PORTRAIT, 22 LEAVES, LONG STEM ENDS DESIGN, 1886-1901.

Designer and Engraver:
Leonard C. Wyon
Composition: .925 silver, .075 copper
Weight: 5.81 grams
Diameter: 23.62 mm
Edge: Reeded
Die Axis: ↑↓

VARIETIES OF 1886 AND 1888. A very interesting and long unrecognized overdate occurs on the 1886 25-cents. The overdate 1886/3 seems unlikely in view of the fact that the 1885 date came in between and the 1883 coins were all produced at The Mint, Birmingham with the H mint mark; however, in an article it is proved conclusively that the overdate here illustrated is indeed 6/3.

1886
6 over 3

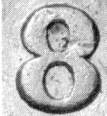

1888
Narrow 8

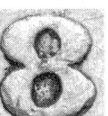

1888
Wide 8

Date, Mint Portrait	Mintage	VG-8	F-12	VF-20	EF-40	AU-50	MS-60	MS-63	MS-65
1886, 6/3-Q5	Included	75.	200.	300.	600.	1,200.	–	–	–
1886-Q5	Included	70.	125.	250.	600.	1,200.	–	–	–
1887-Q5	100,000	175.	325.	650.	1,500.	4,000.	–	–	–
1888, N8-Q5	400,000	35.	75.	150.	300.	500.	1,000.	1,500.	–
1888, W8-Q5	Included	40.	80.	175.	350.	600.	1,000.	1,500.	–
1889-Q5	66,340	200.	550.	900.	1,800.	3,000.	7,000.	20,000.	–
1890H-Q5	200,000	40.	75.	175.	400.	800.	1,500.	3,000.	–
1891-Q5	120,000	125.	200.	500.	900.	1,400.	2,500.	4,500.	15,000.
1892-Q5	510,000	35.	60.	150.	300.	450.	850.	1,500.	6,000.
1893-Q5	100,000	175.	300.	550.	1,100.	1,750.	2,000.	3,000.	15,000.
1894-Q5	220,000	45.	85.	200.	400.	600.	1,200.	2,500.	7,500.
1899-Q5	415,580	18.	40.	80.	200.	400.	850.	1,750.	6,000.
1900-Q5	1,320,000	15.	30.	75.	175.	350.	450.	900.	6,000.
1901-Q5	640,000	15.	30.	65.	200.	350.	800.	1,200.	5,000.

TWENTY-FIVE CENTS
Edward VII 1902-1910

The initial reverse for the Edward VII coins of this denomination has an almost unaltered wreath from the Victorian issues coupled with a small Imperial State crown and a new legend containing "CANADA" (it was formerly on the obverse).

IMPERIAL STATE CROWNED PORTRAIT, MAPLE LEAF, SMALL CROWN DESIGN, 1902-1906.

Designer and Engraver:
  Obv.: George W. DeSaulles
  Rev.: George W. DeSaulles
Composition: .925 silver, .075 copper
Weight: 1902-1910: 5.81 grams
  1910: 5.83 grams
Diameter: 23.62 mm
Edge: Reeded
Die Axis: ↑↓

The Heaton Mint issue of 1902 has an "H" mint mark on the reverse under the wreath. Royal Mint issues have no mint mark.

Small crown reverse
1902-1906

'H' Mint mark

Date and Mint Mark	Mintage	VG-8	F-12	VF-20	EF-40	AU-50	MS-60	MS-63	MS-65
1902	464,000	18.	35.	100.	250.	350.	1,000.	3,000.	10,000.
1902H	800,000	12.	30.	75.	150.	225.	300.	700.	3,000.
1903	846,150	18.	50.	125.	250.	450.	900.	3,000.	6,000.
1904	400,000	50.	80.	275.	500.	1,250.	2,000.	4,000.	10,000.
1905	800,000	20.	45.	200.	400.	750.	2,000.	5,000.	12,500.
1906 Sm. Cr.	237,843	3,000.	4,000.	6,000.	8,000.	10,000.	–	–	–

Note: Fewer than 35 examples of the 1906 Small Crown coin, across all grades, have been recorded.

IMPERIAL STATE CROWNED PORTRAIT, MAPLE LEAF, LARGE CROWN DESIGN, 1906-1910.

The reverse design was modified in 1906, by W. H. J. Blakemore, to improve die life and impart a balanced appearance to the coins. The maple leaf wreath was extensively remodelled and the Imperial State Crown was enlarged, filling the space between the tips of the maple boughs.

Engraver: Rev.: W. H. J. Blakemore
Weight: 1906-1910: 5.81 grams
　　　　　1910: 5.83 grams
Die Axis: 1906-1907 ↑↓
　　　　　1908-1910 ↑↑
Specifications: Same as 1902 issue

Large crown

Small crown

Date and Mint Mark	Mintage	VG-8	F-12	VF-20	EF-40	AU-50	MS-60	MS-63	MS-65
1906 Lg. Cr.	Included	15.	35.	90.	250.	450.	750.	2,000.	12,500.
1907	2,088,000	12.	20.	75.	200.	300.	600.	1,350.	8,500.
1908	495,016	20.	50.	125.	250.	450.	500.	750.	2,000.
1909	1,335,929	15.	35.	100.	225.	375.	800.	2,000.	–
1910	3,577,569	15.	25.	60.	125.	200.	325.	500.	3,500.

TWENTY - FIVE CENTS
George V 1911 - 1936

IMPERIAL STATE CROWNED PORTRAIT, 'GODLESS', MAPLE LEAF, LARGE CROWN DESIGN, 1911. The obverse issued on the 1911 coins provoked public outcry because it lacked reference to the King's ruling "by the grace of God." The coinage tools were modified during the year and a new legend including the Latin abbreviation "DEI GRA:" appeared on the 1912 and subsequent issues. The reverse was a continuation of the Large Crown variety of Edward VII.

Designer and Engraver:
  Obv.: Sir E. B. MacKennal
  Rev.: W. H. J. Blakemore
Composition: .925 silver, .075 copper
Weight: 5.83 grams
Diameter: 23.62 mm
Edge: Reeded
Die Axis: ↑↑

Date and Mint Mark	Mintage	F-12	VF-20	EF-40	AU-50	MS-60	MS-63	MS-65
1911	1,721,341	20.	60.	125.	200.	350.	700.	1,500.

IMPERIAL STATE CROWNED PORTRAIT, 'DEI GRA', MAPLE LEAF, LARGE CROWN DESIGN, 1912-1936

Composition:
  1912-1919: .925 silver, .075 copper
  1920-1936: .800 silver, .200 copper

Specifications: Same as 1911 issue

Date and Mint Mark	Mintage	F-12	VF-20	EF-40	AU-50	MS-60	MS-63	MS-65
1912	2,544,199	12.	30.	75.	200.	475.	1,000.	4,000.
1913	2,213,595	12.	25.	75.	175.	425.	850.	3,500.
1914	1,215,397	12.	35.	85.	275.	600.	1,500.	–
1915	242,382	75.	225.	600.	1,500.	3,500.	9,000.	–
1916	1,462,566	8.	25.	50.	100.	300.	800.	4,000.
1917	3,365,644	6.	20.	50.	80.	175.	275.	1,250.
1918	4,175,649	5.	20.	45.	65.	100.	225.	1,000.
1919	5,852,262*	6.	18.	40.	65.	100.	300.	900.
1920	1,975,278	6.	18.	45.	85.	250.	525.	2,000.
1921	597,337	45.	150.	350.	700.	1,500.	3,500.	12,000.
1927	468,096	75.	150.	325.	550.	1,100.	2,000.	5,000.
1928	2,114,178	8.	25.	50.	90.	200.	400.	2,000.
1929	2,690,562	6.	25.	50.	90.	225.	450.	2,000.
1930	968,748	7.	30.	60.	100.	325.	650.	2,000.
1931	537,815	8.	40.	80.	160.	300.	650.	3,000.
1932	537,994	10.	40.	80.	125.	250.	650.	1,500.
1933	421,282	10.	45.	85.	125.	250.	400.	1,500.
1934	384,350	15.	50.	85.	150.	350.	650.	2,000.
1935	537,772	10.	35.	75.	150.	200.	400.	1,000.
1936	1,125,779	5.	15.	35.	65.	125.	225.	1,250.

Note: *51,494 25¢ pieces, .925 fine and presumably all dated 1919, were melted in 1920.

THE DOT COINAGE OF 1936. Early in 1937, while the Royal Canadian Mint was awaiting the arrival of the master tools for the new coinage for George VI, an emergency issue of 25-cent pieces occurred to satisfy urgent demands for this denomination. To mark the special nature of the coinage the dies bore a small raised dot on the reverse under the wreath. That such an emergency issue had even taken place was generally not known until 1940, when collectors began noticing that some of the 25-cent pieces dated 1936 had a dot under the wreath. It was learned that supposedly 1- and 10-cent pieces were issued also, but no circulated examples of the two latter denominations have been proved genuine.

Physical specifications are as the 1911 issues   1936 With raised dot below
Chemical specifications are as the 1920 issues.   date struck in 1937.

Date and Mint Mark	Mintage	VG-8	F-12	VF-20	EF-40	AU-50	MS-60	MS-63	MS-65
1936 Dot	Included	45.	100.	225.	450.	600.	1,250.	2,500.	6,000.

TWENTY-FIVE CENTS
George VI 1937 - 1952

COINAGE OF GEORGE VI 1937-1952. The design chosen for the reverse of the new George VI coinage in 1937 was Emanuel Hahn's caribou head. This design was part of the government's program of modernizing the coinage. The original master tools were prepared at the Paris Mint because of a heavy work load at the Royal Mint in London at that time.

UNCROWNED PORTRAIT, 'ET IND: IMP:', CARIBOU DESIGN, 1937-1947. The initial obverse bore a legend containing an abbreviation for the Latin phrase, "ET INDIAE IMPERATOR"' meaning "and Emperor of India," referring to the fact that the monarch had held that position since Queen Victoria was made Empress of India in 1876.

Designer and Engraver:
Obv.: T. H. Paget
Rev.: Emanuel Hahn
Composition: .800 silver, .200 copper
Weight: 5.83 grams
Diameter: 23.62 mm
Edge: Reeded
Die Axis: ↑↑

Note: George VI twenty-five cent coinage, except for the key varieties, does not command a premium over silver value for the lower grades.

Date and Mint Mark	Mintage	EF-40	AU-50	MS-60	MS-63	MS-65
1937	2,689,813	10.	15.	20.	35.	300.
1938	3,149,245	15.	40.	90.	150.	750.
1939	3,532,495	15.	25.	75.	125.	450.
1940	9,583,650	9.	12.	16.	45.	250.
1941	6,654,672	6.	10.	20.	35.	275.
1942	6,935,871	6.	10.	20.	40.	325.
1943	13,559,575	6.	10.	20.	45.	350.
1944	7,216,237	6.	12.	30.	50.	400.
1945	5,296,495	6.	10.	25.	60.	350.
1946	2,210,810	15.	35.	60.	100.	475.
1947	1,524,554	12.	35.	60.	85.	1,000.

VARIETIES OF 1947. In early 1948 the Royal Canadian Mint was faced with a problem resulting from India's recent independence. The new obverse coinage tools, with the Latin abbreviation "ET IND: IMP." omitted to indicate that the King's titles had changed, would not arrive for several months, yet there was a great need for all denominations of coins. The mint satisfied the demand by striking coins dated 1947 and bearing outmoded titles on the obverse. To distinguish this issue from the regular strikings of 1947, a tiny maple leaf was placed after the date.

1947 Maple Leaf Issue struck in 1948	1947 Dot Issue

Date and Mint Mark	Mintage	F-12	VF-20	EF-40	AU-50	MS-60	MS-63	MS-65
1947 Maple Leaf	4,393,938	3.	4.	6.	10.	25.	35.	225.
1947 Dot	Included	70.	120.	200.	300.	500.	750.	2,500.

UNCROWNED PORTRAIT, 'DEI GRATIA', CARIBOU DESIGN, 1948-1952. Following the arrival of the master tools with the new obverse legend lacking "ET IND: IMP:" in 1948, production of the 1947 Maple Leaf coinage was suspended. For the remainder of the year coins were produced with the new obverse and the true date, 1948.

Designer and Engraver:
Obv.: T. H. Paget
Rev.: Emanuel Hahn
Composition: .800 silver, .200 copper
Weight: 5.83 grams
Diameter: 23.62 mm
Edge: Reeded
Die Axis: ↑↑

Date and Mint Mark	Mintage	EF-40	AU-50	MS-60	MS-63	MS-65
1948	2,564,424	15.	30.	65.	100.	500.
1949	7,988,830	4.	6.	18.	30.	600.
1950	9,673,335	4.	6.	15.	25.	200.

VARIETIES OF 1951-1952. In an attempt to improve the appearance of the obverse of this denomination a fresh reduction was made to produce an obverse with a slightly larger, lower relief portrait. Both varieties were used in 1951 and 1952. Aside from the difference in relief and the size of the portrait, the two varieties can be distinguished by the lettering. The High Relief variety has a plain lettering style in the legend, and the first "A" in "GRATIA" points to a rim denticle. On the Low Relief variety the letters are more flared and the first "A" in "GRATIA" points between rim denticles.

High Relief Obverse

Low Relief Obverse

Date and Mint Mark	Mintage	VF-20	EF-40	AU-50	MS-60	MS-63	MS-65
1951 High Relief	Included	2.	3.	5.	18.	35.	300.
1951 Low Relief	8,290,719	–	–	500.	1,000.	2,000.	–
1952 High Relief	Included	4.	7.	10.	50.	75.	600.
1952 Low Relief	8,859,642	3.	5.	10.	15.	30.	600.

TWENTY-FIVE CENTS
Elizabeth II 1953 to Date

LAUREATED PORTRAIT, CARIBOU DESIGN, 1953-1964. Two obverse varieties, called the No Shoulder Fold and Shoulder Fold obverses, saw use during 1953 (see 1-cent Elizabeth II, 1953 to date for full explanation). On the 25-cents these obverses are combined with reverses that are readily distinguishable. The No Shoulder Fold obverse comes with a Large Date reverse (carried over from George VI) and the Shoulder Fold was used with a Small Date reverse.

1953 No Shoulder Fold Obverse, Large Date Reverse

1953 Shoulder Fold Obverse Small Date Reverse

Designer: Obv.: Mary Gillick

Engraver: No Shoulder Fold Obverse:
Thomas Shingles, using the
Gillick portrait model;
Composition: .800 silver, .200 copper
Weight: 5.83 grams
Diameter: 1953 Large date: 23.62 mm
1953 Small date-1964: 23.88 mm

Rev.: Small Date: Thomas Shingles,
modifying existing models
Shoulder Fold Obverse:
Thomas Shingles, modifying existing
NSF coinage tools
Edge: Reeded
Die Axis: ↑↑

Date and Mint Mark	Mintage	AU-50	MS-60	MS-63	MS-64	MS-65
1953 LD, NSF	10,456,769	4.	12.	25.	35.	125.
1953 SD, SF	Included	5.	15.	45.	75.	500.
1954	2,318,891	15.	30.	50.	125.	350.
1955	9,552,505	5.	10.	25.	50.	300.
1956	11,269,353	3.	10.	18.	35.	150.
1957	12,770,190	2.	10.	15.	30.	125.
1958	9,336,910	2.	6.	10.	30.	125.
1959	13,503,461	2.	6.	10.	30.	125.
1960	22,835,327	2.	6.	10.	25.	100.
1961	18,164,368	2.	6.	10.	25.	100.
1962	29,559,266	2.	3.	8.	25.	200.
1963	21,180,642	2.	3.	15.	30.	150.
1964	36,479,343	2.	3.	10.	25.	200.

TIARA PORTRAIT, CARIBOU DESIGN, 1965-1966. A new obverse with the Queen showing more mature facial features and wearing a tiara was introduced on all denominations in 1965.

Designer and Engraver:
Obv.: Arnold Machin

Specifications: Same as 1954-1964
issues

Date and Mint Mark	Mintage	MS-60	MS-63	MS-64	MS-65
1965 Medal	44,708,869	2.	5.	20.	75.
1965 Coinage	Included		Only one known		
1966	25,388,892	2.	5.	20.	75.

TIARA PORTRAIT, CENTENNIAL DESIGN, 1967. A reverse design featuring a walking wildcat (bobcat) was selected as part of the commemorative set of coins for this year. During the year, the rising price of silver resulted in reduction of the silver content from .800 to .500. The two varieties are not distinguishable by appearance.

Designer: Rev.: Alex Colville
Engraver: Rev.: Myron Cook
Composition: .800 silver, .200 copper or
    .500 silver, .500 copper
Specifications: Same as 1954-1964
    issues.

Date and Mint Mark	Mintage	MS-60	MS-63	MS-64	MS-65
1967 .800 silver	48,855,500	2.	5.	15.	50.
1967 .500 silver	Included	2.	5.	15.	50.

TIARA PORTRAIT, CARIBOU DESIGN RESUMED, 1968-1972. During 1968 it was necessary to discontinue the use of silver in favour of pure nickel. Nickel coins are darker in colour and are attracted to a magnet.

Designer and Engraver:
    Obv.: Arnold Machin
Composition:
    1968: .500 silver, .500 copper
    1968-1972: 1.00 nickel
Weight: Silver: 5.83 grams
    Nickel: 5.07 grams
Diameter: 23.88 mm
Edge: Reeded
Die Axis: ↑↑

Date and Mint Mark	Mintage	MS-63	MS-64	MS-65	MS-66	MS-67
1968 .500 Silver	71,464,000	5.	15.	50.	–	–
1968 Nickel	88,686,931	1.	2.	5.	–	–
1969	133,037,929	1.	2.	5.	–	–
1970	10,302,010	1.	2.	5.	–	–
1971	48,170,428	1.	2.	5.	–	–
1972	43,743,387	1.	2.	5.	–	–

TIARA PORTRAIT, COMMEMORATING THE CENTENNIAL OF THE FOUNDING OF THE R.C.M.P. DESIGN, NICKEL, 1973. The special reverse on the 1973 25-cent piece commemorates the centennial of the founding of the North West Mounted Police, which later became the Royal Canadian Mounted Police.

Designer: Rev.: Paul Cedarberg
Engraver: Small Bust Obv.:
    Patrick Brindley, modifying the
    existing Machin Portrait
    Rev.: Walter Ott

Specifications: Same as 1968 nickel
    issue

VARIETIES OF 1973. A new obverse with a smaller, more detailed portrait and fewer rim denticles placed farther from the rim was prepared for use with the commemorative reverse. However, a small quantity of coins was struck with the 1972 obverse, creating two varieties for the year. The quantity of the Large Bust variety struck for circulation is believed not to exceed 10,000.

Large Bust   Small Bust

Date and Mint Mark	Mintage	VF-20	EF-40	AU-50	MS-60	MS-63	MS-64	MS-65
1973 Lge. Bust	Included	125.	150.	175.	250.	500.	1,000.	2,500.
1973 Sm. Bust	135,958,589	–	–	–	–	1.	2.	5.

TIARA PORTRAIT, CARIBOU DESIGN RESUMED, NICKEL, 1974-1978. With the return to the caribou reverse for the 25-cent piece in 1974, the use of the Large Portrait obverse was resumed.

Specifications: Same as 1968 nickel issue

Date and Mint Mark	Mintage	MS-63	MS-64	MS-65	MS-66	MS-67
1974	192,360,598	1.	2.	5.	–	–
1975	252,259,000	1.	2.	5.	–	–
1976	86,898,261	1.	2.	5.	–	–
1977	99,634,555	1.	2.	5.	–	–

VARIETIES OF 1978

1978
148 Small Denticles

1978
120 Large Denticles

Date and Mint Mark	Mintage	MS-63	MS-64	MS-65	MS-66	MS-67
1978 Small Denticles	174,475,408	15.	30.	60.	–	–
1978 Large Denticles	Included	1.	2.	5.	–	–

TIARA PORTRAIT MODIFIED, CARIBOU DESIGN, NICKEL, 1979-1989. Beginning with the 1979 issue and as part of a general standardization of the coinage, the portrait of the Queen was reduced. The intention was to make the size of the portrait proportional to the diameter of the coin, regardless of the denomination. This obverse is not the same as that employed in connection with the 1973 R.C.M.P. commemorative.

Designer, Engraver and Specifications:
Same as 1968 nickel issue.

Date and Mint Mark	Mintage	MS-63	MS-64	MS-65	MS-66	MS-67
1979	131,042,905	1.	2.	5.	–	–
1980	76,178,000	1.	2.	5.	–	–
1981	131,583,900	1.	2.	5.	–	–
1982	171,926,000	1.	2.	5.	–	–
1983	13,162,000	1.	2.	5.	–	–
1984	119,212,000	1.	2.	5.	–	–
1985	158,734,000	1.	2.	5.	–	–
1986	132,220,000	1.	2.	5.	–	–
1987	53,408,000	1.	2.	5.	–	–
1988	80,368,473	1.	2.	5.	–	–
1989	19,624,307	1.	2.	5.	–	–

CROWNED PORTRAIT, CARIBOU DESIGN, NICKEL, 1990-1991. A new obverse portrait of the Queen wearing a diamond diadem and jewellery was introduced on all denominations in 1990.

Designers and Engravers:
Obv.: Dora de Pédery-Hunt
Ago Aarand
Rev.: Emanuel Hahn
Composition: 1.00 nickel
Weight: 5.05 grams
Diameter: 23.88 mm
Edge: Reeded
Die Axis: ↑↑

Date and Mint Mark	Mintage	MS-63	MS-64	MS-65	MS-66	MS-67
1990	31,258,000	1.	2.	5.	–	–
1991	459,000	1.	2.	5.	–	–

CROWNED PORTRAIT, 125TH ANNIVERSARY OF CONFEDERATION DESIGNS, NICKEL 1867-1992. During each month of 1992 the Royal Canadian Mint issued a twenty-five cent coin bearing a unique design to represent one of the twelve provinces and territories. Each coin was launched at a special event organized in the capital city of the province or territory commemorated by the design. The designs for the thirteen coins issued to celebrate the 125th birthday (a one dollar coin was issued for Canada Day 1992) were chosen by a national contest.

Designers and Engravers:
Obv.: Dora de Pédery-Hunt
           Ago Aarand
Rev.: See below

Specifications: Same as 1990 issue, however, die axis varieties exist

The obverse and physical specifications are common to all twelve coins

New Brunswick	Northwest Territories	Newfoundland	Manitoba
January 9, 1992	February 6, 1992	March 5, 1992	April 7, 1992
Ronald Lambert	Beth McEachen	Christopher Newhook	Muriel Hope
Sheldon Beveridge	A. Aarand/C. Saffioti	Sheldon Beveridge	Ago Aarand

Yukon	Alberta	Prince Edward Island	Ontario
May 7, 1992	June 4, 1992	July 7, 1992	August 6, 1992
Libby Dulac	Mel Heath	Nigel Roe	Greg Salmela
William Woodruff	William Woodruff	Sheldon Beveridge	Susan Taylor

Nova Scotia	Quebec	Saskatchewan	British Columbia
September 9, 1992	October 1, 1992	November 5, 1992	November 9, 1992
Bruce Wood	Romualdas Bukauskas	Brian Cobb	Carla Egan
Terry Smith	Stanley Witten	Terry Smith	Sheldon Beveridge

Date and Mint Mark	Description	Mintage	MS-63	MS-64	MS-65	MS-66	MS-67
1992	New Brunswick, (↑↑)	2,174,000	1.	2.	5.	–	–
1992	New Brunswick, (↑↓)	Included	150.	200.	–	–	–
1992	New Brunswick. (↑→)	Included	75.	100.	–	–	–
1992	Northwest Territories (↑↑	12,580,000	1.	2.	5.	–	–
1992	Northwest Territories, (↑→)	Included	75.	100.	–	–	–
1992	Newfoundland	11,405,000	1.	2.	5.	–	–
1992	Manitoba	11,349,000	1.	2.	5.	–	–
1992	Yukon	10,388,000	1.	2.	5.	–	–
1992	Alberta	12,133,000	1.	2.	5.	–	–
1992	Prince Edward Island	13,001,000	1.	2.	5.	–	–
1992	Ontario	14,263,000	1.	2.	5.	–	–
1992	Nova Scotia	13,600,000	1.	2.	5.	–	–
1992	Quebec	13,607,000	1.	2.	5.	–	–
1992	Saskatchewan	14,165,000	1.	2.	5.	–	–
1992	British Columbia	14,001,000	1.	2.	5.	–	–

CROWNED PORTRAIT, CARIBOU DESIGN RESUMED, NICKEL, 1993-1996. In 1993 the practice of using a single date was resumed. The transition to beads from rim denticles, which began in 1982 on the one-cent piece, was completed in 1993 with the use of beads on the twenty-five cent coin. No circulating caribou reverse twenty-five cent coins were minted from 1997 to 2000. From 1997 through to 2000, the numismatic department minted caribou reverse twenty-five cent coins for use in the following numismatic sets: "Oh Canada!," "Tiny Treasures" and Specimen. The Winnipeg Mint 1998W twenty-five cent coins are only found in the "Oh Canada!" and "Tiny Treasures" sets, and were not issued for general circulation.

Designers, Engravers and Specifications:
Same as 1990 issue

Date and Mint Mark	Mintage	MS-63	MS-64	MS-65	MS-66	MS-67
1993	73,758,000	1.	2.	5.	–	–
1994	77,670,000	1.	2.	5.	–	–
1995	89,210,000	1.	2.	5.	–	–
1996	28,106,000	1.	2.	5.	–	–

Note: No Caribou reverse design twenty-five cent coins for the years 1997, 1998, 1999 and 2000 were struck for circulation, an example of these 25¢ coins must be obtain from brilliant uncirculated sets for the years in question.

CROWNED PORTRAIT, MILLENNIUM DESIGNS, NICKEL, 1999: Struck to celebrate the millennium, the following series of coins reflect development, milestones, discoveries, inventions and achievements in the past millennium which helped shape today's Canada.

Designers and Engravers:
Obv.: Dora de Pédery-Hunt
Ago Aarand
Rev.: See below

Specifications: Same as 1990 issue.

The obverse and physical specifications are common to all twelve coins

January	February	March	April
A Country Unfolds	Etched in Stone	The Log Drive	Our Northern Heritage
P. Ka-Kin Poon	L. Springer	M. Lavoie	Ken Ojnak Ashevac
Cosme Saffioti	José Osio	Stanley Witten	Sheldon Beveridge

May	June	July	August
The Voyageurs	From Coast to Coast	A Nation of People	The Pioneer Spirit
S. Minenok	G. Ho	M. H. Sarkany	A. Botelho
William Woodruff	William Woodruff	Stanley Witten	Cosme Saffioti

September	October	November	December
Canada Through a	A Tribute to	The Air Plane	This is Canada
Child's Eye	the First Nation	Opens the North	J. L. P. Provencher
C. Bertrand	J. E. Read	B. R. Bacon	Stanley Witten
Stanley Witten	Sheldon Beveridge	Stanley Witten	

MILLENNIUM DESIGNS, 1999, CONTINUED. During production of this series of 25 cent coins, die deterioration appeared to be a major problem for the Mint. Design and font styles used on these coins played an important part in the life of the dies.

Date and Mint Mark	Description	Mintage	MS-63	MS-64	MS-65	MS-66	MS-67
1999	January, A Country Unfolds	12,238,559	1.	2.	5.	–	–
1999	February, Etched in Stone	13,985,195	1.	2.	5.	–	–
1999	March, The Log Drive	15,157,061	1.	2.	5.	–	–
1999	April, Our Northern Heritage	15,214,397	1.	2.	5.	–	–
1999	May, The Voyageurs	14,906,187	1.	2.	5.	–	–
1999	June, From Coast to Coast	19,821,722	1.	2.	5.	–	–
1999	July, A Nation of People	16,537,018	1.	2.	5.	–	–
1999	August, The Pioneer Spirit	17,621,561	1.	2.	5.	–	–
1999	September, A Child's Eye	31,077,650	1.	2.	5.	–	–
1999	October, First Nation	31,964,487	1.	2.	5.	–	–
1999	November, The Air Plane	27,437,677	1.	2.	5.	–	–
1999	December, This is Canada	42,927,482	1.	2.	5.	–	–
1999	Total Issue	258,888,000	–	–	–	–	–

CROWNED PORTRAIT, MILLENNIUM DESIGNS, NICKEL, 2000. The twelve-coin series for the year 2000 focused on the hopes and dreams of the future: Canadians' vision of our culture, exploration, science and technology for the third millennium.

Designers and Engravers:
Obv.: Dora de Pédery-Hunt
Rev.: See below

Specifications: Same as 1990 issue

January	February	March	April
Pride	Ingenuity	Achievement	Health
Donald F. Warkentin	John Jaciw	Daryl Dorosz	Annie Wassef
José Osio	William Woodruff	Stanley Witten	Stanley Witten

May	June	July	August
Natural Legacy	Harmony	Celebration	Family
Randy Trantau	Haver Demirer	Laura Paxton	Wade Stephen Baker
José Osio	José Osio	Stanley Witten	Susan Taylor

MILLENNIUM DESIGNS, 2000, CONTINUED

September	October	November	December
Wisdom	Creativity	Freedom	Community
Cezar Serbanescu	Jerik (Kong Tat) Hui	Kathy Vinish	Michelle Thibodeau
Cosme Saffioti	Susan Taylor	William Woodruff	José Osio

Date and Mint Mark	Description	Mintage	MS-63	MS-64	MS-65	MS-66	MS-67
2000	January, Pride (↑↑)	50,749,102	1.	2.	5.	–	–
2000	January, Pride, (↑→)	Included	75.	100.	–	–	–
2000	February, Ingenuity	35,812,988	1.	2.	5.	–	–
2000	March, Achievement	35,135,154	1.	2.	5.	–	–
2000	April, Health	34,663,619	1.	2.	5.	–	–
2000	May, Natural Legacy	36,416,953	1.	2.	5.	–	–
2000	June, Harmony (↑↑)	34,604,075	1.	2.	5.	–	–
2000	June, Harmony (↑←)	Included	75.	100.	–	–	–
2000	July, Celebration	34,816,329	1.	2.	5.	–	–
2000	August, Family	34,320,111	1.	2.	5.	–	–
2000	September, Wisdom	33,993,016	1.	2.	5.	–	–
2000	October, Creativity	35,102,206	1.	2.	5.	–	–
2000	November, Freedom	33,251,352	1.	2.	5.	–	–
2000	December, Community	34,378,898	1.	2.	5.	–	–
2000	Total Issue	435,751,000	–	–	–	–	–

CROWNED PORTRAIT, CARIBOU DESIGN RESUMED, NICKEL, 2001. The last year for the use of pure nickel blanks in the production of 25-cent coins was 2001. No Caribou reverse coinage was issued for general circulation in 2000.

Designers, Engravers and Specifications:
Same as 1990 issue

Date and Mint Mark	Mintage	MS-63	MS-64	MS-65	MS-66	MS-67
2001	8,415,000	1.	2.	5.	–	–

CROWNED PORTRAIT, CARIBOU DESIGN, MULTI-PLY PLATED STEEL, 1999-2003. In 2001 the Royal Canadian Mint began issuing circulating coinage struck from their new Multi-Ply Plated steel blanks. The process is acid based and electroplates a thin coating of nickel, then copper, then nickel again on to a steel core.

1999P to 2001P, and 2003P

Designers and Engravers:
Obv.: Dora de Pédery-Hunt
     Ago Aarand
Rev.: Emanuel Hahn
Composition: .940 steel, .038 copper,
     .022 nickel
Weight: 4.4 grams
Diameter: 23.58 mm
Thickness: 1.58 mm
Edge: Reeded
Die Axis: ↑↑

Double dates 1952 2002P

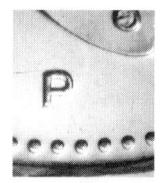

Date and Mint Mark	Mintage	MS-63	MS-64	MS-65	MS-66	MS-67
1999P	Issued for testing	15.	20.	25.	–	–
2000P	Issued for testing	–	7,500.	–	–	–
2001P	64,182,000	1.	2.	5.	–	–
1952-2002P	187,992,000	1.	2.	5.	–	–
2003P	15,905,090	1.	2.	5.	–	–

Note: For the complete Multi Ply Plated Test Coin Set (TTS-3), see page 248.

CROWNED PORTRAIT, CANADA DAY DESIGN, MULTI-PLY PLATED STEEL, 2002. The 2002 Canada Day twenty-five cents celebrates 135 years of National Pride. Presented to new Canadians at their citizenship ceremony during 'Celebrate Canada Day' week, this coin marks an important step for those who make Canada their home. The new 25 cent coins were issued for a three month period beginning July 2002 and ending September 2002.

Designers and Engravers:
Obv.: Dora de Pédery-Hunt
     Ago Aarand
Rev.: Judith Chartier
     Stan Witten
Specifications: Same as 1999P issue

Date and Mint Mark	Mintage	MS-63	MS-64	MS-65	MS-66	MS-67
1952-2002P	30,627,000	1.	2.	5.	–	–

UNCROWNED PORTRAIT, CARIBOU DESIGN, MULTI-PLY PLATED STEEL, 2003-2004. In 2003 a new obverse design was introduced. An uncrowned portrait of Queen Elizabeth II was designed by Susanna Blunt.

Designers and Engravers:
  Obv.: Susanna Blunt, Susan Taylor
  Rev.: Emanuel Hahn

Specifications: Same as 1999P issue

Date and Mint Mark	Mintage	MS-63	MS-64	MS-65	MS-66	MS-67
2003P	66,861,633	1.	2.	5.	–	–
2004P	159,465,000	1.	2.	5.	–	–

400TH ANNIVERSARY OF THE FIRST SETTLEMENT IN NORTH AMERICA, 2004. In 1603, Pierre Dugua, Sieur de Mons, was given the title of Lieutenant General of "La Cadie" (Acadie). The following year, he arrived in Acadie on the flagshop Bonne-Renommée. The ship's company included Samuel de Champlain, a skilled mapmaker and chronicler. In search of a suitable site for settlement, the expedition arrived in the Passamaquoddy Bay in late June. De Mons named the Island Saint Croix and it was there that he tried to establish year-round French settlement in North America, an event that symbolizes the founding of Acadie.

Designers and Engravers:
  Obv.: Susanna Blunt, Susan Taylor
  Rev.: Robert Ralph Carmichael
        Stan Witten

Specifications: Same as 1999P issue

Date and Mint Mark	Mintage	MS-63	MS-64	MS-65	MS-66	MS-67
2004P	15,400,000	2.	4.	10.	–	–

REMEMBRANCE DAY "POPPIES", 2004. This is the first coloured circulating coin issued in Canada.

Designers and Engravers:
  Obv.: Susanna Blunt, Susan Taylor
  Rev.: Cosme Saffioti, Stan Witten

Specifications: Same as 1999P issue,
        Colourized

Date and Mint Mark	Description	Mintage	MS-63	MS-64	MS-65	MS-66	MS-67
2004P	Circulation Issue	28,500,000	1.	4.	10.	–	–
2004P	Mint Roll, 40 coins	Included	–	–	15.	–	–
2004P	First Strike	9,928	30.	–	–	–	–

Note: The issue price of the "First Strike" Poppy twenty-five cents was $19.95. It was issued in a cardboard folder with blister packed coin. See page 249 for the "Poppy" Test Set of 2004.

100TH ANNIVERSARY OF ALBERTA, 2005.

Designers and Engravers:
Obv.: Susanna Blunt, Susan Taylor
Rev.: Michelle Grant, Stan Witten

Specifications: Same as 1999P issue

Date and Mint Mark	Description	Mintage	MS-63	MS-64	MS-65	MS-66	MS-67
2005P	Alberta	N/A	1.	2.	5.	–	–

100TH ANNIVERSARY OF SASKATCHEWAN, 2005.

Designers and Engravers:
Obv.: Susanna Blunt, Susan Taylor
Rev.: Paulette Sapergia, José Osio

Specifications: Same as 1999P issue

Date and Mint Mark	Description	Mintage	MS-63	MS-64	MS-65	MS-66	MS-67
2005P	Saskatchewan	N/A	1.	2.	5.	–	–

UNCROWNED PORTRAIT, CARIBOU DESIGN, MULTI-PLY PLATED STEEL, 2005.

Designers and Engravers:
Obv.: Susanna Blunt, Susan Taylor
Rev.: Emanuel Hahn

Specifications: Same as 1999P issue

Date and Mint Mark		Mintage	MS-63	MS-64	MS-65	MS-66	MS-67
2005P	Circulation Issue	N/A	1.	2.	5.	–	–
2005P	Mint Roll, 50 coins	N/A	13.	–	–	–	–
2005P	First Strike	5,000	15.	–	–	–	–

FIFTY CENTS
Victoria 1870 - 1901

Since the Province of Canada did not issue this denomination, new coinage tools had to be produced when the Dominion placed its first order for coins. For the obverse L.C. Wyon used the same portrait model as he did for the 25-cents: a crowned effigy of Victoria based on a model by William Theed. The reverse featured the St. Edward's crown atop crossed boughs of sweet maple, tied at the bottom by a ribbon. By the end of the reign four major obverses and two reverses had been utilized. A detailed description of the obverses and listing of these varieties by year follow on the next two pages.

VICTORIA OBVERSE PORTRAIT VARIETIES

PORTRAIT: H1
No shamrock behind first jewel of crown.
Without initials LCW.

H1 will be found on the following date:
1870 No LCW

PORTRAIT: H2
With shamrock behind first jewel of crown.
Small space between poorly formed bow
and ribbon at the nape of the neck.

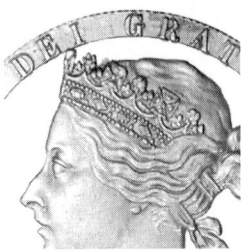

H2 will be found on the following dates:
1870 LCW; 1871; 1871H; 1872H;
1872H A/V; 1888

VICTORIA OBVERSE PORTRAIT VARIETIES

PORTRAIT: H3

With shamrock behind first jewel of crown.
Large space between crudely formed bow
and ribbon at the nape of the neck.

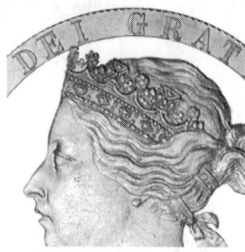

H3 will be found on the following dates:
1881H; 1888; 1890H; 1892

PORTRAIT: H4

With shamrock behind first jewel of crown.
No space between a well defined bow and
ribbon at the nape of the neck.

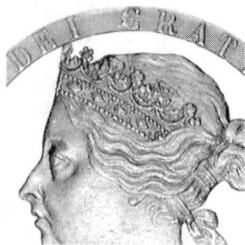

H4 will be found on the following dates:
1890H; 1892; 1894; 1898; 1899; 1900;
1901

VICTORIA REVERSE VARIETIES

Two reverse varieties are used on the Victoria fifty cent series. The first variety, used in 1870, was designed by L. C. Wyon, and consists of crossed boughs of maple leaves, tied with a bow, and topped with the St. Edward's Crown. The Crown and Wreath were re-engraved, thus creating a second variety.

DIADEMED PORTRAIT, MAPLE WREATH DESIGN, 1870.

Designer and Engraver:
        Leonard C. Wyon
Composition: .925 silver,
        .075 copper
Weight: 11.62 grams
Diameter: 29.72 mm
Edge: Reeded
Die Axis: ↑↓

Heaton Mint issues of 1871-1881 and the Birmingham Mint issue of 1890 have an "H" on the reverse under the wreath. Royal Mint strikings have no mint mark.

VARIETIES OF 1870. The initial obverse for this denomination lacked the initial of the designer on the truncation of the queen's neck. The second obverse, also employed for the 1870 coinage, has the "L.C.W.," as well as a shamrock just behind the front cross in the Queen's tiara.

No shamrock behind front cross

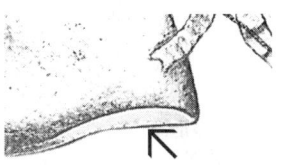

1870 Without L.C.W.

Shamrock behind front cross

1870 L.C.W. on Truncation

Date, Mint Portrait	Mintage	VG-8	F-12	VF-20	EF-40	AU-50	MS-60	MS-63	MS-65
1870 No LCW-H1	450,000	1,100.	1,800.	3,250.	5,000.	10,000.	–	–	–
1870 LCW-H2	Included	70.	125.	250.	500.	1,300.	6,500.	–	–

DIADEMED PORTRAIT, MODIFIED MAPLE WREATH DESIGN, 1871-1901. Numerous repunching varieties exist on the 1872H coinage, but the only one interesting enough to include in this catalogue involves a blundered obverse die. While repunching defective letters in the obverse legend the engraver inadvertently used an "A" punch to repair a defective "V" in "VICTORIA," converting the Queen's name into "∀ICTORIA."

Modified maple leaves

1872 Inverted "A"
in VICTORIA

Date, Mint Portrait	Mintage	VG-8	F-12	VF-20	EF-40	AU-50	MS-60	MS-63	MS-65
1871-H2	200,000	85.	175.	450.	750.	2,000.	8,000.	17,500.	–
1871H-H2	45,000	150.	300.	750.	1,400.	3,000.	–	–	–
1872H-H2	80,000	65.	150.	300.	700.	2,000.	5,000.	11,500.	50,000.
1872H A/V-H2	Included	375.	750.	1,800.	5,000.	–	–	–	–
1881H-H3	150,000	75.	150.	300.	750.	1,750.	–	–	–
1888-H2	60,000	400.	600.	–	–	–	–	–	–
1888-H3	Included	350.	550.	1,000.	2,500.	–	–	–	–
1888-H4	Included	–	600.	–	–	–	–	–	–
1890H-H3	20,000			No examples known					
1890H-H4	Included	1,500.	2,250.	4,000.	6,500.	9,000.	–	–	–
1892-H3	151,000	100.	175.	450.	900.	2,500.	–	–	–
1892-H4	Included	100.	200.	400.	1,000.	–	–	–	–
1894-H4	29,036	450.	750.	1,500.	3,000.	6,000.	20,000.	–	–
1898-H4	100,000	125.	250.	400.	900.	3,000.	12,500.	–	–
1899-H4	50,000	150.	475.	1,350.	2,250.	5,000.	–	–	–
1900-H4	118,000	75.	150.	300.	650.	2,000.	6,000.	17,500.	–
1901-H4	80,000	85.	175.	300.	800.	2,250.	7,500.	–	–

Note: For an indication of the Good-4 (G-4) price, use 50 to 60% of the Very Good-8 (VG-8) value.

FIFTY CENTS
Edward VII 1902 - 1910

A new obverse portrait design was engraved by DeSaulles and used from 1902-1910. The reverse of the Edward VII 50-cents followed the same design as the lower silver denominations: the word "CANADA" was made part of the legend, moved from it's former position at the bottom of the obverse, and the Imperial State crown replaced the St. Edward's crown. The first reverse used the Victorian maple wreath from 1902 to 1910, but the tools were modified by Blakemore in 1910 to accommodate the Royal Canadian Mint.

IMPERIAL STATE CROWNED PORTRAIT, VICTORIAN LEAF DESIGN, 1902-1910.

Designer and Engraver:
  Obv.: G. W. DeSaulles
Engraver:
  Victorian Leaves Reverse:
    G. W. DeSaulles
  Edwardian Leaves Reverse:
    W. H. J. Blakemore
Composition: .925 silver,
              .075 copper
Weight: **1902-1910:** 11.62 grams
         1910: 11.66 grams
Diameter: 29.72 mm
Edge: Reeded
Die Axis: 1902-1907: ↑↓
         1908-1910: ↑↑

The Birmingham Mint issue of 1903 has an "H" mint mark on the reverse under the wreath. Royal Mint issues (1902-1907) and Royal Canadian Mint issues (1908-1910) have no mint mark.

Date and Mint Mark	Mintage	VG-8	F-12	VF-20	EF-40	AU-50	MS-60	MS-63	MS-65
1902	120,000	25.	60.	175.	325.	650.	2,000.	3,500.	17,500.
1903H	140,000	30.	75.	225.	425.	800.	2,000.	5,000.	–
1904	60,000	175.	275.	550.	1,250.	1,750.	3,000.	–	–
1905	40,000	175.	375.	800.	2,500.	4,500.	–	–	–
1906	350,000	20.	60.	125.	350.	1,000.	2,000.	4,000.	–
1907	300,000	18.	50.	100.	325.	800.	5,000.	10,000.	–
1908	128,119	30.	85.	300.	600.	900.	1,500.	2,500.	8,000.
1909	203,118	30.	75.	300.	650.	1,500.	4,000.	6,000.	–
1910	649,521	30.	60.	150.	500.	800.	2,500.	–	–

FIFTY CENTS
Edward VII 1910

IMPERIAL STATE CROWNED PORTRAIT, EDWARDIAN LEAF DESIGN, 1910. Because the Victorian Leaves variety 50-cent pieces being coined at the Ottawa Mint had almost no rim, it was requested that the parent Royal Mint in London make new reverse tools. In addition to a wider rim the new variety (Edwardian Leaves reverse) had several altered leaves and a different cross atop the crown. The most noticeable difference is the two outside leaves at the right side of the date. On the Victorian Leaves reverse these leaves have long points which nearly touch the denticles, but on the Edwardian Leaves reverse these leaves have shorter, more curved points farther from the denticles.

   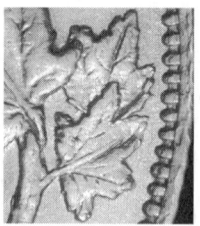

1902-1910 Victorian   1910 Edwardian
Leaves Reverse   Leaves Reverse

Date and Mint Mark	Mintage	VG-8	F-12	VF-20	EF-40	AU-50	MS-60	MS-63	MS-65
1910 Edwardian	Included	20.	65.	100.	400.	1,100.	2,500.	–	–

George V 1911 - 1936

IMPERIAL STATE CROWNED PORTRAIT, "GODLESS", EDWARDIAN LEAF DESIGN, 1911. Public outcry greeted the new George V coins issued in 1911 because the obverse legend lacked reference to the King's ruling "by the grace of God."

Designer and Engraver:
Sir E. B. MacKennal
Composition: .925 silver,
.075 copper
Weight: 11.66 grams
Diameter: 29.72 mm
Edge: Reeded
Die Axis: ↑↑

Date and Mint Mark	Mintage	VG-8	F-12	VF-20	EF-40	AU-50	MS-60	MS-63	MS-65
1911	209,972	30.	75.	350.	750.	1,250.	2,000.	3,500.	–

FIFTY CENTS
George VI 1911 - 1936

IMPERIAL STATE CROWNED PORTRAIT, "DEI GRATIA", EDWARDIAN LEAF DESIGN, 1912-1936. The coinage tools were modified during the year and a new legend containing the Latin abbreviation "DEI GRA:" appeared on the 1912 and subsequent issues. The reverse was a continuation of the Edwardian Leaves variety of the previous reign. In 1920, 144,200 fifty-cent pieces of .925 silver were melted. It is believed they were all dated 1919.

Composition:
1912-1919:
   .925 silver, .075 copper
1920-1936:
   .800 silver, .200 copper

Specifications:
Same as 1911 issue

Date and Mint Mark	Mintage	VG-8	F-12	VF-20	EF-40	AU-50	MS-60	MS-63	MS-65
1912	285,867	9.	40.	150.	325.	600.	2,000.	3,500.	–
1913	265,889	10.	50.	175.	350.	750.	2,000.	5,000.	–
1914	160,128	25.	75.	275.	500.	1,750.	5,000.	–	–
1916	459,070	8.	20.	75.	175.	450.	800.	1,500.	–
1917	752,213	7.	20.	60.	175.	400.	800.	1,500.	5,000.
1918	854,989	7.	18.	40.	125.	275.	800.	1,250.	4,500.
1919	1,113,429	7.	18.	45.	125.	275.	500.	1,000.	7,000.

VARIETIES OF 1920. Two punch spacing varieties of 1920 are known, the final digit '0' is found in two positions, far from and nearer to the '2'.

Wide Date 1920   Narrow Date 1920

1921 FIFTY CENTS

During the early and mid-1920s the demand for 50-cent pieces was very light; only 28,000 pieces were issued between 1921 and 1929. These are assumed to have been almost entirely 1920s. When a greater demand for this denomination arose later in 1929, the Master of the Ottawa Mint decided to melt the stock of 1920 and 1921 coins (amounting to some 480,392 pieces) and recoin the silver into 1929 coins. He took this decision because he feared that the public would suspect they were receiving counterfeits if a large quantity of coins with "old" dates were issued. It is believed that the 75 or so 1921s that have survived came from specimen sets sold to collectors or from circulation strikes sold to Mint visitors.

Date and Mint Mark	Mintage	VG-8	F-12	VF-20	EF-40	AU-50	MS-60	MS-63	MS-65
1920 W0	584,429	12.	30.	75.	250.	500.	850.	1,500.	8,000.
1920 N0	Included	9.	15.	45.	175.	375.	850.	1,500.	8,000.
1921	206,398	25,000.	35,000.	–	–	65,000.	–	–	–
1929	228,328	7.	15.	55.	175.	325.	800.	1,500.	6,000.
1931	57,581	20.	45.	100.	275.	650.	1,000.	2,000.	6,000.
1932	19,213	200.	275.	550.	1,000.	1,750.	5,000.	10,000.	–
1934	39,539	20.	40.	125.	350.	600.	1,000.	1,500.	3,500.
1936	38,550	30.	75.	125.	300.	450.	700.	1,000.	3,500.

Note: Our pricing table will not hold the 1921 MS-63 value of $125,000.

FIFTY CENTS
George VI 1937 - 1952

UNCROWNED PORTRAIT, 'ET IND:IMP:', COAT-OF-ARMS DESIGN, 1937-1947. A stylized Canadian coat-of-arms designed by George Edward Kruger-Gray was selected for the George VI 50-cent piece, first issued in 1937. The initial obverse bore a legend containing an abbreviation for the Latin phrase, "ET INDIAE IMPERATOR," meaning "and Emperor of India," denoting that the King was emperor of that vast country.

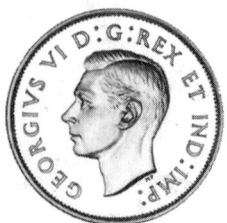 

Designer and Engraver:
Obv.: T.H. Paget
Rev.: G.E. Kruger-Gray
Composition: .800 silver,
.200 copper
Weight: 11.66 grams
Diameter: 29.72 mm
Thickness: 2.00 mm
Edge: Reeded
Die Axis: ↑↑

Date and Mint Mark	Mintage	F-12	VF-20	EF-40	AU-50	MS-60	MS-63	MS-65
1937	192,016	8.	12.	16.	20.	65.	95.	–
1938	192,018	10.	16.	40.	85.	125.	400.	2,500.
1939	287,976	10.	16.	30.	75.	100.	275.	1,750.
1940	1,996,566	4.	5.	10.	18.	45.	90.	1,250.
1941	1,714,874	4.	5.	10.	16.	35.	70.	1,500.
1942	1,974,165	4.	5.	10.	16.	35.	70.	1,500.
1943 Near 3	3,109,583	4.	5.	10.	20.	50.	100.	–
1943 Far 3	Included	4.	5.	10.	20.	50.	100.	–
1944	2,460,205	4.	5.	10.	18.	50.	100.	–
1945	1,959,528	4.	5.	10.	20.	50.	100.	–
1946	950,235	4.	6.	12.	30.	75.	200.	–

VARIETIES OF 1947. There are two styles of 7 for the 1947 issue. The first is a tall figure with a tail curving to the left at the bottom (Straight 7), similar to that on the 1937 issue. The second (Curved 7) has a bottom that curves to the right.

1947 Straight 7   1947 Curved 7

Date and Mint Mark	Mintage	F-12	VF-20	EF-40	AU-50	MS-60	MS-63	MS-65
1947 Straight 7	424,885	4.	7.	20.	45.	125.	250.	–
1947 Curved 7	Included	4.	10.	25.	60.	125.	350.	–

VARIETIES OF THE 1947 MAPLE LEAF ISSUE. With the granting of independence to India, the Royal Canadian Mint was faced with a dilemma in early 1948. The new obverse coinage tools with the Latin abbreviation "ET IND: IMP" omitted would not arrive for several months, yet there was a great need for all denominations of coins. The Mint satisfied the demand by striking coins dated 1947 and bearing an obverse with outmoded titles. To differentiate this issue from the regular strikings of 1947, a tiny maple leaf was placed after the date. Both styles of 7 (see above) were employed for the Maple Leaf coinage, creating four varieties of the 1947 date in all.

1947 Maple Leaf
Straight 7

1947 Maple Leaf
Curved 7

Date and Mint Mark	Mintage	VG-8	F-12	VF-20	EF-40	AU-50	MS-60	MS-63	MS-65
1947 ML, S7	38,433	–	35.	50.	75.	125.	225.	400.	3,000.
1947 ML, C7	Included	1,400.	1,800.	2,500.	3,000.	4,500.	6,000.	15,000.	–

UNCROWNED PORTRAIT, 'DEI GRATIA', COAT-OF-ARMS DESIGN, 1948-1952. In 1948, following the arrival of the master tools with the new obverse legend, production of the 1947 Maple Leaf coinage was suspended. For the remainder of the year coins were produced with the new obverse and true date, 1948.

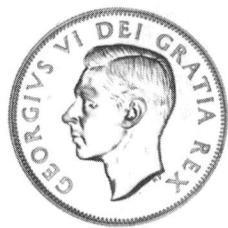

Specifications:
Same as 1937 issue

Date and Mint Mark	Mintage	F-12	VF-20	EF-40	AU-50	MS-60	MS-63	MS-65
1948	37,784	100.	125.	150.	200.	300.	400.	1,200.
1949	858,991	4.	8.	12.	20.	60.	150.	900.
1950	2,384,179	4.	5.	6.	7.	18.	35.	500.
1951	2,421,730	4.	5.	6.	7.	18.	30.	200.
1952	2,596,465	4.	5.	6.	7.	15.	20.	200.

FIFTY CENTS
Elizabeth II 1953 to date

LAUREATED PORTRAIT, COAT-OF-ARMS DESIGN, 1953-1954. During 1953 two obverse varieties were employed. Known as No Shoulder Fold and Shoulder Fold varieties (see 1-cent Elizabeth II, 1953 to date for full description), they were combined with two major reverse varieties. The No Shoulder Fold obverse was used with both Small and Large Date reverses, though only a modest quantity of the latter were struck. The Small Date reverse was carried over from George VI issues. The Shoulder Fold obverse appeared only with the Large Date reverse.

Designer and Engraver:
Obv.: No Shoulder Fold – Thomas Shingles, using the Gillick portrait model
       Shoulder Fold – Thomas Shingles, modifying existing NSF coinage tools
Rev.: Small Date – G. E. Kruger-Gray
      Large Date – Thomas Shingles, copying existing model
Composition: .800 silver, .200 copper
Weight: 11.66 grams
Diameter: 29.72 mm
Thickness: 2.00 mm
Edge: Reeded
Die Axis: ↑↑

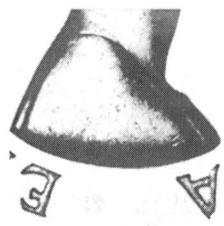

No Shoulder Fold
Obverse 1953

Letters have pronounced flaring

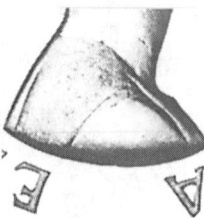

Shoulder Fold Obverse
1953-1964

Letters have subdued flaring

Small Date Reverse
1953

Large Date Reverse
1953-1964

Date and Mint Mark	Mintage	VF-20	EF-40	AU-50	MS-60	MS-63	MS-64	MS-65
1953 SD, NSF	1,630,429	3.	4.	7.	15.	30.	45.	1,000.
1953 LD, NSF	Included	6.	10.	25.	75.	150.	300.	–
1953 LD, SF	Included	5.	7.	12.	30.	50.	1,000.	1,500.
1954	506,305	6.	12.	15.	30.	40.	75.	275.

LAUREATED PORTRAIT, REVISED COAT-OF-ARMS DESIGN, 1955-1958. Continuing difficulties with the coat-of-arms reverse design resulted in the introduction of a major modification in 1955. The problem was the obverse portrait tended to draw away too much metal at the moment the coin was struck, leaving insufficient metal to bring up the design fully on the reverse. Thus, the coins sometimes showed a weakness in the design at and around the crown and top of the shield. This problem was largely solved by a new reverse with a smaller version of the coat-of-arms.

Designer and Engraver:
Thomas Shingles, copying existing models

Specifications:
Same as 1953 issue

Date and Mint Mark	Mintage	VF-20	EF-40	AU-50	MS-60	MS-63	MS-64	MS-65
1955	753,511	6.	8.	10.	18.	30.	50.	250.
1956	1,379,499	5.	6.	7.	15.	20.	40.	175.
1957	2,171,689	5.	6.	7.	10.	15.	30.	200.
1958	2,957,266	5.	6.	7.	10.	15.	30.	175.

Note: In the Elizabeth II laureated portrait series, 1953 to 1964, no fifty cent coin has been graded MS-66 or better by a Canadian grading company.

LAUREATED PORTRAIT, MODIFIED COAT-OF-ARMS DESIGN, 1959-1964. In 1959 the new Canadian coat-of-arms which had received government approval in 1957 was adapted for the 50-cent piece. One of the major changes compared to the previous design was the addition of a ribbon at the bottom bearing "A MARI USQUE AD MARE," meaning "from sea to sea" and making reference to the territorial extent of the country. The 1959 issue had horizontal lines in the bottom panel, indicating the colour incorrectly as blue. To indicate the correct colour, white, these lines were removed from the 1960 and subsequent issues. The obverse continued unchanged.

Designer and Engraver:
  Rev.: Thomas Shingles
Composition: .800 silver,
                      .200 copper
Weight: 11.66 grams
Diameter: 29.72 mm
Thickness: 2.00 mm
Edge: Reeded
Die Axis: ↑↑

Date and Mint Mark	Mintage	MS-60	MS-63	MS-64	MS-65
1959	3,095,535	10.	12.	30.	250.
1960	3,488,897	5.	6.	30.	250.
1961	3,584,417	5.	6.	25.	125.
1962	5,208,030	5.	6.	20.	125.
1963	8,348,871	5.	6.	20.	75.
1964	9,377,676	5.	6.	20.	75.

TIARA PORTRAIT, MODIFIED COAT-OF-ARMS REVERSE, 1965-1966. A new obverse with the Queen showing more mature facial features and wearing a tiara was introduced in 1965.

Designer and Engraver:
  Obv.: Arnold Machin
  Rev.: Thomas Shingles

Specifications:
  Same as 1959 issue

Date and Mint Mark	Mintage	MS-60	MS-63	MS-64	MS-65
1965	12,629,974	5.	6.	18.	75.
1966	7,683,228	5.	6.	18.	75.

TIARA PORTRAIT, CENTENNIAL DESIGN, 1967. A design for the reverse showing a howling wolf was chosen as part of the set of commemorative coins for this year. The obverse continued unchanged.

Designer: Obv.: Arnold Machin
          Rev.: Alex Colville
Engraver: Rev.: Myron Cook

Specifications:
          Same as 1959 issue

Date and Mint Mark	Mintage	MS-60	MS-63	MS-64	MS-65
1967 Confederation	4,211,395.	5.	9.	20.	300.

TIARA PORTRAIT, MODIFIED COAT-OF-ARMS DESIGN RESUMED, REDUCED SIZE NICKEL COINAGE, 1968-1976. When the coat-of-arms reverse design was resumed in 1968, and for ease of striking, the new nickel composition dictated a coin with a smaller diameter.

Designer and Engraver:
          Obv.: Arnold Machin
          Rev.: Thomas Shingles
Composition: 1.00 nickel
Weight: 8.10 grams
Diameter: 27.13 mm
Thickness:
          1968-1979: 1.93 mm
          1980-2000: 1.90 mm
Edge: Reeded
Die Axis: ↑↑

Date and Mint Mark	Mintage	MS-63	MS-64	MS-65	MS-66	MS-67
1968	3,966,932	1.	2.	5.	–	–
1969	7,113,929	1.	2.	5.	–	–
1970	2,429,516	1.	2.	5.	–	–
1971	2,166,144	1.	2.	5.	–	–
1972	2,515,632	1.	2.	5.	–	–
1973	2,546,096	1.	2.	5.	–	–
1974	3,436,650	1.	2.	5.	–	–
1975	3,710,000	1.	2.	5.	–	–
1976	2,646,000	1.	2.	5.	–	–

TIARA PORTRAIT, MODIFIED COAT-OF-ARMS DESIGN, 1977. The 1977 coinage features pronounced changes on both sides. The obverse bears a smaller bust with increased hair detail, smaller lettering, and larger beads placed farther from the rim. The reverse shows a smaller coat-of-arms and, for the first time, beads instead of denticles around the rim.

Engraver:
Obv.: Patrick Brindley,
        modifying the Machin
        portrait
Rev.: Thomas Shingles

Specifications:
Same as 1968 issue

Date and Mint Mark	Mintage	MS-63	MS-64	MS-65	MS-66	MS-67
1977	709,939	1.	2.	5.	–	–

TIARA PORTRAIT, MODIFIED COAT-OF-ARMS DESIGN, 1978-1989. In 1978 the Mint's attempts to settle upon standard designs continued. The beaded motif for the reverse was dropped and a design essentially the same as that for 1968-1976 was restored. Two minor varieties of the 1978 reverse are known. The 1978 obverse was a combination of the 1968-1976 and 1977 designs. The unmodified Machin portrait was restored, but the smaller lettering of 1977 was retained.

Designer and Engraver:
Obv.: Arnold Machin
Rev.: Thomas Shingles

Specifications:
Same as 1968 issue

VARIETIES OF 1978. The modification to the Coat-of-Arms in 1977 was carried into 1978, with the reverse crown undergoing design changes.

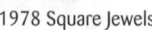

1978 Square Jewels   1978 Round Jewels

Date and Mint Mark	Mintage	MS-63	MS-64	MS-65	MS-66	MS-67
1978 Square Jewels	3,341,892	1.	2.	5.	–	–
1978 Round Jewels	Included	10.	20.	–	–	–
1979	3,425,000	1.	2.	5.	–	–
1980	1,943,155	1.	2.	5.	–	–
1981	2,588,900	1.	2.	5.	–	–

VARIETIES OF 1982, MODIFIED PORTRAIT. In the drive to increase die life in the striking of Canadian coins from nickel planchets, the design of the fifty cent coin was modified by decreasing the relief needed to create the Queen's image.

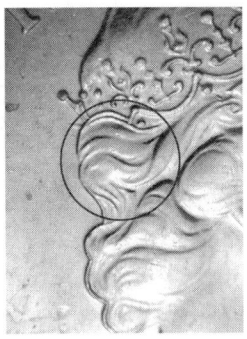

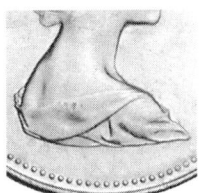

Large Beads

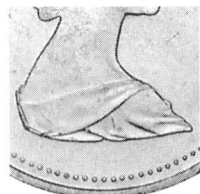

Small Beads

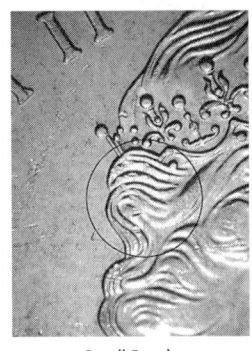

Large Beads
High Relief

Small Beads
Low Relief

Date and Mint Mark	Mintage	VF-20	EF-40	AU-50	MS-60	MS-63	MS-64	MS-65
1982 Large Beads	2,884,572	–	–	–	–	1.	2.	5.
1982 Small Beads	Included	35.	45.	50.	85.	100.	150.	500.

Date and Mint Mark	Mintage	MS-63	MS-64	MS-65	MS-66	MS-67
1983	1,177,000	1.	2.	5.	–	–
1984	1,502,989	1.	2.	5.	–	–
1985	2,188,374	1.	2.	5.	–	–
1986	781,400	1.	2.	5.	–	–
1987	373,000	1.	2.	5.	–	–
1988	220,000	1.	2.	5.	–	–
1989	266,419	1.	2.	5.	–	–

CROWNED PORTRAIT, COAT-OF-ARMS DESIGN, 1990-1991. A new obverse portrait of the Queen wearing a diamond diadem and jewellery was introduced on all denominations in 1990. In 1992 the reverse design was modified to include the dates 1867-1992, to celebrate the 125th birthday of Canada.

| 1990 and 1991 | Common Obverse | Double date 1867 1992 |

Designer and Engraver: Specifications:
   Obv.: Dora de Pédery-Hunt, Ago Aarand   Same as 1968 issue
   Rev. : Thomas Shingles

Date and Mint Mark	Mintage	MS-63	MS-64	MS-65	MS-66	MS-67
1990	207,000	1.	2.	5.	–	–
1991	490,000	1.	2.	5.	–	–
1867-1992	248,000	1.	2.	5.	–	–

CROWNED PORTRAIT, MODIFIED COAT OF ARMS DESIGN RESUMED, 1993-1996. In 1993 the practice of using a single date was resumed. Also, the transition to beads from rim denticles, which began in 1982 on the one cent coin, was completed in 1993 on the fifty cent piece.

Designers and Engravers:
   As for the 1990 issue.

Specifications:
   Same as 1968 issue

Date and Mint Mark	Mintage	MS-63	MS-64	MS-65	MS-66	MS-67
1993	393,000	1.	2.	5.	–	–
1994	987,000	1.	2.	5.	–	–
1995	626,000	1.	2.	5.	–	–
1996	458,000	1.	2.	5.	–	–

CROWNED PORTRAIT, REDESIGNED COAT OF ARMS, 1997-2000. A new coat of arms appeared for the first time in 1997. The new coin incorporates the motto "Desiderantes Meliorem Patriam" ("They desire a better country") on a ribbon behind the shield. The mantling depicts a series of overlapping stylized maple leaves. The arrangement of the English rose, Scottish thistle, Irish shamrock and the French fleur-de-lis has been modified and extends the width of the motto. The Winnipeg Mint Mark (W) is found only on coins from the "Oh Canada!" and "Tiny Treasures" sets issued by the Numismatic Department of the Mint.

Designers and Engravers:
Obv.: Dora de Pédery-Hunt
           Ago Aarand
Rev.: C. Bursey-Sabourin
           William Woodruff

Specifications:
Same as 1968 issue

Date and Mint Mark	Mintage	MS-63	MS-64	MS-65	MS-66	MS-67
1997	387,000	1.	2.	5.	–	–
1998	308,000	1.	2.	5.	–	–
1999	496,000	1.	2.	5.	–	–
2000	573,000	1.	2.	5.	–	–

CROWNED PORTRAIT, REDESIGNED COAT-OF-ARMS, MULTI-PLY PLATED STEEL, 1999-2001. In 2001 the Royal Canadian Mint began issuing circulating coinage struck from their new Multi-Ply Plated steel blanks. The process is acid based and electroplates a thin coating of nickel, then copper, then nickel again to a steel core.

A 50-cent coin, dated 2000P, was incorporated into the cover of a desk clock and presented at the launch of the plating facilities in Winnipeg in 2000. It is believed that fewer than 200 clocks were made with about an equal number of half dollars, which were given in presentation.

In 1992 to commemorate the 50th anniversary of the reign of Queen Elizabeth II, all circulating coinage carried the double dates of her reign, 1952-2002, on the obverse.

Designers and Engravers:
As for the 1997 issue.
Composition: .9325 steel,
                      .0475 copper,
                      .0200 nickel
Weight: 6.9 grams
Diameter: 27.13 mm
Thickness: 1.95 mm
Edge: Serrated
Die Axis: ↑↑

Date and Mint Mark	Mintage	MS-63	MS-64	MS-65	MS-66	MS-67
1999P	Issued for testing	15.	20.	25.	–	–
2000P	Issued for testing			Fewer than ten known		
2001P	389,000	1.	2.	5.	–	–

IMPERIAL STATE CROWNED PORTRAIT, REDESIGNED COAT-OF-ARMS DESIGN, 2002. Using the obverse design of the 1953 Canadian Coronation Medallion, a new 50-cent circulating coin was issued to commemorate the golden jubilee of Her Majesty Queen Elizabeth II. The reverse design features Canada's Coat-of-Arms struck with the dual dates 1952-2002.

Designers and Engravers:
Obv.: Susan Taylor
Rev.: C. Bursey-Sabourin
       William Woodruff

Specifications:
Same as 1999P issue

Date and Mint Mark	Mintage	MS-63	MS-64	MS-65	MS-66	MS-67
1952-2002P	14,440,000	1.	2.	5.	–	–

Note: No fifty cent Multi Ply Plated coins were issued for circulation in 2003-2004. All examples of these dates which are offered for sale are taken from brilliant uncirculated sets issued by the Royal Canadian Mint.

UNCROWNED PORTRAIT, REDESIGNED COAT-OF-ARMS, MULTI-PLY PLATED STEEL, CONTINUED, 2005.

Photograph not
available
at press time

Designers and Engravers:
Obv.: Susanna Blunt,
       Susan Taylor
Rev.: C. Bursey-Sabourin
       William Woodruff

Specifications:
Same as 1999P issue

Issue Price	Description	Mintage	MS-63	MS-64	MS-65	MS-66	MS-67
2005P	Circulation	N/A	1.	2.	5.	–	–
2005P	Mint Roll, 25 coins	N/A	20.	–	–	–	–
2005P	First Strike	5,000	15.	–	–	–	–

ONE DOLLAR - SILVER
George V 1935 - 1936

SILVER JUBILEE COMMEMORATIVE 1935. Canada's first silver dollar for circulation, also the first commemorative coin, marked the 25th anniversary of the accession of King George V. The Bank of Canada $25 bill also commemorated the special event. The reverse of the silver dollar was a modern design by sculptor Emanuel Hahn, showing an Indian and a voyageur, a travelling agent for a fur company, paddling a canoe by an islet on which there are two wind-swept trees. In the canoe are bundles of goods; the bundle at the right has HB, representing the Hudson's Bay Company. The vertical lines in the background represent the northern lights. This modern design began a trend which produced the beautiful reverses for 1937.

The obverse was the commemorative side of the coin with the Latin legend indicating the King was in the 25th year of his reign. The portrait was by Percy Metcalfe and was never used for any other Canadian coinage, but had been used previously for the obverses of some New Zealand and Australian coinages.

Generally, the coins were issued in cardboard tubes of 20.

Designer and Engraver:
    Obv.: Percy Metcalfe
    Rev.: Emanuel Hahn (EH in water left end of canoe)
Composition: .800 silver, .200 copper
Weight: 23.33 grams
Diameter: 36.00 mm
Edge: Reeded
Die Axis: ↑↑

Date and Mint Mark	Mintage	VF-20	EF-40	AU-50	MS-60	MS-63	MS-64	MS-65	MS-66
1935	428,707	30.	40.	50.	60.	100.	125.	300.	750.

STANDARD OBVERSE, 1936. In 1936 the issue of silver dollars continued, with the new reverse remaining unchanged. The obverse was the regular MacKennal design used for 1- to 50-cent pieces of 1912-1936. The tools for this obverse had already been prepared in 1911 for use on the 1911 dollar (see DC-6 in the chapter on Patterns).

Designer and Engraver:
　　Obv.: Sir E.B. MacKennal (B.M. on truncation)
Specifications: Same as 1935 issue

Date and Mint Mark	Mintage	VF-20	EF-40	AU-50	MS-60	MS-63	MS-64	MS-65	MS-66
1936	306,100	20.	25.	30.	55.	100.	175.	500.	2,000.

ONE DOLLAR - SILVER
George VI 1937 - 1952

VOYAGEUR DESIGN, 1937-1938. New reverse designs were under consideration for the 1937 issues; however, it was decided to retain the voyageur design, since it was already modern.

Designer and Engraver:
　　Obv.: T.H. Paget (H.P. below bust)
Composition: .800 silver, .200 copper
Weight: 23.33 grams
Diameter: 36.00 mm
Edge: Reeded
Die Axis: ↑↑

Date and Mint Mark	Mintage	VF-20	EF-40	AU-50	MS-60	MS-63	MS-64	MS-65	MS-66
1937	241,002	15.	18.	24.	50.	115.	275.	—	—
1938	90,304	60.	70.	90.	125.	275.	750.	3,500.	8,000.

COMMEMORATIVE FOR ROYAL VISIT, 1939. Canada's second commemorative coin was created when the reverse of the 1939 silver dollar was used to mark the visit of George VI and Queen Elizabeth to Canada. The design consists of the centre block of the Parliament buildings in Ottawa and the Latin phrase, "FIDE SVORVM REGNAT," meaning "He reigns by the faith of his people."

The usual means of issuing coins was through the Bank of Canada, but for this special coinage it was decided to make them available through the Post Office as well. Consequently, 369,500 of the original mintage of nearly 1.4 million were issued directly to the Post Office. This mintage proved to be larger than public demand and between 1939 and 1945 nearly 160,000 pieces were returned to the Mint and melted.

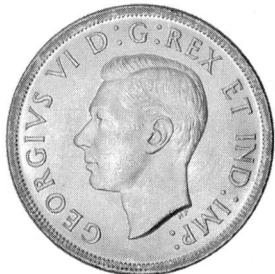 

Designer and Engraver: Reverse: Emanuel Hahn (E H flanked the building in the original model, but was removed by order of Canadian government officials)

Specifications: Same as 1937 issue

Date and Mint Mark	Mintage	VF-20	EF-40	AU-50	MS-60	MS-63	MS-64	MS-65	MS-66
1939	1,363,816*	10.	14.	16.	20.	45.	100.	300.	–

* 158,084 pieces were returned to the Mint and melted between 1939 and 1945.

"ET IND; IMP;" OBVERSE, VOYAGEUR DESIGN RESUMED, 1945-1947. Beginning with the 1945 silver dollar a more brilliant appearance was achieved. This resulted from the use of chromium-plated coinage dies. For previous issues unplated dies with a rougher surface had been used.

Specifications: Same as 1937 issue

Date and Mint Mark	Mintage	VF-20	EF-40	AU-50	MS-60	MS-63	MS-64	MS-65	MS-66
1945	38,391	175.	200.	225.	325.	650.	1,500.	5,000.	–
1946	93,055	40.	60.	100.	125.	350.	1,200.	–	–

ONE DOLLAR

VARIETIES OF THE 1947: POINTED SEVEN. Two styles of 7 were used to date the 1947 dies; a tall figure with the lower tail pointing back to the right (Pointed 7); and a shorter 7 with the lower tail pointing almost straight down (Blunt 7).

The 'dot' after the seven variety is the result of a specimen die being put in service as a working die for business strikes. The dot is the result of an accidental pit on the die.

1947 Pointed 7

1947 Pointed 7
Double punched 4

1947 Pointed 7
Dot

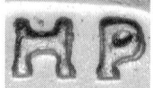

Doubled

Tripled

Quadrupled

Date and Mint Mark	Mintage	VF-20	EF-40	AU-50	MS-60	MS-63	MS-64	MS-65	MS-66
1947 Pt 7	65,595	125.	175.	225.	350.	1,500.	4,000.	–	–
1947 Pt 7 Dot	Included	150.	200.	250.	500.	2,000.	5,000.	–	–
1947 Pt 7 RP4	Included	250.	300.	350.	500.	2,000.	–	–	–
1947 Pt 7 DHP	Included	150.	200.	250.	500.	2,000.	–	–	–
1947 Pt 7 THP	Included	150.	200.	250.	375.	2.000.	–	–	–
1947 Pt 7 QHP	Included	200.	250.	300.	500.	2,000.	–	–	–

VARIETIES OF THE 1947: BLUNT SEVEN. As with the 1947 Pointed Seven, the 1947 Blunt Seven may have doubling of the designer's initials.

1947 Blunt 7

1947 Blunt 7
Doubled HP

Date and Mint Mark	Mintage	VF-20	EF-40	AU-50	MS-60	MS-63	MS-64	MS-65	MS-66
1947 Bl 7	Included	100.	150.	175.	250.	400.	1,000.	–	–
1947 Bl 7 DHP	Included	125.	175.	225.	275.	–	–	–	–

VARIETIES OF THE 1947: MAPLE LEAF ISSUE. In early 1948 the Royal Canadian Mint was faced with a problem. New obverse coinage tools with the Latin abbreviation "ET IND: IMP:" omitted to indicate that the King's titles had been changed to concur with India's recently granted independence would not arrive for several months. Yet, there was a great need for all denominations of coins. The Mint satisfied the demand by striking coins dated 1947 and bearing an obverse with outmoded titles. To differentiate this issue from the regular strikings of 1947, a tiny maple leaf was placed after the date. Only the Blunt 7 was employed for dating this issue.

1947 Maple Leaf Issue,
struck in 1948

1947 Double HP

Date and Mint Mark	Mintage	VF-20	EF-40	AU-50	MS-60	MS-63	MS-64	MS-65	MS-66
1947 ML	21,135	200.	225.	275.	375.	650.	1,700.	–	–
1947 MLDHP	Included	250.	300.	375.	–	–	–	–	–

MODIFIED OBVERSE LEGEND, VOYAGEUR DESIGN, 1948. Following the arrival in 1948 of the master tools with the new obverse legend, production of the 1947 Maple Leaf coinage was suspended. For the remainder of the year coins were produced with the new obverse and the true date, 1948.

Specifications: Same as 1937 issue

Date and Mint Mark	Mintage	VF-20	EF-40	AU-50	MS-60	MS-63	MS-64	MS-65	MS-66
1948	18,780	800.	950.	1,100.	1,400.	2,000.	3,500.	–	–

COMMEMORATIVE FOR ENTRY OF NEWFOUNDLAND INTO CONFEDERATION, 1949. On March 31, 1949 Newfoundland became the tenth province of the Dominion of Canada. This historic event was recognized on the Canadian coinage with a special reverse for the 1949 silver dollar. The design shows the ship "Matthew" in which it is thought John Cabot discovered Newfoundland in 1497. Below it is the Latin phrase, "FLOREAT TERRA NOVA," meaning "May the new found land flourish." The obverse design was taken from a photograph of a model of the "Matthew" provided by Ernest Maunder of St. John's, Newfoundland. The obverse continued unchanged from that of 1948.

The 1949 dollars were struck more carefully than those of previous years and were issued in plastic or cardboard tubes of 20 to protect them. Many of these coins remain in proof-like condition today. Thomas Shingles was the engraver, doing his work entirely by hand, without the aid of a "reducing" machine.

It was decided to strike these coins, dated 1949, as long as there was a demand for them. In 1950 some 40,718 pieces were coined. The 1949 and 1950 strikings have been combined to give the total production for the type.

Designer:
    Rev.:   Thomas Shingles, based upon Ernest Maunder's model of
           the "Matthew"
Engraver:
    Rev.:   Thomas Shingles
Specifications: Same as 1937 issue

Date and Mint Mark	Mintage	VF-20	EF-40	AU-50	MS-60	MS-63	MS-64	MS-65	MS-66
1949	672,218	20.	30.	35.	40.	45.	60.	100.	200.

ARNPRIOR TYPE DOLLAR DIE VARIETIES, 1950-1952; . During the year 1950 a technical problem arose that was to plague the Mint throughout the 1950's. At each end of the canoe are four (not three as is so often claimed) shallow water lines. In the process of polishing or repolishing the dies, parts of these lines tended to disappear, creating differences within a given year's coinage. Collectors have decided arbitrarily that a certain pattern of partial water lines at the right-hand end of the canoe should be collected separately and command a premium over dollars with perfect water lines or other partial lines configurations.

The so-called Arnprior configuration (see One Dollar, Queen Elizabeth II 1955 for more details) consists of 2 ½ (often incorrectly called 1 ½) water lines at the right. Any trace of the bottom water line disqualifies a coin from being an Arnprior. One should also beware of coins that have had part of the water line fraudulently removed.

See page 163 for an explanation of the origin of the term Arnprior Variety.

UNCROWNED PORTRAIT, VOYAGEUR DESIGN RESUMED, 1950-1952.

VARIETIES OF 1950 AND 1951.

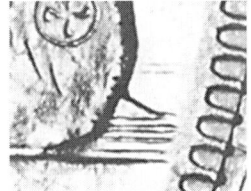  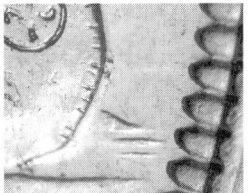

1950-1951 Normal	1950-1951 Arnprior	1950-1951
Full Water Lines at Right	2½ Water Lines at Right	Short Water Lines

Date and Mint Mark	Mintage	VF-20	EF-40	AU-50	MS-60	MS-63	MS-64	MS-65	MS-66
1950 FWL	261,002	12.	16.	20.	30.	60.	125.	175.	400.
1950 SWL	Included	15.	20.	30.	65.	125.	200.	500.	–
1950 Arn.	Included	15.	20.	30.	65.	175.	325.	1,000.	–
1951	416,395	8.	9.	12.	17.	40.	125.	–	–
1951 Arn.	Included	50.	75.	90.	200.	350.	800.	–	–

VARIETIES OF 1952. In 1952 a modified reverse, with no water lines at all, was put into use. In addition to removing the water lines, this reverse differs from the Water Lines variety in having a remodeled (larger) islet tip at the right end of the canoe. This variety is fundamentally different from the Arnpriors in that it is was deliberately, not accidentally created. The Water Lines variety was also used in 1952.

1952 Short Water Lines Variety	1952 No Water Lines Variety

Date and Mint Mark	Mintage	VF-20	EF-40	AU-50	MS-60	MS-63	MS-64	MS-65	MS-66
1952 FWL	406,148	8.	9.	12.	16.	40.	125.	300.	–
1952 SWL	Included	20.	25.	35.	60.	100.	200.	–	–
1952 No Lines	Included	10.	12.	15.	35.	60.	200.	350.	–

ONE DOLLAR - SILVER
Elizabeth II 1953 - 1967

LAUREATED PORTRAIT; VOYAGEUR DESIGN, 1953-1957. As was true of all the lower denominations, the 1953 silver dollars occur with two obverses, called the No Shoulder Fold and Shoulder Fold varieties (see one cent, Queen Elizabeth II, 1953 to date for full explanation). On this denomination these obverses are combined with different reverses. The No Shoulder Fold variety appears with the Wire Edge reverse, the Water Lines reverse of 1950-1952, and the Shoulder Fold obverse with the Wide Border reverse.

 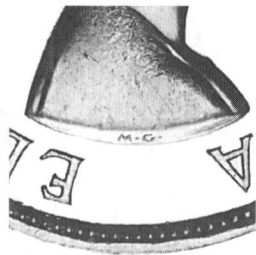 

No Shoulder Fold Obverse 1953
letters have pronounced flaring

 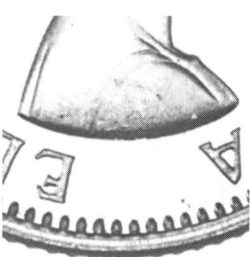 

Shoulder Fold Obverse 1953-1964
letters have subdued flaring

Designer:
   Obv.: Mary Gillick
Engraver:
   Obv.: No Shoulder Fold: Thomas Shingles, using the Gillick portrait
          Shoulder Fold: Thomas Shingles, modifying existing NSF coinage tools
Composition: .800 silver, .200 copper
Weight: 23.33 grams
Diameter: 36.00 mm
Edge: Reeded
Die Axis: ↑↑

Date and Mint Mark	Mintage	VF-20	EF-40	AU-50	MS-60	MS-63	MS-64	MS-65	MS-66
1953 NSF	1,074,578	8.	9.	10.	12.	30.	75.	400.	—
1953 SF	Included	8.	9.	10.	12.	35.	100.	250.	—
1954	246,606	12.	15.	18.	25.	50.	125.	—	—

ARNPRIOR VARIETY OF 1955. In December,1955 the Mint made up an order of 2,000 silver dollars for a firm in Arnprior, Ontario. These coins had 2 ½ water lines at the right of the canoe, similar to the configuration which occurred on some of the 1950 - 1951 dollars. It was the 1955 dollars that first attracted the attention of collectors, but the term Arnprior has been applied to any dollar with a similar configuration of defective water lines. Confirmation of the 1955 Arnprior is given by the die break on the obverse legend, the joining of the "T"and "I" of GRATIA. Arnprior dollars without this die break will command a slightly lower price. See the 1950-1951 silver dollars issues for additional comments.

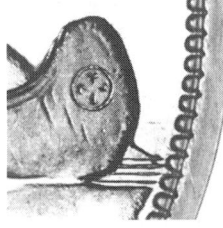
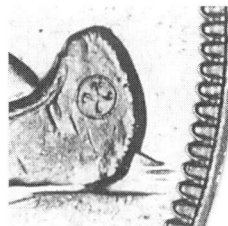
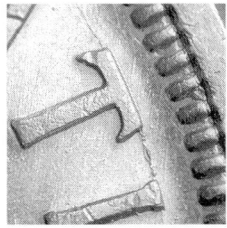

| 1955 Normal | 1955 Arnprior | Obverse die break between |
| 4 Water Lines | 2½ Water Lines | "T" and "I" of GRATIA |

Date and Mint Mark	Mintage	VF-20	EF-40	AU-50	MS-60	MS-63	MS-64	MS-65	MS-66
1955	268,105	11.	15.	16.	25.	60.	150.	–	–
1955 Arn.	Included	60.	70.	80.	100.	175.	400.	–	–
1955 Arn. w/DB	Included	100.	125.	150.	200.	300.	500.	–	–
1956	209,092	12.	16.	20.	35.	90.	175.	–	–

VARIETIES OF 1957. Another Arnprior 'type' variety was created by the polishing of the 1957 reverse dies, resulting in a die with only one water line to the right of the canoe.

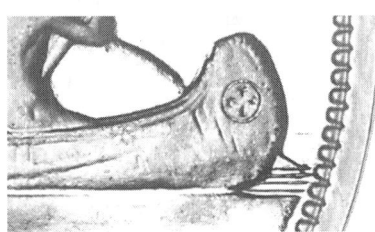
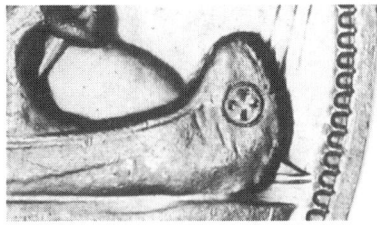

| 1957 Full (4) Water Lines at Right | 1957 One Water Line at Right |

Date and Mint Mark	Mintage	MS-60	MS-63	MS-64	MS-65	MS-66
1957 Full Water Lines	496,389	12.	20.	100.	–	–
1957 One Water Line	Included	15.	50.	200.	–	–

BRITISH COLUMBIA COMMEMORATIVE, 1958. The reverse of the 1958 dollar commemorates the centenary of the Cariboo gold rush and the establishment of British Columbia as a crown colony. The design shows a totem pole section with mountains in the background. The top element in the totem is a raven, used by some Indians to symbolize death. As a result, it was rumoured that those Indians disliked the dollars, causing them to be called "death dollars." The obverse was the same as that on the 1954-1957 issues.

Designer and Engraver: Rev.: Stephan Trenka

Specifications: Same as 1953 issue

Date and Mint Mark	Mintage	MS-60	MS-63	MS-64	MS-65	MS-66
1958	3,039,630	12.	20.	50.	200.	—

VOYAGEUR DESIGN RESUMED, 1959-1963. By 1959 the master dies utilizing the Emanuel Hahn reverse design had been in use for nearly twenty-five years. The 'Northern Lights' and 'water line' details were weakening. In 1960, Thomas Shingles re-engraved the matrix, strengthening the weak design elements.

Designers and Engravers:
   Obv.: Mary Gillick, Thomas Shingles
   Rev.: Emanuel Hahn, Thomas Shingles

Specifications: Same as 1953 issue

Date and Mint Mark	Mintage	MS-60	MS-63	MS-64	MS-65	MS-66
1959	1,443,502	12.	15.	75.	—	—
1960	1,420,486	12.	15.	75.	—	—
1961	1,262,231	12.	15.	75.	—	—
1962	1,884,789	12.	15.	65.	—	—
1963	4,179,981	10.	15.	75.	250.	—

CONFEDERATION MEETINGS COMMEMORATIVE, 1964. The reverse of the 1964 silver dollar carried a special design marking the centennial of the 1864 meetings in Charlottetown, P.E.I. and Quebec City, Quebec which prepared the way for Confederation in 1867. The design depicts, conjoined within a circle, the French fleur-de-lis, the Irish shamrock, the Scottish thistle and the English rose. The obverse coupled with the commemorative reverse was a reworking of the Shoulder Fold variety.

Designer: Rev.: Dinko Vodanovic
Engraver: Obv.: Myron Cook, modifying existing model
              Rev.: Thomas Shingles
Specifications: Same as 1953 issue

Date and Mint Mark	Mintage	MS-60	MS-63	MS-64	MS-65	MS-66
1964	7,296,832	10.	15.	50.	−	−

TIARA PORTRAIT, VOYAGEUR DESIGN, 1965. A new obverse with the Queen showing more mature facial features and wearing a tiara was introduced on all denominations in 1965. The first new obverse for the dollar had to be replaced because it gave such poor die life. The difficulty was caused by a flat field (Small Beads variety). A single trial die (Medium Beads variety) established that an obverse with the field sloping up at the edge was preferable, so new master tools were prepared (Large Beads variety) and those dies became the standard. In addition two reverses, bearing slightly different 5s were employed, creating five varieties in all for 1965.

Designer: Obv.: Arnold Machin
Specifications: As for the 1953 issue

VARIETIES OF 1965. An anomaly was generated with the 1965 varieties. When the silver dollars for 1965 were released the varieties were discovered in the order they are classified: Type 1 through Type 5, not in the order they were struck at the Mint. which is as follows: Type 1, then 2, then 5, then 3 and finally, Type 4. The Type 5 variety was an internal test coin, to investigate whether a sloping field improved die life. The test worked and the dish was extended producing Types 3 and 4.

VARIETY 1 and 2: SMALL BEADS	POINTED and BLUNT FIVE	REAR JEWEL

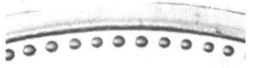

1965 Pointed 5 (at bottom)

1965 Blunt 5 (at bottom)

Small Beads Obverse
1965-1966, rear jewel in
tiara is well attached

VARIETY 5: MEDIUM BEADS	POINTED FIVE	REAR JEWEL

1965 Pointed 5 (at bottom)

Medium Beads Obverse: Rear
jewel in tiara is nearly detached

VARIETY 3 and 4: LARGE BEADS	BLUNT and POINTED FIVE	REAR JEWEL

1965 Blunt 5 (at bottom)

1965 Pointed 5 (at bottom)

Large Beads Obverse: Rear
jewel in tiara is well attached

Date and Mint Mark	Mintage	MS-60	MS-63	MS-64	MS-65	MS-66
1965 SB, P5; T-1	10,768,569	10.	15.	50.	–	–
1965 SB, B5; T-2, Medal	Included	10.	15.	50.	–	–
1965 SB, B5; T-2, Coinage	Included	3,000.	–	–	–	–
1965 LB, B5; T-3	Included	10.	15.	50.	100.	300.
1965 LB, P5; T-4	Included	10.	15.	50.	100.	300.
1965 MB, P5; T-5	Included	25.	50.	200.	–	–

VARIETIES OF 1966. The obverse of the 1966 (normal) dollar remained unchanged from the large beads variety of 1965. The reverse also remained unchanged from the previous year.

The 1966 "Small Beads Obverse" variety is the result of coupling a small beads variety obverse die from 1965 with a reverse dated 1966. This was a muling similar to the 1954 No Shoulder Fold cent and, like that variety, was probably produced only for numismatic sets. The "Small Beads" dollars were therefore officially produced and we have heard of at least one being found in a prooflike set (which presumably was officially issued). All of these pieces were slated for melting. The circumstances of the appearance of the loose coins on the numismatic market suggests that their issue was "unofficial", placing them in a similar category to the double-struck 1967 dollar (see section "Other Silver and Nickel Dollars of Canada"). The mintage of the Small Beads variety has been estimated at about 500, but this cannot be confirmed.

Large Beads (normal)   Small Beads

Date and Mint Mark	Mintage	EF-40	AU-50	MS-60	MS-63	MS-64	MS-65	MS-66
1966 LB	9,912,178	6.	7.	10.	15.	60.	150.	–
1966 SB	Included	–	2,000.	2,500.	3,500.	4,000.	5,000.	–

COMMEMORATIVE FOR CENTENNIAL OF CONFEDERATION, 1967. A design for the reverse showing a Canada goose in flight was chosen as part of the set of commemorative coins for this year. The obverse was the Large Beads variety of 1965-1966.

Designer and Engraver: Rev.: Alex Colville, Myron Cook
Composition: .800 silver, .200 copper
Weight: 23.33 grams
Diameter: 36.00 mm
Edge: Reeded
Die Axis: ↑↑

Date and Mint Mark	Mintage	MS-60	MS-63	MS-64	MS-65	MS-66
1967 Medal	6,767,496	10.	15.	50.	150.	–
1967 Coinage	Included	3,000.	4,000.	–	–	–

Note: In 1967 141,741 pieces were melted.

ONE DOLLAR - NICKEL
Elizabeth II 1968 - 1987

VOYAGEUR DESIGN RESUMED; REDUCED SIZE COINAGE, 1968-1969. When the voyageur reverse design was resumed in 1968, the strikes were in nickel. In order to make coining easier in the harder metal the diameter was reduced considerably.

Engraver: Myron Cook, using existing models
Composition: 1.00 nickel
Weight: 15.62 grams
Diameter: 32.13 mm
Edge: Reeded
Die Axis: ↑↑

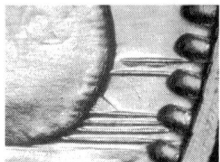 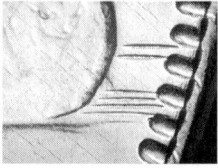 

Island	Small Island	No Island

Date and Mint Mark	Mintage	MS-63	MS-64	MS-65	MS-66	MS-67
1968	5,579,714	2.	3.	6.	–	–
1968 Small Island	Included	10.	12.	14.	–	–
1968 No Island	Included	8.	10.	12.	–	–
1969	4,809,313	2.	3.	6.	–	–

MANITOBA CENTENNIAL COMMEMORATIVE, 1970. The year 1970 saw Canada's first commemorative nickel dollar, with a special reverse featuring a prairie crocus in recognition of the centenary of Manitoba's entry into Confederation. The obverse continued unchanged from the 1968-1969 issues.

Designer:
   Rev.: Raymond Taylor
Engraver:
   Rev.: Walter Ott

Specifications:
   Same as 1968-69 issues

Date and Mint Mark	Mintage	MS-63	MS-64	MS-65	MS-66	MS-67
1970	4,140,058	2.	3.	6.	–	–

BRITISH COLUMBIA CENTENNIAL COMMEMORATIVE, 1971. The nickel dollar for 1971 commemorates the entry of British Columbia into Confederation in 1871. Its design is based on the arms of the province, with a shield at the bottom and dogwood blossoms at the top. The obverse is the same as on previous nickel issues.

Designer and Engraver:
Obv.: Arnold Machin
Rev.: Thomas Shingles
Composition: 1.00 nickel
Weight: 15.62 grams
Diameter: 32.13 mm
Edge: Reeded
Die Axis: ↑↑

Date and Mint Mark	Mintage	MS-63	MS-64	MS-65	MS-66	MS-67
1971	4,260,781	2.	3.	6.	–	–

VOYAGEUR DESIGN RESUMED, 1972. In 1972 the standard voyageur reverse was resumed. The obverse and reverse are the same as for the 1968-1969 issues. The physical and chemical specifications are as for the 1968-1969 issues.

Date and Mint Mark	Mintage	MS-63	MS-64	MS-65	MS-66	MS-67
1972	2,193,000	2.	3.	6.	–	–

P.E.I. CENTENNIAL COMMEMORATIVE, 1973. The special reverse on the nickel dollar of 1973 marks the 100th anniversary of the entry of Prince Edward Island into Confederation. The design depicts the provincial legislature building. A new obverse with a smaller, more detailed portrait, and fewer rim beads placed farther from the rim, is brought into use with this reverse.

Designers and Engravers:
Obv.: Arnold Machin
      Patrick Brindley
Rev.: Terry Manning
      Walter Ott

Composition: 1.00 nickel
Weight: 15.62 grams
Diameter: 32.13 mm
Edge: Reeded
Die Axis: ↑↑

Date and Mint Mark	Mintage	MS-63	MS-64	MS-65	MS-66	MS-67
1973	3,196,452	2.	3.	6.	–	–

WINNIPEG COMMEMORATIVE, 1974. The 1974 issue of nickel dollars commemorates the centenary of the City of Winnipeg, Manitoba. The design consists of a large 100; in the first 0 is a view of Main Street in 1874 and in the second 0 is a view of the same location 100 years later. For the first time the special collectors' issue of silver dollars for that year had the same design.

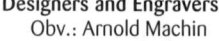

Designers and Engravers:
Obv.: Arnold Machin
       Patrick Brindley
Rev.: Paul Pederson
       Patrick Brindley
Composition: 1.00 nickel
Weight: 15.62 grams
Diameter: 32.13 mm
Edge: Reeded
Die Axis: ↑↑

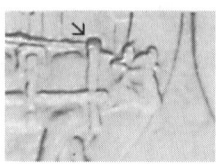

1974 Single Yoke   1974 Doubled Yoke
Variety 2

Date and Mint Mark	Mintage	MS-60	MS-63	MS-64	MS-65	MS-66	MS-67
1974 Single Yoke	2,799,363	–	2.	3.	6.	–	–
1974 Doubled Yoke, Variety 2	Included	150.	200.	250.	350.	–	–

VOYAGEUR DESIGN RESUMED, 1975-1976. The designs employed for the voyageur dollars of 1975-1976 were essentially continuations of previous designs, except for some minor variations on the obverse. The physical and chemical specifications are as for the 1974 issues.

Date and Mint Mark	Mintage	MS-63	MS-64	MS-65	MS-66	MS-67
1975	3,256,000	2.	3.	6.	–	–
1976	2,101,000	2.	3.	6.	–	–

MODIFIED REVERSE, 1977. A major alteration was made on the reverse of the 1977 dollar. A new model was prepared on which the size of the device was reduced and the legend was in small lettering, much farther from the rim. The rim denticles were replaced with beads.

Designers and Engravers:
Obv.: Arnold Machin
       Patrick Brindley
Rev.: E. Hahn
       Terry Smith
Composition: 1.00 nickel
Weight: 15.62 grams
Diameter: 32.13 mm
Edge: Reeded
Die Axis: ↑↑

Date and Mint Mark	Mintage	MS-63	MS-64	MS-65	MS-66	MS-67
1977	1,393,745	2.	3.	6.	–	–

MODIFIED DESIGNS, 1978-1981. Continued major changes occurred in the nickel dollar coinage in 1978. In a reversal of design policy, the Mint returned to designs more like those used prior to 1977. On the obverse the unmodified Machin portrait was restored, but the beads were farther from the rim than on the 1968-1972 issues. The reverse had a design similar to that of 1975-1976, complete with rim denticles instead of beads, but the northern lights were rendered as raised lines, as they were for the 1977 issue.

Designer and Engraver:
  Obv.: Arnold Machin
  Rev.: E. Hahn
Composition: 1.00 Nickel
Weight: 15.62 grams
Diameter: 32.13 mm
Edge: Reeded
Die Axis: ↑↑

Date and Mint Mark	Mintage	MS-63	MS-64	MS-65	MS-66	MS-67
1978	2,948,488	2.	3.	6.	–	–
1979	1,884,789	2.	3.	6.	–	–
1980	2,544,000	2.	3.	6.	–	–
1981	2,778,900	2.	3.	6.	–	–

CONSTITUTION COMMEMORATIVE DOLLAR 1982. On June 10, 1982, a one dollar pure nickel circulating coin was struck to commemorate the new Canadian Constitution. The obverse of the coin depicts the effigy of Queen Elizabeth II and the year 1982. The reverse features a faithful reproduction of the celebrated painting of the Fathers of Confederation. It commemorates the Constitution with the inscription "1867 CONFEDERATION" above the painting and "CONSTITUTION 1982" beneath it. This is the first time a commemorative and a voyageur dollar were issued in the same year for circulation. For the collector's edition of this dollar please see page 300.

Two varieties from the regular 1982 Constitution dollar are known: one with a coinage die axis, the other where the coin was struck on an underweight planchet. The thin planchet variety is the result of purchases of blanks from a private producer. Most of the latter were recovered by the Mint's quality control division.

Designers and Engravers:
  Obv.: Arnold Machin,
        RCM Staff
  Rev.: Ago Aarand,
        RCM Staff
Composition: 1.00 Nickel
Weight: 15.62 grams
Diameter: 32.13 mm
Edge: Reeded
Die Axis: ↑↑, ↑↓

Date and Mint Mark	Mintage	MS-60	MS-63	MS-64	MS-65	MS-66	MS-67
1982 Medal	11,812,000	–	2.	3.	6.	–	–
1982 Coinage	Included	2,000.	–	–	–	–	–
1982 Coinage, thin planchet	Included			Only Two Known			

VOYAGEUR REVERSE, MODIFIED DESIGN, 1982-1983. The modified designs of 1978 were continued for 1982 and 1983.

Date and Mint Mark	Mintage	MS-63	MS-64	MS-65	MS-66	MS-67
1982	1,544,398	2.	3.	6.	–	–
1983	2,267,525	2.	3.	6.	–	–

JACQUES CARTIER COMMEMORATIVE DOLLAR, 1984. The four hundred and fiftieth year of Jacques Cartier's landing at Gaspe, Quebec was honoured on July 24, 1984 by the issuing of a commemorative nickel dollar. Again, as in 1982 a commemorative and a voyageur design were issued for circulation in the same year.

Designers and Engravers:
Obv.: Arnold Machin,
RCM Staff
Rev.: Hector Greville,
Victor Cote
Composition: 1.00 nickel
Weight: 15.62 grams
Diameter: 32.13 mm
Edge: Reeded
Die Axis: ↑↑

Date and Mint Mark	Mintage	MS-63	MS-64	MS-65	MS-66	MS-67
1984 Jacques Cartier	6,141,503	2.	3.	6.	–	–

VOYAGEUR REVERSE, MODIFIED DESIGN, 1984-1987. The modified designs of 1978 were continued between 1984 and 1987. The 1987 issue of the nickel dollar appeared only in uncirculated sets sold by the numismatic department of the Mint (see page 301).

Date and Mint Mark	Mintage	MS-63	MS-64	MS-65	MS-66	MS-67
1984	1,223,486	2.	3.	6.	–	–
1985	3,104,592	2.	3.	6.	–	–
1986	3,089,225	2.	3.	6.	–	–

ONE DOLLAR - NICKEL/BRONZE
Elizabeth II 1987 to date

TIARA PORTRAIT, LOON DESIGN, 1987-1989. The increased costs associated with the production of the one dollar bank note led the Bank of Canada to request from the Mint a high denomination coin that would circulate, eventually replacing the paper note. The previous silver and nickel dollar issues did not. The new loon reverse is of reduced size, eleven-sided and new composition allowing the coin to be easily distinguishable from other circulating denominations. Of course, being lighter in weight it facilitated the use of pocket change. In 1987 two different sizes of dollar coins were issued, the Voyageur and the Loon. See page 303 for the proof loon dollar.

Designers: Obv.: Arnold Machin
          Rev.: Robert R. Carmichael
Composition: .915 nickel, .085 bronze
11-sided: 1987: 26.72 mm
          1988-1989: 26.50 mm
Edge: Plain

Engravers: Obv.: RCM Staff
          Rev.: Terrence Smith
Weight: 7.00 grams
Thickness: 1987: 1.95 mm
          1988-1989: 1.75 mm
Die Axis: ↑↑

Date and Mint Mark	Mintage	MS-63	MS-64	MS-65	MS-66	MS-67
1987	205,405,000	4.	6.	8.	–	–
1988	138,893,539	4.	6.	8.	–	–
1989	184,773,902	4.	6.	8.	–	–

CROWNED PORTRAIT, LOON DESIGN, 1990-1992. A new obverse portrait of the Queen wearing a diamond diadem and jewellery was introduced on all denominations in 1990. In 1992 the reverse design was modified to include the dates 1867-1992 to commemorate the 125th birthday of Canada.

1990 and 1991   Common obverse   Double dates
                                        1867-1992

Designers: Obv.: Dora de Pédery-Hunt
          Rev.: Robert R. Carmichael
Composition: .915 nickel, .085 bronze
11-sided: 26.50 mm
Edge: Plain

Engravers: Obv.: Ago Aarand
          Rev.: Terrence Smith
Weight: 7.00 grams
Thickness: 1.75 mm
Die Axis: ↑↑

Date and Mint Mark	Mintage	MS-63	MS-64	MS-65	MS-66	MS-67
1990	68,402,000	4.	6.	8.	–	–
1991	23,156,000	4.	6.	8.	–	–
1867-1992	4,242,085	4.	6.	8.	–	–

125TH ANNIVERSARY OF CONFEDERATION, 1867-1992. This commemorative dollar was issued as part of the "Canada 125" coin program celebrating Canada's 125th birthday. The design features the centre block of the Parliament Buildings and three children seated on the ground. One child holds a Canadian flag while another points to the Peace Tower clock which reads 1:25. For the collector's issue see page 306.

Designers and Engravers:
Obv.: Dora de Pédery-Hunt
        Ago Aarand
Rev.: Rita Swanson
        Ago Aarand

Specifications: Same as 1990 issue

Date and Mint Mark	Mintage	MS-63	MS-64	MS-65	MS-66	MS-67
1992	23,010,915	4.	6.	8.	–	–

CROWNED PORTRAIT, LOON DESIGN RESUMED, 1993. In 1993 the practice of using the current date was resumed. Between the years 1997 and 2001, no one dollar nickel-bronze coins were issued for circulation. The year 2002 saw the first dollar coins issued to commemorate the 50th anniversary of the reign of Queen Elizabeth II, and like all circulating coinage, the dollars carried the double dates of her reign 1952-2002.

Designers, Engravers and Specifications: Same as 1990 issue

Date and Mint Mark	Mintage	MS-63	MS-64	MS-65	MS-66	MS-67
1993	33,662,000	4.	6.	8.	–	–
1994	40,406,000	4.	6.	8.	–	–

CROWNED PORTRAIT, REMEMBRANCE DESIGN, 1994. The National War Memorial in Ottawa, unveiled by King George VI in May of 1939, commemorates the Canadians who died in WWI. The National War Memorial was rededicated in 1982 for WWII and the Korean War. For the collector's issue see page 308.

Designers and Engravers:
Obv.: Dora de Pédery-Hunt
Ago Aarand
Rev.: RCM Staff

Specifications: Same as 1990 issue

Date and Mint Mark	Mintage	MS-63	MS-64	MS-65	MS-66	MS-67
1994	15,000,000	4.	6.	8.	–	–

CROWNED PORTRAIT, PEACEKEEPING DESIGN, 1995. This coin commemorates Canada's commitment to world peace, and the 50th anniversary of the founding of the United Nations. The reverse depicts the Peacekeeping Monument in Ottawa, unveiled in 1992. For the collector's issue see page 309.

Designers and Engravers:
Obv.: Dora de Pédery-Hunt
Ago Aarand
Rev.: J. K. Harman
R. G. Enriquez
C. H. Oberlander
Susan Taylor

Specifications: Same as 1990 issue

Date and Mint Mark	Mintage	MS-63	MS-64	MS-65	MS-66	MS-67
1995	Included in 1995 Loon mintage	4.	6.	8.	–	–

CROWNED PORTRAIT; LOON DESIGN CONTINUED, 1995-2003. From 1997 to 2001 the One Dollar Loon coins were not issued for general circulation. They were found in the collectors sets for these years.

Designers, Engravers and Specifications: Same as 1990 issue

1995, 1996, and 2003

Double dates 1952 2002

Date and Mint Mark	Mintage	MS-63	MS-64	MS-65	MS-66	MS-67
1995	41,813,100	4.	6.	8.	–	–
1996	17,101,000	4.	6.	8.	–	–
1952-2002	2,301,000	4.	6.	8.	–	–

UNCROWNED PORTRAIT, LOON DESIGN, 2003-2004.

Designer and Engravers:
Obv.: Susanna Blunt
      Susan Taylor
Rev.: Robert R. Carmichael
      Terrence Smith
Composition: Nickel electroplated with bronze
Weight: 7.00 grams
11-sided: 26.50 mm
Thickness: 1.95 mm
Edge: Plain
Die Axis: ↑↑

Date and Mint Mark	Mintage	MS-63	MS-64	MS-65	MS-66	MS-67
2003	5,102,000	4.	6.	8.	–	–
2004	3,409,000	4.	6.	8.	–	–
2005	N/A	4.	6.	8.	–	–

Note: No One Dollar Loon coins were issued for circulation during the years 1997 to 2001. They were, however, issued by the Royal Canadian Mint in Brilliant Uncirculated Sets during these years.

UNCROWNED PORTRAIT, OLYMPIC LUCKY LOONIE, 2005. Carrying on the spirit established in the Winter Olympic Games of 2002, the Royal Canadian Mint issued a Lucky Loon as a good luck symbol for the 2004 Summer Olympic Games in Athens, Greece.

Designer and Engravers:
Obv.: Susanna Blunt,
            Susan Taylor
Rev.:   R. R. Carmichael,
            Susan Taylor, RCM Staff

Specifications: Same as 1990 issue

Date and Mint Mark		Mintage	MS-63	MS-64	MS-65	MS-66	MS-67
2004	Lucky Loonie	6,526,000	4.	6.	8.	–	–
2004	RCM Mint Roll, 25 coins	Included	35.	–	–	–	–
2004	Special Edition	34,234	15.	–	–	–	–

Note: The Special Edition "Lucky Loonie" is housed in a folder and carries an issue price of $14.95.

25TH ANNIVERSARY OF THE MARATHON OF HOPE, 2005. On April 12th, 1980, Terry Fox began his Marathon of Hope in St. John's, Newfoundland. He was not to finish, but his marathon continues. The Terry Fox dollar is the first circulating commemorative to feature a Canadian hero.

Designer and Engravers:
Obv.: Susanna Blunt,
            Susan Taylor
Rev.:   Stan Witten

Specifications: Same as 1990 issue

Date and Mint Mark		Mintage	MS-63	MS-64	MS-65	MS-66	MS-67
2005	Terry Fox	11,000,000	4.	6.	8.	–	–
2005	Fox Mint Roll, 25 coins	Included	35.	–	–	–	–
2005	RCM Mint Roll, 25 coins	Included	35.	–	–	–	–
2005	First Strike	20,000	15.	–	–	–	–

Note: The "First Strike" coin was minted on the first day of production January 18th, 2005, at the Winnipeg Mint. It is specially packaged in a limited edition cover with an issue price of $14.95.

TWO DOLLAR CIRCULATING COINS

TWO DOLLAR BIMETALLIC
Elizabeth II 1996 to 2004

CROWNED PORTRAIT; POLAR BEAR DESIGN, 1996-1999. On February 19, 1996, Canada's new two dollar coin was officially launched. The lifespan of a coin is over twenty years, while that of a bank note is only a year. The economies are obvious. The new coin is bimetallic with a nickel outer ring and an aluminum bronze core. The reverse features a polar bear along the edge of a floe, and the obverse features the effigy of Her Majesty Queen Elizabeth II. See the Collector section on page 324 for collector issues of the two dollar coin. The Winnipeg Mint Mark (W) is found only on coins from the "Oh Canada!" and "Tiny Treasures" sets issued by the Numismatic Department of the Mint.

Designers: Obv.: Dora de Pédery-Hunt		**Engravers:** Obv.: Ago Aarand
Rev.: Brent Townsend		Rev.: Ago Aarand

Composition:
Ring: .99+ nickel
Core: .92 copper, .06 aluminum, .02 nickel

Weight: 7.3 grams   **Thickness:** 1.80 mm
Diameter: Ring: 28.0 mm   **Edge:** Interrupted serration
Core: 16.8 mm   **Die Axis:** ↑↑

Date and Mint Mark	Mintage	MS-63	MS-64	MS-65	MS-66	MS-67
1996	375,483,000	4.	6.	8.	–	–
1997	16,942,000	4.	6.	8.	–	–
1998	5,309,000	4.	6.	8.	–	–

CROWNED PORTRAIT, NUNAVUT DESIGN, 1999. This two dollar coin was issued on May 27, 1999, to commemorate the creation of a third territory in Canada, Nunavut.

Designers and Engravers:
Obv.: Dora de Pédery-Hunt
Rev.: G. Arnaktavyok
José Osio

Specifications: Same as 1996 issue

Date and Mint Mark	Mintage	MS-63	MS-64	MS-65	MS-66	MS-67
1999	25,130,000	4.	6.	8.	–	–

CROWNED PORTRAIT, POLAR BEAR AND CUBS DESIGN, 2000. Issued to commemorate the 2000 Millennium, the Path of Knowledge $2.00 coin was launched July 1, 2000 at a citizenship ceremony at Downsview, Toronto. The coin is inscribed with knowledge - Le Savoir reflecting the experience, wisdom and knowledge that is passed down from generation to generation.

Designer and Engraver:
Obv.: Dora de Pédery-Hunt
Rev.: Tony Bianco

Specifications: Same as 1996 issue

Date and Mint Mark	Mintage	MS-63	MS-64	MS-65	MS-66	MS-67
2000	29,880,000	4.	6.	8.	–	–

CROWNED PORTRAIT, POLAR BEAR DESIGN RESUMED, 2000-2003. With the 2000 millennium celebrations over the Polar Bear design was continued in 2001. The 2002 Jubilee issue commemorates the 50th anniversary of the reign of Queen Elizabeth II. All circulating coinage carries the double dates of her reign 1952-2002.

2001 and 2003   1952-2002 Double dates

Designers, Engravers, and Specifications: Same as 1996 issue

Date and Mint Mark	Mintage	MS-63	MS-64	MS-65	MS-66	MS-67
2001	11,910,000	4.	6.	8.	–	–
1952-2002	27,020,000	4.	6.	8.	–	–
2003	7,123,697	4.	6.	8.	–	–

UNCROWNED PORTRAIT, POLAR BEAR DESIGN, 2003-2004.

Designers: Obv.: Susanna Blunt
          Rev.: Brent Townsend
Composition:
    Ring: .99+ nickel
    Core: .92 copper, .06 aluminum,
    .02 nickel
Weight: 7.3 grams
Diameter: Ring: 28.0 mm
          Core: 16.8 mm

Engravers: Obv.: Susan Taylor
          Rev.: Ago Aarand

Thickness: 1.80 mm
Edge: Interrupted serration
Die Axis: ↑↑

Date and Mint Mark	Mintage	MS-63	MS-64	MS-65	MS-66	MS-67
2003	4,120,104	4.	6.	8.	–	–
2004	12,907,000	4.	6.	8.	–	–
2005	N/A	4.	6.	8.	–	–

FIVE AND TEN DOLLAR SILVER COINS

Montreal was chosen as the site for the XXI Olympiad, the summer Olympics of 1976. Taking the lead from the Munich Olympics in 1972, it was proposed that Canada Post issue Olympic coins to assist in the financing of the Montreal games. The Olympic Coin Program, a marketing arm of Canada Post, was established to assume overall control, with the Royal Canadian Mint being assigned the role of manufacturer for the 28-coin series. The first four coins of the series were issued in two parts: a monitizing issue through the banking system at face value, where no packaging was involved; the second, a more complicated issue, offering two types of finishes, and many different varieties of packaging. Only the circulating coinage is listed here; see page 337 for the uncirculated sets.

Coin No. 1 World Map

Coin No. 3 Montreal Skyline

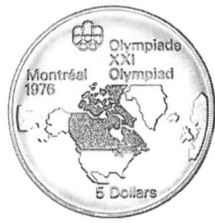

Coin No. 2
Map of North America

Images shown
sre smaller
than actual

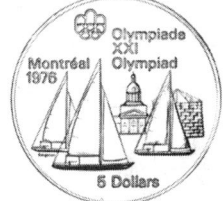

Coin No. 4
Kingston and Sailboats

Designers: Obv.: Arnold Machin
Rev.: Georges Huel, worked by invitation
Engravers: 1. ($10 Map of the World): design was photochemically etched
2. ($5 Map of North America): design was photochemically etched
3. ($10 Montreal Skyline): Ago Aarand
4. ($5 Kingston and Sailboats): Terrance Smith

$5 Coin	$10 Coin
Composition: .925 silver, .075 copper	**Composition:** .925 silver, .075 copper
Weight: 24.30 grams	**Weight:** 48.60 grams
Edge: Reeded	**Edge:** Reeded
Diameter: 38.00 mm	**Diameter:** 38.00 mm
Thickness: 2.35 mm	**Thickness:** 3.15 mm
Die Axis: ↑↑	**Die Axis:** ↑↑

Date	Denom.	Description	Mintage	MS-60	MS-63	MS-64	MS-65
1973	$5	World Map		7.50	–	–	–
1973	$5	Map of NA	Not	7.50	–	–	–
1973	$10	Montreal Skyline	Known	15.00	–	–	–
1973`	$10	Kingston/Sailboats		15.00	–	–	–

OTTAWA MINT SOVEREIGNS

The British £1 pieces (sovereigns) coined at the Ottawa Mint between 1908 and 1919 occupy a controversial position in Canadian numismatics. Some argue that these pieces are Canadian and must be collected as part of the Canadian series, while others claim that they are British and are separate from the decimal series of the Dominion of Canada.

From the time of the opening of the Ottawa Mint it was the intention of the Dominion government to mint decimal gold coins; however, the fact that the Ottawa Mint was a branch of the Royal Mint in London meant it was obligated to mint sovereigns on request. And while sovereigns were legal tender in Canada, so were gold coins of the United States. Neither type of gold circulated to any significant degree in Canada in the 20th century. Most companies who requested the Ottawa Mint to strike sovereigns did so because they wanted the coins for export purposes. Finally, the fact that some sovereigns were coined at the Ottawa Mint does not automatically make them Canadian, any more than other coinages (e.g. Newfoundland or Jamaica) produced there.

ONE POUND (SOVEREIGNS)
Edward VII 1908

As with all other branch mint sovereigns of the period, the Edward VII Canadian sovereigns are identical to the corresponding London mint issues except for the branch mint mark. The 1908 strikes were Specimen coins only and the tiny mintage was struck merely to establish the series.

Designer and Engraver:
  Obv.: George W. DeSaulles
  Rev.: Benedetto Pistrucci
Composition: .917 gold, .083 copper
Weight: 7.99 grams
Diameter: 22.05 mm
Edge: Reeded
Die Axis: ↑↑

The "C" mint mark (for Canada) is on the ground line above the centre of the date.

Date and Mint Mark	Mintage	SP-20	SP-40	SP-50	SP-60	SP-63	SP-64	SP-65	SP-66
1908C	636	2,750.	3,250.	3,750.	4,500.	5,000.	5,500.	6,000.	10,000.

ONE POUND (SOVEREIGNS)
Edward VII 1909 - 1910

The production of sovereigns for circulation began in earnest in 1909.

Photogaph not
available
at press time

Designer and Engraver:
Obv.: George W. DeSaulles
Rev.: Benedetto Pistrucci
Composition: .917 gold, .083 copper
Weight: 7.99 grams
Diameter: 22.05 mm
Edge: Reeded
Die Axis: ↑↑
The "C" mint mark (for Canada) is on the
ground line above the centre of the date.

Date and Mint Mark	Mintage	VF-20	EF-40	AU-50	MS-60	MS-63	MS-64	MS-65	MS-66
1909C	16,273	275.	350.	450.	1,000.	2,500.	4,500.	10,000.	–
1910C	28,012	250.	300.	400.	800.	2,500.	7,500.	–	–

George V 1911 - 1919

The mintages for the Ottawa mint sovereigns of George V continued the modest trend set in the previous reign. The total of all sovereigns from Ottawa barely equalled the yearly mintage at London or one of the Australian branch mints.

The 1916C issue is rare, with about fifty or so pieces known. Most of the small mintage may have been melted, accounting for the rarity, although this is by no means an established fact. Until the last few years the 1916 London issue was also rare, but thousands of them were released from a British bank.

Another tale told about the 1916C sovereign is that the mintage was lost at sea on its way to England during World War I, as part of an inter-country settlement. This is no established fact, only rumour. If there was to be a gold exchange between Canada and England in 1916, the gold needed only to be deposited with the New York Federal Reserve for the account of Great Britain, and not subjected to a perilous sea voyage during a time of war.

The reverse of the George V sovereigns is the same as that for Edward VII.

Designer and Engraver:
Obv.: E. B. Mackennal
Rev.: Benedetto Pistrucci
Composition: .917 gold, .083 copper
Weight: 7.99 grams
Diameter: 22.05 mm
Edge: Reeded
Die Axis: ↑↑

Date and Mint Mark	Mintage	VF-20	EF-40	AU-50	MS-60	MS-63	MS-64	MS-65	MS-66
1911C	256,946	150.	165.	175.	200.	250.	450.	1,500.	3,000.
1913C	3,715	800.	1,000.	1,250.	2,750.	4,500.	6,500.	–	–
1914C	14,891	350.	450.	600.	800.	1,100.	1,500.	–	–
1916C	6,111	–	17,500.	21,500.	25,000.	30,000.	60,000.	–	–
1917C	58,845	150.	165.	175.	300.	400.	–	–	–
1918C	106,516	150.	165.	175.	275.	1,500.	–	–	–
1919C	135,889	150.	165.	175.	225.	450.	–	–	–

FIVE DOLLARS – GOLD
George V 1912 - 1914

From the first year of operation of the Ottawa Mint it was planned that gold should be coined in dollar denominations as well as British sovereigns. The preparations proceeded slowly, however, and it was not until 1911 that final designs were decided upon (see DC-7 and DC-8 in the chapter on patterns) for the $5 and $10 coins. Originally it had been planned to strike denominations of $2.50, $5, $10 and $20, but some time in 1911 these plans were modified to include only the two middle denominations.

Coins for circulation were first issued in 1912. Their production was halted in 1914, when Canada adopted new wartime legislation to restrict the flow of gold. At that time notes issued by the Dominion government ceased to be redeemable in gold. This redeemability was not restored until 1926.

The design for the reverse features the old Canadian coat-of-arms superimposed upon two boughs of maple.

Designer:
    Obv.: Sir E. B. Mackennal
    Rev.: W. H. J. Blakemore
Composition: .900 gold, .100 copper
Weight: 8.36 grams
Diameter: 21.59 mm
Edge: Reeded
Die Axis: ↑↑

Date and Mint Mark	Mintage	VF-20	EF-40	AU-50	MS-60	MS-63	MS-64	MS-65	MS-66
1912	165,680	220.	250.	300.	400.	700.	1,250.	5,000.	–
1913	98,832	220.	250.	300.	500.	1,000.	1,500.	–	–
1914	31,122	425.	475.	650.	1,000.	2,250.	–	–	–

TEN DOLLARS – GOLD
George V 1912 - 1914

The designs of this denomination are the same as those of the $5 except for the change in value.

Designer:
    Obv.: Sir E. B. Mackennal
    Rev.: W. H. J. Blakemore
Composition: .900 gold, .100 copper
Weight: 16.72 grams
Diameter: 26.92 mm
Edge: Reeded
Die Axis: ↑↑

Date and Mint Mark	Mintage	VF-20	EF-40	AU-50	MS-60	MS-63	MS-64	MS-65	MS-66
1912	74,759	425.	525.	575.	800.	1,850.	5,000.	10,000.	–
1913	149,232	425.	525.	575.	1,000.	2,500.	–	–	–
1914	140,068	500.	600.	700.	1,400.	3,000.	–	–	–

SPECIMEN COINS OF CANADA

1858-1967

The sets of Specimen coins produced between 1858 and 1967 are among the most spectacular items in Canadian numismatics and are keenly sought after by collectors. These coins were beautifully struck and represent Canadian coinage at its finest. The finish imparted to specimen coins has varied over the years. During the Victorian period, it consisted of frosted, raised elements with bright, mirror fields. In the reigns of Edward VII and George V an overall satin (sometimes called matte) finish was in vogue. The 1937 coins of George VI came with both finishes. Between 1938 and the mid-1940s the specimen coins tended to have an overall polished appearance.

Specimen sets were often issued in official cases. These cases are sometimes encountered without coins and so are numbered, described and priced as separate entities in the listings that follow.

These prices are only an indication, as specimen coins are the highest example of numismatic art, and with only a few examples known, the final price must be determined between the buyer and seller.

PROVINCE OF NEWFOUNDLAND

SPECIMEN ONE CENT 1864 - 1947

Date and Mint Mark	Description	SP-63 R/B	SP-65 R/B	SP-65 Red
1864	Plain, NF-18	3,500.	5,000.	10,000.
1872H	Plain	400.	1,200.	2,500.
1873	Plain	3,000.	6,000.	12,500.
1880, Oval 0	Plain	3,000.	5,000.	20,000.
1885	Plain	3,000.	5,000.	15,000.
1894	Plain	1,200.	3,000.	7,500.
1896	Plain	1,200.	3,000.	7,500.
1904H	Plain	6,000.	10,000.	15,000.
1917C	Plain	750.	3,500.	6,000.
1919C	Plain	1,250.	3,500.	7,000.
1920	Plain	1,500.	4,000.	9,500.
1929C	Plain	1,250.	3,500.	7,000.
1936	Plain	1,500.	4,000.	9,500.
1938	Plain	750.	2,000.	5,000.
1940	Plain	750.	2,000.	5,000.
1947	Plain	1,500.	3,000.	6,500.

PROVINCE OF NEWFOUNDLAND

SPECIMEN FIVE CENTS 1865 - 1940

Date and Mint Mark	Description	SP-63	SP-65	SP-67
1865	Plain	4,500.	12,500.	25,000.
1870	Plain	4,500.	12,500.	25,000.
1870	Reeded	4,500.	12,500.	25,000.
1873	Reeded	12,500.	30,000.	50,000.
1880	Reeded	6,500.	15,000.	30,000.
1881	Reeded	6,500.	15,000.	30,000.
1882H	Reeded	2,000.	4,500.	12,500.
1885	Reeded	8,000.	20,000.	40,000.
1888	Reeded	8,000.	20,000.	40,000.
1890	Reeded	5,000.	12,000.	25,000.
1894	Reeded	5,000.	12,000.	25,000.
1896	Reeded	5,000.	12,000.	25,000.
1903	Reeded	2,000.	4,500.	10,000.
1904H	Reeded	1,250.	3,000.	7,500.
1912	Reeded	1,500.	6,000.	15,000.
1917C	Reeded	1,500.	6,000.	15,000.
1919C	Reeded	1,500.	6,000.	15,000.
1938	Reeded	1,250.	3,500.	7,500.
1940C	Reeded	1,250.	6,000.	10,000.

SPECIMEN TEN CENTS 1864 - 1946

Date and Mint Mark	Description	SP-63	SP-65	SP-67
1865	Plain	5,000.	15,000.	30,000.
1870	Plain	10,000.	30,000.	50,000.
1870	Reeded	10,000.	30,000.	50,000.
1873	Reeded	10,000.	30,000.	50,000.
1880	Reeded	7,500.	17,500.	35,000.
1882H	Reeded	3,000.	5,500.	12,500.
1885	Reeded	7,500.	20,000.	40,000.
1888	Reeded	7,500.	20,000.	40,000.
1890	Reeded	5,000.	15,000.	30,000.
1894	Reeded	5,000.	15,000.	30,000.
1896	Reeded	5,000.	15,000.	30,000.
1903	Reeded	2,500.	5,000.	12,500.
1904H	Reeded	1,500.	4,000.	10,000.
1912	Reeded	1,750.	7,000.	17,500.
1917C	Reeded	1,750.	7,000.	17,500.
1919C	Reeded	1,750.	7,000.	17,500.
1938	Reeded	2,000.	4,500.	9,000.
1940	Reeded	1,500.	7,000.	11,500.
1946C	Reeded	750.	1,750.	3,500.

PROVINCE OF NEWFOUNDLAND

SPECIMEN TWENTY CENTS 1865 - 1912

Date and Mint Mark	Description	SP-63	SP-65	SP-67
1865	Plain	6,500.	17,500.	35,000.
1865	Reeded	9,000.	25,000.	45,000.
1870	Plain	6,500.	17,500.	30,000.
1870	Reeded	6,500.	17,500.	30,000.
1873	Reeded	10,000.	30,000.	50,000.
1880	Reeded	7,500.	20,000.	40,000.
1881	Reeded	7,500.	20,000.	40,000.
1882H	Reeded	3,500.	10,000.	20,000.
1885	Reeded	10,000.	30,000.	50,000.
1888	Reeded	9,000.	27,500.	50,000.
1890	Reeded	6,500.	17,500.	35,000.
1894	Reeded	6,500.	17,500.	35,000.
1896, L6	Reeded	6,500.	17,500.	35,000.
1900	Reeded	6,500.	17,500.	35,000.
1904H	Reeded	1,500.	5,000.	10,000.
1912	Reeded	2,000.	8,000.	20,000.

SPECIMEN TWENTY-FIVE CENTS 1917 - 1919

Date and Mint Mark	Description	SP-63	SP-65	SP-67
1917C	Reeded	2,000.	8,000.	20,000.
1919C	Reeded	2,000.	8,000.	20,000.

SPECIMEN FIFTY CENTS 1870 - 1919

Date and Mint Mark	Description	SP-60	SP-63	SP-65
1870	Plain	10,000.	25,000.	75,000.
1870	Reeded	12,500.	40,000.	75,000.
1873	Reeded	20,000.	75,000.	150,000.
1874	Reeded	20,000.	50,000.	100,000.
1880	Reeded	20,000.	50,000.	100,000.
1881	Reeded	−	−	150,000.
1882H	Reeded	7,500.	15,000.	35,000.
1885	Reeded	20,000.	50,000.	100,000.
1888	Reeded	20,000.	50,000.	100,000.
1896	Reeded	15,000.	50,000.	100,000.
1904H	Reeded, Matte	4,500.	12,000.	30,000.
1917C	Reeded	3,000.	5,000.	15,000.
1919C	Reeded	3,000.	5,000.	15,000.

PROVINCE OF NEWFOUNDLAND

SPECIMEN TWO DOLLARS 1865 - 1885

Date and Mint Mark	Description	SP-63	SP-64	SP-65
1865	Plain	30,000.	50,000.	100,000.
1870	Reeded	40,000.	75,000.	125,000.
1872	Reeded	25,000.	35,000.	80,000.
1880	Reeded	75,000.	115,000.	175,000.
1882H	Reeded	7,500.	25,000.	80,000.
1885	Reeded	40,000.	60,000.	125,000.

SPECIMEN SETS 1865 - 1940

Date and Mint Mark	Description	Average Grade	Price Indication
1865, Double Set	10 Coins w/box 1¢ - $2	SP-65	275,000.
1870	5 Coins, n/box 5¢ - $2	SP-65	200,000.
1880	6 Coins, n/box 1¢ - $2	SP-65	300,000.
1882H	5 Coins, n/box 5¢ - $2	SP-66	125,000.
1885	6 Coins, n/box 1¢ - $2	SP-65	250,000.
1888	4 Coins, n/box 5¢ - 50¢	SP-65	150,000.
1896	5 Coins, n/box 1¢ - 50¢	SP-65	100,000.
1904H	5 Coins, n/box 1¢ - 50¢	SP-67	85,000.
1912	3 Coins, n/box 5¢ - 20¢	SP-64	13,000.
1917C	6 Coins, n/box 1¢ - 50¢	SP-64	15,000.
1919C	6 Coins, n/box 1¢ - 50¢	SP-64	15,000.
1938C	3 Coins, n/box 1¢ - 10¢	SP-65	9,000.
1940C	3 Coins, n/box 1¢ - 10¢	SP-65	15,000.

CASES ONLY 1864-1865

Charlton Number	Intended Contents	Exterior Colour and Dimensions	Interior Colours	Price For Empty Case
1	Newfoundland 1864(1¢);1865 (others) 1¢, 5¢, 10¢, 20¢, $2 1¢, 5¢, 10¢, 20¢, $2		Details unknown. Possibly same as case #1	2,000.

PROVINCE OF PRINCE EDWARD ISLAND

SPECIMEN ONE CENT 1871

Date	Denom.	Description	SP-63 R/B	SP-65 R/B	SP-65 Red
1871	1¢	Coinage axis	2,500.	4,000.	7,000.
1871	1¢	Medal axis	2,500.	4,000.	7,000.

PROVINCE OF NOVA SCOTIA

SPECIMEN COINAGE OF 1861

Date	Denom.	Description	SP-63 R/B	SP-65 R/B	SP-65 Red
1861	½¢	Mirror	2,000.	4,000.	8,000.
1861	1¢	Large Rosebud, Mirror	2,500.	4,500.	9,000.

PROVINCE OF NEW BRUNSWICK

SPECIMEN COPPER COINAGE OF 1861 AND 1862

Date	Denom.	Description	SP-63 R/B	SP-65 R/B	SP-65 Red
1861	½¢	Plain, Mirror	3,000.	6,000.	10,000.
1861	1¢	Plain, Mirror	3,000.	6,000.	10,000.
1862	1¢	Plain, Mirror	5,000.	8,000.	12,500.

SPECIMEN SILVER COINAGE OF 1862 AND 1864

Date	Denom.	Description	SP-60	SP-63	SP-65
1862	5¢	Plain	2,500.	7,500.	15,000.
1862	10¢	Plain, Normal Date	2,500.	7,500.	20,000.
1862	20¢	Plain	2,000.	7,500.	20,000.
1864	10¢	Plain	3,500.	10,000.	20,000.

CASES ONLY

Charlton Number	Intended Contents	Exterior Colour and Dimensions	Interior Colours	Price for Empty Case
2	New Brunswick, 1862 1¢, 5¢, 10¢, 20¢ 1¢, 5¢, 10¢, 20¢		Details unknown. Possibly same as case #1.	$1,750.
3	New Brunswick, 1862 1¢, 5¢, 10¢, 20¢		Details unknown.	$1,250.

PROVINCE OF CANADA and CANADA

SPECIMEN ONE CENT 1858 - 1967

Date and Mint Mark	Description	SP-63 R/B	SP-65 R/B	SP-65 Red
1858	Plain	1,750.	4,500.	7,500.
1859/9	Plain, DP -9	2,500.	4,000.	8,000.
1859	Plain, Bronze	2,500.	4,000.	8,000.
1876	Plain	3,000.	5,000.	10,000.
1876H	Plain, Copper	2,500.	4,000.	9,500.
1876H	Plain, Nickel	4,000.	7,500.	−
1881H	Plain	2,500.	4,000.	9,000.
1882H	Plain	2,500.	4,000.	9,000.
1898H	Plain	3,000.	6,000.	12,000.
1908	Plain	200.	800.	1,500.
1911	Plain	300.	1,000.	2,500.
1921	Plain	3,000.	5,000.	15,000.
1922	Plain	2,500.	4,500.	15,000.
1923	Plain	3,000.	5,000.	15,000.
1924	Plain	2,500.	4,500.	12,000.
1925	Plain	2,500.	4,500.	12,000.
1926	Plain	2,500.	4,500.	9,000.
1927	Plain	2,500.	4,500.	9,000.
1928	Plain	2,000.	4,000.	9,000.
1929	Plain	1,750.	3,500.	7,000.
1930	Plain	2,500.	4,500.	10,000.
1931	Plain	2,500.	4,500.	10,000.
1934	Plain	5,000.	10,000.	15,000.
1936, Dot	Plain	200,000.	300,000.	450,000.
1937	Plain, Mirror	100.	200.	400.
1937	Plain, Matte	30.	100.	200.
1938	Plain	2,500.	4,000.	7,000.
1944	Plain	2,500.	4,000.	7,000.
1945	Plain	450.	750.	1,500.
1946	Plain	100.	200.	300.
1947	Plain	125.	250.	400.
1947, ML	Plain	100.	200.	300.
1948	Plain	125.	225.	500.
1949	Plain	125.	200.	450.
1950	Plain	75.	150.	250.
1951	Plain	75.	150.	300.
1952	Plain	100.	200.	350.
1953, NSF	Plain	125.	250.	500.
1964	Plain	25.	50.	100.
1965	Plain	25.	50.	100.
1967	Plain	2.	5.	10.

PROVINCE OF CANADA and CANADA

SPECIMEN FIVE CENTS 1858 - 1967

Date and Mint Mark	Description	SP-63	SP-65	SP-67
1858SD	Plain	1,200.	4,000.	10,000.
1858SD	Reeded	1,500.	4,500.	12,500.
1858LD	Plain	3,000.	7,500.	15,000.
1858LD	Reeded	4,000.	10,000.	17,500.
1870WR	Plain	3,000.	10,000.	20,000.
1870WR	Reeded	3,000.	10,000.	20,000.
1870NR	Plain	3,000.	10,000.	20,000.
1870NR	Reeded	3,000.	12,000.	20,000.
1872H	Reeded	5,000.	15,000.	25,000.
1874H, Crosslet 4	Reeded	3,500.	15,000.	25,000.
1875H, SD	Reeded	15,000.	35,000.	70,000.
1875H, LD	Reeded	12,500.	30,000.	60,000.
1880H	Reeded	3,500.	15,000.	25,000.
1881H	Reeded	3,500.	15,000.	25,000.
1882H	Reeded	4,500.	17,500.	30,000.
1884, Near 4	Reeded	15,000.	35,000.	70,000.
1885, Lg 5	Reeded	15,000.	30,000.	50,000.
1886, Sm 6	Reeded	15,000.	30,000.	50,000.
1902H	Reeded	3,500.	6,500.	17,500.
1905	Reeded	3,000.	6,000.	12,500.
1908, L8	Reeded	200.	750.	2,000.
1908, S8	Reeded	–	–	–
1911	Reeded	300.	1,000.	3,000.
1921	Reeded	40,000.	75,000.	150,000.
1922	Plain	600.	1,200.	3,500.
1923	Plain	4,500.	12,000.	20,000.
1924	Plain	1,500.	5,000.	12,500.
1925	Plain	3,500.	10,000.	20,000.
1926, N6	Plain	3,000.	7,500.	20,000.
1927	Plain	2,000.	5,000.	15,000.
1928	Plain	2,500.	5,500.	17,500.
1929	Plain	1,500.	4,000.	10,000.
1930	Plain	2,500.	5,000.	15,000.
1931	Plain	2,500.	5,000.	15,000.
1932	Plain	10,000.	20,000.	50,000.
1934	Plain	2,500.	5,000.	15,000.
1936	Plain	3,000.	7,500.	20,000.
1937	Plain, Mirror	80.	150.	300.
1937	Plain, Matte	50.	125.	200.
1938	Plain	7,500.	15,000.	20,000.
1942	Plain, Nickel	–	25,000.	–
1942	Plain, Tombac	250.	1,000.	2,000.
1943	Plain, Tombac	200.	800.	1,750.
1944	Plain	200.	600.	1,500.
1945	Plain	450.	1,500.	3,000.
1946	Plain	150.	250.	500.
1947	Plain	200.	500.	1,000.
1947, ML	Plain	125.	300.	750.
1948	Plain	175.	350.	1,000.
1949	Plain	175.	300.	750.
1950	Plain	90.	250.	500.
1951, HR	Plain	1,750.	3,500.	8,500.
1951, Comm.	Plain	100.	350.	1,000.
1952	Plain	125.	300.	750.
1953, NSF	Plain	100.	250.	600.
1964	Plain	50.	100.	200.
1965	Plain	50.	100.	200.
1967	Plain	2.	5.	10.

PROVINCE OF CANADA and CANADA

SPECIMEN TEN CENTS 1858 - 1967

Date and Mint Mark	Description	SP-63	SP-65	SP-67
1858	Plain	2,500.	6,500.	15,000.
1858	Reeded	3,000.	7,000.	17,500.
1870, Nar 0	Plain	3,500.	12,500.	25,000.
1870, Nar 0	Reeded	3,500.	12,500.	25,000.
1871	Reeded	7,500.	15,000.	25,000.
1872H	Reeded	6,000.	12,500.	25,000.
1875H	Reeded	15,000.	40,000.	100,000.
1880H	Reeded	4,000.	15,000.	25,000.
1881H	Reeded	5,000.	17,500.	30,000.
1882H	Reeded	4,500.	15,000.	25,000.
1885	Reeded	10,000.	25,000.	50,000.
1886, Lg 6	Reeded	11,000.	30,000.	60,000.
1888	Reeded	7,500.	20,000.	50,000.
1890H	Reeded	9,000.	18,000.	27,500.
1892	Reeded	7,500.	20,000.	50,000.
1894	Reeded	7,500.	20,000.	50,000.
1902H	Reeded	4,000.	10,000.	20,000.
1903H	Reeded	7,500.	15,000.	25,000.
1903	Reeded	7,500.	15,000.	25,000.
1908	Reeded	400.	1,000.	2,500.
1911	Reeded	650.	1,250.	3,500.
1913, SL	Reeded	7,500.	15,000.	25,000.
1921	Reeded	3,500.	10,000.	20,000.
1928	Reeded	2,000.	6,500.	12,500.
1929	Reeded	2,000.	5,000.	10,000.
1930	Reeded	3,500.	10,000.	20,000.
1931	Reeded	3,500.	7,500.	15,000.
1932	Reeded	5,000.	15,000.	25,000.
1934	Reeded	4,500.	10,000.	20,000.
1936, Dot	Reeded	175,000.	225,000.	250,000.
1937	Reeded, Mirror	80.	150.	300.
1937	Reeded, Matte	70.	125.	250.
1938	Reeded	2,500.	5,000.	7,500.
1939	Reeded, Mirror	2,000.	4,500.	7,500.
1944	Reeded	2,250.	4,500.	7,500.
1945	Reeded	300.	2,000.	5,000.
1946	Reeded	300.	600.	1,500.
1947	Reeded	300.	850.	1,700.
1947, ML	Reeded	150.	350.	750.
1948	Reeded	200.	400.	900.
1949	Reeded	350.	600.	1,500.
1950	Reeded	100.	300.	700.
1951	Reeded	100.	400.	800.
1952	Reeded	100.	400.	800.
1953, NSF	Reeded	100.	250.	400.
1964	Reeded	50.	100.	200.
1965	Reeded	50.	100.	200.
1967	Reeded	2.	5.	10.

SPECIMEN TWENTY CENTS 1858 - 1871

Date and Mint Mark	Description	SP-63	SP-65	SP-67
1858	Plain	3,000.	10,000.	30,000.
1858	Reeded	3,500.	12,000.	30,000.
1871	Plain	10,000.	15,000.	35,000.
1871	Reeded	10,000.	15,000.	35,000.

PROVINCE OF CANADA and CANADA

SPECIMEN TWENTY-FIVE CENTS 1870 - 1967

Date and Mint Mark	Description	SP-63	SP-65	SP-67
1870	Reeded	5,000.	15,000.	30,000.
1870	Plain	5,000.	15,000.	30,000.
1871	Reeded	9,000.	20,000.	40,000.
1872H	Reeded	5,000.	20,000.	50,000.
1875H	Reeded	22,500.	45,000.	100,000.
1880H, Wide 0	Reeded	8,500.	25,000.	50,000.
1880H, Nar 0	Reeded	7,500.	25,000.	50,000.
1881H	Reeded	8,500.	25,000.	50,000.
1882H	Reeded	6,500.	25,000.	50,000.
1883H	Reeded	7,000.	17,500.	37,500.
1885	Reeded	15,000.	35,000.	75,000.
1886, 6/3	Reeded	15,000.	35,000.	75,000.
1888	Reeded	10,000.	25,000.	50,000.
1889	Reeded	25,000.	35,000.	75,000.
1892	Reeded	25,000.	35,000.	75,000.
1900	Reeded	9,000.	25,000.	40,000.
1902H	Reeded	4,500.	12,500.	25,000.
1903	Reeded	8,000.	17,500.	30,000.
1908	Reeded	650.	1,500.	5,000.
1911	Reeded	900.	2,000.	5,000.
1921	Reeded	7,500.	20,000.	40,000.
1927	Reeded	7,500.	20,000.	40,000.
1928	Reeded	3,000.	10,000.	20,000.
1929	Reeded	3,000.	8,000.	17,000.
1930	Reeded	3,000.	11,000.	20,000.
1931	Reeded	3,000.	11,000.	20,000.
1934	Reeded	8,000.	15,000.	25,000.
1936, Dot	Reeded	12,500.	40,000.	80,000.
1937	Reeded, Mirror	200.	500.	1,000.
1937	Reeded, Matte	100.	225.	450.
1938	Reeded	3,000.	5,000.	10,000.
1939	Reeded, Mirror	3,000.	5,000.	10,000.
1944	Reeded	3,000.	5,000.	10,000.
1945	Reeded	500.	1,500.	6,000.
1946	Reeded	400.	900.	2,500.
1947	Reeded	400.	1,500.	2,500.
1947, ML	Reeded	250.	600.	1,500.
1948	Reeded	350.	750.	2,000.
1949	Reeded	300.	600.	1,200.
1950	Reeded	150.	450.	1,000.
1951, HR	Reeded	125.	300.	750.
1952, LR	Reeded	125.	300.	750.
1953, NSF	Reeded	150.	350.	700.
1964	Reeded	75.	150.	300.
1965	Reeded	75.	150.	300.
1967	Reeded	2.	5.	10.

PROVINCE OF CANADA and CANADA

SPECIMEN FIFTY CENTS 1870 - 1967

Date and Mint Mark	Description	SP-63	SP-65	SP-67
1870, LCW	Plain	15,000.	55,000.	100,000.
1870, LCW	Reeded	16,000.	60,000.	100,000.
1870, No LCW	Plain	80,000.	120,000.	175,000.
1871	Reeded	30,000.	60,000.	100,000.
1871H	Reeded	30,000.	60,000.	100,000.
1872H	Reeded, Mirror	30,000.	60,000.	135,000.
1872H	Reeded, Semi Matte	25,000.	50,000.	100,000.
1881H	Reeded	15,000.	35,000.	65,000.
1888	Reeded	25,000.	60,000.	100,000.
1908	Reeded	1,500.	3,000.	7,500.
1911	Reeded	3,500.	7,500.	12,500.
1921	Reeded	80,000.	150,000.	300,000.
1929	Reeded	6,500.	12,500.	25,000.
1931	Reeded	7,500.	17,500.	35,000.
1932	Reeded	12,500.	30,000.	60,000.
1934	Reeded	7,500.	20,000.	40,000.
1936	Reeded	10,000.	20,000.	35,000.
1937	Reeded, Mirror	400.	1,000.	2,000.
1937	Reeded, Matte	125.	300.	900.
1938	Reeded	4,000.	7,500.	15,000.
1944	Reeded	4,000.	8,000.	15,000.
1945	Reeded	1,500.	4,000.	10,000.
1946	Reeded	1,250.	3,000.	5,500.
1947, S7	Reeded	1,100.	3,000.	5,500.
1947, C7	Reeded	1,500.	3,500.	7,000.
1947, ML C7	Reeded	4,000.	6,000.	9,000.
1948	Reeded, Convex	750.	2,250.	5,000.
1948	Reeded, Concave	650.	1,750.	5,000.
1949	Reeded	500.	1,000.	2,000.
1950	Reeded	300.	750.	1,500.
1951	Reeded	300.	750.	1,500.
1952	Reeded	300.	750.	1,500.
1953, NSF SD	Reeded	250.	650.	1,500.
1953, NSF LD	Reeded	900.	2,000.	3,500.
1964	Reeded	150.	300.	500.
1965	Reeded	150.	300.	500.
1967	Reeded	2.	5.	10.

CANADA

SPECIMEN ONE DOLLAR 1935 - 1967

Date and Mint Mark	Description	SP-63	SP-65	SP-67
1935	Satin Specimen	2,500.	9,000.	22,500.
1935	Matte Specimen	4,500.	10,000.	25,000.
1936	Satin Specimen	2,500.	10,000.	25,000.
1936	Matte Specimen	5,000.	12,500.	25,000.
1937	Mirror Specimen	1,000.	2,000.	5,000.
1937	Matte Specimen	175.	400.	1,000.
1938	Satin Specimen	5,000.	10,000.	15,000.
1938	Matte Specimen	6,000.	17,500.	40,000.
1939	Mirror Specimen	800.	2,500.	6,000.
1939	Matte Specimen	500.	1,500.	4,000.
1945	Mirror Specimen	1,750.	6,000.	15,000.
1946	Mirror Specimen	1,500.	6,000.	10,500.
1947, BL	Satin Specimen	3,000.	9,500.	25,000.
1947, BL	Mirror Specimen	4,000.	10,000.	25,000.
1947, PT	Mirror Specimen	3,000.	9,000.	21,500.
1947, PT Dot	Mirror Specimen	5,000.	10,000.	15,000.
1947, ML	Mirror Specimen	2,000.	7,000.	20,000.
1948	Mirror Specimen	4,000.	7,500.	22,000.
1949	Mirror Proof	1,500.	5,000.	12,000.
1950	Mirror Specimen	600.	2,000.	3,500.
1950	Matte, one known	–	20,000.	–
1950	Mirror Proof	750.	2,000.	3,500.
1950, SWL	Mirror Specimen	750.	2,000.	3,500.
1950, Arn	Mirror Specimen	2,000.	5,500.	12,500.
1951	Mirror Specimen	750.	1,750.	3,000.
1951, Arn	Mirror Proof	750.	1,500.	3,000.
1952, WL	Mirror Specimen	1,000.	3,500.	7,500.
1952, SWL	Mirror Specimen	750.	1,500.	3,000.
1953, NSF	Mirror Specimen	1,000.	2,000.	5,000.
1953, SF	Mirror Specimen	1,000.	2,000.	5,000.
1964	Mirror Specimen	200.	450.	2,000.
1965, SBP5	Mirror Specimen	200.	400.	2,000.
1965, SBB5	Mirror Specimen	200.	400.	2,000.
1965, LBB5	Mirror Specimen	200.	400.	2,000.
1965, LBP5	Mirror Specimen	200.	400.	2,000.
1966, LB	Mirror Specimen	200.	500.	2,000.
1967	Mirror Specimen	5.	10.	15.

SPECIMEN GOLD COINAGE 1908 - 1912

Date and Mint Mark	Denom.	Description	SP-63	SP-65	SP-67	SP-68
1908C	Sovereign	Satin Specimen	5,000.	7,500.	25,000.	40,000.
1911C	Sovereign	Matte Specimen	4,000.	12,500.	25,000.	35,000.
1912	Five Dollars	Satin Specimen	7,000.	15,000.	27,500.	40,000.
1912	Ten Dollars	Satin Specimen	10,000.	17,000.	32,500.	55,000.

Note: Even though the Royal Canadian Mint claimed they did not have the equipment to strike proof coinage, there exist a very small number of superb examples of the Thomas Shingles 1949 dollar, and a few of subsequent years, with a proof finish. The known number of 1949 proof dollars is fewer than five.

PROVINCE OF CANADA and CANADA

SPECIMEN SETS

Date and Mint Mark	Description	Average Grade	Price Indication
1858	4 Coin, Plain	SP-64	17,500.
1858	4 Coin, Reeded	SP-64	20,000.
1870	4 Coin, Plain w/box	SP-64	70,000.
1870	4 Coin, Reeded w/box	SP-64	70,000.
1875H	3 Coin	SP-66	175,000.
1880H	3 Coin, Wide 0	SP-67	100,000.
1880H	3 Coin, Narrow 0	SP-67	100,000.
1881H	5 Coin	SP-64	65,000.
1902H	3 Coin	SP-67	65,000.
1908	5 Coin	SP-64	4,500.
1911	5 Coin, 1¢ - 50¢	SP-64	8,000.
1911/12	3 Coin, Gold	SP-67	90,000.
1921	5 Coin	SP-65	250,000.
1929	5 Coin	SP-66	40,000.
1930	4 Coin	SP-66	40,000.
1931	5 Coin, Case #8	SP-66	70,000.
1934	5 Coin	SP-65	60,000.
1936, Dot	6 Coin	SP-66	800,000.
1937	6 Coin, Mirror	SP-65	3,500.
1937	12 Coin, Mirror	SP-65	10,000.
1937	6 Coin, Matte	SP-66	1,250.
1938	6 Coin	SP-65	50,000.
1944	5 Coin	SP-65	25,000.
1945	6 Coin	SP-65	13,500.
1946	6 Coin	SP-65	11,000.
1947	6 Coin, Point	SP-65	16,000.
1947	6 Coin, Blunt	SP-65	17,500.
1947, ML	6 Coin, Straight 7	SP-65	13,500.
1947, ML	6 Coin, Curved 7	SP-65	13,500.
1948	6 Coin, Concave	SP-65	12,000.
1948	6 Coin, Convex	SP-65	12,000.
1949	6 Coin	SP-66	10,000.
1950	6 Coin, Mirror	SP-66	4,500.
1950	6 Coin, Arnprior	SP-65	8,500.
1951	7 Coin, High relief	SP-66	10,000.
1951	7 Coin, Low relief	SP-66	4,500.
1952	6 Coin, WL	SP-66	4,000.
1952	6 Coin, NWL	SP-60	3,000.
1953, NS	6 Coin	SP-66	4,000.
1964	6 Coin	SP-67	2,000.
1965	6 Coin	SP-67	2,000.

Note: Average grade means the average condition in which these sets are found.

CASES FOR SPECIMEN COINAGE

CASE FOUR

The existence of this case is not confirmed. The National Currency Collection in Ottawa does not have an example.

Charlton Number	Intended Contents	Exterior Colour and Dimensions	Interior Colours	Price for Empty Case
4	1858 1¢, 5¢, 10¢, 20¢ 1¢, 5¢, 10¢, 20¢	Black 7.5 x 11.5 cm	u: white satin l: dark blue velvet	$5,000.

CASE FIVE

Charlton Number	Intended Contents	Exterior Colour and Dimensions	Interior Colours	Price for Empty Case
5	1870 5¢, 10¢, 25¢, 50¢	Dark brown 6.5 x 10.5 cm	u: white satin l: dark blue velvet	$5,000.

CASE SIX

Case 6c

Struck to commemorate the opening of the Royal Canadian Mint in Ottawa in 1908, this is the first set of specimen coins offered to the general public. The issue price was $2.00. Coins had a matte finish. Impressed red leather strips were mailed separately to customers who possibly were initially sent sets housed in box 6a.

Charlton Number	Intended Contents	Exterior Colour and Dimensions	Interior Colours	Price for Empty Case
6	1908 1¢, 5¢, 10¢, 25¢, 50¢	Maroon, 5.3 x 15.5 cm	u: blue satin, impressed in gold lettering: "First Coinage in Canada/1908/Royal Mint Ottawa" l: purple velvet 5 holes	$250.
6a	1908 1¢, 5¢, 10¢, 25¢, 50¢	Red, 5.3 x 15.5 cm no inscription	u: blue satin l: blue velvet 5 holes no inscription	$250.
6b	1908 1¢, 5¢, 10¢, 25¢, 50¢	Red, 5.3 x 15.5 cm top impressed in gold lettering: "First Coinage of Canadian Mint/Ottawa/1908"	u: purple satin l: purple velvet 5 holes no inscription	$350.
6c	1908 1¢, 5¢, 10¢, 25¢, 50¢	Red, 5.3 X 15.5 cm no inscription	u: blue satin with affixed red leather strip impressed in gold lettering: "First Coinage of Canadian Mint/Ottawa/1908" l: blue velvet 5 holes	$250.

CASE SEVEN

As in 1908 the George V Coronation of 1911 prompted the Mint again to offer sets to the general public. The sets issued were:

1911 Set: 5 coins all dated 1911
    1¢, 5¢, 10¢, 25¢, 50¢
    Issue Price: $2.00

1911-12 Set: 8 coins, 6 dated 1911,
    1¢, 5¢, 10¢, 25¢, 50¢, £1
    2 dated 1912, $5, $10
    Issue Price: $24.00

Case No. 7, which can hold 9 coins, one cent to ten dollars, was never issued.

Case 7a, which can hold 6 coins, one cent to one dollar, was never issued.

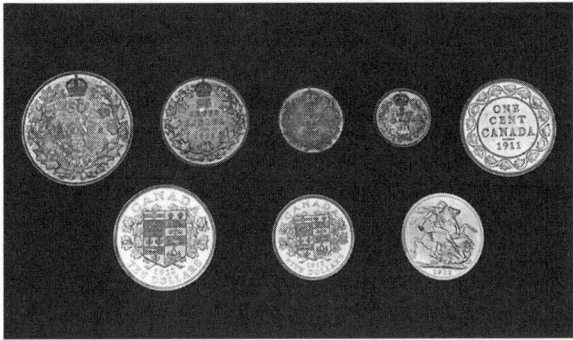

Case 7d

CASE SEVEN (cont.)

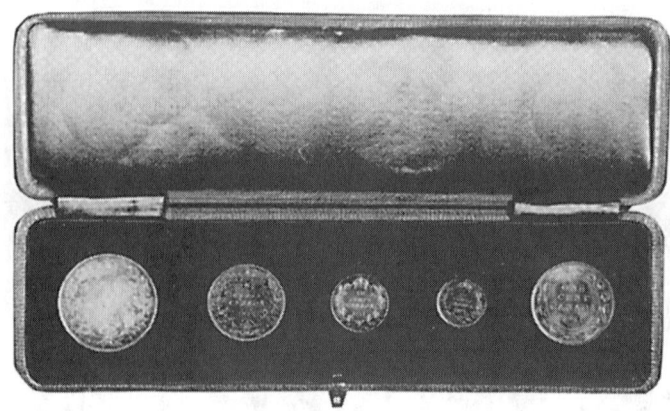

Case 7b

Charlton Number	Intended Contents	Exterior Colour and Dimensions	Interior	Price for Empty Case
7	1911 1¢, 5¢, 10¢, 25¢, 50¢, $1, £1, $5, $10	Red, 8.9 x 19.7 cm top impressed in gold lettering: "Specimen Coins/Ottawa Mint/1911"	u: blue satin l: blue velvet 9 holes no inscription	$1,000.
7a	1911 1¢, 5¢, 10¢, 25¢, 50¢, $1	Red, 5.3 x 19.7 cm top impressed in gold lettering: "Specimen Coins/Silver and Bronze/ Ottawa Mint/1911"	u: blue satin, l: blue velvet 6 holes no inscription	$750.
7b	1911 1¢, 5¢, 10¢, 25¢, 50¢	Red, 5.3 x 19.7 cm top impressed in gold lettering "Specimen Coins Silver and Bronze/ Ottawa Mint/1911"	u: blue satin l: blue velvet 5 holes no inscription	$500.
7c	1911 1¢, 5¢, 10¢, 25¢, 50¢	Red, 5.3 x 19.7 cm top impressed in gold lettering: "Specimen Coins/ Ottawa Mint / 1911"	u: Blue satin l: blue velvet 5 holes no inscription	$500.
7d	1911 1¢, 5¢, 10¢, 25¢, 50¢ £1 and 1912 $5, $10 1911	Red, 8.9 x 19.7 cm top impressed in gold lettering: "Specimen Coins/Ottawa Mint/ 1911-12"	u: Blue satin l: blue velvet 8 holes no inscription	$1,000.

CASE EIGHT

Case 8

This five-hole case is similar to Cases 7b and c, but made to hold the small one cent and five cent nickle coins.

Charlton Number	Intended Contents	Exterior Colour and Dimensions	Interior Colours	Price for Empty Case
8	1931 1¢ (small), 5¢ (nickel), 10¢, 25¢, 50¢	Red, 5.3 x 19.7 cm top impressed in gold lettering: "Specimen Coins/Silver and Bronze/ Ottawa Mint	u: blue satin l: blue velvet 5 holes	$750.

CASE NINE

Case #9 1937

Charlton Number	Intended Contents	Exterior Colour and Dimensions	Interior Colours	Price for Empty Case
9	1937 1¢, 5¢, 10¢, 25¢, 50¢, $1	Red cardboard 10.2 x 15.3 cm with horizontal ridges, crowns and scepters and in black lettering: "Royal Canadian Mint/ 1937/Ottawa, Canada"	u: coarse white cloth 6 holes	$75.

CASE NINE (cont.)

Case 9a or b Lid

Case 9a

Case 9b

Charlton Number	Intended Contents	Exterior Colour and Dimensions	Interior Colours	Price for Empty Case
9a	1937 1¢, 5¢, 10¢, 25¢	As case #7a except date covered by paper Union Jack.	u: blue satin l: blue velvet 4 holes	$750.
9b	1937 1¢, 5¢, 10¢, 25¢, 50¢, $1	As case #7a, except the inscription is covered by a blue leather strip upon which is impressed in gold a view of the centre section of the Royal Canadian Mint surrounded on the sides and bottom by a ribbon; "1937" is below. On the ribbon is "Royal Canadian Mint"	u: blue satin l: blue velvet 6 holes	$275.

CASE NINE (cont.)

Case 9c

Charlton Number	Intended Contents	Exterior Colour and Dimensions	Interior Colours	Price for Empty Case
9c	1937 Double Set 1¢, 5¢, 10¢, 25¢, 50¢, $1	Red, 8.9 x 19.7 cm top impressed in gold on a blue label "Royal Canadian Mint / 1937 / Ottawa / Canada"	u: blue satin l: blue velvet 12 holes	$1,500.
9d	1937 Single Set 1¢, 5¢, 10¢, 25¢, 50¢, $1	Red, 5.3 x 19.7 cm top impressed in gold on a blue label "Royal CanadianMint / 1937 / Ottawa / Canada"	u: blue satin l: blue velvet 6 holes	$500.

CASE TEN

Charlton Number	Intended Contents	Exterior Colour and Dimensions	Interior Colours	Price for Empty Case
10	1938-1953 1¢, 5¢, 10¢, 25¢, 50¢, $1	As case #9b, except for the absence of "1937"	As case #9b	$300.

CASE ELEVEN

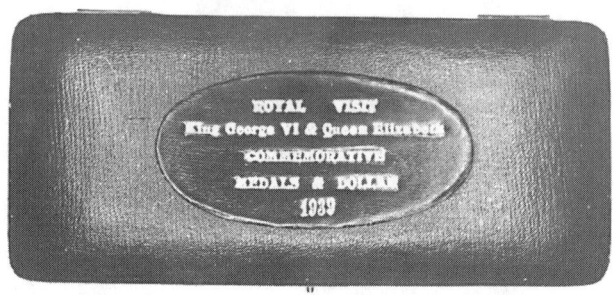

Charlton Number	Intended Contents	Exterior Colour and Dimensions	Interior Colours	Price for Empty Case
11	1939 54mm medal, $1 54mm medal	As case #7, except the inscription is covered by an oval blue patch impressed in gold lettering: "Royal Visit/King George VI & Queen Elizabeth/ Commemorative/Medals & Dollar/1939"	As case #9a	$1,500.

CASE TWELVE

Charlton Number	Intended Contents	Exterior Colour and Dimensions	Interior Colours	Price for Empty Case
12	1953 1¢, 5¢, 10¢, 25¢, 50¢, $1	Red, top impressed in gold with a view of the centre section of the Royal Canadian Mint surrounded on the sides and bottom by a ribbon bearing "Royal Canadian Mint"	u: blue satin l: blue velvet 6 holes	$300.

CASE THIRTEEN

Charlton Number	Intended Contents	Exterior Colour and Dimensions	Interior Colours	Price for Empty Case
13	1953 1¢, 5¢, 10¢, 25¢, 50¢, $1	Large size, Red, top impressed in gold with a view of the centre section of the Royal Canadian Mint surrounded on the sides and bottom by a ribbon bearing "Royal Canadian Mint"	u: blue satin l: blue velvet 6 holes	$1,000.

CASE FOURTEEN

Charlton Number	Intended Contents	Exterior Colour and Dimensions	Interior Colours	Price for Empty Case
14	1967 1¢, 5¢, 10¢, 25¢, 50¢, $1 $20	Black leather, impressed with gold Coat-of-Arms "1867 1967" either side of arms with "Canada" below	u: white satin l: black plush 7 holes	$10.
14a	As above	Brown leather, as above	as above	$50.
14b	As above	Maroon leather, black highlights As above	as above	$50.

PATTERNS, TRIAL PIECES AND OFFICIAL FABRICATIONS

A PATTERN is a piece submitted as a design sample by engravers when a new coinage is contemplated. If the design is adopted for regular coinage with the same date, the piece ceases to be a pattern. If the design is adopted with a later date, the piece remains a pattern. Patterns are usually struck as proofs.

A TRIAL PIECE or ESSAY is from dies already accepted for regular coinage. It may bear a date or mint mark other than on the coins issued for circulation or it may be in a different metal.

AN OFFICIAL FABRICATION is a piece that was created for some special purpose unconnected with design proposals or experiments on coinage design or metals. For example, the New Brunswick pieces bearing the dates 1870, 1871 and 1875 were obviously not connected with an attempt to revive a separate coinage for that province after Confederation.

For many years the best listing of patterns, trial pieces and official fabrications was that published by Fred Bowman in his book Canadian Patterns. The present listing is greatly revised compared to Bowman's and new numbers are used. However, Bowmans original numbers are also included for those pieces which were listed in his book.

PROVINCE OF NOVA SCOTIA

Charlton	Bowman	PATTERNS

NS-1   —

Price Range
Unknown.

Half cent 1860. Reverse – crown surrounded by wreath of roses; date below wreath. (The illustration is from a matrix. It is uncertain whether patterns bearing this date were actually produced.)

NS-2   —

Price Range
Unknown

One cent 1860. Reverse – crown surrounded by wreath of roses; date below wreath. (The illustration is from a matrix. It is uncertain whether patterns bearing this date were actually produced.)

PROVINCE OF NOVA SCOTIA

Charlton   Bowman

NS-3   B-11

Price Range
$2,000. - $5,000.
SP63 to 65

PATTERNS

Half cent 1861, bronze. Specimen; dies ↑↓; wt. 2.85grams; diam. 20.65mm. Obverse - large bust of Victoria by James Wyon. Reverse - pattern design as on NS-1. (National Currency Collection)

NS-4   B-7

Price Range
$2,000. - $5,000.
SP63 to 65

One cent 1861, bronze. Specimen; dies ↑↑; wt. 4.69grams; diam. 25.4mm. Obverse - large bust of Victoria by James Wyon. Reverse - pattern design as on NS-2. (National Currency Collection)

NS-5   B-13

Price Range
$2,500. - $6,000.
SP63 to 65

Half cent 1861, bronze. Specimen; dies ↑↓. Obverse - adopted (small bust) design by L.C. Wyon. Reverse - pattern design as NS-3. (National Currency Collection)

NS-6   B-8

Price Range
$2,500. - $6,000.
MS60 to 63

One cent 1861, bronze. Not a specimen; dies ↑↑; wt. 5.59grams; diam. 25.4mm. Obverse - adopted (small bust) design by L.C. Wyon. Reverse - pattern design as NS-4. (National Currency Collection)

NS-7   B-12

Price Range
$2,500. - $6,000.
SP63 to 65

Half cent 1861, bronze. Specimen; dies ↑↑; wt. 2.78grams; diam. 20.65mm. Obverse - pattern design as on NS-3. Reverse - adopted design (crown and date surrounded by a wreath of mayflowers and roses). (New Netherlands Coin Sale 1960)

PROVINCE OF NOVA SCOTIA

Charlton   Bowman   **PATTERNS**

NS-8   B-10

Price Range
$2,000. - $4,500.
SP63 to 65

One cent 1861, bronze. Specimen; dies ↑↑; wt. 5.65grams; diam. 25.4mm and dies ↑↓; wt. 5.74g; dia. 25.4mm. Obverse - pattern design as on NS-4. Reverse - adopted design (1861), large rose bud variety. (National Currency Collection)

NS-8a   B-10

Price Range
$2,000. - $4,500.
SP63 to 65

One cent 1861, bronze. Specimen; dies ↑↑; wt. 5.80grams; diam. 25.4mm. As NS-8, except the reverse is the small rose bud variety (adopted design for 1861-1864).

NS-9   B-14

Price Range
$3,500. - $7,500.
SP63 to 65

Half cent 186-, bronze. Specimen. As NS-5, except for the incomplete date.

NS-10   B-9

Price Range
$3,500. - $7,500.
SP63 to 65

One cent 186-, bronze. Specimen; dies ↑↑; wt. 5.78grams; diam. 25.4mm. As NS-6, except for the incomplete date.

PROVINCE OF NEW BRUNSWICK

Charlton	Bowman	PATTERNS

NB-1   **B-15**

Price Range
$3,000. - $6,000.
SP63 to 65

One cent 1861, bronze; proof; dies ↑↑; wt. 5.64grams; diam. 25.4mm ; obverse - large bust design by James Wyon as on NS-6, etc. reverse - adopted design. (National Currency Collection)

NB-2   **B-20**

Price Range
$20,000. - $35,000.
SP63 to 65

Ten cents 1862, silver; reeded edge; proof; dies ↑↑; wt. 2.34grams; diam. 18.0mm; obverse - adopted design; reverse - legend and date surrounded by arabesque design somewhat similar to that used for Newfoundland. The arabesque reverse on this piece was also used for a pattern 10-cent piece for Hong Kong. (National Currency Collection)

TRIAL PIECES

NB-3   —

Price Range
$5,000. - $10,000.
SP63 to 65

One cent 1862, bronze; proof. As adopted design, except for the date. Struck to make the date uniform for the 1862 proof sets.

OFFICIAL FABRICATIONS

NB-4   **B-23**

Price Range
$2,500. - $5,000.
SP63 to 65

Twenty cents 1862, silver; plain edge; proof; dies ↑↑; wt. 5.6grams; diam. 22.0 mm; obverse - plain, except for the legend G.W. WYON/OBIT/MARCH 27TH 1862/AETAT/26YEARS. Reverse - adopted design. This is an obituary medalet for George W. Wyon, who was resident engraver at the Royal Mint. The fact that this reverse was chosen for the piece suggests that it was engraved by George Wyon. (National Currency Collection)

PROVINCE OF NEW BRUNSWICK

The following six pieces (NB-5 to NB-10) obviously have nothing to do with contemplated designs for New Brunswick, since they bear dates after Confederation. It is believed they were struck for exhibition purposes where only the type was considered important.

Charlton   Bowman

OFFICIAL FABRICATIONS

NB-5   B-18

Price Range
$25,000. - $40,000.
SP63 to 65

Five cents 1870, silver; plain edge; specimen; dies ↑↑; wt. 1.7grams; diam. 15.5 mm; obverse - adopted design; reverse - adopted design for the Dominion of Canada (wire rim variety). (National Currency Collection)

NB-6   B-21

Price Range
$20,000. - $35,000.
SP63 to 65

Ten cents 1870, silver; reeded edge; specimen; dies ↑↑; wt. 2.3grams; diam. 18.03 mm; plain edge; proof; dies ↑↑, wt. 2.32g; diam. 18.03 mm; obverse - adopted design; reverse - adopted design for the Dominion of Canada and New Brunswick. (National Currency Collection, reeded edge; Norweb Collection, plain edge)

NB-7   B-22

Price Range
$30,000. - $50,000.
SP63 to 65

Ten cents 1871, silver; reeded edge; specimen; dies ↑↑; wt. 2.32grams; diam. 18.03 mm; plain edge; wt. 2.3g; dia. 18.03 mm. As NB-6, except for the date. (National Currency Collection)

NB-8   B-24

Price Range
$12,500. - $35,000.
SP63 to 65

Twenty cents 1871, silver; reeded edge; specimen; dies ↑↑; wt. 5.90grams; diam. 22.5mm; plain edge; proof; wt. 4.7g; diam. 23.27 mm. As the adopted design, except for the date. (National Currency Collection)

NB-9   B-19

Price Range
$35,000. - $55,000.
SP63 to 65

Five cents 1875, silver; reeded edge; specimen; dies ↑↑, wt. 1.16grams; diam. 15.5; obverse - adopted design; reverse - adopted design for the Dominion of Canada. (National Currency Collection)

NB-10   —

Price Range
$35,000. - $55,000.
SP63 to 65

Five cents 1875H, silver; reeded edge; specimen; dies ↑↑. As NB9, except for the H mint mark.

PROVINCE OF NEWFOUNDLAND

The following five patterns (NF-1 to NF-5) are the result of a directive given by the master of the Royal Mint, Thomas Graham, in which he stated that the designs for the reverses of the Newfoundland coins should be those of New Brunswick. This was later altered.

Charlton   Bowman   **PATTERNS**

NF-1   —

Price Range
Unknown

One cent 1864; reverse - similar to the design adopted for the New Brunswick cent. Unknown at present as a struck piece, but may exist.

NF-2   **B-28**

Price Range
$25,000. - $40,000.
SP63 to 65

Five cents 1864, bronze; plain edge; specimen; dies ↑↓; wt. 1.40grams; diam. 15.5 mm; obverse - adopted design; reverse - crown and wreath design adopted for New Brunswick. (W.W.C. Wilson Sale 1925)

NF-3   **B-29**

Price Range
$25,000. - $40,000.
SP63 to 65

Ten cents 1864, bronze; plain edge; specimen; obverse - adopted design; reverse - crown and wreath design adopted for New Brunswick. (British Museum)

NF-4   **B-32**

Price Range
$25,000. - $40,000.
SP63 to 65

Twenty cents 1864, bronze; indented corded edge; specimen; dies ↑↓; wt. 6.2grams; diam. 22.95 mm; obverse - adopted design; reverse - crown and wreath design adopted for New Brunswick. (National Currency Collection)

NF-5   **B-31**

Price Range
$50,000. - $75,000.
SP63 to 65

Two dollars 1864, bronze; plain edge; specimen; dies ↑↓; wt. 2.4grams; diam. 17.1 mm; obverse - adopted design; reverse - crown and wreath for New Brunswick. 10 cents with the legend "TWO/DOLLARS/1864" in the centre. (National Currency Collection)

PROVINCE OF NEWFOUNDLAND

Charlton	Bowman	PATTERNS

NF-6   **B-25**

Price Range
$3,500. - $7,500.
SP63 to 65

One cent 1864, bronze; specimen; dies ↑↑; wt. 5.69 grams; diam. 25.4 mm; obverse - similar to adopted design, except the legend reads VICTORIA QUEEN. Reverse - similar to adopted design, except one leaf is missing from the top of each side of the wreath. (National Currency Collection)

NF-7   **B-27**

Price Range
$4,000. - $10,000.
SP63 to 65

One cent 1865, bronze; specimen; dies ↑↓; wt. 5.45 grams; diam. 25.4 mm; obverse - adopted design for Nova Scotia and New Brunswick. Reverse - pattern design as for NF-6, except for the date. (National Currency Collection)

NF-8   **—**

Price Range
$4,000. - $10,000.
SP63 to 65

Five cents 1865, silver; plain edge; specimen; dies ↑↓; wt. 0.9 grams; diam. 15.5 mm; obverse - adopted design; reverse - similar to the adopted design, except the arches are thinner. (National Currency Collection)

NF-9   **—**

Price Range
$5,000. - $12,500.
SP63 to 65

Ten cents 1865, silver; plain edge; specimen; dies ↑↓; obverse - adopted design; reverse - similar to the adopted design, except the arches are much thinner. (National Currency Collection)

PROVINCE OF NEWFOUNDLAND

Charlton	Bowman	PATTERNS

NF-10 —

Price Range
$5,000. - $17,500.
SP63 to 65

Twenty cents 1865, silver; plain edge; specimen; dies ↑↓; wt. 4.6 grams; diam. 23.19mm; obverse - adopted design; reverse - similar to the adopted design, except the arches are much thinner. (National Currency Collection)

NF-11 —

Price Range
$4,000. - $10,000.
SP63 to 65

Five cents 1865, silver; plain edge; specimen; dies ↑↓; wt. 1.10 grams; diam. 15.5mm; obverse - adopted design; reverse - as the adopted design, except the arches and dots have raised edges. (National Currency Collection)

NF-12 —

Price Range
$5,000. - $12,500.
SP63 to 65

Ten cents 1865, silver; plain edge; specimen; dies ↑↓; wt. 2.3 grams; diam. 18.03 mm; obverse - adopted design; reverse - as the adopted design, except the arches and dots have raised edges. (National Currency Collection)

NF-13 —

Price Range
$5,000. - $17,500.
SP63 to 65

Twenty cents 1865, silver; plain edge; specimen; dies ↑↓; wt. 4.5 grams; diam. 23.19 mm; obverse - adopted design; reverse - similar to the adopted design, except for some details of the arches and the presence of a raised line just inside the rim denticles. (National Currency Collection)

PROVINCE OF NEWFOUNDLAND

Charlton	Bowman	PATTERNS

NF-14 **B-33**

Price Range
$75,000. - $125,000.
SP63 to 65

Two dollars 1865, gold; plain edge; specimen; dies ↑↑; wt. 3.3 grams; diam. 17.6 mm; obverse - adopted design; reverse - similar to the adopted design, except the legend and date are in block type. (National Currency Collection)

NF-15 **B-34**

Price Range
$75,000. - $125,000.
SP63 to 65

Two dollars 1865, gold; plain edge; specimen; dies ↑↓; wt. 3.36 grams; diam. 17.98 mm; obverse - small bust of Victoria (from the 5 cents) in beaded circle with the legend VICTORIA D:G REG:/NEWFOUNDLAND. Reverse - pattern design as on NF-14.

NF-16 **B-35**

Price Range
$25,000. - $75,000.
SP63 to 65

Fifty cents 1870, bronze; plain edge; specimen; dies ↑↑; wt. 9.4 grams; diam. 29.6 mm; obverse - adopted design; reverse - as the adopted design, except the denticles are longer and touch the device. (National Currency Collection)

NF-17 —

Price Range
$75,000. - $125,000.
SP63 to 65

Two dollars 1870, gold; plain edge; specimen; obverse - pattern designs as on NF-15; reverse - adopted design.

PROVINCE OF NEWFOUNDLAND

Charlton   Bowman

TRIAL PIECES

NF-18   **B-26**

Price Range
$3,500. - $7,500.
SP63 to 65

One cent 1864, bronze; specimen; dies ↑↑; wt. 5.6 grams; diam. 25.4 mm. As the adopted design, except for the date. This is the piece that is believed to have been included in the specimen sets of 1864-1865. Proofs of the adopted design of the cent dated 1865 seem not to have been produced. (National Currency Collection)

NF-19   —

Price Range
$60,000. - $100,000.
SP63 to 65

Fifty cents 1882, silver; reeded edge; specimen. As the adopted design, except for the absence of the H mint mark. (British Museum)

NF-20   —

Price Range
None
Mint Error

Ten cents 1945 C, nickel. Struck on a thin blank; not a proof. This piece is rather weakly struck because of the thinness of the blank, suggesting that it is nothing more than a mint error. (National Currency Collection)

NF-21   —

Price Range
$25,000. - $40,000.
SP63 to 65

Twenty cents 1865, bronze; plain edge; specimen; dies ↑↑; wt. 5.16grams, diam. 23.1 mm as adopted design. (Norweb Collection)

PROVINCE OF BRITISH COLUMBIA

Charlton   Bowman   **PATTERNS**

BC-1   B-37

Price Range
$30,000. - $50,000.
SP63 to 65

Ten dollars 1862, silver; specimen; dies ↑↓; wt. 11.2grams; diam. 27.0mm; obverse - crown and legend; reverse - wreath, denomination and date. (National Currency Collection)

BC-1a   B-37

Price Range   Ten dollars 1862, silver; reeded edge; specimen; dies ↑↑. Design as above.
$30,000. - $50,000.   (Brand Sale 1983)
SP63 to 65

BC-2   B-36

Price Range
$40,000. - $60,000.
SP63 to 65

Twenty dollars 1862, silver; specimen; dies ↑↓; obverse - crown and legend; reverse - wreath, denomination and date. (Brand Sale 1983).

BC-2a   B-36

Price Range   Twenty dollars 1862, silver; reeded edge; specimen; dies ↑↑; wt. 23.6grams;
$40,000. - $60,000.   diam. 34.0mm. Design as above. (National Currency Collection)
SP63 to 65

BC-3   B-37

Price Range   Ten dollars 1862, gold. Design and specifications as BC-1. (B.C. Provincial
$300,000. - $400,000. Archives)
SP63 to 65

BC-4   B-36

Price Range   Twenty dollars 1862, gold. Design and specifications as BC-2. (B.C. Provincial
$350,000. - $500,000. Archives)
SP63 to 65

Note: The ten and twenty dollar gold patterns of British Columbia were designed by George Albert Ferdinand Kuner (1819-1906)

PROVINCE OF CANADA

Charlton	Bowman	**TRIAL PIECES**
PC-1	**B-4**	

Price Range
$15,000. - $20,000.
SP63 to 65

One cent 1858, bronze; specimen; wt. 5.7grams; diam. 23.7mm; uniface - obverse blank; reverse - wreath of maple leaves and seed pods with beaded circle containing ONE/CENT/1858. (National Currency Collection)

PC-2　　**B-4**

Price Range
$15,000. - $20,000.
SP63 to 65

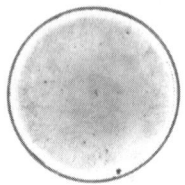 

One cent 1858, bronze; specimen; wt. 4.0 - 5.4grams; diam. 23.7mm; uniface - obverse blank; reverse - similar to PC-1 except the date is more closely spaced and the device is farther from the inner beaded circle. (National Currency Collection)

PC-3　　**B-3**

Price Range
$20,000. - $30,000.
SP63 to 65

One cent 1858, bronze; specimen; dies ↑↓; wt. 3.88grams; diam. 23.7mm; obverse - adopted legend with diademed bust of Victoria. Reverse - pattern design as on PC-2. (Wayte Raymond Sale 1928)

PC-4　　**B-6**

Price Range
$10,000. - $35,000.
SP63 to 65

Twenty cents 1858, silver; plain edge; specimen; dies ↑↑; wt. 4.50grams; diam. 23.7mm; dies ↑↓; wt. 4.03grams; diam. 23.27mm; obverse - adopted design; reverse - adopted design for New Brunswick. (National Currency Collection)

PROVINCE OF CANADA

Charlton	Bowman	PATTERNS
PC-5	B-5	

Price Range
$25,000. - $35,000.
SP63 to 65

One cent 1859 (in Roman numerals), bronze; specimen; obverse - adopted design; reverse - Britannia reverse for a pattern British halfpenny. (Parsons Collection 1936. The Norweb Collection contained an example struck in copper-nickel; wt. 5.63grams; diam. 25.4mm.)

Charlton	Bowman	TRIAL PIECES
PC-6	—	

Price Range
$15,000. - $25,000.
SP63 to 65

One cent 1858, cupro-nickel; specimen; dies ↑↑; wt. 9.11grams; diam. 25.4mm. Adopted design; struck from proof dies on an unpolished blank of double thickness. (National Currency Collection)

PC-7 —

Price Range
$5,000. - $15,000.
SP63 to 65

One cent 1858, cupro-nickel; specimen; dies ↑↑; wt. 4.42grams; diam. 25.4mm. Adopted design; normal thickness. (National Currency Collection)

CANADA

Charlton   Bowman

DC-1   B-38

Price Range
$12,500. - $20,000.
SP63 to 65

One cent 1876H, bronze; specimen; dies ↑↑; diam. 25.45mm; obverse - adopted laureated head design for the Province of Canada. Reverse - adopted design. The existence of this pattern suggests that the government of the Dominion of Canada initially considered using the Province of Canada laureated obverse for its new cent. (National Currency Collection)

DC-2   –

Price Range
$7,500. - $15,000.
SP63 to 65

 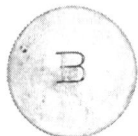

Ten cents (no date), bronze; reeded edge; specimen; wt. 2.1grams; diam. 17.85mm; obverse - adopted design (Haxby Obv. 6); reverse - plain, except for a B engraved on the piece after it was struck. Probably unique. (National Currency Collection)

DC-3   –

Price Range
$75,000. - $125,000.
SP63 to 65

Fifty cents 1870, bronze; plain edge; specimen; dies ↑↑; wt. 9.2grams; diam. 29.72mm; obverse - no L.C.W. on the truncation, but otherwise very similar to Obv. H-2. Reverse - slight differences in some leaves compared to the adopted design. (National Currency Collection)

DC-4   –

Price Range
$65,000. - $150,000.
SP63 to 65

Images as above

As DC-3, but silver. Specimen; dies ↑↓; wt. 11.2grams; diam. 29.72mm.

CANADA

Charlton　　**Bowman**

DC-5　　　–

Price Range
$25,000. - $40,000.
SP63 to 65

One cent 1911, bronze; specimen; dies ↑↑; wt. 5.6grams; diam. 25.4mm. As the adopted design for 1912-1920, except for the date; i.e. the obverse legend has DEI GRA:. (Royal Mint Collection)

DC-6　　**B-40**

Price Range
$1,250,000.
SP63 to 65

One dollar 1911, silver; reeded edge; specimen; dies ↑↑; obverse - the standard MacKennal design later adopted for the 1936 dollar. Reverse - crown, wreath, legend and date.

In the Dominion of Canada Currency Act of 1910, which received royal assent on May 4, 1910, provision was made for the striking of a Canadian silver dollar. The schedule appended to the act specified a coin of 360 grains weight and a standard fineness of .925 silver. The Dominion Government, having decided to add a silver dollar to the coinage, purchased a new coining-press from Taylor and Challen of Birmingham, England, for the express purpose of striking coins of this size. A pair of dies for the new coin was prepared by the Die and Medal Department of the Royal Mint, London, and at least two specimens were struck. When cases were prepared for the specimen sets of the first Canadian coinage of George V, a space was left for the dollar. Later, however, the Dominion authorities decided against the issue of a silver dollar at that time, although no reason was given for this decision.

Only two specimens of the 1911 silver dollar are known to exist; one is in the National Currency Collection and the other was sold at auction in 2003 for $690,000 U.S.F., at the Heritage Belzberg Sale.

CANADA

Charlton   Bowman   **PATTERNS**

DC-6a   —

Price Range
$250,000.
SP63 to 65

One dollar 1911, lead. As DC-6, except for the metal. Probably unique. This piece was only recently discovered by the numismatic world, having been in storage in Ottawa since 1911. It is believed to be a sample piece struck at the Ottawa mint to be used for gaining approval to proceed with the production of coins for circulation. (National Currency Collection)

DC-7   B-41

Price Range
$75,000. - $125,000.
SP63 to 65

Five dollars 1911, gold; reeded edge specimen; dies ↑↑; diam. 21.6mm. As the adopted design for 1912-1914, except for the date. (Royal Mint Collection)

DC-8   B-42

Price Range
$75,000. - $125,000.
SP63 to 65

Ten dollars, 1911, gold; reeded edge specimen; dies ↑↑; diam. 26.9mm. As the adopted design for 1912-1914, except for the date. (Royal Mint Collection)

In 1926 Dominion notes (the treasury notes issued by the Government of the Dominion of Canada) were made redeemable in gold for the first time since 1914. Since the time of the production of the gold $5 and $10 of 1912-1914, it had been concluded that the coat-of-arms borne on their reverses was incorrect. Therefore, new reverses were engraved in the event that a gold coinage should again be struck. Bronze patterns were produced to provide samples of the designs. A few of these, probably made for the designer, G.E. Kruger-Gray, have the obverse design machined off, SPECIMEN punched in instead, and the entire piece acid-etched.

CANADA

Charlton   Bowman   PATTERNS

DC-9   –

Price Range
$25,000. - $40,000.
SP63 to 65

Five dollars 1928, bronze; reeded edge; specimen; dies ↑↑; wt. 4.2grams; diam. 21.6mm; obverse - as the adopted design for the 1912-1914 issues. Reverse - modified Canadian arms by G.E. Kruger-Gray. (National Currency Collection)

DC-10   –

Price Range
$27,500. - $50,000.
SP63 to 65

Ten dollars 1928, bronze; reeded edge; specimen; dies ↑↑; wt. 8.49grams; diam. 26.92mm; obverse - as the adopted design for the 1912-1914 issues. Reverse - modified Canadian arms by G.E. Kruger-Gray. (National Currency Collection)

DC-11   –

Price Range
$15,000. - $30,000.
SP63 to 65

Five dollars 1928, bronze; reeded edge; wt. 3.7grams; diam. 21.6mm; obverse - planed off flat just inside the denticles after striking; SPECIMEN has been punched in by hand. Reverse - pattern design as on DC-9. The entire piece has been acid-etched (officially) giving it a light brown colour. (National Currency Collection)

DC-12   –

Price Range
$15,000. - $35,000.
SP63 to 65

Ten dollars 1928, bronze; reeded edge; wt. 7.2grams; diam. 26.92mm; obverse - planed off flat just inside denticles after striking; SPECIMEN has been punched in by hand. Reverse - pattern design as on DC-10. The entire piece has been etched as for DC-11. (National Currency Collection)

CANADA

Charlton	Bowman	TRIAL PIECES

DC-13 —

Price Range
$10,000. - $15,000.
MSP63 to 65

One dollar 1964, tin; plain edge, struck on a thick planchet; not a proof; wt. 26.9grams; diam. 35.5mm; obverse - blank, except for small symbol ʃ. Reverse - similar to the adopted design, except for being higher in relief and having thin rounded rim denticles instead of wide square ones. Unique. This unusual piece is a matrix trial. (National Currency Collection)

DC-14 —

Price Range
$17,500. - $22,500.
MS63 to 65

One dollar 1967, silver; reeded edge; not a specimen. Similar to the adopted design, except the fields on both sides are flat instead of concave and the rim beads differ slightly in size and position.

DC-15 —

Price Range
$5,000. - $7,500.
SP63 to 65

Fifty cents (no date), white metal. Trial impression of portrait of Victoria only; as on Haxby Obv.2, 1870-1888. (National Currency Collection)

DC-16 —

Price Range
$40,000. - $60,000.
SP63 to 65

Five cents 1875, silver; reeded edge; specimen; dies ↑↓; wt. 1.20grams; diam. 15.45mm. As the adopted design, except for the absence of the H mint mark. (National Currency Collection)

CANADA

Charlton Bowman	**TRIAL PIECES**

DC-17 —

Price Range
$3,500. - $7,500.
SP63 to 65

One cent 1876H, cupro-nickel; specimen; dies ↑↓; wt. 5.81grams; diam. 25.4mm. As the adopted design. These pieces are believed to have been struck for exhibition purposes, without regard to the fact that there was no currency issue corresponding exactly to them. (American Numismatic Society)

DC-18 —

Price Range
$3,500. - $7,500.
SP63 to 65

One cent 1876, bronze; specimen; dies ↑↑; wt. 5.6grams; diam. 25.4mm. As the adopted design, except for the absence of the H mint mark. (National Currency Collection)

The five brass pieces listed below (DC-19 to DC-23) were produced at the Paris mint. It is there that the original matrices for these denominations were engraved as the Royal Mint was too busy producing coins for Great Britain.

DC-19 —

Price Range
$4,000. - $6,000.
SP63 to 65

One cent 1937, brass; specimen; dies ↑↓; wt. 3.1grams; diam. 19.05mm. As the adopted design. Slightly thicker than normal. (National Currency Collection)

DC-20 —

Price Range
$5,000. - $9,000.
SP63 to 65

Five cents 1937, brass; specimen; dies ↑↓; wt. 4.98grams; diam. 21.5mm. As the adopted design. Slightly thicker than normal. (National Currency Collection)

CANADA

Charlton	Bowman	**TRIAL PIECES**

DC-21   —

Price Range
$5,000. - $9,000.
SP63 to 65

Ten cents 1937, brass; reeded edge; specimen; dies ↑↓; wt. 2.46grams; diam. 18.03mm. As the adopted design. Slightly thicker than normal. (National Currency Collection)

DC-22   —

Price Range
$5,000. - $9,000.
SP63 to 65

Twenty-five cents 1937, brass; reeded edge; specimen; dies ↑↓; wt. 6.1grams; diam. 23.9mm. As the adopted design. Slightly thicker than normal. (National Currency Collection)

DC-23   —

Price Range
$6,000. - $10,000.
SP63 to 65

Fifty cents 1937, brass; reeded edge; specimen; dies ↑↓; wt. 14.9g; diam. 30.0mm. As the adopted design. Thicker than normal. (National Currency Collection)

DC-24   —

Price Range
$6,500. - $10,000.
SP63 to 65

Twenty-five cents 1937, bronze; reeded edge; specimen; dies ↑↑; wt. 5.5grams; diam. 23.62mm. As the adopted design. Normal thickness. (National Currency Collection)

CANADA

Charlton	Bowman	TRIAL PIECES
DC-25	—	

Price Range
$7,500. - $10,000.
MS63 to 65

Five cents 1942, nickel; not a specimen; dies ↑↑; wt. 5.5grams; diam. 23.62mm. As the 12-sided design adopted for the tombac pieces. (National Currency Collection)

DC-26 —

One cent 1943, copper-plated steel; not a specimen; dies ↑↑; wt. 3.0grams; diam. 19.05mm. As the adopted design. (National Currency Collection)

DC-26a — One cent 1943, steel; not a specimen; dies ↑↑; wt 3.1grams; diam. 19.05mm. As the adopted design. (National Currency Collection)

DC-27 — Five cents 1943, steel; specimen. As the design adopted for the tombac pieces. (Piece seen, but composition not confirmed.)

DC-28 — Five cents 1944, tombac. See page 89.

DC-29 —

Price Range
$5,000. - $7,500.
SP63 to 65

Five cents 1951, chrome-plated steel; specimen; dies ↑↑; wt. 4.6g; diam. 21.3mm. As the commemorative design struck in nickel. (National Currency Collection)

Note: Where the only known examples are in institutional collections the prices are not shown.

CANADA

Charlton   Bowman

TRIAL PIECES

DC-30   −

Price Range
$2,500. - $5,000.
SP63 to 65

Five cents 1952, composition unknown; specimen; dies ↑↑; wt. 3.80 grams; diam. 21.3mm. As the adopted designs. (National Currency Collection)

DC-31   −

Price Range
$7,500. - $10,000.
MS63 to 65

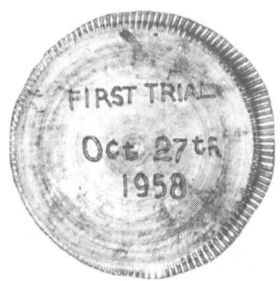 

Fifty cents 1959, tin; uniface on thick, oversize blank; obverse - blank except for the engraved inscription (added after the piece was struck) FIRST TRIAL/Oct 27th/1958. Reverse - as the adopted design, except lacks rim denticles. Unique. (National Currency Collection)

DC-32   −

Price Range
$1,500. - $2,500.
MS63 to 65

One cent 1966, nickel; dies ↑↑; wt. 3.50grams; diam. 19.05mm. As the adopted designs.

DC-33   −

Price Range
$3,000. - $5,000.
MS63 to 65

Ten cents 1967, nickel; dies ↑↑; wt. 2.07grams; diam. 18.03mm. As the adopted designs.

CANADA

Charlton Bowman

DC-34 –

Price Range
$3,000. - $5,000.
MS63 to 65

TRIAL PIECES

Twenty-five cents 1967, nickel; dies ↑↑; wt. 5.07grams; diam. 23.62mm. As the adopted designs.

DC-35 –

Price Range
$10,000. - $15,000.
VF to EF

Photograph not
available
at press time

Fifty cents 1881H, Copper; reeded edge; circulation strike; dies ↑↑; wt. 9.74grams; diam. 29.72mm. As the adopted design.

Charlton Bowman

DC-50 –

Price Range
$7,500. - $30,000.
SP63 to 65

OFFICIAL FABRICATION

Twenty cents 1871, silver; reeded edge; specimen; dies ↑↓; wt. 4.62grams; diam. 23.3mm. As the adopted design, see below. As the adopted design for the Province of Canada, except for the date. This piece does not represent a proposed 20 cents for the Dominion of Canada. It is believed to have been struck for exhibition to show the Province of Canada 20 cents. Only the type was important; no concern was given to using a date corresponding to the coins actually issued for circulation. (National Currency Collection).

DC-51 –

Price Range
$7,500. - $30,000
SP64 to 65

Twenty cents 1871, silver; plain edge; specimen; dies ↑↑; wt. 4.70grams; diam. 23.3mm.

CANADA — TEST TOKENS

As far back as 1907, test tokens have been used during the various stages of production to ensure a flawless final product. Test tokens are utilized for die and die coating testing, for plating process modifications, for dimensional testing, for metal tolerance, for the edge profile process, for coin collars, for the conformity of the electromagnetic signature in coins, as well as for other uses.

Test tokens have been officially offered by the Royal Canadian Mint only in 1996, 2000 and 2004. Other test tokens listed have found their way into collections via other routes.

ONE CENT TEST TOKENS

ROUND COPPER TOKEN, THREE MAPLE LEAVES WITH BEADS, FULL WEIGHT, 1976.

Weight: 3.24 grams
Diameter: 19.05 mm
Thickness: 1.42 mm
Edge: Plain
Die Axis: ↑↓

TT-1.1   English/English legends

Cat. No.	Description	Price Range
TT-1.1	Round copper, full weight	75.-125.

ROUND COPPER TOKEN, REDUCED SIZE AND WEIGHT, 1977. The Royal Canadian Mint issued a one-cent test token on December 15, 1977; however, because it was almost identical in diameter to tokens used by the Toronto Transit Commission, it was withdrawn.

 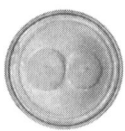

Weight: 1.87 grams
Diameter: 16.0 mm
Thickness: 1.35 mm
Edge: Plain
Die Axis: ↑↑

TT-1.2   Obverse and reverse design only

Cat. No.	Description	Price Range
TT-1.2	Round copper, reduced size and weight	75.-125.

ONE CENT TEST TOKENS

ROUND COPPER TOKEN, THREE MAPLE LEAVES WITH BEADS, REDUCED WEIGHT, 1979. In August 1979 another test token was introduced. This time the weight of the copper planchet was reduced.

Weight: 2.80 grams
Diameter: 19.05 mm
Thickness: 1.38 mm
Edge: Plain
Die Axis: ↑→

TT-1.3A   English/English legends "TEST TOKEN ROYAL CANADIAN MINT"

Specifications: Same as TT-1.3A

TT-1.3B   French/French legends "EPREUVE MONNAIE ROYALE CANADIENNE"

Specifications: Same as TT-1.3A

TT-1.3C   English/French legends "TEST TOKEN ROYAL CANADIAN MINT /
           EPREUVE MONNAIE ROYALE CANADIENNE"

Cat. No.	Description	Price Range
TT-1.3A	Round, With Beads, English/English Lengends	150.-200.
TT-1.3B	Round, With Beads, French/French Lengends	150.-200.
TT-1.3C	Round, With Beads, English/French Lengends	30.-50.

ONE CENT TEST TOKENS

ROUND COPPER TOKEN, THREE MAPLE LEAVES WITHOUT BEADS, 1979

Weight: 2.50 grams
Diameter: 19.05 mm
Thickness: 1.38 mm
Edge: Plain
Die Axis: ↑↑

TT-1.4A   English/English legends "TEST TOKEN ROYAL CANADIAN MINT"

Specifications: Same as TT-1.4A

TT-1.4B   French/French legends "EPREUVE/MONNAIE ROYALE CANADIENNE"

Specifications: Same as TT-1.4A

TT-1.4C   English/French legends "TEST TOKEN ROYAL CANADIAN MINT /
EPREUVE MONNAIE ROYALE CANADIENNE"

Cat No.	Description	Price Range
TT-1.4A	Round, Without beads, English/English Legends	Rare
TT-1.4B	Round, Without beads, French/French Legends	150.-200.
TT-1.4C	Round, Without beads, English/French Legends	Rare

ROUND COPPER-ZINC TOKEN, THREE MAPLE LEAVES WITH BEADS, 1979.

Weight: 2.70 grams
Diameter: 19.20 mm
Thickness: 1.30 mm
Edge: Plain
Die Axis: ↑↑

TT-1.5A   English/English legends "TEST TOKEN ROYAL CANADIAN MINT

Weight: 2.68 grams
Diameter: 19.05 mm
Thickness: 1.85 mm
Edge: Plain
Die Axis: ↑↑

TT-1.5B   English/French legends "TEST TOKEN ROYAL CANADIAN MINT"/
"EPREUVE MONNAIE ROYALE CANADIENNE"

Cat. No.	Description	Price Range
TT-1.5A	Round, With Beads English/English Legends	150.-200.
TT-1.5B	Round, With Beads English/French Legends	150.-200.

ONE CENT TEST TOKENS

7-SIDED COPPER TOKEN, THREE MAPLE LEAVES, CIRCA 1980

Weight: 2.3 grams
Diameter: 18.7 mm
Thickness: 1.3 mm
Edge: Plain
Die Axis: ↑↑

TT-1.6   English/French legends "TEST TOKEN ROYAL CANADIAN MINT" /
"EPREUVE MONNAIE ROYALE CANADIENNE"

Cat. No.	Description	Price Range
TT-1.6	7-sided, English/French Legends	175.-225.

11-SIDED COPPER TOKEN, THREE MAPLE LEAVES, SHARP CORNERS, 1981.
The 11-sided Mark I test token was issued on July 12, 1981, but because of its sharp corners it was rejected.

Weight: 2.60 grams
Diameter:
  Across corners: 18.95 mm
  Across flat: 18.40 mm
Thickness: 1.50 mm
Edge: Plain
Die Axis: ↑↑

TT-1.7A   English/English legends "TEST TOKEN ROYAL CANADIAN MINT"

Specifications: Same as TT-1.6A

TT-1.7B   French/French legends "EPREUVE/MONNAIE ROYALE CANADIENNE"

Specifications: Same as TT-1.6A

TT-1.7C   English/French legends "TEST TOKEN ROYAL CANADIAN MINT / EPREUVE
MONNAIE ROYALE CANADIENNE"

Cat. No.	Description	Price Range
TT-1.7A	11-sided, Sharp Corners, English/English Legends	175.-225.
TT-1.7B	11-sided, Sharp Corners, French/French Legends	175.-225.
TT-1.7C	11-sided, Sharp Corners, English/French Legends	75.-125.

ONE CENT TEST TOKENS

12-SIDED COPPER TOKEN, THREE MAPLE LEAVES, ROUNDED CORNERS, 1981. This 12-sided test token (mark II) was a success, and a new one cent coin went into production spring 1982.

Weight: 2.50 grams
Diameter:
    Across corners: 19.10 mm
    Across flat: 18.80 mm
Thickness: 1.45 mm
Edge: Plain
Die Axis: ↑↑

TT-1.8A   English/English legends "TEST TOKEN ROYAL CANADIAN MINT" / "TEST TOKEN ROYAL CANADIAN MINT"

Specifications: Same as TT-1.8A

TT-1.8B   French/French legends "EPREUVE MONNAIE ROYALE CANADIENNE" / "EPREUVE MONNAIE ROYALE CANADIENNE"

Specifications: Same as TT-1.8A

TT-1.8C   English/French legends "TEST TOKEN ROYAL CANADIAN MINT" / "EPREUVE MONNAIE ROYALE CANADIENNE"

Cat. No.	Description	Price Range
TT-1.8A	12-sided, Round Corners, English/English Legends	175.-225.
TT-1.8B	12-sided, Round Corners, French/French Legends	175.-225.
TT-1.8C	12-sided, Round Corners, English/French Legends	75.-125.

ROUND MULTI-PLY PLATED TOKEN, THREE MAPLE LEAVES, 2004. This test token was issued as part of the "Poppy Test Token" set, TTS-4.

Composition: Two-ply plated
    steel/copper
Weight: 2.35 grams
Diameter: 19.05 mm
Thickness: 1.45 mm
Edge: Plain
Die Axis: ↑↑

TT-1.9   English/French legends "TEST TOKEN ROYAL CANADIAN MINT" / "EPREUVE MONNAIE ROYALE CANADIENNE"

Cat. No.	Description	Price Range
TT-1.9	Round, Two-ply plated, English/French Legends	15.-20.

FIVE CENT TEST TOKENS

ROUND NICKEL TOKEN, THREE MAPLE LEAVES WITH BEADS, 1976

Weight: 4.30 grams
Diameter: 21.9 mm
Thickness: 1.71 mm
Edge: Plain
Die Axis: ↑↑

TT-5.1A   English/English legends "TEST TOKEN - ROYAL CANADIAN MINT"

Specifications: Same as TT-5.1A

TT-5.1B   French/French legends "EPREUVE/MONNAIE ROYALE CANADIENNE"

Specifications: Same as TT-5.1A

TT-5.1C   English/French legends "TEST TOKEN ROYAL CANADIAN MINT /
EPREUVE MONNAIE ROYALE CANADIENNE"

Cat. No.	Description	Price Range
TT-5.1A	Round, Beads, English/English Legends	75.-125.
TT-5.1B	Round, Beads, French/French Legends	75.-125.
TT-5.1C	Round, Beads, English/French Legends	75.-125.

FIVE CENT TEST TOKENS

ROUND TOKENS, VARIOUS COMPOSITIONS, 1983. The letters or numbers given in quotation marks, for example "S", are punched into the test tokens. The different composition test tokens are not priced because of lack of market activity.

Photographs not available at press time

TT-5.2 to 5.6 English/French legends "TEST TOKEN ROYAL CANADIAN MINT / EPREUVE MONNAIE ROYALE CANADIENNE"

Edge: Plain   Die Axis: ↑↑

Cat. No.	Description	Weight Grams	Diam. mm	Thickness mm	Price Range
TT-5.2	Stainless Steel, "430" Incused	3.50	21.1	1.7	200.-300.
TT-5.4	Nickel bonded Steel 6%, "NBS" Incused	4.09	21.2	1.7	200.-300.
TT-5.5	Steel, "S" Incused	4.00	21.1	1.8	200.-300.
TT-5.6	Nickel, "T" Incused	4.07	21.1	1.8	200.-300.

ROUND MULTI-PLY PLATED TOKEN, THREE MAPLE LEAVES, 2004. This test token was issued as part of the "Poppy Test Token" set, TTS-4.

Composition: Multi-ply plated steel/copper/nickel
Weight: 3.95 grams
Diameter: 21.2 mm
Thickness: 1.76 mm
Edge: Plain
Die Axis: ↑↑

TT-5.7   English/French legends "TEST TOKEN ROYAL CANADIAN MINT / EPREUVE MONNAIE ROYALE CANADIENNE"

Cat. No.	Description	Price Range
TT-5.7	Round, Multi-ply plated, English/French Legends	15.-20.

TEN CENT TEST TOKENS

ROUND NICKEL TOKEN; BOUQUET OF FLOWERS AND FLEUR-DE-LIS; 1965.

Weight: 2.09 grams
Diameter: 17.8 mm
Thickness: 1.2 mm
Edge: Reeded
Die Axis: ↑↑

TT-10.1A   Legend "R.C.M. TEN TOKENS 1965"

Specifications: Same as TT-10.1A

TT-10.1B   Legend "TEN TOKENS 1965"

Cat. No.	Description	Price Range
TT-10.1A	Round, "R.C.M. TEN TOKENS"	40.-60.
TT-10.1B	Round, "TEN TOKENS"	40.-60.

ROUND NICKEL TOKEN; THREE MAPLE LEAVES; 1976.

Weight: 1.75 grams
Diameter: 17.95 mm
Thickness: 1.2 mm
Edge: Reeded
Die Axis: ↑↑

TT-10.2   Legend "TEST TOKEN/ROYAL CANADIAN MINT / EPREUVE/MONNAIE
ROYAL CANADIENNE"

Cat. No.	Date	Description	Price Range
TT-10.2		Round, nickel, English/French Legends	75.-125.

TEN CENT TEST TOKENS

ROUND TEST TOKENS; VARIOUS COMPOSITION; 1983. The letters or numbers given in quotation marks, for example "S", are punched on the test token, indicating the composition of that token.

TT-10.3 to 10.9 English/French legends "TEST TOKEN / ROYAL CANADIAN MINT / EPREUVE MONNAIE ROYALE CANADIENNE"

Edge: Reeded   **Die Axis:** ↑↑

Cat. No.	Description	Weight Grams	Diam. mm	Thickness mm	Price Range
TT-10.3	Stainless Steel, "430" Incused	1.92	17.9	1.0	200.-300.
TT-10.4	Stainless Steel, "304" Incused	1.98	17.9	1.0	200.-300.
TT-10.5	Nickel Bonded Steel 6.3%, "SHERRITT" incused	1.78	17.9	1.0	200.-300.
TT-10.6	Steel, "S" Incused	2.00	17.9	1.0	200.-300.
TT-10.7	Nickel, "T" Incused	2.00	17.9	1.0	200.-300.
TT-10.8	Nickel Bonded, Steel 6%, "NBS" Incused	1.80	17.9	1.0	200.-300.
TT-10-9	Unknown, None	1.78	17.9	1.0	200.-300.

ROUND MULTI-PLY PLATED TOKEN; THREE MAPLE LEAVES; 2004. This test token was issued as part of the "Poppy Test Token" set, TTS-4.

Composition: Multi-ply plated steel/copper/nickel
Weight: 1.75 grams
Diameter: 18.06 mm
Thickness: 1.22 mm
Edge: Reeded
Die Axis: ↑↑

TT-10.10   Englis/French legends "TEST TOKEN / ROYAL CANADIAN MINT / EPREUVE/MONNAIE ROYAL CANADIENNE"

Cat. No.	Description	Price Range
TT-10.10	Round, Multi-ply plated, English/French Legends	15.-20.

TWENTY-FIVE CENT TEST TOKENS

ROUND NICKEL TOKEN; THREE CANADA GEESE; 1965. These test tokens were struck to provide an example of the quality of coins produced by the Royal Canadian Mint and to provide a piece for adjusting vending machines for nickel coins.

Weight: 5.01 grams
Diameter: 23.7 mm
Thickness: 1.6 mm
Edge: Reeded
Die Axis: ↑↑

TT-25.1A   Legend "TWENTY FIVE TOKENS/1965/R.C.M."

Specifications: Same as TT-25.1A

TT-25.1B   Legend "TWENTY FIVE TOKENS/1965"

Cat. No.	Description	Price Range
TT-25.1A	Round, "TWENTY FIVE TOKENS/1965/R.C.M.	65.-85.
TT-25.1B	Round, "TWENTY FIVE TOKENS/1965"	65.-85.

ROUND COPPER TOKEN; THREE CANADA GEESE; 1965.

Weight: 5.16 grams
Diameter: 23.7 mm
Thickness: 1.6 mm
Edge: Plain
Die Axis: ↑↑

TT-25.2A   Legend "TWENTY FIVE TOKENS/1965"

Cat. No.	Description	Price Range
TT-25.2A	Round, "TWENTY FIVE TOKENS"	65.-85.

TWENTY-FIVE CENT TEST TOKENS

ROUND CUPRO-NICKEL TOKEN; CONJOINED BUSTS OF KING GEORGE VI AND QUEEN ELIZABETH / THREE CANADA GEESE; 1965.

Weight: 5.02 grams
Diameter: 23.7 mm
Thickness: 1.3 mm
Edge: Reeded
Die Axis: ↑↑; ↑↓

TT-25.3A; TT-25.3B   Legend Rev.: "TWENTY FIVE TOKENS/1965/CANADA"

Cat. No.	Description	Price Range
TT-25.3A	Royal Visit Obverse ↑↑	800.-1,200.
TT-25.3B	Royal Visit Obverse ↑↓	800.-1,200.
TT-25.3B	Royal Visit Obverse, Magnetic ↑↓	800.-1,200.
TT-25.3B	Royal Visit Obverse, Non magnetic ↑↓	800.-1,200.

ROUND STAINLESS STEEL 304; THREE CANADA GEESE; 1965 (1977). In 1977 these test tokens were struck to support a tender to supply circulating coinage to the Government of Bangladesh. These tokens are not magnetic.

Weight: 5.82 grams
Diameter: 23.6 mm
Thickness: 1.7 mm
Edge: Plain
Die Axis: ↑↑

TT-25.4   Legend Obv.: "TWENTY FIVE TOKENS/1965/R.C:M."
               Legend Rev.: "TWENTY FIVE TOKENS/1965/CANADA"

Cat. No.	Description	Price Range
TT-25.4	304 Stainless Steel	800.-1,200.

TWENTY-FIVE CENT TEST TOKENS

ROUND, VARIOUS COMPOSITION TEST TOKENS, THREE MAPLE LEAVES, 1983. The following test tokens are round. Letters are used to identify the test tokens' composition. The different composition test tokens are not priced because of lack of market activity; however a price indication may be in the $150.00 to $250.00 range.

TT-25.5 to 25.17 English/French legends "TEST TOKEN/ROYAL CANADIAN MINT" / "EPREUVE/MONNAIE ROYALE CANADIENNE"

Edge: Plain   Die Axis: ↑↑

Cat. No.	Description	Weight Grams	Diam. mm	Thickness mm	Price Range
TT-25.5	Aluminum, "T" Raised	1.47	23.9	1.65	150.-250.
TT-25.6	Brass, "H" Raised	5.25	23.8	1.70	150.-250.
TT-25.7	Copper, "O" Raised	5.02	23.8	1.65	150.-250.
TT-25.8	Copper, "V" Raised	4.72	23.8	1.55	150.-250.
TT-25.9	Copper-Nickel, "I" Raised	5.08	23.8	1.65	150.-250.
TT-25.10	Copper-Nickel, "U" Raised	5.11	23.8	1.70	150.-250.
TT-25.11	Nickel, "T" Incused	4.53	23.8	1.30	150.-250.
TT-25.12	Nickel, "W" Raised	5.16	23.9	1.65	150.-250.
TT-25.13	Nickel Bonded Steel 6%, "NBS" Incused	4.50	23.9	1.10	150.-250.
TT-25.14	Nickel Bonded, Steel 6.3% "Sherritt" Incused	4.79	23.9	1.40	150.-250.
TT-25.15	Stainless Steel, "304" Incused	4.07	23.8	1.10	150.-250.
TT-25.16	Stainless Steel, "430" Incused	4.24	23.4	1.10	150.-250.
TT-25.17	Steel, "S" Incused	4.55	23.8	1.10	150.-250.

12-SIDED ALUMINUM TOKEN, THREE MAPLE LEAVES, 1983.

Photograph not
available
at press time

Weight: 1.78 grams
Diameter: 24.0 mm
Thickness: 1.30 mm
Edge: Plain
Die Axis: ↑↑

TT-25.18   English/French legends "TEST TOKEN/ROYAL CANADIAN MINT" / "EPREUVE/MONNAIE ROYALE CANADIENNE"

Cat. No.	Description	Price Range
TT-25.18	"M" Raised, Aluminum	200.-250.

TWENTY-FIVE CENT TEST TOKENS

ROUND, UNKNOWN COMPOSITION TEST TOKEN, THREE MAPLE LEAVES, DATE UNKNOWN.
This test token is magnetic and may have been used to test multi-ply plated blanks.

Weight: 4.5 grams
Diameter: 23.7 mm
Thickness: 1.20 mm
Edge: Reeded
Die Axis: ↑↑

TT-25.19   English/French legends "TEST TOKEN/ROYAL CANADIAN MINT" /
             "EPREUVE/MONNAIE ROYALE CANADIENNE"

Cat. No.	Description	Price Range
TT-25.19	Magnetic	200.-250.

ROUND MULTI-PLY PLATED TOKEN; ROYAL CANADIAN MINT LOGO, UNCOLOURED POPPY REVERSE, 2004. This test token was issued as part of the "Poppy Test Token" set, (TTS-4). The token does not carry the red colour of the "Poppy" circulating coin.

Composition: Multy-ply plated
                steel/copper/nickel
Weight: 4.40 grams
Diameter: 23.8 mm
Thickness: 1.58 mm
Edge: Reeded
Die Axis: ↑↑

TT-25.20   "TEST TOKEN EPREUVE / CANADA 2004 REMEMBER / SOUVENIR"

Cat. No.	Description	Price Range
TT-25.20	Round, RCM logo, Poppy Reverse	15.-20.

FIFTY CENT TEST TOKENS

ROUND BRONZE TOKEN; 1907. This piece was struck to adjust the coining presses prior to the first production of Canadian coins at the new Ottawa branch of the Royal Mint.

Weight: N/A
Diameter: 30.6 mm
Thickness: 2.0 mm
Edge: Reeded
Die Axis: ↑↑

TT-50.1   Legend "OTTAWA MINT/TRIAL RUN/NOVEMBER/1907"

Cat. No.	Description	Price
TT-50.1	Round, bronze	7,500.

ROUND NICKEL TOKEN; STANDING RAM; 1965. This test token provides an example of the quality of coins produced at the Royal Canadian Mint.

Weight: N/A
Diameter: N/A
Thickness: N/A
Edge: Reeded
Die Axis: ↑↑

TT-50.2   Legend "50 TOKENS/R.C. MINT/1965"
ROUND BRASS TOKEN; STANDING RAM; 1965

Weight: N/A
Diameter: N/A
Thickness: N/A
Edge: Reeded
Die Axis: ↑↑

TT-50.3   Legend "50 TOKENS/R.C. MINT/1965"

Cat. No.	Date	Description	Price Range
TT-50.2	1965	Round, nickel	1,000.-1,500.
TT-50.3	1965	Round, brass	1,000.-1,500.

ONE DOLLAR TEST TOKENS

ROUND TOKEN (VARIOUS COMPOSITIONS); THREE MAPLE LEAVES; 1983. When the decision was made to retire the one dollar bank note, tests were conducted with various compositions of the standard dollar blank. Legends and the individual specifications listed are common to all round 1983 tokens. Each token is counterstamped with the composition's initials such as "N.B.S." for Nickel Bonded Steel.

Legend: English/French Legends "TEST TOKEN/ROYAL CANADIAN MINT/(counterstamp)" / "EPREUVE/MONNAIE ROYALE CANADIENNE/ (counterstamp)"

Edge: Plain   **Die Axis:** ↑↑

Cat. No.	Description	Weight Grams	Diam. mm	Thickness mm	Price Range
TT-100.1	Nickel Bonded Steel, "N.B.S."	13.2	2.31	32.8	150.-200.
TT-100.3	Coloured bronze, "C.Br."	12.4	2.13	32.8	150.-200.
TT-100.4	Stainless Steel, "S.S."	10.2	1.92	32.8	150.-200.
TT-100.5	Bronze, "BR."	12.8	2.13	32.8	150.-200.
TT-100.6	Nickel, "NI."	14.0	2.25	32.8	150.-200.
TT-100.7	Gold Plated Nickel, "AV.PL.NI"	14.0	2.32	32.8	150.-200.
TT-100.8	Copper Nickel, "CU.NI"	12.4	2.00	32.8	150.-200.
TT-100.9	Unknown, "92/8"	13.0	2.11	32.8	150.-200.
TT-100.10	Aluminum, "AL. 5454"	4.0	2.13	32.8	150.-200.

11-SIDED TOKEN (COMPOSITION UNKNOWN); THREE MAPLE LEAVES; 1984. The following one dollar test token is the preliminary testing for the Loon dollar that was adopted in 1987.

Legend: English/French legends "TEST TOKEN/ROYAL CANADIAN MINT" / "EPREUVE/ MONNAIE ROYALE CANADIENNE"

Weight: 7.0 to 7.1 grams   **Edge:** Plain   **Diameter:** 26.5 mm

Cat. No.	Description	Thickness mm	Die Axis	Price Range
TT-100.11	Unknown, Unknown Composition, wide rims	1.43	↑↓	75.-125.

ONE DOLLAR TEST TOKENS

11-SIDED TOKEN (VARIOUS COMPOSITIONS); THREE MAPLE LEAVES, 1985.

Legend: English/French legends "TEST/ROYAL CANADIAN MINT" / "EPREUVE/ MONNAIE ROYALE CANADIENNE"

Weight: 7.0 to 7.1 grams   **Edge:** Plain   **Diameter:** 26.5 mm

Cat. No.	Description	Thickness mm	Die Axis	Price Range
TT-100.12	Int'l. Nickel, Gold plated on nickel, narrow rims	1.90	↑↑	175.-225.
TT-100.13	Sherritt, Nickel plated bronze, narrow rims	1.80	↑↑	175.-225.

11-SIDED TOKEN, BRONZE PLATED NICKEL, THREE MAPLE LEAVES, 2005.

Legend: English/French legends "TEST TOKEN/ROYAL CANADIAN MINT" / "EPREUVE/ MONNAIE ROYALE CANADIENNE"

Weight: 7.0 to 7.1 grams   **Edge:** Plain   **Diameter:** 26.5 mm

Cat. No.	Description	Thickness mm	Die Axis	Price Range
TT-100.14	Bronze Plated Nickel	1.80	↑↑	15.-20.

TWO DOLLAR TEST TOKENS

ROUND, VARIOUS COMPOSITIONS AND EDGES, THREE MAPLE LEAVES, 1994-1995.
Between 1994 and 1995, during the preparation period for the two dollar coin which would soon replace the two dollar note, the Royal Canadian Mint tested many different sizes, shapes and compositions of two dollar blanks. Table One contains a listing of bimetal planchets, while Table Two lists trimetal planchets.

TWO DOLLARS

Legend: English/French legends "TEST TOKEN/ROYAL CANADIAN MINT" / "EPREUVE/
MONNAIE ROYALE CANADIENNE"

Thickness: 2.46 mm   **Die Axis:** ↑↑

Cat. No.	Description / Edge	Weight Grams	Diam. mm	Price Range
TT-200.1	12-sided, Copper-zinc / Scalloped smooth	4.0	22.5 mm	100.-125.
TT-200.2	6-sided, Copper-zinc / Scalloped smooth	4.0	22.5 mm	100.-125.
TT-200.3	12-sided, Stainless steel / Scalloped smooth	4.0	22.5 mm	100.-125.
TT-200.4	6-sided, Copper-nickel /Scalloped smooth	4.0	22.5 mm	100.-125.
TT-200.5	Round, Copper-zinc / Reeded	7.5	22.5 mm	100.-125.
TT-200.6	Round, Copper-zinc / Reeded	9.3	24.6 mm	100.-125.
TT-200.7	7-sided, Copper-zinc / Plain	5.8	22.5 mm	100.-125.

BIMETALLIC TWO DOLLAR TEST TOKENS.

TT-200.9

Cat. No.	Description / Edge	Weight Grams	Diam. mm	Price Range
TT-200.8	Round, Aluminum-bronze ring, Nickel Centre / Interrupted reeded	5.0	22.50	150.-200.
TT-200.9	Round, Nickel ring, Copper-tin-zinc centre / Interrupted reeded	6.2	25.25	150.-200.
TT-200.10	Round, Nickel ring, Aluminum-bronze centre / Interrupted reeded	6.2	25.25	150.-200.
TT-200.11	Round, Ring unknown, centre unknown / Plain	7.7	27.1	150.-200.
TT-200.12	7-sided, Copper nickel ring, Aluminum-bronze centre / Smooth	7.7	28.0	150.-200.
TT-200.13	8-sided, Copper-nickel ring, Aluminum-bronze centre / Smooth	8.5	28.0	150.-200.
TT-200.14	9-sided, Copper-nickel ring, Aluminum-bronze centre / Smooth	8.5	28.0	150.-200.

TRIMETALLIC TWO DOLLAR TEST TOKENS.

Cat No.	Description /	Edge	Weight Grams	Diam. mm	Price Range
TT-200.15	11-sided, Aluminum-bronze ring, Aluminum-bronze centre, Copper-nickel inner ring	N/A	9.6	29.0	200.-300.
TT-200.16	11-sided, Copper-nickel outer ring, Copper-nickel centre Aluminum-bronze inner ring	N/A	9.6	29.0	200.-300.

ROUND BIMETALLIC TOKEN; THREE MAPLE LEAVES; 1996. Bimetallic test tokens were made available to the public for the first time in 1996.

Composition: Nickel ring; copper, aluminum nickel core
Weight: 7.30 grams
Diameter: 28 mm
Thickness: 1.7 mm
Edge: Interrupted serration
Die Axis: ↑↑

TT-200.17   English/French legends "TEST TOKEN/ROYAL CANADIAN MINT" / "EPREUVE/ MONNAIE ROYALE CANADIENNE"

Cat. No.	Description	Price Range
TT-200.17	Round bimetallic	75.-100.

TEST TOKEN SETS

TTS-1   1984: ONE DOLLAR, TWO DOLLAR, ONE CENT AND TEST TOKEN SET

Cat. No.	Date	Description	Price Range
TTS-1	1973	Round one cent	150.-250.
	1984	12-sided one cent	
	1984	Voyageur dollar	
	Undated	11-sided test token	

TTS-2   1986: ONE DOLLAR AND TWO DOLLAR TEST TOKEN SETS

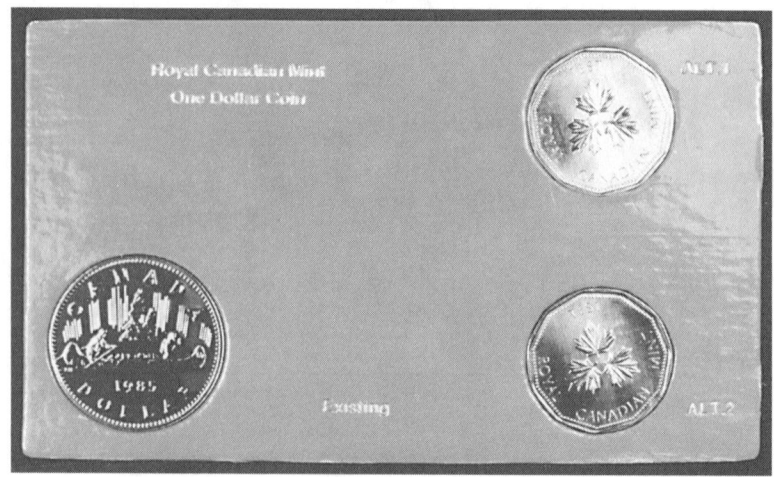

Cat. No.	Date	Description	Price Range
TTS-2	1985	Voyageur dollar	350.-450.
		Gold plate on nickel test token	
		Bronze plate on nickel test token	

TTS-3   FIVE COIN MULTI-PLY PLATED STEEL BRILLIANT UNCIRCULATED SET, 1999

Multi-Ply Plated coinage was issued to the vending industry for test purposes in 1999. The industry's request was for "actual coins" that would be used in circulation, not "test" coinage that may or may not be issued. Five denominations, one cent through to the fifty cents, were issued to the industry on a deposit basis. Naturally not all were returned, for some found their way into the numismatic market. Finding superior demand for the legal tender "test coinage," the mint issued a six-piece set containing five multi-ply plated steel coins and a medallion for sale to the numismatic market. The finish is brilliant relief on a brilliant background.

Date	Description	No. of Pieces	Issue Price	Mintage	BRILLIANT UNCIRCULATED (MS)			
					65	66	67	68
1999P	Pliofilm set	5 coins / Medallion	99.95	20,000	55.	—	—	—

TEST TOKEN SETS

TTS-4   2004 TEST TOKEN "POPPY" SET

This set is a manufacturing tribute to Canada's first coloured circulating coins. The set contains one coin, a twenty-five cent Poppy, and six test tokens. All except the one and two dollar test tokens are made of multi-ply plated steel. The finish is brilliant relief on a brilliant background.

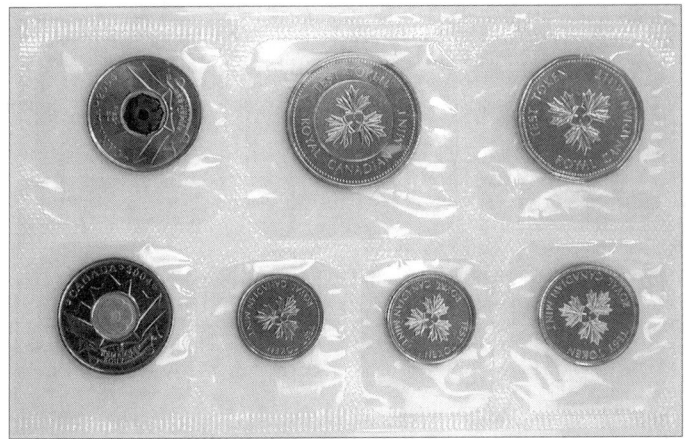

Test Token	Cat. No.	Description
One cent	TT-1.9	Multi-ply plated, two ply
Five cents	TT-5.7	Multi-ply plated
Ten cents	TT-10.10	Multi-ply plated
Twenty-five	TT-25.20	Multi-ply plated, RCM Logo/Poppy reverse
One Dollar	TT-100.13	Nickel plated bronze
Two Dollar	TT-200.17	Nickel ring; copper/ aluminum/nickel ring
Set	TTS-4	Six tokens, "Poppy" twenty-five cents

Date	Description	No. of Pieces	Issue Price	Mintage	BRILLIANT UNCIRCULATED (MS) 65	66	67	68
2004	Pliofilm set	6 tokens / 25¢ Poppy	49.95	9,534	50.	–	–	–

COLLECTOR COINS

Introduction to Modern Finishes

The finish refers to the appearance or surface texture of a coin's relief and field.

Modern numismatic coin production began in 1954 with the Royal Canadian Mint offering for public sale a set of coins (1¢ to the $1) for that year. It was not until 1959, in the Mint Report for that year, that the Royal Canadian Mint officially recognized the sale of "uncirculated coins" by the "Numismatic Section" to the general public. However, the term "uncirculated set" was not mentioned until the 1961 Mint Report. It was early in this seven year period that the term "proof-like" was originated by J. E. Charlton. For over fifty years the finish on Canadian coins has been in evolution, until today when we have seven or more different finishes in use. It is important that the collector have a clear understanding of the finishes and the date sequences for which they occur on the various coins and sets that the Mint has issued.

CIRCULATING COINAGE: Circulating coins are struck on high speed coinage presses with volume handling equipment to move coins from the presses at the rate of over 700 coins per minute. The finish is brilliant relief on a brilliant background. It is at this stage the term brilliant uncirculated or mint state condition is applicable. When the coins are placed into circulation and wear disturbs or removes the finish the coins enter the circulated grades.

NUMISMATIC BRILLIANT UNCIRCULATED FINISH: The finish applied to nickel or plated coinage from 1968 to 2005 is brilliant relief on a brilliant background. The method of production differs only in minor degrees from the production of circulating coinage. The coins are struck on numismatic presses at a slower rate and under greater pressure. The quality of the blanks is higher, the dies are changed more often, and the handling system is such that the struck coins are not allowed to fall into bins, but are handled individually.

PROOF-LIKE FINISH: The finish was applied to silver and copper coinage. This is a collector term that the Royal Canadian Mint failed to recognize for the finish used on their uncirculated sets from 1954 to 1967. The proof-like finish varies from frosted relief on a brilliant background to brilliant relief on a brilliant background, depending on the state of the die when the coin was struck. Used dies were acid cleaned, polished and rechromed. The planchets were selected, polished and specially handled to prevent contact. The coins were struck on numismatic presses with special handling as they were removed from the press, and then sent to the packaging department.

The difference in finish between silver uncirculated sets (1954-1967) and the nickel uncirculated sets (1968-2000) is at times indistinct. Nickel is a hard metal, but with new dies, good blanks and a well set up press, the quality of the finish may vary from brilliant uncirculated to proof-like even though nickel blanks are used.

SPECIMEN FINISH: Specimen finish on Canadian coins has been in use since 1858 and is one of the most confusing of numismatic terms. However, in the era of modern coin finishes, 1954-2005, it is characterized by frosted relief on a brilliant background (1954-1980), and brilliant relief on a parallel lined background (1981-2005). The manufacture of specimen coinage is superior to that of proof-like coinage: better blanks, dies, handling, and more pressure on the numismatic presses lead to a higher quality finish. Specimen was the highest quality finish the Mint offered on Canadian coin products until 1981, with the exception of the Montreal Olympic Coin Programme (1972-1976).

PROOF FINISH: This is the highest quality finish on coins offered by the Royal Canadian Mint. The finish is a frosted relief on a mirror-like reflective field. Special blanks, hand polished dies, multiple strikes, more frequent die replacement, coins passing through the presses individually, special handling, and rigorous quality control all contribute to this high finish. Proof coinage has been offered by the Royal Canadian Mint since 1981.

Condition

The pricing tables have been expanded in response to current collector demand for certified coins, including mint products. In the absence of sufficient market data, only the consensus condition (average condition when received from the Mint) prices are listed at this time.

Mint Items	Consensus Condition	
	Numismatic	Bullion
Brilliant Uncirculated	65	66
Proof-like	65	Not issued
Specimen	66	66
Proof	67	67

ONE CENT

SELECTIVELY GOLD PLATED ONE CENT, 2003. This one cent coin is the first of a series of six coins, one of which will be included each year with the Annual Mint Report, leading up to the Royal Canadian Mint's centennial in 2008. See the One Cent Derivatives listed below.

Designers: Obv.: Dora de Pédery-Hunt
            Rev.: G. E. Kruger-Gray
Composition: Copper plated zinc
Diameter: 19.05 mm
Thickness: 1.45 mm
Finish: Proof, Selectively gold plated
Case of Issue: See Derivatives

Engravers: Obv.: Ago Aarand
           Rev.: G. E. Kruger-Gray
Weight: 2.25 grams
Edge: Plain
Die Axis: ↑↑

Date	Description	Issue Price	Mintage	65	PROOF (PR) 66	67	68
2003	Selectively gold plated	N.I.I.	10,000	–	–	25.	–

Note: N.I.I. denotes Not issued individually, see derivatives.

ONE CENT DERIVATIVES

Date	Description	Condition	Issue Price / Issuer	Mintage	Price
2003	**2003 ANNUAL MINT REPORT** One cent coin, selectively gold plated	PR-67	19.95 RCM	7,746	25.
2003	**CORONATION COIN AND STAMP SET**, two one cent coins, 1953 and 2003; two fifty cent coins, 2002 Jubilee and 2003 Uncrowned Portrait; two mint and two cancelled stampes of Her Majesty's Jubilee and Coronation, Presentation Case	MS-65	NA / RCM	14,743	30.

THREE CENTS

150TH ANNIVERSARY OF CANADA'S FIRST POSTAGE STAMP, 2001. Sir Sandford Fleming's (1851) Three Pence Beaver was Canada's first postage stamp and a symbol of the transfer of postal authority from Britain to Canada.

Designers: Obv.: Dora de Pédery-Hunt
Rev.: Sir Sandford Fleming
Composition: .925 silver, .075 copper,
24-karat gold covered
Diameter: 21.3 mm
Thickness: 1.9 mm
Case of Issues: See Derivatives

Engravers: Obv.: Dora de Pédery-Hunt
Rev.: Cosme Saffioti
Weight: 5.35 grams
Edge: Plain
Die Axis: ↑↑
Finish: Proof

Date	Description	Issue Price	Mintage	65	66	PROOF (PR) 67	68
2001	3 Cent Beaver	N.I.I. See deriv.	59,573	–	–	15.	–

THREE CENTS DERIVATIVES

Date	Description	Condition	Issue Price / Issuer	Mintage	Price
2001	**THREE CENTS** Medallion, Stamp set Maroon leatherette case, COA	PR-67	39.95 RCM, CP	59,573	17.50

Note: CP denotes Canada Post
RCM denotes Royal Canadian Mint
N.I.I. denotes Not issued individually

FIVE CENTS

COMMEMORATING THE LES VOLTIGEURS de QUEBEC, 2000. Since 1862 the first French-Canadian Regiment served with dignity and honour. The reverse of the 5-cent proof sterling silver coin features a baton, drums, and a sash of the Regimental Insignia of Les Voltigeurs de Québec.

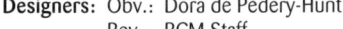

Designers: Obv.: Dora de Pédery-Hunt
          Rev.: RCM Staff
Composition: .925 silver, .075 copper
Weight: 5.3 grams
Diameter: 21.3 mm
Finish: Proof

Engravers: Obv.: Dora de Pédery-Hunt
          Rev.: RCM Staff
Thickness: 1.85 mm
Edge: Plain
Die Axis: ↑↑

Case of Issue: Black leatherette clam case; green insert and sleeve; encapsulated coin

Date	Description	Issue Price	Mintage	65	PROOF (PR) 66	67	68
2000	Les Voltigeurs de Québec	16.95	34,024	–	–	10.	–

ROYAL MILITARY COLLEGE OF CANADA COMMEMORATIVE, 2001. The second sterling silver commemorative five-cent coin honours the Royal Military Colleges in Canada that train our officers for the Armed Forces.

Designers: Obv.: Dora de Pédery-Hunt
          Rev.: Gerald T. Locklin

Engravers: Obv.: Dora de Pédery-Hunt
          Rev.: Susan Taylor

Specifications: Same as 2000 issue
Finish: Proof
Case of Issue: Black leatherette clam case; green insert, encapsulated coin; multicoloured sleeve

Date	Description	Issue Price	Mintage	65	PROOF (PR) 66	67	68
2001	Royal Military College	16.95	25,834	–	–	10.	–

85TH ANNIVERSARY OF THE BATTLE FOR VIMY RIDGE, 2002. On April 9th, 1917, the Canadian Army launched an assault on a small hill in France during World War I. Six days later the Canadians took Vimy Ridge, which was the turning point in the war.

Designers: Obv.: Dora de Pédery-Hunt   Engravers: Obv.: Dora de Pédery-Hunt
           Rev.: S. A. Allward   Rev.: Susan Taylor

Specifications: Same as 2000 issue   Finish: Proof
Case of Issue: Black leatherette clam case; maroon insert; encapsulated coin; multicoloured sleeve.

Date	Description	Issue Price	Mintage	65	PROOF (PR) 66	67	68
2002	Vimy Ridge	16.95	22,646	–	–	28.	–

60TH ANNIVERSARY OF D-DAY, 2004. On June 6th, 1944, the Canadian Army and its Allies mounted the greatest seaborne invasion in history against Nazi held Europe. This coin commemorates the event which took place on the beaches of Normandy.

Designers: Obv.: Susanna Blunt   Engravers: Obv.: Susan Taylor
           Rev.: Thomas Shingles   Rev.: RCM Engravers
Specifications: 12-sided, same as 2000 issue
Finish: Proof
Case of Issue: See Derivatives, page 255

Date	Description	Issue Price	Mintage	65	PROOF (PR) 66	67	68
2004	D-Day	N.I.I.	20,000	–	–	65.	–

60TH ANNIVERSARY OF VE-DAY, 2005. On May 8th, 1945, victory in Europe was declared over Nazi Germany, thus ending the second World War in Europe.

Designer:　Obv.: Thomas Shingles　　　**Engravers:** Obv.: Thomas Shingles
　　　　　　　Rev.: Thomas Shingles　　　　　　　　　Rev.: Christie Paquet
Specifications: 12-sided, same as 2000 issue
Finish: Proof
Case of Issue: See Derivatives

Date	Description	Issue Price	Mintage	PROOF (PR) 65	66	67	68
2005	1945 Victory Five Cents	N.I.I.	N/A	–	–	30.	–

FIVE CENTS DERIVATIVES

Date	Description	Condition	Issue Price / Issuer	Mintage	Price
2004	**VICTORY FIVE CENTS** 1944-2004, sterling silver Medallion, CD, Folder	PR-67	29.95 RCM	19,977	60.
2005	**VICTORY FIVE CENTS** 1945-2005, sterling silver Medallion and Booklet	PR-67	29.95 RCM	N/A	30.

TEN CENTS

500TH ANNIVERSARY OF CABOTO'S FIRST TRANSATLANTIC VOYAGE 1997. Giovanni Caboto sailed from Bristol, England, in 1497, sighting "Newfoundland" weeks later. He is credited with opening North America for settlement. The "Matthew" is depicted in full sail approaching the rocky coast of Newfoundland.

Designer: Obv.: Dora de Pédery-Hunt	**Engravers:** Obv.: Dora de Pédery-Hunt
Rev.: Donald H. Curley	Rev.: Stan Witten
Composition: .925 silver, .075 copper	**Thickness:** 1.2 mm
Weight: 2.4 grams	**Edge:** Reeded
Diameter: 18.0 mm	**Die Axis:** ↑↑
Finish: Proof	

Case of Issue: Clear plastic case with black insert, white sleeve. See derivatives.

Date	Description	Issue Price	Mintage	65	PROOF (PR) 66	67	68
1997	The "Matthew"	10.95	49,848	–	–	20.	–

100TH ANNIVERSARY OF THE BIRTH OF CREDIT UNIONS IN NORTH AMERICA, 2000. In 1900 Alphonse Desjardins founded Canada's Savings and Credit Union in Lévis, Quebec. His house "Maison Desjardins", illustrated on the ten cent coin, was the site of the first Caisse Populaire.

Designer: Obv.: Dora de Pédery-Hunt	**Engravers:** Obv.: Dora de Pédery-Hunt
Rev.: Jean-Guy Lebel	Rev.: William Woodruff
Specifications: Same as for 1997	**Finish:** Proof

Case of Issue: Green printed card folder with encapsulated coin

Date	Description	Issue Price	Mintage	65	PROOF (PR) 66	67	68
2000	Caisse Populaire	14.95	69,791	–	–	10.	–

INTERNATIONAL YEAR OF THE VOLUNTEERS, 2001. This coin celebrates the contributions of millions of Canadians who volunteered their time and energy towards making this country and our provinces better places for all.

Designers: Obv.: Dora de Pédery-Hunt
Rev.: R.C.M. Design
Specifications: Same as 1997 issue
Case of Issue: Multicoloured printed card folder with encapsulated coin

Engravers: Obv.: Dora de Pédery-Hunt
Rev.: Stan Witten
Finish: Proof

Date	Description	Issue Price	Mintage	65	PROOF (PR) 66	67	68
2001	Volunteers	14.95	40,634	–	–	10.	–

100TH ANNIVERSARY OF THE CANADIAN OPEN GOLF CHAMPIONSHIP, 2004. The Canadian Open, first played in 1904, is the third oldest National Open in the world.

Designers: Obv.: Susanna Blunt
Rev.: Cosme Saffioti
Composition: Three ply nickel
Weight: 1.75 grams
Diameter: 18.03 mm
Finish: Brilliant Uncirculated
Case of Issue: See Derivatives

Engravers: Obv.: Susan Taylor
Rev.: Cosme Saffioti
Thickness: 1.22 mm
Edge: Serrated
Die Axis: ↑↑

Date	Description	Issue Price	Mintage	65	BRILLIANT UNCIRCULATED (MS) 66	67	68
2004	Putting	N.I.I.	31,744	15.	–	–	–

TEN CENTS DERIVATIVES

Date	Description	Condition	Issue Price / Issuer	Mintage	Price
1997	**JOHN CABOTO** Ten cents, sterling Canada 45¢ stamp and Italy 1300 Lira stamp, Multicoloured card folder	PR-67	19.95 / RCM, CP	N/A	20.
2000	**TALL SHIPS** Ten cents, sterling (.925) Two cancelled 46¢ stamps Blue presentation case	PR-67	19.95 / RCM, CP	15,000	10.
2004	**TEN CENT** and **FIVE DOLLAR COINS**, framed with two.48¢ circular stamps	MS-65 PR-67	49.95 / RCM, CP	25,000	50.
2004	**TEN CENT COINS** Two coins, one Golf, one Bluenose, framed with two golf tees and a divot tool	MS-65	39.95 / RCM, CP	16,121	20.

Note: CP denotes Canada Post
RCM denotes Royal Canadian Mint

TWENTY-FIVE CENTS

125TH ANNIVERSARY OF CANADA SILVER PROOF SET, 1992. Issued by the Royal Canadian Mint, in silver, the twelve different designs represent a familiar scene from each of the twelve provinces and territories of Canada. This is the first issue of sterling silver twenty-five cent coins since 1919. For illustrations and more information on these issues see page 129 for the companion circulating issue.

Designers and Engravers: See page 129
Composition: .925 silver, .075 copper
Weight: 5.9 grams
Diameter: 23.9 mm
Thickness: 1.7 mm
Edge: Reeded
Die Axis: ↑↑
Finish: Proof

Case of Issue: (A) Royal blue flocked single coin case
(B) Royal blue flocked case, 13 coins. Twelve 25¢ coins; one $1.00 coin

Date	Description	Issue Price	Mintage	PROOF (PR) 65	66	67	68
1992	N.B.	9.95	Total	–	–	8.	–
1992	N.W.T.	9.95	mintage	–	–	8.	–
1992	Nfld.	9.95	of silver	–	–	8.	–
1992	Manitoba	9.95	individual	–	–	8.	–
1992	Yukon	9.95	25-cents	–	–	8.	–
1992	Alberta	9.95	651,812	–	–	8.	–
1992	P. E.I.	9.95		–	–	8.	–
1992	Ontario	9.95		–	–	8.	–
1992	N.S.	9.95		–	–	8.	–
1992	Quebec	9.95		–	–	8.	–
1992	Saskatchewan	9.95		–	–	8.	–
1992	B.C.	9.95		–	–	8.	–
1992	13 Coin Set	129.45	84,397 sets	–	–	75.	–

125TH ANNIVERSARY OF CANADA NICKEL UNCIRCULATED SET, 1992. Released October 7th, 1992, this collection is mounted in a brilliantly coloured map of Canada, with each twenty-five cent coin placed in the province or territory commemorated by its design. The Canada Day dollar is the central point of a compass. Each twenty-five cent coin is nickel and issued in "Brilliant uncirculated" condition.

Designers, Engravers: See page 129
Composition: 1.0 Nickel
Weight: 5.05 grams
Diameter: 23.88 mm
Thickness: 1.60 mm
Edge: Reeded
Die Axis: ↑↑
Finish: Brilliant Uncirculated

Date	Description	Issue Price	Mintage	BRILLIANT UNCIRCULATED (MS) 65	66	67	68
1992	13 Coin Set with "Map" Holder	17.25	448,178	10.	–	–	–

1867-1992, 125TH ANNIVERSARY MULE. An 1867-1992 obverse is muled with a Caribou reverse. The coin was reportedly issued in a brilliant uncirculated set of 1993.

Designers and Engravers:
Obv.: Dora de Pédery-Hunt
Rev.: Emanuel Hahn
Specifications: Same as 1992 Nickel issue
Finish: Brilliant Uncirculated

Date	Description	BRILLIANT UNCIRCULATED (MS) 65	66	67	68
1867-1992	Mule		Only one known.		

MILLENNIUM SILVER PROOF COMMEMORATIVE SET, 1999.

Designers and Engravers: See page 131
Specifications: Same as 1992 Silver issue
Finish: Proof

Case of Issue: (A) Gold plastic single hole, oval case, royal blue flocked insert
(B) Gold plastic 12-hole, oval case, royal blue flocked insert

Date	Description	Issue Price	Mintage	PROOF (PR) 65	66	67	68
1999	January	14.95	9,190	–	–	9.	–
1999	February	14.95	8,691	–	–	9.	–
1999	March	14.95	8,765	–	–	9.	–
1999	April	14.95	9,040	–	–	9.	–
1999	May	14.95	9,315	–	–	9.	–
1999	June	14.95	11,004	–	–	9.	–
1999	July	14.95	8,899	–	–	9.	–
1999	August	14.95	8,570	–	–	9.	–
1999	September	14.95	9,169	–	–	9.	–
1999	October	14.95	8,243	–	–	9.	–
1999	November	14.95	8,813	–	–	9.	–
1999	December	14.95	11,715	–	–	9.	–
1999	Set of 12 Coins	149.45	60,245	–	–	95.	–

MILLENNIUM NICKEL SOUVENIR SET, 1999. The twelve 25-cent nickel coins of 1999 were issued along with a 1999 millennium medallion, inserted in a replica of a 1785 map of Canada. Two different medallions were issued, one with a maple leaf obverse, the other carried the Nestlé logo; both have the common Royal Mint logo reverse. They were only available in the millennium set. All coins are brilliant uncirculated.

It is in this set that the "No Denomination" coins of September and November are found. During the Fall of 1999, a Queen Elizabeth II Caribou obverse die became paired with the reverse dies of September and November millennium twenty-five cents coins creating two mules. The interesting result of this pairing is that for the first time Canada has a non-denominated legal tender coin.

Queen Elizabeth II / Caribou Twenty-five Cents Obverse	1999 September Reverse	1999 November Reverse
1999 RCM Medallion Obv.	1999 Medallion Rev.	1999 Nestlé logo Obv.

For the **Designers and Engravers**, see page 131, for the **Specifications** see page 259.

Date	Description	Issue Price	Mintage	BRILLIANT UNCIRCULATED (MS)			
				63	64	65	66
1999	12 coins/R.C.M.	24.95	1,499,973	–	–	10.	–
1999	12 coins/Nestlé	–	Included	–	–	15.	–
1999	RCM Medallion	–	N.I.I.	–	–	5.	–
1999	Nestlé Medallion	–	N.I.I.	–	–	10.	–
1999	Sept., no denom.	–	Included	–	–	150.	–
1999	Nov., no denom.	–	Included	–	–	150.	–

MILLENNIUM SILVER PROOF COMMEMORATIVE SET, 2000.

Designers and Engravers: See page 132
Specifications: Same as 1992 Silver issue
Finish: Proof

Case of Issue: (A) Black plastic single-hole, oval case, royal blue flocked insert, encapsulated
(B) Black plastic 12-hole, oval case, royal blue flocked insert, encapsulated
(C) Red Plush presentation case, light brown inserts, encapsulated, 24 coins and a 2000 Medal. This set was issued for the Chinese market.

Date	Description	Issue Price	Mintage	PROOF (PR) 65	66	67	68
2000	January	14.95	N/A	–	–	10.	–
2000	February	14.95	N/A	–	–	10.	–
2000	March	14.95	N/A	–	–	10.	–
2000	April	14.95	N/A	–	–	10.	–
2000	May	14.95	N/A	–	–	10.	–
2000	June	14.95	N/A	–	–	10.	–
2000	July	14.95	N/A	–	–	10.	–
2000	August	14.95	N/A	–	–	10.	–
2000	September	14.95	N/A	–	–	10.	–
2000	October	14.95	N/A	–	–	10.	–
2000	November	14.95	N/A	–	–	10.	–
2000	December	14.95	N/A	–	–	10.	–
2000	12-coin set	149.95	37,940	–	–	10.	–
1999 & 2000	24-coin set	N/A	6,888	–	–	100.	–
2000	Double 24-coin set	N/A	N/A	–	–	250.	–

MILLENNIUM NICKEL SOUVENIR SET, 2000. The 2000 Souvenir Set features all twelve 25 cent nickel coins in brilliant uncirculated condition plus the 2000 commemorative medallion which was only issued with the souvenir set. The coins are displayed on an easel featuring an aerial photograph of Canada.

February" Twenty-five cent coin   2000 RCM Medallion

2000 Mule, Coin Obverse/Medallion Obverse   2000 Nestle Medallion

Designers and Engravers: See page 132
Specifications: Same as 1992 Nickel issue
Finish: Brilliant Uncirculated
Case of Issue: (A) 13 hole, Map of Canada
                      (B) 13 hole, plastic case

Date	Description	Issue Price	Mintage	BRILLIANT UNCIRCULATED (MS) 63	64	65	66
2000	12 coins / RCM	24.95	876,041	–	–	10.	–
2000	12 coins / Plastic display case	49.55	Included	–	–	30.	–
2000	R.C.M. Medallion	–	N.I.I.	–	–	5.	–
2000	Nestlé Medallion	–	N.I.I.	–	–	10.	–
2000	12 coins / Nestlé	–	Included	–	–	15.	–
2000	Coin / Medallion Mule	–	Unknown	500.	600.	–	–

MILLENNIUM, JANUARY, NICKEL, COLOURIZED, 2000. Issued to celebrate the year 2000, this was the first colourized coin issued by the Royal Canadian Mint.

Designers: Obv.: Dora de Pédery-Hunt   **Engravers:** Obv.: Dora de Pédery-Hunt
              Rev.: Donald F. Warkentin   Rev.: Jose Osio
Specifications: Same as 1992 Nickel issue   **Finish:** Brilliant Uncirculated, Colourized

Case of Issue: Blister packed on information card.

Date	Description	Issue Price	Mintage	BRILLIANT UNCIRCULATED (MS) 63	64	65	66
2000	Millennium	8.95	49,719	–	–	20.	–

CANADA DAY SERIES

CANADA DAY, COLOURIZED, 2000. The following series of twenty-five cent coins were issued to celebrate the Canada Day celebrations that take place during the last week of June, leading up to July 1st.

Designers: Obv.: Dora de Pédery-Hunt	Engravers: Obv.: Dora de Pédery-Hunt
Rev.: Laura Paxton	Rev.: Stan Witten

Designers: Obv.: Dora de Pédery-Hunt
    Rev.: Laura Paxton
Composition: 1.00 nickel
Weight: 5.05 grams
Diameter: 23.88 mm

Engravers: Obv.: Dora de Pédery-Hunt
    Rev.: Stan Witten
Thickness: 1.6 mm
Die Axis: ↑↑
Finish: Brilliant Uncirculated, Colourized

Case of Issue: Blister packed on information card.

Date	Description	Issue Price	Mintage	BRILLIANT UNCIRCULATED (MS) 65	66	67	68
2000	Canada Day	8.95	26,106	75.	−	−	−

CANADA DAY, COLOURIZED, 2001.

Designers: Obv.: Dora de Pédery-Hunt
    Rev.: Silke Ware
Composition: Multi Ply Plated, .940 steel
    .038 copper, .022 nickel
Weight: 4.4 grams
Finish: Brilliant Uncirculated, Colourized

Engravers: Obv.: Dora de Pédery-Hunt
    Rev.: William Woodruff
Diameter: 23.58 mm
Thickness: 1.58 mm
Die Axis: ↑↑

Case of Issue: Encapsulated coin fastened to an information card

Date	Description	Issue Price	Mintage	BRILLIANT UNCIRCULATED (MS) 65	66	67	68
2001P	Canada Day	9.95	96,352	10.	−	−	−

CANADA DAY SERIES

CANADA DAY, COLOURIZED, 2002. The 2002 Canada Day twenty-five cents celebrates 135 years of National Pride. Presented to new Canadians at their citizenship ceremony during 'Celebrate Canada Day' week, this coin marks an important step for those who make Canada their home.

Designers:
 Obv.: Dora de Pédery-Hunt
 Rev.: Judith Chartier
Engravers:
 Obv.: Ago Aarand
 Rev.: Stan Witten
Specifications: See Canada Day 2001
Finish: Brilliant Uncirculated, Colourized
Case of Issue: Folder

Date	Description	Issue Price	Mintage	BRILLIANT UNCIRCULATED (MS) 65	66	67	68
1952-2002P	Canada 2002	9.95	49,901	10.	–	–	–

CANADA DAY, COLOURIZED, 2003.

Designers:
 Obv.: Dora de Pédery-Hunt
 Rev.: Jade Pearen
Engravers:
 Obv.: Ago Aarand
 Rev.: Stan Witten
Specifications: See Canada Day 2001
Finish: Brilliant Uncirculated, Colourized
Case of Issue: Folder

Date	Description	Issue Price	Mintage	BRILLIANT UNCIRCULATED (MS) 65	66	67	68
2003P	Canada 2003	9.95	63,511	10.	–	–	–

CANADA DAY, COLOURIZED, 2004.

Designers:
 Obv.: Susanna Blunt
 Rev.: Cosme Saffioti
Engravers:
 Obv.: Susan Taylor
 Rev.: Stan Witten
Specifications: See Canada Day 2001
Finish: Brilliant Uncirculated, Colourized
Case of Issue: Folder

Date	Description	Issue Price	Mintage	BRILLIANT UNCIRCULATED (MS) 65	66	67	68
2004P	Canada 2004	9.95	44,759	10.	–	–	–

CANADA DAY SERIES

CANADA DAY, MULTI-PLY PLATED STEEL, 2004. Five thousand of these coins were given to new Canadians during "Canada Week Celebrations," June 25 to July 1, 2004. The balance, 27,000, were offered in a "walking bundle."

Designers:
    Obv.: Susanna Blunt
    Rev.: Nick Wooster
Engravers:
    Obv.: Susan Taylor
    Rev.: William Woodruff
Specifications: See Canada Day 2001
Finish: Brilliant Uncirculated
Case of Issue: See Derivatives, page 269

Date	Description	Issue Price	Mintage	BRILLIANT UNCIRCULATED (MS) 65	66	67	68
2004P	Canada Day	N.I.I. (See Deriv.)	29,762	25.	–	–	–

CANADA DAY, COLOURIZED, 2005.

Designers:
    Obv.: Susanna Blunt
    Rev.: Stan Witten
Engravers:
    Obv.: Susan Taylor
    Rev.: Stan Witten
Specifications: See Canada Day 2001
Finish: Brilliant Uncirculated, Colourized
Case of Issue: Folder

Date	Description	Issue Price	Mintage	BRILLIANT UNCIRCULATED (MS) 65	66	67	68
2005P	Canada Day	9.95.	N/A	10.	–	–	–

CHRISTMAS DAY, COLOURIZED, 2004. The twenty five cent colourized Santa Claus of 2004 was issued as part of the Holiday Gift Set for 2004.

Designers:
Obv.: Susanna Blunt
Rev.: N/A
Engravers:
Obv.: Susan Taylor
Rev.: José Osio
Specifications: See Canada Day 2001
Finish: Brilliant Uncirculated, Colourized
Case of Issue: See Brilliant Uncirculated Sets, page 410

Date	Description	Issue Price	Mintage	BRILLIANT UNCIRCULATED (MS)			
				65	66	67	68
2004P	Santa Claus	N.I.I.	60,965	30.	–	–	–

SILVER POPPY, SELECTIVELY GOLD PLATED, 2004. This coin is the second in the Royal Canadian Mint Annual Report series.

Designers:
Obv.: Susanna Blunt
Rev.: Cosme Saffioti
Engravers:
Obv.: Susan Taylor
Rev.: Stan Witten
Composition: Sterling silver
Specifications: Same as 1992 Silver issue, Selectively gold plated
Finish: Proof, Selectively gold plated
Case of Issue: See Derivatives, Page 269

Date	Description	Issue Price	Mintage	PROOF (PR)			
				65	66	67	68
2005	Poppy	N.I.I. (See Deriv.)	15,000	–	–	25.	–

60TH YEAR OF LIBERATION: THE NETHERLANDS AND CANADA, 2005. The Canadian Armed Forces played a leading role in the liberation of the Netherlands that was completed May 5th, 1945. This coin is issued in an eight-coin, brilliant uncirculated set.

Designers:
Obv.: Susanna Blunt
Rev.: N/A
Engravers:
Obv.: Peter Mossman
Rev.: José Osio

Specifications: Same as 1999P issue

Date	Description	Issue Price	Mintage	BRILLIANT UNCIRCULATED (MS)			
				65	66	67	68
2005P	Liberation	N.I.I.	N/A	25.	–	–	–

TWENTY FIVE CENT DERIVATIVES

The following were issued by the Royal Canadian Mint in credit card format, with a twenty five cent coin encapsulated into the card. A different card was issued for each month during 1999 and 2000.

Date	Description	Condition	Issue Price / Issuer	Mintage	Price
1999	JANUARY "A Country Unfolds"	MS-65	N/A / RCM	N/A	2.
	FEBRUARY "Etched in Stone"	MS-65	N/A / RCM	N/A	2.
	MARCH "The Log Drive"	MS-65	N/A / RCM	N/A	2.
	APRIL "Our Northern Heritage"	MS-65	N/A / RCM	N/A	2.
	MAY "The Voyageurs"	MS-65	N/A / RCM	N/A	2.
	JUNE "From Coast to Coast"	MS-65	N/A / RCM	N/A	2.
	JULY "A Nation of People"	MS-65	N/A / RCM	N/A	2.
	AUGUST "The Pioneer Spirit"	MS-65	N/A / RCM	N/A	2.
	SEPTEMBER "Canada Through a Child's Eye	MS-65	N/A / RCM	N/A	2.
	OCTOBER "A Tribute to the First Nation"	MS-65	N/A / RCM	N/A	2.
	NOVEMBER "The Airplane Opens the North	MS-65	N/A / RCM	N/A	2.
	DECEMBER "This is Canada"	MS-65	N/A / RCM	N/A	2.
2000	JANUARY - Pride "Tomorrow Today"	MS-65	N/A / RCM	N/A	2.
	FEBRUARY - Ingenuity "Building for Tomorrow"	MS-65	N/A / RCM	N/A	2.
	MARCH - Achievement "The Power to Excel"	MS-65	N/A / RCM	N/A	2.
	APRIL - Health "Quest for a Cure"	MS-65	N/A / RCM	N/A	2.
	MAY - Natural Legacy "Our Natural Treasures"	MS-65	N/A / RCM	N/A	2.
	JUNE - Harmony "Hand in Hand"	MS-65	N/A / RCM	N/A	2.
	JULY - Celebration "Celebrating our Future"	MS-65	N/A / RCM	N/A	2.
	AUGUST - Family "The Ties That Bind"	MS-65	N/A / RCM	N/A	2.
	SEPTEMBER - Wisdom "The Legacy"	MS-65	N/A / RCM	N/A	2.
	OCTOBER - Creativity "Expression For All Time"	MS-65	N/A / RCM	N/A	2.
	NOVEMBER - Freedom "Strong and Free"	MS-65	N/A / RCM	N/A	2.
	DECEMBER - Community "Canada in the World"	MS-65	N/A / RCM	N/A	2.

TWENTY FIVE CENT DERIVATIVES

Date	Description	Condition	Issue Price / Issuer	Mintage	Price
2000	APRIL, CIBC "Run For The Cure" Credit Card	MS-65	NA / RCM, CIBC	N/A	2.
2004	WALKING BUNDLE Twenty-five cent 'Moose' coin, T-shirt, waterbottle, bag	MS-65	19.95 / RCM	29,762	30.
2004	2004 ANNUAL REPORT Twenty-five cent "Poppy" coin, selectively gold plated	PR-67	24.95 / RCM	15,000	25.
2005	60TH ANNIV. 1945-2005 Liberation Set	MS-65	49.95 / RCM	17,500	50.

FIFTY CENTS

DISCOVERING NATURE SERIES
1995 - 2000

BIRDS OF CANADA, STERLING SILVER 50¢, 1995. The first set in the Discovering Nature Series commemorates birds that are native to Canada. This is the first of eight sets totalling 32 coins. They are the first sterling silver fifty cents to be issued since 1919.

Designers: Obv.: Dora de Pédery-Hunt
Rev.: Jean Luc Grondin
Engravers: Obv.: Dora de Pédery-Hunt
Rev.: Coin 1: Sheldon Beveridge
Coin 2: Stan Witten
Coin 3: Sheldon Beveridge
Coin 4: Cosme Saffioti
Composition: .925 silver, .075 copper
Weight: 9.30 grams
Diameter: 27.13 mm
Thickness: 2.08 mm
Edge: Reeded (serrated)
Die Axis: ↑↑
Finish: Proof, Frosted relief on mirror background

Coin No. 1
Atlantic Puffins

Coin No. 2
Whooping Crane

Coin No. 3
Gray Jays

Coin No. 4
White Tailed Ptarmigans

Case of Issue: Encapsulated coin in presentation box with illustrated booklet.

Date	Description	Issue Price	Mintage	PROOF (PR) 65	66	67	68
1995	Puffin) two coin	–	Total	–	–	20.	–
1995	Crane) set	29.95	mintage	–	–	20.	–
1995	Jays) two coin	–	of all	–	–	20.	–
1995	Ptarmigans) set	29.95	coins	–	–	20.	–
1995	Set, 4 coins	56.95	172,377	–	–	75.	–

DISCOVERING NATURE SERIES
1995 - 2000

LITTLE WILD ONES, STERLING SILVER 50¢, 1996. The second set commemorates the young wildlife of Canada in their natural habitat.

Designers:
    Obv.: Dora de Pédery-Hunt
    Rev. : Dwayne Harty
Engravers:
    Obv.: Dora de Pédery-Hunt
    Rev.: Coin 5: Ago Aarand
           Coin 6: Sheldon Beveridge
           Coin 7: Stan Witten
           Coin 8: Sheldon Beveridge
Specifications: See page 270
Finish: Proof

Case of Issue: (A) Two coin set; encapsulated coins
                (B) Four coin set; encapsulated coins

Coin No. 5
Moose Calf

Coin No. 6
Wood Ducklings

Coin No. 7
Cougar Kittens

Coin number 8
Black Bear Cubs

Date	Description	Issue Price	Mintage	PROOF (PR) 65	66	67	68
1996	Calf) two coin	–	Total	–	–	20.	–
1996	Ducklings) set	29.95	mintage	–	–	20.	–
1996	Kittens) two coin	–	of all	–	–	20.	–
1996	Cubs) set	29.95	coins	–	–	20.	–
1996	Set, 4 coins	56.95	206,552	–	–	75.	–

DISCOVERING NATURE SERIES
1995 - 2000

CANADA'S BEST FRIENDS, STERLING SILVER 50¢, 1997. The silver 50¢ set of 1997 honours the friendship and loyalty of four of Canada's favourite canine companions.

Designers:
  Obv.: Dora de Pédery-Hunt
  Rev.: Arnold A. Nagy
Engravers:
  Obv.: Dora de Pédery-Hunt
  Rev.: Coin 9: William Woodruff
        Coin 10: Stan Witten
        Coin 11: Sheldon Beveridge
        Coin 12: Cosme Saffioti
Specifications: See page 270
Finish: Proof

Case of Issue: Encapsulated coin in presentation box, plus illustrated booklet.

Coin No. 9
Newfoundland

Coin No. 10
Nova Scotia Duck
Tolling Retriever

Coin No. 11
Labrador Retriever

Coin No. 12
Canadian Eskimo Dog

Date	Description	Issue Price	Mintage	PROOF (PR) 65	66	67	68
1997	Newfoundland	19.95	Total	–	–	10.	–
1997	Retriever	19.95	mintage	–	–	10.	–
1997	Labrador	19.95	of all	–	–	10.	–
1997	Eskimo Dog	19.95	coins	–	–	10.	–
1997	Set, 4 coins	59.95	184,536	–	–	40.	–

DISCOVERING NATURE SERIES
1995 - 2000

CANADA'S OCEAN GIANTS, STERLING SILVER 50¢, 1998. The silver 50¢ set of 1998 shows the grace and beauty of the whales that are seen off our coasts.

Designers:
   Obv.: Dora de Pédery-Hunt
   Rev.: Pierre Leduc
Engravers:
   Obv.: Dora de Pédery-Hunt
      Coin 13: William Woodruff
      Coin 14: Sheldon Beveridge
      Coin 15: Cosme Saffioti
      Coin 16: Stan Witten
Specifications: See page 270
Finish: Proof

Case of Issue: Encapsulated coin in presentation box, plus illustrated booklet.

Coin No. 13
Killer Whale

Coin No. 14
Humpback Whale

Coin No. 15
Beluga Whale

Coin No. 16
Blue Whale

Date	Description	Issue Price	Mintage	PROOF (PR) 65	66	67	68
1998	Killer Whale	19.95	Total	–	–	10.	–
1998	Humpback Whale	19.95	mintage	–	–	10.	–
1998	Beluga Whale	19.95	of all	–	–	10.	–
1998	Blue Whale	19.95	coins	–	–	10.	–
1998	Set, 4 coins	59.95	133,310	–	–	40.	–

DISCOVERING NATURE SERIES
1995 - 2000

CATS OF CANADA, STERLING SILVER 50¢, 1999. This set, issued in 1999, honours four species of domestic and wild felines found in Canada, a salute to our rich Canadian wildlife.

Designers:
    Obv.: Dora de Pédery-Hunt
    Rev.: John Crosby
Engravers:
    Obv.: Dora de Pédery-Hunt
    Rev.: Coin 17: Susan Taylor
          Coin 18: Susan Taylor
          Coin 19: Susan Taylor
          Coin 20: Susan Taylor
Specifications: See page 270
Finish: Proof

Case of Issue: Encapsulated coin in presentation box, plus illustrated booklet.

Coin No. 17
Tonkinese

Coin No. 18
Lynx

Coin No. 19
Cymric

Coin No. 20
Cougar

Date	Description	Issue Price	Mintage	65	66	67	68
					PROOF (PR)		
1999	Tonkinese	19.95	Total	–	–	30.	–
1999	Lynx	19.95	mintage	–	–	30.	–
1999	Cymric	19.95	of all	–	–	30.	–
1999	Cougar	19.95	coins	–	–	30.	–
1999	Set, 4 coins	59.95	83,423	–	–	125.	–

DISCOVERING NATURE SERIES
1995 - 2000

CANADIAN BIRDS OF PREY, STERLING SILVER 50¢, 2000. The sixth and last set of the series features the hunting birds indigenous to Canada.

Designers:
  Obv.: Dora de Pédery-Hunt
  Rev. : Coin 21, 23, Jean-Luc Grondin
        Coin 22, 24, Pierre Leduc
Engravers:
  Obv.: Dora de Pédery-Hunt
  Rev.: Coin 21: William Woodruff
       Coin 22: Susan Taylor
       Coin 23: Susan Taylor
       Coin 24: Stanley Witten
Specifications: See page 270
Finish: Proof

Case of Issue: Encapsulated coin in presentation box, plus illustrated booklet.

Coin No. 21
Bald Eagle

Coin No. 22
Osprey

Coin No. 23
Great Horned Owl

Coin No. 24
Red-Tailed Hawk

Date	Description	Issue Price	Mintage	PROOF (PR) 65	66	67	68
2000	Bald Eagle	19.95	Total	–	–	20.	–
2000	Osprey	19.95	mintage	–	–	20.	–
2000	Great Horned Owl	19.95	of all	–	–	20.	–
2000	Red-Tailed Hawk	19.95	coins	–	–	20.	–
2000	Set, 4 coins	59.95	123,628	–	–	80.	–

CANADIAN SPORTS SERIES
1998 - 2000

CANADIAN SPORTS FIRSTS, STERLING SILVER 50¢, 1998. A new sport series of sterling silver 50¢ coins began in 1998 with the issue of the following four coins. The series comprises a total of twelve coins, four issued each of the years 1998, 1999 and 2000.

Designers:
   Obv.: Dora de Pédery-Hunt
   Rev.: Friedrich G. Peter
Engravers:
   Obv.: Dora de Pédery-Hunt
   Rev.: Coin 1: Sheldon Beveridge
           Coin 2: Ago Aarand
           Coin 3: Stan Witten
           Coin 4: Cosme Saffioti
Specifications: See page 270
Finish: Proof

Case of Issue: Singles: Lithographed metal box, black flocked insert, encapsulated coin.
                 Set: Twelve coin metal container.

Coin No.1
First Official Amateur Figure Skating
Championships of 1888

Coin No. 2
First Canadian Ski Running and Ski
Jumping Championships of 1898

Coin No. 3
First Overseas Canadian Soccer
Tour of 1888

Coin No. 4
Gilles Villeneuve; Victory in the Grand
Prix of Canada for F1 Auto Racing 1978

Date	Description	Issue Price	Mintage	65	PROOF (PR) 66	67	68
1998	Skating	19.95	Total	–	–	22.50	–
1998	Skiing	19.95	mintage	–	–	22.50	–
1998	Soccer	19.95	of all	–	–	22.50	–
1998	Auto Racing	19.95	coins	–	–	22.50	–
1998	Set, 4 coins	59.95	56,428	–	–	85.00	–

CANADIAN SPORTS SERIES
1998 - 2000

CANADIAN SPORTS FIRSTS, STERLING SILVER 50¢, 1999. The 1999 50¢ sterling silver coin set commemorates important dates in the history of Canadian sports. The designs reflect both the history of the sport and the growth and development into national pastimes.

Designers:
    Obv.: Dora de Pédery-Hunt
    Rev.: Donald H. Curley
Engravers:
    Obv.: Dora de Pédery-Hunt
    Rev.: Coin 5: William Woodruff
          Coin 6: Stan Witten
          Coin 7: Cosme Saffioti
          Coin 8: Sheldon Beveridge
Specifications: See page 270
Finish: Proof

Case of Issue: Singles: Lithographed metal box, black flocked insert, encapsulated coin.
            Set: Twelve coin metal container.

Coin No. 5
1904-1999 First Canadian Open
Golf Championship of 1904

Coin No. 6
1874-1999 First International Yacht Race
between Canada and U.S.A. in 1874

Coin No. 7
1909-1999 First Grey Cup in
Canadian Football

Coin No. 8
1891-1999 Invention of Basketball
by Canadian James Naismith

Date	Description	Issue Price	Mintage	PROOF (PR) 65	66	67	68
1999	Golf	19.95	Total	–	–	22.50	–
1999	Yachting	19.95	mintage	–	–	22.50	–
1999	Football	19.95	of all	–	–	22.50	–
1999	Basketball	19.95	coins	–	–	22.50	–
1999	Set, 4 coins	59.95	52,115	–	–	85.00	–

CANADIAN SPORTS SERIES
1998 - 2000

CANADIAN SPORTS FIRSTS, STERLING SILVER 50¢, 2000. The 2000 50¢ Sterling Silver coin set celebrates the first competitions in Hockey, Curling, Steeplechase and Five Pin Bowling held in Canada. This is the last set in the twelve coin series.

Designers:
 Obv.: Dora de Pédery-Hunt
 Rev.: Brian Hughes
Engravers:
 Obv.: Dora de Pédery-Hunt
 Rev.: Coin 9: Stanley Witten
   Coin 10: Cosme Saffioti
   Coin 11: Susan Taylor
   Coin 12: William Woodruff
Specifications: See page 270
Finish: Proof

Case of Issue: Singles: Lithographed metal box, black flocked insert, encapsulated coin.
      Set: Twelve coin metal case.

Coin No. 9
1875-2000 First
Recorded Hockey Game

Coin No. 10
1760-2000 Introduction
of Curling to North America

Coin No. 11
1840-2000 First Steeplechase
Race in British North America

Coin No. 12
1910-2000 Birth of the
First 5-Pin Bowling League

Date	Description	Issue Price	Mintage	PROOF (PR) 65	66	67	68
2000	Hockey	19.95	Total	—	—	22.50	—
2000	Curling	19.95	mintage	—	—	22.50	—
2000	Steeplechase	19.95	of all	—	—	22.50	—
2000	Bowling	19.95	coins	—	—	22.50	—
2000	Set, 4 coins	59.95	50,091	—	—	85.00	—

CANADIAN FESTIVALS SERIES
2001 - 2003

CANADIAN FESTIVALS, STERLING SILVER 50¢, 2001. The Royal Canadian Mint introduced a new series of sterling silver 50-cent coins in 2001 commemorating Canadian Festivals. Each coin represents a Canadian Province, Territory or Community, celebrating it's culture, history and traditions with colourful festivals. The 13-coin set was issued over three years, starting in 2001 and ending 2003. and was available by subscription in 2001 for $249.95 with coins being shipped as they became available.

Designers:
 Obv.: Dora de Pédery-Hunt
 Rev.: See below
Engravers:
 Obv.: Dora de Pédery-Hunt
 Rev.: See below
Specifications: See page 270
Finish: Proof

Case of Issue: A: Singles; Multicoloured printed card folder with encapsulated coin.
     B: Thirteen coin set; Canadian Festivals subscription coffee table book.

Coin No. 1
Quebec Winter Carnival (Quebec)
Sylvie Daigneault, Stan Witten

Coin No. 2
Toonik Tyme (Nunavut)
John Mardon, José Osio

Coin No. 3 Newfoundland and Labrador
Folk Festival (Newfoundland)
David Craig, Cosme Saffioti

Coin No. 4 Festival of Fathers
(Prince Edward Island)
Brenda Whiteway, William Woodruff

Date	Description	Issue Price	Mintage	PROOF (PR) 65	66	67	68
2001	Quebec	21.95	Total	–	–	20.	–
2001	Nunavut	21.95	mintage	–	–	20.	–
2001	Newfoundland	21.95	all coins	–	–	20.	–
2001	P.E.I.	21.95	58,123	–	–	20.	–

CANADIAN FESTIVALS SERIES
2001-2003

CANADIAN FESTIVALS, STERLING SILVER 50¢, 2002. The second issue in the 13-coin set Canadian Festival series commemorates the various festivals across Canada.

Designers:
> Obv.: Dora de Pédery-Hunt
> Rev.: See below

Engravers:
> Obv.: Dora de Pédery-Hunt
> Rev.: See below

Specifications: See page 270
Finish: Proof

Case of Issue: A: Singles; Multicoloured printed card folder with encapsulated coin.
B: Thirteen coin set; Canadian Festivals subscription coffee table book.

Coin No. 5
Annapolis Valley Blossom Festival
(Nova Scotia)
Bonnie Ross, José Osio

Coin No. 6
Stratford Festival of Canada
(Ontario)
Laurie McGaw, Susan Taylor

Coin No. 7
Folklorama
(Manitoba)
William Woodruff

Coin No. 8
Calgary Stampede
(Alberta)
Michelle Grant
Stan Witten

Coin No. 9
Squamish Days
Logger Sports
(British Columbia)
José Osio

Date	Description	Issue Price	Mintage	65	66	PROOF (PR) 67	68
2002	Nova Scotia	21.95	Total	–	–	20.	–
2002	Ontario	21.95	mintage	–	–	20.	–
2002	Manitoba	21.95	for all	–	–	20.	–
2002	Alberta	21.95	coins	–	–	20.	–
2002	British Columbia	21.95	61,900	–	–	20.	–

CANADIAN FESTIVALS SERIES
2001-2003

CANADIAN FESTIVALS, STERLING SILVER 50¢, 2003. The third issue in the 13-coin set commemorates festivals across Canada.

Designers:
 Obv.: Dora de Pédery-Hunt
 Rev.: See below
Engravers:
 Obv.: Dora de Pédery-Hunt
 Rev.: See below
Specifications: See page 270
Finish: Proof

Case of Issue: A: Singles; Multicoloured printed card folder with encapsulated coin.
 B: Thirteen coin set; Canadian Festivals subscription coffee table book.

Coin No. 10
Yukon Festival
(Yukon)
Ken Anderson, José Osio

Coin No. 11
Back to Batoche
(Manitoba)
David Hannan, Stan Witten

Coin No. 12
Great Northern Arts Festival
(Inuvik)
Dawn Oman, Susan Taylor

Coin No. 13
Festival Acadien de Caraquet
(New Brunswick)
Hudson Design Group, Susan Taylor

Date	Description	Issue Price	Mintage	PROOF (PR) 65	66	67	68
2003	Yukon	21.95	Total	–	–	20.	–
2003	Manitoba	21.95	mintage	–	–	20.	–
2003	Inuvik	21.95	for all	–	–	20.	–
2003	New Brunswick	21.95	coins	–	–	20.	–
2001/03	Set, 13 coins	249.95	26,451	–	–	250.	–

CANADIAN FOLKLORE AND LEGENDS SERIES
2001 - 2002

CANADA'S FOLKLORE AND LEGENDS, STERLING SILVER 50¢, 2001-2002. A new series of 50-cent sterling silver coins celebrates Canadian Folklore and Legends. Official release date was April 11, 2001.

Designers:
    Obv.: Dora de Pédery-Hunt
    Rev.: See below
Engravers:
    Obv.: Dora de Pédery-Hunt
    Rev.: See below
Specifications: See page 270
Finish: Proof

Case of Issue: Multicoloured printed card folder with encapsulated coin.

Coin No. 1	Coin No. 2	Coin No. 3
The Sled	The Maiden's Cave	Les Petits Sauteux
Valentina Hotz-Entin	Peter Kiss	Miyuki Tanobe
Susan Taylor	Susan Taylor	José Osio

Coin No. 4	Coin No. 5	Coin No. 6
The Pig That Wouldn't	Shoemaker in Heaven	Le Vaisseau Fantome
Get Over the Stile	Francine Gravel	Colette Boivin
Laura Jolicoeur / José Osio	Cosme Saffioti	William Woodruff

Date	Description	Issue Price	Mintage	PROOF (PR) 65	66	67	68
2001	The Sled	24.95	Total mintage	–	–	22.50	–
2001	Maiden's Cave	24.95	of 2001 coins	–	–	22.50	–
2001	Petits Sauteux	24.95	28,979	–	–	22.50	–
2002	Pig / Stile	24.95	Total mintage	–	–	22.50	–
2002	Shoemaker	24.95	of 2002 coins	–	–	22.50	–
2002	Fantome	24.95	19,789	–	–	22.50	–

SELECTIVELY GOLD PLATED

50TH ANNIVERSARY OF THE CANADIAN TULIP FESTIVAL, 2002. After World War II and the Dutch Royal Family's stay in Ottawa, Princess Juliana thanked Canadians for their hospitality with a personal gift of 20,000 tulip bulbs. The gift became the foundation for what was to become the annual Tulip Festival held in Ottawa.

Designers:
Obv.: Dora de Pédery-Hunt
Rev.: Anthony Testa
Engravers:
Obv.: Dora de Pédery-Hunt
Rev.: Stan Witten
Specifications: See page 270, selectively gold plated
Finish: Proof, selectively gold plated

Case of Issue: Folder dated 2002, encapsulated coin

Date	Description	Issue Price	Mintage	65	66	67	68
					PROOF (PR)		
2002	Golden Tulip	24.95	19,986	–	–	70.	–

GOLDEN DAFFODIL, SYMBOL OF HOPE, 2003. The daffodil is the Canadian Cancer Society's symbol of hope. The Royal Canadian Mint donated $2.00 from the sale of each coin to the Cancer Society, with all funds going to support cancer research.

Designers:
Obv.: Dora de Pédery-Hunt
Rev.: Christie Paquet
Engravers:
Obv.: Dora de Pédery-Hunt
Rev.: Stan Witten
Specifications: See page 270, Selectively gold plated
Finish: Proof, Selectively gold plated

Case of Issue: Folder dated 2003, encapsulated coin

Date	Description	Issue Price	Mintage	65	66	67	68
					PROOF (PR)		
2003	Golden Daffodil	34.95	36,293	–	–	30.	–

SELECTIVELY GOLD PLATED

GOLDEN EASTER LILY, 2004. First introduced in North America over 200 years ago, the white flower naturally blossoms at Easter.

Designers:
  Obv.: Susanna Blunt
  Rev.: Christie Paquet
Engravers:
  Obv.: Susan Taylor
  Rev.: Stan Witten
Specifications: See page 270,
  Selectively gold plated
Finish: Proof, Selectively gold
  plated

Case of Issue: Folder dated 2004, encapsulated coin

Date	Description	Issue Price	Mintage	PROOF (PR) 65	66	67	68
2004	Easter Lily	34.95	23,486	–	–	30.	–

GOLDEN ROSE, 2005. First discovered in China in 1899, Father Hugo Scallion sent the golden rose plants to Great Britain.

Designers:
  Obv.: Susanna Blunt
  Rev.: Christie Paquet
Engravers:
  Obv.: Susan Taylor
  Rev.: Christie Paquet
Specifications: See page 270,
  Selectively gold plated
Finish: Proof, Selectively gold
  plated

Case of Issue: Red plastic display case, black plastic insert, encapsulated coin, COA

Date	Description	Issue Price	Mintage	PROOF (PR) 65	66	67	68
2005	Golden Rose	N/A	23,000	–	–	35.	–

COAT OF ARMS OF CANADA

The Coat of Arms of Canada, which graced the George VI fifty-cent coin in 1937, has evolved over the years. This four coin set, besides tracing that evolution, records the portrait changes of Elizabeth II.

Obverse Portraits:
1953-1964 Mary GIllick
1965-1989 Arnold Machin
1990-2003 Dora de Pédery-Hunt
2003-2006 Susanna Blunt

Reverse: Arms of Canada

1953 Small date: G. E. Kruger-Gray
      Large date: Thomas Shingles
1954-1958 Thomas Shingles after
      G. E. Kruger-Gray
1959-1996 Thomas Shingles
1997-2006 C. Bursey-Sabourin

Specifications: See page 270
Finish: Proof

Case of Issue: Maroon leatherette case, black flocked interior, encapsulated coins, COA

1953-1964   1953

1965-1989   1954-1958

1990-2003   1959-1996

2003-2005   1997-2005

Date	Description	Issue Price	Mintage	PROOF (PR) 65	66	67	68
2004	Arms of Canada	79.95	11,707	—	—	80.	—

CANADIAN BUTTERFLY COLLECTION 2004-2005

CANADIAN TIGER SWALLOWTAIL BUTTERFLY, HOLOGRAM, 2004. This is the first in a series on Canada's butterflies, and also the first hologram fifty cent coin.

Designers:
  Obv.: Susanna Blunt
  Rev.: Jianping Yan
Engravers:
  Obv.: Susan Taylor
  Rev.: RCM Staff
Specifications: See page 270
  Hologram
Finish: Proof, Hologram
Case of Issue: Red leatherette clam case, black flocked insert, encapsulated coin, COA

CANADIAN CLOUDED SULPHUR BUTTERFLY, SELECTIVE GOLD PLATING, 2004. This is the second in the series on Canada's butterflies.

Designers:
  Obv.: Susanna Blunt
  Rev.: Susan Taylor
Engravers:
  Obv.: Susan Taylor
  Rev.: Susan Taylor
Specifications: See page 270
  Selectively gold plated
Finish: Proof, Selectively gold plated
Case of Issue: Red leatherette clam case, black flocked insert, encapsulated coin, COA

MONARCH BUTTERFLY, COLOURED, 2005. One of the more interesting butterflies whose migration path from Canada to the southern part of California and northern Mexico covers thousands of kilometers.

Designers:
  Obv.: Susanna Blunt
  Rev.: Susan Taylor
Engravers:
  Obv.: Susan Taylor
  Rev.: Susan Taylor
Specifications: See page 270, Coloured
Finish: Proof, Colourized
Case of Issue: Red plastic display case, black plastic insert, encapsulated coin, COA

Date	Description	Issue Price	Mintage	PROOF (PR) 65	66	67	68
2004	Tiger Swallowtail	39.95	19,910	–	–	40.	–
2004	Clouded Sulphur	39.95	15,281	–	–	40.	–
2005	Monarch	39.95	20,000	–	–	40.	–

THE CANADIAN QUEST FOR PEACE AND FREEDOM DURING THE SECOND WORLD WAR
1945-2005

The 60th anniversary of the end of World War II, 1945-2005, and the part Canada played, are commemorated in a six coin sterling silver set.

Obverse

Designers:
    Obv.: Susanna Blunt
    Rev.: Peter Mossman
Engravers:
    Obv.: Susan Taylor
    Rev.: José Osio
Specifications: See page 270
Finish: Specimen

	Photograph not available at press time	Photograph not available at press tim
Battle of Britain	Battle for the Atlantic	Raid on Dieppe

Photograph not available at press tim	Photograph not available at press tim	Photograph not available at press tim
Conquest of Sicily	Liberation of the Netherlands	Battle of the Scheldt

Case of Issue: Red leatherette case, black flocked insert, encapsulated coin, COA

Date	Description	Issue Price	Mintage	65	SPECIMEN (SP) 66	67	68
2005	World War II	149.95	20,000	—	150.	—	—

FIFTY CENT DERIVATIVES

Date	Description	Condition	Issue Price / Issuer	Mintage	Price
2001	**CANADA PROVINCIAL CREST** Credit Card Type	MS-65	NA / RCM	N/A	2.
2003	**CORONATION COIN AND STAMP SET**, two one cent coins, 1953 and 2003; two fifty cent coins, 2002 Jubilee and 2003 Uncrowned Portrait; two mint and two cancelled stampes of Her Majesty's Jubilee and Coronation; Presentation Case	MS-65	NA / RCM	14,743	30.

ONE DOLLAR

The following pages list the commemorative silver, nickel and nickel bronze dollars issued by the numismatic department of the Royal Canadian Mint over the past years. The characteristics of these issues are itemized below.

COMMEMORATIVE DOLLAR SPECIFICATIONS

Specifications	Specimen Nickel Dollars 1968-1976 1982, 1984	Specimen/ Proof Silver Dollars 1971-1991	Proof Nickel/ Bronze Dollars 1987-date	Proof Silver Dollars 1992-2002	Proof Silver Dollars 2003 to date
Composition:	1.00 Nickel	.500 Silver .500 Copper	Nickel Plated with Bronze	.925 Silver .075 Copper	99.99 Silver
Weight (grams):	15.62	23.30	7.00	25.175	25.175
Diameter:					
Round (mm)	32.13	36.07	–	36.07	36.07
11-sided (mm)	–	–	26.50	36.07	–
Thickness:			1.90	2.95	3.02
Edge:	Reeded	Reeded	11-Sided Plain	Reeded	Reeded
Die axis:	↑↑	↑↑	↑↑	↑↑	↑↑

VOYAGEUR NICKEL DOLLAR 1968 AND 1969: A cased 1968 and 1969 nickel dollar was available from the numismatic department of the Mint during 1968-69. The department did not aggressively market this product until 1970. Thus the years 1968 and 1969 saw the development of the "cased dollar" line with the evolution of a "clam" style case.

Designers: Obv.: Arnold Machin   **Engravers:** Obv.: Patrick Brindley
              Rev.: Raymond Taylor   Rev.: Walter Ott
Finish: Proof-like
Case of Issue: Black leatherette with gold side trim. Gilt Royal Mint Building as crest. Blue inside with black insert and gilt Coat of Arms of Canada

Date	Description	Issue Price	Mintage	65	SPECIMEN (SP) 66	67	68
1968	Voyageur	N/A	N/A	–	3.	–	–
1969	Voyageur	N/A	N/A	–	3.	–	–

MANITOBA CENTENNIAL NICKEL DOLLAR 1970. Canada's first commemorative nickel dollar has a special reverse featuring a prairie crocus in recognition of the centenary of Manitoba's entry into Confederation.

Designers: Obv.: Arnold Machin   **Engravers:** Obv.: Patrick Brindley
          Rev.: Raymond Taylor   Rev.: Walter Ott
Specifications: See page 289
Finish: Specimen
Cases of Issue:
    (A) Black leatherette, gilt RCM crest, blue insert.
    (B) Maroon leatherette, gold stamped crest of Canada, red inside with black insert.
    (C) Black leatherette case, gold stamped with the Japanese characters, Maple Leaf, Canada. Red interior with black insert. Card insert. (Sold at the Canada pavillion in Japan, during 1970.)

Date	Description	Issue Price	Mintage	65	SPECIMEN (SP) 66	67	68
1970	Man., Case A	2.00	349,120	–	3.	–	–
1970	Man., Case B	N/A	Included	–	3.	–	–
1970	Man., Case C	N/A	Included	–	3.	–	–

BRITISH COLUMBIA CENTENNIAL NICKEL DOLLAR 1971. The nickel dollar for 1971 commemorates the entry in 1871 of British Columbia into Confederation. Its design is based on the arms of the province, with a shield at the bottom and dogwood blossoms at the top. The design of the specimen nickel dollar is identical to that of the circulating issue. See page 169.

Designers: Obv.: Arnold Machin   **Engravers:** Obv.: Patrick Brindley
        Rev.: Thomas Shingles   Rev.: Thomas Shingles
Specifications: See page 289   **Finish:** Specimen
Case of Issue: Blue leatherette case, coat of arms of Canada stamped in silver, blue and black insert

Date	Description	Issue Price	Mintage	65	SPECIMEN (SP) 66	67	68
1971	B.C. Centennial	2.00	181,091	–	3.	–	–

BRITISH COLUMBIA CENTENNIAL SILVER DOLLAR 1971. The first non-circulating silver dollar was issued to the public in 1971. It commemorates the entry of British Columbia into Confederation in 1871, with the design based upon the provincial arms. The obverse features a modification of the Machin portrait in which the portrait of the Queen was reduced slightly and her hair extensively redone.

Designers: Obv.: Arnold Machin   **Engravers:** Obv.: Patrick Brindley
        Rev.: Patrick Brindley   Rev.: Patrick Brindley
Specifications: See page 289   **Finish:** Specimen
Cases of Issue:
    (A) Black leatherette, coat of arms, maroon and black insert
    (B) Black leatherette, coat of arms, white and black insert.

Date	Description	Issue Price	Mintage	65	SPECIMEN (SP) 66	67	68
1971	B.C. Centennial	3.00	585,217	–	7.	–	–

VOYAGEUR NICKEL DOLLAR 1972. The specimen nickel dollar issued by the numismatic department of the Royal Canadian Mint has the same design as the circulating dollar.

Designers: Obv.: Arnold Machin   **Engravers:** Obv.: Patrick Brindley
             Rev.: Emanuel Hahn   Rev.: Terry Smith
Specifications: See page 289   **Finish:** Specimen
Case of Issue: Blue leatherette case, blue and black insert.

Date	Description	Issue Price	Mintage	65	SPECIMEN (SP) 66	67	68
1972	Voyageur	2.00	143,392	–	3.	–	–

VOYAGEUR SILVER DOLLAR 1972. The reverse of the 1972 silver dollar is the voyageur design somewhat modified from its last use on the 1966 silver dollar. One of the most noticeable differences is the substitution of beads for denticles at the rim.

Designers and Engravers: Same as Nickel issue
Specifications: See page 289
Finish: Specimen
Case of Issue: Black leatherette case, maroon and black insert.

Date	Description	Issue Price	Mintage	65	SPECIMEN (SP) 66	67	68
1972	Voyageur	3.00	341,581	–	7.	–	–

PRINCE EDWARD ISLAND CENTENNIAL NICKEL DOLLAR 1973. The 100th anniversary of the entry of Prince Edward Island into Confederation is commemorated with the reverse design depicting the provincial legislature building in Charlottetown.

 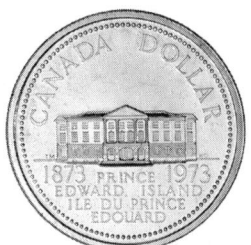

Designers: Obv.: Arnold Machin   Engravers: Obv.: Patrick Brindley
         Rev.: Terry Manning   Rev.: Walter Ott
Specifications: See page 289   Finish: Specimen
Case of Issue: Blue leatherette case, coat of arms, blue and black insert.

Date	Description	Issue Price	Mintage	65	SPECIMEN (SP) 66	67	68
1973	P.E.I. Centennial	2.00	466,881	–	3.	–	–

ROYAL CANADIAN MOUNTED POLICE CENTENNIAL SILVER DOLLAR 1973. The reverse of the 1973 silver dollar recognizes the founding of the North West Mounted Police which later became the Royal Canadian Mounted Police.

Designers: Obv.: Arnold Machin   Engravers: Obv.: Patrick Brindley
         Rev.: Paul Cedarberg   Rev.: Patrick Brindley
Specifications: See page 289   Finish: Specimen
Case of Issue:
    (A) Black leatherette case, coat of arms, maroon and black insert.
    (B) Blue leatherette case, gilt RCMP crest, maroon and black insert.

Date	Description	Issue Price	Mintage	65	SPECIMEN (SP) 66	67	68
1973	Case A	3.00	904,723	–	7.	–	–
1973	Case B	3.00	Included	–	7.	–	–

WINNIPEG CENTENNIAL NICKEL DOLLAR 1974. The 1974 cased specimen nickel dollar carries the same design as the circulating dollar. See page 170.

Designers: Obv.: Arnold Machin   Engravers: Obv.: Patrick Brindley
           Rev.: Paul Pederson   Rev.: Patrick Brindley
Specifications: See page 289   Finish: Specimen
Case of Issue: Blue leatherette case, coat of arms, blue and black plastic insert.

Date	Description	Issue Price	Mintage	65	SPECIMEN (SP) 66	67	68
1974	Nickel	2.00	363,786	–	3.	–	–

WINNIPEG CENTENNIAL SILVER DOLLAR 1974. The 100th anniversary of the establishment of Winnipeg, Manitoba, as a city is marked by the reverse of the 1974 silver dollar. The design is identical to that of the nickel dollar.

Designers: Obv.: Arnold Machin   Engravers: Obv.: Patrick Brindley
           Rev.: Paul Pederson   Rev.: Patrick Brindley
Specifications: See page 289   Finish: Specimen
Case of Issue: Black leatherette case, coat of arms, maroon and black plastic insert.

Date	Description	Issue Price	Mintage	65	SPECIMEN (SP) 66	67	68
1974	Silver	3.50	628,183	–	7.	–	–

VOYAGEUR NICKEL DOLLAR 1975. The numismatic department of the Royal Canadian Mint issued this specimen quality example of the circulating nickel dollar.

Designers: Obv.: Arnold Machin   **Engravers:** Obv.: Patrick Brindley
             Rev.: Emanuel Hahn   Rev.: Terry Smith
Specifications: See page 289   **Finish:** Specimen
Case of Issue: Blue leatherette case, coat of arms, blue and black insert.

Date	Description	Issue Price	Mintage	65	SPECIMEN (SP) 66	67	68
1975	Voyageur	2.50	88,102	–	3.	–	–

CALGARY CENTENNIAL SILVER DOLLAR 1975. For the centenary of the founding of Calgary, Alberta, the silver dollar of 1975 bears a special reverse showing a cowboy atop a bucking bronco. Oil wells and the modern city skyline appear in the background.

Designers: Obv.: Arnold Machin   **Engravers:** Obv.: Patrick Brindley
             Rev.: D. D. Paterson   Rev.: Patrick Brindley
Specifications: See page 289   **Finish:** Specimen
Case of Issue: Black leatherette case, coat of arms, maroon and black insert.

Date	Description	Issue Price	Mintage	65	SPECIMEN (SP) 66	67	68
1975	Calgary Cent.	3.50	833,095	–	7.	–	–

VOYAGEUR NICKEL DOLLAR 1976. This coin was issued by the numismatic department of the Royal Canadian Mint in specimen quality. This was the last year of issue for a single cased voyageur nickel dollar.

Designers: Obv.: Arnold Machin   Engravers: Obv.: Patrick Brindley
          Rev.: Emanuel Hahn   Rev.: Terry Smith
Specifications: See page 289   Finish: Specimen
Case of Issue: Blue leatherette case, coat of arms, blue and black insert.

Date	Description	Issue Price	Mintage	65	SPECIMEN (SP) 66	67	68
1976	Voyageur	2.50	74,209	–	3.	–	–

LIBRARY OF PARLIAMENT CENTENNIAL SILVER DOLLAR 1976. The reverse of the 1976 silver dollar commemorates the 100th anniversary of the completion of the Library of Parliament. This attractive building was the only part of the original centre block of the Parliament Buildings that was saved during the disastrous fire of 1916. It is still in use and is a popular tourist attraction in Ottawa.

Designers: Obv.: Arnold Machin   Engravers: Obv.: Patrick Brindley
          Rev.: Walter Ott   Rev.: Walter Ott
               Patrick Brindley   Finish: Specimen
Specifications: See page 289
Cases of Issue:
     (A) Black leatherette case, coat of arms, maroon and black insert.
     (B) Blue leatherette case, coat of arms, light blue insert with purple satin cloth printed
          "Library of Parliament - Bibliotheque du Parlement 1876-1976."

Date	Description	Issue Price	Mintage	65	SPECIMEN (SP) 66	67	68
1976	Case A	4.00	483,722	–	7.	–	–
1976	Case B	4.00	Included	–	7.	–	–

QUEEN ELIZABETH II SILVER JUBILEE SILVER DOLLAR 1977. During 1977 the Queen celebrated the 25th anniversary of her accession to the throne. Many countries, including Canada, recognized the event with a special commemorative coin. The design on the reverse depicts the throne of the Senate of Canada, which is used by the Queen or the Governor General for ceremonial occasions. The obverse was specifically designed for this coin and bears a special legend and the dates 1952-1977.

Designers: Obv.: Arnold Machin   **Engravers:** Obv.: Royal Mint Staff
           Rev.: Raymond Lee   Rev.: Ago Aarand
Specifications: See page 289   **Finish:** Specimen
Cases of Issue:
    (A) Black leatherette case, coat of arms, maroon and black plastic insert.
    (B) Maroon leatherette case, coat of arms, maroon and black plastic insert.
    (C) Maroon velveteen case, coat of arms, maroon velveteen insert.

Date	Description	Issue Price	Mintage	65	SPECIMEN (SP) 66	67	68
1977	Jubilee, Case A	4.25	744,848	–	7.	–	–
1977	Jubilee, Case B	–	Included	–	15.	–	–
1977	Jubilee, Case C	–	Included	–	15.	–	–

COMMONWEALTH GAMES SILVER DOLLAR 1978. The 1978 silver dollar commemorates the 11th Commonwealth Games, held in Edmonton, Alberta, August 3-12 of that year. The reverse design features the symbol of the Games in the centre, and the official symbols of the ten sports which comprise the Games along the perimeter. The obverse was made specifically for this issue.

Designers: Obv.: Arnold Machin
         Rev.: Raymond Taylor
Specifications: See page 289
Case of Issue: Black leatherette case, Coat of Arms, maroon and black plastic insert.

Engravers: Obv.: Royal Mint Staff
         Rev.: Victor Coté
Finish: Specimen

Date	Description	Issue Price	Mintage	SPECIMEN (SP) 65	66	67	68
1978	Comm. Games	4.50	640,000	–	7.	–	–

GRIFFON TRICENTENNIAL SILVER DOLLAR 1979. The 300th anniversary of the first voyage by a commercial ship on the Great Lakes is commemorated on the reverse of the 1979 silver dollar.

Designers: Obv.: Arnold Machin
         Rev.: Walter Schluep
Specifications: See page 289
Case of Issue: Black leatherette case, maroon insert, encapsulated coin.

Engravers: Obv.: Patrick Brindley
         Rev.: Terry Smith
Finish: Specimen

Date	Description	Issue Price	Mintage	SPECIMEN (SP) 65	66	67	68
1979	Griffon	5.50	688,671	–	7.	–	–

ARCTIC TERRITORIES CENTENNIAL SILVER DOLLAR 1980. The 1980 commemorative silver dollar marks the centenary of the transfer of the Arctic islands from the British Government to the Government of the Dominion of Canada.

Designers: Obv.: Arnold Machin   **Engravers:** Obv.: Patrick Brindley
            Rev.: D. D. Paterson   Rev.: Walter Ott
Specifications: See page 289   **Finish:** Specimen
Case of Issue: Black leatherette case, maroon insert, encapsulated coin.

Date	Description	Issue Price	Mintage	65	SPECIMEN (SP) 66	67	68
1980	Arctic	22.00	389,564	–	25.	–	–

TRANS-CANADA RAILWAY CENTENNIAL SILVER DOLLAR 1981. The 1981 silver dollar commemorates the 100th anniversary of the approval by the Canadian government to build the Trans-Canada Railway. This is the first year of issue by the Mint of two different qualities of silver dollars.

Designers: Obv.: Arnold Machin   **Engravers:** Obv.: Patrick Brindley
            Rev.: Christopher Gorey   Rev.: Walter Ott
Specifications: See page 289
Finish: (A) Proof, frosted relief against a parallel lined background
          (B) Brilliant Uncirculated, brilliant relief on a brilliant background
Cases of Issue:
          (A) Black leatherette case, maroon insert, encapsulated coin, COA
.   (B) Clear plastic outer case, black plastic insert, silver sleeve

Date	Descrip.	Issue Price	Mintage	Finish	65	GRADE 66	67	68
1981	Railway	18.00	353,742	PR	–	–	20.	–
1981	Railway	14.00	148,647	MS	10.	–	–	–

CONSTITUTION NICKEL DOLLAR 1982. The reverse features a faithful reproduction of the celebrated painting of the Fathers of Confederation. This nickel dollar commemorates the Constitution with the inscription "1867 CONFEDERATION" above the painting and "CONSTITUTION 1982" beneath it. The condition of this dollar is "select uncirculated" as offered by the Mint.

Designers: Obv.: Arnold Machin
Rev.: Ago Aarand

Engravers: Obv.: Royal Mint Staff
Rev.: Royal Mint Staff

Specifications: See page 289

Finish: Proof

Case of Issue: Maroon case with maple leaf logo, maroon insert, encapsulated coin.

Date	Description	Issue Price	Mintage	PROOF (PR) 65	66	67	68
1982	Constitution	9.75	107,353	–	–	9.	–

REGINA CENTENNIAL SILVER DOLLAR 1982. This silver dollar commemorates the centennial of the founding of Regina in 1882.

Designers: Obv.: Arnold Machin
Rev.: Huntley Brown

Engravers: Obv.: Patrick Brindley
Rev.: Walter Ott

Specifications: See page 289

Finish: (A) Proof, frosted relief against a parallel lined background
(B) Brilliant Uncirculated, brilliant relief on a brilliant background

Cases of Issue:
(A) Black leatherette case, maroon insert, encapsulated coin, COA
(B) Clear plastic outer case, black plastic insert, silver sleeve

Date	Descrip.	Issue Price	Mintage	Finish	GRADE 65	66	67	68
1982	Regina Cent.	15.25	577,959	PR	–	–	12.	–
1982	Regina Cent.	10.95	144,989	MS	10.	–	–	–

WORLD UNIVERSITY GAMES SILVER DOLLAR 1983. This coin commemorates the World University Games held in Edmonton, Alberta, during July of that year.

Designers: Obv.: Arnold Machin   **Engravers:** Obv.: Patrick Brindley
            Rev.: Carola Tietz   Rev.: Walter Ott
Specifications: See page 289
Finish: (A) Proof, frosted relief against a parallel lined background
         (B) Brilliant Uncirculated, brilliant relief on a brilliant background
Cases of Issue:
         (A) Black leatherette case, maroon insert, encapsulated coin, COA
.   (B) Clear plastic outer case, black plastic insert, silver sleeve

Date	Descrip.	Issue Price	Mintage	Finish	65	66	67	68
						GRADE		
1983	Univ. Games	16.15	340,068	PR	–	–	9.	–
1983	Univ. Game	10.95	159,450	MS	7.	–	–	–

JACQUES CARTIER NICKEL DOLLAR 1984. The 450th year of Jacques Cartier's landing at Gaspé, Quebec, was honoured on July 24, 1984, by the issuing of a commemorative nickel dollar.

Designers: Obv.: Arnold Machin   **Engravers:** Obv.: Royal Mint Staff
            Rev.: Hector Greville   Rev.: Victor Coté
Specifications: See page 289
Finish: Proof
Case of Issue: Green velvet case, green insert, encapsulated coin.

Date	Description	Issue Price	Mintage	65	66	67	68
					PROOF (PR)		
1984	Jacques Cartier	9.75	87,776	–	–	6.	–

TORONTO SESQUICENTENNIAL SILVER DOLLAR 1984. This coin commemorates the 150th anniversary of the incorporation of the City of Toronto in 1834.

Designers: Obv.: Arnold Machin   **Engravers:** Obv.: Patrick Brindley
       Rev.: D. J. Craig   Rev.: Walter Ott
Specifications: See page 289
Finish: (A) Proof, frosted relief against a parallel lined background
         (B) Brilliant Uncirculated, brilliant relief on a brilliant background
Cases of Issue:
         (A) Black leatherette case, maroon insert, encapsulated coin, COA
.   (B) Clear plastic outer case, black plastic insert, silver sleeve

Date	Descrip.	Issue Price	Mintage	Finish	65	66	67	68
1984	Toronto Sesq.	17.50	571,079	PR	–	–	12.	–
1984	Toronto Sesq.	11.40	133,563	MS	13.	–	–	–

NATIONAL PARKS CENTENNIAL SILVER DOLLAR 1985. The 1985 silver dollar commemorates the 100th anniversary of an important part of Canada's heritage, the National Parks.

Designers: Obv.: Arnold Machin   **Engravers:** Obv.: Patrick Brindley
       Rev.: Karel Rohlicek   Rev.: Walter Ott
Specifications: See page 289
Finish: (A) Proof, frosted relief against a parallel lined background
         (B) Brilliant Uncirculated, brilliant relief on a brilliant background
Cases of Issue:
         (A) Black leatherette case, maroon insert, encapsulated coin, COA
.   (B) Clear plastic outer case, black plastic insert, silver sleeve

Date	Descrip.	Issue Price	Mintage	Finish	65	66	67	68
1985	National Parks	17.50	537,297	PR	–	–	12.	–
1985	National Parks	12.00	162,873	MS	10.	–	–	–

VANCOUVER CENTENNIAL SILVER DOLLAR 1986. This coin commemorates the 100th anniversary of the founding of Vancouver and the arrival of the first trans-Canada train in Vancouver. Canadian Pacific Engine No. 371 was the first to arrive, in 1886.

Designers: Obv.: Arnold Machin   **Engravers:** Obv.: Patrick Brindley
          Rev.: Elliott John Morrison   Rev.: Victor Coté
Specifications: See page 289   Rev.: Walter Ott
Finish: (A) Proof, frosted relief against a parallel lined background
       (B) Brilliant Uncirculated, brilliant relief on a brilliant background
Cases of Issue:
       (A) Black leatherette case, maroon insert, encapsulated coin, COA
.   (B) Clear plastic outer case, black plastic insert, silver sleeve

Date	Descrip.	Issue Price	Mintage	Finish	65	66	67	68
						GRADE		
1986	Vancouver	18.00	496,418	PR	–	–	13.	–
1986	Vancouver	12.25	124,574	MS	18.	–	–	–

THE LOON NICKEL/BRONZE DOLLAR 1987. A proof striking of the loon dollar was issued by the numismatic department of the Royal Canadian Mint in 1987.

Designers: Obv.: Arnold Machin   **Engravers:** Obv.: Patrick Brindley
          Rev.: R. R. Carmichael   Rev.: Terry Smith
Specifications: See page 289   **Finish:** Proof
Case of Issue: Blue velvet case, blue velvet insert, encapsulated coin.

Date	Description	Issue Price	Mintage	65	66	67	68
					PROOF (PR)		
1987	Loon	13.50	178,120	–	–	10.	–

JOHN DAVIS SILVER DOLLAR 1987. The 400th anniversary of John Davis' historic expedition in search of the North West Passage is commemorated on the 1987 silver dollar.

Designers: Obv.: Arnold Machin   **Engravers:** Obv.: Patrick Brindley
           Rev.: Christopher Gorey   Rev.: Victor Coté
Specifications: See page 289
Finish: (A) Proof, frosted relief against a parallel lined background
        (B) Brilliant Uncirculated, brilliant relief on a brilliant background
Cases of Issue:
        (A) Black leatherette case, maroon insert, encapsulated coin, COA
        (B) Clear plastic outer case, black plastic insert, silver sleeve

Date	Descrip.	Issue Price	Mintage	Finish	GRADE 65	66	67	68
1987	John Davis	19.00	405,688	PR	–	–	12.	–
1987	John Davis	14.00	118,722	MS	10.	–	–	–

SAINT-MAURICE IRONWORKS SILVER DOLLAR 1988. The 250th anniversary of the Saint-Maurice Ironworks, Canada's first heavy industry, is commemorated on the 1988 silver dollar.

Designers: Obv.: Arnold Machin   **Engravers:** Obv.: Patrick Brindley
           Rev.: R. R. Carmichael   Rev.: Sheldon Beveridge
Specifications: See page 289
Finish: (A) Proof, frosted relief against a parallel lined background
        (B) Brilliant Uncirculated, brilliant relief on a brilliant background
Cases of Issue:
        (A) Black leatherette case, maroon insert, encapsulated coin, COA
        (B) Clear plastic outer case, black plastic insert, silver sleeve

Date	Descrip.	Issue Price	Mintage	Finish	GRADE 65	66	67	68
1988	Ironworks	20.00	259,230	PR	–	–	20.	–
1988	Ironworks	15.00	106,702	MS	20.	–	–	–

MACKENZIE RIVER BICENTENNIAL SILVER DOLLAR 1989. The bicentennial of the first full length voyage of the Mackenzie River by Alexander Mackenzie and his European crew, all the way to the Arctic Ocean, is commemorated on the 1989 silver dollar.

Designers: Obv.: Arnold Machin   **Engravers:** Obv.: Patrick Brindley
            Rev.: John Mardon   Rev.: Sheldon Beveridge
Specifications: See page 289
Finish: (A) Proof, frosted relief against a parallel lined background
          (B) Brilliant Uncirculated, brilliant relief on a brilliant background
Cases of Issue:
          (A) Black leatherette case, maroon insert, encapsulated coin, COA
          (B) Clear plastic outer case, black plastic insert, silver sleeve

Date	Descrip.	Issue Price	Mintage	Finish	65	66	67	68
1989	Mackenzie	21.75	272,319	PR	–	–	30.	–
1989	Mackenzie	16.25	110,650	MS	20.	–	–	–

HENRY KELSEY TRICENTENNIAL SILVER DOLLAR 1990. The 300th anniversary of Henry Kelsey's ventures into the Canadian West is commemorated on the 1990 silver dollar.

Designers: Obv.: Dora de Pédery-Hunt   **Engravers:** Obv.: Dora de Pédery-Hunt
            Rev.: D. J. Craig   Rev.: Ago Aarand
Specifications: See page 289
Finish: (A) Proof, frosted relief against a parallel lined background
          (B) Brilliant Uncirculated, brilliant relief on a brilliant background
Cases of Issue:
          (A) Black leatherette case, maroon insert, encapsulated coin, COA
          (B) Clear plastic outer case, black plastic insert, silver sleeve

Date	Descrip.	Issue Price	Mintage	Finish	65	66	67	68
1990	Henry Kelsey	22.95	222,983	PR	–	–	32.	–
1990	Henry Kelsey	16.75	85,763	MS	14.	–	–	–

FRONTENAC SILVER DOLLAR 1991. This coin commemorates the 175th anniversary of the first steamship to sail on the Great Lakes. Built by a partnership of Kingston merchants in 1815, the Frontenac established a regular passenger and freight route between Prescott and Burlington by 1817, thus becoming the first Canadian built steamship to operate on Lake Ontario.

Designers: Obv.: Dora de Pédery-Hunt   **Engravers:** Obv.: Dora de Pédery-Hunt
           Rev.: D. J. Craig   Rev.: Sheldon Beveridge
Specifications: See page 289
Finish: (A) Proof, frosted relief against a parallel lined background
        (B) Brilliant Uncirculated, brilliant relief on a brilliant background
Cases of Issue:
        (A) Black leatherette case, maroon insert, encapsulated coin, COA
.   (B) Clear plastic outer case, black plastic insert, silver sleeve

Date	Descrip.	Issue Price	Mintage	Finish	GRADE 65	66	67	68
1991	Frontenac	22.95	222,892	PR	–	–	45.	–
1991	Frontenac	16.75	82,642	MS	13.	–	–	–

125TH ANNIVERSARY OF CANADA NICKEL/BRONZE DOLLAR 1992. This coin is part of the "125" coin program by the numismatic department of the Mint. This proof coin is the companion piece to the circulating issue of the same design. For more information on this coin see page 174.

Designers: Obv.: Dora de Pédery-Hunt   **Engravers:** Obv.: Dora de Pédery-Hunt
           Rev.: Rita Swanson   Rev.: Ago Aarand
Specifications: See page 289   **Finish:** Proof
Case of Issue: Royal blue flocked case, blue insert, encapsulated coin.

Date	Description	Issue Price	Mintage	PROOF (PR) 65	66	67	68
1992	125th Anniv.	19.95	24,227	–	–	12.	–

KINGSTON TO YORK STAGECOACH SILVER DOLLAR 1992. This coin commemorates the 175th anniversary of the first stage coach service between Kingston and York in January 1817. Samuel Purdy was only able to maintain regular service during the winter months, hence the sleigh with runners. This is the first issue of a dollar coin in sterling silver since the pattern dollar was struck in London by the Royal Mint in 1911.

Designers: Obv.: Dora de Pédery-Hunt   **Engravers:** Obv.: Dora de Pédery-Hunt
            Rev.: Karsten Smith   Rev.: Susan Taylor
Specifications: See page 289
Finish: (A) Proof   (B) Brilliant Uncirculated
Cases of Issue:
    (A) Black leatherette case, maroon insert, encapsulated coin, COA
.   (B) Clear plastic outer case, black plastic insert, silver sleeve

Date	Descrip.	Issue Price	Mintage	Finish	65	66	GRADE 67	68
1992	Stagecoach	23.95	187,612	PR	–	–	24.	–
1992	Stagecoach	17.50	78,160	MS	13.	–	–	–

STANLEY CUP SILVER DOLLAR 1893-1993. This coin commemorates the 100th anniversary of the Stanley Cup, first presented during the 1892 - 1893 season to the Montreal Amateur Athletic Association team by Lord Stanley.

Designers: Obv.: Dora de Pédery-Hunt   **Engravers:** Obv.: Dora de Pédery-Hunt
            Rev.: Stewart Sherwood   Rev.: Sheldon Beveridge
Specifications: See page 289
Finish: (A) Proof   (B) Brilliant Uncirculated
Cases of Issue:
    (A) Black leatherette case, maroon insert, encapsulated coin, COA
.   (B) Clear plastic outer case, black plastic insert, silver sleeve

Date	Descrip.	Issue Price	Mintage	Finish	65	66	GRADE 67	68
1993	Stanley Cup	23.95	294,314	PR	–	–	22.	–
1993	Stanley Cup	17.50	88,150	MS	12.	–	–	–

RCMP NORTHERN DOG TEAM PATROL SILVER DOLLAR 1994. This coin commemorates the 25th anniversary of the last RCMP Northern Dog Team Patrol.

Designers: Obv.: Dora de Pédery-Hunt   **Engravers:** Obv.: Dora de Pédery-Hunt
              Rev.: Ian D. Sparkes   Rev.: Ago Aarand
Specifications: See page 289
Finish: (A) Proof, frosted relief against a parallel lined background
        (B) Brilliant Uncirculated, brilliant relief on a brilliant background
Cases of Issue:
        (A) Black leatherette case, maroon insert, encapsulated coin, COA
        (B) Clear plastic outer case, black plastic insert, silver sleeve

Date	Descrip.	Issue Price	Mintage	Finish	GRADE 65	66	67	68
1994	Dog Team	24.50	178,485	PR	–	–	39.	–
1994	Dog Team	17.95	65,295	MS	25.	–	–	–

REMEMBRANCE NICKEL/BRONZE DOLLAR 1994. The war memorial was built to commemorate the participation of all Canadians in the First World War. The memorial was rededicated in 1982 to include veterans of the Second World War and the Korean War. For the circulating issue please see page 175.

Designers: Obv.: Dora de Pédery-Hunt   **Engravers:** Obv.: Dora de Pédery-Hunt
              Rev.: Royal Canadian Mint Staff   Rev.: T. Smith, Ago Aarand
Specifications: See page 289   **Finish:** Proof
Case of Issue: Royal blue flocked case, blue insert, encapsulated coin, COA.

Date	Description	Issue Price	Mintage	PROOF (PR) 65	66	67	68
1994	Remembrance	16.95	54,524	–	–	12.	–

325TH ANNIVERSARY OF THE FOUNDING OF THE HUDSON'S BAY COMPANY SILVER DOLLAR 1995. From 1670 to the current day the history of the Hudson's Bay Company has been intertwined with that of Canada.

Designers: Obv.: Dora de Pédery-Hunt   **Engravers:** Obv.: Dora de Pédery-Hunt
            Rev.: Vincent McIndoe   Rev.: Susan Taylor
Specifications: See page 289
Finish: (A) Proof, frosted relief against a parallel lined background
         (B) Brilliant Uncirculated, brilliant relief on a brilliant background
Cases of Issue:
         (A) Black leatherette case, maroon insert, encapsulated coin, COA
.   (B) Clear plastic outer case, black plastic insert, silver sleeve

Date	Descrip.	Issue Price	Mintage	Finish	65	66	67	68
1995	H.B. Co.	24.50	166,259	PR	–	–	39.	–
1995	H.B. Co.	17.95	61,819	MS	15.	–	–	–

PEACEKEEPING IN CONJUNCTION WITH THE 50TH ANNIVERSARY OF THE UNITED NATIONS NICKEL/BRONZE DOLLAR 1995. This coin commemorates Canada's role in the United Nations peacekeeping forces. For circulating issue see page 175.

Designers: Obv.: Dora de Pédery-Hunt   **Engravers:** Obv.: Dora de Pédery-Hunt
            Rev.: J. K. Harman,   Rev.: Susan Taylor, Ago Aarand
                 R. G. Henriguez
                 C. H. Oberlander
Specifications: See page 289   **Finish:** Proof
Case of Issue: Royal blue flocked display case, blue insert, encapsulated coin, COA

Date	Description	Issue Price	Mintage	65	66	67	68
1995	Peacekeeping	17.95	43,293	–	–	10.	–

200TH ANNIVERSARY OF JOHN MCINTOSH, SILVER DOLLAR 1996. John McIntosh arrived in Canada in 1796 and settled in Ontario. This dollar pays tribute to the originator of Canada's most important commercial apple.

Designers: Obv.: Dora de Pédery-Hunt   **Engravers:** Obv.: Dora de Pédery-Hunt
         Rev.: Roger Hill   Rev.: Sheldon Beveridge
Specifications: See page 289
Finish: (A) Proof, frosted relief against a parallel lined background
       (B) Brilliant Uncirculated, brilliant relief on a brilliant background
Cases of Issue:
       (A) Black leatherette case, maroon insert, encapsulated coin, COA
       (B) Clear plastic outer case, black plastic insert, silver sleeve

Date	Descrip.	Issue Price	Mintage	Finish	GRADE 65	66	67	68
1996	McIntosh	29.95	133,779	PR	–	–	42.50	–
1996	McIntosh	19.95	58,834	MS	21.00	–	–	–

25TH ANNIVERSARY OF THE 1972 CANADA/RUSSIA HOCKEY SERIES, SILVER DOLLAR 1997. Paul Henderson's winning goal won the 1972 series for Canada. In 1997 two gift packages were offered: (1) A sterling silver Pin / uncirculated dollar. (2) A numbered colour reproduction print / uncirculated dollar.

Designers: Obv.: Dora de Pédery-Hunt   **Engravers:** Obv.: Dora de Pédery-Hunt
         Rev.: Walter Burden   Rev.: Stan Witten
Specifications: See page 289
Finish: (A) Proof, frosted relief against a parallel lined background
       (B) Brilliant Uncirculated, brilliant relief on a brilliant background
Cases of Issue:
       (A) Black leatherette case, maroon insert, encapsulated coin, COA
       (B) Clear plastic outer case, black plastic insert, silver sleeve

Date	Descrip.	Issue Price	Mintage	Finish	GRADE 65	66	67	68
1997	Can./Russia	29.95	184,965	PR	–	–	42.50	–
1997	Can./Russia	19.95	155,252	MS	13.00	–	–	–

10TH ANNIVERSARY OF THE ONE DOLLAR LOON 1997. The Flying Loon (nickel-bronze) one dollar coin was issued only in "Oh Canada!" and Specimen Sets of 1997. The sterling silver Flying Loon was issued singly. All were sold by the Numismatic Department of the Royal Canadian Mint as limited editions during 1997.

STERLING SILVER FLYING LOON

NICKEL BRONZE FLYING LOON

Designers: Obv.: Dora de Pédery-Hunt   **Engravers:** Obv.: Dora de Pédery-Hunt
           Rev.: Jean-Luc Grondin   Rev.: Sheldon Beveridge

Specifications: See page 289
Finish: See below
Cases of Issue:
    (A) Sterling silver: Black clam style case with maroon flock interior, encapsulated coin, COA
    (B) Nickel bronze: Single coins are obtained from the 1997 "Oh Canada!" or Specimen Sets: see pages 408 and 418

Date	Descrip.	Issue Price	Mintage	Finish	GRADE 65	66	67	68
1997	Silver	49.95	24,995	PR	–	–	125.	–
1997	Ni.-Br.	N.I.I.	–	SP	–	25.	–	–
1997	Ni.-Br.	N.I.I.	–	MS	25.	–	–	–

Note: N.I.I. = Not issued individually

125TH ANNIVERSARY OF THE ROYAL CANADIAN MOUNTED POLICE, SILVER DOLLAR, 1998.
The design by Adeline Halvorson features a mounted police officer in a 1900s uniform.

Designers: Obv.: Dora de Pédery-Hunt   **Engravers:** Obv.: Dora de Pédery-Hunt
            Rev.: Adeline Halvorson   Rev.: Sheldon Beveridge
Specifications: See page 289
Finish: (A) Proof, frosted relief against a parallel lined background
       (B) Brilliant Uncirculated, brilliant relief on a brilliant background
Cases of Issue:
       (A) Multicoloured sleeve, dark green clam display case, green insert, encapsulated
           coin, COA.
       (B) Multicoloured plastic slide case, encapsulated coin.

Date	Descrip.	Issue Price	Mintage	Finish	65	66	67	68
1998	RCMP	29.95	130,795	PR	–	–	32.50	–
1998	RCMP	19.95	81,376	MS	18.00	–	–	–

225th ANNIVERSARY OF THE VOYAGE OF JUAN PEREZ AND THE SIGHTING OF THE QUEEN CHARLOTTE ISLANDS, SILVER DOLLAR 1999. In 1774 Juan Perez led an expedition which made the first documented sighting of the Queen Charlotte Islands. The reverse of this coin illustrates the 225-ton frigate 'The Santiago,' one of the Queen Charlotte Islands and the Haida canoes approaching the ship.

Designers: Obv.: Dora de Pédery-Hunt   **Engravers:** Obv.: Dora de Pédery-Hunt
            Rev.: D. J. Craig   Rev.: Stanley Witten
Specifications: See page 289
Finish: (A) Proof, frosted relief against a parallel lined background
       (B) Brilliant Uncirculated, brilliant relief on a brilliant background
Cases of Issue:
       (A) Multicoloured sleeve, dark green clam display case, green insert, encapsulated
           coin, COA.
       (B) Multicoloured plastic slide case, encapsulated coin.

Date	Descrip.	Issue Price	Mintage	Finish	65	66	67	68
1999	Perez	29.95	126,435	PR	–	–	37.50	–
1999	Perez	19.95	67,655	MS	14.00	–	–	–

INTERNATIONAL YEAR OF OLDER PERSONS, SILVER DOLLAR, 1999. The United Nations, in October 1999, declared 1999 as the International Year of Older Persons. This coin supports Canada's concept of "A Society for All Ages."

Designers: Obv.: Dora de Pédery-Hunt   Engravers: Obv.: Dora de Pédery-Hunt
    Rev.: S. Armstrong-Hodgson   Rev: William Woodruff
Specifications: See page 289   Finish: Proof
Case of Issue: Multicoloured case, black insert, encapsulated coin, COA.

Date	Description	Issue Price	Mintage	65	66	67	68
					PROOF (PR)		
1999	Older Persons	49.95	24,976	–	–	42.50	–

VOYAGE OF DISCOVERY, SILVER DOLLAR, 2000. Poised on the launch pad to the next millennium, Canada's voyage of discovery promises to be one of energy, ability and achievement.

Designers: Obv.: Dora de Pédery-Hunt   Engravers: Obv.: Dora de Pédery-Hunt
    Rev.: D. F. Warkentine   Rev.: Cosme Saffioti
Specifications: See page 289
Finish: (A) Proof, frosted relief against a parallel lined background
   (B) Brilliant Uncirculated, brilliant relief on a brilliant background
Cases of Issue:
   (A) Multicoloured sleeve, dark green clam display case, green insert, encapsulated
     coin, COA.
   (B) Multicoloured plastic slide case, encapsulated coin.

Date	Descrip.	Issue Price	Mintage	Finish	65	66	67	68
						GRADE		
2000	Discovery	29.95	121,575	PR	–	–	30.00	–
2000	Discovery	19.95	62,975	MS	22.50	–	–	–

50TH ANNIVERSARY OF THE NATIONAL BALLET OF CANADA, SILVER DOLLAR, 2001. The National Ballet of Canada, a company with more than 50 dancers and its own full symphony orchestra, is Canada's premier dance company, which ranks as one of the world's top international companies. Founded in 1951 by English dancer Celia Franca, the classical company is the only Canadian company to present a full range of traditional full evening ballet classics.

Designers: Obv.: Dora de Pédery-Hunt Engravers: Obv.: Scott McKowen
Rev.: Dora de Pédery-Hunt Rev.: Susan Taylor
Specifications: See page 289
Finish: (A) Proof, frosted relief against a parallel lined background
(B) Brilliant Uncirculated, brilliant relief on a brilliant background
Cases of Issue:
(A) Multicoloured sleeve, dark green clam display case, green insert, encapsulated coin, COA.
(B) Multicoloured plastic slide case, encapsulated coin.

Date	Descrip.	Issue Price	Mintage	Finish	65	GRADE 66	67	68
2001	National Ballet	30.95	89,390	PR	–	–	30.	–
2001	National Ballet	20.95	53,668	MS	12.	–	–	–

90TH ANNIVERSARY OF THE STRIKING OF CANADA'S 1911 SILVER DOLLAR 2001. The 1911 Canadian silver dollar is the most valuable Canadian coin. Only three examples exist, two sterling silver trial strikes and one lead strike.

Designers: Obv.: Dora de Pédery-Hunt Engravers: Obv.: Dora de Pédery-Hunt
Rev.: W. H. J. Blakemore Rev.: Cosme Saffioti
Specifications: See page 289 Finish: Proof
Case of Issue: Unknown

Date	Description	Issue Price	Mintage	65	PROOF (PR) 66	67	68
2001	90th Anniv.	49.95	24,996	–	–	75.	–

50TH ANNIVERSARY OF HER MAJESTY QUEEN ELIZABETH II'S ACCESSION TO THE THRONE, SILVER DOLLAR, 2002. For the first time a silver dollar carries a double date (1952-2002) on the obverse.

Designers: Obv.: Dora de Pédery-Hunt   **Engravers:** Obv.: Dora de Pédery-Hunt
                Rev.: Royal Canadian Mint Staff   Rev.: Susan Taylor
Specifications: See page 289
Finish: (A) Proof, frosted relief against a parallel lined background
        (B) Brilliant Uncirculated, brilliant relief on a brilliant background
Cases of Issue:
        (A) Multicoloured sleeve, dark green clam display case, green insert, encapsulated coin, COA.
        (B) Multicoloured plastic slide case, encapsulated coin.

Date	Descrip.	Issue Price	Mintage	Finish	65	66	67	68
							GRADE	
2002	Silver	33.95	29,688	PR	–	–	30.	–
2002	Silver	24.95	65,410	MS	20.	–	–	–
2002	Gold-plated	N.I.I.	65,315	PR	–	–	75.	–

Note: A 24 karat gold plated variety was issued in a special edition proof set: see page 421.

15TH ANNIVERSARY OF THE ONE DOLLAR LOON, 2002. First struck in 1987, the one dollar coin with the image of a solitary Common Loon soon became Canada's most popular coin, affectionately called the "Loonie." This commemorative dollar, depicting a loon family, was issued only in special edition specimen sets for 2002. Single coins are removed from sets. (See page 418).

Designers: Obv.: Dora de Pédery-Hunt   **Engravers:** Obv.: Dora de Pédery-Hunt
                Rev.: Dora de Pédery-Hunt   Rev.: Cosme Saffioti
Specifications: See page 289   **Finish:** Specimen
Case of Issue: See Specimen Sets, page 418

Date	Description	Issue Price	Mintage	65	66	67	68
					SPECIMEN (SP)		
1952-2002	Anniv. Loons	N.I.I.	67,672	–	40.	–	–

CENTRE ICE, LOON, 2002. A "Centre Ice" 22-karat gold-plated loon dollar coin was issued as part of a souvenir album, entitled "Going For Gold," jointly offered by the Mint, Post Office and MacLean's Magazine to commemorate the Olympic gold medals for hockey won by Canadian teams in 2002.

Designers: Obv.: Dora de Pédery-Hunt   **Engravers:** Obv.: Dora de Pédery-Hunt
          Rev.: R. R. Carmichael   Rev.: Cosme Saffioti
Specifications: See page 289, but 22 karat gold plated, with privy mark.
Finish: Proof
Case of Issue: Souvenir Album

Date	Description	Issue Price	Mintage	65	66	67	68
					PROOF (PR)		
2002	Centre Ice	N.I.I.	25,000	–	–	35.	–

QUEEN ELIZABETH THE QUEEN MOTHER, SILVER DOLLAR, 2002. Available only in proof condition this silver dollar honours the life of Queen Elizabeth the Queen Mother.

Designers: Obv.: Dora de Pédery-Hunt   **Engravers:** Obv.: Dora de Pédery-Hunt
          Rev.: RCM Staff   Rev.: Susan Taylor
Specifications: See page 289   **Finish:** Proof
Case of Issue: Not known

Date	Description	Issue Price	Mintage	65	66	67	68
					PROOF (PR)		
2002	Queen Mother	49.95	9,994	–	–	400.	–

100TH ANNIVERSARY OF THE COBALT SILVER DISCOVERY, SILVER DOLLAR, 2003. This coin marks 100 years since Fred LaRose, a blacksmith, threw his hammer at a fox, of course missing the fox, but striking a rock revealing a gleaming vein of silver. This is the first issue of a pure silver (.9999 fine) dollar by the Royal Canadian Mint.

Designers: Obv.: Dora de Pédery-Hunt
           Rev.: John Mardon
Specifications: See page 289
Finish: (A) Proof
Cases of Issue:
    (A) Multicoloured sleeve, dark green clam display case, green insert, encapsulated coin, COA.
    (B) Multicoloured plastic slide case, encapsulated coin.

Engravers: Obv.: Dora de Pédery-Hunt
          Rev.: William Woodruff

    (B) Brilliant Uncirculated

Date	Descrip.	Issue Price	Mintage	Finish	65	66	67	68
							GRADE	
2003	Cobalt	36.95	88,536	PR	–	–	40.	–
2003	Cobalt	28.95	51,130	MS	25.	–	–	–

50TH ANNIVERSARY OF THE CORONATION, ACCESSION TO THE THRONE, OF HER MAJESTY QUEEN ELIZABETH II, GOLD DOLLAR, 2003. Unique gold issue based on the 1952-2002 reverse design of the silver dollar, and the new obverse design for 2003. This coin was sold on eBay, September 25th, 2003, with 100% of the proceeds being donated to charities.

Designers: Obv.: Susanna Blunt
          Rev.: RCM Staff
Composition: .9999 gold
Weight: 25.175 grams
Diameter: 36.07 mm
Case of Issue: Not known

Engravers: Obv.: Susan Taylor
          Rev.: Susan Taylor
Thickness: 2.66 mm
Die Axis: ↑↑
Finish: Proof, frosted relief on mirror background

Date	Description	Issue Price	Mintage	65	66	67	68
					PROOF (PR)		
2003	Coronation	Auction	One		Realized $62,600.		

50TH ANNIVERSARY OF THE CORONATION OF QUEEN ELIZABETH II, SILVER DOLLAR, 1953-2003. This silver dollar is a reissue of the dollar first struck during the coronation year, 1953. The design is differentiated by the double dates 1953-2003 on the obverse, as opposed to the single date on the reverse of the 1953 dollar.

Designers: Obv.: Mary Gillick
         Rev.: Emanuel Hahn
Specifications: See page 289
Case of Issue: See page 421

Engravers: Obv.: Thomas Shingles
        Rev.: Emanuel Hahn
Finish: Proof, Frosted relief on a mirror
      background

Date	Description	Issue Price	Mintage	65	66	67	68
1953– 2003	Double dates	N.I.I.	21,400	–	–	50.	–

50TH ANNIVERSARY OF THE CORONATION OF QUEEN ELIZABETH II, SILVER DOLLAR, 2003. A special edition commemorates 50 years on the throne, with the reverse honouring the "Voyageurs" design of Canada's first circulating silver dollar. A fine gold (.9999) example of this design was struck by the Royal Canadian Mint and sold on eBay with the proceeds going to charities.

Designers: Obv.: Susanna Blunt
         Rev.: Emanuel Hahn
Specifications: Silver, see page 289
      Gold, see page 317
Case of Issue: Silver: Unknown
      Gold: Unknown

Engravers: Obv.: Susan Taylor
        Rev.: Emanuel Hahn
Finish: Proof

Date	Descrip.	Issue Price	Mintage	65	66	67	68
2003	50th/Silver	51.95	29,586	–	–	50.	–
2003	50th/Gold	Auction	One		Realized $55,100. USF		

400TH ANNIVERSARY OF THE FIRST FRENCH SETTLEMENT IN NORTH AMERICA, SILVER DOLLAR, 1604-2004. In 1604 a tiny island, in what was to be called the St. Croix River, became the first French settlement in North America. A 2004 Ile Sainte-Croix coin and stamp set was issued containing this silver dollar counterstamped with a fleur-de-lis privy mark: see page 323. Images shown below are reduced in size.

                        Common Obverse   Privy Mark Reverse

Designers: Obv.: Susanna Blunt   **Engravers:** Obv.: Susan Taylor
           Rev.: R.R. Carmichael   Rev.: Stan Witten
Specifications: For .9999 silver, see page 289
Finish: See below
Case of Issue:
    (A) Multicoloured sleeve, dark green clam display case, green insert, encapsulated coin, COA.
    (B) Multicoloured plastic slide case, encapsulated coin.
    (C) Privy Mark Dollar: See derivatives

Date	Descrip.	Issue Price	Mintage	Finish	65	66	67	68
2004	Settlement	36.95	81,355	PR	–	–	32.50	–
2004	Settlement	28.95	41,934	MS	25.00	–	–	–
2004	Settlement / privy mark	N.I.I.	8,315	MS	100.00	–	–	–

CANADA GOOSE, BRONZE DOLLAR, 2004. This bronze dollar was issued only in the 2004 specimen set as a tribute to Jack Miner, one of the world's most influential conservationists. Miner founded a bird sanctuary near Kingsville, Ontario, in 1904. Not issued individually, single coins have been removed from sets.

Designers: Obv.: Susanna Blunt   **Engravers:** Obv.: Susan Taylor
           Rev.: Susan Taylor   Rev.: Susan Taylor
Specifications: See page 289
Finish: Specimen
Case of Issue: See Specimen Sets, page 418

Date	Description	Issue Price	Mintage	65	66	67	68
2004	Canada Goose	N.I.I.	–	–	40.00	–	–

ELUSIVE LOON, 2004. This dollar coin was issued only as part of the Elusive Loon "$1 Limited Edition Stamp and Coin Set", a joint venture between the Royal Canadian Mint and Canada Post. The Elusive Loon coin, which carries a maple leaf privy mark, was issued in a wooden presentation case along with mint and cancelled $1.00 Loon stamps. Not issued individually, single coins have been removed from sets.

Designers: Obv.: Susanna Blunt
          Rev.: N/A
Specifications: See page 289
Case of Issue: See One Dollar Derivatives, page 323

Engravers: Obv.: Susan Taylor
          Rev.: Christie Paquet
Finish: Proof

		Issue		PROOF (PR)			
Date	Description	Price	Mintage	65	66	67	68
2004	Elusive Loon	N.I.I.	25,105	–	–	30.	–

"LUCKY LOON" SPECIAL COLLECTOR'S EDITION, SILVER DOLLAR, 2004. This silver dollar celebrates Canada's olympic athletes, underscoring their commitment to excellence. For the circulating "Lucky Loonie" one dollar coin see page 177.

Designers: Obv.: Susanna Blunt
          Rev.: R. R. Carmichael, RCM Staff
Specifications: See page 289
Finish: Proof
Cases of Issue: Not known

Engravers: Obv.: Susan Taylor
          Rev.: Terry Smith, Susan Taylor

		Issue			PROOF (PR)			
Date	Descrip.	Price	Mintage	Finish	65	66	67	68
2004	Silver	39.95	19,941	PR	–	–	60.	–

"THE POPPY" SPECIAL COLLECTOR'S EDITION, SILVER DOLLAR, 2004. Throughout the world the poppy has become one of the most powerful symbols that honours the men and women who gave their lives for freedom. For the circulating "Poppy" twenty-cents coin see page 135.

Designers: Obv.: Susanna Blunt   Engravers: Obv.: Susan Taylor
          Rev.: Cosme Saffioti   Rev.: Cosme Saffioti
Specifications: See page 289   **Finish:** Proof
Case of Issue: Red leatherette clam style case, black flocked insert, encapsulated coin, COA

Date	Description	Issue Price	Mintage	PROOF (PR) 65	66	67	68
2004	Poppy	49.95	24,527	–	–	50.	–

40TH ANNIVERSARY OF CANADA'S NATIONAL FLAG, SILVER DOLLAR, 2005. The Canadian flag, which is composed of the symbolic maple leaf and the national colours first proclaimed in 1921, was raised the the first time February 15th, 1965, on Parliament Hill. The 2005 brilliant uncirculated silver dollar was also issued in a gift set which included an interactive CD-Rom.

Designers: Obv.: Susanna Blunt   Engravers: Obv.: Susan Taylor
          Rev.: William Woodruff   Rev.: William Woodruff
Specifications: See page 289
Finish: 1. Proof   2. Proof, selectively gold plated   3. Brilliant Uncirculated
Cases of Issue: Proof and Brilliant Uncirculated: Red plastic slide case, black plastic insert, encapsulated coin, COA

Date	Descrip.	Issue Price	Mintage	Finish	GRADE 65	66	67	68
2004	Silver	34.95	N/A	PR	–	–	35.	–
2004	Gold plated	N.I.I.	–	PR	–	–	75.	–
2004	Silver	24.95	N/A	MS	25.	–	–	–

Note: The Anniversary of Canada's National Flag proof silver dollar which is contained in the 2005 proof set is a variety with selective gold plating {see page 421}.

TUFTED PUFFIN, NICKEL BRONZE, 2005. Issued only in the 2005 specimen set, the limited edition one dollar coin features one of British Columbia's most captivating sea birds. Coins sold singly have been removed from specimen sets. (See page 418).

Designers: Obv.: Susanna Blunt   Engravers: Obv.: Susan Taylor
           Rev.: N/A   Rev.: Christie Paquet
Specifications: See page 289   Finish: Specimen
Case of Issue: See Specimen Sets, page 418.

Date	Description	Issue Price	Mintage	SPECIMEN (SP) 65	66	67	68
2005	Tufted Puffin	N.I.I.	40,000	–	35.	–	–

ONE DOLLAR DERIVATIVES

Date	Description	Condition	Issue Price / Issuer	Mintage	Price
1997	HOCKEY, SILVER DOLLAR Two 45¢ mint stamps, $5 phone card, Multicoloured folder	MS-65	$29.95 / RCM, CP	N/A	20.
1997	HOCKEY, SILVER DOLLAR with pin	MS-65	29.95 / RCM	N/A	15.
1997	HOCKEY, SILVER DOLLAR with print	MS-65	24.95 / RCM	N/A	15.
1997	HOCKEY, SILVER DOLLAR with phone card and stamp set	MS-65	N/A / RCM	N/A	15.
1998	LOON DOLLAR, Mint and cancelled one dollar stamps, Blue presentation case	MS-65	17.99 / RCM, CP	N/A	10.
1998	ONE DOLLAR 125th Anniv. R.C.M.P. with pin	MS-65	29.95 / RCM	N/A	20.
1999	SILVER DOLLAR, 25th Anniv. Juan Perez, Journal Gift Set Multicoloured folder	MS-65	N/A / RCM, CP	N/A	15.
2000	LOON DOLLAR Mint and cancelled one dollar stamps, Blue presentation case	MS-65	17.99 / RCM, CP	N/A	10.
2000	LOON DOLLAR Encapsulated in a credit card	MS-65	N/A / RCM	N/A	5.
2001	LOON DOLLAR encapsulated in credit card	MS-65	N/A / RCM	N/A	10.
2001	LOON / SACAGAWEA DOLLARS, Folder	MS-65	N/A / RCM, USM	N/A	10.
2004	FRENCH SETTLEMENT 2004 Silver Dollar with privy mark, 2004 silver ¼ Euro, Canada 49¢ stamps, mint/cancelled France .90 Euro stamps, mint/cancelled wooden box, blue insert, encapsulated coins, COA	MS-65	99.95/ RCM, CP	8,315	125.
2004	ELUSIVE LOON Coin and stamp set, Wooden presentation case	PR-67	25.22/ RCM, CP	25,105	40.
2005	SILVER DOLLAR 40th Anniversary of Canadian Flag, selective gold plating, CD-Rom, Card folder	MS-65	34.95 / RCM	N/A	35.

Note: CP = Canada Post; RCM = Royal Canadian Mint; USM = United States Mint

TWO DOLLARS

The two dollar coin was issued in 1996 by the Numismatic Department of the Royal Canadian Mint to commemorate the introduction of the coin which replaced the two dollar bank note. Four different compositions were used to produce the numismatic two dollar coins of 1996.

SPECIFICATIONS OF THE TWO DOLLAR BIMETALLIC NUMISMATIC ISSUES

In order to identify the compositions of the two dollar coins, liberty has been taken with the bimetallic term for category D which is an alloy/alloy composition.

A. BIMETALLIC, NICKEL RING – ALUMINUM BRONZE CORE. This composition will be found in brilliant uncirculated, specimen and proof coinage.

Composition:
    Ring: .990 Ni
    Core: .092 Cu, .060 Al, .020 Ni
Weight: 7.3 g
    Ring: 5.09 g
    Core: 2.39 g
Edge: Interrupted Serration

Diameter:
    Ring: 28 mm
    Core: 16.8 mm
Thickness: 1.80 mm

Die Axis: ↑↑

B. BIMETALLIC, NICKEL RING – ALUMINUM BRONZE, GOLD PLATED CORE.
Specifications: As for "A", except the core (aluminum bronze) is 24kt gold plated.

C. BIMETALLIC, STERLING SILVER RING – GOLD-PLATED STERLING SILVER CORE.

Composition:
    Ring: 92.5 Ag, 7.5 Cu
    Core: 7.5 Cu, 92.5 Ag, 24kt Au-pltd
Weight:
Normal: 8.83 g
    Ring: 5.86 g
    Core: 2.97 g
Piedfort: 17.66 gms
    Ring: 11.72 g
    Core: 5.94 g

Diameter:
    Ring: 28.07 mm
    Core: 16.8 mm
Thickness:
    Standard: 1.8 mm
    Piedfort: 3.6 mm
Edge: Interrupted Serration
Die Axis: ↑↑

D. BIMETALLIC, GOLD RING, GOLD CORE. The two dollar gold coin was issued only in proof finish. The obverse core of the 1996, 1999 and 2000 coins carry the 22kt designation and the Royal Canadian Mint mark.

Composition:
    Ring: .172 Au, .776 Ag,
        .052 Cu (4.1 kt)
    Core: .917 Au, .041 Ag,
        .042 Cu (22kt)
Weight: 11.4 g
    Ring: 6.314 g
    Core: 5.09 g

Diameter:
    Ring: 28.0 mm
    Core: 16.80 mm
Thickness: 1.80 mm
Edge: Interrupted Serration
Die Axis: ↑↑

POLAR BEAR TWO DOLLAR COIN, 1996. The 1996 two dollar Piedfort was not issued singly; it was issued as part of a set. See the Two Dollar Derivatives, page 330.

Obverse: Gold - Gold

Designers:	Obv.: Dora de Pédery-Hunt	Engravers:	Rev.: Dora de Pédery-Hunt
	Rev.: Brent Townsend		Rev.: Ago Aarand

Specifications:	Finish:	Cases of Issue:
Bronze; Page 324-A	Specimen	Presentation folder
Bronze, gilt; Page 324-C	Proof	Black leatherette case, blue inside, encapsulated coin, COA multicoloured sleeve
Silver. gilt; Page 324-C	Proof	Black suede case, blue flock inside, encapsulated coin
Silver, gilt; Piedfort; Page 324-C	Proof	See Sets, page 330
Gold; Page 324-D	Proof	Blue ultrasuede case, blue inside, encapsulated coin

		Issue					GRADE	
Date	Descrip.	Price	Mintage	Finish	65	66	67	68
1996	Bronze	10.95	74,669	SP	–	9.	–	–
1996	Bronze, gilt	24.95	66,843	PR	–	–	20.	–
1996	Silver	N/A	N/A	PR	–	–	25.	–
1996	Silver, Piedfort	N.I.I.	11,526	PR	–	–	100.	–
1996	Gold	299.95	5,000	PR	–	–	300.	–

Note: The 1996 Two Dollar Polar Bear coin sold singly in the presentation folder was offered as "brilliant uncirculated"; however, it is actually a specimen finish.

NUNAVUT TWO DOLLAR PROOF COMMEMORATIVE, 1999. This coin commemorates the formation of Nunavut, Canada's third territory, in 1999.

Obverse: Gold - Gold

Designers: Obv.: Dora de Pédery-Hunt   **Engravers:** Obv.: Dora de Pédery-Hunt
Rev.: G. Arnaktauyok   Rev.: Ago Aarand, José Osio

VARIETIES OF 1999. The ring varieties of the Nunavut reverse design appear to be a function of the alloy and its flow characteristics. Three different reverse dies are used on three finishes of two dollar coins.

Narrow Ring
Brilliant Uncirculated
Issue

Wide Ring
Specimen Issue

No Ring
Proof Issue

1999 NUNAVUT MULE. The brilliant uncirculated $2 Nunavut mule is found only in brilliant uncirculated sets.

Nickel-aluminum bronze, narrow ring obverse

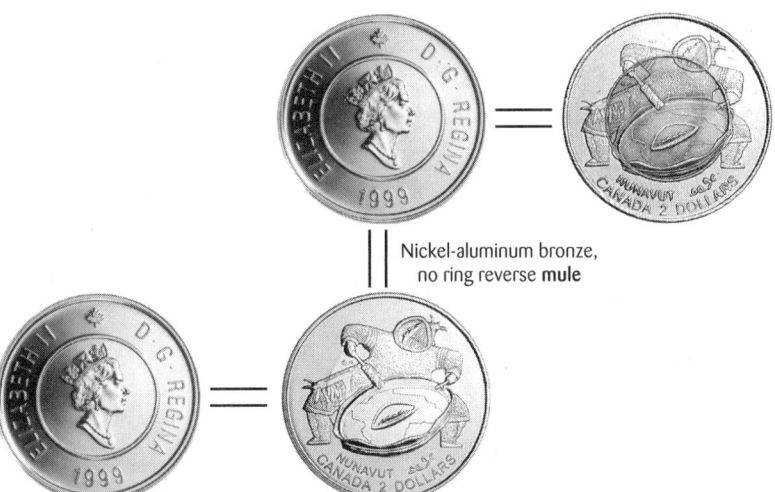

Nickel-aluminum bronze, no ring reverse **mule**

Sterling silver, goldplated sterling, no ring reverse

Specifications	Finish	Case of Issue
Bronze; Page 324-A	Uncirculated	Presentation folder
Bronze; Page 324-A	Specimen	Maple wood case, encapsulated coin multicoloured sleeve
Silver; Page 324-C	Proof	Green leatherette oval clam style case, black insert, encapsulated coin, COA, white box within a black shipping box
Gold; Page 324-D	Proof	Antique oval clam style case with black suede

Date	Descrip.	Issue Price	Mintage	Finish	GRADE 65	66	67	68
1999	Bronze	N/A	N/A	MS	10.	–	–	–
1999	Bronze	N/A	20,000	SP	–	15.	–	–
1999	Silver	24.95	39,873	PR	–	–	25.	–
1999	Gold	299.95	4,298	PR	–	–	200.	–
1999	Mule	N.I.I.	Unknown	MS	200.	–	–	–

POLAR BEARS TWO DOLLAR COMMEMORATIVE 2000. This coin commemorates the Path of Knowledge reflected in experience, wisdom and knowledge that is passed down from generation to generation.

Obverse: Gold - Gold

Designers: Obv.: Dora de Pédery-Hunt
           Rev.: Tony Bianco

Engravers: Obv.: Dora de Pédery-Hunt
           Rev.: Cosme Saffioti

Specifications	Finish	Case of Issue
Bronze; Page 324-A	Specimen	Maple wood case, encapsulated coin
Silver; Page 324-C	Proof	Green leatherette oval clam style case, black insert, encapsulated coin, COA, white box within a blackshipping box
Gold; Page 324-D	Proof	Antique oval clam style case with black suede

Date	Descrip.	Issue Price	Mintage	Finish	GRADE 65	66	67	68
2000	Bronze	N/A	1,500	SP	–	15.	–	–
2000	Silver, Gilt	24.95	39,768	PR	–	–	20.	–
2000	Gold	299.95	5,881	PR	–	–	200.	–

POLAR BEAR, 2000-2001.

Designers: Obv.: Dora de Pédery-Hunt
           Rev.: Brent Townsend

Engravers: Obv.: Dora de Pédery-Hunt
           Rev.: Ago Aarand

Specifications: Bronze; See page 324-A
Finish: Specimen
Case of Issue: Maple wood case, encapsulated coin

Date	Descrip.	Issue Price	Mintage	SPECIMEN (SP) 65	66	67	68
2000	Bronze	N/A	20,000	–	50.	–	–
2001	Bronze	N/A	20,000	–	50.	–	–

Note: Mintages are estimated

PROUD POLAR BEAR, 2004. Issued jointly by the Royal Canadian Mint and Canada Post, the $2 Proud Polar Bear Stamp and Coin Set contains the first single metal two dollar Canadian coin. The set comprises mint and cancelled $2.00 stamps, along with the $2.00 sterling silver coin. The two dollar coin is unusual in that it carries two privy marks.

| Designer: | Obv.: Susanna Blunt | Engraver: | Obv.: Susan Taylor |
| | Rev.: N/A | | Rev.: Stan Witten |

Composition: .925 silver, .075 copper **Thickness:** 1.7 mm
Weight: 8.8 grams **Die Axis:** ↑↑
Diameter: 27.95 mm **Finish:** Proof
Case of Issue: See Two Dollar Derivatives, page 330

Date	Description	Issue Price	Mintage	65	PROOF (PR) 66	67	68
2004	Polar Bear	N.I.I.	25,208	–	–	40.	–

TWO DOLLAR DERIVATIVES

The following single coins, coin and note sets, or coin and stamp sets are based on the numismatic two dollar coin.

Date	Description	Condition	Issue Price / Issuer	Mintage	Price
1996	**TWO DOLLAR COIN** and Bank note Presentation folder	SP-66	29.95 / RCM	91,427	10.
1996	**TWO DOLLAR COIN** Replacement note Presentation folder	PR-67	79.95 / RCM	27,103	25.
1996	**TWO DOLLAR PIEDFORT COIN** Pair of uncut replacement notes Blue leatherette display case	PR-67	179.95 / RCM	11,526	90.
1996	**TWO DOLLAR COIN** Bank note 45¢ mint stamp Presentation case	MS-65	N/A / RCM, CP	N/A	10.
1998W	**TWO DOLLAR COIN** Mint and cancelled $2 stamps Blue presentation case	MS-65	N/A / RCM, CP	N/A	10.
1999	**TWO DOLLAR NUNAVUT COIN** Mint and cancelled 46¢ stamps Blue presentation case	MS-65	17.95 / RCM, CP	N/A	10.
2000W	**TWO DOLLAR COIN** Mint and cancelled $2 stamps Blue presentation case	MS-65	19.99 / RCM, CP	N/A	20.
2000	**TWO DOLLAR COIN THREE BEARS** in credit card-like holder	MS-65	N/A / RCM	N/A	15.
2001	**TWO DOLLAR COIN** in credit card-like holder	MS-65	N/A / RCM	N/A	8.
2004	**TWO DOLLAR SILVER COIN** and stamp set, Wooden presentation case	PR-67	29.22 / RCM, CP	25,208	40.

Note: "W" is the mint mark for coins struck at the Winnipeg Mint.

NUMISMATIC FIVE DOLLARS

NORMAN BETHUNE FIVE DOLLAR COIN, 1998. In 1998 the Royal Canadian Mint produced a $5 silver coin to commemorate the 60th anniversary of Dr. Norman Bethune's arrival in China. The coin was issued as part of a two coin set, in conjunction with China Gold Coin Incorporation (CGCI).

Designers:	Obv.: Dora de Pédery-Hunt	Engravers:	Obv.: Dora de Pédery-Hunt
	Rev.: Harry Chan		Rev.: Ago Aarand, Stan Witten

Mint	Composition	Weight (g)	Diameter	Edge	Thickness
CGCI	.9999 silver	31.10	40.0	Reeded	3.2 mm
RCM	.9999 silver	31.39	38.0	Reeded	3.3 mm

Finish: Proof
Case of Issue: Brown plastic two-hole red insert, encapsulated coin, COA, box cover in Chinese brocade

Date	Description	Issue Price	Mintage	65	PROOF (PR) 66	67	68
1998	Bethune - CGCI	–	–	–	–	20.	–
1998	Bethune - RCM	–	–	–	–	20.	–
1998	2 coin set	98.00	65,831	–	–	35.	–

THE VIKING SETTLEMENT FIVE DOLLAR COIN, 1999. This coin commemorates the Vikings landing at L'Anse-aux-Meadows, Newfoundland, circa 1000 A.D. Norway issued a 20 Kroner coin in 1999 also commemorating the same Viking Landing. These two coins were offered as a set.

Designers:	Obv.: Dora de Pédery-Hunt	Engravers:	Obv.: Dora de Pédery-Hunt
	Rev.: Donald Curley		Rev.: Stan Witten

Composition: .810 Copper
.090 Nickel
.100 Zinc

Thickness: 2.5 mm
Weight: 9.9 grams
Diameter: 27.0 mm

Edge: Plain
Finish: Proof
Case of Issue: Oval imitation resin stone case, two-holes; brown insert, encapsulated coins, printed cardboard outer sleeve.

Date	Description	Issue Price	Mintage	PROOF (PR) 65	66	67	68
1999	Canada $5	–	–	–	–	17.50	–
1999	Norway 20KR	–	–	–	–	17.50	–
1999	Set of 2 coins	N/A	28,450	–	–	30.00	–

100TH ANNIVERSARY OF THE FIRST WIRELESS TRANSMISSION FIVE DOLLAR COIN, 1901-2001. On December 12th, 1901, Gugliemo Marconi (1874-1937) successfully transmitted the first wireless message across the Atlantic from Poldhu in Cornwall, England, to Signal Hill in St. John's, Newfoundland. To commemorate this anniversary the Royal Canadian Mint, in conjunction with the Royal Mint, issued this two-coin set.

	CANADA $5	**BRITISH £2**
Designers:	Obv.: Dora de Pédery-Hunt	Ian Rank-Bradley
	Rev.: Cosme Saffioti	Robert Evans
Engravers:		
	Obv.: Dora de Pédery-Hunt	Royal Mint Staff
	Rev.: Cosme Saffioti	Robert Evans

Composition:

	CANADA $5	BRITISH £2
	Coin: .925 silver, .075 copper	Coin: .925 silver, .075 copper
	Cameo: 24-karat gold plate	Outer circle: Plated 22kt gold
		Inner disc: .925 silver, .075 copper
Weight:	16.96 grams	24.0 grams
Diameter:	28.40 mm	28.40 mm
Thickness:	N/A	N/A
Edge:	Serrated	Lettering
Die Axis:	↑↑	↑↓
Finish:	Proof (frosted relief, brilliant background)	Reverse proof (brilliant relief, frosted background)

Case of Issue: Brown resin oval case with a Marconi stamp on upper lid, brown flock insert, encapsulated coin, COA, brown printed cardboard box.

Date	Description	Issue Price	Mintage	PROOF (PR) 65	66	67	68
2001	Canada $5	–	–	–	–	25.	–
2001	U.K. £2	–	–	–	–	25.	–
2001	Set of 2 coins	99.95	15,011	–	–	50.	–

2006 F.I.F.A. WORLD CUP, FIVE DOLLAR COIN, 2003. The Canadian Soccer Association, founded in 1912, has been affiliated with the Federation International de Football Association since 1913. The next World Cup championship is to be held in Germany in 2006.

Designers: Obv.: Susanna Blunt
            Rev.: Utszula Walerzak
Composition: .9999 silver
Weight: 31.3 grams
Diameter: 38.1 mm
Finish: Proof

Engravers: Obv.: Susan Taylor
            Rev.: José Osio
Thickness: 3.1 mm
Die Axis: ↑↑
Edge: Serrated

Case of Issue: Black case, black flock interior, encapsulated coin, COA, multicoloured sleeve

Date	Description	Issue Price	Mintage	65	66	67	68
					PROOF (PR)		
2003	Soccer	39.95	19,519	–	–	40.	–

THE MAJESTIC MOOSE FIVE DOLLAR COIN, 2004. This five dollar stamp and coin set, issued jointly by the Royal Canadian Mint and Canada Post, pays homage to Canada's diverse wildlife. This is the first in the series, and comes with two $5 stamps, one mint and the other cancelled.

Designers: Obv.: Susanna Blunt
            Rev.: David Preston-Smith
Specifications: See 2003 issue
Finish: Proof

Engravers: Obv.: Susan Taylor
            Rev.: Stan Witten

Case of Issue: See Five Dollar Derivatives, page 336

Date	Description	Issue Price	Mintage	65	66	67	68
					PROOF (PR)		
2004	Majestic Moose	N.I.I.	25,553	–	–	150.	–

Note: N.I.I. denotes Not issued individually.

100TH ANNIVERSARY CANADIAN OPEN CHAMPIONSHIP, 2004. Issued jointly by the Royal Canadian Mint and Canada Post to celebrate the 100th anniversary of the tournament, this limited edition framed set contains both a five dollar and ten cent coin, which were not issued singly.

Designers: Obv.: Susanna Blunt   **Engravers:** Obv.: Susan Taylor
Rev.: Cosme Saffioti   Rev.: Cosme Saffioti
Specifications: See 2003 issue   **Finish:** Proof
Case of Issue: See Five Dollar Derivatives page 336

Date	Description	Issue Price	Mintage	65	PROOF (PR) 66	67	68
2004	Golfer	N.I.I.	15,623	–	–	25.	–

60TH ANNIVERSARY OF THE END OF THE SECOND WORLD WAR, 2005. In the six years of conflict Canada had enlisted more than one million men and women in His Majesty's Armed Forces. Of these, more than 45,000 gave their lives in the cause of peace.

Royal Canadian Mint Reverse   British Royal Mint Reverse

Designers: Obv.: Susanna Blunt   **Engravers:** Obv.: Susan Taylor
Rev.: Peter Mossman   Rev.: Christie Paquet
Specifications: See 2003 issue
Finish: Specimen, Brilliant relief against a parallel lined background
Case of Issue: Red plastic display case, black plastic insert, encapsulated coin, COA

Date	Description	Issue Price	Mintage	65	SPECIMEN (SP) 66	67	68
2005	60th Anniv.	39.95.	25,000	–	40.	–	–
2005	60th Anniv./ With Privy Mark Maple Leaf	N.I.I.	10,000	–	100.	–	–

FIVE DOLLAR DERIVATIVES

Date	Description	Condition	Issue Price / Issuer	Mintage	Price
2004	**FIVE DOLLAR COIN,** Majestic Moose Two postage stamps, Wooden presentation case	PR-67	39.95 / RCM, CP	25,553	40.
2004	**FIVE DOLLAR COIN,** Canadian Open Chmpshp Framed limited edition along with a 10 cent coin, medallion, two mint stamps	PR-67	49.99 / RCM, CP	15,623	50.
2005	**ALLIED FORCES SILVER PROOF SET,** six coins Australia, Canada, Russia U.S.A. and U.K.	PR-67	£245. / RCM, BRM	10,000.	500.

FIVE AND TEN DOLLARS

MONTREAL SUMMER OLYMPICS, SILVER ISSUES, 1973-1976. In 1976, Montreal, Quebec, hosted the XXI Olympiad. To commemorate and help finance Canada's first Olympics, the federal government agreed to produce a series of twenty-eight silver and two gold coins (see section following for the $100 gold coins). There are seven series of silver coins. Each series has two $5 and two $10 coins, making a total of fourteen coins of each denomination. Each series depicts different Olympic themes on the reverse and has a common design (except for the date) on the obverse. The date on the coins is usually the year of minting. Orders for the Olympic coins were accepted up to the end of December 1976, so a small unit continued to function into 1977 on the Olympic Coin Program. Mintage by series was never recorded, but the annual reports of the Royal Canadian Mint give the following figures by year: 1973 - 537,898 $10, 543,098 $5; 1974 - 3,949,878 $10, 3,981,140 $5; 1975 - 4,952,433 $10, 3,970,000 $5; 1976 - 3,970,514 $10, 3,775,259 $5. These figures do not necessarily coincide with the actual post office sales figures for the coins.

The Olympic coins were offered to the collector in two finishes, brilliant uncirculated and proof. The uncirculated issues were packaged and offered for sale in four different formats: (1) encapsulated (single coins only in styrene crystal capsules); (2) one-coin "standard" case (single coins in black case with red interior); (3) four-coin "custom" set (two $5 and two $10 coins by series in black case with gold trim and red insert); and (4) four-coin "prestige" set (two $5 and two $10 coins by series in matte black leatherette case with blue insert).

The proof coins were only offered in sets, and the "deluxe" case of issue was made of Canadian white birch with a specially tanned steer hide cover with a black insert.

Because of the fluctuating price of silver during the years of the program (1973 to 1976), the original issue prices varied somewhat from series to series.

SERIES I TO VII

The following information is common to all twenty-eight $5.00 and $10.00 silver coins. Naturally, the date changes with the year of issue.

$5 Obverse
Designer: Arnold Machin
Engraver: Patrick Brindley

$10 Obverse
Designer: Arnold Machin
Engraver: Patrick Brindley

SPECIFICATIONS

FIVE DOLLARS
Composition: .925 silver, .075 copper
Weight: 24.30 grams; **Edge:** Reeded
Diameter: 38.00 mm; **Die Axis:** ↑↑
Thickness: 2.35 mm
Finish: Proof and Uncirculated
Case of Issues: See page above

TEN DOLLARS
Composition: .925 silver, .075 copper
Weight: 48.60 grams; **Edge:** Reeded
Diameter: 45.00 mm; **Die Axis:** ↑↑
Thickness: 3.15 mm

Original Issue Prices

Package Type	Series I	Series II	Series III-VII
$5 Encapsulated	6.00	7.50	8.00
$10 Encapsulated	12.00	15.00	15.75
Set of 4 Encapsulated	36.00	45.00	47.50
$5 in Standard Case	7.50	9.00	9.00
$10 in Standard Case	14.00	17.00	17.00
Set of 4 in Standard Case	43.00	52.00	52.00
Custom Set	45.00	55.00	55.00
Prestige Set	50.00	60.00	60.00
Deluxe Proof Set	72.50	82.50	82.50

MONTREAL OLYMPICS — SERIES I

Coin No. 1
World Map

Coin No. 2
Map of North America

Coin No. 3
Montreal Skyline

Coin No. 4
Kingston and Sailboats

Theme: Geographic
Official Release Date:
        December 13, 1973. The Series I issuing period began in late 1973 and was
        carried over into 1974.

Designer of Reverse:
Georges Huel, worked by invitation.
Engravers:
1 ($10 Map of the World): design was photochemically etched
2 ($5 Map of North America): design was photochemically etched
3 ($10 Montreal Skyline): Ago Aarand
4 ($5 Kingston and Sailboats): Terrence Smith
Finish: Proof and Brilliant Uncirculated

Date	Description	Issue Price	Mintage	Finish	65	66	67	68
1973	$5 N. America		537,898	MS	7.50	–	–	–
1973	$5 N. America		Included	PR	–	–	7.50	–
1973	$5 Sailboats	See	Included	MS	7.50	–	–	–
1973	$5 Sailboats	Page	Included	PR	–	–	7.50	–
1973	$10 World	338	543,098	MS	15.00	–	–	–
1973	$10 World		Included	PR	–	–	15.00	–
1973	$10 Skyline		Included	MS	15.00	–	–	–
1973	$10 Skyline		Included	PR	–	–	15.00	–

MONTREAL OLYMPICS – 1973-1974 Mule

During the latter half of 1974, a dated obverse die - possibly made in advance for the Series II coins - was paired inadvertently with a Series I reverse die of the Map of the World resulting in the production and release of a Series I-Series II mule dated 1974. The 1973-1974 Mule was found in the 1973 four-coin custom sets, and mostly those with a European release location.

Date	Description	Issue Price	Mintage	BRILLIANT UNCIRCULATED (MS)			
				65	66	67	68
1973-74	$10 1974 Obv. 1973 Map Rev.	N.I.I.	Unknown	350.	–	–	–

Note: Mintage numbers are simply estimates based on the 1974 Royal Canadian Mint report.

MONTREAL OLYMPICS – SERIES II

Coin No. 5
Head of Zeus

Coin No. 6
Athlete with Torch

Coin No. 7
Temple of Zeus

Coin No. 8
Olympic Rings and Wreath

Theme: Olympic Motifs
Official Release Date: September 16, 1974
Designer of Reverse: Anthony Mann, winner of an invitational competition.
Engravers:

    5 ($10 Head of Zeus): Patrick Brindley
    6 ($5 Athlete with Torch): Patrick Brindley
    7 ($10 Temple of Zeus): Walter Ott
    8 ($5 Olympic Rings and Wreath): Walter Ott

Finish: Proof and Brilliant Uncirculated

Date	Description	Issue Price	Mintage	Finish	GRADE 65	66	67	68
1974	$5 Torch		1,990,570	MS	7.50	–	–	–
1974	$5 Torch		Included	PR	–	–	7.50	–
1974	$5 Rings	See	Included	MS	7.50	–	–	–
1974	$5 Rings	Page	Included	PR	–	–	7.50	–
1974	$10 Zeus	338	1,974,939	MS	15.00	–	–	–
1974	$10 Zeus		Included	PR	–	–	15.00	–
1974	$10 Temple		Included	MS	15.00	–	–	–
1974	$10 Temple		Included	PR	–	–	15.00	–

MONTREAL OLYMPICS — SERIES III

Coin No. 9
Lacrosse

Coin No. 10
Canoeing

Coin No. 11
Cycling

Coin No. 12
Rowing

Theme: Early Canadian Sports
Official Release Date: April 16, 1975
Designer of Reverse: Ken Danby, winner of an invitational competition.
Engravers:
9 ($10 Lacrosse): Walter Ott
10 ($5 Canoeing): Patrick Brindley
11 ($10 Cycling): Ago Aarand
12 ($5 Rowing): Terrence Smith
Finish: Proof and Brilliant Uncirculated

Date	Description	Issue Price	Mintage	Finish	65	66	67	68
1974	$5 Canoe		1,990,570	MS	7.50	–	–	–
1974	$5 Canoe		Included	PR	–	–	7.50	–
1974	$5 Rowing	See	Included	MS	7.50	–	–	–
1974	$5 Rowing	Page	Included	PR	–	–	7.50	–
1974	$10 Lacrosse	338	1,974,939	MS	15.00	–	–	–
1974	$10 Lacrosse		Included	PR	–	–	15.00	–
1974	$10 Cycling		Included	MS	15.00	–	–	–
1974	$10 Cycling		Included	PR	–	–	15.00	–

MONTREAL OLYMPICS – SERIES IV

Coin No. 13
Men's Hurdles

Coin No. 14
Marathon

Coin No. 15
Women's Shot Put

Coin No. 16
Women's Javelin

Theme: Olympic Track and Field Sports
Official Release Date: August 12, 1975
Designer of Reverse: Leo Yerxa, winner of an invitational competition.
Engravers:
      13 ($10 Men's Hurdles): Patrick Brindley
      14 ($5 Marathon): Walter Ott
      15 ($10 Women's Shot Put): Patrick Brindley
      16 ($5 Women's Javelin): Walter Ott
Finish: Proof and Brilliant Uncirculated

Date	Description	Issue Price	Mintage	Finish	65	66	67	68
1975	$5 Marathon		1,985,000	MS	7.50	–	–	–
1975	$5 Marathon		Included	PR	–	–	7.50	–
1975	$5 Javelin	See	Included	MS	7.50	–	–	–
1975	$5 Javelin	Page	Included	PR	–	–	7.50	–
1975	$10 Hurdles	338	2,476,217	MS	15.00	–	–	–
1975	$10 Hurdles		Included	PR	–	–	15.00	–
1975	$10 Shot Put		Included	MS	15.00	–	–	–
1975	$10 Shot Put		Included	PR	–	–	15.00	–

MONTREAL OLYMPICS – SERIES V

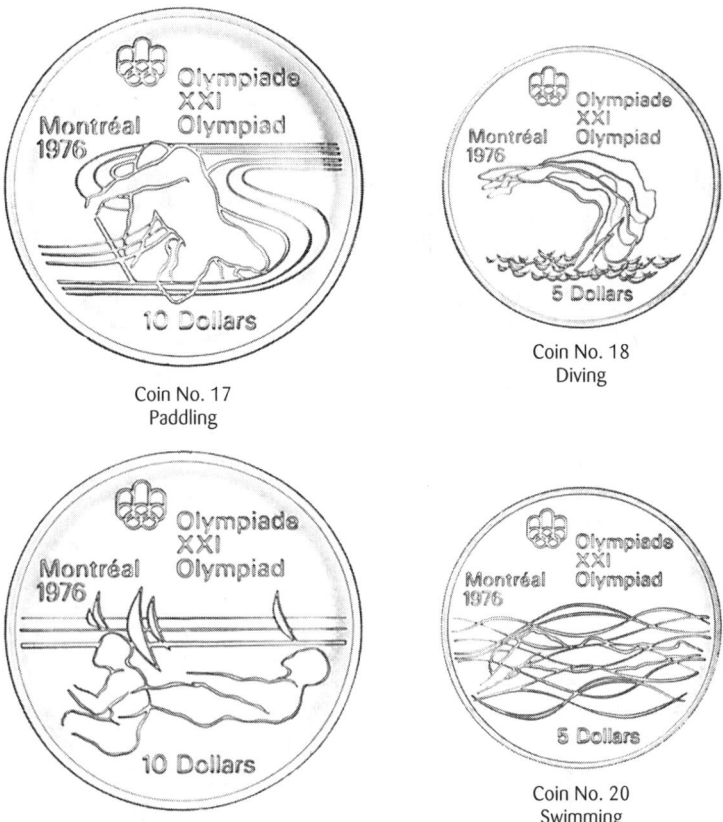

Coin No. 17
Paddling

Coin No. 18
Diving

Coin No. 19
Sailing

Coin No. 20
Swimming

Theme: Olympic Summer Sports
Official Release Date: December 1, 1975
Designer of Reverse: Lynda Cooper, winner of an open national competition.
Engravers:
  17 ($10 Paddling): design was photochemically etched
  18 ($5 Diving): design was photochemically etched
  19 ($10 Sailing): design was photochemically etched
  20 ($5 Swimming): design was photochemically etched
Finish: Proof and Brilliant Uncirculated

Date	Description	Issue Price	Mintage	Finish	65	66	67	68
1975	$5 Diving		1,985,000	MS	7.50	–	–	–
1975	$5 Diving		Included	PR	–	–	7.50	–
1975	$5 Swimming	See	Included	MS	7.50	–	–	–
1975	$5 Swimming	Page	Included	PR	–	–	7.50	–
1975	$10 Paddling	338	2,476,216	MS	15.00	–	–	–
1975	$10 Paddling		Included	PR	–	–	15.00	–
1975	$10 Sailing		Included	MS	15.00	–	–	–
1975	$10 Sailing		Included	PR	–	–	15.00	–

MONTREAL OLYMPICS – SERIES VI

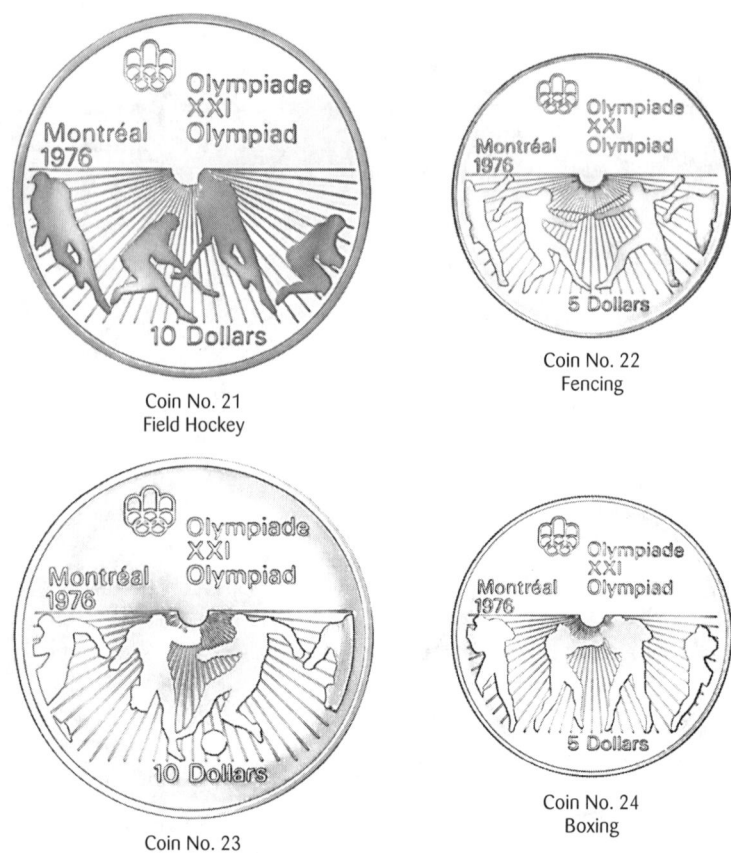

Coin No. 21
Field Hockey

Coin No. 22
Fencing

Coin No. 23
Soccer

Coin No. 24
Boxing

Theme: Olympic Team and Body Contact Sports
Official Release Date: March 1, 1976
Designer of Reverse: Shigeo Fukada, winner of an open international competition.
Engravers:
    21 ($10 Field Hockey): design was photochemically etched
    22 ($5 Fencing): design was photochemically etched
    23 ($10 Soccer): design was photochemically etched
    24 ($5 Boxing): design was photochemically etched
Finish: Proof and Brilliant Uncirculated

Date	Description	Issue Price	Mintage	Finish	65	66	67	68
1976	$5 Fencing		1,887,630	MS	7.50	–	–	–
1976	$5 Fencing		Included	PR	–	–	7.50	–
1976	$5 Boxing	See	Included	MS	7.50	–	–	–
1976	$5 Boxing	Page	Included	PR	–	–	7.50	–
1976	$10 Hockey	338	1,985.257	MS	15.00	–	–	–
1976	$10 Hockey		Included	PR	–	–	15.00	–
1976	$10 Soccer		Included	MS	15.00	–	–	–
1976	$10 Soccer		Included	PR	–	–	15.00	–

SERIES VII

Coin No. 25
Olympic Stadium

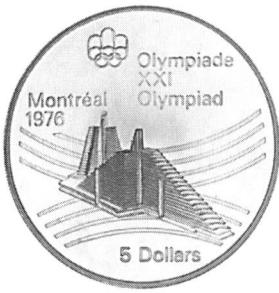

Coin No. 26
Olympic Village

Coin No. 27
Olympic Velodrome

Coin No. 28
Olympic Flame

Theme: Olympic Games Souvenir Designs
Official Release Date: June 1, 1976
Designer of Reverse: Elliott John Morrison, winner of an invitational competition.
Engravers:
    25 ($10 Olympic Stadium): Ago Aarand
    26 ($5 Olympic Village): Sheldon Beveridge
    27 ($10 Olympic Velodrome): Terrence Smith
    28 ($5 Olympic Flame): Walter Ott
Finish: Proof and Brilliant Uncirculated

Date	Description	Issue Price	Mintage	Finish	65	66	67	68
1976	$5 Village		1,887,629	MS	7.50	–	–	–
1976	$5 Village		Included	PR	–	–	7.50	–
1976	$5 Flame	See	Included	MS	7.50	–	–	–
1976	$5 Flame	page	Included	PR	–	–	7.50	–
1976	$10 Stadium	338	1,985,257	MS	15.00	–	–	–
1976	$10 Stadium		Included	PR	–	–	15.00	–
1976	$10 Velodrome		Included	MS	15.00	–	–	–
1976	$10 Velodrome		Included	PR	–	–	15.00	–

EIGHT DOLLARS

GREAT GRIZZLY, 2004.

Designers: Obv.: Susanna Blunt	**Engravers:** Obv.: Susan Taylor
Rev.: N/A	Rev.: Susan Taylor
Composition: .925 silver, .075 copper	**Weight:** 28.8 grams
Diameter: 39.0 mm	**Thickness:** 2.75 mm
Edge: Reeded (serrated)	**Die Axis:** ↑↑
Finish: Proof	

Case of Issue: See Eight Dollar Derivatives, page 348

		Issue			PROOF (PR)		
Date	**Description**	**Price**	**Mintage**	**65**	**66**	**67**	**68**
2004	Great Grizzly	N.I.I.	25,883	–	–	75.	–

120TH ANNIVERSARY OF THE CANADIAN PACIFIC RAILWAY, 2005. A set of two eight dollar coins was ssued in 2005: one honours the Chinese workers in Canada for their enormous contributions; the other commemorates the opening of the Transcontinental Railway in 1885.

RAILWAY BRIDGE

CHINESE MEMORIAL

Designers: Obv.: Susanna Blunt
           Rev.: RCM Staff
Composition: .9999 silver with gold
           plated inner core
Thickness: N/A
Die Axis: ↑↑
Case of Issue: N/A

Engravers: Obv.: Susan Taylor
         Rev.: RCM Staff
Weight: 32.15 grams
Diameter: 40.0 mm
Edge: Reeded (serrated)
Finish: Proof

Date	Description	Issue Price	Mintage	65	66	67	68
						PROOF (PR)	
2004	Railway Bridge	–	–	–	–	65.	–
2005	Chinese Mem.,		–	–	–	65.	–
	Set, 2 coins	120.00	20,000	–	–	120.	–

EIGHT DOLLAR DERIVATIVES

Date	Description	Condition	Issue Price / Issuer	Mintage	Price
2004	**EIGHT DOLLAR GREAT GRIZZLY,** Two postage stamps, Wooden presentation case	PR-67	48.88 RCM, CP	25,883	85.

FIFTEEN DOLLARS

100TH ANNIVERSARY OF THE OLYMPIC MOVEMENT, 1996. The International Olympic Committee initiated a commemorative coin programme to mark the centennial of the modern Olympic movement in 1996. Five mints, Canada, Australia, France, Austria and Greece participated by issuing one gold and two silver coins over a five year period. The total collection comprises five gold and ten silver coins.

The Royal Canadian Mint issued the first three coins in 1992. The silver fifteen dollar coins are listed here, the gold on page 385.

The standard catalogue lists only the coins issued by RCM.

Designers:
  Obv.: Dora de Pédery-Hunt
  Rev.: Coin 1: David Craig
    Coin 2: Stewart Sherwood
Engravers:
  Obv.: Coin 1: Dora de Pédery-Hunt
  Rev.: Coin 1: Sheldon Beveridge
    Coin 2: Terry Smith
Composition: .925 silver, .075 copper
Thickness: 3.1 mm
Weight: 33.63 grams
Edge: Lettering: Citius, Altius, Fortius
Diameter: 40.0 mm
Die Axis: ↑↑
Finish: Proof

Coin No. 1
Speed Skater, Pole Vaulter, Gymnast

Coin No. 2
The Spirit Of the Generations

Case of Issue:
  Single Coin: Burgundy leatherette case
  Set: Wooden display case

Date	Description	Issue Price	Mintage	PROOF (PR) 65	66	67	68
1992	Skater	46.95	105,645	–	–	30.	–
1992	No edge lettering	46.95	Included	–	–	500.	–
1992	Spirit	46.95	Included	–	–	30.	–
1992	No edge lettering	46.95	Included	–	–	500.	

CHINESE LUNAR CALENDAR STERLING SILVER COIN SERIES, 1998-2009. Starting in 1998 with the year of the Tiger, the mint embarked on issuing a twelve year series of Chinese Lunar calendar coins. The twelve sterling silver coins are being issued one per year to commemorate the start of each new year of the twelve year cycle. The coins are available singly or by subscription. The subscription was for a five year period beginning in 1999 and ending in 2003. The five coins, shipped one per year, were offered at a fixed price of $428.28 including a sterling silver medallion housed in a 13-hole presentation box made of embossed red velvet and gold moiré. The single presentation box is a smaller version of the larger one, red and gold moiré.

YEAR OF THE TIGER 1998

YEAR OF THE RABBIT 1999

Designers: Obv.: Dora de Pédery-Hunt
        Rev.: Harvey Chain
Composition: .925 silver, .075 copper
        24-karat gold plated cameo
Weight: 34.00 grams
Diameter: 40.0 mm
Finish: Proof

Engravers: Obv.: Dora de Pédery-Hunt
        Rev.: **1998:** Stan Witten
        1999-2004: José Osio
Thickness: 3.35 mm
Edge: Reeded (serrated)
Die Axis: ↑↑

Case: A. A thirteen-hole embossed red velvet presentation box with gold moiré sides. Included is a sterling silver medallion carrying the twelve signs of the zodiac.
       B. A single-hole embossed red velvet presentation box as above, encapsulated, COA

Date	Description	Issue Price	Mintage	PROOF (PR) 65	66	67	68
1998	Tiger	68.88	68,888	–	–	400.	–
1999	Rabbit	72.88	77,791	–	–	60.	–
1998	13 coin case	–	–	–	–	100.	–

YEAR OF THE DRAGON 2000

YEAR OF THE SNAKE 2001

YEAR OF THE HORSE 2002

Date	Description	Issue Price	Mintage	65	66	PROOF (PR) 67	68
2000	Dragon	72.88	88,634	–	–	150.00	–
2001	Snake	78.88	60,754	–	–	47.50	–
2002	Horse	78.88	59,395	–	–	75.00	–

YEAR OF THE SHEEP 2003

YEAR OF THE MONKEY 2004

YEAR OF THE ROOSTER 2005

Date	Description	Issue Price	Mintage	PROOF (PR) 65	66	67	68
2003	Sheep	78.88	53,714	–	–	75.	–
2004	Monkey	83.88	46,182	–	–	100.	–
2005	Rooster	83.88	N/A	–	–	80.	–

LUNAR FIFTEEN DOLLAR DERIVATIVES

Date	Description	Condition	Issue Price / Issuer	Mintage	Price
1998	Year of the Tiger Fifteen dollar coin Souvenir stamp sheet Presentation album	PR-67	88.88 / RCM, CP	8,000	450.
1999	Year of the Rabbit as 1998	PR-67	88.88 / RCM, CP	8,000	90.
2000	Year of the Dragon as 1998	PR-67	88.88 / RCM, CP	10,000	175.
2000	Year of the Dragon 18kt gold stamp Mint stamp Presentation case	PR-67	N/A / RCM, CP	N/A	300.
2001	Year of the Snake as 1998	PR-67	94.88 / RCM, CP	8,000	95.
2002	Year of the Horse as 1998	PR-67	98.88 / RCM, CP	8,000	100.
2003	Year of the Sheep as 1998	PR-67	98.88 / RCM, CP	8,000	100.
2004	Year of the Monkey as 1998	PR-67	98.88 / RCM, CP	8,000	100.
2005	Year of the Rooster as 1998	PR-67	98.88 / RCM, CP	8,000	100.

TWENTY DOLLAR COINS

CALGARY WINTER OLYMPICS, 1985-1988. In 1988, Calgary, Alberta, hosted the XV Olympic Winter Games. To commemorate the event, and assist in the financing, the Federal Government, through the Royal Canadian Mint, agreed to produce a series of ten sterling silver coins and one gold coin. The silver coins were issued in sets of two $20.00 coins over the period September 1985 through September 1987. Unlike the 1976 Olympic coins, the Calgary Winter Olympic coins were issued in proof quality only.

The date on the coins (obverse) is the year of minting while the reverse carries the date 1988, the year of the games. Mintage was limited to a total of 5,000,000 coins, resulting if minted in equal numbers, in 500,000 complete sets of the ten coins. The first offering of the coins for sale by the Royal Canadian Mint was based on 350,000 complete sets at $370.00 per set. By the fifth series the complete set was being offered at $420.00.

Edge lettering was used for the first time on Canadian silver coins. "XV OLYMPIC WINTER GAMES - JEUX OLYMPIQUES D'HIVER" appeared on all ten silver coins. There are existing varieties that have missed the edge lettering process.

Designer: Arnold Machin
**Reverse Designers and Sculpture
  Engravers:** See each coin
Composition: .925 silver, .075 copper
Weight: 34.07 grams
Diameter: 40 mm
Edge: Lettered
Die Axis: ↑↑
Finish: Proof
Case: Green velvet, Olympic Logo, one or two coin display.

CALGARY OLYMPICS – FIRST SERIES

Coin No. 1 Downhill Skiing
Ian Stewart, Terrence Smith

Coin No. 2 Speed Skating
Friedrich Peter, Ago Aarand

Official Release Date: September 16, 1985

Date	Description	Issue Price	Mintage	PROOF (PR)			
				65	66	67	68
1985	Downhill Skiing	37.00	406,360	–	–	25.	–
1985	Speed Skating	37.00	354,222	–	–	25.	–
1985	Speed Skating, no edge lettering	37.00	Included	–	–	200.	–
1985	Set of 2 coins	74.00	Included	–	–	48.	–

CALGARY OLYMPICS – SECOND SERIES

Coin No. 3 Hockey
Ian Stewart,Victor Coté

Coin No. 4 Biathlon
John Marden, Sheldon Beveridge

Official Release Date: February 25, 1986

Date	Description	Issue Price	Mintage	65	66	PROOF (PR) 67	68
1986	Hockey	37.00	396,602	–	–	25.	–
1986	Hockey, no edge lettering	37.00	Included	–	–	200.	–
1986	Biathlon	37.00	308,086	–	–	25.	–
1986	Biathlon, no edge lettering	37.00	Included	–	–	200.	–
1986	Set of 2 coins	79.00	Included	–	–	48.	–

CALGARY OLYMPICS – THIRD SERIES

Coin No. 5 Cross-Country Skiing
Ian Stewart, Terrence Smith

Coin No. 6 Free-Style Skiing
Walter Ott, Walter Ott

Official Release Date: August 18, 1986

Date	Description	Issue Price	Mintage	65	66	PROOF (PR) 67	68
1986	Cross-Country	39.50	303,199	–	–	25.	–
1986	Free-Style Skiing	39.50	294,322	–	–	25.	–
1986	Free-Style Skiing, no edge lettering	39.50	Included	–	–	200.	–
1986	Set of 2 coins	79.00	Included	–	–	48.	–

CALGARY OLYMPICS – FOURTH SERIES

Coin No. 7 Figure Skating
Raymond Taylor, Walter Ott

Coin No. 8 Curling
Walter Ott, Sheldon Beveridge

Official Release Date: March 14, 1987

Date	Description	Issue Price	Mintage	PROOF (PR) 65	66	67	68
1987	Figure Skating	39.50	334,875	–	–	25.	–
1987	Curling	39.50	286,457	–	–	25.	–
1987	Set , 2 coins	79.00	Included	–	–	48.	–

CALGARY OLYMPICS – FIFTH SERIES

Coin No. 9 Ski-Jumping
Raymond Taylor, David Kierans

Coin No. 10 Bobsleigh
John Mardon, Victor Coté

Official Release Date: August 11, 1987

Date	Description	Issue Price	Mintage	PROOF (PR) 65	66	67	68
1987	Ski-Jumping	42.00	290,954	–	–	25.	–
1987	Bobsleigh	42.00	274,326	–	–	25.	–
1987	Set, 2 coins	84.00	Included	–	–	48.	–

AVIATION SERIES

AVIATION COMMEMORATIVES, 1990-1999. Canada's aviation heroes and achievements are commemorated on this series of twenty dollar sterling silver coins. The series consists of ten coins issued two per year over five years. For the first time each coin design contains a 24 karat gold covered oval cameo portrait of the aviation hero commemorated. All coins were issued in proof quality and a maximum of 50,000 of each coin was offered for sale during the program. Specifications common to the series are:

Designer and Engravers:
  Obv.: Dora de Pédery-Hunt
  Rev.: See below
Composition: .925 silver, .075 copper
  with 24 karat gold cameo
Weight: 31.103 grams
Diameter: 38 mm
Edge: Interrupted serration
Thickness: 3.5 mm
Die Axis: ↑↑
Finish: Proof
Case of Issue: Aluminum case in the shape of a wing. Two and ten coin display cases. The issue price of the ten coin case was $37.00

AVIATION – FIRST SERIES

Coin No. 1
Avro Anson and the
North American Harvard
Robert Leckie

Coin No. 2
Avro Lancaster
J. E. Fauquier

Official Release Date: September 15, 1990
Reverse Designers: 1: Geoff Bennett   2: R.R. Carmichael
Engravers: 1: Sheldon Beveridge   2: Ago Aarand
Portrait Engravers: 1: Terrence Smith   2: Sheldon Beveridge

Date	Description	Issue Price	Mintage	PROOF (PR) 65	66	67	68
1990	Anson/Harvard	55.50	41,844	–	–	50.	–
1990	Lancaster	55.50	43,596	–	–	175.	–

AVIATION – FIRST SERIES (cont.)

Coin No. 3
A.E.A. Silver Dart
F.W. Baldwin and
John A.D. McCurdy

Coin No. 4
de Havilland Beaver
Phillip C. Garratt

Official Release Date: May 16, 1991
Reverse Designers: 3: George Velinger 4: Peter Mossman
Engravers: 3: Sheldon Beveridge 4: Ago Aarand
Portrait Engravers: 3: Terrence Smith 4: William Woodruff

Coin No. 5
Curtiss JN-4 (Canuck)
Sir Frank Wilton Baillie

Coin No. 6
de Havilland Gipsy Moth
Murton A. Seymour

Official Release Date: August 13, 1992
Reverse Designers: 5: George Velinger 6: John Mardon
Engravers: 5: Sheldon Beveridge 6: Ago Aarand
Portrait Engravers: 5: Terry Smith 6: Susan Taylor

		Issue		PROOF (PR)			
Date	Description	Price	Mintage	65	66	67	68
1991	Silver Dart	55.50	35,202	–	–	50.	–
1991	Beaver, Garratt	55.50	36,197	–	–	50.	–
1992	Curtiss, Baillie	55.50	33,105	–	–	50.	–
1992	Gipsy Moth	55.50	32,537	–	–	50.	–

AVIATION – FIRST SERIES (cont.)

Coin No. 7
Fairchild 71c
James A Richardson

Coin No. 8
Lockheed 14 Super Electra
Zebulon Lewis Leigh

Official Release Date: May 3, 1993
Reverse Designers: 7: R. R. Carmichael   8: R. R. Carmichael
Engravers: 7: Susan Taylor   8: Sheldon Beveridge
Portrait Engravers: 7: Susan Taylor   8: Sheldon Beveridge

Coin No. 9
Curtiss HS-2L
Stuart Graham

Coin No. 10
Canadian Vickers Vedette
Wilfred T. Reid

Official Release Date: March 24, 1994
Reverse Designers: 9: John Mardon   10: R. R. Carmichael
Engravers: 9: Sheldon Beveridge   10: Sheldon Beveridge
Portrait Engravers: 9: Susan Taylor   10: Sheldon Beveridge

Date	Description	Issue Price	Mintage	PROOF (PR) 65	66	67	68
1993	Fairchild	55.50	32,199	–	–	50.	–
1993	Lockheed 14	55.50	32,550	–	–	50.	–
1994	Curtiss HS-2L	55.50	31,242	–	–	50.	–
1994	Vedette	55.50	30,880	–	–	50.	–
1990-94	Series One, Set, 10 coins	–	–	–	–	500.	–

AVIATION – SECOND SERIES

This is the second series of the aviation cameo coins of Canada. The theme of this series is "Powered Flight in Canada – Beyond World War II." The obverses, physical and chemical specifications are the same as the first series.

Coin No. 1
Fleet 80 Canuck
J. Omer (Bob) Noury

Coin No. 2
DHC-1 Chipmunk
W. C. Russell Bannock

Official Release Date: September 16, 1995
Reverse Designers: 1: Robert Bradford   2: Robert Bradford
Engravers: 1: Cosme Saffioti   2: William Woodruff
Portrait Engravers: 1: Cosme Saffioti   2: Ago Aarand

Coin No. 3
Avro Canada CF-100 Canuck
Janus Zurakowski

Coin No. 4
Avro Canada CF-105 Arrow
James A. Chamberlin

Official Release Date: July 25, 1996
Reverse Designers: 3: Jim Bruce   4: Jim Bruce
Engravers: 3: Stan Witten   4: William Woodruff
Portrait Engravers: 3: Cosme Saffioti   4: Sheldon Beveridge

Date	Description	Issue Price	Mintage	PROOF (PR) 65	66	67	68
1995	Fleet 80 Canuck	57.95	17,438	–	–	60.	–
1995	DHC-1 Chipmunk	57.95	17,722	–	–	60.	–
1996	CF- 100 Canuck	57.95	18,508	–	–	60.	–
1996	CF-105 Arrow	57.95	27,163	–	–	120.	–

AVIATION – SECOND SERIES (cont.)

Coin No. 5
Canadair F-86 Sabre
Fern Villeneuve

Coin No. 6
Canadair CT-114 Tutor
Edward Higgins

Official Release Date: August 15, 1997
Reverse Designers: 5: Ross Buckland   6: Ross Buckland
Engravers: 5: William Woodruff 6: Stan Witten
Portrait Engravers: 5: Cosme Saffioti   6: Ago Aarand

Coin No. 7
Canadair CP-107 Argus
William S. Longhurst

Coin No. 8
Canadair CL-215 Waterbomber
Paul Gagnon

Official Release Date: June 5, 1998
Reverse Designers: 7: Peter Mossman   8: Peter Mossman
Engravers: 7: Sheldon Beveridge 8: Stan Witten
Portrait Engravers: 7: Cosme Saffioti   8: William Woodruff

Date	Description	Issue Price	Mintage	PROOF (PR) 65	66	67	68
1997	F86 Sabre	57.95	16,440	–	–	60.	–
1997	Tutor Jet	57.95	18,414	–	–	75.	–
1998	Argus	57.95	14,711	–	–	75.	–
1998	Waterbomber	57.95	15,237	–	–	75.	–

Note: In 1998 a special issue of a two-coin set (coin 7 and 8) boxed with a cardboard model was offered. See Derivatives, page 370.

AVIATION – SECOND SERIES (cont.)

Coin No. 9
de Havilland DHC-6 Twin Otter
George A. Neal

Coin No. 10
de Havilland DHC-8 Dash 8
Robert H. (Bob) Fowler

Official Release Date: April 15, 1999
Reverse Designers: 9: Neil Aird   10: Neil Aird
Engravers: 9: Cosme Saffioti   10: William Woodruff
Portrait Engravers: 9: Cosme Saffioti   10: Cosme Saffioti

Date	Description	Issue Price	Mintage	65	66	PROOF (PR) 67	68
1999	Twin Otter	57.95	14,173	–	–	125.	–
1999	Dash 8	57.95	14,138	–	–	125.	–
1995-99	Series Two, Set, 10 coins			–	–	800.	–

TRANSPORTATION ON LAND, SEA AND RAIL, 2000-2003. Canada's first sterling silver hologram cameo twenty dollar coins were issued in 2000. This new series of twelve coins commemorates Canadian achievements in transportation. Each coin bears a 24-karat gold-plated holographic cameo of famous Canadian methods of transportation.

COMMON CHARACTERISTICS

The following are common to the transportation commemorative series.

Designers: Obv.: Dora de Pédery-Hunt   **Engravers:** Obv. Dora de Pédery-Hunt
  Rev.: See below   Rev.: See below
Composition: .925 silver, .075 copper   **Weight:** 31.103 grams
Diameter: 38.0 mm   **Thickness:** 3.5 mm
Edge: Interrupted serration   **Die Axis:** ↑↑
Finish: Proof (frosted relief on a brilliant background)
Case: Charcoal coloured anodized aluminum case with RCM logo, black flocked insert, COA.

LAND, SEA AND RAIL 2000

Obverse

Coin No. 1
H.S. Taylor Steam Buggy
John Mardon / Cosme Saffioti

Coin No. 2
The Bluenose
J. Franklin Wright / Stanley Witten

Coin No. 3
The Toronto
J. Mardon / S. Witten / C. Saffioti

Official Release Date: April 18, 2000

Date	Description	Issue Price	Mintage	PROOF (PR) 65	66	67	68
2000	Steam Buggy	59.95	Total	–	–	80.	–
2002	The Bluenose	59.95	mintage	–	–	200.	–
2000	The Toronto	59.95	all coins	–	–	80.	–
2000	Set, 3 coins	179.85	44,367	–	–	300.	–

LAND, SEA AND RAIL 2001

Obverse

Coin No. 4
The Russell "Light Four"
Model L Touring Car
John Mardon / José Osio

Coin No. 5
The Marco Polo
J. Franklin Wright / Stan Witten

Coin No. 6
The Scotia
Don Curley/ William Woodruff

Official Release Date: April 17, 2001

Date	Description	Issue Price	Mintage	65	66	67	68
					PROOF (PR)		
2001	Russell	59.95	Total	–	–	60.	–
2001	The Marco Polo	59.95	mintage	–	–	60.	–
2001	The Scotia	59.95	all coins	–	–	60.	–
2001	Set of 3 coins	179.85	41,828	–	–	175.	–

LAND, SEA AND RAIL 2002

Obverse

Coin No. 7
The Gray-Dort
John Mardon / Cosme Saffioti

Coin No. 8
The William Lawrence
Bonnie Ross / William Woodruff

Coin No. 9
D-10 Locomotive
Dan Fell / William Woodruff

Official Release Date: April 17th, 2002

Date	Description	Issue Price	Mintage	65	66	67	68
					PROOF (PR)		
2002	Gray-Dort	59.95	Total	–	–	60.	–
2002	Lawrence	59.95	mintage	–	–	60.	–
2002	D-10 Locomotive	59.95	all coins	–	–	60.	–
2002	Set of 3 coins	195.00	35,944	–	–	175.	–

Note: The 2002 Land, Sea and Rail collection was offered with matching COA in a limited edition of 2,500.

LAND, SEA AND RAIL 2003

Obverse

Coin No. 10
HMCS Bras d'Or
Hydrofoil designed by
DeHavilland in 1967
Donald Curley, Stan Witten

Coin No. 11
C.N.R. FA-1 Diesel Electric
Locomotive - No. 9400
John Mardon, William Woodruff

Coin No. 12
Bricklin SV-1 (Land)
designed by Malcolm in 1974
Brian Hughes, José Osio

Official Release Date: April 7th, 2003

Date	Description	Issue Price	Mintage	65	PROOF (PR) 66	67	68
2003	HMCS Bras d'or	59.95	Total	–	–	65.	–
2003	C.N.R. FA-1	59.95	mintage	–	–	70.	–
2003	Bricklin SV-1	59.95	all coins	–	–	75.	–
2003	Set of 3 coins	195.00	31,997	–	–	175.	–

NATURAL WONDERS COLLECTION, 2003-2004. The Royal Canadian Mint, in 2003, introduced a new series of twenty-dollar commemorative coins. Each coin will carry a holographic, colourized or selective gold plating image of one of Canada's natural wonders.

COMMON CHARACTERISTICS

Designers: See below   **Engravers:** See below
Composition: .9999 silver   **Weight:** 31.39 grams
Diameter: 38.0 mm   **Thickness:** 3.5 mm
Edge: Reeded   **Die Axis:** ↑↑
Finish: Proof (frosted relief on a brilliant background)
Cases of Issue:
    (A) Veneer, wooden clam style case, light brown flock interior, encapsulated coin, COA
    (B) Red leatherette clam style case, flocked black insert, encapsulated coin, COA

NIAGARA FALLS, 2003. Located between Canada and the United States, Niagara Falls literally means "thundering waters."

NIAGARA FALLS - Hologram Issue

Coin No. 1   Coin No. 1
Designer: Dora de Pédery-Hunt   Designer: Gary Corcoran
Engraver: Dora de Pédery-Hunt   Engraver: Gary Corcoran

ROCKY MOUNTAINS, 2003. The Canadian Rockies, with some of the world's most spectacular mountain scenery, are the largest mountain range in North America.

ROCKY MOUNTAINS - Colourized Issue

Coin No. 2   Coin No. 2
Designer: Dora de Pédery-Hunt   Designer: José Osio
Engraver: Dora de Pédery-Hunt   Engraver: José Osio

Date	Description	Issue Price	Mintage	PROOF (PR) 65	66	67	68
2003	Niagara Falls	79.95	29,967	–	–	85.	–
2003	Rocky Mountains	69.95	28,793	–	–	70.	–

NATURAL WONDERS COLLECTION (cont.)

ICEBERGS, 2004. The great islands of ice that gradually break away from the polar cap are carried by the ocean currents to the coast of Newfoundland.

ICEBERGS – Hologram Issue

<table>
<tr><td align="center">Coin No. 4
Designer: Susanna Blunt
Engraver: Susan Taylor</td><td align="center">Coin No. 4
Designer: RCM Staff
Engraver: RCM Staff</td></tr>
</table>

NORTHERN LIGHTS, 2004. The Aurora Borealis, an awe-inspiring ribbon of colours, fills the night skies of Canada's northern region.

NORTHERN LIGHTS – Double Image Hologram

<table>
<tr><td align="center">Coin No. 3
Designer: Susanna Blunt
Engraver: Susan Taylor</td><td align="center">Coin No. 3
Designer: Gary Corcoran
Engraver: Stan Witten</td></tr>
</table>

Date	Description	Issue Price	Mintage	65	66	PROOF (PR) 67	68
2004	Icebergs	69.95	24,879	–	–	70.	–
2004	Northern Lights	79.95	34,135	–	–	80.	–

NATURAL WONDERS COLLECTION (cont.)

HOPEWELL ROCKS, 2004. Located in the Bay of Fundy, the Hopewell Rocks are exposed as the tide ebbs in the bay.

HOPEWELL ROCKS – Selectively Gold Plated

Coin No. 5	Coin No. 5
Designer: Susanna Blunt	**Designer:** Stan Witten
Engraver: Susan Taylor	**Engraver:** Stan Witten

DIAMONDS, 2005. The proof design in the background reveals the landscape surrounding Lac de Gras, home to the finest, most brilliant diamonds in the world.

DIAMONDS – Double Image Hologram

Coin No. 6	Coin No. 6
Designer: Susanna Blunt	**Designer:** José Osio
Engraver: Susan Taylor	**Engraver:** José Osio

Date	Description	Issue Price	Mintage	PROOF (PR) 65	66	67	68
2004	Hopewell Rocks	69.95	16,918	–	–	70.	–
2005	Diamonds	69.95	35,000	–	–	70.	–

TWENTY DOLLAR DERIVATIVES

Date	Description	Condition	Issue Price / Issuer	Mintage	Price
1998	**TWENTY DOLLARS** Argus and Waterbomber boxed with cardboard model	PR-67	N/A, RCM	N/A	125.
2004	**TWENTY DOLLARS** "Northern Lights" coin mounted in a frame with a large image of the Northern Lights	PR-67	399.00, RCM	N/A	400.

GOLD 20 DOLLAR COIN

CENTENNIAL OF CONFEDERATION COMMEMORATIVE, 1967. The highlight of the coins issued in 1967 to mark the centenary of Canadian Confederation was a $20 gold coin. It was issued only as part of a $40.00 specimen set (see page 424 for the set listing), but many were later removed from the sets for separate trading. The reverse design is an adaption of the Canadian coat of arms, as on the 50-cent piece of 1960-1966. It is the only coin in the Centennial set that bears the single date 1967 instead of 1867-1967.

Designers: Obv.: Arnold Machin
Rev.: RCM staff
Engravers: Obv.: Myron Cook, using the
Machin portrait model
Rev.: Myron Cook, using the
Thomas Shingles model
of the Canadian
Coat-of-Arms
Composition: .900 gold, .100 copper
Weight: 18.27 grams
Diameter: 27.05 mm
Edge: Reeded
Die Axis: ↑↑
Finish: Specimen

Case of Issue: Black leather with black flock insert

Date	Description	Issue Price	Mintage	65	SPECIMEN (SP) 66	67	68
1967	Confederation	N.I.I.	334,288	–	300.	–	–

GOLD 100 DOLLAR COINS (14kt)

OLYMPIC COMMEMORATIVES, 1976. As part of the series of collectors coins struck to commemorate and help finance the XXI Olympiad, two separate $100 gold coins were issued in 1976. The reverse design for each shows an ancient Grecian athlete being crowned with laurel by the goddess Pallas Athena. The uncirculated edition (brilliant relief/brilliant background) is 14k gold and has rim denticles. The proof edition (frosted relief, mirror background) is 22k gold, slightly smaller, and lacks rim denticles.

Designers: Obv.: Arnold Machin
Rev.: Dora de Pédery-Hunt
Engravers: Obv.: Walter Ott, using the
Machin portrait model
Rev.: Dora de Pédery-Hunt
Walter Ott
Composition: .583 gold, .417 copper alloy
Weight: 13.338 grams
Diameter: 27.00 mm
Edge: Reeded
Die Axis: ↑↑
Finish: Brilliant Uncirculated

Case of Issue: Plastic flip in a brown cardboard sleeve.

Date	Description	Issue Price	Mintage	65	BRILLIANT UNCIRCULATED (MS) 66	67	68
1976	Olympic 14kt	105.00	650,000	150.	–	–	–

GOLD 100 DOLLAR COINS (22kt) 1976-1986

Designers and Engravers: As previous
Composition: .917 gold, .083 copper alloy
Weight: 16.966 grams
Diameter: 25.00 mm
Edge: Reeded
Die Axis: ↑↑
Finish: Proof

Case of Issue: Cowhide and wood with black suede insert, COA

Date	Description	Issue Price	Mintage	65	PROOF (PR) 66	67	68
1976	Olympic 22kt	150.00	350,000	–	–	295.	–

ELIZABETH II SILVER JUBILEE COMMEMORATIVE, 1977. Following the sales success of the Olympic $100 coins, the government decided to embark upon a program of issuing a $100 coin every year. The 1977 coin formed part of a two-coin set - the other coin was the silver dollar, issued in recognition of the Queen's Silver Jubilee. The special reverse shows a bouquet of flowers made up of the official flowers of the provinces and territories. All were issued in proof quality, with mirror fields and matte devices and legends.

Designers: Obv.: Arnold Machin
Rev.: Raymond Lee
Engravers: Obv.: RCM Staff
Rev.: Walter Ott
Composition: .917 gold, .083 silver
Weight: 16.965 grams
Diameter: 27.00 mm
Edge: Reeded
Die Axis: ↑↑
Finish: Proof

Case of Issue: Black leatherette case with maroon insert and plastic coin holder, COA

Date	Description	Issue Price	Mintage	65	PROOF (PR) 66	67	68
1977	Silver Jubilee	140.00	180,396	–	–	295.	–

CANADIAN UNITY COIN, 1978. The reverse of the proof $100 gold coin for 1978 depicts twelve Canada geese flying in formation. The image represents the ten provinces and two territories, and so promotes Canadian unity.

Designers: Obv.: Arnold Machin
Rev.: Roger Savage
Engravers: Obv.: RCM staff, using the
Machin model
Rev.: Ago Aarand
Specifications: Same as 1977 issue
Finish: Proof

Case of Issue: Black leatherette case with blue insert and plastic coin holder, COA

Date	Description	Issue Price	Mintage	65	PROOF (PR) 66	67	68
1978	Canadian Unity	150.00	200,000	–	–	295.	–

INTERNATIONAL YEAR OF THE CHILD COMMEMORATIVE, 1979. Children playing hand in hand beside a globe adorn the reverse of the 1979 $100 gold coin struck in honour of the International Year of the Child.

Designers: Obv.: Arnold Machin
             Rev.: Carola Tietz
Engravers: Obv.: RCM staff using the
                 Machin model
             Rev.: Victor Coté
Specifications: Same as 1977 issue
Finish: Proof

Case of Issue: Brown leatherette case with brown flocked insert, plastic coin holder, COA

Date	Description	Issue Price	Mintage	PROOF (PR) 65	66	67	68
1979	Year of the Child	185.00	250,000	–	–	295.	–

ARCTIC TERRITORIES COMMEMORATIVE, 1980. The gold $100 coin for 1980 is a commemorative marking the 100th anniversary of the transfer of the Arctic Islands from the British Government to the Government of the Dominion of Canada. Its reverse shows an Inuk paddling a kayak near a small iceberg and has no lettering or date. The obverse features the Machin bust of Queen Elizabeth, with the legend and date.

Designers: Obv.: Arnold Machin
             Rev.: Arnaldo Marchetti
Engravers: Obv.: RCM staff using the
                 Machin model
             Rev.: Sheldon Beveridge
Specifications: Same as 1977 issue
Finish: Proof

Case of Issue: See 1979 issue.

Date	Description	Issue Price	Mintage	PROOF (PR) 65	66	67	68
1980	Arctic Territories	430.00	130,000	–	–	295.	–

"O CANADA" COMMEMORATIVE, 1981. The $100 gold coin for 1981 marks the decision of the Canadian Parliament, on July 1, 1980, to adopt the song "O Canada" as our national anthem.

Designers: Obv.: Arnold Machin
             Rev.: Roger Savage
Engravers: Obv.: RCM staff using the
                 Machin model
             Rev.: Walter Ott
Specifications: Same as 1977 issue
Finish: Proof

Case of Issue: See 1979 issue.

Date	Description	Issue Price	Mintage	PROOF (PR) 65	66	67	68
1981	National Anthem	300.00	100,950	–	–	295.	–

PATRIATION OF THE CANADIAN CONSTITUTION, 1982. The $100 gold coin for 1982 commemorates the patriation of the Constitution of Canada. The reverse of the coin portrays this historical event by a page turning in an open book bearing the coat of arms of Canada and a maple leaf. The obverse of this coin, the seventh in the 22 karat $100 series, depicts Arnold Machin's effigy of Her Majesty Elizabeth II and the legend "100 Dollars" and "Elizabeth II."

Designers: Obv.: Arnold Machin
Rev.: Friedrich Peter
Engravers: Obv.: RCM staff using the Machin model
Rev.: Walter Ott
Specifications: Same as 1977 issue
Finish: Proof

Case of Issue: See 1979 issue

Date	Description	Issue Price	Mintage	65	PROOF (PR) 66	67	68
1982	Constitution	290.00	121,706	–	–	295.	–

SIR HUMPHREY GILBERT'S LANDING IN NEWFOUNDLAND, 1983. The $100 gold coin for 1983 commemorates Gilbert's landing in Newfoundland to proclaim it as Britain's first overseas colony. The word "CANADA" appears on the edge for the first time in Canadian coinage.

Designers: Obv.: Arnold Machin
Rev.: John Jaciw
Engravers: Obv.: RCM staff using the Machin model
Rev.: Walter Ott
Edge: Lettered, Reeded
Specifications: Same as 1977 issue
Finish: Proof

Case of Issue: See 1979 issue

Date	Description	Issue Price	Mintage	65	PROOF (PR) 66	67	68
1983	Gilbert's Landing	310.00	83,128	–	–	295.	–

JACQUES CARTIER'S VOYAGE OF DISCOVERY, 1984. The $100 gold coin for 1984 commemorates Cartier's landing at Gaspé, Bonaventure in 1534. The reverse portrays a profile of Jacques Cartier and a ship of his era. Arnold Machin's effigy of Her Majesty Queen Elizabeth II is continued. The edge security lettering of 1983 was not continued in 1984.

Designers: Obv.: Arnold Machin
Rev.: Carola Tietz
Engravers: Obv.: RCM staff using the Machin model
Rev.: Walter Ott
Specifications: Same as 1977 issue
Finish: Proof

Case of Issue: See 1979 issue

Date	Description	Issue Price	Mintage	65	PROOF (PR) 66	67	68
1984	Jacques Cartier	325.00	67,662	–	–	295.	–

NATIONAL PARKS CENTENARY, 1985. The $100 gold coin of 1985 commemorates the centennial of an important part of Canada's heritage, the National Parks. The reverse of the coin portrays a bighorn sheep poised on a cliff in the Canadian Rockies.

Designers: Obv.: Arnold Machin
Rev.: Hector Greville
Engravers: Rev.: Walter Ott
Specifications: Same as 1977 issue
Finish: Proof

Case of Issue: Brown leatherette book type case, with maple leaf emblem. Interior: Beige satin, encapsulated coin. All enclosed in a brown plastic box, COA

Date	Description	Issue Price	Mintage	65	PROOF (PR) 66	67	68
1985	National Parks	325.00	58,520	–	–	295.	–

INTERNATIONAL YEAR OF PEACE, 1986. The $100 gold coin for 1986 signifies Canada's support for world peace. The reverse depicts a branch of maple leaves intertwined with a branch of olive leaves, symbols of Canada and Peace coming together. The words "Peace-Paix" forming a circle are superimposed on the design.

Designers: Obv.: Arnold Machin
Rev.: Dora de Pédery-Hunt
Engravers: Obv.: RCM staff
Rev.: Dora de Pédery-Hunt
Specifications: Same as 1977 issue
Finish: Proof

Case of Issue: See 1985 issue.

Date	Description	Issue Price	Mintage	65	PROOF (PR) 66	67	68
1986	Year of Peace	325.00	76,255	–	–	295.	–

GOLD 100 DOLLAR COINS (14kt) 1987 TO DATE

XV OLYMPIC WINTER GAMES, 1987. The $100 gold coin for 1987 commemorates the XV Olympic Winter Games held in Calgary in 1988. The reverse portrays a hand holding the Olympic Torch with a stylized flame forming an image of the Canadian Rocky Mountains. This is the second $100 gold coin to have a lettered edge. The inscription reads "XV Olympic Winter Games - XVes Jeux Olympiques D'Hiver."

Designers: Obv.: Arnold Machin
Rev.: Friedrich Peter
Engravers: Rev.: Ago Aarand
Composition: .583 gold, .417 silver
Weight: 13.338 grams
Diameter: 27.00 mm
Thickness: 2.15 mm
Edge: Lettered
Die Axis: ↑↑
Finish: Proof

Case of Issue: See 1985 issue

Date	Description	Issue Price	Mintage	PROOF (PR) 65	66	67	68
1987	Winter Games	255.00	145,175	–	–	150.	–

THE BOWHEAD WHALE (BALAENA MYSTICETUS), 1988. The $100 gold coin for 1988 celebrates a precious national treasure, the Bowhead whale. The reverse of this coin portrays a bowhead whale and her calf enclosed in a circle.

Designers: Obv.: Arnold Machin
Rev.: Robert R. Carmichael
Engravers: Rev.: Ago Aarand
Composition: 0.583 gold, .4167 silver
Weight: 13.338 grams
Diameter: 27.00 mm
Thickness: 2.15 mm
Edge: Reeded
Die Axis: ↑↑
Finish: Proof

Case of Issue: See 1985 issue

Date	Description	Issue Price	Mintage	PROOF (PR) 65	66	67	68
1988	Bowhead Whale	255.00	52,239	–	–	150.	–

Note: Canadian gold coins, due to the large number issued, trade at a small premium over gold value. Please refer to the bullion value for pricing if there is a major change in the price of gold.

SAINTE-MARIE, 1639-1989. In 1639 the French Jesuits founded a fortified mission village near Midland, Ontario, which they named Sainte-Marie among the Hurons. 1989 was the 350th anniversary of this first self-sufficient settlement in Ontario, where one-fifth of the European population of Canada lived.

Designers: Obv.: Arnold Machin
　　　　　　Rev.: David J. Craig
Engravers: Obv.: Patrick Brindley
　　　　　　Rev.: Ago Aarand
Specifications: Same as 1988 issue
Finish: Proof

Case of Issue:　See 1985 issue

Date	Description	Issue Price	Mintage	65	PROOF (PR) 66	67	68
1989	Sainte-Marie	245.00	63,881	–	–	160.	–

INTERNATIONAL LITERACY YEAR, 1990. The General Assembly of the United Nations declared 1990 as the International Year of Literacy, setting the stage for the eradication of illiteracy around the world by the year 2000.

Designers: Obv.: Dora de Pédery-Hunt
　　　　　　Rev.: John Mardon
Engravers: Obv.: Dora de Pédery-Hunt
　　　　　　Rev.: Ago Aarand
　　　　　　　　　Susan Taylor
Specifications: Same as 1988 issue
Finish: Proof

Case of Issue:　See 1985 issue

Date	Description	Issue Price	Mintage	65	PROOF (PR) 66	67	68
1990	Literacy	245.00	49,940	–	–	160.	–

EMPRESS OF INDIA, 1991. This coin commemores the 100th anniversary of the Empress of India's first arrival in Vancouver from Yokohama, Japan. The Canadian Pacific's trans-Pacific Empress ships were among the world's first cruise ships.

Designers: Obv.: Dora de Pédery-Hunt
　　　　　　Rev.: Karsten Smith
Engravers: Obv.: Dora de Pédery-Hunt
　　　　　　Reverse: Sheldon Beveridge
Specifications: Same as 1988 issue
Finish: Proof

Case of Issue:　See 1985 issue

Date	Description	Issue Price	Mintage	65	PROOF (PR) 66	67	68
1991	Empress of India	245.00	33,966	–	–	160.	–

CITY OF MONTREAL, 350TH ANNIVERSARY, 1642-1992. On May 17, 1642, three vessels arrived from France landing Maisonneuve and his men on an island in the St. Lawrence River. They called the island Ville-Marie which was renamed Montreal in the early 1700's.

Designers: Obv.: Dora de Pédery-Hunt
            Rev.: Stewart Sherwood
Engravers: Obv.: Dora de Pédery-Hunt
            Rev.: Ago Aarand,
                  Cosme Saffioti
Specifications: Same as 1988 issue
Finish: Proof
Case of Issue: See 1985 issue

Date	Description	Issue Price	Mintage	65	PROOF (PR) 66	67	68
1992	Montreal	239.85	28,190	–	–	160.	–

1893 THE ERA OF THE HORSELESS CARRIAGE, 1993. The five vehicles pictured on the reverse of the 1993 gold coin are, clockwise from the left, the French Panhard-Levassor's Daimler, the American Duryea, the German Benz Victoria, the Simmonds Steam Carriage and, in the centre, the first Canadian built electric car, the Featherstonhaugh

Designers: Obv.: Dora de Pédery-Hunt
            Rev.: John Mardon
Engravers: Obv.: Dora de Pédery-Hunt
            Rev.: Ago Aarand
                  William Woodruff
Specifications: Same as 1988 issue
Finish: Proof
Case of Issue: See 1985 issue

Date	Description	Issue Price	Mintage	65	PROOF (PR) 66	67	68
1993	Horseless Carriage	239.85	25,971	–	–	180.	–

THE HOME FRONT, 1994. This coin is part of the Remembrance & Peace Issue. The design was taken from a 1945 painting by P. Clark, entitled "Maintenance Jobs in the Hangar."

Designers: Obv.: Dora de Pédery-Hunt
            Rev.: Paraskeva Clark
Engravers: Obv.: Dora de Pédery-Hunt
            Rev.: Susan Taylor,
                  Ago Aarand
Specifications: Same as 1988 issue
Finish: Proof
Case of Issue: See 1985 issue

Date	Description	Issue Price	Mintage	65	PROOF (PR) 66	67	68
1994	Home Front	249.95	17,603	–	–	195.	–

275TH ANNIVERSARY OF THE FOUNDING OF LOUISBOURG, 1995. Louisbourg, built in 1720 as a strategic centre for the French military in North America, is commemorated on the $100.00 gold coin of 1995.

Designers: Obv.: Dora de Pédery-Hunt
Rev.: Lewis Parker
Engravers: Obv.: Dora de Pédery-Hunt
Rev.: Sheldon Beveridge
Specifications: Same as 1988 issue
Finish: Proof
Case of Issue: See 1985 issue

Date	Description	Issue Price	Mintage	65	PROOF (PR) 66	67	68
1995	Louisbourg	249.95	16,916	–	–	195.	–

100TH ANNIVERSARY OF THE FIRST MAJOR GOLD DISCOVERY IN THE KLONDIKE, 1996. In 1896 the Gold Rush began when George and Kate Carmack, Skookum Jim and Dawson Charlie made the Klondike's first major gold find. 1996 was the last year in which $100.00 gold coins were packaged in the book-type cases.

Designers: Obv.: Dora de Pédery-Hunt
Rev.: John Mantha
Engravers: Obv.: Dora de Pédery-Hunt
Rev.: Cosme Saffioti
Specifications: Same as 1988 issue
Finish: Proof
Case of Issue: See 1985 issue

Date	Description	Issue Price	Mintage	65	PROOF (PR) 66	67	68
1996	Klondike	259.95	17,973	–	–	210.	1

150TH ANNIVERSARY OF ALEXANDER GRAHAM BELL'S BIRTH, 1997. The $100 gold coin of 1997 honours the creative genius of Alexander Graham Bell. He was born in Scotland in 1847. In 1874, while in Ontario, he carried out the experiments that led to the invention of the telephone. The $100 gold coin was offered for the first time with an optional case.

Designers: Obv.: Dora de Pédery-Hunt
Rev.: Donald H. Curley
Engravers: Obv.: Dora de Pédery-Hunt
Rev.: Sheldon Beveridge
Specifications: Same as 1988 issue
Finish: Proof
Original Issue Price: With case: $259.95
Without case: $254.95

Case of Issue: Black suede clam type case, black suede inside, encapsulated coin

Date	Description	Issue Price	Mintage	65	PROOF (PR) 66	67	68
1997	Bell	See above	14,030	–	–	235.	–

75TH ANNIVERSARY OF THE NOBEL PRIZE FOR THE DISCOVERY OF INSULIN, 1998. The discovery of insulin by Frederick Banting and John MacLeod earned them the Nobel Prize for Physiology and Medicine in 1923.

Designers: Obv.: Dora de Pédery-Hunt
Rev.: Robert R. Carmichael
Engravers: Obv.: Dora de Pédery-Hunt
Rev.: Stan Witten
Specifications: Same as 1988 issue
Finish: Proof
Original Issue Price: With case: $259.95
Without case: $254.95
Case of Issue: See 1997 issue

Date	Description	Issue Price	Mintage	PROOF (PR) 65	66	67	68
1998	Nobel Prize	See above	11,220	–	–	245.	–

50TH ANNIVERSARY OF NEWFOUNDLAND'S CONFEDERATION WITH CANADA IN 1949, 1999. The 50th anniversary of Newfoundland's union with Canada on March 31, 1949 is celebrated.

Designers: Obv.: Dora de Pédery-Hunt
Rev.: J. Gale-Vaillancourt
Engravers: Obv.: Dora de Pédery-Hunt
Rev.: William Woodruff
Specifications: Same as 1988 issue
Finish: Proof
Original Issue Price: With case: $259.95
Without case: $254.95
Case of Issue: Black suede clam type case, black suede inside, encapsulated coin

Date	Description	Issue Price	Mintage	PROOF (PR) 65	66	67	68
1999	Newfoundland	See above	10,242	–	–	285.	–

150TH ANNIVERSARY OF THE SEARCH FOR THE NORTHWEST PASSAGE IN 1850, 2000. The Franklin Expedition, which was lost on its voyage to discover a Northwest passage to the far East, is commemorated on the 100 dollar gold coin for 2000.

Designers: Obv.: Dora de Pédery-Hunt
Rev.: John Mardon
Engravers: Obv.: Dora de Pédery-Hunt
Rev.: Stan Witten
Specifications: Same as 1988 issue
Finish: Proof
Original Issue Price: With case: $269.95
Without case: $254.95
Case of Issue: Metal presentation case with wood insert, COA

Date	Description	Issue Price	Mintage	PROOF (PR) 65	66	67	68
2000	NWT Passage	See above	10,547	–	–	285.	–

125TH ANNIVERSARY OF THE LIBRARY OF PARLIAMENT, 2001. The Library of Parliament is one of the most famous symbols of the Canadian Confederation. "This beautiful building is an architectural marvel, and a treasure for all Canadians to cherish."

Designers: Obv.: Dora de Pédery-Hunt
                  Rev.: Robert R. Carmichael
Engravers: Obv.: Dora de Pédery-Hunt
                   Rev.: Susan Taylor
                         William Woodruff
Specifications: Same as 1988 issue
Finish: Proof
Original Issue Price: With case $274.95
                            Without case $260.95
Case of Issue: See 2000 issue

Date	Description	Issue Price	Mintage	65	PROOF (PR) 66	67	68
2001	Library of Parliament	See above	8,080	–	–	265.	–

COMMEMORATING CANADA'S OIL INDUSTRY, 2002. This coin commemorates the major economic importance of oil to the Canadian economy and Canada's place as one of the major oil producers of the world. The sea of 'black gold' at the foot of the oil rig commemorates the major discovery of the Leduc oil field on February 13, 1947.

Designers: Obv.: Dora de Pédery-Hunt
                  Rev.: John Mardon
Engravers: Obv.: Dora de Pédery-Hunt
                   Rev.: Stan Witten
Specifications: Same as 1988 issue
Finish: Proof, colourized
Original Issue Price: With case $274.95
                            Without case $260.95
Case of Issue: See 2000 issue

Date	Description	Issue Price	Mintage	65	PROOF (PR) 66	67	68
2002	Leduc	See above	9,994	–	–	450.	–

100TH ANNIVERSARY OF THE DISCOVERY OF MARQUIS WHEAT, 2003. After 10 years of experiments, Dr. William Saunders and his sons Percy and Charles discovered the marquis wheat variety, making Canada forever known as the world's bread basket.

Designers: Obv.: Dora de Pédery-Hunt
                  Rev.: Thom Nelson
Engravers: Obv.: Dora de Pédery-Hunt
                   Rev.: Stan Witten
Specifications: Same as 1988 issue
Finish: Proof
Original Issue Price: With case $289.95
                            Without case $277.95
Case of Issue: See 2000 issue

Date	Description	Issue Price	Mintage	65	PROOF (PR) 66	67	68
2003	Marquis Wheat	See above	9,993	–	–	290.	–

50TH ANNIVERSARY OF THE COMMENCEMENT OF THE ST. LAWRENCE SEAWAY CONSTRUCTION, 2004. On August 10, 1954, a sod turning ceremony signalled the start of a mammoth project by Canada and the United States.

Designers: Obv.: Susanna Blunt
                  Rev.: Susan Taylor
Engravers: Obv.: John Mardon
                   Rev.: José Osio
Composition: .5833 gold, .4167 silver
Weight: 12.0 grams
Diameter: 27.0 mm
Edge: Reeded
Die Axis: ↑↑
Finish: Proof
Original Issue Price: With case $289.95
                      Without case $277.95
Case of Issue: See 2000 issue

Date	Description	Issue Price	Mintage	65	66	67	68
					PROOF (PR)		
2004	St. Lawrence Seaway	See above	7,123	–	–	290.	–

130TH ANNIVERSARY OF THE SUPREME COURT OF CANADA, 2005. On April 8, 1875, Canada's "Court of Last Resort" was founded. It has been an essential component of Canadian justice for 130 years.

Designers: Obv.: Susanna Blunt
                  Rev.: Suzanne Duranceau
Engravers: Obv.: Susan Taylor
                   Rev.: José Osio
Specifications: Same as 2004 issue
Finish: Proof
Case of Issue: Red plastic slide case,
               black plastic incert, encapsulated
               coin, COA

Date	Description	Issue Price	Mintage	65	66	67	68
					PROOF (PR)		
2005	Supreme Court	329.95	9,000	–	–	330.	–

GOLD HOLOGRAM 150 DOLLAR COINS

YEAR OF THE DRAGON, 2000. This coin commemorates the coincidence of the year of the Dragon and the dawn of a New Millennium, an occurrence that happens once every three thousand years. This is the second holographic coin issued and the first of the Chinese Lunar series of gold coins.

Designers:
  Obv.: Dora de Pédery-Hunt
  Rev.: Harvey Chan
Engravers:
  Obv.: Harvey Chan
  Rev.: RCM Engineering Staff
Finish: Proof, with hologram

Composition: .750 gold, .250 silver   **Thickness:** 1.81 mm
Weight: 11.84 grams   **Edge:** Reeded (serrated)
Diameter: 28.0 mm   **Die Axis:** ↑↑
Case of Issue: Gold satin clam case, taupe flocked insert. encapsulated coin, COA.

Date	Description	Issue Price	Mintage	PROOF (PR) 65	66	67	68
2000	Dragon	388.88	8,874	–	–	1,200.	–

YEAR OF THE SNAKE, 2001. To celebrate the arrival of the year of the Snake in the Chinese Lunar Calendar, the Royal Canadian Mint introduced the second in the series of $150 Holographic gold coins.

Designers, Engravers and Specifications: Same as 2000 issue
Finish: Proof, with hologram
Case of Issue: See 2000 issue

Date	Description	Issue Price	Mintage	PROOF (PR) 65	66	67	68
2001	Snake	388.88	6,571	–	–	300.	–

YEAR OF THE HORSE, 2002. The seventh sign of the Chinese lunar calendar is the Horse. This is the third holographic gold coin in the series.

Designers, Engravers and Specifications: Same as 2000 issue
Finish: Proof, with hologram
Case of Issue: See 2000 issue

Date	Description	Issue Price	Mintage	PROOF (PR) 65	66	67	68
2002	Horse	388.88	6,843	–	–	375.	–

YEAR OF THE SHEEP, 2003. The eighth sign of the Chinese lunar calendar is the Sheep. This is the fourth holographic gold coin in the series.

Designers and Engravers:
Same as 2004 issue
Specifications:
Same as 2000 issue
Finish: Proof, with hologram
Case of Issue: See 2000 issue

Date	Description	Issue Price	Mintage	PROOF (PR)			
				65	66	67	68
2003	Sheep	398.88	3,927	–	–	375.	–

YEAR OF THE MONKEY, 2004. The ninth sign of the Chinese lunar calendar is the Monkey. This is the fifth holographic gold coin in the series.

Designers:
Obv.: Susanna Blunt
Rev.: Harvey Chan
Engravers:
Obv.: Susan Taylor
Rev.: RCM Staff
Composition: .75 gold, .25 silver
Weight: 11.84 grams
Diameter: 28.0 mm
Thickness: 1.60 mm
Edge: Reeded (serrated)
Die Axis: ↑↑
Finish: Proof, with hologram
Case of Issue: See 2000 issue

Date	Description	Issue Price	Mintage	PROOF (PR)			
				65	66	67	68
2004	Monkey	398.88	3,318	–	–	400.	–

YEAR OF THE ROOSTER, 2005. The tenth sign of the Chinese lunar calendar is the Rooster. This is the sixth holographic gold coin in the series.

Designers and Engravers:
Same as 2004 issue
Specifications:
Same as 2004 issue
Finish: Proof, with Hologram
Case of Issue: See 2004 issue

Date	Description	Issue Price	Mintage	PROOF (PR)			
				65	66	67	68
2005	Rooster	398.88	4,888	–	–	400.	–

GOLD 175 DOLLAR COIN

100TH ANNIVERSARY OF THE OLYMPIC MOVEMENT,1992-1996. Commemorating the 100th anniversary of the Olympic movement in 1996, Canada and four other countries, Australia, France, Austria and Greece, issued three-coin sets, consisting of one gold and two silver coins. One set was issued each year beginning with Canada's in 1992. See page 349 for the Royal Canadian Mint silver issues. Only the Royal Canadian Mint issued coins are listed in the Standard Catalogue.

Designers: Obv.: Dora de Pédery-Hunt
          Rev.: Stewart Sherwood
Composition: .916 Gold, .084 Copper
Diameter: 28.00 mm
Edge: Lettering: Citius, altius, fortius
Finish: Proof
Case of Issue: Not known

Engravers: Obv.: Dora de Pédery-Hunt
          Rev.: Ago Aarand
Weight: 16.97g
Thickness: 2.00 mm
Die Axis: ↑↑

Date	Description	Issue Price	Mintage	PROOF (PR) 65	66	67	68
1992	Flame	429.75	22,092	–	–	300.	–

GOLD 200 DOLLAR COINS

CANADA FLAG SILVER JUBILEE, 1990. The 25th anniversary of the proclamation approving Canada's flag is commemorated.

Designers:
  Obv.: Dora de Pédery-Hunt
  Rev.: Stewart Sherwood
Engravers:
  Obv.: Dora de Pédery-Hunt
  Rev.: Ago Aarand
Composition: .916 gold, .083 silver
Weight: 17.13 grams
Diameter: 29.0 mm
Thickness: 2.0 mm
Edge: Reeded
Die Axis: ↑↑

Finish: Proof, frosted relief on brilliant background
Case of Issue: Woven Jacquard clam style case, encapsulated coin, COA.

Date	Description	Issue Price	Mintage	PROOF (PR) 65	66	67	68
1990	Canada Flag	395.00	20,980	–	–	325.	–

A NATIONAL PASSION, 1991. The 1991 two hundred dollar proof gold coin was issued as a tribute to the spirit and vitality of Canadian youth and the national game of hockey.

Designers:
  Obv.: Dora de Pédery-Hunt
  Rev.: Stewart Sherwood
Engravers:
  Obv.: Dora de Pédery-Hunt
  Rev.: Susan Taylor
Specifications: Same as 1990 issue
Finish: Proof
Case of Issue: See 1990 issue

Date	Description	Issue Price	Mintage	PROOF (PR) 65	66	67	68
1991	National Passion	425.00	10,215	–	–	325.	–

NIAGARA FALLS, 1992. The 1992 two hundred dollar gold coin was issued as a tribute to the beauty and majesty of Niagara Falls. The coin features two children playing near the falls.

Designers:
  Obv.: Dora de Pédery-Hunt
  Rev.: John Mardon
Engravers:
  Obv.: D. De Pédery-Hunt
  Rev.: Susan Taylor
Specifications: Same as 1990 issue
Finish: Proof
Case of Issue: See 1990 issue

Date	Description	Issue Price	Mintage	PROOF (PR) 65	66	67	68
1992	Niagara Falls	389.65	9,465	–	–	325.	–

ROYAL CANADIAN MOUNTED POLICE, 1993. The 1993 issue of the two hundred dollar gold coin pays tribute to the unique contribution of the R.C.M.P. to Canadian history.

Designers:
  Obv.: Dora de Pédery-Hunt
  Rev.: Stewart Sherwood
Engravers:
  Obv.: Dora de Pédery-Hunt
  Rev.: Susan Taylor
Specifications: Same as 1990 issue
Finish: Proof
Case of Issue: See 1990 issue

Date	Description	Issue Price	Mintage	65	PROOF (PR) 66	67	68
1993	R.C.M.P.	389.65	10,807	–	–	325.	–

ANNE OF GREEN GABLES, 1994. Issued as a tribute to the famous character in the novel by Canadian writer Lucy Maud Montgomery, this is the last coin in the youth and heritage series.

Designers:
  Obv.: Dora de Pédery-Hunt
  Rev.: Pheobe Gilman
Engravers:
  Obv.: Dora de Pédery-Hunt
  Rev.: Susan Taylor
Specifications: Same as 1990 issue
Finish: Proof
Case of Issue: See 1990 issue

Date	Description	Issue Price	Mintage	65	PROOF (PR) 66	67	68
1994	Anne of Green Gables	399.95	10,655	–	–	325.	–

THE SUGAR BUSH, 1995. This coin celebrates the time-honoured rite of spring known in Canada as "sugaring off."

Designers:
  Obv.: Dora de Pédery-Hunt
  Rev.: J.D. Mantha
Engravers:
  Obv.: Dora de Pédery-Hunt
  Rev.: Sheldon Beveridge
Specifications: Same as 1990 issue
Finish: Proof
Case of Issue: See 1990 issue

D Date	Description	Issue Price	Mintage	65	PROOF (PR) 66	67	68
1995	Sugar Bush	399.95	9,579	–	–	325.	–

TRANSCONTINENTAL LANDSCAPE, 1996. The railway, a central symbol of national life, is commemorated.

Designers:
 Obv.: Dora de Pédery-Hunt
 Rev.: Suzanne Duranceau
Engravers:
 Obv.: Dora de Pédery-Hunt
 Rev.: Cosme Saffioti
Specifications: Same as 1990 issue
Finish: Proof
Case of Issue: See 1990 isse

Date	Description	Issue Price	Mintage	65	PROOF (PR) 66	67	68
1996	Transcontinental	414.95	8,047	–	–	360.	–

HAIDA "RAVEN BRINGING LIGHT TO THE WORLD," 1997. This coin is the first issue of a four year program, celebrating Canadian Native cultures and traditions. The 1997 $200 gold coin was available with or without a case because the mint offered a four-coin case to house the set.

Designers:
 Obv.: Dora de Pédery-Hunt
 Rev.: Robert Davidson
Engravers:
 Obv.: Dora de Pédery-Hunt
 Rev.: C. Saffioti, A. Aarand
Specifications: Same as 1990 issue
Finish: Proof
Original Issue Price:
 With case: $414.95
 Without case: $409.95

Case of Issue: Metal trimmed presentation case, encapsulated coin, COA.

Date	Description	Issue Price	Mintage	65	PROOF (PR) 66	67	68
1997	Haida	See above	11,610	–	–	625.	–

THE LEGEND OF THE WHITE BUFFALO, 1998. The second issue of the four year program celebrates Canadian Native cultures and traditions. The $200 gold coin was available with or without a case.

Designers:
 Obv.: Dora de Pédery-Hunt
 Rev.: Alex Janvier
Engravers:
 Obv.: Dora de Pédery-Hunt
 Rev.: Cosme Saffioti
Specifications: Same as 1990 issue
Finish: Proof
Original Issue Price:
 With case: $414.95
 Without case: $409.95
Case of Issue: See 1997 issue

Date	Description	Issue Price	Mintage	65	PROOF (PR) 66	67	68
1998	Buffalo	See above	7,149	–	–	350.	–

MIKMAQ BUTTERFLY, 1999. This is the third in the four-coin series celebrating Canadian Native cultures and traditions. The coin depicts a butterfly in the traditional Mikmaq double curve, symbolic of the balance between the physical and spiritual worlds.

Designers:
  Obv.: Dora de Pédery-Hunt
  Rev.: Alan Syliboy
Engravers:
  Obv.: Dora de Pédery-Hunt
  Rev.: Cosme Saffioti
Specifications: Same as 1990 issue
Finish: Proof
Original Issue Price:
  With case: $414.95
  Without case: $409.95
Case of Issue: See 1997 issue

Date	Description	Issue Price	Mintage	65	66	67	68
					PROOF (PR)		
1999	Mikmaq Butterfly	See above	6,510	–	–	350.	–

MOTHER AND CHILD, 2000. This is the fourth and last coin in the four-coin Native Cultures and Traditions series.

Designers:
  Obv.: Dora de Pédery-Hunt
  Rev.: Germaine Arnaktauyok
Engravers:
  Obv.: Dora de Pédery-Hunt
  Rev.: Susan Taylor
Specifications: Same as 1990 issue
Finish: Proof
Original Issue Price:
  With Case: $414.95
  Without case: $409.95
Case of Issue: See 1997 issue

Date	Description	Issue Price	Mintage	65	66	67	68
					PROOF (PR)		
2000	Mother and Child	See above	7,410	–	–	360.	–

Note: A special collector case designed by Maryanne Barkhouse for the "Canadian Native Cultures and Traditions" series was issued in 1998. The box was made of imitation stone resin, with the Arctic Fox as the central panel, and on each side an animal on which the native aboriginal depended. The four-coin case was available directly from the Mint, priced at $79.95. The complete four-coin set in case was issued at $1,600.00.

CORNELIUS KRIEGHOFF, 2001. The 2001 $200 gold coin is the first in a four-coin series featuring Canadian art and artists. Cornelius Krieghoff's famous painting "The Habitant Farm," (1856) is featured on the reverse.

Designers:
  Obv.: Dora de Pédery-Hunt
  Rev.: Cornelius Krieghoff
Engravers:
  Obv.: Dora de Pédery-Hunt
  Rev.: Susan Taylor
Specifications: Same as 1990 issue
Finish: Proof
Original Issue Price:
  With case: $424.95
  Without case: $412.95
Case of Issue: See 1997 issue

Date	Description	Issue Price	Mintage	65	66	67	68
					PROOF (PR)		
2001	Krieghoff	See above	5,406	–	–	360.	–

TOM THOMPSON, 2002. The 2002 $200 gold coin is the second coin of the four-coin series honouring Canada's famous painters. Thompson's (1877-1917) "The Jack Pine," painted in 1916 in Algonquin Park, is one of Canada's most familiar images.

Designers:
  Obv.: Dora de Pédery-Hunt
  Rev.: Tom Thompson
Engravers:
  Obv.: Dora de Pédery-Hunt
  Rev.: Susan Taylor
Specifications: Same as 1990 issue
Finish: Proof
Original Issue Price:
  With case: $424.95
  Without case: $412.95
Case of Issue: See 1997 issue

Date	Description	Issue Price	Mintage	65	66	67	68
					PROOF (PR)		
2002	Thompson	See above	5,754	–	–	420.	–

LIONEL LEMOINE FITZGERALD 2003. The third gold coin in the Canadian Art series features Fitzgerald's "Houses," painted in 1929. The rural life of the small prairie towns is the theme of this magnificent painting.

Designers:
Obv.:   Dora de Pédery-Hunt
Rev.:   L. LeMoine Fitzgerald
Engravers:
Obv.:   Dora de Pédery-Hunt
Rev.:   Cosme Saffioti
Specifications: Same as 1990 issue
Finish: Proof
Original Issue Price:
With case: $424.95
Without case: $412.95
Case of Issue: See 1997 issue

Date	Description	Issue Price	Mintage	PROOF (PR) 65	66	67	68
2003	Fitzgerald	See above	4,118	–	–	425.	–

ALFRED PELLAN, 2004. The fourth and last gold coin in the Canadian Art series, Alfred Pellan's "Fragments" makes him one of the most fascinating figures in Canadian Art.

Designers:
Obv.:   Susanna Blunt
Rev.:   Alfred Pellan
Engravers:
Obv.:   Susan Taylor
Rev.:   Christie Paquet
Composition: .917 gold, .083 silver
Weight: 16.0 grams
Diameter: 29.0 mm
Thickness: 1.75 mm
Edge: Reeded
Die Axis: ↑↑

Finish: Proof
Original Issue Price: With case: $424.95
                  Without case: $412.95
Case of Issue: See 1997 issue

Date	Description	Issue Price	Mintage	PROOF (PR) 65	66	67	68
2004	Pellan	See above	3,699	–	–	425.	–

HISTORICAL COMMERCE - FUR TRADERS, 2005. The fur traders (voyageurs) travelled thousands of kilometres exchanging goods with Natives.

Designers:
  Obv.: Susanna Blunt
  Rev.: John Mardon
Engravers:
  Obv.: Susan Taylor
  Rev.: José Osio
Specifications: Same as 2004 issue
Finish: Proof
Case of Issue: Red plastic display case, black plastic insert, encapsulated coin, COA

Date	Description	Issue Price	Mintage	PROOF (PR) 65	66	67	68
2005	Fur Traders	489.95	4,500	—	—	490.	—

GOLD 300 DOLLAR COINS

The first two $300 gold coins were issued as part of the Royal Canadian Mint's commemorative issues marking the Golden Jubilee and Coronation of Queen Elizabeth II.

TRIPLE CAMEO PORTRAITS OF QUEEN ELIZABETH II, 2002. This silver (.9999) coin bears triple cameo, 14kt gold portraits of Queen Elizabeth II: 1953-1964 portrait by Mary Gillick; 1965-1989 portrait by Arnold Machin; 1990-2003 portrait by Dora de Pédery-Hunt.

Designers: Obv.: Dora de Pédery-Hunt   Engravers: Obv.: Stan Witten
        Rev.: Sheldon Beveridge   Rev.: Cosme Saffioti
              Cosme Saffioti
Composition: .999 gold, 38.67 grams   Weight: 60.0 grams
             .9999 silver, 26.33 grams   Thickness: N/A
Total weight: 65.00 grams   Fineness: 0.594
Die Axis: ↑↑   Finish: Proof
Case of Issue: Purple laminated wood presentation case, cream insert, encapsulated coin, COA, purple and gold outer box

Date	Description	Issue Price	Mintage	65	PROOF (PR) 66	67	68
2002	Triple Cameo	1,095.95	999	–	–	1,400.	–

GREAT SEAL OF CANADA, 2003. The Royal Seal, or Great Seal of Canada, is the official stamp used to bring the Queen's authority to any documents produced on her behalf.

Designers: Obv.: Susanna Blunt   Engravers: Obv.: Susan Taylor
            Rev.: RCM Staff   Rev.: RCM Staff
Specifications: Same as 2002 issue   Finish: Proof
Case of Issue: Black leatherette clam case with RCM plaque, black flocked insert,
                 encapsulated coin, COA; black and gold outer case

Date	Description	Issue Price	Mintage	65	66	67	68
					PROOF (PR)		
2003	Great Seal	1,099.95	998	–	–	1,200.	–

QUADRUPLE CAMEO PORTRAITS, 2004. The four coinage portraits of Queen Elizabeth II are featured on the Obverse of the $300 coin for 2004. Each is struck in 24kt gold.

Designers: Obv.: As per portrait
     Rev.: Christie Paquet
Specifications: Same as 2002 issue
Case of Issue: Black leatherette clam case with RCM plaque, black flocked insert, encapsulated coin, COA; black and gold outer case

Engravers: Obv.: As per portrait
     Rev.: Christie Paquet
Finish: Proof

BRITANNIA, 2005. Commemorating the twenty-five cent note issue of 1870, which featured a vignette of Britannia.

Designers: Obv.: Susanna Blunt
     Rev.: R. R. Carmichael
Specifications: Same as 2002 issue
Case of Issue: Black leatherette clam case with RCM plaque, black flocked insert, encapsulated coin, COA; black and gold outer case

Engravers: Obv.: Susan Taylor
     Rev.: José Osio
Finish: Proof

Date	Description	Issue Price	Mintage	PROOF (PR) 65	66	67	68
2004	Cameo Portraits	N/A	994	–	–	1,450.	–
2005	Britannia	N/A	1,250	–	–	1,300.	–

GOLD 350 DOLLARS

THE FLORAL GOLD COIN SIGNATURE SERIES, 1998-2004. Begun in 1998 and issued annually, the $350 gold coin bears either a national or provincial flower.

COMMON CHARACTERISTICS

Composition: .99999 gold
Diameter: 34.0 mm
Thickness: 1998-2003: 2.75 mm
          2004-2005: N/A
Finish: Proof

Weight: 1998-2003: 38.05 grams
       2004-2005: 35.0 grams
Edge: Serrated
Die Axis: ↑↑

Case of Issue:
    (A) 1998 to 2004: Anodized gold-coloured aluminum box with cherry wood stained siding, encapsulated coin, COA.
    (B) 2005: Red plastic display case, black plastic insert, encapsulated coin, COA

90TH ANNIVERSARY OF THE ROYAL CANADIAN MINT, 1998

Designer: Dora de Pédery-Hunt
Engraver: Dora de Pédery-Hunt

Designer: Pierre Leduc
Engraver: Ago Aarand

THE GOLDEN SLIPPER, PRINCE EDWARD ISLAND'S FLORAL EMBLEM, 1999

Designer: Dora de Pédery-Hunt
Engraver: Dora de Pédery-Hunt

Designer: Henry Purdy
Engraver: José Osio

Date	Description	Issue Price	Mintage	PROOF (PR) 65	66	67	68
1998	90th Anniv.	999.99	1,999	–	–	1,600.	–
1999	Golden Slipper	999.99	1,990	–	–	950.	–

THE PACIFIC DOGWOOD, BRITISH COLUMBIA'S FLORAL EMBLEM, 2000.

Photograph not
available
at press time

Designer: Dora de Pédery-Hunt
Engraver: Dora de Pédery-Hunt

Designer: Caren Heine
Engraver: José Osio

THE MAYFLOWER, NOVA SCOTIA'S FLORAL EMBLEM, 2001

Photograph not
available
at press time

Designer: Dora de Pédery-Hunt
Engraver: Dora de Pédery-Hunt

Designer: Bonnie Ross
Engraver: Susan Taylor

THE WILD ROSE, ALBERTA'S FLORAL EMBLEM, 2002

Designer: Dora de Pédery-Hunt
Engraver: Dora de Pédery-Hunt

Designer: Dr. A. K. Hellum
Engraver: William Woodruff

Date	Description	Issue Price	Mintage	65	PROOF (PR) 66	67	68
2000	Pacific Dogwood	999.99	1,971	–	–	1,600.	–
2001	The Mayflower	999.99	1,988	–	–	1,100.	–
2002	The Wild Rose	1,099.99	2,001	–	–	1,100.	–

THE WHITE TRILLIUM, ONTARIO'S FLORAL EMBLEM, 2003

Designer: Dora de Pédery-Hunt
Engraver: Dora de Pédery-Hunt

Designer: Pamela Stagg
Engraver: William Woodruff

THE FIREWEED, YUKON TERRITORY FLORAL EMBLEM, 2004

Photograph not
available
at press time

Designer: Susanna Blunt
Engraver: Susan Taylor

Designer: Catherine Ann Deer
Engraver: William Woodruff

THE WESTERN RED LILY, SASKATCHEWAN'S FLORAL EMBLEM, 2005

Designer: Susanna Blunt
Engraver: Susan Taylor

Designer: Chris Jordison
Engraver: José Osio

Date	Description	Issue Price	Mintage	PROOF (PR)			
				65	66	67	68
2003	White Trillium	1,099.99	1,865	–	–	1,100.	–
2004	Fireweed	1,099.99	1,836	–	–	1,100.	–
2005	Western Red Lily	1,295.95	2,005	–	–	1,200.	–

COLLECTOR SETS
PROOF-LIKE AND BRILLIANT UNCIRCULATED SETS
1954-2005
SIX COIN SILVER PROOF-LIKE SETS 1954-1960

1953 saw the first use of the white cardboard six-coin holder that in 1954 became the package for public sale of sets. The holder with the coins included was wrapped in cellophane. The finish on the coins offered acquired the name proof-like.

Date.	Issue Price	Mintage	63	64	PROOF-LIKE (PL) 65	66	67	68
1954 NSF	2.50	3,000	–	–	1,200.	–	–	–
1954 SF	2.50	Included	–	–	500.	–	–	–
1955	2.50	6,300	–	–	400.	–	–	–
1955 Arn.	2.50	Included	–	–	600.	–	–	–
1956	2.50	6,500	–	–	225.	–	–	–
1957	2.50	11,862	–	–	150.	–	–	–
1957 1WL	2.50	Included	–	–	200.	–	–	–
1958	2.50	18,259	–	–	100.	–	–	–
1959	3.00	31,577	–	–	60.	–	–	–

Note: The 1954 No Shoulder Fold designation applies only to the one cent coin; the balance of the coins (5) are of the Shoulder Fold variety.

SIX COIN SILVER PROOF-LIKE SETS 1960

In 1960 the white carboard holders appeared with a Royal Canadian Mint domicile. Three varieties of stamps exist. A sealed wooden box containting 250 proof-like sets was available directly from the Mint in 1960.

Stamp One

ROYAL CANADIAN MINT
OTTAWA   CANADA

Stamp Two

ROYAL CANADIAN MINT
OTTAWA   CANADA

Stamp Three

Date.	Issue Price	Mintage	63	64	PROOF-LIKE (PL) 65	66	67	68
1960	3.00	64,097	–	–	50.	–	–	–

SIX COIN SILVER PROOF-LIKE SETS 1961-1967

This is a continuation of the set offered previously. It contains one of each denomination (for a total of six coins) packaged in a flat pliofilm pouch, inserted in a brown kraft envelope.

The 1961 set, which of course was the first set packaged under the system, did not come without problems. The one cent coin was prone to discolouring, making a brilliant, red PL-65 cent a scarcity.

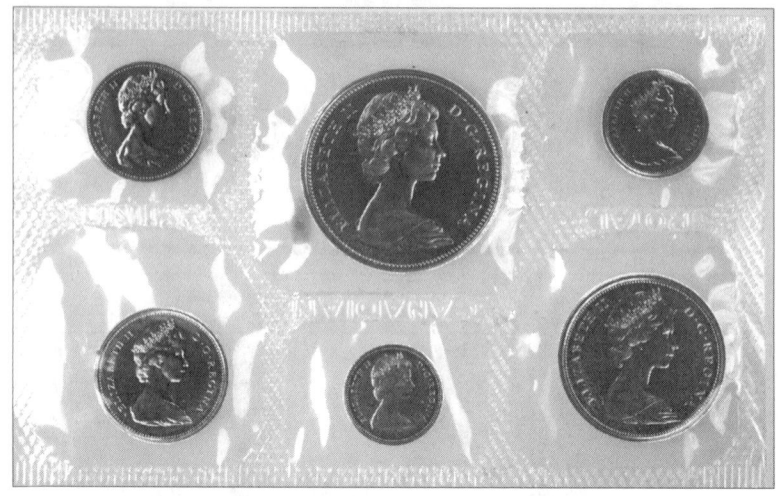

Date.	Issue Price	Mintage	PROOF-LIKE (PL)					
			63	64	65	66	67	68
1961	3.00	98,373	–	–	35.	–	–	–
1962	3.00	200,950	–	–	20.	–	–	–
1963	3.00	673,006	–	–	12.	–	–	–
1964	3.00	1,653,162	–	–	12.	–	–	–
1965 Type 1	4.00	2,904,352	–	–	12.	–	–	–
1965 Type 2	4.00	Included	–	–	12.	–	–	–
1966 L.B.	4.00	672,514	–	–	12.	–	–	–
1967	4.00	963,714	–	–	15.	–	–	–

Note: 1.   Types Three, Four and Five of the 1965 silver dollar were not packaged by the Mint for issue in proof-like sets.

      2.   Since they were not officially released, no 1966 small bead dollars were issued in proof-like sets.

SIX COIN NICKEL BRILLIANT UNCIRCULATED SETS 1968-1976

This is a continuation of the sets previously offered, except that the 10 cents through one dollar coins are now nickel in composition. Naturally, the one cent and five cents remained the same, and the pliofilm packaging continued, the outer envelope is white with blue printing. The finish on the coins in the sets is brilliant uncirculated, brilliant relief on brilliant background.

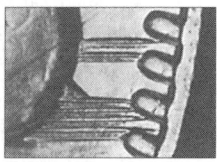

1968 Double Waterlines
Doubled Die (DD)

Pliofilm packaging

1974 Double Yoke
Doubled Die
Variety 1

Date.	Issue Price	Mintage	PROOF-LIKE (PL)					
			63	64	65	66	67	68
1968	4.00	521,641	–	–	3.25	–	–	–
1968 S. Is.	4.00	Included	–	–	12.00	–	–	–
1968 No Is.	4.00	Included	–	–	10.00	–	–	–
1968 DD	4.00	Included	–	–	65.00	–	–	–
1969	4.00	326,203	–	–	4.00	–	–	–
1970	4.00	349,120	–	–	5.00	–	–	–
1971	4.00	253,311	–	–	4.00	–	–	–
1972	4.00	224,275	–	–	4.00	–	–	–
1973 L.B.	4.00	243,695	–	–	275.00	–	–	–
1973 S.B.	4.00	Included	–	–	6.00	–	–	–
1974	5.00	213,589	–	–	5.00	–	–	–
1974 DD	5.00	Included	–	–	450.00	–	–	–
1975	5.00	197,372	–	–	4.00	–	–	–
1976	5.15	171,737	–	–	5.00	–	–	–

SIX COIN NICKEL BRILLIANT UNCIRCULATED SETS, 1977-1980

In 1977 the quality of the pliofilm sets began to improve, probably as a result of purchase of numismatic presses in 1972 to produce Canada's first officially recognized proof coins for the Montreal Olympic sets. The finish on the coins in the sets was now advertised by the Royal Canadian Mint as brilliant relief against a brilliant background.

Date.	Issue Price	Mintage	BRILLIANT UNCIRCULATED (MS)					
			63	64	65	66	67	68
1977	5.15	225,307	–	–	5.00	–	–	–
1977 SWL	5.15	Included	–	–	10.00	–	–	–
1978 SJ	5.25	260,000	–	–	4.00	–	–	–
1978 RJ	5.25	Included	–	–	15.00	–	–	–
1979	6.25	187,624	–	–	7.50	–	–	–
1979 Ptd	6.25	Included	–	–	7.50	–	–	–
1980	8.00	169,390	–	–	5.00	–	–	–

SIX COIN NICKEL BRILLIANT UNCIRCULATED SETS 1981-1987

In 1980 the Mint's marketing department began a restructuring of the selection of coins offered to collectors. The old issue of Proof-like sets (not a term recognized by the R.C.M.) was officially replaced by a new issue called "The Brilliant Uncirculated Set." This set features one coin of each denomination issued for circulation in Canada.

The quality improvement which began in 1977 continued with the 1981 introduction of a confirmed finish on the pliofilm set of "brilliant relief on brilliant background."

In 1985 the Mint experimented with a clear hard plastic package to replace the soft pliofilm package used in previous years. As it did not prove to be practical the experimental package was not adopted.

1987 was the last year the nickel voyageur dollar was used in the brilliant uncirculated sets.

Date.	Issue Price	Mintage	BRILLIANT UNCIRCULATED (MS)					
			63	64	65	66	67	68
1981	5.00	186,250	–	–	5.	–	–	–
1982	5.00	203,287	–	–	5.	–	–	–
1983	5.00	190,838	–	–	9.	–	–	–
1984	5.00	181,415	–	–	8.	–	–	–
1985 Pliofilm	6.95	173,924	–	–	9.	–	–	–
1985 Plastic	N/A	Included	–	–	30.	–	–	–
1986	6.95	167,338	–	–	10.	–	–	–
1987	6.95	212,136	–	–	8.	–	–	–

SIX COIN NICKEL BRILLIANT UNCIRCULATED SETS 1988-1995

In 1987 the nickel Voyageur dollar was retired and in 1988 the bronze Loon dollar was introduced into the brilliant uncirculated set. The finish on the coins in these sets was brilliant relief on a brilliant background.

Date.	Issue Price	Mintage	63	64	BRILLIANT UNCIRCULATED (MS) 65	66	67	68
1988	6.95	182,048	–	–	8.00	–	–	–
1989	7.70	158,636	–	–	12.00	–	–	–
1990	7.70	170,791	–	–	12.00	–	–	–
1991	8.50	147,814	–	–	45.00	–	–	–
1992	9.50	217,597	–	–	17.50	–	–	–
1993	9.50	171,680	–	–	6.00	–	–	–
1993 CNA	9.50	Included	–	–	13.00	–	–	–
1994	9.75	141,676	–	–	8.00	–	–	–
1995	9.75	143,892	–	–	11.00	–	–	–

Note:. The 1993 CNA set is packaged in a commemorative envelope.

SIX COIN NICKEL SPECIMEN SET 1996

In 1996 the finish on the coins was changed to brilliant relief against a parallel lined background. This finish was first developed for the bullion maple leaf program, and in 1981 used on the Specimen sets issued by the Mint for that year.

Date	Issue Price	Mintage	63	64	SPECIMEN (SP) 65	66	67	68
1996	11.95	120,217	–	–	–	27.50	–	–

Note: The 1996 Brilliant Uncirculated set contains the 5¢ NR 6 variety.

SEVEN COIN NICKEL SPECIMEN SET 1997

In 1997 the two dollar Polar Bear coin was added to the set. In mid-1997 the RCM transferred production of the uncirculated sets to Winnipeg. The Ottawa and Winnipeg issues of 1997 can be distinguished by the method of packaging, not by the finish of the coins. They are indicated by (O) for Ottawa and (W) for Winnipeg in the listings. No mint marks appear on 1997-dated coins. The finishes on both sets (1997) are technically equal, which is Brilliant Relief - Parallel Finish on background.

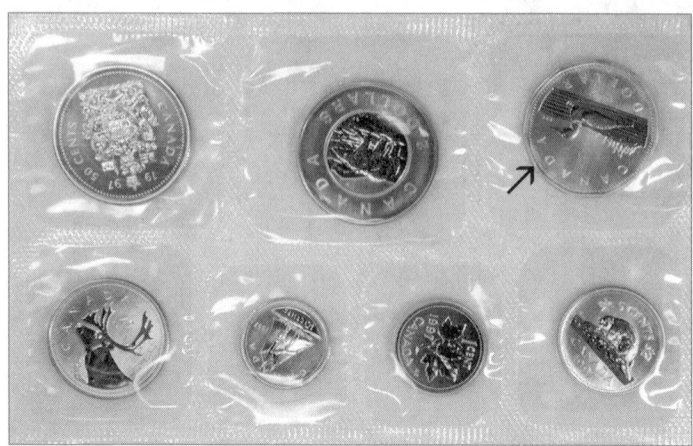

1997 Ottawa Uncirculated Set – The $1.00 Loon coin is at top right
with the $2.00 reverse at top centre

1997 Winnipeg Uncirculated Set – The $1.00 Loon coin is at top left
with the $2.00 reverse at top centre

Date and		Issue		SPECIMEN (SP)			
Mint Mark	Description	Price	Mintage	65	66	67	68
1997 (O)	Loon/Polar Bear	13.95	174,692	–	27.50	–	–
1997 (W)	Loon/Polar Bear	13.95	Included	–	12.00	–	–

SEVEN COIN NICKEL BRILLIANT UNCIRCULATED SETS 1998-2000

In 1998 the finish on the coins returned to a brilliant relief with a brilliant background, and this was continued until 2000. To distinguish the coins produced at the Winnipeg mint in 1998, a "W" was added to all coins from the one cent through to the two dollar coin. This is the first time the Canadian mint placed a mint mark on Canadian coins. When the set production was moved back to Ottawa, in mid-1998, the coins were struck without a mint mark. In 2000, the mint mark appeared again as set production was moved back to the Winnipeg mint. The packaging of the sets in transparent plastic film was continued, and 2000 was the last year of issue for sets containing pure nickel coinage. The Winnipeg mint mark 'W' is found on the obverse, to the lower left of the portrait.

"W" Mint Mark

Date and		Issue		BRILLIANT UNCIRCULATED (MS)			
Mint Mark	Description	Price	Mintage	65	66	67	68
1998	Loon/Polar Bear	13.95	145,439	20.00	–	–	–
1998 W	Loon/Polar Bear	13.95	Included	27.50	–	–	–
1999	Loon/Polar Bear	13.95	117,318	12.00	–	–	–
1999	Loon/Nunavut	13.95	74,821	12.00	–	–	–
1999	Loon/Nun. Mule	13.95	Included	350.00	–	–	–
2000	Loon/Polar Bears	15.95	186,985	12.00	–	–	–
2000 W	Loon/Polar Bear	15.95	Included	12.00	–	–	–

Note: See page 327 for the Brilliant Uncirculated images of the 1999 Nunavut Mule.

FIVE COIN MULTI-PLY PLATED STEEL TEST SET FOR 1999

This set is a Royal Canadian Mint test token set (TTS-3); see page 248 for the complete listing.

SEVEN COIN MULTI-PLY PLATED STEEL BRILLIANT UNCIRCULATED SETS 2001-2005

The first issue of the new multi-ply plated steel, brilliant uncirculated sets took place in 2001. Five coins, one cent through fifty cents, all carried the new composition mark "P". The $1.00 and $2.00 coins did not; they were struck on the standard planchets for those denominations. The finish on the multi-ply plated steel coins is brilliant relief on a brilliant background, continuing from the 2000 nickel sets.

In 2002, to commemorate the Golden Jubilee of Queen Elizabeth II, the Mint issued double dated (1952-2002) plated steel coinage for circulation. These coins were used in the collectors' sets, and are identical to those of the previous year except for the double dates. Special Edition Jubilee Sets are found on page 407.

Mid year 2003 the tiara portrait of Elizabeth II, which had been used since 1990, was replaced with the new uncrowned portrait by Susanna Blunt. The first set issued was 2004.

Date	Description	Issue Price	Mintage	BRILLIANT UNCIRCULATED (MS)			
				65	66	67	68
2001P	Loon/Bear	15.95	115,897	15.	–	–	–
1952-2002P	Loon/Bear	15.95	100,467	16.	–	–	–
2003P	Loon/Bear	15.95	94,126	20.	–	–	–
2004P	Loon/Bear	15.95	90,658	15.	–	–	–
2005P	Loon/Bear	15.95	N/A	16.	–	–	–

SPECIAL EDITION SEVEN COIN BRILLIANT UNCIRCULATED SETS
QUEEN ELIZABETH II, JUBILEE,
MULTI-PLY PLATED STEEL, 1952-2002 and 2003

The Special Edition Uncirculated set of 1952-2002 contains the Golden Jubilee 50-cent piece and the 1952-2002 Canada Day 25-cent coin; the balance of the coins are the regular double-dated Jubilee 1952-2002P issue.

In mid-year 2003, the "Tiara Portrait" of Queen Elizabeth, by Dora de Pédery-Hunt, was replaced by a more mature portrait by Susanna Blunt. The special edition uncirculated set of 2003 contains the seven circulating denominations, with the new effigy of Queen Elizabeth II. This set was struck at the Winnipeg Mint, and naturally carries the mint mark W (WP). The lower denominations, one cent to fifty cents also carry the composition mark "P".

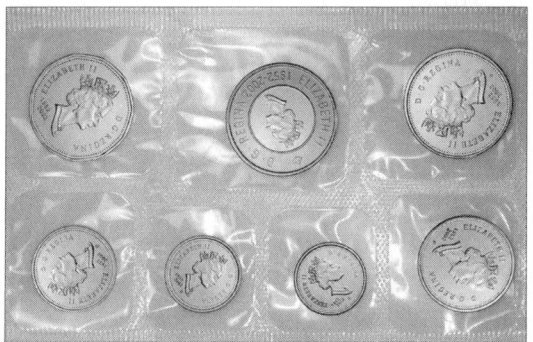

Date	Description	Issue Price	Mintage	BRILLIANT UNCIRCULATED (MS)			
				65	66	67	68
1952-2002P	Accession	15.95	49,869	16.00	–	–	–
2003WP	Coronation	15.95	71,142	16.00	–	–	–

SEVEN COIN NICKEL CUSTOM SETS 1971-1976

The custom set contains one of each denomination, with an extra cent to show the obverse. The finish of the coins is identical to the equivalent year of brilliant uncirculated, brilliant relief on a brilliant background.

Cases: 1971: Coins in black vinyl-covered case with Canada's coat of arms and The word "CANADA" stamped in gold on the top.

1972-1973: as 1971, except the outer case is red.

1974-1976: as 1971, except the outer case is maroon.

Date	Description	Issue Price	Mintage	65	PROOF-LIKE (PL) 66	67	68
1971		6.50	33,517	7.50	–	–	–
1972		6.50	38,198	7.50	–	–	–
1973	LB 25¢	6.50	49,376	300.00	–	–	–
1973	SB 25¢	6.50	Included	7.50	–	–	–
1974		8.00	44,296	7.50	–	–	–
1975		8.00	36,581	7.50	–	–	–

"OH CANADA!" NICKEL BRILLIANT UNCIRCULATED SETS 1994-2000

First issued in 1994, this set includes the nickel-bronze dollar current in that year. In 1997 this set was expanded to include the two dollar polar bear coin. In 1998 the packaging of the "Oh Canada!" sets changed from card displays to clear plastic display units. The coins of the "Oh Canada!" set are identical in finish to the equivalent year of the brilliant uncirculated set.

Date	Description	Issue Price	Mintage	65	BRILLIANT UNCIRCULATED (MS) 66	67	68
1994	Loon/–	16.95	18,794	20.00	–	–	–
1995	Peacekeeping/–	16.95	50,927	19.00	–	–	–
1996	Loon/–	16.95	31,083	20.00	–	–	–
1997	Flying Loon/ Bear	21.95	84,124	42.50	–	–	–
1998	Loon/Bear	21.95	42,710	25.00	–	–	–
1998W	Loon/Bear	21.95	24,792	30.00	–	–	–
1999	Loon/Bear	21.95	82,754	22.50	–	–	–
2000	Loon/Bear	21.95	107,884	10.00	–	–	–
2000W	Loon/Bear	21.95	Included	20.00	–	–	–

"OH CANADA!" MULTI-PLY PLATED STEEL SEVEN COIN BRILLIANT UNCIRCULATED SETS 2001-2005

In 2001 the five subsidiary coins of the "Oh Canada!" set were replaced by the five multi-ply plated steel coins. In the 2002 set all coins bear the double dates 1952-2002 to commemorate the 50th anniversary of Her Majesty Queen Elizabeth II's accession to the throne.

Beginning in 2004 the coins carry the new Susanna Blunt effigy of Queen Elizabeth II. The coins in the "Oh Canada!" set are identical in finish to the brilliant uncirculated set of that year.

Date	Description	Issue Price	Mintage	65	BRILLIANT UNCIRCULATED (MS) 66	67	68
2001P	Loon/Bear	22.95	66,726	10.00	–	–	–
1952-2002P	Loon/Bear	22.95	61,484	22.50	–	–	–
2003P	Loon/Bear	23.95	51,146	22.50	–	–	–
2004P	Loon/Bear	23.95	53,329	20.00	–	–	–
2005P	Loon/Bear	19.95	N/A	20.00	–	–	–

"BUNDLE OF JOY/TINY TREASURES" NICKEL BRILLIANT UNCIRCULATED SETS 1995 - 2000

First issued in 1995, the brilliant uncirculated set of coins was specially packaged for the gift market using the six coins from the brilliant uncirculated set of that year. In 1997 this set was expanded to include the two dollar polar bear coin. In 1998 the name changed from "Bundle of Joy" to "Tiny Treasures" uncirculated sets. Also in the same year the packaging of the sets of "Tiny Treasures" changed from card displays to clear plastic display units. The movement of set production to Winnipeg and back to Ottawa that occurred in 1998 also affected the "Oh Canada!" and "Tiny Treasures" sets. In 2000 production of the sets occurred in both the Ottawa and Winnipeg mints.

Date	Description	Issue Price	Mintage	BRILLIANT UNCIRCULATED (MS) 65	66	67	68
1995	Loon	19.95	36,443	18.00	–	–	–
1996	Loon	19.95	56,618	27.50	–	–	–
1997	Loon/Bear	21.95	55,199	20.00	–	–	–
1998	Loon/Bear	21.95	46,139	20.00	–	–	–
1998W	Loon/Bear	21.95	12,625	27.50	–	–	–
1999	Loon/Bear	21.95	67,694	22.50	–	–	–
2000	Loon/Bear	21.95	82,964	10.00	–	–	–
2000W	Loon/Bear	21.95	Included	20.00	–	–	–
2000	Loon/Bears	21.95	Included	10.00	–	–	–

"TINY TREASURES" MULTI-PLY PLATED STEEL BRILLIANT UNCIRCULATED SETS 2001-2003

As with the uncirculated sets of 2001 the nickel coinage of the previous year was replaced with the new patented multi-ply plated steel coins. In the 2002 set all coins bear the double dates 1952-2002 to commemorate the 50th anniversary of Her Majesty Queen Elizabeth II's accession to the throne. In 2003 two effigys are to be found on the Tiny Treasures coin set, crowned and uncrowned. 2003 was the last year of issue for the "Tiny Treasures" sets.

Date	Description	Issue Price	Mintage	BRILLIANT UNCIRCULATED (MS) 65	66	67	68
2001P	Loon/Bear	22.95	52,085	10.00	–	–	–
1952-2002P	Loon/Bear	22.95	51,491	22.50	–	–	–
2003P	Loon/Bear	22.95	43,197	25.00	–	–	–

BRILLIANT UNCIRCULATED SET DERIVATIVES

GIFT AND HOLIDAY SETS

In 2004 the Royal Canadian Mint introduced a series of brilliant uncirculated, seven-coin sets designed for the gift market. Each set features packaging designed especially for the market for which it is intended.

Date and Mint Mark	Description	Issue Price	Mintage	MS-65
1983	1¢ to $1.00 in a Folder Packaged and sold by the BRM	N/A	N/A	150.
1998	"OH CANADA!" for CIBC, Smart Start	21.95	N/A	10.
2001P	BRILLIANT UNCRICULATED SET with Canada 2001 Medallion	N/A	N/A	25.
2001P	"OH CANADA!" for			
	Banff	22.95	N/A	10.
	Calgary	22.95	N/A	10.
	Halifax	22.95	N/A	10.
	Montreal, regular	22.95	N/A	10.
	Niagara Falls	22.95	N/A	10.
	Quebec City	22.95	N/A	10.
	R.C.M.	22.95	N/A	10.
	St. John's	22.95	N/A	10.
	Vancouver	22.95	N/A	10.
	Whistler	22.95	N/A	10.
2004P	BABY Gift Set	19.95	53,136	20.
	BIRTHDAY Gift Set	19.95	N/A	20.
	GRADUATION Gift Set	19.95	22,751	20.
	WEDDING Gift Set	19.95	19,156	20.
2004P	SANTA CLAUS Colourized twenty-five cents with six other coins in a festive folder	19.95	60,965	20.
2005P	BABY Gift Set	19.95	N/A	20.
	BIRTHDAY Gift set	19.95	N/A	20.
	GRADUATION Gift Set	19.95	N/A	20.
	WEDDING Gift Set	19.95	N/A	20.

Note: BRM denotes British Royal Mint.

SINGLE COINS REMOVED FROM PROOF-LIKE
and BRILLIANT UNCIRCULATED SETS

During the last fifty years, for one reason or another, collectors of Canadian coins have resorted to stripping individual coins from sets issued by the Numismatic Department of the Mint. Besides condition at times being the driving force, there developed in the 1990s another need. Business strikes were just not available if a series were to be maintained. For example, the 1992 Caribou twenty-five cents was not issued as a business strike; therefore, collectors who wished to maintain that series had to extract a brilliant uncirculated coin from a set.

PROOF-LIKE SINGLES 1950-1953

All proof-like singles, 1¢ – $1.00, originated from sets, either sold by the Mint on request or given by the Mint Master to individuals during a visit to the Mint. Of course, on special government occasions coins were struck as presentation gifts to visiting dignitaries. These sets came in either a brown kraft envelope, with the coins enclosed in cellophane packets, approximately 2" x 3", or in a small white cardboard box of the same dimensions.

Early singles prior to 1953 exist but not in sufficient quantities to merit listing. The sets were surprise packages because there was no condition consistency in their contents. More often than not the quality of the six coins was mixed from brilliant uncirculated to specimen. We must remember these sets were considered gifts and thus there was no uniform quality requirement.

The coins listed below all originated from the Mint via this route. The quality of the coins listed is proof-like (PL-65). Set prices are not listed simply because they are seldom found, and if available they were more than likely assembled after the fact.

Finish: Proof-like

Date and Mint Mark	1¢	5¢	PROOF-LIKE (PL-65) 10¢	25¢	50¢	$1
1950	–	–	–	–	–	375.
1950 Arn.	–	–	–	–	–	1,000.
1950 SWL	–	–	–	–	–	650.
1951	2,500.	–	–	150.	350.	325.
1951 Arn.	–	–	–	–	–	2,000.
1952 WL	–	–	–	500.	350.	600.
1952 NWL	–	–	–	–	–	350.
1952 SWL	–	–	–	–	–	2,000.
1953 NSF	300.	500.	300.	450.	1,250.	1,300.
1953 SF	200.	350.	150.	200.	400.	850.

PROOF-LIKE SILVER DOLLARS 1954-1964

In 1954 the Royal Canadian Mint began a program of selling specially struck dollar coins to collectors. These proof-like dollars were packaged in cellophane envelopes between the years 1954 and 1961, and from 1962 to 1964 in pliofilm pouches. Listed below are the issue prices and mintages for each year. For prices see page 412.

Date	Issue Price	Mintage	Date	Issue Price	Mintage
1954	1.25	5,300	1959	1.25	13,583
1955	1.25	7,950	1960	1.25	18,631
1955 Arn	1.25	Included	1961	1.25	22,555
1956	1.25	10,212	1962	1.25	47,591
1957	1.25	15,490	1963	1.25	290,529
1958	1.25	33,237	1964	1.25	1,209,279

SINGLE NICKEL DOLLARS

Nickel dollars were issued for collectors in 1968 and 1969. They were packaged by the Royal Canadian Mint in pliofilm strips of five coins per strip. This method of packaging was discontinued in 1969.

Date and Description	Issue Price	Mintage	BRILLIANT UNCIRCULATED (MS)		
			63	64	65
1968	1.25	885,124	2.	3.	6.
1969	1.25	211,112	2.	3.	6.

PROOF-LIKE SINGLES 1954-1967

As in the previous listing all single proof-like coins are from sets. However, beginning in 1954 the sets were sold to the public, and quality became consistent throughout the set, meaning all coins were proof-like. The Mint never recognized this term, selling the coins as brilliant uncirculated "business strikes." In order to avoid complaints regarding quality the premium over face value was minimal – 59 cents, leaving no room to engage in a discussion over quality.

It is in this series that cameo coins are found. Struck from a silver-copper alloy, they were easier to strike than the later pure nickel coinage. The ease of striking, coupled with new dies, produced cameo coins. The newer the die the greater the potential for cameo strikes. Cameo prices are multiples of the prices listed below.

Finish: Proof-like, see page 413

Date and Mint Mark	PROOF-LIKE (PL- 65)					
	1¢	5¢	10¢	25¢	50¢	$1
1954 NSF	1,000.	–	–	–	–	–
1954 SF	55.	50.	35.	65.	75.	250.
1955 NSF	500.	–	–	–	–	–
1955 SF	30.	25.	25.	45.	55.	150.
1955 Arn	–	–	–	–	–	265.
1956	30.	25.	20.	25.	40.	125.
1957	20.	15.	20.	20.	30.	60.
1957 One WL	–	–	–	–	–	200.
1958	15.	15.	15.	20.	25.	45.
1959	15.	15.	10.	15.	20.	35.
1960	10.	12.	10.	15.	20.	25.
1961	10.	12.	10.	10.	20.	25.
1962	10.	10.	10.	10.	20.	20.
1963	10.	10.	10.	10.	15.	20.
1964	10.	10.	10.	10.	15.	20.
1965 Var. 1 (1¢ SB, P5)	10.	10.	10.	10.	15.	–
1965 Var. 2 (1¢ SB, B5)	10.	–	–	–	–	–
1965 Var. 3 (1¢ LB, B5)	150.	–	–	–	–	–
1965 Var. 1 ($1 SB, PT5)	–	–	–	–	–	20.
1965 Var. 2 ($1 SB, B5)	–	–	–	–	–	35.
1965 Var. 3 ($1 LB, B5)	–	–	–	–	–	150.
1965 Var. 4 ($1 LB, P5)	–	–	–	–	–	150.
1966	10.	10.	10.	10.	15.	20.
1967	10.	10.	10.	10.	15.	20.

Note: The 1965 Variety 5 dollar does not exist in proof-like condition.

CERTIFIED SILVER PROOF-LIKE DOLLARS 1954 TO 1967

Proof-like coins were struck by specially prepared dies on specially prepared blanks with special handling from striking to packaging.

The frosted obverse relief that may be found on proof-like coins has been classified by ICCS in four categories.

The cameo effect is produced by fresh new polished and treated dies. The first few coins will be an ultra heavy cameo with the finish on the relief wearing quickly as striking continues. There may be no more than 500 coins struck from a pair of dies that will be classed as cameos.

Ultra Heavy Cameo: Full frosting across the relief of the coin, both effigy and legend, when viewed from all directions under full lighting conditions. A good example of ultra heavy cameo can be found on the 1953-2003 proof Coronation set.

Heavy Cameo: The frosting is not full and evenly applied across the relief of the coin. In fact, some areas may appear bright when viewed under full lighting conditions.

Cameo: Touches of frosting appear on the relief of the coin. There will be bright areas when the coin is viewed under full lighting conditions.

No Cameo: No frosting, all relief areas will appear bright. There is no difference in contrast between the bright field and a bright relief.

Date	Finish	PL-63	PL-64	PL-65	PL-66	PL-67
1954	Ultra Heavy Cameo	–	–	–	–	–
	Heavy Cameo	–	–	350.	600.	–
	Cameo	–	–	275.	–	–
	No Cameo	125.	165.	200.	400.	600.
1955	Ultra Heavy Cameo	–	–	–	–	–
	Heavy Cameo	100.	160.	275.	–	–
	Cameo	75.	110.	175.	350.	–
	No Cameo	70.	100.	150.	300.	425.
1955 Arn	No Cameo	200.	250.	275.	–	1,700.
1956	Ultra Heavy Cameo	–	275.	–	1,200.	–
	Heavy Cameo	100.	150.	200.	350.	–
	Cameo	75.	85.	125.	175.	–
	No Cameo	65.	75.	100.	150.	–
1957	Ultra Heavy Cameo	–	–	–	–	–
	Heavy Cameo	–	–	–	–	–
	Cameo	40.	45.	175.	–	–
	No Cameo	35.	40.	60.	125.	–
1957 One WL	No Cameo	–	–	–	–	–
1958	Ultra Heavy Cameo	–	–	–	–	–
	Heavy Cameo	50.	70.	150.	150.	–
	Cameo	20.	35.	50.	100.	–
	No Cameo	15.	30.	45.	80.	200.
1959	Ultra Heavy Cameo	–	–	–	–	–
	Heavy Cameo	75.	125.	150.	–	–
	Cameo	20.	30.	40.	–	–
	No Cameo	15.	20.	35.	55.	–
1960	Ultra Heavy Cameo	–	–	–	–	–
	Heavy Cameo	35.	45.	65.	175.	–
	Cameo	25.	25.	35.	75.	–
	No Cameo	20.	25.	30.	50.	–

CERTIFIED SILVER PROOF-LIKE DOLLARS 1954 TO 1967 (cont.)

Date	Finish	PL-63	PL-64	PL-65	PL-66	PL-67
1961	Ultra Heavy Cameo	–	–	–	–	–
	Heavy Cameo	20.	30.	65.	–	–
	Cameo	10.	20.	30.	50.	–
	No Cameo	10.	20.	30.	50.	–
1962	Ultra Heavy Cameo	–	–	–	–	–
	Heavy Cameo	20.	25.	35.	50.	–
	Cameo	10.	20.	30.	40.	–
	No Cameo	10.	15.	25.	35.	–
1963	Ultra Heavy Cameo	100.	145.	185.	–	–
	Heavy Cameo	15.	20.	35.	–	–
	Cameo	10.	15.	20.	35.	–
	No Cameo	10.	15.	20.	35.	200.
1964	Ultra Heavy Cameo	–	–	65.	–	–
	Heavy Cameo	25.	30.	40.	–	–
	Cameo	10.	15.	20.	125.	–
	No Cameo	10.	15.	25.	50.	–
1964 Missing Dot	No Cameo	40.	50.	60.	–	175.
1965 T-1	Ultra Heavy Cameo	–	–	–	–	–
	Heavy Cameo	30.	40.	50.	–	–
	Cameo	15.	20.	30.	–	–
	No Cameo	10.	15.	20.	–	–
1965 T-2	Ultra Heavy Cameo	–	–	–	–	450.
	Heavy Cameo	20.	25.	35.	215.	–
	Cameo	–	–	–	–	–
	No Cameo	15.	20.	35.	60.	300.
1965 T-3	Ultra Heavy Cameo	–	–	–	–	–
	Heavy Cameo	–	–	–	–	–
	Cameo	–	–	–	–	–
	No Cameo	65.	75.	100.	150.	300.
1965 T-4	Ultra Heavy Cameo	–	–	–	–	450.
	Heavy Cameo	–	–	150.	–	300.
	Cameo	–	–	–	–	–
	No Cameo	65.	75.	100.	150.	300.
1965 T-5	Ultra Heavy Cameo	–	–	–	–	–
	Heavy Cameo	–	50.	150.	–	–
	Cameo	–	–	–	–	–
	No Cameo	–	–	–	–	–
1966	Ultra Heavy Cameo	–	–	–	–	–
	Heavy Cameo	15.	20.	45.	–	–
	Cameo	10.	15.	20.	–	–
	No Cameo	10.	15.	20.	70.	–
1966 SB	Ultra Heavy Cameo	–	–	–	–	–
	Heavy Cameo	–	–	–	–	–
	Cameo	–	–	–	–	–
	No Cameo	–	2,900.	3,600.	–	–
1967	Ultra Heavy Cameo	–	–	–	–	–
	Heavy Cameo	25.	35.	40.	125.	–
	Cameo	15.	20.	25.	50.	–
	No Cameo	15.	20.	25.	50.	–

BRILLIANT UNCIRCULATED SINGLES 1968-2005

The average condition of brilliant uncirculated issues is Mint State-65 (MS-65). Coins, when removed from sets may grade higher or lower than the average. However, just to complicate matters it is in this category that the finish on the coins may vary slightly, with the finish moving from brilliant uncirculated to proof-like. It is very difficult for the average collector to make this distinction, in fact even the most sophisticated grading companies may have problems. It is best to think of brilliant uncirculated sets as containing all mint state coins. If, however, proof-like coins do emerge and are certified as such they will command a premium over mint state coins.

Brilliant Uncirculated: 1968 to 2005 Brilliant relief on brilliant background

Prices for Certified MS-65 Coins

Date	1¢	5¢	Denominations 10¢	25¢	50¢	1.00	2.00
1968-2005	10.	10.	10.	12.	15.	20.	20.

Coins found only in Brilliant Uncirculated Sets

Date	Denom	Type	CERTIFIED MS-63	MS-64	MS-65
1997	.25¢	Caribou	–	–	10.
1997	1.00	Loon	–	–	15.
1997	1.00	Flying Loon	–	–	40.
1998	.25¢	Caribou	–	–	20.
1998	1.00	Loon	–	–	15.
1999	.25¢	Caribou	–	–	15.
1999	1.00	Loon	–	–	15.
1999	1.00	Nunavut Mule	–	–	200.
2000	.25¢	Caribou	–	–	15.
2000	1.00	Loon	–	–	15.
2000	2.00	Bear	–	–	18.
2001	1.00	Loon	–	–	20.
2002P	.50¢	Coat of Arms	–	–	20.
2003P	.50¢	Coat of Arms	–	–	20.

Brilliant Uncirculated Coins with "W" Mint Mark

Date and Mint Marks	1¢	5¢	CERTIFIED MS-65 10¢	25¢	50¢	1.00	2.00
1998W	10.	10.	10.	15.	10.	15.	15
2000W	15.	10.	10.	15.	10.	15.	15.
2003WP	15.	10.	10.	10.	20.	20.	15.

SPECIMEN SETS
1970-2005

SIX COIN SPECIMEN SET 1970

In 1968 the Royal Canadian Mint began to study the feasibility of offering for sale six-coin specimen sets to the public. The 1967 specimen set was extremely successful and opened the way for expanded offerings. Trial cases were prepared and a small number of specimen nickel and bronze coins of the years 1968 and 1969 were struck. These coins were not made available to the public.

In 1970 the Royal Canadian Mint provided special specimen sets to Prime Minister Pierre Trudeau for presentation purposes during his trip to China that year. A quantity of specimen sets in anrrow cases were made up. After Trudeau's trip, some of these sets were sold to the public for $13 each. The total quantity of 1970 speciment sets issued in Canada is believed to be fewer than 1,000 and the only way 1970 specimen coins were available was in these sets. When the Mint made specimen sets available to the public starting in 1971, they were house in larger, eight-coin cases. These sets are listed under prestige sets 1971-1980 on page 419.

In the early 1970's empty narrow specimen cases became available. The coins that could be housed in them were taken from prestige sets of the year.

Finish: Specimen, Brilliant relief on brilliant background

Date	Description	SP-65
1970	Specimen set in black case	$1,000.

SPECIMEN SETS

SEVEN COIN CUSTOM SPECIMEN SETS 1976-1980

With the end of the 1976 Montreal Olympic Coin program, and with a new numismatic production facility now in place, the Mint staff turned their attention to improving the quality of their numismatic product line. The quality of the custom sets was upgraded to specimen. The packaging remained constant except for the modifications listed below.

Finish: Specimen, Brilliant relief on a parallel lined background

Cases: 1976-1978: Coins in maroon vinyl-covered case with Canada's coat of arms and the word "CANADA" stamped in gold on the top.

1979-1980: As 1977, except a gold maple leaf replaces the coat of arms and "CANADA"

Date	Description	Issue Price	Mintage	65	SPECIMEN (SP) 66	67	68
1976	Voyageur	8.15	28,162	–	8.50	–	–
1977	Voyageur	8.15	44,198	–	8.50	–	–
1977 SWL	Voyageur	8.15	Included	–	12.00	–	–
1978	Voyageur	8.75	41,000	–	8.50	–	–
1978 RB 50¢	Voyageur	8.75	Included	–	15.00	–	–
1979	Voyageur	10.75	31,174	–	8.50	–	–
1980	Voyageur	12.50	41,447	–	9.50	–	–

SIX COIN SPECIMEN SETS 1981-1996

1981 saw the first official issue of specimen coinage. The package was redesigned, and the coins were marketed as being of specimen quality. The number of coins in the set was reduced to six. The finish on the coins from 1981 to 1995 was brilliant relief on a brilliant background, and in 1996 was changed to brilliant relief against parallel background.

Finish: 1981-1995: Specimen, Brilliant relief on a brilliant background

1996: Specimen, Brilliant relief on a parallel lined background

Cases: 1981-1987: Blue leatherette, booklet type (103 mm x 141 mm), inside a hinged blue plastic frame housing, six encapsulated coins. All enclosed in a silver box.

1988-1996: Blue leatherette, wallet type, (96 mm x 153 mm) silver stamped mint crest, inside clear plastic frame with blue plastic insert. All enclosed in a silver sleeve.

Date	Description	Issue Price	Mintage	65	SPECIMEN (SP) 66	67	68
1981	Voyageur	10.00	71,300	–	9.00	–	–
1982	Voyageur	11.50	62,298	–	9.00	–	–
1983	Voyageur	12.75	60,329	–	9.00	–	–
1984	Voyageur	12.95	60,030	–	9.00	–	–
1985	Voyageur	12.95	61,533	–	10.00	–	–
1986	Voyageur	12.95	67,152	–	9.00	–	–
1987	Voyageur	14.00	74,441	–	10.00	–	–
1988	Loon	14.00	70,205	–	15.00	–	–
1989	Loon	16.95	66,855	–	20.00	–	–
1990	Loon	17.95	76,611	–	20.00	–	–
1991	Loon	17.95	68,552	–	45.00	–	–
1992	Loon	18.95	78,328	–	25.00	–	–
1993	Loon	18.95	77,351	–	20.00	–	–
1994	Loon	19.25	75,973	–	22.50	–	–
1995	Loon	19.25	77,326	–	20.00	–	–
1996	Loon	19.25	62,125	–	30.00	–	–

SEVEN COIN SPECIMEN SETS 1997-2000

In 1997 the two dollar coin was added to the set, raising the number of coins back to seven. The set continued as specimen quality with the packaging being revised in 1998.

Finish: Brilliant relief on a parallel lined background

Case of Issue: **1997:** as 1996 and previous
1998 to Date: Green leatherette outer cover with RCM logo. All enclosed in a multicoloured box.

Date	Description	Issue Price	Mintage	65	SPECIMEN (SP) 66	67	68
1997	Flying Loon/Bear	26.95	97,595	–	40.00	–	–
1998	Loon/Bear	26.95	67,697	–	27.50	–	–
1999	Loon/Bear	26.95	46,786	–	25.00	–	–
1999	Loon/Nunavut	26.95	45,104	–	37.50	–	–
2000	Loon/Bear	34.95	87,965	–	17.50	–	–
2000	Loon/Bears	34.95	Included	–	35.00	–	–

SEVEN COIN MULTI-PLY PLATED STEEL SPECIMEN SETS, 2001 TO DATE

The 2002 specimen set is a double anniversary set issued to commemorate the Golden Jubilee of Queen Elizabeth II, and the 15th anniversary of the Loon dollar coin which was introduced in 1987. This is the only set which contains the "Family of Loons."

The 2004 issue carries the new uncrowned effigy of Queen Elizabeth II, by Susanna Blunt.

Finish: Brilliant relief on a parallel lined background

Date	Description	Issue Price	Mintage	65	SPECIMEN (SP) 66	67	68
2001P	Loon/Bear	39.95	54,613	–	17.50	–	–
1952-2002P	Loon Family/Bear	39.95	67,672	–	40.00	–	–
2003P	Loon/Bear	39.95	41,640	–	40.00	–	–
2004P	Goose/Bear	44.95	44,310	–	40.00	–	–
2005P	Puffin/Bear	39.95	N/A	–	40.00	–	–

SPECIMEN SINGLES

The average condition for specimen issues is Specimen-66 (SP-66). Coins, when removed from sets may grade higher or lower than the average.

Specimen Finish:
1970 to 1980: Brilliant relief on brilliant background
1981 to 2005: Brilliant relief on a parallel lined background

Prices for Certified SP-66 Coins

Date	1¢	5¢	Denominations 10¢	25¢	50¢	1.00	2.00
1970 to 1980	10.	10.	10.	15.	15.	15.	15.
1981 to 2005	10.	10.	10.	15.	15.	15.	15.

Coins found only in Specimen Sets.

Date	Denom	Type	CERTIFIED SP-66
2002	$1	Family of Loons	40.
2004	$1	Canada Goose	40.
2005	$1	Tufted Puffin	40.

PRESTIGE SETS
1971-1980

When it was first introduced in 1971, the prestige set (double dollar set) contained two nickel dollars, with the second nickel dollar being used to display the obverse. This was also true for the 1972 set; however, from 1973 on the second nickel dollar was replaced with a silver dollar. The coins in the prestige sets are of specimen quality until 1980, and proof quality thereafter.

Finish: Brilliant relief on a brilliant background

Cases: **1971-1973:** Crest of Canada; black leather, book type with clasp. Red satin inside red flocked 7-hole stationary display - coloured flocked jackets.

1974-1978: Crest of Canada; black leather, book type with clasp. Red satin inside, hinged black plastic 7-hole display - coloured flocked jackets.

1979-1980: Maple Leaf; black cardboard box, book type with clasp. Red satin inside, hinged black plastic 7-hole display - coloured flocked jackets.

PRESTIGE SETS 1971-1980

Date	Description	Issue Price	Mintage	65	SPECIMEN (SP) 66	67	68
1971	B.C./B.C.	12.00	66,860	–	18.50	–	–
1972	Voyageur/Voyageur	12.00	36,349	–	30.00	–	–
1973 LB 25¢	P.E.I./R.C.M.P.	12.00	119,891	–	300.00	–	–
1973 SB 25¢	P.E.I./R.C.M.P.	12.00	Included	–	22.50	–	–
1974	Winnipeg/Winnipeg	15.00	85,230	–	17.50	–	–
1975	Voyageur/Calgary	15.00	97,263	–	17.50	–	–
1976	Voyageur/Parliament	16.00	87,744	–	17.50	–	–
1977	Voyageur/Jubilee	16.00	142,577	–	17.50	–	–
1977 SWL	Voyageur/Jubilee	16.00	Included	–	18.00	–	–
1978	Voyageur/Edmonton	16.50	147,000	–	16.00	–	–
1978 RB	Voyaguer/Edmonton	16.50	Included	–	28.00	–	–
1979	Voyageur/Griffon	18.50	155,698	–	16.50	–	–
1980	Voyageur/Polar Bear	36.00	162,875	–	27.50	–	–

PROOF SETS 1981-2005

In the product mix reorganization of 1981 the prestige set of previous years was upgraded to proof status.

Finish: Proof, frosted relief against a mirror background

Cases: 1981-1985: Maple Leaf; black cardboard box, book type with clasp. Red satin inside, hinged black plastic 7-hole display - coloured flocked jackets.
1986-1997: Maple leaf; black plastic box, wallet type. Red satin inside, hinged black plastic 7-hole display - coloured flocked jacket.
1998 to date: Mint logo; dark green leather case with black plastic 8-hole insert, green interior with outer box

SEVEN COIN NICKEL / SILVER PROOF SETS 1981-1995

Date	Description	Issue Price	Mintage	65	66	PROOF (PR) 67	68
1981	Voyageur/Train	36.00	199,000	–	–	22.50	–
1982	Voyageur/Skull	36.00	180,908	–	–	17.50	–
1983	Voyageur/Games	36.00	166,779	–	–	22.50	–
1984	Voyageur/Toronto	40.00	161,602	–	–	22.50	–
1985	Voyageur/Parks	40.00	153,950	–	–	25.00	–
1986	Voyageur/Vancouver	40.00	176,224	–	–	22.50	–
1987	Voyageur/Davis Strait	43.00	175,686	–	–	20.00	–
1988	Loon/Ironworks	43.00	175,259	–	–	25.00	–
1989	Loon/MacKenzie	46.95	154,693	–	–	35.00	–
1990	Loon/Kelsey	48.00	158,068	–	–	37.50	–
1991	Loon/Empress	48.00	131,888	–	–	80.00	–
1992	Loon/Stagecoach	49.75	147,061	–	–	32.50	–
1993	Loon/Hockey	49.75	143,065	–	–	35.00	–
1994	Loon/Dogsled Team	50.75	104,485	–	–	42.50	–
1995	Loon/Hudson's Bay	50.75	101,560	–	–	42.50	–

SPECIAL LIMITED EDITION PROOF SETS, 1994-1995

First issued in 1994, these proof sets were limited to 50,000. They contained the silver dollar commemorative, along with the bronze/nickel commemorative of the year. The other five coins are the same as contained in the proof set of that year.

Finish: Proof, frosted relief against a mirror background

Case: Burgundy display case, wallet type, dated on spine with year of issue.
Interior: White satin with brown plastic display frame - burgundy plastic box.

Date	Description	Issue Price	Mintage	65	66	PROOF (PR) 67	68
1994	Remembrance/ Dog Team Patrol	59.50	49,222	–	–	42.50	–
1995	Peacekeeping/ Hudson's Bay	66.95	49,802	–	–	42.50	–

SEVEN COIN SILVER PROOF SETS 1996

Beginning in 1996 the five cent, ten cent, twenty-five cent and fifty cent coins were struck in sterling silver (92.5% Ag and 7.5% Cu). All other specifications remained the same. The composition of sterling silver and loon dollars, along with the one cent coin, remained unchanged.

Finish: Proof, frosted relief against a mirror background

Date	Description	Issue Price	Mintage	65	66	PROOF (PR) 67	68
1996	Loon/McIntosh	66.25	112,835	–	–	60.00	–

EIGHT COIN SILVER PROOF SETS 1997-2003

In 1997 the two dollar coin was added to the set, raising the total to eight coins. The two dollar coin, following the practice established in 1996, was made of sterling silver with a gold plated centre. The one cent coin up to and including 2003, is not the multi-ply plated steel variety, but of bronze composition.

Finish: Proof, frosted relief against a mirror background

Date	Description	Issue Price	Mintage	65	PROOF (PR) 66	67	68
1997	Loon/Hockey/Bear	79.95	113,647	–	–	65.00	–
1997	CNA Edition signed Cournoyer / Ferguson	N/A	N/A	–	–	150.00	–
1997	ANA Edition, signed Gilbert / Park	N/A	N/A	–	–	150.00	–
1998	Loon/R.C.M.P./Bear	79.95	93,632	–	–	90.00	–
1999	Loon/ Queen Charlotte/Bear	79.95	95,113	–	–	135.00	–
2000	Loon/Discovery/Bear	79.95	90,921	–	–	90.00	–
2001	Loon/Ballet/Bear	81.95	74,194	–	–	55.00	–
2001	ANA Edition	69.95	750	–	–	200.00	–
2001	CNA Edition	89.95	N/A	–	–	100.00	–
1952-2002	Loon/Queen Elizabeth II/Bear	81.95	65,315	–	–	80.00	–
1952-2002	ANA Edition	69.95	500	–	–	175.00	–
2003	Loon/Cobalt/Bear	81.95	62,007	–	–	90.00	–
2003	ANA Edition	74.95	500	–	–	175.00	–

Note: ANA and CNA sets contain a numbered Certificate of Authenticity.

SPECIAL LIMITED EDITION PROOF SETS 2002-2003

The Special Edition Proof Set, 1952-2002, contains a commemorative silver dollar and 50-cent coin, both gold plated; the balance of the coins are the regular proof set issue of 1952-2002.

The Special Edition Proof Set, 1953-2003, carries the laureated portrait of Queen Elizabeth II, first issued in 1953. This set commemorates Queen Elizabeth II's Coronation in 1953, and her Jubilee in 2003, with the double dates 1953-2003.

Finish: Proof, frosted relief against a mirror background

Date	Description	Issue Price	Mintage	65	PROOF (PR) 66	67	68
1952-2002	Accession	99.95	33,490	–	–	95.00	–
1953-2003	Coronation	99.95	21,537	–	–	95.00	–

EIGHT COIN SILVER PROOF SETS 2003-2005

Mid year 2003 the tiara portrait of Elizabeth II, which had been used since 1990, was replaced with the new uncrowned portrait by Susanna Blunt. The first set issued was 2004.

Finish: Proof, frosted relief against a mirror background

Date	Description	Issue Price	Mintage	65	PROOF (PR) 66	67	68
2004	Loon/Champlain/Bear	83.95	56,925	–	–	80.00	–
2004	ANA Edition	74.95	500	–	–	100.00	–
2005	Loon/Flag/Bear	81.95	N/A	–	–	85.00	–

PROOF SINGLES

The average condition for proof issues is Proof-67 (PR-67). Coins, when removed from sets may grade higher or lower than the average.

Proof Finish: While this finish was first used on the Montreal Olympic coins it was not incorporated into the general issues until 1981. Please remember that all proof issues carry as part of their finish definition the term of **ultra heavy cameo**.

Finish: Frosted relief on mirror background

Prices for Certified PR-67 Coins

Date	1¢	5¢	10¢	25¢	50¢	1.00	2.00
				Denominations			
1981-1995	15.	15.	15.	20.	20.	20.	–
1996-2005	15.	15.	15.	20.	20.	20.	20.

Coins found only in Proof Sets

Date	Denom	Type	CERTIFIED PR-67
2002	50¢	Gold plated	25.
2002	1.00	Commemmorative silver dollar gold plated	75.
2003	1¢	Laureated Portrait	20.
2003	5¢	Laureated Portrait	20.
2003	10¢	Laureated Portrait	20.
2003	25¢	Laureated Portrait	20.
2003	50¢	Laureated Portrait	25.
2003	$1	Laureated Portrait	50.

SPECIAL ISSUE SETS

100TH ANNIVERSARY OF CONFEDERATION 1867-1967

In 1967 the Royal Canadian Mint produced two special cased coins sets to mark the 100th anniversary of Confederation. The silver medallion set in the red leather-covered case contained one each of the 1¢ to $1 (proof-like finish) and a sterling silver medallion designed and modelled by Thomas Shingles. The gold presentation set contained a $20 gold coin and one each of the 1¢ to $1, all of specimen finish. This set was housed in a black leather presentation case.

Date	Description	Issue Price	Mintage	Finish	65	GRADE 66	67	68
1967	Medallion	12.00	72,463	Proof-like	25.	–	–	–
1967	Gold	40.00	337,687	Specimen	–	350.	–	–

90th ANNIVERSARY OF THE ROYAL CANADIAN MINT 1908-1998

Issued to commemorate the 90th Anniversary of the Royal Canadian Mint, this five coin set features the same reverse designs as the original 1908 coins, except for the double date 1908-1998. The set was issued in two finishes, matte and mirror proof. The matte set cent does not carry the country of origin, "Canada." This error was corrected on the mirror proof cent.

Matte   Mirror

Designers: Obv.: Dora de Pédery-Hunt   Engravers: Obv.: Dora de Pédery-Hunt
           Rev.: Ago Aarand   Rev.: 1¢ – G. W. DeSaulles
                                     5¢, 10¢, 25¢, 50¢ –
                                     W. H. J. Blakemore

Specifications:

Coin	Composition	Weight	Diameter	Edge	Die Axis
1¢	Copper plated on .925 silver, .075 copper	5.67	25.40	Plain	↑↑
5¢	.925 silver, .075 copper	1.17	15.49	Reeded	↑↑
10¢	.925 silver, .075 copper	2.23	18.03	Reeded	↑↑
25¢	.925 silver, .075 copper	5.81	23.62	Reeded	↑↑
50¢	.925 silver, .075 copper	11.62	29.72	Reeded	↑↑

Finish: Proof, matte or mirror
Case of Issue: Burgundy leather clam style case, bronze Mint logo, white lining, five-hole plastic insert, COA

Date	Description	Issue Price	Mintage	Finish	65	PROOF (PR) 66	67	68
1998	W/O"Canada"	99.00	24,893	Matte proof	–	–	50.	–
1998	W/"Canada"	99.00	18,376	Mirror proof	–	–	40.	–

FIVE AND TEN DOLLAR GOLD COMMEMORATIVES 1912-2002

Issued to mark the 90th anniversary of Canada's first five and ten dollar gold coins in 1912, the double-dated 1912-2002 coins carry on a commemorative series which began in 1998, with the issue recalling the first set of coins struck at the Ottawa Mint. Basing the overall design on the 1912 specimen coins from the Bank of Canada collection, the 1912-2002 gold coins differ only in the date and, of course, the obverse effigy.

Designers: Obv.: Dora de Pédery-Hunt
            Rev.: W. H. J. Blakemore

Engravers: Obv.: Dora de Pédery-Hunt
            Rev.: Cosme Saffioti

Physical and chemical specifications:

Denomination:	$5.	$10.
Weight: (grams)	8.36	16.72
Diameter: (mm)	21.59	26.92
Thickness: (mm)	N/A	N/A

Composition: .900 gold, .100 copper
Edge: Reeded
Die Axis: ↑↑
Finish: Proof

Case of Issue: Two-coin clam style case.

Date	Description	Issue Price	Mintage	65	66	67	68
					PROOF (PR)		
1912-2002	$5.00	–	–	–	–	300.	–
1912-2002	$10.00	–	–	–	–	500.	–
1912-2002	Set, 2 coins	749.95	1998	–	–	800.	–

CANADIAN WILDLIFE SERIES
PROOF PLATINUM SETS 1990 - 1994

POLAR BEARS PLATINUM SET 1990. In 1990 the Royal Canadian Mint entered the luxury market for high quality collector coins. Canada's "Monarch of the North" has been transferred by Robert Bateman from the sparkling Arctic environment to the gleaming surface of pure platinum coins.

Designers: Obv.: Dora de Pédery-Hunt
Rev.: Robert Bateman

Engravers: Obv.: Dora de Pédery-Hunt
Rev.: $300 - Terry Smith
$150 - William Woodruff
$ 75 - Ago Aarand
$ 30 - Sheldon Beveridge

Physical and chemical specifications:
Denomination: $300 $150 $75 $30
Weight: (oz) 1.000 .500 .250 .100
Diameter: (mm) 30.0 25.0 20.0 16.0
Thickness: (mm) 2.6, 2.12, 1.65, 1.08

Composition: .9995 platinum
Edge: Reeded
Die Axis: ↑↑
Finish: Proof

Case of Issue: Walnut case with a black suede four hole insert, encapsulated, COA.

Date	Description	Issue Price	Mintage	65	PROOF (PR) 66	67	68
1990	4-coin set	1,990.00	2,629	–	–	2,100.	–

SNOWY OWLS PLATINUM SET 1992. This is the second set in the series of proof platinum coins dedicated to Canadian wildlife.

Designers: Obv.: Dora de Pédery-Hunt
Rev.: Glen Loates
Specifications: Same as 1990 issue
Finish: Proof
Case of Issue: See 1990 issue

Engravers: Obv.: Dora de Pédery-Hunt
Rev.: $300 - Sheldon Beveridge
$150 - Ago Aarand
$ 75 - Terry Smith
$ 30 - William Woodruff

Date	Description	Issue Price	Mintage	65	PROOF (PR) 66	67	68
1991	4-coin set	1,990.00	1,164	–	–	2,200.	–

CANADIAN WILDLIFE SERIES (cont.)

COUGARS PLATINUM SET 1992. This is the third set in the series of proof platinum coins dedicated to Canadian wildlife.

Designers: Obv.: Dora de Pédery-Hunt	**Engravers:** Obv.: Dora de Pédery-Hunt

Designers: Obv.: Dora de Pédery-Hunt
Rev.: George McLean
Specifications: Same as 1990 issue
Finish: Proof
Case of Issue: See 1990 issue

Engravers: Obv.: Dora de Pédery-Hunt
Rev.: $300 - A. Aarand, C.Saffioti
$150 - Susan Taylor
$ 75 - Sheldon Beveridge
$ 30 - Ago Aarand

Date	Description	Issue Price	Mintage	65	66	67	68
					PROOF (PR)		
1992	4-coin set	1,955.00	1,081	–	–	2,200.	–

ARCTIC FOXES PLATINUM SET 1993. This is the fourth set in the series of proof platinum coins dedicated to Canadian wildlife.

Designers: Obv.: Dora de Pédery-Hunt
Rev.: Claude D'Angelo
Specifications: Same as 1990 issue
Finish: Proof
Case of Issue: See 1990 issue

Engravers: Obv.: Dora de Pédery-Hunt
Rev.: $300 - Susan Taylor
$150 - Sheldon Beveridge
$ 75 - Ago Aarand
$ 30 - Ago Aarand

Date	Description	Issue Price	Mintage	65	66	67	68
					PROOF (PR)		
1993	4-coin set	1,955.00	1,033	–	–	2,200.	–

CANADIAN WILDLIFE SERIES (cont.)

SEA OTTERS PLATINUM SET 1994. This is the fifth and last set in the series of proof platinum coins dedicated to Canadian wildlife.

Designers: Obv.: Dora de Pédery-Hunt
           Rev.: Ron S. Parker
Specifications: Same as 1990 issue
Finish: Proof
Case of Issue: Same as 1990,
           except burgundy case

Engravers: Obv.: Dora de Pédery-Hunt
Reverse: $300 - Sheldon Beveridge
          $150 - William Woodruff
          $ 75 - Terry Smith
          $ 30 - Susan Taylor

Date	Description	Issue Price	Mintage	65	PROOF (PR) 66	67	68
1994	4-coin set	1,995.00	766	–	–	2,200.	–

ENDANGERED WILDLIFE SERIES
PROOF PLATINUM SETS 1995 - 2002

CANADA LYNX PLATINUM SET 1995. This is the first set in the series of proof platinum coins commemorating Canada's endangered wildlife.

Designers: Obv.: Dora de Pédery-Hunt
        Rev.: Michael Dumas
Specifications: Same as 1990
Finish: Proof
Case of Issue:
    1/10 oz coin: Leather display case, encapsulated coin
    ½ oz coin: mahogany case, encapsulated coin
    Set, 4 coins: mahogany case, inside green satin, coins individually encapsulated

Engravers: Obv.: Dora de Pédery-Hunt
        Rev.: $300 - Susan Taylor
            $150 - Cosme Saffioti
            $ 75 - Stanley Witten
            $ 30 - Ago Aarand

Date	Description	Issue Price	Mintage	PROOF (PR) 65	66	67	68
1995	30 Dollars	179.95	620	–	–	125.	–
1995	150 Dollars	599.95	226	–	–	600.	–
1995	4-coin set	1,950.00	682	–	–	2,300.	–

PEREGRINE FALCON PLATINUM SET 1996. This is the second set in the series of proof platinum coins commemorating Canada's endangered wildlife.

Designers: Obv.: Dora de Pédery-Hunt
        Rev.: Dwayne Harty
Specifications: Same as 1990 issue
Finish: Proof
Case of Issue: See 1995 issue

Engravers: Obv.: Dora de Pédery-Hunt
        Rev.: $300 - Sheldon Beveridge
            $150 - Stanley Witten
            $ 75 - Cosme Saffioti
            $ 30 - Ago Aarand

Date	Description	Issue Price	Mintage	PROOF (PR) 65	66	67	68
1996	30 Dollars	179.95	910	–	–	125.	–
1996	150 Dollars	599.95	196	–	–	600.	–
1996	4-coin set	2,095.95	675	–	–	2,300.	–

ENDANGERED WILDLIFE SERIES (cont.)

WOOD BISON PLATINUM SET 1997. This is the third set in the series of proof platinum coins commemorating Canada's endangered wildlife.

Designers: Obv.: Dora de Pédery-Hunt
          Rev.: Chris Bacon
Specifications: Same as 1990 issue
Finish: Proof
Case of Issue: See 1995 issue

Engravers: Obv.: Dora de Pédery-Hunt
          Rev.: $300 - Sheldon Beveridge
                $150 - William Woodruff
                $ 75 - Stanley Witten
                $ 30 - Ago Aarand

Date	Description	Issue Price	Mintage	65	PROOF (PR) 66	67	68
1997	30 Dollars	179.95	469	–	–	125.	–
1997	150 Dollars	599.95	116	–	–	600.	–
1997	4-coin set	1,950.00	413	–	–	2,300.	–

GREY WOLF PLATINUM SET 1998. This is the fourth set in the series of proof platinum coins commemorating Canada's endangered wildlife.

Designers: Obv.: Dora de Pédery-Hunt
          Rev.: Kerr Burnett

Specifications: Same as 1990 issue
Finish: Proof
Case of Issue: See 1995 issue

Engravers: Obv.: Dora de Pédery-Hunt
          Rev.: $300 - Sheldon Beveridge
                $150 - Cosme Saffioti
                $ 75 - William Woodruff
                $ 30 - Ago Aarand,
                    José Osio

Date	Description	Issue Price	Mintage	65	PROOF (PR) 66	67	68
1998	30 Dollars	179.95	664	–	–	125.	–
1998	150 Dollars	599.95	194	–	–	600.	–
1998	4-coin set	2,095.00	661	–	–	2,300.	–

ENDANGERED WILDLIFE SERIES (cont.)

MUSKOX PLATINUM SET 1999. This is the fifth set in the series of proof platinum coins commemorating Canada's endangered wildlife.

Designers: Obv.: Dora de Pédery-Hunt
           Rev.: Mark Hobson

Specifications: Same as 1990 issue
Finish: Proof
Case of Issue: See 1995 issue

Engravers: Obv.: Dora de Pédery-Hunt
          Rev.: $300 - William Woodruff
                $150 - Stanley Witten
                $ 75 - Cosme Saffioti
                $ 30 - Sheldon Beveridge

Date	Description	Issue Price	Mintage	65	PROOF (PR) 66	67	68
1999	30 Dollars	179.95	999	–	–	125.	–
1999	4-coin set	2,095.95	495	–	–	2,650.	–

PRONGHORN PLATINUM SET 2000. This is the sixth set in the series of proof platinum coins commemorating Canada's endangered wildlife.

Designers: Obv.: Dora de Pédery-Hunt
           Rev.: Mark Hobson

Specifications: Same as 1990 issue
Finish: Proof
Case of Issue: See 1995 issue

Engravers: Obv.: Dora de Pédery-Hunt
          Rev.: $300 - José Osio
                $150 - Susan Taylor
                $ 75 - Stanley Witten
                $ 30 - William Woodruff

Date	Description	Issue Price	Mintage	65	PROOF (PR) 66	67	68
2000	4-coin set	2,095.95	599	–	–	2,400.	–

ENDANGERED WILDLIFE SERIES (cont.)

HARLEQUIN DUCK PLATINUM SET 2001. This is the seventh set in the series of proof platinum coins commemorating Canada's endangered wildlife.

Designers: Obv.: Dora de Pédery-Hunt
      Rev.: Cosme Saffioti,
          Susan Taylor
Specifications: Same as 1990 issue
Finish: Proof
Case of Issue: See 1995 issue

Engravers: Obv.: Dora de Pédery-Hunt
      Rev.: $300 - Stan Witten
          $150 - Susan Taylor
          $ 75 - Cosme Saffioti
          $ 30 - Susan Taylor

Date	Description	Issue Price	Mintage	65	PROOF (PR) 66	67	68
2001	4-coin set	2,395.95	448	–	–	2,250	–

GREAT BLUE HERON PLATINUM SET 2002. This is the eighth set in the series of proof platinum coins commemorating Canada's endangered wildlife.

Designers: Obv.: Dora de Pédery-Hunt
      Rev.: John-Luc Grondin
Specifications: Same as 1990
Finish: Proof
Case of Issue: See 1995 issue

Engravers: Obv.: Dora de Pédery-Hunt
      Rev.: $300 - Stan Witten
          $150 - Susan Taylor
          $ 75 - Stan Witten
          $ 30 - José Osio

Date	Description	Issue Price	Mintage	65	PROOF (PR) 66	67	68
2002	4-coin set	2,495.95	344	–	–	2,300.	–

ENDANGERED WILDLIFE SERIES (cont.)

ATLANTIC WALRUS PLATINUM SET 2003. This is the ninth set in the series of proof platinum coins commemorating Canada's endangered wildlife.

Designers: Obv.: Dora de Pédery-Hunt
            Rev.: John-Luc Grondin

Specifications: Same as 1990 issue
Finish: Proof
Case of Issue: Same as 1995

Engravers: Obv.: Dora de Pédery-Hunt
            Rev.: $300 - Susan Taylor
                    $150 - José Osio
                    $ 75 - Stan Witten
                    $ 30 - Stan Witten

Date	Description	Issue Price	Mintage	65	66	67	68
					PROOF (PR)		
2003	4-coin set	2,995.95	365	–	–	3,000.	–

GRIZZLY BEAR PLATINUM SET 2004. This is the tenth and last set in the Endangered Wildlife proof platinum series, and it commemorates Canada's Great Grizzly bears.

Designers: Obv.: Susanna Blunt
            Rev.: N/A

Specifications: Same as 1990 issue
Finish: Proof
Case of Issue: See 1995 issue

Engravers: Obv.: Susan Taylor
            Rev.: $300 - José Osio
                    $150 - José Osio
                    $ 75 - José Osio
                    $ 30 - José Osio

Date	Description	Issue Price	Mintage	65	66	67	68
					PROOF (PR)		
2004	4-coin set	2,995.95	376	–	–	3,000.	–

MAPLE LEAF BULLION COINS

In 1979 the Canadian Government introduced a gold bullion coin to compete with similar coins issued by other countries (such as the Krugerrand of South Africa). From 1979 to 1981 only the 50 dollar coin (Maple Leaf) in the one troy ounce size was produced. The Maple Leaf during this period was issued with a gold fineness of .999. During November 1982 the range of the gold Maple Leaf bullion coins being offered was expanded to three sizes. Now included in the offering were the five dollar or 1/10 maple and the ten dollar or ¼ maple. With the addition of the two fractional Maple Leafs all sizes were upgraded in gold content to .9999 fine. July of 1986 saw the offering range expanded once again to include the 20 dollar or ½ maple. All four coins are produced from .9999 fine gold and are legal tender coinage of Canada. In 1988 the Royal Canadian Mint, again expanding on their bullion program, introduced five new coins; four platinum (1/10, ¼, ½ and one maple) and one silver (one maple). In 1990 the reverse hub of the one ounce gold Maple Leaf was re-engraved, enhancing veins in the maple leaf design. Other changes included a more slender stem on the maple leaf and wider spacing of the letters in the legend "Fine Gold 1 oz Or Pur." In 1993 the Royal Canadian Mint added to the series of bullion coin by issuing a 1/20 of an ounce ($1.00) size in gold and platinum. Again in 1994 the $2.00 denomination was added to the bullion coin series (1/15 of an ounce) in both platinum and gold. The $2.00 - 1/15 Maple denomination was discontinued in 1995.

The original finish developed by the Mint in 1979 for the Maple Leaf Gold Program was "The Bullion Finish" a brilliant relief on a parallel lined background.

FINISHES USED BY THE BULLION DEPARTMENT OF THE ROYAL CANADIAN MINT

Bullion:	Brilliant relief against a parallel lined background
	As above / Coloured
	As above / Hologram
Proof:	Frosted relief against a mirror background
	As above / Coloured
	As above / Hologram
Specimen:	Brilliant relief on a satin background
(Reverse Proof)	As above / Coloured
	As above / Hologram

GUIDE TO THE CLASSIFICATION OF MAPLE LEAF COINS

GOLD MAPLE LEAFS		PLATINUM MAPLE LEAFS		SILVER MAPLE LEAFS	
Bullion Issues	434	Bullion Issues	443	Bullion Issues	446
Special Issues		Special Issues		Special Issues	
Singles	436	Sets	444	Singles	448
Sets	438	Hologram Issues		Sets	450
Privy Mark Issues		Sets	445	Privy Mark Issues	
Singles	439			Singles	451
Sets	440			Sets	452
Coloured Issues				Coloured Issues	
Sets	440			Singles	454
Hologram Issues				Hologram Issues	
Singles	441			Singles	455
Bimetallic Issues				Sets	456
Sets	442			Derivatives	457
Derivatives					

GOLD MAPLE LEAFS

BULLION ISSUES

Obverses

Tiara Portrait
1979-1989

Crowned Portrait
1990-2003

Uncrowned Portrait
2004-2005

Reverses

.999 Fine
1979-1982

.9999 Fine
1983-1989

.9999 Fine
Re-engraved
1990-2005

Note: Images illustrated are smaller than actual size.

Designers and Engravers:

Obv.:	1979-1989	Arnold Machin	Walter Ott
	1990-2003	Dora de Pédery-Hunt	Dora de Pédery-Hunt
	2004-2005	Susanna Blunt	Susan Taylor
Rev.:	1979-1982	Walter Ott	R.C.M. Staff
	1983-1989	Walter Ott	R.C.M. Staff
	1990-2005	Walter Ott	R.C.M. Staff

1999 marked the 20th anniversary of the Maple Leaf program. To commemorate this event a privy mark was incorporated into the design of all regular issue Maple Leafs.

A special issue of maple leafs was produced for January 1st, 2000. These were given a double date, 1999-2000, and a Fireworks privy mark.

To celebrate the millennium year, the privy mark added to all maple leaf denominations was Fireworks above the numerals 2000.

1999
20 YEARS ANS

1999-2000
Fireworks

2000
Fireworks 2000

Specifications	$1.00 1/20	$2.00 1/15	Dollar Value and Ounces $5.00 1/10	$10.00 1/4	$20.00 1/2	$50.00 1.0
Fineness (1979-1982)	–	–	–	–	–	.999
Fineness (1982 to date)	.9999	.9999	.9999	.9999	.9999	.9999
Weight (grams)	1.555	2.070	3.131	7.797	15.575	31.150
Diameter (mm)	14.1	15.0	16.0	20.0	25.0	30.0
Thickness (mm)	0.92	0.98	1.22	1.70	2.23	2.93
Edge:	Reeded	Reeded	Reeded	Reeded	Reeded	Reeded
Die Axis:	↑↑	↑↑	↑↑	↑↑	↑↑	↑↑

Finish: Bullion, Brilliant relief against a parallel lined background

MINTAGES: The production (quantity minted) of regular issue gold maple leaf bullion coins is on a demand basis. As coins are ordered by the distributors they are struck and shipped by the Mint.

Composition	Date	$1.00 1/20	$2.00 1/15	Dollar Value and Ounces $5.00 1/10	$10.00 1/4	$20.00 1/2	$50.00 Maple
Gold	1979	N/I	N/I	N/I	N/I	N/I	1,000,000
	1980	N/I	N/I	N/I	N/I	N/I	1,215,000
	1981	N/I	N/I	N/I	N/I	N/I	863,000
	1982	N/I	N/I	184,000	246,000	N/I	883,000
	1983	N/I	N/I	224,000	130,000	N/I	695,000
	1984	N/I	N/I	226,000	355,200	N/I	1,098,000
	1985	N/I	N/I	476,000	607,200	N/I	1,747,500
	1986	N/I	N/I	483,000	879,200	386,400	1,093,500
	1987	N/I	N/I	459,000	376,800	332,800	978,000
	1988	N/I	N/I	412,000	380,000	521,600	800,500
	1989	N/I	N/I	539,000	328,800	259,200	856,000
	1990	N/I	N/I	476,000	253,600	174,400	815,000
	1991	N/I	N/I	322,000	166,400	96,200	290,000
	1992	N/I	N/I	384,000	179,600	116,000	368,900
	1993	37,080	N/I	248,630	158,452	99,492	321,413
	1994	78,860	3,540	313,150	148,792	104,766	180,357
	1995	85,920	N/I	294,890	127,596	103,162	208,729
	1996	56,520	N/I	179,220	89,148	66,246	143,682
	1997	59,720	N/I	188,540	98,104	63,354	478,211
	1998	44,260	N/I	301,940	85,472	65,366	593,704
	1999	62,820	N/I	709,920	98,928	64,760	627,067
	1999-2000	Included	N/I	Included	Included	Included	Included
	2000	31,280	N/I	52,970	31,688	24,404	86,375
	2001	20,720	N/I	63,470	35,168	26,556	138,878
	2002	17,140	N/I	45,020	42,940	28,706	344,883
	2003	3,890	N/I	26,940	23,228	23,470	194,631
	2004	2,470	N/I	33,480	18,296	13,160	253,978
	2005	N/A	N/I	N/A	N/A	N/A	N/A

Note: N/I denotes Not Issued.

PRICING: Buying and selling prices are based on the interday spot price of bullion plus a small percentage premium for the striking and handling. The smaller the unit the larger the percentage premium charged on buying; however, in later selling the premium could very well disappear.

Note: The one-time issue of the 1994 two dollar, 1/15 gold maple, with a mintage of 3,540 pieces has become, at the moment, a one year type bullion coin, with a catalogue value for 2005 of $100.00

GOLD MAPLE LEAF SPECIAL ISSUES

SPECIAL ISSUE SINGLES

10TH ANNIVERSARY OF THE MAPLE LEAF BULLION COINS 1989. To commemorate the 10th anniversary of the maple leaf bullion coin program in 1989 the Royal Canadian Mint issued a series of proof quality silver, gold and platinum coins individually and in sets. The single coins and sets were packaged in solid maple wood presentation cases with brown velvet liners.

Designer and Engraver: See page 434
Specifications: See page 435
Finish: Proof, frosted relief against a mirror background
Case of Issue: Maple wood case, black flocked insert, encapsulated coin, COA

Date	Description	Issue Price	Mintage	65	66	67	68
					PROOF (PR)		
1989	1 ounce maple	B.V.	6,817	–	–	600.	–

125TH ANNIVERSARY OF THE R.C.M.P. 1997. In 1997 the Royal Canadian Mint issued a $50.00 gold (1oz .9999 fine) coin with a guaranteed value of U.S. $310.00 in effect until January 1st, 2000. Since that date the coin has traded at the market price of gold bullion.

Designer: Ago Aarand
Composition: Gold (.9999)
Weight: 31.15 grams, 1 oz
Diameter: 30.00 mm
Edge: Plain, 10-sided
Nominal Value: $50.00

Engraver: Stan Witten
Thickness: 3.25 mm
Die Axis: ↑↑
Finish: Bullion, Brilliant relief against a parallel lined background

Date	Description	Issue Price	Mintage	65	66	67	68
					BRILLIANT UNCIRCULATED (MS)		
1997	Musical Ride	310. USF	12,913	750.	–	–	–

GOLD MAPLE LEAF SPECIAL ISSUES

SPECIAL ISSUE SINGLES

25TH ANNIVERSARY OF THE GOLD MAPLE LEAF COIN, 1979-2004: A special commemorative design for the one ounce maple celebrating Canada's 25 years as a world leader in bullion coin production was issued in 2004, at the A.N.A. World's Fair of Money.

Designers:
   Obv.: Susanna Blunt
   Rev.: Walter Ott
Specifications: See page 435
Case of Issue: Plastic

Engravers:
   Obv.: Susan Taylor
   Rev.: Walter Ott
Finish: Bullion, Brilliant relief against a
   parallel lined background

Date	Description	Issue Price	Mintage	BRILLIANT UNCIRCULATED (MS)			
				65	66	67	68
2004	25th Anniv.	B.V.	10,000	600.	–	–	–

25TH ANNIVERSARY OF THE GOLD MAPLE LEAF COIN, 1979-2004: The majestic moose is featured on this 1/25 oz gold coin, the smallest ever produced by the Royal Canadian Mint.

Image shown twice actual size

Designers:
   Obv.: Susanna Blunt
   Rev.: Cosme Saffioti
Composition: Gold (.9999)
Weight: 1.27 grams
Thickness: 0.63 mm
Finish: Proof, Frosted relief against a mirror background
Case of Issue: Maroon leatherette clam case, black flocked insert, encapsulated coin, COA

Engravers:
   Obv.: Susan Taylor
   Rev.: Cosme Saffioti
Edge: Serrated
Diameter: 13.92 mm

Date	Description	Issue Price	Mintage	PROOF (PR)			
				65	66	67	68
2004	50-cent Moose	69.95	24,991	–	–	100.	–

GOLD MAPLE LEAF SPECIAL ISSUES

SPECIAL ISSUE SETS

10TH ANNIVERSARY OF THE GOLD MAPLE LEAF COIN, 1979-1989. The three sets detailed below were issued for the tenth anniversary of the maple leaf bullion program.

Designers: and Engravers: See page 434
Specifications: See page 435
Finish: Proof, Frosted relief against a mirror background
Case of Issue: Maple wood presentation box, black flocked insert, encapsulated coin, COA

Date	Description	Issue Price	Mintage	PROOF (PR) 65	66	67	68
1989	3-coin set 1oz gold 1oz silver 1oz platinum	1,795.00	3,966	–	–	1,950.	–
1989	3-coin set 1/10 oz gold 1/10 oz platinum 1 oz silver	195.00	10,000	–	–	200.	–
1989	4-coin gold set 1, 1/2, 1/4, 1/10 oz maples	1,395.00	6,998	–	–	1,200.	–

GOLD MAPLE LEAFS WITH PRIVY MARKS

PRIVY MARK SINGLES

GOLD MAPLE LEAF PRIVY MARKS. In 1997, the Royal Canadian Mint began adding privy marks to specific gold maple leaf denominations to commemorate special events. These privy mark maples were commissioned by different organizations and struck by the Royal Canadian Mint.

$5 — 1/10 oz Maple Leaf Privy Marks

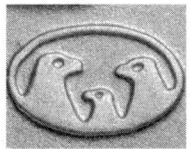

1997
Family
Dillion Gage

1998
Eagles
Dillion Gage

$10 — 1/4 oz Maple Leaf Privy Marks

2000
Expo
Hannover

2001
Basle Coin
Fair

2005
Liberation
Royal Dutch Mint

Date	Denom.	Minage	Issue Price	Case of Issue	Finish	65	GRADE 66	67	68
1997	$5, 1/10 oz	100,730	N/A	Plastic case	SP	–	60.	–	–
1998	$5, 1/10 oz	51,440	N/A	Plastic case	SP	–	65.	–	–
2000	$10, 1/4 oz	N/A	N/A	N/A	SP	–	200.	–	–
2001	$10, 1/4 oz	750	N/A	N/A	SP	–	250.	–	–
2005	$10, 1/4 oz	1,000	E299	N/A	SP	–	475.	–	–

GOLD MAPLE LEAFS WITH PRIVY MARKS

PRIVY MARK SETS

GOLD MAPLE LEAF PRIVY MARK SET, 2001. Each of the five coins in this set carries the bow of a Viking ship as a privy mark. The maples in this set are: 1 oz, 1/2 oz, 1/4 oz, 1/10 oz and 1/20 oz.

Photograph not available at press time

2001 Viking

Designers and Engravers: See page 434
Specifications: See page 435
Finish: Specimen (reverse proof), Brilliant relief against a satin background
Case of Issue: Red mahogany wooden case, black insert, encapsulated coins, green velour with metal trim box.

Date	Description	Prive Mark	Issue Price	Mintage	65	SPECIMEN (SP) 66	67	68
2001	5 coin set	Viking	N/A	850	—	1,500.	—	—

GOLD MAPLE LEAFS COLOURED ISSUES

COLOURED SETS

20TH ANNIVERSARY OF THE MAPLE LEAF PROGRAM, 1979-1999. This limited edition five-coin set, (1 oz, 1/2 oz, 1/4 oz, 1/10 oz and 1/20 oz) struck by the Royal Canadian Mint and coloured in Balerna, Switzerland, was issued with a mintage of 500. They are the first coloured Canadian coins.

Designers and Engravers: See page 434
Specifications: See page 435
Finish: Bullion, Brilliant relief against a parallel lined background, coloured maple leaf
Case of Issue: Wooden maple display case, black leatherette sleeve, black flocked insert, encapsulated coins, COA, red and gold outer box.

Date	Description	Issue Price	Mintage	65	BRILLIANT UNCIRCULATED (MS) 66	67	68
1999	5 coin set	N/A	500	1,500.	—	—	—

GOLD MAPLE LEAFS HOLOGRAM ISSUES

HOLOGRAM SINGLES

$10 GOLD MAPLE LEAF HOLOGRAM 2001. A distinctive maple leaf design appears as a high resolution dot matrix hologram, which is struck directly into the coin.

Designers and Engravers: Obv.: See page 434
Specifications: See page 435
Finish: Specimen (reverse proof), Brilliant relief against a satin background, Hologram
Case: Presentation case

Date	Description	Issue Price	Mintage	65	SPECIMEN (SP) 66	67	68
2001	$10, ¼ oz	195.	14,614	–	200.	–	–

HOLOGRAM SETS

GOLD MAPLE LEAF HOLOGRAM SETS 1999-2001. The Hologram gold maple leaf set of 1999 was the first official issue of hologram coins in Canada.

Designers and Engravers: See page 434
Specifications: See page 435
Finish: Bullion, Brilliant relief against a parallel lined background, Hologram
Case: Presentation case

Date	Description	Issue Price	Mintage	65	BRILLIANT UNCIRCULATED (MS) 66	67	68
1999	5 coin set	1,995.	500	3,750.	–	–	–
2001	5 coin set	1,995.	600	3,150.	–	–	–

BIMETALLIC MAPLE LEAFS

SETS

25TH ANNIVERSARY OF THE GOLD MAPLE LEAF, 1979-2004. To celebrate 25 years as an international standard in bullion coins, a new bimetallic maple leaf set was issued. The six-coin set is the first to include the 1/25 oz maple leaf denomination. Each coin is double-dated 1979-2004, and the 1 ounce coin features a commemorative privy mark.

Designers and Engravers: RCM Staff

Specifications:

Face Value	$0.50	$1.00	$5.00	$10.00	$20.00	$50.00
Ounces (Maple)	1/25	1/20	1/10	1/4	1/2	Maple
Composition						
Ring – fine silver	.9999	.9999	.9999	.9999	.9999	.9999
Core – fine gold	.9999	.9999	.9999	.9999	.9999	.9999
Weight (grams)	1.270	1.581	3.136	7.802	15.589	31.650
Diameter (mm)	16.00	18.03	20.00	25.00	30.00	36.07
Thickness (mm)	N/A	N/A	N/A	N/A	N/A	N/A
Edge	Plain	Plain	Plain	Plain	Plain	Plain
Axis	↑↑	↑↑	↑↑	↑↑	↑↑	↑↑

Finish: Bullion, Brilliant relief against a parallel lined background
Case: Black leather presentation case, black velour insert, encapsulated coins, COA

Date	Description	Issue Price	Mintage	BRILLIANT UNCIRCULATED (MS)			
				65	66	67	68
1979-2004	6 coin set	2,495.95	801	2,350.	—	—	—

PLATINUM MAPLE LEAFS

BULLION ISSUES

$50.00 Platinum

Designers:
Obv.: 1988-1989 Arnold Machin
        1990-1999 Dora de Pédery-Hunt
Rev.: 1988-1999 Walter Ott
Engravers:
Obv.: 1988-1989 Walter Ott
        1990-1999 Dora de Pédery-Hunt
Rev.: 1990-1999 Re-engraved R.C.M.
                 Staff
        1988-1989 RCM Staff

Specifications:

Face value	$1.00	$2.00	$5.00	$10.00	$20.00	$50.00
Ounces (Maple)	1/20	1/15	1/10	1/4	1/2	Maple
Fineness	.9995	.9995	.9995	.9995	.9995	.9995
Weight (grams)	1.555	2.070	3.131	7.797	15.575	31.150
Diameter (mm)	14.10	15.0	16.00	20.00	25.00	30.00
Thickness (mm)	0.92	0.94	1.01	1.50	2.02	2.52
Edge	Reeded	Reeded	Reeded	Reeded	Reeded	Reeded
Die Axis:	↑↑	↑↑	↑↑	↑↑	↑↑	↑↑

Finish: Bullion, Brilliant relief against a parallel lined background

MINTAGES: The production of platinum maple leafs was on an order basis, unlike the production of coinage for circulation where the Mint will anticipate the number of coins required to fulfill the needs of the economy. Maple leafs are not struck unless ordered.

				Mintages			
		$1.00	$2.00	$5.00	$10.00	$20.00	$50.00
Composition	Date	1/20	1/15	1 /10	1/4	1/2	Maple
Platinum	1988	N/I	N/I	46,000	87,200	23,600	26,000
	1989	N/I	N/I	18,000	3,200	4,800	10,000
	1990	N/I	N/I	9,000	1,600	2,600	31,900
	1991	N/I	N/I	13,000	7,200	5,600	31,900
	1992	N/I	N/I	16,000	11,600	12,800	40,500
	1993	2,120	N/I	14,020	8,048	6,022	17,666
	1994	4,260	1,625	19,190	9,456	6,710	36,245
	1995	460	N/I	8,940	6,524	6,308	25,829
	1996	1,640	N/I	8,820	6,160	5,490	62,273
	1997	1,340	N/I	7,050	4,552	3,990	25,480
	1998	2,000	N/I	5,710	3,816	5,486	10,403
	1999	4,000	N/I	4,080	2,092	788	3,248

Note: 1. N/I denotes Not Issued.
2. No platinum bullion coins have been issued since 1999.

PRICING: Buying and selling prices are based on the interday spot price of bullion plus a small percentage premium for the striking and handling. The smaller the unit the larger the percentage premium charged on buying, however, in later selling the premium could very well disappear.

Note: The one-time issue of the 1994 two dollar, 1/15 platinum maple, with an estimated adjusted mintage of 600 pieces has become, at the moment, a one year type bullion coin, with a catalogue value for 2005 of $400.00

PLATINUM MAPLE LEAF SPECIAL ISSUES

SPECIAL ISSUE SETS

10TH ANNIVERSARY OF MAPLE LEAF BULLION COINS, 1989. This four-coin proof platinum set was issued to commemorate the 10th anniversary of the first maple leaf coins issued in 1979.

Designers and Engravers: See page 443
Specifications: See page 443
Finish: Proof, frosted relief against a mirror background
Case of Issue: Wooden maple presentation case, black flocked insert, encapsulated coin, COA

Date	Description	Issue Price	Mintage	65	66	67	68
					PROOF (PR)		
1989	4 coin set	1,995.	1,999	–	–	2,650.	–

POLAR BEAR ISSUE, 1999. In 1999 the Royal Canadian Mint issued a special set of platinum Maple Leafs, at the request of a distributor, MTB Bank. They are legal tender coins issued in five denominations with the same specifications as the bullion issues but with a polar bear reverse design. The reverse design is a modification of the two dollar polar bear reverse by Brent Townsend.

Designers:
    Obv.: Dora de Pédery-Hunt
    Rev.: Brent Townsend

Engravers:
    Obv.: Dora de Pédery-Hunt
    Rev.: Ago Aarand

Specifications: See page 443
Finish: Bullion, Brilliant relief against a parallel lined background
Case of Issue: N/A

Date	Description	Issue Price	Mintage	65	66	67	68
				BRILLIANT UNCIRCULATED (MS)			
1999	$1.00 - 1/20 oz	N/A	1999	75.	–	–	–
1999	$5.00 - 1/10 oz	N/A	1999	150.	–	–	–
1999	$10.00 - ¼ oz	N/A	500	350.	–	–	–
1999	$20.00 - ½ oz	N/A	1999	1,000.	–	–	–
1999	$50.00 - 1 oz	N/A	1999	1,350.	–	–	–
1999	Set, 5 coins	N/A	500	2,650.	–	–	–

PLATINUM MAPLE LEAF HOLOGRAM ISSUES

HOLOGRAM SETS

PLATINUM MAPLE LEAF PROOF HOLOGRAM FIVE-COIN SET 2002. In this set the distinctive maple leaf appears as a high-resolution dot matrix hologram which has been struck directly onto regular issues of each of the five coins. The five coins, one ounce, one-half ounce, one-quarter ounce, one-tenth ounce, and one-twentieth ounce are struck with the same specifications and denominations as the regular issues of 1988-1999 see page 443.

Designers: **Engravers:**
    Obv.: Dora de Pédery-Hunt   Obv.: Dora de Pédery-Hunt
    Rev.: RCM Staff   Rev.: RCM Staff
Specifications: See page 443
Finish: Specimen (reverse proof), Brilliant relief on a satin background, Hologram
Case of Issue: Red mahogany wooden case, black insert, encapsulated coins, green velour
          with metal trim box.

Date	Description	Issue Price	Mintage	65	SPECIMEN (SP) 66	67	68
2002	5-coin set	2,895.95	500	–	3,250.	–	–

SILVER MAPLE LEAFS

BULLION ISSUES

The first silver one ounce maple leaf was issued in 1988. The design is a continuation of that first conceived for the gold maples in 1979. The 1999-2000, and the 2000-dated silver maple leaf $5.00 coins carry the fireworks privy mark for 1999-2000, and the millennium privy mark for 2000. See page 447 for privy marks.

Obverses

Tiara Portrait	Crowned Portrait	Uncrowned Portrait
1988-1989	1990-2003	2004-2005

Reverse

1988-2005

Designers and Engravers:

1988-1989: Obv.: Arnold Machin, Walter Ott   Rev.: Walter Ott, R.C.M. Staff
1989-2003: Obv.: Dora de Pédery Hunt   Rev.: Walter Ott, R.C.M. Staff
2004-2005: Obv.: Susanna Blunt, Susan Taylor   Rev.: Walter Ott, R.C.M. Staff

Specifications: See below

Face value Ounces (Maple)	$1.00 1/20	$2.00 1/10	$3.00 1/4	$4.00 1/2	$5.00 Maple
Fineness	.9999	.9999	.9999	.9999	.9999
Weight (grams)	1.63	3.23	7.96	15.87	31.39
Diameter (mm)	16.00	20.00	27.00	34.00	38.00
Thickness (mm)	1.10	1.30	1.80	2.10	3.15
Edge	Reeded	Reeded	Reeded	Reeded	Reeded
Die Axis:	↑↑	↑↑	↑↑	↑↑	↑↑

Finish: Bullion, Brilliant relief against a parallel lined background
Cases of Issue: 1988: (A) Single coin sealed in clear mylar pouch
                           (B) Plastic tubes of 20 coins
          1999-2005: Sealed singly in clear mylar pouches, in strips of 10 coins

Note: Images shown are reduced from actual size.

SILVER MAPLE LEAFS

BULLION ISSUES

The two privy marks illustrated below appear on all silver maple leafs for that particular year.

Dated 1999-2000
"Fireworks"

Dated 2000
"Fireworks 2000"

Date	Privy Marks	Mintage	65	MINT STATE (MS) 66	67	68
1988		1,062,000	–	16.	–	–
1989		3,332,200	–	13.	–	–
1990		1,708,800	–	15.	–	–
1991		644,300	–	17.	–	–
1992		343,800	–	16.	–	–
1993		1,133,900	–	15.	–	–
1994		889,946	–	15.	–	–
1995		326,244	–	16.	–	–
1996		250,445	–	50.	–	–
1997		100,970	–	30.	–	–
1998		591,359	–	16.	–	–
1999		1,229,442	–	15.	–	–
1999-2000	Fireworks	Included	–	16.	–	–
2000	Fireworks 2000	403,652	–	16.	–	–
2001		398,563	–	16.	–	–
2002		576,196	–	16.	–	–
2003		684,750	–	16.	–	–
2004		680,925	–	14.	–	–
2005		N/A	–	12.	–	–

PRICING: Please remember that the above silver maple leaf prices are linked to the price of silver and may be priced higher, or lower, than prices shown depending on market conditions. Unlike gold and platinum maple leafs, silver leafs do experience a collector demand which will result in price differentials between dates. The price is affected by the total mintage and the pattern of distribution during year of issue.

SILVER MAPLE LEAF SPECIAL ISSUES

SINGLES

10TH ANNIVERSARY OF THE SILVER MAPLE LEAF, 1998. In 1998 the Royal Canadian Mint issued the 10 ounce silver maple leaf in celebration of the 10th anniversary of the silver maple leaf bullion coin. This coin is the largest legal tender Canadian coin ever produced, and is accompanied by a sterling silver plaque of authenticity. This coin is shown smaller than its actual size.

Designers and Engravers:
    Obv.: Dora de Pédery-Hunt
    Rev.: Royal Canadian Mint Staff
Composition: Silver (.9999)
Weight: 311.04 grams, 10 oz
Nominal Value: $5.00

Diameter: 65.0 mm
Thickness: 11 mm
Edge: Lettered, 10th Anniversary
    10e Anniversaire
Finish: Bullion, Brilliant relief against a
    parallel lined background

Date	Description	Issue Price	Mintage	BRILLIANT UNCIRCULATED (MS) 65	66	67	68
1998	10 oz	200.00	13,533	250.	—	—	—

SILVER MAPLE LEAF SPECIAL ISSUES

SINGLES

10TH ANNIVERSARY OF MAPLE LEAF BULLION COINS, 1989. This coin was issued in 1989 in proof finish to commemorate the 10th anniversary of the introduction of the maple leaf in 1979.

Designers, Engravers and Specifications: See page 446.

Case of issue: Maple wood presentation box, black flocked insert, encapsulated coins, COA, outer maple leaf printed box.

Date	Description	Issue Price	Mintage	65	66	67	68
					PROOF (PR)		
1989	1 ounce	39.00	29,999	–	–	50.	–

SAMBRO ISLAND LIGHTHOUSE, 2004. This silver maple was issued to commemorate the oldest working lighthouse in North America. Sambro Lighthouse has guided ships in and out of Halifax Harbour for over 200 years.

Designers: Obv.: Susanna Blunt   Engravers: Obv.: Susan Taylor
           Rev.: Hedley Doty   Rev.: William Woodruff

Specifications: See page 446
Finish: Proof, Frosted relief against a mirror background
Case of Issue: Maroon leather clam case, black flocked insert, encapsulated coin, COA

Date	Description	Issue Price	Mintage	65	66	67	68
					PROOF (PR)		
2004	Sambro Island	69.95	17,515	–	–	70.	–

Note: See page 457 for Sambro Island Lighthouse derivatives.

TORONTO ISLAND LIGHTHOUSE, 2005. The Toronto Island Lighthouse built in 1809 on Gibraltar Point, on what is now Toronto Island, guided ships into the Port of York (Toronto). It is the oldest existing lighthouse on the Great Lakes.

Designers: Obv.: Susanna Blunt   **Engravers:** Obv.: Susan Taylor
           Rev.: Brian Hughes   Rev.: William Woodruff
Specifications: See page 446
Finish: Proof, Frosted relief against a mirror background
Case of Issue: Red plastic display case, black plastic insert, encapsulated coin, COA

Date	Description	Issue Price	Mintage	65	66	PROOF (PR) 67	68
2005	Toronto Island	69.95	20,000	–	–	70.	–

SILVER MAPLE LEAF SPECIAL ISSUES

SETS

ARCTIC FOX FINE SILVER COIN SET, 2004. The first fractional fine silver coins feature wildlife designs that were originally created for platinum proof coins. The Arctic Fox first appeared on the Platinum proof coins of 1993.

Designers: Obv.: Susanna Blunt   **Engravers:** Obv.: Susan Taylor
           Rev.: Claude D'Angelo   Rev.: $5 – Susan Taylor
                                               $4 – Sheldon Beveridge
                                                 $3 – Ago Aarand
                                                 $2 – Ago Aarand

Specifications: See page 446
Finish: Proof, Frosted relief against a mirror background
Case of Issue: Black case, multicoloured outer sleeve

Date	Description	Issue Price	Mintage	65	66	PROOF (PR) 67	68
2004	Arctic Fox	89.95	13,694	–	–	90.	–

Note: Arctic Fox coins are illustrated smaller than actual size.

SILVER MAPLE LEAF WITH PRIVY MARKS

SINGLES

$5 SILVER MAPLE LEAFS WITH PRIVY MARKS 1998-2005. Beginning in 1998 the Royal Canadian Mint started a special issue of the $5.00 - 1 oz silver Maple Leafs. Privy marks were added to the reverses, commemorating special events for each year. For Designers, Engravers and Specifications see page 446.

1998 Titanic
Dillon - Gage

1998 Tiger
MTB Bank

1998 R.C.M.P.
Post Office

1908-1998 Anniv.
R.C.M.

1999 Rabbit
MTB Bank

2000 Dragon
MTB Bank

2000 Expo Hanover
R.C.M.

2001 Snake
R.C.M.

2002 Horse
R.C.M.

2003 Sheep
R.C.M.

2004 Monkey
R.C.M.

2004 'D' Day
R.C.M.

2004 Desjardins
R.C.M.

2005 Rooster
R.C.M.

2005 Liberation
of the Netherlands
R.D.M.

PRIVY MARK SINGLES (cont.)

Date	Description	Mintage	Issue Price	Case of Issue	Finish	GRADE 65	66	67	68
1998	Titanic	26,000	N/A	Mylar pouch	SP	–	30.	–	–
1998	Tiger	25,000	N/A	Mylar pouch	SP	–	30.	–	–
1998	R.C.M.P.	25,000	N/A	Mylar pouch	SP	–	40.	–	–
1998	90th Anniv.	13,025	N/A	Mylar pouch	SP	–	35.	–	–
1999	Rabbit	25,000	N/A	Mylar pouch	SP	–	40.	–	–
2000	Dragon	25,000	N/A	Mylar pouch	SP	–	60.	–	–
2000	Expo	15,000	N/A	Mylar pouch	SP	–	150.	–	–
2001	Snake	25,000	N/A	Mylar pouch	SP	–	35.	–	–
2002	Horse	25,000	N/A	Mylar pouch	SP	–	25.	–	–
2003	Sheep	25,000	N/A	Mylar pouch	SP	–	22.	–	–
2004	Monkey	25,000	N/A	Mylar pouch	SP	–	22.	–	–
2004	D Day	12,485	39.95	Red display	SP	–	40.	–	–
2004	Desjardins	15,000	39.95	Red display	MS	40.	–	–	–
2005	Rooster	15,000	24.95	Mylar pouch	SP	–	30.	–	–
2005	Liberation	3,500	E45.95	N/A	SP	–	125.	–	–

MS = Brilliant uncirculated, Brilliant relief on a brilliant background
SP = Specimen (reverse proof), Brilliant relief on a satin background
PR = Proof, Frosted relief against a mirror background

Note: Silver maple leafs are found, at times, in black or red clam style cases. These are not official cases.

PRIVY MARK SETS

ROYAL CANADIAN MINT PRIVY MARK SET, 2004. This five coin, 1, 1/2, 1/4, 1/10, and 1/20 maple ($5, $4, $3, $2 and $1) set carries the Royal Canadian Mint privy mark on each coin.

Privy Mark

Designers: Obv.: Susanna Blunt   **Engravers:** Obv.: Susan Taylor
Rev.: RCM Staff   Rev.: RCM Staff

Specifications: See page 446
Finish: Specimen (reverse proof), Brilliant relief on a satin background
Case of Issue: Dark blue leatherette clam style case, black insert, encapsulated coin, COA, silver sleeve

Date	Description	Issue Price	Mintage	SPECIMEN (SP) 65	66	67	68
2004	Set, 5 coins	99.95	13,859	–	100.	–	–

ZODIAC PRIVY MARK SET, 2004. This twelve coin set was struck by the Royal Canadian Mint, and issued jointly by Gatewest Coin Ltd. and Universal Coins. Each coin carries one of the twelve signs of zodiac as a privy mark.

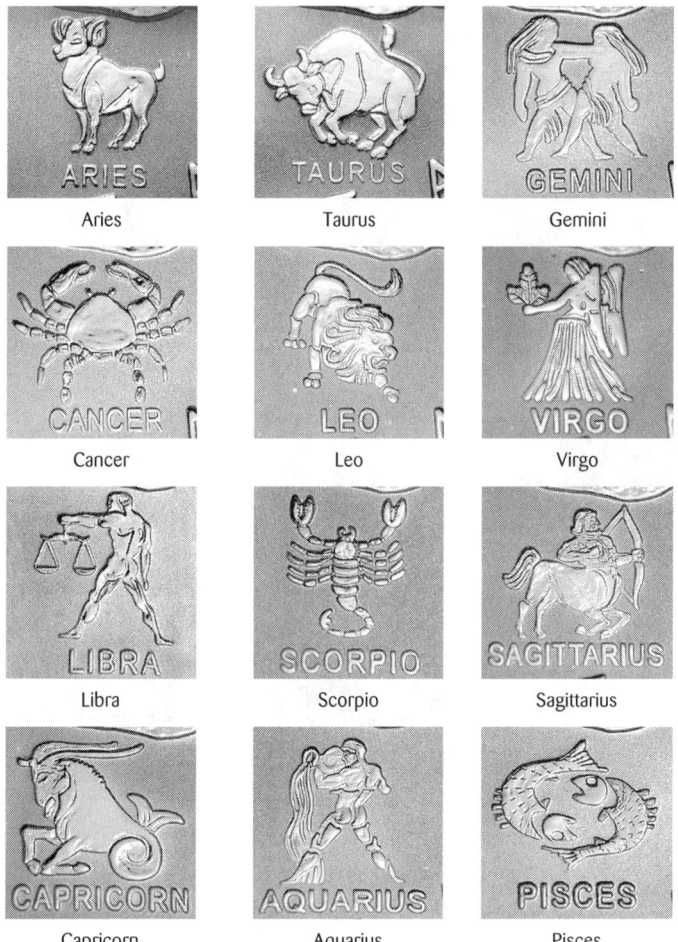

Aries	Taurus	Gemini
Cancer	Leo	Virgo
Libra	Scorpio	Sagittarius
Capricorn	Aquarius	Pisces

Designers: Obv.: Susanna Blunt   **Engravers:** Rev.: Susan Taylor
                         RCM Staff   RCM Staff

Specifications: See page 446
Finish: Specimen (reverse proof), Brilliant relief on a satin background
Case of Issue: Plastic pouch

Date	Description	Issue Price	Mintage	65	SPECIMEN (SP) 66	67	68
2004	12-coin set	368.88	5,000	–	375.	–	–
2004	Single coin	39.95	Included	–	40.	–	–

COLOURED SILVER MAPLES

SINGLE COINS

$5 SILVER MAPLE LEAFS, COLOURED, 2001-2004. This four-coin issue, depicting the seasons of the year, was first issued in 2001.

Obverse 2001 to 2003   Obverse 2004

Obverse:
  Designers:
    2001 Dora de Pédery-Hunt
    2004 Susanna Blunt
  Engravers:
    2001 Dora de Pédery-Hunt
    2004 Susan Tyalor
Reverse:
  Designers:
    2001 Debbie Adams
    2002 N/A
    2003 Stan Witten
    2004 Stan Witten
  Engravers:
    2001 N/A
    2002 N/A
    2003 Stan Witten
    2004 Stan Witten

Autumn 2001   Spring 2002

Finish: Bullion - Brilliant relief against a parallel lined background, colourized
Case of Issue:
  Dark green or red clam case, black flocked insert, encapsulated coin, COA

Summer 2003   Winter 2004

Date	Description	Issue Price	Mintage	BRILLIANT UNCIRCULATED (MS)			
				65	66	67	68
2001	Autumn	34.95	49,709	60.	–	–	–
2002	Spring	34.95	29,509	60.	–	–	–
2003	Summer	34.95	29,416	40.	–	–	–
2004	Winter	39.95	26,848	40.	–	–	–

Note: Images shown smaller than actual size.

SILVER MAPLE LEAFS WITH HOLOGRAMS

SINGLES

"MAPLE OF GOOD FORTUNE" HOLOGRAMS, 2001 and 2003. First issued in 2001, the $5 Maple Leaf coin carries a privy mark of Chinese characters, meaning Maple of Good Fortune, or Hope, as part of the hologram.

Photograph not
available
at press time

Privy Mark 2001

2001 Obverse   2001 Reverse

2003 Obverse   2003 Reverse   Privy Mark 2003

2005 Obverse   2005 Reverse   Privy Mark 2005

Specifications: See page 446
Finish: Specimen (reverse proof), Brilliant relief on satin background, hologram
Case of Issue: Red oval clam case, taupe flocked insert, encapsulated coin, COA

Date	Description	Issue Price	Mintage	65	SPECIMEN (SP) 66	67	68
2001	Good Fortune	59.99	29,817	–	100.	–	–
2003	Good Fortune	39.99	29,731	–	60.	–	–
2005	Hope	39.95	25,000	–	40.	–	–

SILVER MAPLE LEAF WITH HOLOGRAM

SINGLES

15TH ANNIVERSARY OF THE ONE DOLLAR LOON 2002. These maple leaf coins were struck to commemorate the 15th anniversary of the one dollar loon coin issued in 1987. No other coin has caught the imagination of Canadians as much as the "Loonie."

Designers: Obv.: Dora de Pédery-Hunt   Engravers: Obv.: Dora de Pédery-Hunt
        Rev.: RCM Staff   Rev.: RCM Staff
Specifications: See page 446
Finish: Specimen (reverse proof), Brilliant relief on a satin background, hologram
Case of issue: Black leatherette clam case, hunter green interior, encapsulated coin, COA

| Date | Description | Issue Price | Mintage | SPECIMEN (SP) | | | |
				65	66	67	68
2002	$5 Loon	39.95	29,970	–	55.	–	–

SETS

15TH ANNIVERSARY OF THE SILVER MAPLE LEAF 2003. Issued to commemorate the 15th anniversary of the silver maple leaf, 1988-2003. This five coin set contains two new denominations for Canadian coinage, a $3 and $4 coin, and all coins are struck with a maple leaf hologram.

Designers: Obv.: Dora de Pédery-Hunt   Engravers: Obv.: Dora de Pédery-Hunt
        Rev.: RCM Staff   Rev.: RCM Staff
Specifications: See page 446
Finish: Bullion, Brilliant relief against a parallel lined background, Hologram
Case of Issue: Red wooden case, black flocked insert, encapsulated coin, COA, silver outer box

| Date | Description | Issue Price | Mintage | BRILLIANT UNCIRCULATED (MS) | | | |
				65	66	67	68
2003	Set, 5 coins	149.95	28,947	150.	–	–	–

SILVER MAPLE LEAF DERIVATIVES

$5 SILVER MAPLE LEAF SETS, 2001. Three varieties of silver maples (colourized, hologram and regular) were combined with the seven proof coins, 1¢ to $2.00, of the 2001 Prestige Set to form the following Premium Proof sets:

Date	Description	Condition	Issue Price / Issuer	Mintage	Price
1998	**125th Anniv. of R.C.M.P.** Silver maple with R.C.M.P. privy mark Souvenir sheet Dark blue presentation case COA, booklet	SP-66	47.95 RCM, CP	25,000	50.
2001	**Proof Set of 2001** Seven proof coins, Specimen, hologram maple leaf	PR-67	150.00 RCM	3,000	150.
2001	**Specimen Set of 2001** Seven specimen coins, Brilliant uncirculated, coloured maple leaf	SP-66	100.00 RCM	Included above	100.
2001	**Brilliant Uncirculated Set of 2001** Seven brilliant uncirculated coins, Brilliant uncirculated maple leaf	MS-65	75.00 RCM	Included above	75.
2004	**Sambro Island** Framed image and Twenty dollar coin	PR-67	249.00 RCM	N/A	250.
2004	**Sambro Island** Ltd. Ed. Comm. Plate	–	29.95 RCM	2,000	30.

VARIETY SECTION

The third section of the "Charlton-Zoell Variety Catalogue" has arrived with the 60th edition of "Canadian Coins." In the previous two chapters the many different types of varieties were explored, focussing on die varieties and only touching on planchet and strike varieties. These were intentionally left to a later time. It is our hope that, after having read the first two sections, the collector will realize that varieties offer an interesting and complicated branch of numismatics. In the third section on varieties we now begin to build the main chapters of the "Charlton-Zoell Variety Catalogue" dealing with dollar varieties, both silver and nickel. The following 90 pages are devoted solely to listing dollar varieties. Our next chapter, accompanying the 61st edition, will enumerate the varieties of the fifty cent coins.

Numbering System

The reference number has three main components: the denomination/date, the surface of the coin on which the variety appears (obverse, reverse or edge), and the assignment of the variety number as a function of the finish. The following reference numbers have been assigned to the various finishes:

> .001 to .499 Brilliant Uncirculated
> .500 to .599 Proof-like Finish
> .600 to .699 Specimen Finish
> .700 to .799 Proof Finish
> .800 to .849 Bullion Mint State
> .850 to .899 Bullion Specimen or Reverse Proof
> .900 to .949 Bullion Proof

Within each category the first number assigned will be to the normal or standard coin with the remaining numbers being available for numbering the varieties as they are discovered. The system visualized is a simple first come, first served listing. The variety that arrives first is listed first, the second, second, and so on. No attempt will be made to classify the variety type within the catalogue numbering system; there are just too many different types. At some point in the future a comprehensive index will have to be created to cross-reference all the variety types within the numbering system.

Using a 1953NSF silver dollar, the reference numbers will be:

1953NSF Obv.-001 – The Obverse side of the Normal (or standard) coin is number .001
1953NSF Rev.-001 – The Reverse side of the Normal (or standard) coin is number .001

Assuming the first variety of the 1953NSF dollar submitted has an obverse die break in "GRATIA", and a "Voyageur" reverse with Short Water Lines two variety listings would be generated:

1953NSF Obv.-002   Die Break in "GRATIA"
1953NSF Rev.-002   Short Water Lines

If the variety submitted did not have the die break (and thus a normal obverse), but only a Voyageur reverse with Short Water Lines, the classification would be:

1953NSF Rev.-002 Short Water Lines

As all die cracks and die breaks will vary, the reference number will be taken from the first recorded appearance for each particular date/denomination, obverse or reverse for that coin. As more varieties come to light the numbering system will grow, and the rules will expand along with the listings.

ONE DOLLAR

1935 OBVERSE VARIETIES

MACHINE DOUBLING DAMAGE (MDD) VARIETIES

This is an after strike doubling as defined by Herbert in Section V-B-1, Machine Doubling Damage.

DOUBLING OF XXV.

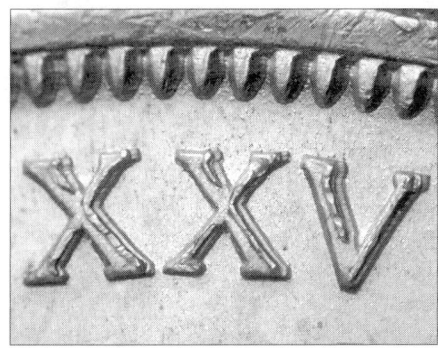

Ref. No.	Description	VF-20	EF-40	AU-50	MS-60	MS-63
1935 Obv.-001	Normal	30.	40.	50.	60.	100.
1935 Obv.-002	Doubling of "XXV"	35.	45.	55.	65.	110.

DIE CRACKS AND BREAKS

Die cracks and breaks are the result of wear and tear on the tools that produce the coins. See Herbert Sections 11-D and 11-E.

CRACK THROUGH "ANNO REGNI"

Ref. No.	Description	VF-20	EF-40	AU-50	MS-60	MS-63
1935 Obv.-001	Normal	30.	40.	50.	60.	100.
1935 Obv.-003	Crack through "ANNO REGNI"	35.	45.	55.	65.	110.

ONE DOLLAR

1935 REVERSE VARIETIES

MACHINE DOUBLING DAMAGE (MDD) VARIETIES

DOUBLING OF "RIGHT TREE"

Doubling of "Right Tree"
Zoell No. R501k

Ref. No.	Description	VF-20	EF-40	AU-50	MS-60	MS-63
1935 Rev.-001	Normal	30.	40.	50.	60.	100.
1935 Rev.-002	Doubling of "Right Tree"	35.	45.	55.	65.	110.

DOUBLING OF "VOYAGEUR AND INDIAN"

Doubling of Voyageur and Indian
Zoell No. R501g

Ref. No.	Description	VF-20	EF-40	AU-50	MS-60	MS-63
1935 Rev.-001	Normal	30.	40.	50.	60.	100.
1935 Rev.-003	Doubling "Voyageur and Indian"	35.	45.	55.	65.	110.

ONE DOLLAR

1935 REVERSE VARIETIES

COUNTERSTAMPED "J.O.P"

Joseph Oliva Patenaude, of Nelson, B.C., counterstamped silver dollars starting in 1935, and the practice continued into the early 1950s. Various styles of punches were used over this period. Such coins are discussed in Herbert IV-B, as counterstamps and revalued coins.

INITIALS ONLY (INCUSED)

OVAL WITH SMALL INITIALS (RAISED)

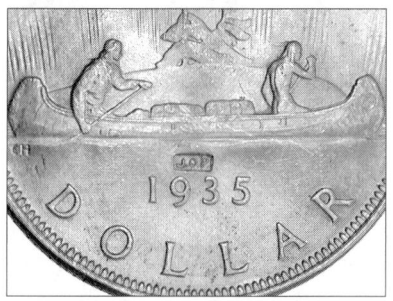 

OVAL WITH LARGE INITIALS (RAISED)

Submitted by: Scott Cornwell

Ref. No.	Description	VF-20	EF-40	AU-50	MS-60	MS-63
1935 Rev.-001	Normal	30.	40.	50.	60.	100.
1935 Rev.-004	Initials JOP only	–	175.	350.	450.	–
1935 Rev.-005	Oval, Small Initals J.O.P	–	175.	350.	450.	–
1935 Rev.-006	Oval, Large Initals J.O.P	–	–	–	–	–

ONE DOLLAR

1936 REVERSE VARIETIES

COUNTERSTAMPED "J.O.P"

The most authoritative history of Joseph Oliva Patenaude and his counterstamped "J.O.P." dollars is Larry Gingras' article on the subject published in the Canadian Numismatic Journal of October 1959. From this article two important points emerge: (1) a time line for the J.O.P. dollar, 1935 when the first dollar was counterstamped, to 1950 when he sold his business in Nelson, B.C., and then to his death in 1956, and (2) the fact that he was a perfectionst.

These two points must be used concurrently when assessing the rumours that fake counterstamped "JOP" dollars were supposedly produced in the early 1960s.

An important point in the fake counterstamps discussion concerns the fate of the punches used by Patenaude. Were they sold as part of the business in 1950, and, if so, were they used between 1950 and 1956, the date of his death? Were these 1950-56 examples produced by fake punches or were the original Patenaude punches used with his consent? Following is a table of four different punches and the dollars on which they appear. Counterstamps One and Two are recorded in books and articles published in or before1961. Stamps Three and Four do not fit the "perfectionists" label, and thus should be suspect, but nothing has yet been confirmed.

Initials (1)	Oval Small Initials (2)		Oval Large Initials (3)	Rectangle Initials (4)
1935	1935	1947 ML	1936	1947 Bl
1947 Bl	1936	1950	1947 Bl	
1949	1937	1951		
	1938	1952 WL		
	1939	1952 NWL		
	1946	1953 NSF		
	1947 Bl	1954		

Note: A 1948 J.O.P. dollar was recorded by Gingras in his CNA Journal article of October, 1959.

OVAL WITH SMALL INITIALS (RAISED)

Submitted by: Scott Cornwell

Ref. No.	Description	VF-20	EF-40	AU-50	MS-60	MS-63
1936 Rev.-001	Normal	20.	25.	30.	55.	100.
1936 Rev.-002	Oval, small initials J.O.P	–	175.	350.	450.	–

ONE DOLLAR

1937 OBVERSE VARIETIES

MACHINE DOUBLING DAMAGE (MDD) VARIETIES

DOUBLING OF "HP" TO THE NORTH WEST

DOUBLING OF "HP" TO THE WEST

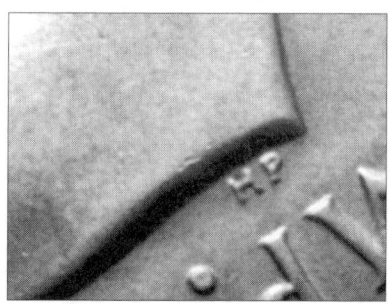 

Submitted by: Kerry Pinette

Ref. No.	Description	VF-20	EF-40	AU-50	MS-60	MS-63
1937 Obv.-001	Normal	15.	18.	24.	50.	115.
1937 Obv.-002	North West "H.P."	20.	25.	30.	60.	125.
1937 Obv.-003	West "HP"	20.	25.	30.	60.	125.

ONE DOLLAR

1937 REVERSE VARIETIES

COUNTERSTAMPED "J.O.P"

OVAL WITH SMALL INITIALS (RAISED)

Submitted by: Scott Cornwell

Ref. No.	Description	VF-20	EF-40	AU-50	MS-60	MS-63
1937 Rev.-001	Normal	15.	18.	24.	50.	115.
1937 Rev.-002	Oval, Small Initials J.O.P	–	175.	350.	450.	–

ONE DOLLAR

1938 OBVERSE VARIETIES

DIE DETERIORATION DOUBLING

See Herbert, Section II-G-3. The letter cavities of the die will enlarge with use causing wear that will distort the shapes of the letters.

DOUBLING OF "HP"

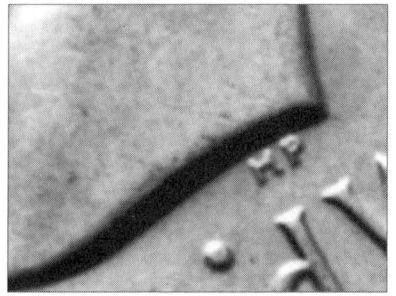 

Ref. No.	Description	VF-20	EF-40	AU-50	MS-60	MS-63
1938 Obv.-001	Normal	60.	70.	90.	125.	275.
1938 Obv.-002	Doubling of "HP"	65.	75.	95.	135.	285.

1938 REVERSE VARIETIES

COUNTERSTAMPED "J.O.P"

OVAL WITH SMALL INTIALS (RAISED)

Submitted by: Scott Cornwell

Ref. No.	Description	VF-20	EF-40	AU-50	MS-60	MS-63
1938 Rev.-001	Normal	60.	70.	90.	125.	275.
1938 Rev.-002	Oval, Small Initials J.O.P	–	175.	350.	450.	–

ONE DOLLAR

1939 OBVERSE VARIETIES

PUNCH DOUBLED

Eight different Hub (punch) Doubled varieties are explained in Herbert's Section II-B.

PUNCH QUADRUPLED "HP"

Submitted by: Kerry Pinette

Ref. No.	Description	VF-20	EF-40	AU-50	MS-60	MS-63
1939 Obv.-001	Normal	10.	14.	16.	20.	45.
1939 Obv.-002	Quadrupled "HP"	25.	30.	35.	40.	65.

1939 REVERSE VARIETIES

COUNTERSTAMPED "J.O.P"

OVAL WITH SMAL LETTERS (RAISED)

Submitted by: Scott Cornwell

Ref. No.	Description	VF-20	EF-40	AU-50	MS-60	MS-63
1939 Rev.-001	Normal	10.	14.	16.	20.	45.
1939 Rev.-002	Oval, Small Letters J.O.P	–	175.	350.	450.	–

ONE DOLLAR

1945 OBVERSE VARIETIES

DIE DETERIORATION DOUBLING

DOUBLING OF "HP"

Submitted by: Kerry Pinette

Ref. No.	Description	VF-20	EF-40	AU-50	MS-60	MS-63
1945 Obv.-001	Normal	175.	200.	225.	325.	650.
1945 Obv.-002	Doubling of "HP"	180.	225.	250.	350.	750.

ONE DOLLAR

1946 OBVERSE VARIETIES

PUNCH DOUBLED

PUNCH QUADRUPLED "HP"

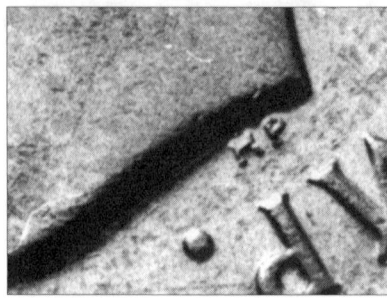 

Submitted by: Kerry Pinette

Ref. No.	Description	VF-20	EF-40	AU-50	MS-60	MS-63
1946 Obv.-001	Normal	40.	60.	100.	125.	350.
1946 Obv.-002	Quadrupled "HP"	60.	70.	125.	150.	375.

ONE DOLLAR

THE "WATER LINE" YEARS

The years 1946 to 1957 are the "water line" variety years for Canadian silver dollars. Currently there are 25 different varieties in the eleven year period, and there is no reason to believe that this will be the final number. The water line varieties form an interesting collection.

Below is a Die Usage table of the "water line" years illustrating the difficulty the Mint experienced with die, and most likely punch, life.

DIE USAGE

Date	Obverse Dies	Reverse Dies	Coins Per Die Pair
1946	48	35	2,215
1947	11	17	4,685
1948	9	6	5,322
1949	48	94	8,894
1950	69	52	4,987
1951	111	65	4,971
1952	82	58	5,971
1953	166	82	8,666
1954	20	15	14,092
1955	25	11	14,338
1956	52	28	5,227
1957	12	6	55,154

Averages

	Obverse Dies	Reverse Dies	Coins Per Die Pair
1946-1956	54.6	42.6	7,215
1946-1957	54.4	39.1	11,210

During the war years, World War II and then the Korean War, all high quality tool steel was needed for the war effort. Between the wars, it was required for economic reconstruction.

Poor quality tool steel will make poor quality dies. Averaging 7,215 coins per pair of dies, the dies did not have a long life span. Die failure was the rule of the day, and any procedure that would keep the die working was used.

Poor dies also meant poor punches, for more than likely the same tool steel that was used to produce the dies was used to produce the punches. Punches, producing large quantities of dies, fail in the same manner as dies. The polishing and refinishing of punches may also be a source of die varieties.

ONE DOLLAR

1946 REVERSE VARIETIES

ABRADED DIES

Refer to Herbert, Section II-I, on Die Scratches, Polished and Abraded Dies.

SHORT WATER LINES

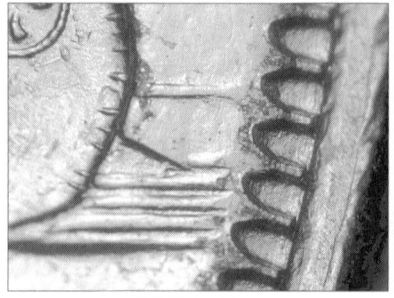 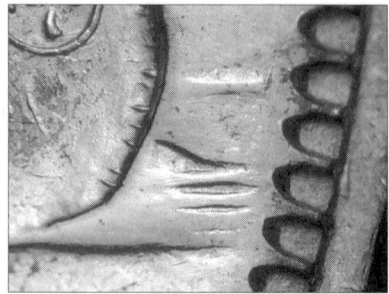

Full Water Lines · Short Water Lines

Submitted by: Ray Fishlock and Kerry Pinette

Ref. No.	Description	VF-20	EF-40	AU-50	MS-60	MS-63
1946 Rev.-001	Normal, Full Water Lines	40.	60.	100.	125.	350.
1946 Rev.-002	Short Water Lines	50.	70.	110.	150.	400.

COUNTERSTAMPED "J.O.P"

OVAL WITH SMALL LETTERS (RAISED)

Submitted by: Scott Cornwell

Ref. No.	Description	VF-20	EF-40	AU-50	MS-60	MS-63
1946 Rev.-001	Normal, Full Water Lines	40.	60.	100.	125.	350.
1946 Rev.-003	Oval, Small Letters J.O.P	–	175.	350.	450.	–

ONE DOLLAR

1947 POINTED 7 OBVERSE VARIETIES

PUNCH DOUBLED, TRIPLED, QUADRUPLED AND DIE DETERIORATION DOUBLING

"HP"

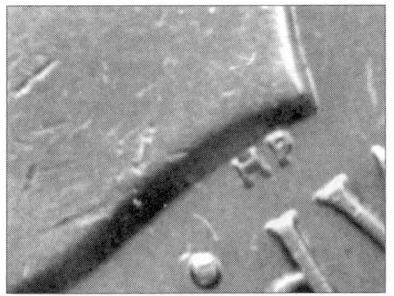

Normal "HP"

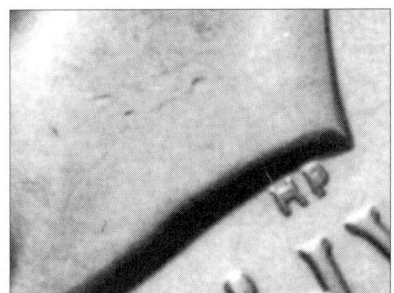

Punch Doubled "HP"

Punch Quadrupled "HP"

Die Deterioration Doubling of "HP"

Ref. No.	Description	VF-20	EF-40	AU-50	MS-60	MS-63
1947 Pt Obv.-001	Normal	125.	175.	225.	350.	1,500.
1947 Pt Obv.-002	Doubled "HP"	150.	200.	250.	500.	2,000.
1947 Pt Obv.-003	Tripled "HP"	150.	200.	250.	375.	2,000.
1947 Pt Obv.-004	Quadrupled "HP"	200.	250.	300.	500.	2,000.
1947 Pt Obv.-005	Die Deterioration "HP"	135.	185.	235.	375.	2,000.

ONE DOLLAR

1947 POINTED 7 REVERSE VARIETIES

DOT AFTER 7

Conflicting views exist on this variety. Zoell claimed it is an intermediate coin coming between the "1947 Pointed 7" and the "1947 Maple Leaf" varieties. Dushnik suggested that a specimen die became marked by a small piece of metal, with the die being put in to service to produce business strike coins for the remainder of its life.

| No Dot After 7 | Dot after 7 |
| Zoell No. 511E replace with X508c ??? | Zoell No. B508d |

Ref. No.	Description	VF-20	EF-40	AU-50	MS-60	MS-63
1947 Pt Rev.-001	Normal	125.	175.	225.	350.	1,500.
1947 Pt Rev.-002	Dot After 7	150.	200.	250.	400.	2,000.

DOUBLE PUNCHED DIGIT

DOUBLED "4"

The last two digits of the date were added to the working die by hand, with the use of a mallet and a steel punch. It took at least two strikes to form a digit. If the second strike was not in line, doubling occurred. See Herbert, Section II-A-3.

Punch doubled 4 in date
Zoell No. R508F

Ref. No.	Description	VF-20	EF-40	AU-50	MS-60	MS-63
1947 Pt Rev.-001	Normal	125.	175.	225.	350.	1,500.
1947 Pt Rev.-003	Doubled "4"	250.	300.	350.	500.	2,000.

ONE DOLLAR

1947 POINTED 7 REVERSE VARIETIES

FULL WATER LINES, SHORT WATER LINES

Full Water Lines

Short Water Lines

Ref. No.	Description	VF-20	EF-40	AU-50	MS-60	MS-63
1947 Pt Rev.-001	Normal, Full Water Lines	125.	175.	225.	350.	1,500.
1947 Pt Rev.-004	Short Water Lines	150.	200.	250.	375.	1,600.

ONE DOLLAR

1947 BLUNT 7 OBVERSE VARIETIES

PUNCH DOUBLED

DOUBLED "HP"

Photograph not
available
at press time

Ref. No.	Description	VF-20	EF-40	AU-50	MS-60	MS-63
1947 Bl Obv.-001	Normal	100.	150.	175.	250.	400.
1947 Bl Obv.-002	Doubled "HP"	125.	175.	225.	275.	—

ONE DOLLAR

1947 BLUNT REVERSE VARIETIES

PUNCH SPACING

The last two digits of the date were added to the working die by punching. If the digits were not aligned correctly, variations in punch spacing occurred.

LOW "47"

Normal 47

Low 47, Narrow Date

DOUBLE PUNCHED DIGIT

DOUBLED "7"

The punching of digits took two or more blows with the mallet on the punch. If the second positioning of the punch on the first impression was not correct, doubling of the numbers occurred. See Herbert, Section II-A-9.

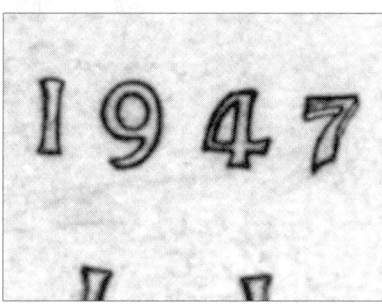

Repunched 7 over 7
Zoell No. R508a

Ref. No.	Description	VF-20	EF-40	AU-50	MS-60	MS-63
1947 Bl Rev.-001	Normal	100.	150.	175.	250.	400.
1947 Bl Rev.-002	Low "47"	200.	250.	275.	350.	500.
1947 Bl Rev.-003	Doubled "7"	200.	250.	275.	350.	500.

ONE DOLLAR

1947 BLUNT 7 REVERSE VARIETIES

COUNTERSTAMPED "J.O.P"

OVAL WITH SMALL INITIALS (RAISED)

OVAL WITH LARGE INITIALS (RAISED)

RECTANGLE WITH INITIALS (RAISED)

Submitted by: Scott Cornwell

Ref. No.	Description	VF-20	EF-40	AU-50	MS-60	MS-63
1947 Bl Rev.-001	Normal	100.	150.	175.	250.	400.
1947 Bl Rev.-004	Oval, Small, Initials J.O.P	–	300.	475.	650.	–
1947 Bl Rev.-005	Oval, Large Initials J.O.P	–	–	–	–	–
1947 Bl Rev.-006	Rectangle with initials J.O.P.	–	–	–	–	–

Note: Counterstamps, Oval with Large Initials and Rectangle with Initials are in question as to their authenticity.

ONE DOLLAR

1947 MAPLE LEAF OBVERSE VARIETIES

PUNCH DOUBLED

DOUBLED "HP"

Ref. No.	Description	VF-20	EF-40	AU-50	MS-60	MS-63
1947 ML Obv.-001	Normal	200.	225.	275.	375.	650.
1947 ML Obv.-002	Doubled"HP"	250.	300.	375.	–	–

1947 MAPLE LEAF REVERSE VARIETIES

COUNTERSTAMPED "J.O.P"

OVAL WITH SMALL INITIALS (RAISED)

Submitted by: Scott Cornwell

Ref. No.	Description	VF-20	EF-40	AU-50	MS-60	MS-63
1947 ML Rev.-001	Normal	200.	225.	275.	375.	650.
1947 ML Rev.-003	Oval, Small Letters "J.O.P"	–	375.	575.	775.	–

ONE DOLLAR

1948 REVERSE VARIETIES

FULL WATER LINES, SHORT WATER LINES

Full Water Lines

Short Water Lines

Ref. No.	Description	VF-20	EF-40	AU-50	MS-60	MS-63
1948 Rev.-001	Normal, Full Water Lines	800.	950.	1,100.	1,400.	2,000.
1948 Rev.-002	Short Water Lines	800.	950.	1,100.	1,400.	–

LOW 4 WITH LARGE 8

In the Low 4, Large 8 variety the digit "8" resembles an "S".

Normal 8

Low 4 with Large 8

Ref. No.	Description	VF-20	EF-40	AU-50	MS-60	MS-63
1948 Rev.-001	Normal	800.	950.	1,100.	1,400.	2,000.
1948 Rev.-003	Low 8	900.	1,050.	1,200.	1,500.	–

ONE DOLLAR

1949 REVERSE VARIETIES

CLASH DIES

HALF MOON

Clash dies are defined by Herbert in Section II-G, Worn and Damaged Dies, Collars and Hubs (Punches).

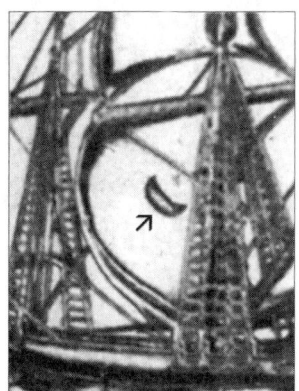

Half Moon
Zoell No. C511c

Ref. No.	Description	VF-20	EF-40	AU-50	MS-60	MS-63
1949 Rev.-001	Normal	20.	30.	35.	40.	45.
1949 Rev.-002	Half Moon	25.	35.	40.	45.	50.

COUNTERSTAMPED "J.O.P"

INITIALS ONLY (INCUSED)

This counterstamp is suspicious because the incused letters lack uniformity. It should be remembered that Patenande was a jeweller who took pride in his work. (He also took credit for having the silver dollar struck).

Submitted by: Scott Cornwell

Ref. No.	Description	VF-20	EF-40	AU-50	MS-60	MS-63
1949 Rev.-001	Normal	20.	30.	35.	40.	45.
1949 Rev.-003	Counterstamped, Initials Only	—	175.	350.	450.	—

ONE DOLLAR

1950 REVERSE VARIETIES

FULL, SHORT AND ARNPRIOR WATER LINES

Full Water Lines

Short Water Lines

Arnprior
Zoell K512b

Ref. No.	Description	VF-20	EF-40	AU-50	MS-60	MS-63
1950 Rev.-001	Normal, Full Water Lines	12.	16.	20.	30.	60.
1950 Rev.-002	Short Water Lines	15.	20.	30.	65.	125.
1950 Rev.-003	Arnprior	15.	20.	30.	65.	175.

ONE DOLLAR

1950 REVERSE VARIETIES

MACHINE DOUBLING DAMAGE (MDD)

Herbert defines machine doubling damage (V-B-I), as the result of die bounce, chatter or die displacement. It constitutes damage to the coin after it has been struck. Machine doubling damage is the most common form of doubling found.

DOUBLING OF "VOYAGEUR"

Doubling of "Voyageur" Zoell No. R512Q	Photograph not available at press time 1950 Arnprior Doubled Voyageur

Ref. No.	Description	VF-20	EF-40	AU-50	MS-60	MS-63
1950 Rev.-001	Normal, Full Water Lines	12.	16.	20.	30.	60.
1950 Rev.-004	FWL, Doubled Voyageur	18.	25.	30.	40.	70.
1950 Rev.-005	Arnprior, Doubled Voyageur	20.	25.	35.	75.	200.

COUNTERSTAMPED "J.O.P"

OVAL WITH SMALL INITIALS (RAISED)

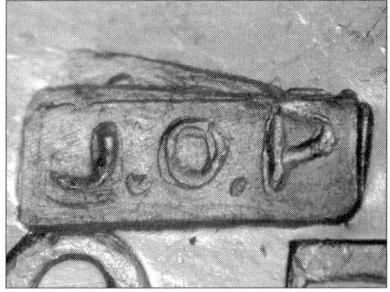

1950 Counterstamp Dollar   Counterstamp

Submitted by: Scott Cornwell

Ref. No.	Description	VF-20	EF-40	AU-50	MS-60	MS-63
1950 Rev.-001	Normal	12.	16.	20.	30.	60.
1950 Rev.-006	Oval, Small Initials "J.O.P"	–	175.	350.	450.	–

ONE DOLLAR

1950 REVERSE VARIETIES

WITH "ISLAND LOGS", FULL WATER LINES

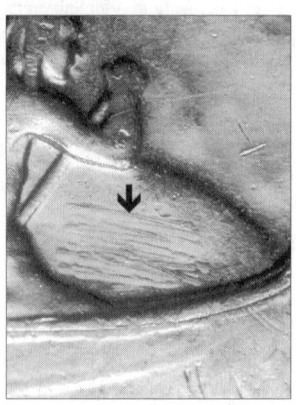

Submitted by: Ray Fishlock

Ref. No.	Description	VF-20	EF-40	AU-50	MS-60	MS-63
1950 Rev.-001	Normal, Full Water Lines	12.	16.	20.	30.	60.
1950 Rev.-007	"Island Logs"	18.	25.	30.	40.	70.

SHORT WATER LINES REVERSE, REPUNCHED LOW "0"

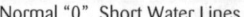

Normal "0", Short Water Lines   Repunched Low "0", Short Water Lines

Submitted by: Scott Cornwell

Ref. No.	Description	VF-20	EF-40	AU-50	MS-60	MS-63
1950 Rev.-002	Short Water Lines	15.	20.	30.	65.	125.
1950 Rev.-008	SWL, Repunched Low "0"	30.	40.	60.	125.	250.

ONE DOLLAR

1950 REVERSE VARIETIES

REENGRAVED DIE

ISLAND AND WATER LINES REENGRAVED

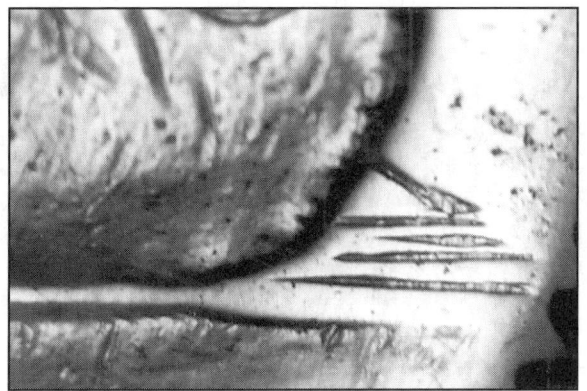

Submitted by: Steve Olter, Ken Potter

Ref. No.	Description	VF-20	EF-40	AU-50	MS-60	MS-63
1950 Rev.-001	Normal, Full Water Lines	12.	16.	20.	30.	60.
1950 Rev.-009	Reengraved Island, Water Lines	60.	80.	100.	125.	150.

ARNPRIOR WITH MISSING RAYS

Arnprior with "Rays"

Arnprior Without "Rays"

Ref. No.	Description	VF-20	EF-40	AU-50	MS-60	MS-63
1950 Rev.-003	Arnprior	15.	20.	30.	65.	175.
1950 Rev.-010	Arnprior, Without "Rays"	50.	75.	100.	125.	200.

ONE DOLLAR

1951 OBVERSE VARIETIES

PUNCH DOUBLED

DOUBLED "HP" OBVERSE – FULL WATER LINES REVERSE

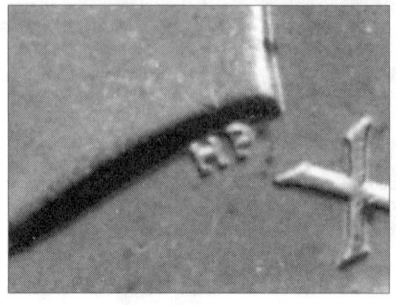

Punch Doubled "HP"

Ref. No.	Description	VF-20	EF-40	AU-50	MS-60	MS-63
1951 Obv.-001	Normal – FWL Reverse	8.	9.	12.	17.	40.
1951 Obv.-002	Punch Doubled "HP"	50.	60.	75.	100.	125.

DIE DETERIORATION DOUBLING

DOUBLING OF "HP" OBVERSE – SHORT WATER LINES REVERSE

Doubling of "HP"

Ref. No.	Description	VF-20	EF-40	AU-50	MS-60	MS-63
1951 Obv.-001	Normal – SWL Reverse	20.	30.	50.	75.	150.
1951 Obv.-003	Doubling of "HP"	25.	35.	55.	80.	160.

ONE DOLLAR

1951 REVERSE VARIETIES

FULL, SHORT AND ARNPRIOR WATER LINES

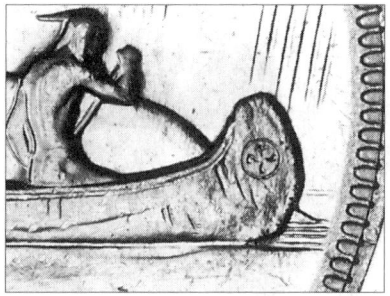

Full Water Lines

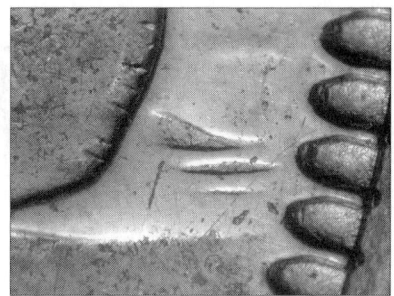

Short Water Lines

Arnprior
Zoell No. K513b

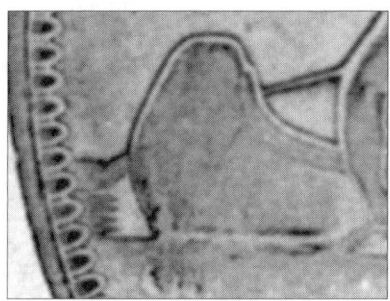

Short Water Lines
Behind Canoe
Zoell No. K513d

Ref. No.	Description	VF-20	EF-40	AU-50	MS-60	MS-63
1951 Rev.-001	Normal, Full Water Lines	8.	9.	12.	17.	40.
1951 Rev.-002	Short Water Lines	20.	30.	50.	75.	150.
1951 Rev.-003	Arnprior	50.	75.	90.	200.	350.
1951 Rev.-004	Short Rear Lines	20.	30.	50.	75.	150.

ONE DOLLAR

1951 REVERSE VARIETIES

PUNCH DOUBLED "I"

DIGIT PUNCH DOUBLED "I"

Punch Doubled "1"
Zoell No. FR513a

Ref. No.	Description	VF-20	EF-40	AU-50	MS-60	MS-63
1951 Rev.-001	Normal	8.	9.	12.	17.	40.
1951 Rev.-005	Punch Doubled "1"	10.	15.	20.	25.	50.

DOT ABOVE FRONT OF CANOE

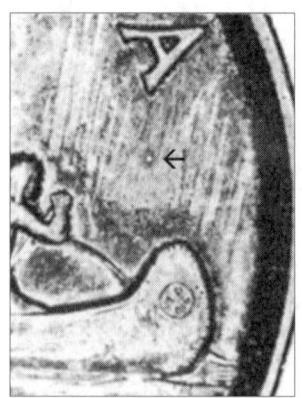

Dot above Canoe
Zoell No. B513a

Ref. No.	Description	VF-20	EF-40	AU-50	MS-60	MS-63
1951 Rev.-001	Normal	8.	9.	12.	17.	40.
1951 Rev.-006	Dot above Canoe	10.	15.	20.	25.	50.

ONE DOLLAR

1951 REVERSE VARIETIES

COUNTERSTAMPED "J.O.P"

OVAL WITH SMALL INITIALS (RAISED)

Submitted by: Scott Cornwell

Ref. No.	Description	VF-20	EF-40	AU-50	MS-60	MS-63
1951 Rev.-001	Normal	8.	9.	12.	17.	40.
1951 Rev.-007	Oval, Small Letters "J.O.P"	–	175.	350.	450.	–

ONE DOLLAR

1952 OBVERSE VARIETIES

DIE CRACKS AND BREAKS

Dies fail from fatigue, and cracks are the first sign of failure. Small cracks become larger until they turn into breaks. They are progressive; thus, no two are exactly alike. The two images below are interesting in that failure of the obverse die may have taken place over two different reverse dies. The number 1952 Obv.-002 has been assigned to the Die Cracks vareity of the 1952 dollar and 1952 Obv.-003 has been assigned to Die Breaks.

DIE CRACK OBVERSE — FULL WATER LINE REVERSE
DIE BREAK OBVERSE — SHORT WATER LINE REVERSE

Obverse Die Crack with
Full Water Lines Reverse

Obverse Die Break with
Short Water Lines Reverse

Ref. No.	Description	VF-20	EF-40	AU-50	MS-60	MS-63
1952 Obv.-001	Normal, Full Water Lines	8.	9.	12.	16.	40.
1952 Obv.-002	Obv. Die Crack — FWL Reverse	12.	15.	20.	25.	50.
1952 Obv.-003	Obv. Die Break — SWL Reverse	25.	30.	40.	75.	125.

DIE DETERIORATION DOUBLING

DOUBLING OF "HP" OBVERSE — SHORT WATER LINES REVERSE

Ref. No.	Description	VF-20	EF-40	AU-50	MS-60	MS-63
1952 Obv.-001	Normal, SWL Reverse	20.	25.	35.	60.	100.
1952 Obv.-004	Doubling of "HP" — SWL Reverse	25.	30.	40.	75.	125.

ONE DOLLAR

1952 OBVERSE VARIETIES

DIE CLASH

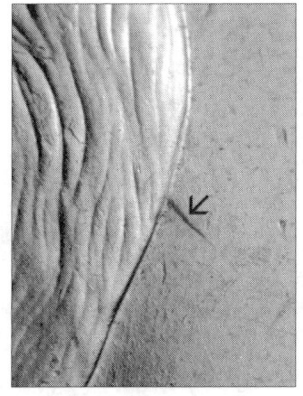 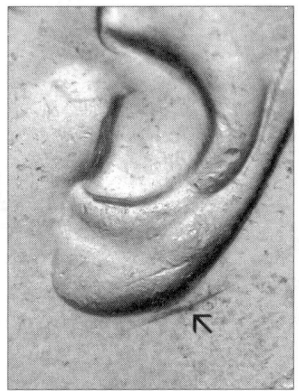

Submitted by: Ray Fishlock

Ref. No.	Description	VF-20	EF-40	AU-50	MS-60	MS-63
1952 Obv.-001	Normal	8.	9.	12.	16.	40.
1952 Obv.-005	Die Clash	12.	15.	20.	25.	50.

ONE DOLLAR

1952 REVERSE VARIETIES

ABRADED DIES

FULL, SHORT, ARNPRIOR, AND NO WATERLINES

1952 Full Water Lines
Zoell No. A514

1952 Short Water Lines
Zoell No. S514o

1952 Arnprior
Zoell No. K514b

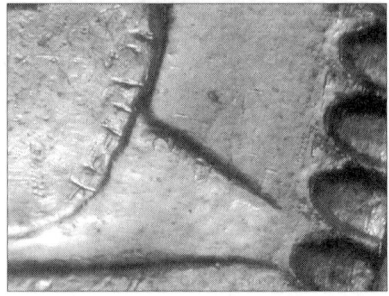

1952 No Water Lines
Zoell No. K514n and S514h

Ref. No.	Description	VF-20	EF-40	AU-50	MS-60	MS-63
1952 Rev.-001	Normal, Full Water Lines	8.	9.	12.	16.	40.
1952 Rev.-002	Short Water Lines	20.	25.	35.	60.	100.
1952 Rev.-003	Arnprior	20.	30.	45.	75.	150.
1952 Rev.-004	No Water Lines	10.	12.	15.	35.	60.

ONE DOLLAR

1952 REVERSE VARIETIES

ABRADED DIES

SHORT WATER LINES, WITHOUT RAYS

Short Water Lines With Rays

Short Water Lines Without Rays

Submitted by: Ray Fishlock

Ref. No.	Description	VF-20	EF-40	AU-50	MS-60	MS-63
1952 Rev.-002	Short Water Lines, With Rays	20.	25.	35.	60.	100.
1952 Rev.-005	Short Water Lines, Without Rays	30.	35.	45.	75.	125.

ONE DOLLAR

1952 REVERSE VARIETIES

COUNTERSTAMPED "J.O.P"

FULL WATER LINES, OVAL WITH SMALL INITIALS (RAISED)

1952 Full Water Lines Reverse
Counterstamped "J.O.P"

Counterstamped "J.O.P"

NO WATER LINES, OVAL WITH SMALL INITIALS (RAISED)

1952 No Water Lines Reverse
Counterstamped "J.O.P"

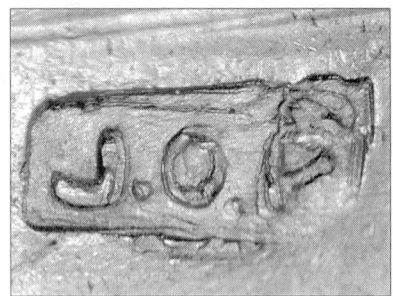

Counterstamped "J.O.P"

Submitted by: Scott Cornwell

Ref. No.	Description	VF-20	EF-40	AU-50	MS-60	ms-63
1952 Rev.-001	Normal, Full Water Lines	8.	9.	12.	16.	40.
1952 Rev.-006	FWL, Oval, Small Initials "J.O.P"	–	175.	350.	450.	–
1952 Rev.-004	No Water Lines	10.	12.	15.	35.	60.
1952 Rev.-007	NWL, Oval, Small Initials "J.O.P"	–	175.	350.	450.	–

ONE DOLLAR

1952 REVERSE VARIETIES

The coin illustrated is a double variety. The "5" is a repunched 5, while the doubling of the "2" is the result of die deterioration. The varieties are listed separately with the understanding that a single variety Repunched "5" will be found.

DOUBLE PUNCHED DIGIT

DOUBLED "5"

Repunched "5"

Submitted by: Kerry Pinette

Ref. No.	Description	VF-20	EF-40	AU-50	MS-60	MS-63
1952 Rev.-001	Normal, Full Water Lines	8.	9.	12.	16.	40.
1952 Rev.-008	Doubled "5", Full Water Lines	15.	20.	30.	40.	60.

DIE DETERIORATION DOUBLING

DOUBLING OF "2"

Die Break on "2"

Submitted by: Kerry Pinette

Ref. No.	Description	VF-20	EF-40	AU-50	MS-60	MS-63
1952 Rev.-001	Normal, Full Water Lines	8.	9.	12.	16.	40.
1952 Rev.-009	Doubling of "2", Full Water Lines	20.	25.	40.	75.	125.

ONE DOLLAR

1952 REVERSE VARIETIES

DIE BREAKS

DIE BREAKS IN LEGEND AND DIGIT, NO WATER LINES REVERSE

No Water Lines, Die Breaks
Zoell No. FL514q

Ref. No.	Description	VF-20	EF-40	AU-50	MS-60	MS-63
1952 Rev.-004	No Water Lines	10.	12.	15.	35.	60.
1952 Rev.-010	Die Breaks	15.	18.	20.	40.	75.

Note: See the previous page for an earlier version of the doubling of the "2". 1952 Rev.-010 has been assigned the number for the 1952 Reverse Die Break variety.

ONE DOLLAR

1953 NO SHOULDER FOLD VARIETIES

NO SHOULDER FOLD – WIRE BORDER

No Shoulder Fold, Wire Border Obverse
Flared "II"

Wire Border Reverse

Ref. No.	Description	VF-20	EF-40	AU-50	MS-60	MS-63
1953 NSF Obv.-001/Rev.-001	NSF, Wire Border, Normal	8.	9.	10.	12.	30.

1953 NO SHOULDER FOLD OBVERSE VARIETIES

DIE CRACKS

The most common failure of the obverse die occurs throughout the letters of the legend "ELIZABETH II DEI GRATIA REGINA".

DIE BREAK THROUGH "LEGEND"

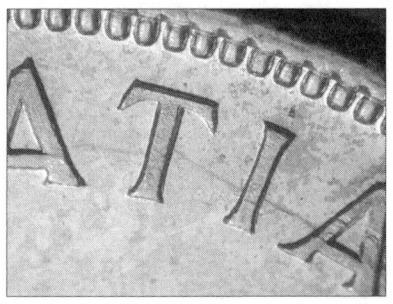 

Ref. No.	Description	VF-20	EF-40	AU-50	MS-60	MS-63
1953 NSF Obv.-001	Normal	8.	9.	10.	12.	30.
1953 NSF Obv.-002	Die Crack through Legend	10.	12.	15.	18.	35.

ONE DOLLAR

1953 NO SHOULDER FOLD REVERSE VARIETIES

FULL AND SHORT WATER LINES

NSF, Full Water Lines
Zoell No. K515c

NSF, Short Water Lines

Ref. No.	Description	VF-20	EF-40	AU-50	MS-60	MS-63
1953 NSF Rev.-001	Normal, Full Water Lines	8.	9.	10.	12.	30.
1953 NSF Rev.-002	Short Water Lines	15.	20.	25.	30.	40.

COUNTERSTAMPED "J.O.P"

OVAL WITH SMALL INITIALS (RAISED)

Submitted by: Scott Cornwell

Ref. No.	Description	VF-20	EF-40	AU-50	MS-60	MS-63
1953 NSF Rev.-001	Normal	8.	9.	10.	12.	30.
1953 NSF Rev.-003	Oval, Small Letters "J.O.P"	—	175.	350.	450.	—

ONE DOLLAR

1953 SHOULDER FOLD VARIETIES

SHOULDER FOLD – FLAT BORDER

Shoulder Fold, Flat Border Obverse
Straight "II"

Flat Border Reverse

Ref. No.	Description	VF-20	EF-40	AU-50	MS-60	MS-63
1953 SF Obv.-001/Rev.-001	Normal, Flat Border	8.	9.	10.	12.	30.

ONE DOLLAR

1953 SHOULDER FOLD OBVERSE VARIETIES

DIE CRACKS

DIE CRACK THROUGH "REGINA" OBVERSE – SHORT WATER LINE REVERSE

Submitted by: Ray Fishlock

Ref. No.	Description	VF-20	EF-40	AU-50	MS-60	MS-63
1953 SF Obv.-001/Rev.-002	Short Water Line Reverse	15.	20.	25.	30.	40.
1953 SF Obv.-002	Die Crack "REGINA", SWL	18.	25.	30.	35.	45.

DIE DETERIORATION DOUBLING

DOUBLING OF "EL" OF "ELIZABETH"

Doubling of "EL" of ELIZABETH
Zoell No. R515b

Ref. No.	Description	VF-20	EF-40	AU-50	MS-60	MS-63
1953 SF Obv.-001	Normal	8.	9.	10.	12.	35.
1953 SF Obv.-003	Doubling of "EL"	10.	15.	20.	25.	40.

ONE DOLLAR

1953 SHOULDER FOLD REVERSE VARIETIES

ABRADED DIES

FULL AND SHORT WATER LINES

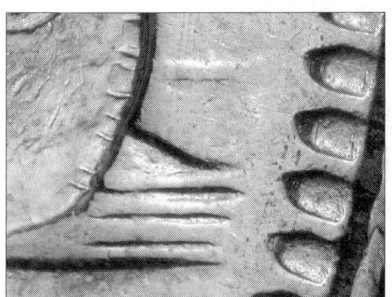

Shoulder Fold
Full Water Lines

Shoulder Fold
Short Water Lines

Ref. No.	Description	VF-20	EF-40	AU-50	MS-60	MS-63
1953 SF Rev.-001	Normal, Full Water Lines	8.	9.	10.	12.	35.
1953 SF Rev.-002	Short Water Lines	15.	20.	25.	30.	40.

ONE DOLLAR

1954 OBVERSE VARIETIES

WIDE AND NARROW BORDERS

Top: Normal Wide Border, Zoell No. A516
Bottom: Narrow Border. Zoell No. K516c

Ref. No.	Description	VF-20	EF-40	AU-50	MS-60	MS-63
1954 Obv.-001	Normal, Wide Border	12.	15.	18.	25.	50.
1954 Obv.-002	Narrow Border	15.	18.	20.	30.	60.

DIE CRACK

DIE CRACK THROUGH "GRATIA"

Ref. No.	Description	VF-20	EF-40	AU-50	MS-60	MS-63
1954 Obv.-001	Normal	12.	15.	18.	25.	50.
1954 Obv.-003	Die Crack "GRATIA"	15.	18.	20.	30.	60.

ONE DOLLAR

1954 REVERSE VARIETIES

FULL AND SHORT WATER LINES

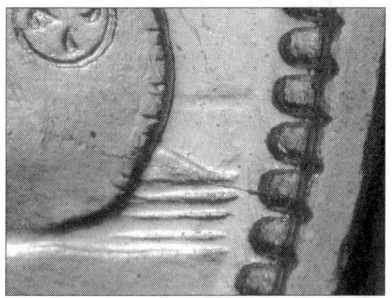

Full Water Lines   Short Water Lines

Ref. No.	Description	VF-20	EF-40	AU-50	MS-60	MS-63
1954 Rev.-001	Normal, Full Water Lines	12.	15.	18.	25.	50.
1954 Rev.-002	Short Water Lines	20.	25.	30.	40.	75.

COUNTERSTAMPED "J.O.P"

OVAL WITH SMALL INITIALS (RAISED)

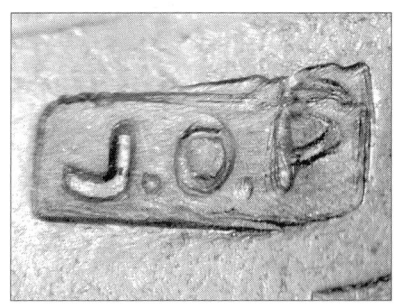

Submitted by: Scott Cornwell

Ref. No.	Description	VF-20	EF-40	AU-50	MS-60	MS-63
1954 Rev.-001	Normal	12.	15.	18.	25.	50.
1954 Rev.-003	Oval, Small Initials "J.O.P"	–	175.	350.	450.	–

ONE DOLLAR

1955 OBVERSE VARIETIES

DIE CRACKS

DIE CRACK THROUGH OBVERSE LEGEND – FULL WATER LINES REVERSE

Ref. No.	Description	VF-20	EF-40	AU-50	MS-60	MS-63
1955 Obv.-001	Normal	11.	15.	16.	25.	60.
1955 Obv.-002	Die Crack through Legend	14.	16.	18.	30.	65.

ONE DOLLAR

1955 REVERSE VARIETIES

FULL, SHORT AND ARNPRIOR WATER LINES

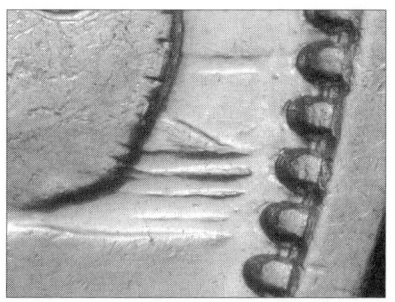

Full Water Lines

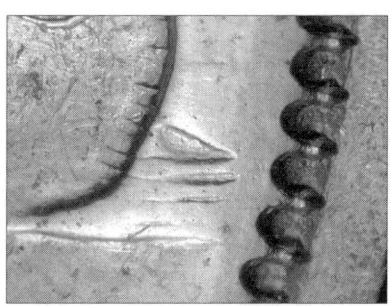

Short Water Lines

Arnprior
2 ½ Water Lines

Ref. No.	Description	VF-20	EF-40	AU-50	MS-60	MS-63
1955 Rev.-001	Normal, Full Water Lines	11.	15.	16.	25.	60.
1955 Rev.-002	Short Water Lines	20.	25.	35.	45.	75.
1955 Rev.-003	Arnprior	60.	70.	80.	100.	175.
1955 Rev.-003/Obv.-002	Arnprior with Die Break	100.	125.	150.	200.	300.

ONE DOLLAR

1956 REVERSE VARIETIES

ABRADED DIES

FULL AND SHORT WATER LINES

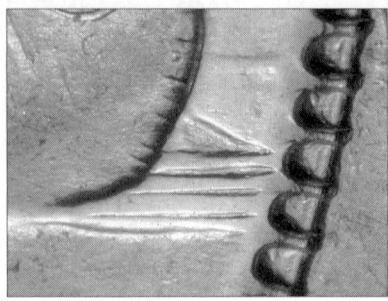

Full Water Lines

Short Water Lines

Ref. No.	Description	VF-20	EF-40	AU-50	MS-60	MS-63
1956 Rev.-001	Normal, Full Water Lines	12.	16.	20.	35.	90.
1956 Rev.-002	Short Water Lines	20.	25.	30.	45.	125.

ONE DOLLAR

1957 REVERSE VARIETIES

ABRADED DIES

FULL AND 1½ WATER LINES

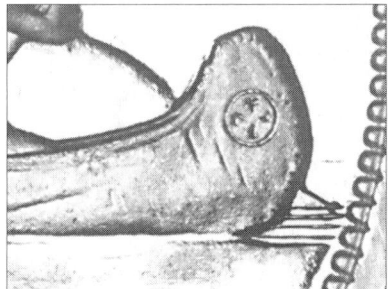

Full Water Lines

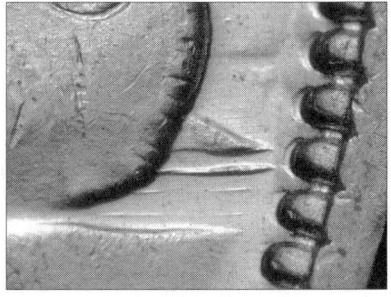

1½ Water Lines
Zoell No. K519b

Ref. No.	Description	VF-20	EF-40	AU-50	MS-60	MS-63
1957 Rev.-001	Normal, Full Water Lines	–	–	–	12.	20.
1957 Rev.-002	1½ Water Lines	–	–	–	15.	50.

ONE DOLLAR

1958 REVERSE VARIETIES

MACHINE DOUBLING DAMAGE (MDD)

DOUBLING OF 1858 1958

Double 1858-1959
Zoell No. R520o

Ref. No.	Description	VF-20	EF-40	AU-50	MS-60	MS-63
1958 Rev.-001	Normal	–	–	–	12.	20.
1958 Rev.-002	Doubling of 1858 1958	–	–	–	20.	30.

ONE DOLLAR

1960 REVERSE VARIETIES

Thomas Shingles reworked the matrix in 1960, adding two horizon lines in front of the canoe.

DOUBLE PUNCHED DIGIT

DOUBLED "0"

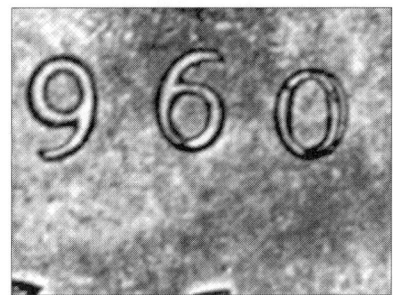

Repunched "0" over "0"
Zoell No. R522c

Ref. No.	Description	VF-20	EF-40	AU-50	MS-60	MS-63
1960 Rev.-001	Normal	–	–	–	12.	15.
1960 Rev.-002	Repunched "0"	–	–	–	20.	30.

ONE DOLLAR

1961 REVERSE VARIETIES

DIE CLASH

ARROW HEADS ON INDIAN'S BACK

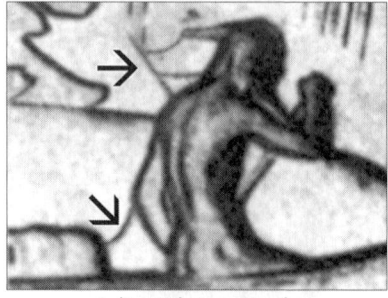

Indian Without Arrow Head

Indian With Arrow Heads
Zoell No. C523o

Ref. No.	Description	VF-20	EF-40	AU-50	MS-60	MS-63
1961 Rev.-001	Normal	–	–	–	12.	15.
1961 Rev.-002	Arrow Head	–	–	–	20.	30.

ONE DOLLAR

1962 REVERSE VARIETIES

DIE CLASH

ARROW HEADS ON INDIAN'S BACK

Indian Without Arrow Head
Zoel No. C524n

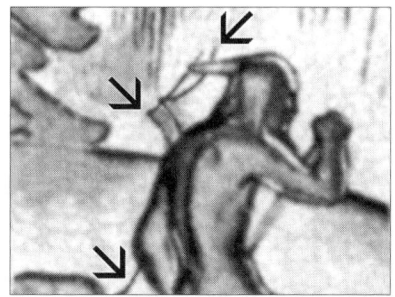

Indian With Double Arrow Heads
Zoell No. C524o

Ref. No.	Description	VF-20	EF-40	AU-50	MS-60	MS-63
1962 Rev.-001	Normal	–	–	–	12.	15.
1962 Rev.-002	Arrow Head	–	–	–	20.	30.
1962 Rev.-003	Double Arrow Head	–	–	–	30.	50.

ONE DOLLAR

ONE DOLLAR, 1963, REVERSE

DIE CLASH

ARROW HEADS ON INDIAN'S BACK

Indian Without Arrow Head

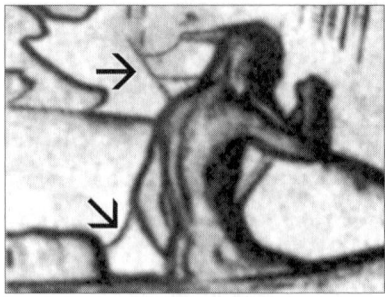
Indian With Arrow Heads

Ref. No.	Description	VF-20	EF-40	AU-50	MS-60	MS-63
1963 Rev.-001	Normal	–	–	–	10.	15.
1963 Rev.-002	Arrow Head	–	–	–	20.	30.

ONE DOLLAR

1964 REVERSE VARIETIES

MISSING DOT

With Dot after "T"

Missing Dot after "T"
Zoell No. S526o

Ref. No.	Description	VF-20	EF-40	AU-50	MS-60	MS-63
1964 Rev.-001	Normal	–	–	–	10.	15.
1964 Rev.-002	Missing Dot	–	–	–	15.	20.

ONE DOLLAR

1965 OBVERSE VARIETIES

VARIETIES 1 and 2: SMALL BEADS

Small Beads
Obverse

VARIETY 5: MEDIUM BEADS

Medium Beads
Obverse

VARIETIES 3 and 4: LARGE BEADS

Large Beads
Obverse

Ref. No.	Description	VF-20	EF-40	AU-50	MS-60	MS-63
1965 SB Obv.-001	Normal	–	–	–	10.	15.
1965 MB Obv.-002	Normal	–	–	–	25.	50.
1965 LB Obv.-003	Normal	–	–	–	10.	15.

ONE DOLLAR

1965 OBVERSE REVERSE VARIETIES

ROTATED DIES

COINAGE AXIS ALIGNMENT OF VARIETY 2, SMALL BEADS, BLUNT 5

Small Beads Blunt 5

Ref. No.	Description	VF-20	EF-40	AU-50	MS-60	MS-63
1965 Obv.-001/Rev.-001	Medal	–	–	–	10.	15.
1965 Obv.-001/Rev.-004	Coinage	–	–	–	3,000.	–

1965 REVERSE VARIETIES

FONT STYLES

POINTED AND BLUNT 5

1965 Pointed 5 (at bottom)   195 Blunt 5 (at bottom)

Ref. No.	Description	VF-20	EF-40	AU-50	MS-60	MS-63
1965 Rev.-001	Pointed 5	–	–	–	10.	15.
1965 Rev.-002	Blunt 5	–	–	–	10.	15.

ONE DOLLAR

1966 OBVERSE VARIETIES

LARGE BEADS, CONCAVE FIELD; SMALL BEADS, FLAT FIELD

LARGE BEADS (CONCAVE FIELD)
This obverse design was carried forward from Variety 3 or 4 of 1965.

Large Beads (Concave Field)

SMALL BEADS (FLAT FIELD)
This obverse design was carried forward from Variety 1 or 2 of 1965.

Small Beads (Flat Field)

Ref. No.	Description	VF-20	EF-40	AU-50	MS-60	MS-63
1966 Obv.-001	Large Beads	—	—	7.	10.	15.
1966 Obv.-002	Small Beads	—	—	2,000.	2,500.	3,500.

ONE DOLLAR

1966 REVERSE VARIETIES

PUNCH DOUBLED

DOUBLED HORIZON LINES

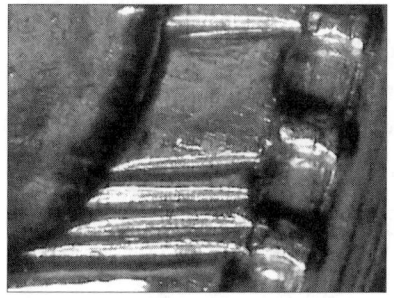

Doubled Horizon Lines

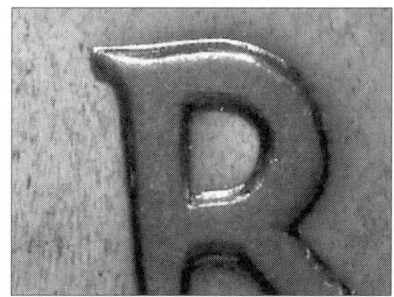

Doubled "R" in DOLLAR

Submitted by: Ray Fishlock

Ref. No.	Description	VF-20	EF-40	AU-50	MS-60	MS-63
1966 Rev.-001	Normal	–	–	–	10.	15.
1966 Rev.-002	Double Horizon Lines	–	–	–	50.	75.

ONE DOLLAR

1967 OBVERSE VARIETIES

The flat field 1967 dollar was a trial piece struck in 1966, for design testing of the 1967 reverse. The obverse design of 1965, Variety 3 or 4 was carried forward into 1967.

LARGE BEADS (CONCAVE FIELD)

Large Beads (Concave Field)

SMALL BEADS (FLAT FIELD)

The obverse design of 1965, Variety 1 or 2 was used as a test obverse with the 1967 reverse (Goose) design.

Small Beads (Flat Field)

Ref. No.	Description	VF-20	EF-40	AU-50	MS-60	MS-63
1967 Obv.-001	Concave field, Normal	—	—	—	10.	15.
1967 Obv.-002	Flat field		Only One Known			

ONE DOLLAR

1967 OBVERSE AND REVERSE VARIETIES

DOUBLE STRIKE

DOUBLE STRIKE

TRIPLE AND FLIPFLOP STRIKES

Images of
Triple Strike
and Flip Flop Strike
not available
at press time

Ref. No.	Description	VF-20	EF-40	AU-50	MS-60	MS-63
1967 Obv.-001/Rev.-001	Normal	–	–	–	10.	15.
1967 Obv.-003/Rev.-002	Double Strike	–	–	–	300.	500.
1967 Obv.-004/Rev.-003	Triple Strike	–	–	–	400.	600.
1967 Obv.-005/Rev.-004	Flip Flop	–	–	–	–	–

ONE DOLLAR

1967 OBVERSE and REVERSE VARIETIES

ROTATED DIES

DIVING GOOSE – 45 DEGREE DIE ROTATION

Ref. No.	Description	VF-20	EF-40	AU-50	MS-60	MS-63
1967 Obv.-001/Rev.-001	Medal Axis	–	–	–	10.	15.
1967 Obv.-001/Rev.-005	Diving Goose	–	–	–	550.	650.

ROTATED DIES

COINAGE AXIS ALIGNMENT – 180 DEGREE DIE ROTATION

Ref. No.	Description	VF-20	EF-40	AU-50	MS-60	MS-63
1967 Obv.-001/Rev.-001	Medal Axis	–	–	–	10.	15.
1967 Obv.-001/Rev.-006	Coinage Axis	–	–	–	3,000.	4,000.

ONE DOLLAR

1968 OBVERSE VARIETIES

FLAT FIELD DOUBLING

DOUBLING ON THE BEADS AND "REGINA"

Doubling on "REGINA"

Ref. No.	Description	63	64	65	SPECIMEN (SP-66) 66	67
1968 Obv.-600	Normal	–	–	–	15.	–
1968 Obv.-601	Doubling of "REGINA"	–	–	–	25.	–

ONE DOLLAR

1968 REVERSE VARIETIES

ABRADED DIE

ISLAND VARIETIES

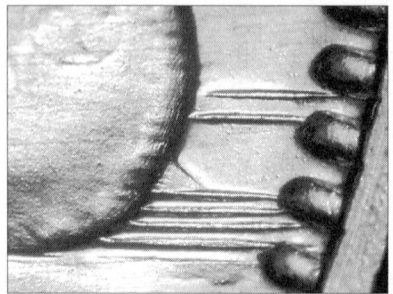

Island

Small Island

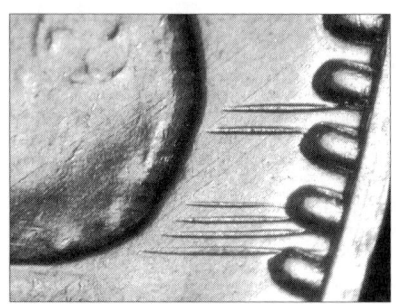

No Island

Ref. No.	Description	BRILLIANT UNCIRCULATED (MS)				
		63	64	65	66	67
1968 Rev.-001	Normal, Island	2.	3.	6.	–	–
1968 Rev.-002	Small Island	10.	12.	14.	–	–
1968 Rev.-003	No Island	8.	10.	12.	–	–

ONE DOLLAR

1968 REVERSE VARIETIES

ISLAND WITH DOUBLED HORIZON LINES, VARIETY 1

Confirmation of the doubled horizon lines (Cat. No. 1968 Rev.-010 / 010), 1968 dollar is found in the doubled "68" of 1968 and "AR" of DOLLAR. Other punch doubled dies exist but none offer stronger confirmation than this; see following variety.

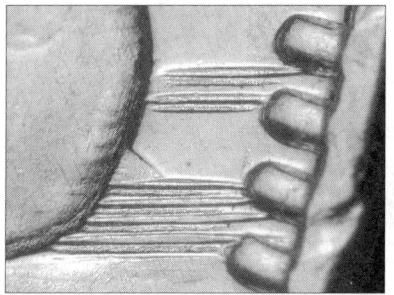

Ref. No.	Description	BRILLIANT UNCIRCULATED (MS)				
		63	64	65	66	67
1968 Rev.-001	Normal, Island	2.	3.	6.	–	–
1968 Rev.-004	Doubled Lines Var. 1	50.	75.	100.	–	–

ONE DOLLAR

1968 REVERSE VARIETIES

ISLAND WITH DOUBLED HORIZON LINES, VARIETY 2

Another variety of "Doubled Horizon Lines" this coin lacks the confirming doubled "68" and "AR" of DOLLAR.

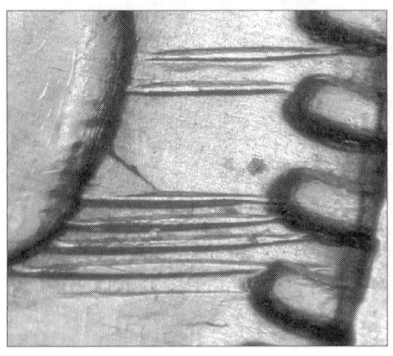

Ref. No.	Description	BRILLIANT UNCIRCULATED (MS)				
		63	64	65	66	67
1968 Rev.-001	Normal, Island	2.	3.	6.	–	–
1968 Rev.-005	Doubled Lines Var. 2	15.	20.	25.	–	–

ONE DOLLAR

1969 OBVERSE VARIETIES

FLAT FIELD DOUBLING

DOUBLING OF BEADS and LEGEND

This is a classic example of flat field doubling. The doubling extends through the full legend.

Submitted by: Ray Fishlock

Ref. No.	Description	63	64	SPECIMEN (SP) 65	66	67
1969 Obv.-600	Normal	–	–	–	15.	–
1969 Obv.-601	Doubling of Beads and Legend	–	–	–	15.	–

ONE DOLLAR

1970 OBVERSE VARIETIES

FLAT FIELD DOUBLING

DOUBLING OF BEADS AND LEGEND

Ref. No.	Description	SPECIMEN (SP)				
		63	64	65	66	67
1970 Obv.-600	Normal	–	–	–	15.	–
1970 Obv.-601	Doubling of "REGINA"	–	–	–	15.	–

ONE DOLLAR

1972 REVERSE VARIETIES

MACHINE DOUBLING DAMAGE (MDD)

DOUBLING OF "1972" and "DOLLAR"

Submitted by: Ray Fishlock

Ref. No.	Description	63	64	SPECIMEN (SP) 65	66	67
1972 Rev.-600	Normal	–	–	–	15.	–
1972 Rev.-601	Doubling of "1972" and "Dollar"	–	–	–	15.	–

ONE DOLLAR

1973 OBVERSE VARIETIES

FLAT FIELD DOUBLING

DOUBLING OF DATE AND BEADS

Submitted by: Randy Ash.

Ref. No.	Description	SPECIMEN (SP)				
		63	64	65	66	67
1973 Obv.-600	Normal	–	–	–	15.	–
1973 Obv.-601	Doubling of "Date" and "Beads"	–	–	–	15.	–

ONE DOLLAR

1974 OBVERSE VARIETIES

DIE CRACK

Die cracks are progressive and no two coins are identical. From the right hand image and the image below, you can readily see how the crack progressed as the die was used. Pricing is difficult, for the more dramatic the crack the greater the premium placed on the coin.

DIE CRACK LINKING BEADS

 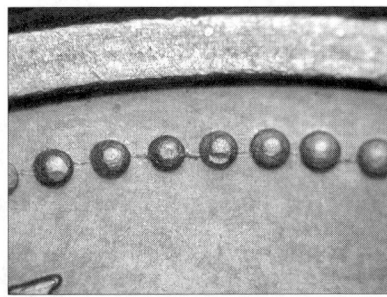

Minor Die Crack Linking Beads

Major Die Crack Linking Beads

Submitted by: Charles Daigle

Ref. No.	Description	BRILLILANT UNCIRCULATED (MS)				
		63	64	65	66	67
1974 Obv.-001	Normal	2.	3.	6.	—	—
1974 Obv.-002	Die Crack "Linking Beads"	Price Range $5. - $500.				

ONE DOLLAR

1974 REVERSE VARIETIES

PUNCH DOUBLED YOKE

DOUBLED YOKE, VARIETY 1: Second Yoke is located directly North of Main Yoke

Submitted by: Ken Potter

Ref. No.	Description	BRILLIANT UNCIRCULATED (MS)				
		63	64	65	66	67
1974 Rev.-001	Normal	2.	3.	6.	–	–
1974 Rev.-002	Doubled Yoke, Var. 1	350.	450.	600.	–	–

Note: As of May 31, 2005 fifteen different punch doubled varieties of the 1974 Winnipeg dollar have been recorded. For a full explanation and listing of all varieties visit www.kionpro.com.

ONE DOLLAR

1974 REVERSE VARIETIES

PUNCH DOUBLED YOKE

DOUBLED YOKE, VARIETY 2: Second Yoke is located North West of Main Yoke

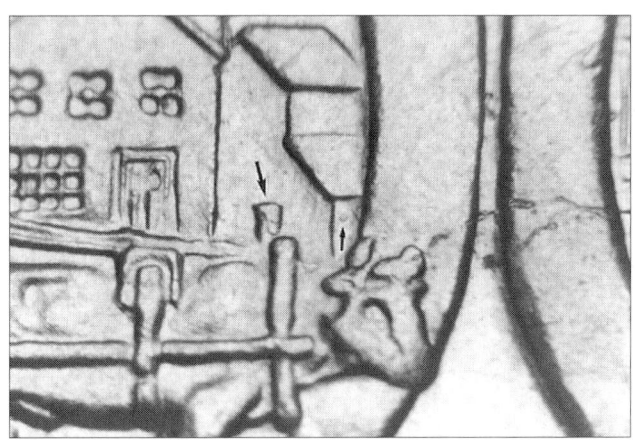

Submitted by: Ken Potter

Ref. No.	Description	BRILLIANT UNCIRCULATED (MS)				
		60	63	64	65	66
1974 Rev.-001	Normal	–	2.	3.	6.	–
1974 Rev.-003	Doubled Yoke, Var. 2	150.	200.	250.	350.	–

ONE DOLLAR

1974 REVERSE VARIETIES

PUNCH DOUBLED YOKE

DOUBLE YOKE, VARIETY 3: Second Yoke is located East of Main Yoke

Submitted by: Ken Potter

Ref. No.	Description	BRILLIANT UNCIRCULATED (MS)				
		63	64	65	66	67
1974 Rev.-001	Normal	2.	3.	6.	–	–
1974 Rev.-004	Doubled Yoke, Var. 3	175.	275.	400.	–	–

ONE DOLLAR

1975 OBVERSE VARIETIES

ABRADED DIES

ATTACHED AND DETACHED JEWELS, FULL WATER LINES

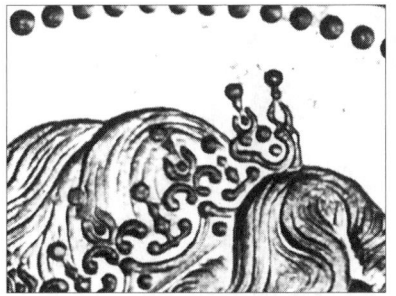

Attached Jewels

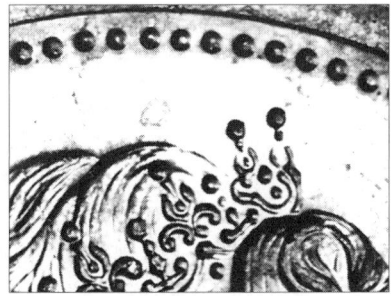

Detached Jewels

Ref. No.	Description	BRILLIANT UNCIRCULATED (MS)				
		63	64	65	66	67
1975 Obv.-001	Normal, Attached Jewel	2.	3.	6.	–	–
1975 Obv.-002	Detached Jewel	5.	8.	12.	–	–

Ref. No.	Description	SPECIMEN (SP)				
		63	64	65	66	67
1975 Obv.-601	Normal, Attached Jewel	–	–	–	15.	–
1975 Obv.-602	Detached Jewel	–	–	–	15.	–

ONE DOLLAR

1975 REVERSE VARIETIES

FULL WATER LINES, ATTACHED AND DETACHED JEWELS

While this is not a variety listing it does set the stage for the upcoming "short water line" varieties that follow and, perhaps the 1975 SWL which is yet to be found.

Ref. No.	Description	BRILLIANT UNCIRCULATED (MS)				
		63	64	65	66	67
1975 Rev.-001	Normal, Full Water Lines	2.	3.	6.	–	–

DIE DETERIORIATION DOUBLING

DOUBLING OF 1975

Submitted by: Scott Cornwell

Ref. No.	Description	BRILLIANT UNCIRCULATED (MS)				
		63	64	65	66	67
1975 Rev.-001	Normal	2.	3.	6.	–	–
1975 Rev.-002	Doubling of "1975"	8.	10.	15.	–	–

Ref. No.	Description	SPECIMEN (SP)				
		63	64	65	66	67
1975 Rev.-600	Normal	–	–	–	15.	–
1975 Rev.-601	Doubling of "1975"	–	–	–	15.	–

ONE DOLLAR

1975 REVERSE VARIETIES

DIE CLASH

ISLAND LIGHTNING, FULL WATER LINES

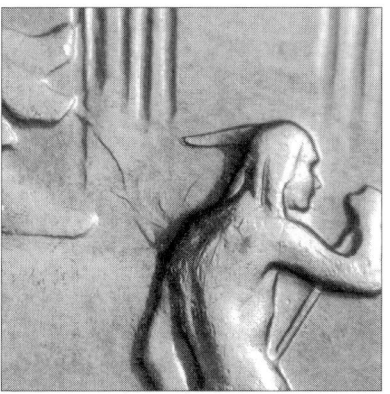

Submitted by: Ray Fishlock

Ref. No.	Description	BRILLIANT UNCIRCULATED (MS)				
		63	64	65	66	67
1975 Rev.-001	Normal, Full Water Lines	2.	3.	6.	–	–
1975 Rev.-003	Die Clash "Island Lightning"	10.	15.	20.	–	–

DIE CRACK

DIE CRACK THROUGH "DOLLAR"

 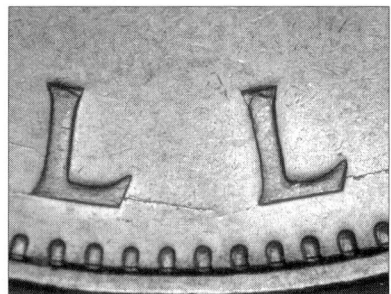

Ref. No.	Description	BRILLIANT UNCIRCULATED (MS)				
		63	64	65	66	67
1975 Rev.-001	Normal, FWL	2.	3.	6.	–	–
1975 Rev.-004	Die Crack "Dollar"	3.	5.	8.	–	–

ONE DOLLAR

1976 OBVERSE VARIETIES

ABRADED DIES
ATTACHED AND DETACHED JEWELS, FULL WATER LINES

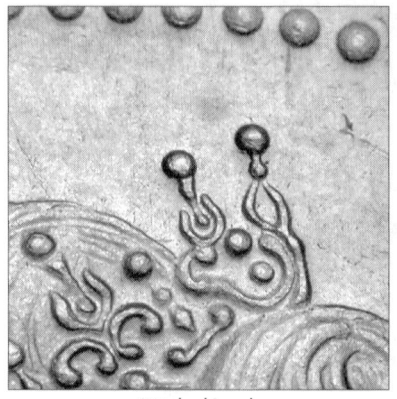 

Attached Jewels   Detached Jewels

Ref. No.	Description	BRILLIANT UNCIRCULATRED (MS)				
		63	64	65	66	67
1976 Obv.-001	Normal, Attached Jewel	2.	3.	6.	–	–
1976 Obv.-002	Detached Jewel	2.	3.	6.	–	–

Ref. No.	Description	SPECIMEN (SP)				
		63	64	65	66	67
1976 Obv.-601	Normal, Attached Jewel	–	–	–	15.	–
1976 Obv.-602	Detached Jewel	–	–	–	15.	–

ONE DOLLAR

1976 REVERSE VARIETIES

FULL WATER LINES, ATTACHED AND DETACHED JEWELS

As in the 1975 Reverse listing, the 1976 Full Water Line reverse is just for keeping order, no Short Water Line variety has been found.

		BRILLIANT UNCIRCULATED (MS)				
Ref. No.	Description	63	64	65	66	67
1976 Rev.-001	Normal, Full Water Lines	2.	3.	6.	–	–

DIE DETERIORIATION DOUBLING

DOUBLING OF "1976"

Doubling of "1976"

		BRILLIANT UNCIRCULATED (MS)				
Ref. No.	Description	63	64	65	66	67
1976 Rev.-001	Normal, Full Water Lines	2.	3.	6.	–	–
1976 Rev.-002	Doubling of "1976"	8.	10.	15.	–	–

ONE DOLLAR

1977 OBVERSE VARIETIES

ABRADED DIES

ATTACHED AND DETACHED JEWELS

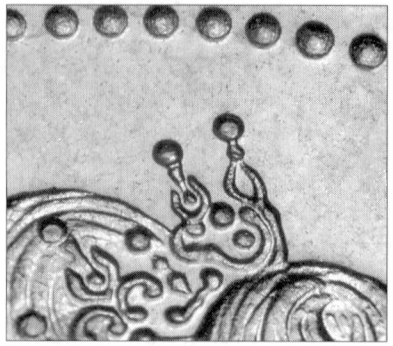
Attached Jewel

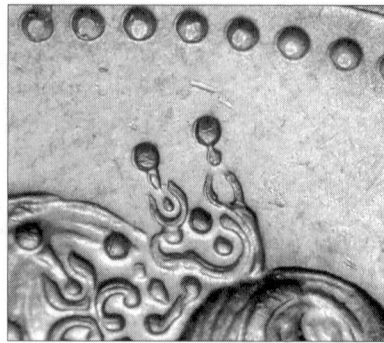
Detached Jewel

Ref. No.	Description	BRILLIANT UNCIRCULATRED (MS)				
		63	64	65	66	67
1977 Obv.-001	Normal, Attached Jewel	2.	3.	6.	–	–
1977 Obv.-002	Detached Jewel	5.	8.	12.	–	–

Ref. No.	Description	SPECIMEN (SP)				
		63	64	65	66	67
1977 Obv.-601	Normal, Attached Jewel	–	–	–	15.	–
1977 Obv.-602	Detached Jewel	–	–	–	15.	–

ONE DOLLAR

1977 REVERSE VARIETIES

ABRADED DIES

FULL AND SHORT WATER LINES

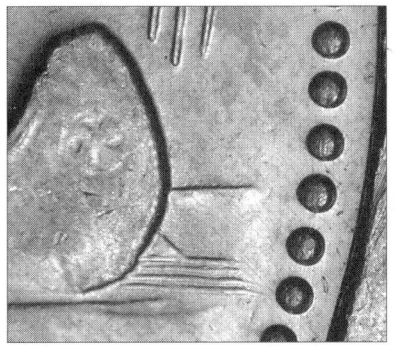

Full Water Lines

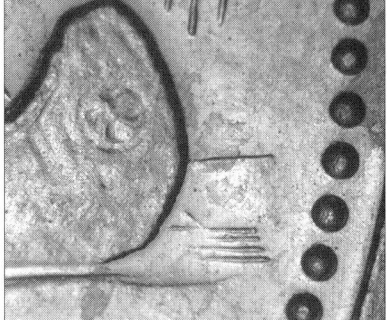

Short Water Lines

		BRILLIANT UNCIRCULATRED (MS)				
Ref. No.	**Description**	**63**	**64**	**65**	**66**	**67**
1977 Rev.-001	Normal, Full Water Lines	2.	3.	6.	–	–
1977 Rev.-002	Short Water Lines	2.	3.	6.	–	–

		SPECIMEN (SP)				
Ref. No.	**Description**	**63**	**64**	**65**	**66**	**67**
1977 Rev.-600	Normal, Full Water Lines	–	–	–	15.	–
1977 Rev.-601	Short Water Lines	–	–	–	15.	–

FOUR COMBINATION VARIETIES

The following four combinations are possible and could be found in either Mint State or Specimen.

1977 Obv.-001/Rev.-001
1977 Obv.-001/Rev.-002
1977 Obv.-002/Rev.-001
1977 Obv.-002/Rev.-002

ONE DOLLAR

1977 REVERSE VARIETIES

ABRADED DIES

FULL WATER LINES WITH FLAT ISLAND

The Flat Island, Full Water Lines Reverse is paired with 1977 Obv.-002 Detached Jewel Obverse.

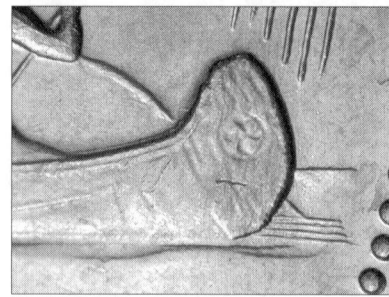

Raised Island with Full Water Lines

Flat Island with Full Water Lines

Ref. No.	Description	BRILLIANT UNCIRCULATED (MS)				
		63	64	65	66	67
1977 Rev.-001	Normal, Full Water Lines	2.	3.	6.	–	–
1977 Rev.-003	Flat Island, Full Water Lines	5.	10.	15.	–	–

SHORT WATER LINES WITH FLAT ISLAND

The Flat Island, Short Water Lines Reverse is paired with 1977 Obv.-001 Attached Jewel Obverse.

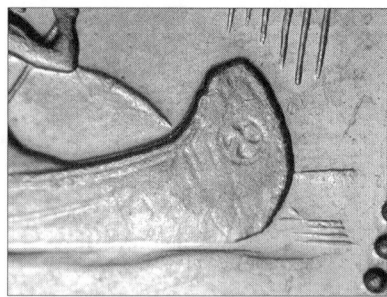

Raised Island with Short Water Lines

Flat Island with Short Water Lines

Ref. No.	Description	BRILLIANT UNCIRCULATED (MS)				
		63	64	65	66	67
1977 Rev.-001	Normal, Short Water Lines	2.	3.	6.	–	–
1977 Rev.-004	Flat Island, Short Water Lines	5.	10.	15.	–	–

ONE DOLLAR

1978 REVERSE VARIETIES

ABRADED DIES

ISLAND, SMALL ISLAND, NO ISLAND

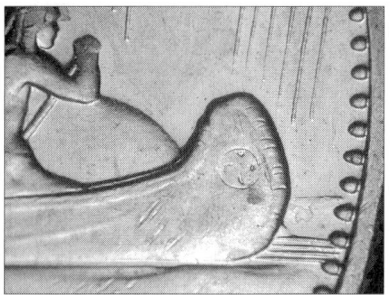

Island, Full Water Lines

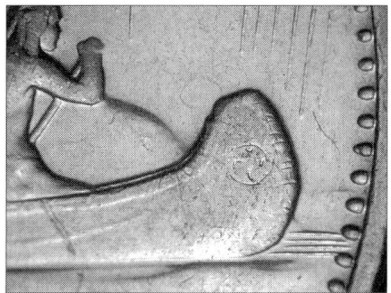

Small Island, Full Water Lines

No Island, Full Water Lines

Note: "No Island" variety is also
         missing the horizon line

Submitted by: Andrew McKaig

		BRILLIANT UNCIRCULATED (MS)				
Ref. No.	Description	63	64	65	66	67
1978 Rev.-001	Normal Island, Full Water Lines	2.	3.	6.	–	–
1978 Rev.-002	Small Island, Full Water Lines	3.	5.	8.	–	–
1978 Rev.-003	No Island, Full Water Lines	3.	5.	8.	–	–

		SPECIMEN (SP)				
Ref. No.	Description	63	64	65	66	67
1978 Rev.-600	Normal Island, Full Water Lines	–	–	–	15.	–
1978 Rev.-601	No Island, Full Water Lines	–	–	–	15.	–

ONE DOLLAR

ONE DOLLAR, 1978, REVERSE

ISLAND AND SMALL ISLAND WITH BROKEN WATER LINE

The "Broken Water Line", Full Water Line is paired with 1978 Obv.-001, as is the "Broken Water Line", Short Water Line.

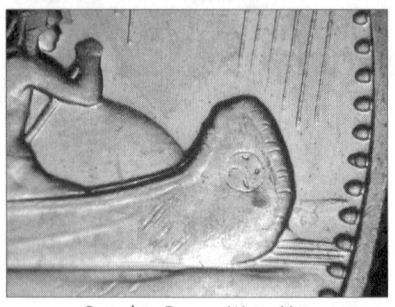

Complete Bottom Water Line

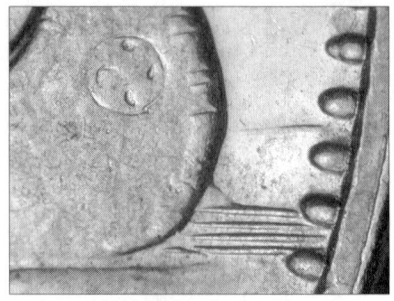

Large Island, Broken Bottom Water Line

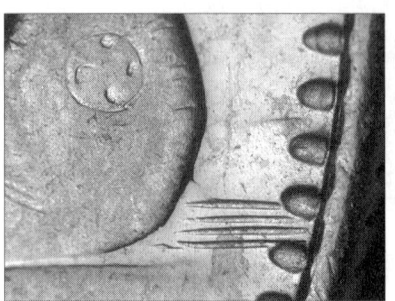

Small Island, Broken Bottom Water Line

Submitted by: Andrew McKaig

Ref. No.	Description	BRILLIANT UNCIRCULATED (MS)				
		63	64	65	66	67
1978 Rev.-001	Normal, Island, Full Water Lines	2.	3.	6.	–	–
1978 Rev.-004	Large Island, Broken Line	5.	10.	15.	–	–
1978 Rev.-005	Small Island, Broken Line	5.	10.	15.	–	–

ONE DOLLAR

1978 REVERSE VARIETIES

MAJOR DIE BREAK

SECOND ISLAND, FORMED BY HORIZON LINES DISAPPEARING INTO A DIE BREAK

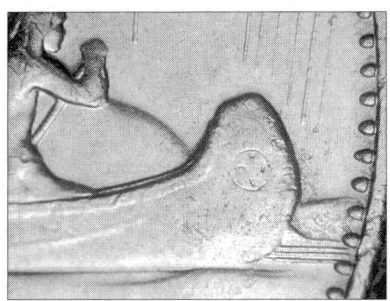
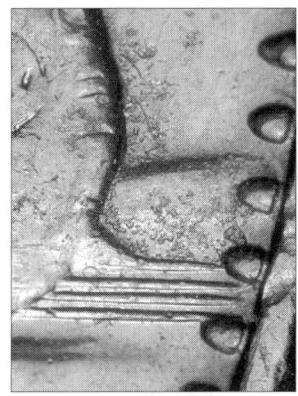

| Ref. No. | Description | BRILLIANT UNCIRCULATED (MS) | | | | |
		63	64	65	66	67
1978 Rev.-001	Normal, Full Water Lines	2.	3.	6.	–	–
1978 Rev.-006	Die Break, Second Island	5.	10.	15.	–	–

ONE DOLLAR

1982 OBVERSE VARIETIES

FLAT FIELD DOUBLNG

DOUBLING OF DATE AND LEGEND

| Ref. No. | Description | | | SPECIMEN (SP) | | |
		63	64	65	66	67
1982 Obv.-600	Normal	–	–	–	15.	–
1982 Obv.-601	Doubling of Date and Legend	–	–	–	15.	–

ONE DOLLAR

1982 OBVERSE AND REVERSE VARIETIES

ROTATED DIES

COINAGE AXIS ALIGNMENT, 180 DEGREES

Ref. No.	Description	BRILLIANT UNCIRCULATED (MS)				
		60	63	64	65	66
1982 Obv.-001/Rev.-001	Medal	–	2.	3.	6.	–
1982 Obv.-001/Rev.-002	Coinage	2,000.	–	–	–	–

ONE DOLLAR

1982 PLANCHET VARIETIES

THIN PLANCHET

The 1982 nickel dollar exists on a rolled thin blank or planchet. See Herbert I-B-3.

Weight: 15.62 grams
Diameter: 32.13 mm
Thickness: 2.50 mm

Normal planchet
full reeding,
thickness, weight

Weight: 7.78 grams
Diameter: 31.82 mm
Thickness: 1.50 mm

Thin planchet
incomplete reeding,
thickness, weight

Ref. No.	Description	Price Range
1982	Normal Planchet	$2. – $10.
1982	Thin Planchet	$1,800. – $2,500.

ONE DOLLAR

1985 OBVERSE AND REVERSE VARIETIES

DEFECTIVE STRIKES AND MISMATCHED DIES

NEW ZEALAND / CANADA MULE

For a description of Mismatched Dies, see Herbert III-P-2.

Ref. No.	Description	Price Range
1985 Obv./Rev.	Normal	$2. − $10.
1985 Obv./Rev.	New Zealand / Canada Mule	$3,000. − $5,000.

ONE DOLLAR

1995 LOON REVERSE VARIETIES

DIE CHIPS

 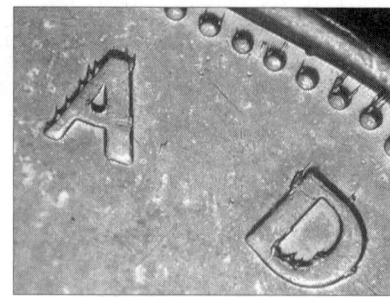

Submitted by: Marion Krause

Ref. No.	Description	BRILLIANT UNCIRCULATED (MS)				
		63	64	65	66	67
1995 Loon Rev.-001	Normal	4.	6.	8.	–	–
1995 Loon Rev.-002	Die Chips "Legend"	5.	7.	10.	–	–

ONE DOLLAR

1995 PEACEKEEPING REVERSE VARIETIES

DIE CHIPS

 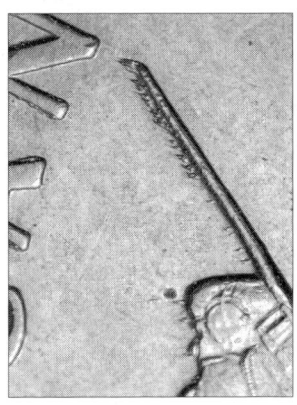

Submitted by: Marion Krause

		BRILLIANT UNCIRCULATED (MS)				
Ref. No.	Description	63	64	65	66	67
1995 Peacekeeping Rev.-001	Normal	4.	6.	8.	–	–
1995 Peacekeeping Rev.-002	Die Chips	5.	7.	10.	–	–

Application for Membership/Subscription

Applications for membership/subscription in the Canadian Numismatic Association may be made by any reputable party upon payment of the required dues.

(check one of each group)

☐ New ☐ Renewal _____ ☐ Reinstatement
(member number)

☐Regular ☐Junior ☐Family

☐Corporate ☐Life Membership

☐Mr. ☐Mrs. ☐Ms. ☐Club

Name:

Street: *Address may be published in the Journal* ☐ yes ☐ no

City: Province/State Postal Code/Zip

Country Birthdate

Signature of applicant Signature of Sponsor

Signature of guardian (if under 18 years of age)

Dues

Dues shown are in Canadian dollars to Canadian addresses and in U.S. dollars to all other addresses. Payment may be made by money order, bank draft or personal cheque. We regret that we are unable to offer credit card services. Postage stamps are not acceptable. Currency (U.S. or Canadian only) is acceptable and should be sent by security registered mail only. Membership is not Goods and Services taxable.

REGULAR* - Applicants 18 years of age or over **$33.00**

JUNIOR - Applicants under 18 years of age **$16.50**
  Persons under 18 must be sponsored by a parent or guardian

FAMILY - Husband, wife and children at home, under 18 years of age
  One Journal only **$44.00**

CORPORATE - Clubs, Societies, Libraries and other non-profit
  organizations...**$33.00**

LIFE MEMBERSHIP **$495.00**

(After one year of regular membership. Details on payment plan available on request.)

First class mailing of the Journal is available on remittance of $9.00 (Cdn.) to Canadian addresses, $7.50 (U.S.$) to U.S.A. addresses and $15.00 (U.S.$) to all other addresses. Addresses of all new members are published in the Journal.

Please mail application and payment to the Canadian Numisimatic Association, 4936 Yonge St., Suite 601, North York, Ontario, Canada, M2N 6S3 Tel.: (416) 223-5980 Fax: (416) 223-6782 E-mail: cnainfo@look.ca

Application must be complete and accompanied by full dues to be accepted. Please photocopy and mail.